ENGLISH RECUSANT LITERATURE
1558–1640

Selected and Edited by
D. M. ROGERS

Volume 146

ROGER BAYNES
The Baynes of Aquisgrane
1617

THOMAS FITZHERBERT
A Defence of the Catholyke Cause
1602

ROGER BAYNES

The Baynes of Aquisgrane
1617

1756347

The Scolar Press
1973

ISBN 0 85417 961 5

Published and Printed in Great Britain by
The Scolar Press Limited, 20 Main Street,
Menston, Yorkshire, England

NOTE

The following works are reproduced (original size), with permission:

1) Roger Baynes, *The Baynes of Aquisgrane*, 1617, from a copy in the library of Trinity College, Cambridge, by permission of the Librarian.
References: Allison and Rogers 76; STC 1650.

2) Thomas Fitzherbert, *A defence of the catholyke cause*, 1602, from a copy in Cambridge University Library, by permission of the Syndics. Leaf R4 in this copy has a lacuna, and this leaf from a copy in the library of Downside Abbey is included as an appendix, by permission of the Abbot and Community.
References: Allison and Rogers 310; STC 11016.

THE
BAYNES OF
AQVISGRANE,

The I. Part, & I. Volume,

INTITVLED

VARIETY.

Contayning Three Bookes, in the forme of Dialogues,
vnder the Titles following, Viz.

PROFIT, PLEASVRE, HONOVR.

Furnished with diuers things, no lesse delightfull, then beneficiall to be knowne, and obserued.

Related by ROG. BAYNES GENT. *a long Exile
out of England, not for any temporall respects.*

Qui nihil sperat, nihil desperat.

¶ Printed at Augusta in Germany. M.DC.XVII.

The Printer to the Reader.

THIS *present Volume, and the rest that are to follow,*
though they haue not come to the Presse till now, yet
haue they byn written some yeares ago, in the tyme of
the late Queene Elizabeth.

THE
GENERAL PROEME
MADE BY THE RELATOR
OF THIS WORKE,

Vnto the firſt Part therof, intituled

VARIETY,

Dedicated in the Names of the Authors themſelues,
vnto the future Poſterity of ENGLAND.

NOT only novv, but alſo for the tyme to come, ſome in ENGLAND may be taken to be Learned vvho are not, and ſome may neither be Learned, nor yet taken ſo to be. Againe ſome may be Learned vvho are not ſo

taken

taken, and some others may be both Learned and taken so to be; vvhereunto may be added a fift sort of such, as take themselues to be Learned, vvhen indeed they be not. And vnto this last sort of Men, for certaine reasons (not needfull heere to be related) this Worke is but reseruedly dedicated; I meane so far forth only, as they shall vouchsafe to regard it : but principally and directly it is presented vnto the first and second sortes of men aboue mentioned; that is to say, it is directed first vnto those vvho be neither Learned, nor yet taken to be so, to the end they may be able to knovv somevvhat; and next vnto those others vvho be indeed Learned, though they take not themselues so to be; vvho also may esteeme it as presented to them, to the end they may better their supposed Knovvledge : For vvhich respects I presume that this Worke vvillbe gratefull to them both.

And

And therfore if any of thofe others,
vnto vvhome it is not directly dedicated
should perhaps go about to calumniate
the fame, or any part therof; he may vvith
more reafon and reputation faue that labour: becaufe neither is the Worke dedicated vnto him, nor yet compofed by
men of his rank, or degree in Learning,
but by certaine curious Trauailers, as the
follovving difcourfe vvill more plainly
declare, vvho being indeed Courtiers,
make no profeffion of any other Science
but Humanity only: and therfore for a
man of his skill to make any competence
at all vvith thefe, or to controle or blemish their Endeauours, this he ought not
in reafon to do, nor yet permit others to
do it. And fo much alfo the leffe, becaufe
in Dialogues it is not to be expected, that
all vvhich is vvritten, is to be continuate
doctrine, but that fome Interlocutions
are to enter betvvixt; the vvhich being
paffed ouer, then the matter of doctrine

returneth

returneth againe.

This trace hath *Count Baltazar Castiglio* in his *Courtier*, and *Boetius* in his *Consolation* directly follovved; and *Plato* in his Compofitions more then any other. The vvhich Interlocutions though perhaps they may not fall out ftill to be fo pleafing as the doctrine it felfe;yet fo long as they be not vnproportionable to the matter vvhich they concerne, they may be permitted to paffe: becaufe vvhen all is done, he vvho vvill haue good ftore of corne, muft be content vvithall to take fome chaffe. Yet I cannot vvell deny,but that fome motions I haue had, to diminish heere and there fome difcourfes of the Interlocutors, had I not confidered vvithall, that one thing it is to publish a Booke, and another thing to publish but a Pamphlet; and alfo a Booke or Bookes of fuch particuler titles, as vvithout fome amplification made, fome of them doe render of themfelues but fmall difcourfe

of

of matter.

And therfore I haue refolued to let the Bookes paffe vvith all , and the very fame fpeaches , vvhich the Authors them-felues, haue vpon different occafions, in-terpofed : becaufe it vvill eafily be confi-dered , that Argumentations made by vvord of mouth , cannot fo clofely be compacted togeather, as may things more confiderately fet dovvne by pen ; though I hope it vvill appeare vvithall , that com-parably vnto other English Workes, no vvant of doctrine vvill heare be found. All vvhich is done for the inftruction of thofe only , vvho albeit they do not afpire to be counted Learned, may yet haue a defire to knovv the fcope of all Sciences, befides much Morality, & fome Oecono-my alfo, vvhich they may find here. So as vvith a fevv dayes reading they may know much , and vvith the price of one only volume quit the coft of many . To con-clude, diuers queftions no leffe pleafant

then

THE PROEME.

then profitable, not handled in thefe tvvo Volumes (as namely touching Policy, and many other curious matters) are referued for the other Volumes enfuing; to the end it may be feene in the meane vvhile, hovv gratefully thefe firft vvilbe accepted.

Qui nihil fperat, nihil defperat.

THE

THE BAYNES OF
A Q V I S G R A N E.

The I. Part, and I. Booke,

INTITVLED PROFIT.

The Dedication of the Relator, to the Profef-
fors in England of THRIFT.

IVERS there are amongst the variety of
men, who though they defire to haue Wealth
do not know how to get it. Others there are,
who though they know how to get it, haue not
either the patience, or will to take the paynes
to do it. And other fome alfo there are, who
when they haue it either left them by others,
or gotten by their owne inauftry, do not know how to keep it.
So that the way vnto Thrift, is not only to get, or to haue
Wealth gotten, but alfo to know how to gouerne & conferue it:
not couetoufly, aboue the ftynt of their conuenient need, as diuers

A   do;

do ; but temperately, proportionatly, and decently : since Thrift *ought to be the meane betwixt Liberality and Auarice, like as Liberality is the meane betwixt Auarice and Prodigality; though yet by errour or false interpretation, the one of these is sometimes taken for the other . As the couetous Gamester, by his continuall loosing, either at Dice or Cardes, may be thought to be prodigall though he be not : And on the other side the thriuing Merchant opressed at home with children more then he can well prouide for, may be taken to be couetous when he is not : Since, according to the old Saying,*He who hath a daughter to marry, hath need of money; & he likewise who hath two daughters to marry, hath need of more; but he who hath many daughters to marry, hath need of a great deale. *The which to get, some do vse publike violence, and these are commonly depriued therof againe (either they, or theirs) by the speciall prouidence of God : and some others hauing got their wealth with equity and vpright dealing, do prudently conserue and spend it; and these be only they, who may truely be termed* Thrifty . *Vnto which sort there needeth no more to be said, becaufe they haue the Lawes both of God and Men concurring with them . And therefore vnto those other two forts of Getters before mentioned, this first Booke of the first Volume of my Relation, is only intended, who though they pretend to be followers also of* Thrift; *yet is it no thriuing to get & conserue their goods, by such culpable meanes, as assuredly resteth punishable, as well by diuine, as by humane Iustice .*

Qui nihil sperat, nihil desperat.

INTER-

INTERLOCVTORS.

Aquilonius . Fauonius . Subſolanus .

RELATOR.

THE Intentions of men being by the di-
uerſity of Diſcourſe , and imbecillity of
nature, ſubiect vnto mutation; a difficult
thing it is to imagine, and much more to
determine , what reſolution to make of
purpoſes, and deſignes premeditated : be-
cauſe no ſooner is any one thing in tearmes to be reſolued,
but ſtraight there is wont to riſe a kind of feare, that ſome
errour may be committed therin . Whereupon I haue eft-
ſoones ſaid to my ſelfe (ſince I accepted the enterprize of
this worke in hand) that if I erre in any thing , it would
ſeeme to be in this, to haue taken vpon me to ſet downe
in writing the words of other mens diſputation and ſpea-
ches, not put together perhaps with ſuch care , nor with
that correctedneſ of ſtile , as things better thought of ,
might haue beene . Whereat, though I my ſelfe were preſent ; yet was I no more but a behoulder, as an allied Aſſi-
ſtant by name vnto one of the company, & chiefly drawen
therto by my owne curioſity, and for my priuate vſe only
to keep in record ſome remembrance of that which paſſed
amongſt them : gathering vp ſo well as my memory might

ſerue

ferue me to do, and but one alone to colleA all the arguments of three difputers ; making ftill this account with
my felfe, that if the matter fell not out to my lyking, nor
to be worth my paynes taken, then I might keep my loffe
fecret vnto my felfe without any blame at all : and that
if it happened to fall out otherwife; then I might poffibly
get fome further recompence of thankes, by imparting
the fame vnto others, fuch as would be glad to fee fo many
particularities of things, as this worke contayneth, treated
of in their owne language. So that now at laft the waight
of all that cogitation of myne, is come to depend vpon
this other poynt : to wit, Whether my labour may be any
whit gratefull vnto others, or no, if not for the manner of
handling (which is but by the way of Conference) yet
for the diuerfity of things heere handled? The which I wil
not vndertake to determine, becaufe I wil not preiudicate
either the Readers, or the worke it felfe: the one in refpeA
of the variety of mens Iudgments, and the other in refpeA
of my owne intereft, not to cenfure that which hath fo
voluntarily paffed through my owne handes. And therfore as one wel perfwaded of the beft, I will put thefe con-
fiderations, as it were, in a ballance, to counterpoife one a-
nother, & leaue them to ftriue as they will amongft themfelues, whiles I begin to performe fo much of my duty
as vnto me belongeth, by fupplying the office of a true Relator.

¶ Thou fhalt therfore vnderftand, good Reader, that
there happened of late to meet togeather in the auncient
Citty of *Aquifgrane,* three men of one nation, and of one
language, but of different Prouinces, & of diuers difpofiti-
ons. The firft a dexterous Northern-man, who being the
conduAer of a certaine Gentlemans fonne of thofe quarters, and a Politician by profeffion, was come thither only
for

for ſtipend and remuneration of his ſeruice, whome we will cal for the preſent by the name of A Q V I L O N I V S, according to the title of the Climate towards which he was borne. The ſecond was a far borne Weſtern-man, & by profeſſion a Proteſtant , but of the ciuiller ſort , come thither only, as trauellers be wont to do , for curioſity to ſee the place, whome for the like reſpect before alledged, we will call by the name of F A V O N I V S. And the laſt a middle dwelling Eſtern-man, who being a Catholike exiled, was come thither only by reaſon of ſicknes, to take in that place the commoditie of the Baynes (more vulgar-ly called Bathes) and him we will call, for the former reſ-pect, by the name of S V B S O L A N V S. Theſe three per-ſons, being wont, at one of their lodgings, to meet togea-ther often, were fallen one day into a more ſerious debate-ment then at any tyme before. Wherupon my ſelfe (who was lodged in a chamber of the ſame houſe) hearing them grow ſomewhat lowder then they were wont to be, reſol-ued to go in vnto them: & euen as I was entring into the chamber, I heard *Aquilonius* ſay theſe very words.

A Q V I L O N I V S. The world being a wonderfull machine of variety, of greatnes , and of admiration, con-tayneth in it diuers ſorts of creatures, but all of them con-ditioned and qualified like vnto it ſelfe; that is to ſay, full of intereſt, and rapine: the birdes of the aire by flying, the fiſhes of the water by ſwymming ; and the beaſts of the earth by running, to catch and deuoure whatſoeuer they can ouertake : why then alone ſhould man be blamed, for ſeeking in like manner to prouide for himſelfe, aſwell as the reſt; vnleſſe you would thinke it conuenient continu-ally to ſtriue againſt kind, as the Giants be ſaid by *Cicero* to haue done, when they ſtroue againſt the Heauens , the which would be no ſmall infelicity? Or that on the other

A 3

ſide

fide it fhould be good for vs by labouring all to be Angells
heere on earth, to derogate from the celeftiall fpirits their
due , and to vfurpe vnto our felues their bleffednes before
our time,which I thinke may be done foone inough,when
we ariue vnto the place where they be liuing:in the meane
while , in fuch fort, and with fuch an intermixture of cogitations and actions,as not depriuing vs alltogeather of
the way to Heauen, we may not alfo loofe the fruition of
thofe benefits which the world is ftill ready to beftow vpo
vs.   F A V O N I V S . Your manner of fpeach is fomwhat extrauagant,but yet to make therof the moft fauourable conftruction, my meaning was not in that which I
faid a little before to taxe the world in fuch a general fort,
as by this your anfwere it feemeth you vnderftand me to
haue done : but only to inferre vpon your owne words
fpoken in the behalfe of your mentioned friend, that the
world was like to haue inough to do, to fatisfy the worldlines of fuch fwelling fpirits , as he that thought himfelfe
to be another *Mercurius* . And this chiefly for only hauing
had the happe to vncipher a fimple ciphered Letter , and
no more : the which by all likelihood , either a follicitous
Merchant, or a common Notarie might well inough haue
beene able to do , no leffe then he .   A Q V I L O N I V S .
Though you make but light accompt therof;yet I do attri-
bute much vnto the mind of fuch a man, who being fo
well perfwaded of his owne doing, doth redouble therby
the force of all his other fufficiency . The which alone
were able to pricke him potently forward vnto fome notable degree of Excellency , in whatfoeuer profeffion he
fhould betake himfelfe vnto: fince the greateft operations
hitherto doneby any of the moft famous men of the world,
haue for the moft part been feen to take their beginning
from a good opinion of themfelues .   F A V O N I V S·
                                                                          So

So that , to be a notable well-weaner of himſelfe, and his owne doings, you take to be a principall ſtimulator vnto Excellency . A QV IL O N I V S . I ſee as yet no contrary reaſon, why, to alter my opinion therein . F A V O - N I V S . You put me in remembrance hereby , of a certayne Grecian Prince called *Clitus,* who for hauing ouerthrowne by ſea ſome three or foure little Barkes, gloryed ſo much therof, as he vſurped the name of the *God of the Waters,* & cauſed himſelfe to be called *Neptune* . A QV I - L O N I V S . If *Amaſis* the Egyptian had not had in him a great mind, and a greater opinion of himſelfe, & his owne doings , then his fortune would ſeeme by birth to haue allotted him , he had neuer riſen to be King of Egypt . F A V O N I V S . That ſame art of riſing, as I perceiue by your words, is a very principall and materiall point, which greatly occupieth and troubleth your mind . A - QV I L O N I V S . I know but few who either are not for the preſent, or haue not bene contented heeretofore , to trouble themſelues ſometimes with ſuch cogitations as theſe . F A V O N I V S . An old Philoſopher being asked by ſuch an aſpiring wordling , as you haue ſpoken of, what *Iupiter* was doing in heauen? anſwered: He doth nothing els but make ladders for ſome to aſcend, and ſome to deſcend by . A QV I L O N I V S . And what of this, I pray you? F A V O N I V S . His blindnes notwithſtanding was ſuch, as it rather increaſed his folly the other wiſe, by giuing him occaſion to perplexe himſelfe about the aſcending ladder only, but nothing at all about the deſcending . A QV I L O N I V S . I expect to heare the end of your intention . F A V O N I V S . My meaning herein is this , that ſuch worldly cogitations, be for the moſt part greater in the imagination , then they happen to prooue in effect . A QV I L O N I V S . Then belike you will reſemble

ble a worldly man vnto King *Agiau* his fhoomaker, who
was wont to make great fhooes for little feete.

¶ Heere *Subfolanus* interrupting a little their talke,
began to fay thus.   S v b s o l a n v s. In thefe myfti-
call reckonings of yours, me thinks you pay one another
like as a fouldier of *Ægipt* did, who only withthe found of
his money paid a brawling Cook, for the fmel of his roft-
meate ; fince what with variety, and what with obfcuri-
ty you determine of nothing.   A q v i l o n i v s. Indeed, as you fay, we Northern borderers be very obfcure
fellowes, for that we call a Hare a Hare, and a Dogge a
Dogge, when we talke togeather in our owne dome-
ftcalilanguage.   Favonivs. So that you leaue, I perceaue, vnto me (faid *Fauonius*) to anfwer vnto the imputed variety of our talke, as alfo to the not determining of
our things fomewhat better. And therfore to follow our
propofition a little more ftriclly then before, I fay now :
That whereas worldlines tranfgrefleth moft of all in exceffe, if it be on your part amended, & temperately moderated, the rekconing will be eafily made vp betwixt vs.
A q v i l o n i v s. As though in fuch a man (layd *Aquilonius*) as followeth the world attentiuely, there might
not be tolerated, fometimes, an once of exceffe in his a-
ctions, to get thereby a pound of credit.   Favonivs.
This kind of merchandize I do not well vnderftand.
A q v i l o n i v s. As for example, to commit fome fort
of exceffe, eyther in extending fomewhat too far the opinion of his owne fufficiency, or by vndertaking the execution of fome greater enterprize, then he is well able to
performe.   Favonivs. But what if his debility in
eyther of thefe cafes, fhould be afer difcouered ; would
not this be rather a difcredit, then a credit vnto him ?
A q v i l o n i v s. The difcredit were like inough to
be

be attributed to his attentiue forwardnes in the affaires
of the world, and the credit,if any happē,would fall vnto
himfelfe,aduancing him thereby not a little.　F A V O-
N I V S. So that forwardnes in worldly affaires , you
take to be a fufficient warrant to excufe any morall error
whatfoeuer.　A Q V I L O N I V S. I do fo indeed,*Fauonius*. But what if a man by louing the world ouer well,
fhould vtterly loofe himfelfe,yet his worldlines will not
fo eafely loofe herfelfe in him .　FAVONIVS. It feemeth
hereby you haue not yet confidered this other point, that
there is not fcarcely any thing in the world to be found fo
dangerous to be dealt withall,as worldlines it felfe,which
as fayth an old Doctour of your owne Schoole, in his
booke *De Ciuitate Dei*, leadeth men vnto things that be
vaine, hurtfull ,full of biting thoughts , perturbations ,
afflictions, feares , foolifh delights , difcords , quarrells,
warres , intrapments , wrath, enimity, falfity, flattery,
deceipt, ftealth, rapine , obftinacy , pride , ambition ,
enuy, flaughters of men, of parents, of friends, of kinfe-
men , cruelty ,malignity, carnalty, bouldnes , vnfhame-
faftnes,violence, pouerty,fornicatiō,adultery of all forts,
and other filthines,which are not fit to be fpoken of:fa-
criledge, herefies, periuries, oppreffions , calumniations,
preuarications , falfe teftimonies , iniuft Iudgments, in-
forcements, theeuery, and fuch like. And therefore not
without caufe is it elfewhere faid , That the world , with
her worldlings,is an affembly of wicked men a flaughter-
houfe of good men, a nourifher of vice, an oppreffor of
vertue , an enemy of peace, a freind of contention and
warre , a fweet receptacle of wicked men , a bitter inter-
tayner of good men , a defender of lies ,an inuentor of
nouelties,an vnquietnes of ignorant men, a Martyrdome
of euill men, a table of glottons, an ouen of concupif-

B　　　　　　　　fence,

fence, a *Carybdes* and a *Scylla* of fuffocating thoughts: Whereupon it is faid further by another, that the world doth hate thofe that do loue it, deceaue thofe that truft it, perfecute thofe that ferue it, afflict thofe that efteeme it, difhonor thofe that honor it, & forget thofe who do moft of all remember it: Whofe conuerfation is full of affli-ction, whofe myrth full of melancholy, whofe pleafure full of remorfe, whofe confolation full of fcruple, and whofe profperity is full of feare: Liberall it is in promi-fing, and fcarce in performing, producing many euills; and is the occafion of many miferable effects, beginning without any prudence, & ending with bitter repentance. And therfore it is to be beheld a far off, like a monftrous and rauenous beaft, leaft he that commeth too neere it, be deuoured by it. For the more familiar any man is with the world, the more perillous it is: vfing thofe men worfe who do fauour it, then thofe who do abhorre it: And to loue it, & not to perifh in it, is a thing impoffible, becaufe making fhew of one thing, it deceaueth men with another, like as *Iezabel* would haue deceaued *Iehu*, 4. *Reg*. 9. fhewing to him her fine platted head, but fought to hyde from him her further abhominations: So as many it de-ceaueth, and many alfo it vtterly blindeth. A Q V I-LO N I V S. Then to begin with your felfe for one; the world me thinkes would feeme to haue alfo blinded you, in not letting you fee whome you calumniate heerein. For who made the world, I pray you, that you will needs inueigh fo much againft worldlings? and that with fuch great exageration, as you haue vfed, to impeach the fame?

¶ Heere *Subfolanus* interpofing himfelfe betwixt them againe, fpake in this manner. S V B S O L A-N V S. Not fo hoatly, *Aquilonius*: this matter would be tal-ked of betwixt you a little more calmely. And therfore

to allay fomewhat your earneftnes , a conuenient occafion of fome little paufe is profered . We haue now talked
ftanding a good while : let vs therfore take thefe chaires
and fit downe , for that this Conference I doubt me, may
continue long . No ceremonies at all, I pray you . In this
lodging of myne , you muft be content to be ruled by me.
Take you the patience to fit heere , and you there : this o-
ther more vneafie feate you fhall giue me leaue to take to
my felfe . And let this be our cuftome ftill without any
more adoe , fo often as heerafter we fhall meet togeather,
admitting alfo this other allied Affiftant of myne , to be
prefent in the hindmoft place , to fupply all occafions
which may happen , & likewife for his owne inftruction
if he thinke good , to note downe any thing that fhalbe
faid , for he hath inke and paper there by him : who to
the end he may know, before hand , the fcope whereunto
our Conference hath to tend , and we alfo keep amongft
our felues the better accompt of our owne indeauours , it
will not perhaps be amiffe , if I do here begin (by your
good leaues and liking) to fet downe fome argumentes
fit to be fpoken of, during the twentie and feauen dayes ,
which we haue to abide in this Citty . And becaufe three
things do chiefly prefent themfelues to be heere confidered , namely the Variety of the World , the Subordination therof , and the Folly of the fame ; therfore the
firft nyne dayes we will treate of Variety ; the fecond
nyne dayes of Subordination ; and the laft nyne dayes of
the Folly of the world . And fo to begin firft with the
Variety of the World , becaufe , touching the fame, there
occurre three things to be confidered , namely Humane
Nature , the Mynd of man , and the Body of man (from
the which all Variety doth proceed :) therfore as concerning the firft branch , we will the firft three dayes debate

of *Profit*, of *Pleafure*, and of *Honour*: the fecond three dayes we will debate of *Ignorance*, of *Opinion*, and of *Science*: and the laft three dayes our Conference fhall be concerning *Education*, *Trauaile*, and *Repofe*. And now becaufe *Aquilonius* a little before hath fo earneftly asked, who made the world; I my felfe will take vpon me this burthen to tel it you, if you will but lend a little patience to heare the fame. So it is therfore that about the creation of the world, the Poets firft had two fictions, the one, that it was done by *Demogorgon*, *Eternity*, *Chaos*, and *Erebus*; and the other that it was made by *Iupiter*, *Hebe*, *Prometheus*, and *Epimetheus*, wherof the one is very foolifh and fond, and the other ridiculous. Alfo the Philofophers had diuers opinions therof. *Ariftotle* was of the mynd, that the world was *ab æterno*, & that confequently it fhould endure for euer. *Democritus* held, that it was created of infeparable *Atomi*: And *Plato* faith, that the primitiue matter therof was *ab æterno*, but that the world it felfe had a beginning, though it fhall haue no end. Finally our Deuins (who teach the infallible truth, as well concerning this point, as other matters of Faith) hold, that the world it felfe & the primitiue matter therof were both created, and therfore fubiect to corruption: all I meane faue the *Intellectuall fpirits*, and *Celeftiall bodyes* only, the which according to fome Deuines are eterniz'd by the excellency of their formes, and alfo of the matter that God hath giuen them; yet fo, as they are certainly to be tranfmuted, and purified againe, more then as yet they are. But whether the *Intellectuall*, the *Celeftiall*, & *Terreftriall* worlds were all created at once, fome diuerfity of opinions is found euen amongft the Deuins themfelues. For S. *Auguftine*, S. *Thomas*, S. *Bonauenture*, and all the other Doctors of the Scholes do generally hould, that there was of them all, but one creation: and this is taken for the

only

only true opinion. Though otherwise out of the doctrine
of some of the ancient Fathers, some thinke it may be
probably gathered that God created first the *Intellectuall,*
and *Incorporeall* world, that is to say, the Angels or Intelli-
gences. Secondly the *Cœlestiall* corporall world , contayning the *Spheres* of all the Heauens : and thirdly this *Ele-
mentall* corporall world of ours, and all things therin
contayned. Which doctrine may more particulerly be
drawne out of S. *Damascen , de orthodoxa fide, lib. 1. cap. 14.*
then out of any of the rest, where he saith : that the good,
and all good, and excelling good, that is to say Almighty
God , being Goodnes it selfe , would not suffer his sayd
Goodnes to remayne sole in himselfe, without communication therof to others; and therefore created first the
Angelicall world, next the Celestiall, and lastly the Ele-
mentall world . And according to this sense, some also do
expound the words of S. *Iohn* in his Ghospell, the first
Chapter, where he saith , *In mundo erat* , meaning therby
the Angelicall world : *Et mundus per ipsum factus est* , therby vnderstanding the Celestiall world, *Et mundus cum non
cognouit,* speaking of this Elemental world of ours; wherof Christ himselfe also spake when he said , *Regnum meum
non est de hoc mundo .* And heere haue I set downe these o-
pinions concerning the creation of the world , to the end
that the verity of the first may be distinguished from the
curiosity of the second . Now then to descend vnto the
subdiuision of this Terrestriall world , and the contents
therof. First it contayneth the soule of the same , with all
the primitiue procreable matters: Secondly it contayneth
the foure Elements of Fier , Aire, Water, and Earth, the
which are all corruptible , but yet of themselues perfect
and vnmixt: Thirdly the mixed Meteors of Haile , Snow,
and the like , the which are imperfect : Fourthly the

more perfect bodyes of Mettals and Stones, the which are without life : Fiftly the vitall bodyes of Hearbes, Plants , and Trees , the which are without fenfe : Sixtly the fenfible bodyes of Fifhes, Foules, and Beaftes , the which are without Reafon . And laftly it conteyneth the vitall, fenfible , and alfo reafonable Creature , to wit Man , whom God hath conftituted and appoynted to be Lord and Maifter ouer all the reft .   A QV I L O N I V S . Not ouer all ; for that the woodes and deferts , he hath conftituted for the habitation of wild beaftes : The paftures and meddowes for the feeding of cattell : The ayre for that habitation of birdes : and the feas and waters for the feeding of fifhes .   S V B S O L A N V S. This doth not alter the cafe at all , for euen as in a magnificent Pallace , although the Kitchin, Stable, and other like places are more to be inhabited by the feruants , then by the Lord and Patron himfelfe; yet the Pallace cannot be faid to be made for the feruants , but for the Patron only . And fo we may likewife fay of the vniuerfall World : That though the wild Beaftes , Cattell , Birdes , and Fifhes do inhabite a great part therof ; yet both they themfelues, and all the reft is made for the benefit of Man only. And that this to be true, what more manifeft argument can you haue , then that out of the woods and deferts the ftrongeft Lions , the fwifteft Tigers , and the moft monftrous Elephantes are taken , and tamed by Men, yea ledde vp and downe the world vnder the obedience and gouerment of Man ? Out of the paftures and meddowes he draweth to his yoke , the moft vntamed Bull : and vnto his bridle the moft fierce Horfe ; and vnto his trap the moft rauening Beare , or Wolfe . Out of the aire he bringeth into his fnares the wildeft fort of birdes , and maketh them after fo tame, that though he turne them

loofe

loofe abroad they obay his voice , and returne againe
vnto his lure . And out of the deepeſt ſeas he draweth into
his nets innumerable ſorts of fiſhes,yea the Whale himſelfe
falleth many tymes to his Prey,though he be ſometimes ſo
bigg,as an hundred men may ſtand hewing with their axes
the fleſh of his back . A QVILONIVS. Suppoſing
it to be as you ſay , that man may do great things in the
world , yet this would ſtill (me thinkes) be vnderſtood,
not by his contemning the world , but by his more and
more addicting himſelfe therunto ; otherwiſe, either he for
his part ſhould ſeeme to haue byn made in vayne , or the
world it ſelfe , touching temporall things , to haue been
made to ſmall effect. SVBSOLANVS. It is no mar-
uell at all, though the world, with her temporall ſmall effects, do herin deceaue you , ſince the ſame long before ,
with the only effect of the beauty of the prohibited apple
in Paradiſe , deceaued our firſt Mother *Eue*, before, by the
Serpent , the reaſons were yet giuen her to eate therof,*Gen.*
cap. 3. A QVILONIVS. My meaning is not to reach
ſo high , as vnto things done in Paradiſe , for that the caſe
ſince then is altered with vs not a little; only hereupon I
relye me , and no more; That the temporall wealth of the
world , to thoſe who liue in the ſame, is not to be contemned . SVBSOLANVS. To come downe therfore
ſomewhat lower ; the world with her glittering temporall
wealth , like as now it deceaueth you ; ſo heretofore , in o-
ther kinds, it hath done the like vnto others, as it deceaued
the children of *Iſraël* with the *Moabites* , *Num.* 25. *Sampſon*
with *Dalida* , *Iud.* 16 . *Acab* with 400 . falſe Prophets , 3.
Reg. 22. and *Naboth* with the falſe promiſe made by *Acab*
of a better vineyard then his owne , 3. *Reg.* 21 . the which
while *Naboth* attended to belieue , he was not only depriued of his vineyard,but alſo of his life . So that,the deceauing

uing fnares of the world, be *Auarice*, *Pleafure*, *Senfuality*,
Flatterie, and *Fallehood*: wherof, the Auarice corrupteth,
the Pleafure infecteth, the Senfuality wafteth, the Flattery fwelleth, and the Fallehood betrayeth: according as
in the world, it is eafie inough fo to do; for that the world
it felfe is like a Citty without a wall, a Houfe without a
dore, a Shippe without a helme, a Pot without a couer,
and a Horfe without a bridle.   A QVILONIVS.
None of all this though it cannot be well denied; yet we
alfo our felues, being more or leffe of the fame condition
that the world is, muft be contented to take the temporall
euill with the good.   SVBSOLANVS. Some temporall good, no doubt, there is in the world, though more
be the euill, and more frequently appearing then the good
it felfe. And therfore in the world there is not any ioy
without dolour, any peace without difcord, any quietnes without feare, any health without infirmity, any
bread without labour, nor any paftime without difcontentment: and which is worfe, ech where the wicked do
perfecute the good, as *Cain* did *Abel*, *Gen.* 4. *Ifmael*, *Ifaac*,
Gen. 21. *Efau*, *Iacob*, *Gen.* 27. *Saul*, *Dauid*, 1. *Reg.* 19. and
Iezabel; *Elias*, 3. *Reg.* 19. who againe for their labour, fo
foone as they, or any fuch other, be waxen rich, the
world doth make them poore, and thofe that be poore,
it maketh them rich, like as an Houre-glaffe putteth the
fand out of one cruet into another. So as no worldly man,
can haue in the world any animofity at all, for the inftability of his owne eftate, readier then to come downe
when he is at the higheft: and therfore, all the animofity of the world, remayneth with vertue, whofe ftate and
dominion is high and full of generofity, while being as it
is in the world, yet it pretendeth nothing of it. For which
refpeƈt, better it were for a worldly man, to the end he
may

may the more rely vpon vertue , to quit himfelfe of his
Wealth of his owne accord , rather then to be corrupted
therby, or to fee it confume away of it felfe , to his owne
greater dolour in the end .   A Q V I L O N I V S. This
counfell of yours is not vnlike vnto his , who aduifed his
friend , becaufe a tooth of his had bitten his tongue , to
pull out the tooth that did it, in reuenge of the dolour receaued therby ; though yet of the two, better a man may
liue without teeth , then he may liue without wealth ,
which muft nourifh the teeth, the tongue, and all the reft.
S V B S O L A N V S. If men were not feene , to become
by occafion of their wealth, worfe and worfe, according
as *Pharao, Saul*, and *Ieroboam* did , you might haue fome
colour to defend it: but this being fo, much better it were,
to be vnto vertue a poore flaue , then to be a rich free-
man to the world : fince the worldly man , while he followeth attentiuely his worldlines , doth togeather with
his worldly Pride loofe God , togeather with his worldly
Enuie loofe his neyghbour , and togeather with his
worldly Wealth loofe himfelfe : making a falfe fhew therby to haue in him that vertue which he hath not , and
therby couering withall thofe vices which he hath , becaufe he is afhamed of them . And yet for all this , he is
not able if he would , to rid himfelfe of his worldlines ,
vntill he become fo bare againe , as when into the world
he entred firft : and then , like as if all before had byn but
a dreame, he may well refemble himfelfe vnto *Ionas* , who
when he fell a fleep , he was couered with a greene Y uy ,
and when he waked , the Y uy being dried vp, he was left
wide open in the parching funne , *Ion . cap*. 4. Therfore
fee in what vnftable ftate , the meere worldly man doth
liue and wallow in the world , when he thinketh himfelfe
at the beft : though yet ftill it cannot be denied , but that,

C   as

as hath byn said before, all whatsoeuer is in the world,
either flying in the aire, or swimming in the water, or resi-
ding vpon the earth, God, indeed, hath made them all for
man, and all to be vnder his rule and commaundement,
as Lord and Maiſter of all.   A Q V I L O N I V S. Then
if God at leaſtwiſe, who made this terreſtriall world, haue
appointed man, as you ſay, to be Maiſter and Lord of all,
what reaſon is it, that he ſhould not loue the ſame?   S V B-
S O L A N V S. Let *Fauonius* anſwere to this if he will, for
that it moſt of all concerneth himſelfe, I hauing already
performed ſo much as my promiſe was.   F A V O N I V S.
I haue not (quoth *Fauonius*) directly ſaid as yet, that the
World is not to be loued, but that the exceſſe in louing it
is to be hated.   A Q V I L O N I V S. By this which now
you ſay, you affirme neither the one, nor the other, ſince
whatſoeuer is indifferent betwixt Loue and Hate, cannot
properly be ſaid either to be loued, or hated.   F A V O-
N I V S. Perhaps in this you deceaue your ſelfe, and ſo
much the rather, becauſe a great Deuine in his Booke of
Sentences ſaith : That the world is both to be loued and
hated ; meaning belike, that it is to be loued as the
worke of the Creator, and to be hated as the iuſtrument
of temptation vnto ſinne.   A Q V I L O N I V S. Your
citation of Diuinity, knowing as I do of what Schoole you
be, moueth me not ſo much, as the reaſon it ſelfe of your
argument; whereby ſtill you would make it a ſinfull thing,
I perceaue, for a man to liue in the world, like a worldly
man ; and yet not yong men alone, but old men alſo, do by
their actions argue the contrary ; while as none do proue
more worldly then old men themſelues, who you know are
the wiſer ſort of men.   F A V O N I V S. For all your
making ſo little accompt of my Diuinity, a daungerous
point I can tell you, it is, to determine what is ſinne, and
what

what is not, by this or that mans proceeding only, be he young or old. AQVILONIVS. I fpeake of multitudes both of the oldeft & wifeft fort of men, and not of any one particuler perfon alone. FAVONIVS. Let them be as old and as wife as they will, it is nether their age, nor their wit (but fome other higher myfterie) that can keep them from ftraying out of the true beaten path of difcipline. AQVILONIVS. Then belike old men, and the wifer fort of men, do not know what they do. FAVONIVS. As though it were not poffible for an old Wife man, fometymes to play the Foole? AQVILONIVS. If he play the Foole in any thing, it is in this, for not to attend to the World, and to his Profit, fo much as he ought to do; confidering the diuers wantes, to the which Age is dayly more, and more fubiect, as Eafe, Seruice, Aboundance of clothes, Extraordinary fuftenance, and the like, which cannot well be had without fome ftore of money. FAVONIVS. Nay rather the contrary, for that the more he attendeth in his age to worldlines and Profit, the more he may be faid to be ouerfeene therin; becaufe hauing, as then, but a little while to liue, the fame world which bringeth all, carryeth with it all away againe. And therfore fo long as old men be moderate in their defires, and cheerfull of Nature, their age, albeit it be not accompanied with any great ftore of Wealth, will not be very noyfome vnto them: but if they be immoderate & with all melancholy, their age wilbe dolorous vnto them, notwithftanding they be rich. And not only age, but youth alfo it felfe, in that cafe, would be no leffe, becaufe it is not the wealth, but the mind which maketh the well contented, either youth or age. AQVILONIVS. Me thinkes in this accompt you reft deceaued much, fince of the two, the immodeft Poore man, who

by

by reafon of his bouldnes can fhitt for himfelfe well inough, would feeme better able to fupport his age then may the modeft Poore man, whofe fhamefaftnes may be an occafion to make him indure much want. Befides that, being on the one fide afflicted with neceffity, and on the other fide with feare of his approaching death, he cannot but paffe a moft miferable age : And therfore I do repute the hauing of wealth, to be a very neceffary thing, not only for all forts of men, but chiefly for old men.   F A- V O N I V S . Yet it feemeth that in this point you forget your felfe greatly, fince old men be of nature fo couetous. that when they haue wealth, they be loath to fpend it : fo that it were allmoft as good not to haue it, as to liue befides it, and to feele the affliction of pouerty, no leffe then pooremen themfelues do, or rather more then they, by reafon of the care and folicitude that rich men haue to keep their wealth from being robbed or purloyned from them, which the poore old men be voide of. So that Pouerty and Age would better feeme to agree togeather, then age and welthines; & the rather becaufe when the houre of death approacheth, the poorer fort of men haue leffe anxiety to leaue their pouerty, then haue the more wealthy to forfake their riches .   A Q V I L O N I V S . You pleafe me with this point very well, and fay in effect as I would haue you : for that an old man without money, may be likened to a foule without a body . And therfore no meruaile if he defire euery houre to be rather out of the world then in it : And fo much the more, becaufe fuch a poore and needy old man carrieth for the moft part his eyes in his pocket, his eares in his belly, his teeth in his girdle, and his legges in his hands, which is but a miferable ftate to liue in . All which myferies may in an old man that is welthy be fupplied, by hauing others to read and write for him, with-

out

out vfing his fpectacles : and alfo by hauing others to tell
him what a clocke it is , without ayming at his dinner
tyme by his hungry ftomake: Likewife to haue others
to cut & carue his meate for him without carying about
him any knife of his owne : And laftly by hauing others
to beare him abroad either in his chaire or his coach;
without vfing the help either of ftaffe, or crutches : and
therfore of the two , yong men might better want the
wealth of the world , then old men ; though yet on the o-
ther fide a yong man without money may in a contrary
fimilitude to that before of an old man , be likened to a
body without a foule, wifhing rather in that cafe to haue
neuer come into the world, then fo to liue in it. And therfore for ought I can perceaue , it is neceffary for youth af-
well as for age , to attend alfo vnto Worldlines and Profit , fome by one kind of trade , & fome by another. And
he who hath no trade , nor reuenew to liue by , may v-
furpe the title of a Phifitian, or elfe of a Lawyet , for that
thefe men get money by bare words only, if others do but
conceaue an opinion of them , though they haue no skill
at all .   F A V O N I V S . Your counfell were good ,
and found if it would worke effect in deeds , fo well as it
feemeth to do in words : but though an vnskilfull Phifitian may fometymes get money, by practifing with men
leffe skilfull then himfelfe ; yet how an vnskilfull Lawyer
may be able to do the like , I cannot well perceaue : becaufe he may happen many tymes to contend with other
fuch Lawers as be skilfull indeed .   A Q V I L O N I V S.
This me thinks might be remedied by two or three ways,
according as I haue noted , by obferuing the proceedings
of our owne Countrey : to wit, either by a firme, and re-
folute boldnes (the which may many tymes put a fober
learned man to filence) or elfe by beftowing fome part

of his owne fees, to get the fauour of the Iudge : or otherwife by making friendfhip with his fellow Lawiers, to
fauour one another vnderhand, though they make fhew
to be great aduerfaries. FAVONIVS. Then by
meanes of thefe helps an vnskilfull Lawier, you fuppofe,
might be able well inough to make his Profit by the Law:
As if it were no greater a matter, to become a Lawier,
then to become a Clarke of a Market, whofe office it is,
whenfoeuer he is called vpon, to fee due meafure to be
made of Corne. AQVILONIVS. And what more
I pray you, hath to do the Lawier, then to fee good meafure to be made of Contracts, by alledging that, and no
more which his Clients euidences and teftimonies haue
already made knowne vnto him, without further medling
with the Law. FAVONIVS. This feemeth ftrange
vnto me, how a Lawier may fo quite himfelfe from
knowing the Law, who hath for his profit to excer-
cife the fame; when as it is neceffary for an ordinary fubiect, that hath but only to obay the Law, to be able after
a fort to know it. AQVILONIVS. It muft be
(you may fuppofe)but a very filly knowledg of the Law,
that a common Subiect may attaine vnto, and the rather
for that the grounds, not only of fome old forren Lawes
abroad, but alfo of fome newer Lawes vfed in certaine
parts of England, be fo intricate and obfcure, that one
Law is contrary to another, and yet both of them houlden
for good. As for example concerning old Lawes : The
Carthaginians had a Law, that in the tyme of peace no
fouldiar might fteale, becaufe he might liue by any ma-
nuall trade: but in the tyme of warre he might fteale, to
prouide both for his prefent need, and alfo for the tyme
to come. The *Ægiptians* had a contrary Law, that in
time of warre no fouldiar might fteale, for not hindring
therby

therby his Military difcipline; but in tyme of peace he might, becaufe he had not then any pay ; yet with this condition , that he fhould write his name for a Theefe in the booke of the hygh Prieft , and prefent vnto him alfo a note of the ftolne goods,to the end, that if the owner redemanded them , they might be reftored him , excepting only the fourth part, which was to remayne to the theefe, as alfo the whole, if it were not redemanded . Were not thefe Lawes , thinke you , one contrary to another ? F A-V O N I V s. Contrary they were, and fo perhaps the people, who made them, were no leffe côtrary of nature then their Lawes. A Q V I L O N I V S . What fay you then to the *Athenians* , who had amongft them an old Law , That euery man fhould take two wiues , to the end that no man for variety of pleafure fhould either keep concubynes , or pra& ife with other mens wiues : wheras on the other fide their Neighbours the *Lacedemonians* , had a contrary old Law, to wit, That euery woman fhould take two husbáds , to the end that one of them fhould be ftill at home, to prouide for the houfe, while the other was at the warres . Can there any thing be more contrary then thefe? F A V O-N I V S. You muft confider , that thofe Lawes were made in tyme of Gentility , and alfo by Cittyes of feuerall Iurifdictions , that were emulators in all things one to another. A Q V I L O N I V S. I propound you then another example at home amongft our felues , That in one Lordfhip the eldeft Sonne is to be heyre , becaufe he is fuppofed beft able to ferue his Prince; and in another Lordfhip the yongeft Sonne is to inherite all , becaufe he is leaft able to prouide for himfelfe : be not thefe alfo contrary Lawes the one to the other, and yet both of them houlden to be good? F A-V O N I V S. If both thefe Lawes were in vfe in two diftinct Lordfhipes houlden alike by Kinghts feruice , they might

import

import fome contrariety as you fay : but your latter cafe, is only for Landes which are houlden in Socage Tenure, according to our Law terme; and not for all fuch Landes neither, but for the fmalleft pait therof, and for that part alfo permitted only by the particuler cuftomes of fome Mannours, and not fo cōmaunded by the Law; the which Law may be knowne, no doubt, well inough vnto all, or the moft part of thofe who haue to obay it, notwith-ftanding your alledged contradiction . A Q V I L O-N I V S . Let vs then confider this other reafon, Whether ordinary fubiects fhould be bound fo ftrictly to know the Law, when as that which was Law the laft yeare, may this yeare be no Law at all, by occafion of fome new Sta-tute made againft it ? F A V O N I V S . Then by this accompt, becaufe the laft yeare there was peace and this yeare warre, the fubiects fhould not be bound to know when it is peace, and when warre ; not that I will infer hereof, that euery common Subiect fhould know the Law, fo exactly and particulerly as Lawiers themfelues, who make their profit of it ; but only to know the fame fuperficially and in generall : that is to fay, partly by Tra-dition, and partly by naturall Reafon . A Q V I L O-N I V S . Then naturall Reafon by your owne confeffion is halfe inough of it felfe in fubiects, to make them to know fo much of the Law as is neceffary for their voca-tion . F A V O N I V S . You fay very well, for fo much haue I confeffed already indeed . A Q V I L O-N I V S . But he who doth know any part of the Law by naturall Reafon, may he not execute by naturall Reafon fo much therof in his practife as he knoweth? F A V O-N I V S . I will not greatly deny, but that naturall Reafon alone may ferue well inough the turne to execute all forts of priuate Iuftice, the which extendeth it felfe no further

then

therby his Military difcipline; but in tyme of peace he might,becaufe he had not then any pay ; yet with this condition, that he fhould write his name for a Theefe in the booke of the hygh Prieft , and prefent vnto him alfo a note of the ftolne goods,to the end, that if the owner redemanded them, they might be reftored him, excepting only the fourth part,which was to remayne to the theefe,as alfo the whole, if it were not redemanded . Were not thefe Lawes , thinke you , one contrary to another ?   F A-V O N I V S. Contrary they were,and fo perhaps the people, who made them,were no leffe côtrary of nature then their Lawes.   A Q V I L O N I V S. What fay you then to the *Athenians* , who had amongft them an old Law , That euery man fhould take two wiues, to the end that no man for variety of pleafure fhould either keep concubynes ,or practife with other mens wiues : wheras on the other fide their Neighbours the *Lacedemonians* ,had a contrary old Law,to wit,That euery woman fhould take two husbâds, to the end that one of them fhould be ftill at home, to prouide for the houfe,while the other was at the warres.Can there any thing be more contrary then thefe?   F A V O-N I V S. You muft confider , that thofe Lawes were made in tyme of Gentility , and alfo by Cittyes of feuerall Iurifdictions , that were emulators in all things one to another. A Q V I L O N I V S. I propound you then another example at home amongft our felues , That in one Lordfhip the eldeft Sonne is to be heyre , becaufe he is fuppofed beft able to ferue his Prince; and in another Lordfhip the yongeft Sonne is to inherite all , becaufe he is leaft able to prouide for himfelfe : be not thefe alfo contrary Lawes the one to the other,and yet both of them houlden to be good?   F A-V O N I V S. If both thefe Lawes were in vfe in two diftinct Lordfhipes houlden alike by Kinghts feruice , they might

import

import some contrariety as you say : but your latter case, is only for Landes which are houlden in Socage Tenure, according to our Law terme; and not for all such Landes neither, but for the smallest part therof, and for that part also permitted only by the particuler customes of some Mannours, and not so cõmaunded by the Law; the which Law may be knowne, no doubt, well inough vnto all, or the most part of those who haue to obay it, notwith-standing your alledged contradiction.　A Q V I L O-N I V S. Let vs then consider this other reason, Whether ordinary subiects should be bound so strictly to know the Law, when as that which was Law the last yeare, may this yeare be no Law at all, by occasion of some new Sta-tute made against it ?　F A V O N I V S. Then by this accompt, because the last yeare there was peace and this yeare warre, the subiects should not be bound to know when it is peace, and when warre ; not that I will infer hereof, that euery common Subiect should know the Law, so exactly and particulerly as Lawiers themselues, who make their profit of it ; but only to know the same superficially and in generall : that is to say, partly by Tra-dition, and partly by naturall Reason.　A Q V I L O-N I V S. Then naturall Reason by your owne confession is halfe inough of it selfe in subiects, to make them to know so much of the Law as is necessary for their voca-tion.　F A V O N I V S. You say very well, for so much haue I confessed already indeed.　A Q V I L O-N I V S. But he who doth know any part of the Law by naturall Reason, may he not execute by naturall Reason so much therof in his practise as he knoweth?　F A V O-N I V S. I will not greatly deny, but that naturall Reason alone may serue well inough the turne to execute all sorts of priuate Iustice, the which extendeth it selfe no further

then

then for one Neighbour to render to another his dew , so
far forth as Humanity , and Charity do oblige him therunto : But for the practise of publike Iustice in Courts of
Record , there is required the help of more art , according
as hath been said before .   A Q V I L O N I V S . Then
by this I perceaue you will now allot vs two sorts of Iustice , wherof the one hath to proceed from the morality
of the mynd , and the other from the equity of the Law .
F A V O N I V S . Not only from the equity of the Law ,
which consisteth in the Reason therof; but also from the
force of the Law , which consisteth in the authority of
the same : the first being to be called the Body , and the
second the Soule; and both of them tending togeather ,
to teach as well what is good, as to prohibite what is euil;
without which two helps (as saith *Plutarke* , in his Mo-
rals) it were hard for vs to inioy the benefits which God
hath bestowed vpon the world . And therfore not without cause it is said by *Plato* , in the ninth of his Laws, That
men without Law, *nihil à feris atrocissimis discreparent.* A-
Q V I L O N I V S . And yet I haue heard it said, That those
men be better that haue no Lawes at all , then those
that haue good Lawes , and do not keep them .   F A-
V O N I V S . The reason is , because good Lawes vnkept
do in some sort extenuate the ordinary Law of Nature;
for that with such as haue no written Lawes at all, the
Law of Nature is seene to be more of force .   A Q V I-
L O N I V S . In all places where I haue been the Law of
Nature is much extenuated , for that euery where I find
good Lawes inough, but very few of them executed, except against poore men only : wheras the rich by force of
their wealth , do escape all penalty ; like as the great flies
do passe through the Cobwebs , but the little ones , not
being able, do rest intrapped .   F A V O N I V S . But do
you

you take this to be the fault of the Law, or of thofe who
fhould better execute the fame?   A QV I L O N I V S.
Of the executors therof, and not of the Law ; for that the
Law it felfe is always good, and profitable, if it be executed accordingly.   F A V O N I V S . All thefe things
being well confidered, then how may your ignorant Lawier, before mentioned, be able by his Ignorance to make
any profit to himfelfe, in the practife and execution of the
Law, without knowing the fame?   A QV I L O N I V S.
His faid practife alone, if not in the principall Courtes of
Record, yet in their inferiour Courtes of Iuftice, wilbe
able in a little while to teach him fo much knowledg of
the Law, as he may make a competent profit of it.   F A-
V O N I V S . Then you will haue him at the firft to fell that
v nto others, which he hath not himfelfe, vntill at their
charges and alfo loffes, his faid ignorant practife may haue
yielded him both knowledg and profit : which were as
much to fay, as for the following of his worldlines, to become a publick deceauer, and a betrayer of Iuftice.   A-
QV I L O N I V S. Me thinks you go a little to farre in applying thofe vndecent Termes, vnto fuch a ciuill way of
getting money, as is the trade of Lawiers.   F A V O-
N I V S. Then what haue you to fay to the words of *Laer-
tius* : *Quod damnum potius, quàm turpe lucrum eligendum eft* ?
A QV I L O N I V S . As much as you can be able to fay to
the words of *Iunenall: Lucri bonus odor ex re qualibet*. Let vs
fet the Hares head vnto the Goofe giblets, and fo make vp
the quittance.   F A V O N I V S . I fee by this, you be
apt inough inclined to proportion the meafure of honefty
by the meafure of riches, and not the meafure of riches by
the meafure of honefty.   A QV I L O N I V S. I can
tell you, that to talke now adayes too much of honefty,
chiefly amongft young men who attend vnto Profit, is a
                                                    thing

thing that euery where offendeth the ftomake; and the
rather, for that to fhunne any kind of commodity, for
fcrupuloufnes of honefty, wilbe attributed to folly more
then to wifdome.　F A V O N I V S. Do you not know
that euery commodity bringeth with it her incommodi-
ty, and that commonly, accordirg to the Prouerbe, *Ill
gotten goods, are ill ſpent* .　A Q V I L O N I V S. Let
them be ſpent as ill as they will, while at the leaftwiſe,
this I do know well inough, that he who ſpeaketh againft
Commodity and Profit, ſpeaketh againſt Induſtrie, a-
gainſt Sodality, yea againſt Iuftice it ſelfe : for that if
Iuftice were not commodious and profitable, who would
extoll her to be the Queene of the World, according as
commonly ſhe is reputed euery where to be ?

　¶　Heere *Subſolanus* perceauing that *Fauonius* began
to make ſome ſhew of wearines, ſaid vnto *Aquilonius*,
fomewhat angerly.　S V B S O L A N V S. O ſacred
Iuftice, how many be there, that doe calumniate thy
Name, and how few on the other ſide, that do ſeeke to
defend thee !　A Q V I L O N I V S. *Aliud ex alio malum:*
there is now another ftone fallen into the well, which is
like to difturbe all the water. What cauſe haue you (ſaid
Aquilonius) to make any ſuch exclamation in fauour of
Iuftice ; when as nothing hath yet been ſpoken, that may
any way found to her derogation ?　S V B S O L A N V S.
As though it were no derogation vnto her to be extolled
more for the mercenarie Commodity that may be made
of her, then for her owne proper integrity.　A Q V I-
L O N I V S. Hould your ſelfe contented, for I haue only
made mention of her, comfortably vnto that her externall part, which is moſt appropriated vnto vs, and to
our particuler good, leauing her internall integrity vnto
her ſelfe, as a part of her owne Eſſence.　S V B S O L A-

N V S. Then belike you take the Eſſence of Iuſtice to be made of many mixtures, ſince you impute integrity to be one of them .   A QV I L O N I V S. Whether integrity be her whole Eſſence, or but a part therof, I will not much ſtand vpon it; ſince vnto me it ſhall ſuffice, that ſhe be only voyd of paſſion, becauſe the ſame obſcureth the true vnderſtanding of Controuerſies betwixt partie and party .   S V B S O L A N V S . Altogeather without paſſion ſhe cannot well be, for then ſhe ſhould haue in her no anger wherwith to puniſh the wicked , nor yet on the other ſide, no affectionate loue, wherewith to incite her to reward the good .   A QV I L O N I V S . By this it would ſeeme to follow, ſince you begin to reckon vp appetites , that it were requiſite alſo for her to be ſomewhat ſuſpitious, to the end ſhe may penetrate into the maliⅽe of all falſe meaſures and meanings.   S Y B S O L A N V S. Your meaning ſeemeth to be good, but your termes agree not therewith , ſince the ſame appetite or paſſion, which in men of little wit is called Suſpition, may be called in the wiſer ſort , by the name of Circumſpection; the which of it ſelfe may ſuffice vnto the doing of Iuſtice well inough betwixt party and party; becauſe no Iudge is bound to proceed beyond that which is produced , except in Criminall Cauſes only : for that in theſe, it is requiſite, to proceed ſometimes by due coniectures; I meane in cauſes touching life and death , at the leaſt touching the preuention of diuers ſorts of euills , the which might grow too farre, if nothing ſhould be attempted againſt the contriuers therof, vntill the commenced crime might be iuridically proued .   A QV I L O N I V S. If all this be true , that in ciuill cauſes a Iudge hath not to proceed any further by his art, then according to the proofe produced , and that alſo in Criminall Cauſes he may leaue,

if

if he will, all art a fide, and proceed by conie&ures : then
as little Law, for the getting of his liuing may ferue vnto
a Iudge, as may haue ferued our forefaid praétifing Lawier, fince naturall reafon alone, is able ftill in Criminall
Caufes to penetrate far inough by conie&ure, as alfo to
diſtinguiſh the right from the wronge in Ciuill Caufes,
wḥen fufficient euidence is giuen on both fides, and he
not to paffe any further, then according to the fame.
SVBSOLANVS. Then any man that hath not meanes
to liue by, may counterfait himfelfe for his prcfit to be
of what Trade he will, and fo by little and little afcend
vnto the higheft degree of his countertaite profeffion.
AQVILONIVS You fay very well herein, for fuch is
now the practife of the world. As for example how many fimple Apothecaries haue afcended by that meanes to
be formall Phifitians? How many petty Scholemaifters
haue mounted to be preachers in Diuinity, as if they had
been Doctours of that art? and how many crafty Scribes
in vnder Offices haue growne to be eftemed for fubftan-
tiall Lawiers? and alfo of thefe, how many haue afterwards become to be Stewards vnto Noble men of their
Lands, and fo by fitting there as Iudges, to render iuftice
betwixt partie and partie, perhaps with as little Law in
their heads, as they had abftinence in their hands, from
taking of bribes? SVBSOLANVS. Then a man
that hath no skill in the Law at all, may not only for his
profit be a practifing Lawier, as you haue faid, but may
now alfo rife vp to be a certaine kind of Iudge, and fo to
know in that office how to execute Iuftice. AQVI-
LONIVS. Albeit you fpeake this in derogation of that
vnskilfull Iudge of myne; yet fo long as he with the good
liking and fatisfaction of others, can know how to make
to himfelfe a fufficient cōmodity of his faid profeffion,

what

what more skill fhould he need to require? S v b s o-
L a n v s. So that this Iudge of yours, if he haue fufficient
skill to fell Iuftice for money , which is a reproachfull
thing , you thinke him for all the reft , to be able inough to
execute that office . As if to know how to make his owne
profit , were to know how to execute Iuftice . .   A-
q̃ v i l o n i v s. Though you feeme to make the execution of Iuftice fo hard a matter , yet I cannot fee why fuch
an vnlearned Iudge may not do it very wel, only by knowing how to abftaine from doing Iniuftice . S v b s o-
l a n v s. This is a new kind of learning , fcarcely heard
of before, and therfore not thought of by many . A-
q̃ v i l o n i v s. It is not fo new as you imagine; for it is
the doctrine of *Socrates* , who faid (as *Xenophon* reporteth)
that the very abftayning from doing Iniuftice, is Iuftice it
felfe . S v b s o l a n v s. If this were true, as you
fay (that to abftaine from Iniuftice , were Iuftice) then
to abftaine from not committing any foolifh Act , fhould
be Prudence; and to abftaine from not doing any temera-
rious enterprize, fhould be Fortitude ; and alfo to abftaine
from not eating of poyfon, fhould be Temperance. But
Vertue it felfe being otherwife agreed vpon by the Philofophers , not to confift at all in the leauing of any euill
thing vndone , but in the voluntary doing of good things,
therfore none of tho e former abftinences in manner and
former as they be related , can be truly reckoned for Vertues . As alfo againe , they cannot yet be Vertues , for another reafon ; to wit , becaufe whatfoeuer is equally diftant
from payne and reward , cannot be either Vice or Vertue; fuch I meane, as may be either offenfiue , or helping
vnto others . For if it merit not to be punifhed, it is no fuch
criminal!Vice as the Law taketh care of; and on the other
fide , if it merit no reward , it is no fuch eminent Vertue as
                                                          is

is had in any eftimation. For where do you find, that any
State or Citty did euer reward any man, becaufe he was
a Drunkard? or did euer receaue any one to be a Cittizen amongft them, becaufe he was a Glutton? or did
euer prefer any man to be an Arbitrator in Controuerfies,
becaufe he was a fluggard? But to the end this may yet appeare vnto you more plainely, I will propound you another example The famous *Ariftides* of *Athens*, a man of
great authority but very poore, was fent by the Senators
of that Citty, vnto certaine their Confederate Ilanders,
partly to moderate their exceffe of payments (becaufe
they tended to Rebellion) & partly to gather vp certaine
old Tributes. This *Ariftiae* hauing by his wifdome fet all
things in good order amongft them, returned home a-
gaine, more poore then he went forth, without hauing
benehted himfelfe any thing at all by that office, as many
others would haue done. Heere I fay, if any one fhould
haue gone about to haue perfwaded the Cittizens of
Athen, that *Ariftides* did merit to be receaued home with
great Triumph and Honour, becaufe in executing the office committed vnto his charge. he had not taken, to fuftaine his pouerty, any vnlawfull bribe at all: would not
this, thinke you, haue been rather laughed at, then graunted? Wheras on the other fide, if it fhould haue been faid
vnto them, that *Ariftides* did merit to be receaued home
with Triumph and Honour for as much as hauing wife-
ly moderated the exceffe of thofe payments, and reduced
downe the old tributes vnto the ability of the people, who
were before oppreffed therby, and that he had fo preuented a generall reuolt of all thofe mifcontented Ilanders
from the confederation of the *Athenians*: Heere in this fecond cafe, I fay, the fame being thus propounded the Cittizens could hardly haue thought him vnworthy, either
of

of Triumph, or of fome other Honour, becaufe by his iuft
operation in that action he had ftood them in great fteed,
and done them great feruice; wheras in the fame very cafe
as it was propounded before, no fuch Triumph or Honour
could well be graunted him, becaufe nothing therein was
faid to be done by him, worthy of the Honour demaunded,
but fomewhat only left vndone, touching his owne particuler, which merited no publike remuneration. And
therfore for all thefe reafons put togeather, I may now
conclude againft your former affertion, that the not doing
of Iniuftice, is no worke of Iuftice at all, becaufe Iuftice
confifteth not in the leauing of any vniuft thing vndone,
but in the skilfull executing of that which is iuft. A-
QVILONIVS. Notwithftanding all this, if on the o-
ther fide it may be truly faid, as all the morall Writers do
affirme, that the firft part of Vertue, is to abftaine from
Vice; why then may it not be faid as well, that the firft
part of Iuftice, is to abftaine from Iniuftice? SVB-
SOLANVS. Thefe be different manners of fpeaking, to
fay, that the firft part of Iuftice is to abftaine from Iniuftice, and to fay, that to abftaine from Iniuftice, is Iuftice:
for though the extremity of one contrary, may be the beginning of another; yet they cannot enter the one into the
other. As for Example, the extremity of too much Liberty, may be the beginning of Seruitude, but yet not part of
Seruitude, for that Liberty & Seruitude can haue no affinity togeather, no more then Iuftice and Iniuftice : and
therfore though a man, altogeather vnlearned, may leaue
fometimes to do Iniuftice, yet can he hardly be a good Iu-
fticer, nor know how to do Iuftice, without fpeciall skill
in the Law : fo that the doing of Iuftice is a thing of greater moment, then the leauing of Iniuftice vndone; for
that this may be common vnto euery man, whereas the o-
ther

ther is but proper vnto Lawiers only . A Q V I L O-
N I V S. So as your meaning is , that Iuſtice doth not con-
ſiſt in leauing any vniuſt thing vndone , but in doing of
that which is iuſt , not according to euery skilfull mans
conceipt therof , but as the Law it ſelfe ordaineth , the
which ordaineth nothing but that which Iuſtice doth determine and commaund. S V B S O L A N V S. You ſay
well , and according to my meaning : wherupon it would
follow , that if to do that which the Law commaundeth ,
ſhould be Iuſtice , then the reſiſtance and not doing of that
which the Law commaundeth, ſhould be Iniuſtice . A-
Q V I L O N I V S. It may be well inough as you ſay, though
yet your ſpeach be ſomewhat too ſtrict, and not according
to the common vnderſtanding therof . S V B ‘ O L A-
N V S. Then you haue belike ſome ſcruple in your head
whether it be ſo , or no . A Q V I L O N I V S. As
touching my ſcruples, take you no care , for when they be
of any moment, they ſhallbe ſufficiently made knowne vnto you . S V B S O L A N V S . So that without any
ſcruple of yours herein , you will haue me to vnderſtand
that Iuſtice & Iniuſtice, may be ſaid to be contraries. A-
Q V I L O N I V S. According as you haue laied them ſo
oppoſite one to another, they would ſeeme at the leaſt wiſe
ſo to be. S V B S O L A N V S. Then belike they be not
ſo indeed. A Q V I L O N I V S. Since you will needs
vrge me ſo farre , I muſt tell you , that as contrary as you
ſeeme to make them , yet diuers tymes it happeneth , that
one and the ſame man, may be both iuſt and vniuſt as well
as one and the ſame man may be a Niggard and Prodigall;
the which if they were meerly contraries , could not come
ſo to paſſe S V B S O L A N V S. I do not vnderſtand
you well, in neither of theſe caſes. A Q V I L O-
N I V S . Tell me then , I pray you , He that is a Niggard

E

in eating, or in apparrelling, or in paying his feruantes wages ; may he not be Prodigall either in building, or in furniture of houfhould, or in beftowing vpon flatterers? S v b s o l a n v s. I do not deny but that fo it may be. A qv i l o n i v s. And fo on the other fide, he that is iuft to his friends, may he not be vniuft to his enemies, as diuers be feene now a dayes to be?   S v b s o l a n v s. I will not greatly ftand vpon it.   A qv i l o n i v s. Then hereby it would appeare, that Iuftice and Iniuftice are not fo meerly contraryes as you fuppofe them to be. S v b s o l a n v s. To the end you may the better know what my conceyt is herein, let me aske you ere we go any further this other queftion; That fame worldly Profit of yours, wherof you haue fpoken fo much before, fhall we fay, that it is contrary to Difprofit, or that it is not?   A-qv i l o n i v s. I like fo little of Difprofit, and fo well of Profit, that I am content to admit them for contraries. S v b s o l a n v s. So that no Difprofit can be profitable, nor no Profit difprofitable.   A qv i l o n i v s. You fay very truely herein.   S v b s o l a n v s. For, if Difprofit could be profitable, or Profit difprofitable, they fhould not be contraryes.   A qv i l o n i v s. We agree hitherto very well.   S v b s o l a n v s. And yet it hapeneth fometimes, that the giuing of ten fhillings to a poore friend, that would borrow ten pounds, is a pro-fitable Difprofit: as on the other fide, the taking a horfe in gift of one that intrudeth therby to foiourne fome while at his houfe, is a difprofitable Profit.   A qv i l o-n i v s. What will you inferre hereupon?   S v b s o-l a n v s. I inferre, that as Profit and Difprofit are merely contraryes, by your owne confeffion, and yet one and the felfe fame thing may be profitable & difprofitable; fo alfo one man may be iuft and vniuft, though Iuftice and Iniu-ftice

ſtice be contraries ; which Conſequence you ſeemed to
deny before, affirming, that if Iuſtice and Iniuſtice were
meerly contraries , one man could not be both iuſt and
iuiuſt . A QVILONIVS . Whatſoeuer I haue ſaid
before concerning this point according to the vulgar
opinion , that which I wiſhed to be debated , and do
now affirme , is , that Iuſtice, and Iniuſtice may be both
of them profitable , and diſprofitable. As firſt , concerning their Diſprofit , I ſay , that as well Iuſtice as Iniuſtice may be diſprofitable to ſuch Iudges , or Magiſtrates,
as do runne too apparantly without any artificiall moderation, either vnto the one extremity, or the other, wherby they become to be either of them poore : the violent
Iniuſticer by his infamie, and the violent Iuſticer by
his ſcrupuloſity ; the one of which cauſes may be exemplified in the perſon of *Hyperbolus* , and the other in the
perſon of the allready ſpecified *Ariſtides* , both of them
Cittizens of *Athens* ; the firſt the iniuſteſt, and the ſecond
the iuſteſt of the times they liued in , and acknowledged
of all men to be ſuch ; who died both of them alike, that is
to ſay very poore , and in vtter diſgrace of the people.
SVBSOLANVS . Touching thoſe two men, I ſhall tell
you my mynd , when you ſhall haue made a full end of
your narration . A QVILONIVS . And now on
the other ſide, I ſay againe vnto you , that Iuſtice and Iniuſtice may be both of them ſaid to be profitable , ſpecially vnto ſuch kind of Iudges , or Magiſtrates , as do know
how to runne a middle courſe betwixt the extremities of
Iuſtice and Iniuſtice, wherby ſecretly, and couertly, making their Profit the one of his Iuſtice, the other of his Iniuſtice, they become both of them Rich: the firſt of which
cauſes may be exemplified in *Pericles* and *Alcibiades* in
Athens , and the ſecond may be in *Lyſander* , and *Ageſilaus*
E 2 in

in *Lacedemonia*, who knew the way so well to runne the middle courte betwixt scrupulous Iustice & defamed Iniustice, as all of them died very rich, & not only well esteemed in their Cittyes, but famous also to the world abroad: which hap befell not in *Rome* it selfe, neither to *Graccus*, nor yet to *Cato*, notwithstanding they were reputed of all other, the iustest men of their tyme, who, as I haue said, not knowing how to runne this myddle courfe, died both of them miserably.   S v b s o l a n v s. You haue here alledged thefe examples in regard of the fucceffes happened, not as they were indeed : but yet you do not penetrate aright into the true caufes of the fame. For that the Citty of *Athens*, in the tyme of *Hyperbolus*, had great fame for the integrity of Iustice praĉtised therin, and therfore no meruaile, though fuch an iniust man was there of no reputation; wheras after, in the tyme of *Aristides*, *Athens* was become to be infamous for Iniustice according as *Rome* was also in the tyme of *Graccus* and *Cato*; and therefore as little meruaile it is, that fuch iust men as they, could not thriue there amongst them : but when *Lysander* and *Agesilaus* liued in *Lacedemonia*, and *Pericles* and *Alcibiades* in *Athens*, both of thefe Cittyes were neither apparantly iust, nor apparantly iniust; and therfore for men of their conditions to grow to be great in fuch Cittyes, as were allready like vnto themfelues, it is also no great meruaile : fo as that artificiall Iustice, and Iniustice, wherof you haue fpoken, be not alwayes fure to profper, or to paffe vnreprehended, if not alfo punished; chiefly if the gouerment vnder which thofe men do liue, be iust and vpright of it felfe : and therfore your reafons before alledged in the behalfe of thofe particulers, be not altogeather fo firme as you fuppofed.   A q v i l o n i v s. Thefe be no more but diftinĉtions of ages and places, when & where Iustice

and

and Iniuſtice may be more or leſſe profitable or diſprofitable; but do not therfore diſproue, that Iniuſtice ſometimes may not be profitable, and Iuſtice diſprofitable;
nor yet on the other ſide, that Iniuſtice ſometimes may
not be diſprofitable, and Iuſtice profitable: I meane at
leaſtwiſe vnto ſuch a Iudge, or Magiſtrate, as knoweth
how to ſell the ſame for money, which yet it may be, you
will alſo reckon togeather with the reſt to be a kind of Iniuſtice.   Svbsolanvs. You ſay well, and according as I do reckon it indeed; but yet to be ſuch a kind
of Iniuſtice, as is farre more tolerable then is the violating of Iuſtice, by the doing of Iniquity and Wrong : and
therfore taking Iuſtice to be commodious in the trueſt
ſenſe, as when it is executed for Equity, and not for Gaines, in this ſort I ſay, my meaning is not to diſproue at all
(as you before would ſeeme to ſuppoſe) that either Iuſtice is profitable, or Iniuſtice diſprofitable : but rather
the contrary, to wit, that Iniuſtice may be profitable, or
Iuſtice any way diſprofitable, either to the publicke, or
elſe in particuler.   Aqvilonivs. Then all the
difficulty reſteth ſtill (I perceaue) touching thoſe two
latter points, wherin leauing aſide for a while to ſpeake
of diſprofitable Iuſtice, till better place may ſerue for the
ſame, I cannot for the reſt but meruaile with my ſelfe,
how you haue not yet perceaued out of my former Examples, that Iniuſtice ſometymes may be profitable.
Svbsolanvs. You muſt vnderſtand, that I haue
perceaued ſo much the leſſe for theſe conſiderations following ; becauſe if Iniuſtice may be profitable, it muſt be
profitable either to the whole State in general (the which
I thinke you will not ſay) or els to the Executor therof
in particuler; and this alſo but in ſome reſerued ſort of
proceeding only, ſince in Cauſes of publike and apparant

Iniquity

Iniquity by your owne confeſſion, it cannot be ſo; vnto which reſerued ſort I do now begin to anſwere you , that though by deceipt of vnderſtanding, ſuch a cunning corrupted Iudge may ſuppoſe to gaine therby, yet in the end when he commeth to put togeather his reckoning , and to make vp his whole accompt , he will not find it to be ſo.   A Q V I L O N I V S . What better accompt will you haue him, or can he deſire to make for himſelfe herein (I meane according to the preſent ſtate of the world, and his better meanes alſo to be able to withſtand the miſeries therof) then to find himſelfe prouided therby of all kind of neceſſaryes belonging to the maintenance of his degree and ſtate, the which ſome other of his owne profeſſion and trade, either for too much ſcrupuloſity , or els for too little dexterity do many times want .   S V B S O L A N V S . So that you would haue him (I perceaue) at one and the very ſame time, to ſerue himſelfe not only of Iniuſtice, but alſo of Iuſtice , vſing the one fraudulently , and vnderhand for his ſecret gaine, and exteriourly vſing the other for his reputation only , and to colour therby the Iniquity of Iniuſtice.   A Q V I L O N I V S . The cuſtome of the world now a dayes is come, I can tell you, but vnto little better paſſe .   S V B S O L A N V S . Then all thoſe Iudges , who will not after this manner be vniuſt , may be accompted for ſilly men. A Q V I L O N I V S . For ſilly men you may be ſure , and the rather becauſe,by the art and authority of the ſaid vniuſt ſort of Iudges, the Iuſtice of the Iuſt is many times reputed to be counterfait,and ſuborned Iniuſtice.   S V B S O L A N V S .So that the iniuſt Magiſtrate by this meanes getteth not only wealth,but alſo reputation to be accompted an adminiſtrator of Iuſtice, while the iuſt Magiſtrate liueth poorly, and is with all reputed to be iniuſt by the

falſe

falſe ſuggeſtion of his fraudulent Aduerſaries. A-
QVILONIVS. We ſee it for the moſt part to come ſo
to paſſe. SVBSOLANVS. Wherupon it followeth
that to learne to be a cunning Iniuſticer, were a very profitable kind of art? AQVILONIVS. Our inten-
tion being heere to ſpeake of Profit, I cannot alledge you
any Art that may be more profitable; and that profitable
Artes are not to be neglected, is not my thinking alone,
but the opinion of *Plato* (in the eight of his Lawes) who
ſaith, *Omnes complectuntur artes ex quibus lucrum conſequi
poteſt.* SVBSOLANVS. Though *Plato* ſignifyed in
thoſe words that men be prone to imbrace any profitable
Art; yet meant he not that all profitable Artes, are to be
imbraced (but only ſuch as are lawfull) and leaſt of all
any Art that tendeth to the corruption of publicke Iuſtice, as it euidently appeareth throughout all his Workes,
and eſpecially in his Bookes *de Republica,* and of his Lawes,
wherin all his doctrine tendeth to nothing els, but to frame
a moſt happy Common Wealth by the adminiſtration of
ſincere Iuſtice: and therfore he ſpecially endeauoreth to
make moſt iuſt and vertuous Magiſtrates. AQVI-
LONIVS. But what ſay you then to *Cicero?* Was he not
held for a good Magiſtrate, and yet he ſaith in the third of
his *Offices, cùm aliqua ſpecies vtilitatis obiecta eſt, nos commo-
ueri neceſſe eſt.* And againe: *Omnes appetimus vtilitatem, &
ad eam rapimur.* SVBSOLANVS. He ſaith not this
to incite men to the practiſe of all kind of Profit, but only
to ſhew the imbecillity of man, deſirous of that which
impayreth his Condition; & that Profit and Wealth do ſo,
we may gather by the *Philoſopher,* in the third of his *Politiques,* where he ſaith; *Lucrum facit homines deteriores* : the
which is confirmed by *Deip. apud Volat.* where he alſo
ſaith; *Niſi lucrum eſſet, nemo fuiſſet improbus* : and all this
the

the rather , becaufe (as faith another moderne Writer)
Wealth is a great nourifher of Vice , and Pouerty of Vertue . And
albeit this were not fo , yet the too much defire of Profit is
the rather to be bridled , becaufe though the manner of
gayning may be neuer fo honeft : yet faith *Seneca* (*Epift.*
95.) *Lucrum fine damno alterius fieri non poteft* . And fo much
alfo the more , when Iniuftice it felfe is fraudulently violated for caufe of lucre : *Nam tale turpe lucrum accufatio natu-*
ræ eft , as we read *apud Strobæum.*　　A Q V I L O N I V S.
If Nature be accufed therby , it is rather for taking too
much delight therin , then for any mifliking at all it hath
of the fame .　　S V B S O L A N V S. If your fraudulent
Iniuftice be not only fo good and fo profitable a thing as
you make it , but with all fo agreable vnto Nature it felfe ,
as you fay , we may then (me thinkes) do well to place
the fame amongft the number of Vertues .　　A Q V I-
L O N I V S. If it were not for one exception only , which
occurreth to me at this prefent , it might be a thing (I can
tell you) to be thought on , but that indeed the words of
Cicero (in the fifth of his *Tufculans*) are plainely againft it ,
where he faith ; *Nulla poteft effe virtus nifi gratuita.*　　S V B-
S O L A N V S. You haue done well to thinke of that exception your felfe, for otherwife you muft haue byn made
to remember it out of *Pontanus* (*lib. 2. de Prud.*) where he
faith; *Virtus nihil,quod extra fe eft, quærit* .　　A Q V I L O-
N I V S. It is fo much the worfe for her felfe , you may be
fure, fince therby fhe liueth in fuch continuall penury and
pouerty as fhe doth .　　S V B S O L A N V S. But yet at
the leaft wife by you owne confeffion , we may fay , that
Iuftice though fhe be neuer fo poore , yet hath fhe alwayes
her place amongft the Vertues .　　A Q V I L O N I V S.
We may fo .　　S V B S O L A N V S. And that Iniuftice
confequently though fhe be neuer fo rich , is alwayes to be
placed

placed amongſt the Vices.   A Q V I L O N I V S. By
rigour of ſpeach , you may ſay your pleaſure thereof ,
though on the other ſide for the Profit that riſeth therby ,
more gentle and more moderate words might be vſed of
it .   S V B S O L A N V S . Then you ſuppoſe (I perceaue) that for theſe former reſpeĉts it were ſomewhat
too rigorous a kind of ſpeaking to ſay, that Iniuſtice were
a vicious thing .   A Q V I L O N I V S. I do ſo indeed,
as alſo becauſe , whereas no man knoweth well how to
be able to liue in the world , except he haue Fortunes fauour , Iniuſtice of it ſelfe alone , and without any other
help at all , can get him the goods of Fortune ; the which
on the other ſide, if we will credit him, who commenteth
vpon the ſeauenth Booke of the *Politiques*, the firſt Chapter, Iuſtice of her ſelfe is not able ſo to do .   S V B-
S O L A N V S. So as Iuſtice and Vertue , you will haue
them to giue place vnto Riches and Fortune .   A-
Q V I L O N I V S. It is not my cenſure alone , for *Horace*
himſelfe (*Satyr. 3. lib. 2.*) is alſo of the ſame opinion ,
where he ſaith , That he who is rich , *Erit vtique clarus, fr-
tis ,ſapiens ,etiam Rex , & quicquid volet* .   S V B S O-
L A N V S . That is to ſay , he may ſeeme perhappes to be
ſuch , but not ſo indeed .   A Q V I L O N I V S. Do
you call it but a ſeeming ſo to be , when as in flat termes
the ſaid Author ſaith further in the ſame place , That vnto Riches, *Non ſolùm Virtus , ſed etiam Fama, Decus , Diuina
Humanaꝗ parent* .   S V B S O L A N V S. He ſpeaketh
it as a *Satyrical* Poet, only to carpe at the abuſe of the time,
as by theſe other his words elſewhere we may well diſcouer , *In pretio pretium nunc eſt* , and not that he thinketh, it
ought to be ſo indeed , but that the corruption of manners had then brought it ſo to paſſe : the which corruption of manners , is wont ſpecially to raigne amongſt the
      F   followers

followers of Riches , as we may gather by *Lactantius* (*de
falsa Relig* .) where he faith : *Voluntas fingendi, & mentiun-
di est eorum qui opes appetunt , & lucra desiderant* ; and therefore it were better for you to giue eare vnto *Horace* himfelfe , when he speaketh serioufly , faying : *Quòd pecunia
studium fidem , probitatem , ceterasque bonas artes subuertit :*
also vnto *Saluft* , where he faith , *Domat omnia Virtus :* and
againe ; *Quicquid homines arant , nauigant, ædificant, Virtuti
omnia parent* : the which is confirmed likewife by *Plautus* ,
who faith , *Virtuti Fortuna cedit :* fo that not Vertue vnto
Riches , but Riches vnto Vertue ftoupeth and obaieth.
In which refpect *Cicero* faith , *Virtute qui præditi funt , foli
funt diuites* , becaufe thofe that be truly vertuous be allwayes firme and ftable , and out of all feare of Fortunes
checkes ; *quia nihil eripit Fortuna, nifi quod ipfa dedit* , as faith
Seneca (*de tranquil* .) Now then of all the morall Vertues,
none is either more gratefull to God , or neceffary and
profitable to Man , then Iuftice , without the which no
Comon Wealth can ftand : as alfo on the other fide , no
Vice is either more hateful vnto God and pernicious vnto
man , then Iniuftice , which deftroyeth all Common
wealths and Ciuill Societies by the iuft iudgment of God,
who, as the holy Scripture teftifieth (*Deut*. 25 .) *Auerfatur
omnem Iniuftitiam:* wherof I will fpeake more amply in the
Conclufion of this dayes Conference ; meaning firft to
heare all that you meane to fay, before I will much preffe
you with Diuine Authority,which (as I prefume) you do
not meane to contradict.

¶   Heere *Fauonius* fuppofing that *Aquilonius* had
well neere forgotten himfelfe of the latter part of his former partition, began to fay thus vnto him . F A-
V O N I V S . What haue you now I pray you , after this
your defence of profitable Iniuftice, to fay further touching

ching that other point of difprofitable Iuſtice, wherof you
alſo promiſed to treate ?　A Q V I L O N . I haue to ſay
more perhappes , then you be aware of , and therefore to
deſcend now into this other branch , I muſt firſt tell you ,
That two wayes Iuſtice may be difprofitable, the one Priuate , the other Publick : and as for the former , to wit ,
how Iuſtice may ſometimes be priuately difprofitable , I
haue already declared it by the example of *Ariſtides* , of
Graccus, and of *Cato* : and how alſo it may be publikely diſprofitable , that is to ſay , by determinate ſentence giuen
betwixt party and party , I will now ſhew you by other
examples .　F A V O N I V S . I like it well that you
meane to proceed by examples , rather then by argument.
A Q V I L O N I V S .　To content you then according to
your owne liking : What Profit I pray you, did riſe to the
Troyans of the ſentence pronounced by *Paris* , about the di-
ſtribution of the goulden Apple , in the Vale of *Ida* ; when
as the ruine of *Paris* himſelfe, and of his whole Country
enſued therby ?　F A V O N I V S . This in effect was
no more but a Poeticall fiction , and not any formall ſentence of Iuſtice ; ſo that it ſerueth your purpoſe nothing at
all .　A Q V I L O N I V S . What ſay you then to the
ſentence giuen in the cauſe of a Scholler and his Maiſter ,
who being promiſed twenty crownes when he had taught
him the Art of perſwading, ſued him for his money. Vnto
whome the Scholler ſaid : If I can perſwade the Iudge that
I owe thee nothing , then nothing thou art to haue ; and if
I cannot perſwade him ſo, then nothing alſo is dew vnto
thee , becauſe thou haſt not taught me the Art of perſwading . Whereupon the Maiſter replied ; If thou canſt perſwade the Iudge , that thou oweſt me nothing , then art
thou to pay me , becauſe thou haſt learned of me the Art of
perſwading : and if thou canſt not perſwade him ſo , then

ſo

ſo much the more thou art to pay me, for that the ſentence will fall on my ſide. So that whether thou perſwade him, or not perſwade him, thou art ſtill to pay me. Heere I ſay in this cauſe, the ſentence being giuen for the Scholler, what Profit could come vnto him thereof: when as by hauing perſwaded the Iudge to belieue him, he diſcouered to haue learned of his Maiſter, ſo much as he had promiſed to teach him, and therfore reſted ſtill bound to pay him for the ſame? F A V O N I V S. This is rather a Paradoxe then a ſentence, and therfore can auaile you as little as that other before. A Q V I L O N I V S. Let vs then conſider the ſentence of *Cyrus*, while he was but yet young, about the taking from a little boy, a Coate which was too long for him, and from a great boy, another Coate which was too ſhort for him, cauſing them to be veſted with ech others coates: which ſentence what Profit could it bring vnto either of them, when as neither was contented with that exchange? F A V O N I V S. This was but a Childes play, and therfore by the Tutor vnto *Cyrus* it was preſently reuoked, and ſo ſerueth you alſo but vnto ſmall effect. A Q V I L O N I V S. I would then know, what you will ſay vnto the ſentence of *Xerxes* King of *Aſia*, who to ſaue his owne life, in a Tempeſt at ſea, was perſwaded by his Pilot to caſt ouer board all his chiefe Gentlemen, and when he came on ſhore, he ordeyned a Crowne of Gould to be giuen to the Pilot, for hauing ſaued his life, & incontinently after, iudged him to be hanged, for hauing byn the cauſe of the death of ſo many worthy Gentlemen: wherupon I would know, what Profit grew either to the State, or to the Pilot by this kind of ſentence, when as the one lamented ſtill the loſſe of their Nobility, and the other with his owne death, paid the ſauing of the Kinges life? F A V O N I V S. This was no more

but

but the will and fantaſie of a King ,and not any formall
ſentence giuen by the way of proceſſe , and therfore not
auaylable.   A QVILONIVS. Let vs then conſider this other ſentence, in the cauſe of a poore Tyler,
who falling downe from a houſe brake his legge, and killed another man vpon whom he fell; whoſe Sonne ſuing
for Iuſtice, receaued this Iudgement,that he ſhould go vp
to the toppe of the ſame houſe,and fall vpon the Tyler &
kill him if he could , as the Tyler fell vpon his Father : of
which ſentence, what Profit I pray you,enſued either to
the one man for breaking of his legge , or vnto the other
for his Fathers death.   FAVONIVS. This was
but a ſhift of a cũning Iudge, to make an end of an impertinent quarrell,with a more impertinent arbitrement,and
therfore as little to the purpoſe,as the reſt before .   A-
QVILONIVS. What ſay you then to the ſentence concerning an Inhabitant of one of the old Cittyes in *Greece*,
who hauing deliuered his Country from a notorious pe-
rill, was by a particuler Law of theirs to be graunted any
one petition he would aske, and ſo he demanding another
mans wife , had her : whoſe firſt husband hauing ſhortly
after done ſuch another like ſeruice to his Country , demanded his owne wife againe,wherin was giuen this ſentence ; *Let the Law take place* . If the Law do take place ,
ſaid the firſt husband, ſhe is wholy myne , for that I haue
wonne her : and if the Law do not take place , then alſo
is ſhe myne, becauſe ſhe was myne before. Wherunto the
ſecond husband replied thus: If ſo the Law take place,ſhe
is wholy mine , becauſe the ſame Law hath already giuen
her me; and if the Law do not take place , then can ſhe
not be thine , becauſe thou haſt no Law to claime her
from me that haue receaued her by the Law . Wherupon
by a ſecond ſentence ſhe was ſequeſtred from them both ,

F 3   to

to the great difcontentment of the one & the other : therfore tell me now , if you can, what Profit did grow vnto
any of them , by either of thefe fentences ?   F A V O-
N I V S. This is a kind of Riddle rather then a cafe of Law,
and therfore to be reiected with the reft .   A Q V I L O-
N I V S. What fay you then to the fentence that was giuen not many yeares ago, at home in our owne Country , againft the Maiefty of *Mary* the late moft Memorable Queene of *Scotland*; was it not a difprofitable thing
to the State, to fentéce in fuch fort, fuch an abfolute Prin-
cefle, as was no way fubiect to the iurifdiction of thofe
who gaue that fentence againft her ?   F A V O N I V S.
You be now defcended indeed into fo notorious a cafe of
our owne , that may not well be fo eafily reiected, as haue
been your other before. Concerning the which , for as
much as my felfe do know certaine good and affured particulers , fuch as may giue you fome fatisfaction , if they
might be related, I will not therfore fticke to fay , and
affirme vnto you, that hitherto at the leaft no difprofit hath
enfued therof, neither vnto our State, nor vs .   A Q V I-
L O N I V S. Do you thinke that Dishonour and vniuerfall foule Imputation to haue committed therin fuch an
act of Incongruity as was neuer yet heard of before, nor
will euer be left to be fpoken of to the worlds end; do you
thinke (I fay) that it is no Difprofit vnto your State?
F A V O N I V S. Was fhe not , I pray you, found culpable
of all the contriued crymes that were brought in euidence
againft her, the which being true, as it cannot well be denied , what caufe then haue you to crie out fo much , as
you do , vpon the Incongruity of that Sentence giuen?
A Q V I L O N I V S. Can there be any greater Incongruity , then to execute the rigour of the Law vpon one who
by prerogatiue is not tryable by the fame ?   For either it
                                                    muft

muſt be , that thoſe contryued crimes you ſpeake of, were
committed before ſhe came into England , or after ; if
before , cleare it is, that by the Law, and Reaſon of State
her abſolute Soueraignty acquiteth her therof : & if after,
then muſt you ſhew (if you will try her by Engliſh Laws)
how ſhe came to be depriued of that her Soueraigne freedome of birth ; the liberty whereof in the cauſe of a priuate
perſon (and much more of an abſolute Queene) cannot
be taken from him , without either preſcription, conſent,
or forfaite : but of any ſuch preſcription concerning the
Queenes Maieſty of *Scotland* , we ſee no Record of Conſent, no Act , nor any forfait, neither yet any ſuch crime
committed , as might depriue her of her Principality, the
which remayning in her ſtill, how could ſhe (who vnder
no Poſitiue Law was borne) be brought to be tried and
executed in a forraine Country, by the rigour of any ſuch
Law ? FAVONIVS. She was a priſoner, and all
priſoners be ſubiect to their Lawes whoſe Priſoners they
be. AQVILONIVS. Then *Iohn* & *Francis* Kings
of *France* , the one priſoner in *England* , and the other in
Spaine , might haue byn brought to the barre of Tranſ-
greſſors , and tried , by either of thoſe Country Lawes ,
but neither of them were ſo handled ; therfore belike the
Congruity of proceeding would not permit it . FA-
VONIVS. If Congruity , as you ſaid , would not permit it , how happened it then that *Charles* the firſt King
of Naples , did in like manner put to death by ſentence of
the Lawes of that Kingdome , his priſoner *Conradine*, who
ſucceeding the Emperour *Fredericke* the ſecond in the
Dukedome of *Sweuia* , made alſo pretenſe to the Kingdome of *Naples* ?. AQVILONIVS. This alſo was
houlden for ſuch an Incongruous Act (*Cùm nec Par in Pa-
rem poteſtatem habet , nec inferior in Superiorem . Leg.* 3 . & 4.
                                                                  de

de arbitr.) as all the world cried out vpon the fame . And
particulerly *Robert* Count of *Flanders*, Sonne-in Law to
the faid *Charles*, did for the great indignity therof, run his
fword through the Protonotary *Robert de Bary*, who read
the fentence of *Conradines* death. He alfo who ftroke off his
head, had prefently after by another, his owne head ftro-
ken off in the fame place. And this Act was the more grieuoufly condemned, becaufe the faid *Charles* himfelfe hauing
byn taken prifoner before by the *Saracens*, in the Warres of
the holy Land, was by them honorably entertained, and
Royally releafed. Whereupon *Peter* King of *Aragon*, in an
opprobrious letter of his written about this Act, and fent
to the faid *Charles*, fayth to him amongft other things :
Tu Nerone neronior, & Saracenis crudelior .   F A V O-
N I V S. It was only iealofy of State, that made the faid
Charles more cruell therein, then otherwife perhapps he
would haue byn, becaufe *Conradine* not long before was
come with a potent armie to take from him his Kingdome
of *Naples* : and the fame reafon may alfo feeme to excufe
the putting to death of the Queene of *Scotland*, becaufe fhe
likewife as then made claime to the Crowne of *England*,
and Crownes, I can tell you, may comport no Competi-
tors .   A Q V I L O N I V S. And yet the forfaid *Peter*
King of *Aragon*, who by the right of *Conftance* his wife Co-
fen-german to the beheaded *Conradine*, hauing from the
faid *Charles* the firft King of *Naples* the Kingdome of *Sicilia* , and alfo taken Prifoner the Sonne of that *Charles* called
Charles the fecond, who ftill made claime to *Sicilia*, did notwithftanding not put him to death, neither in refpect of
that claime of his, nor yet in reuenge of the death of *Conradine* his Cofen, but with Honorable conditions he was
after fet at liberty by *Iames* Sonne to the faid *Peter*, at the
inftance of *Edward* the firft King of *England* : and all this
ftill

ftill vnto the greater obloquy of the forfaid Jncongruity of *Charles* the firft : therfore fee now what little caufe you had to bring in him for an example to approue the like vfed in England againft the Queenes Maiefty of *Scotland*, when fhe was not taken Prifoner by any Law of Armes , as thefe other Princes were , but comming into England of her owne accord, yea and inuited, was retayned there by force: and therfore put the cafe , that fhe had confpired againft the Queene of *England* and her State (as fhe was charged to haue done) fhe did no more then fhe might lawfully do, to redeeme her owne vniuft vexation, and to procure her liberty wherof fhe was moft vniuftly depriued . For which refpects her condemnation was, as I haue faid , moft incongruous and fo much the more for that fhe was a Woman , a Widdow , the neareft Ally vnto the Crowne of *England* , an inuited Gueft , an Exile out of her Kingdome,and fled into *England* for fuccour; and finally in fuch a ftate, that our State could pretend no lawfull caufe of feare : for that being indurance fhe could neither attempt any thing of her felfe , nor yet practife with any others further then the State of *England* would permit and wincke at . And therfore by doing as they did , they derogated from the Lawes of Nature , of Charity , of Iurifdiction and Maiefty , of Parentage , of Hofpitality , of Protection , and finally from the Law of Nations , and confequently from humaine Intelligence and reafon . And thus much concerning the Incongruity of the fact it felfe , togeather with the difprofit of that fentence giuen : not only in refpect of the Vniuerfall obliquy rifen therby, but alfo of the future harmes which by occafion of that euill example left in memory , may happen to grow hereafter vnto fome Prince of *England* in the like cafe .

G ¶ Heere

¶ Heere *Subsolanus* interrupting their further talke
began to say vnto *Aquilonius*.   S v B S O L A N V S. It
may suffice herein that we be better content to admit your
example of disprofitable Iustice, then your proofes of profitable Iniustice, though there be place inough left of exception to be made vnto the one, as well as to the other,
were it not that other matters do yet occure to be also spoken of : and therfore hauing hitherto treated of Worldlines and Profit, in old men, in young men, in Lawiers, in
Iudges, and in other Magistrates, some by ouer-weening
of themselues. some by excesse of forwardnes, some by ignorance some by skill, some by Iniustice, some by Iustice; me thinkes it were now tyme, that we should begin
to determine what Profit is, and how many sorts of Profit there may be said to be.   A Q V I L O N I V S. Take
you then the care therof vpon your selfe to do it, & for the
rest we be already agreed.   S v B S O L A N V S. May
we not then do well to say, That Profit is a thing which is
either desired for it selfe, or else for some other thing to
follow therby?   A Q V I L O N I V S. Me thinkes not,
becaufe this would seeme to haue relation rather vnto the
vtility rising from the thing it selfe, then to the gaine to
be made therof, by any Industry annexed.   S v B S O-
L A N V S. We may then perhaps do better to say, That
Profit is an Act which may be reputed to confist in buying
good cheape, and in selling deere.   A Q V I L O N I V S.
This on the other side would seeme to haue relation altogeather to the gaine which is to be made of things, and
not at all vnto the Vtility rising of the thing it selfe.
S v B S O L A N V S It may be, that then this other will content you best, to say, That Profit is no more but a certaine
kind of skill, how to turne the vse of all things vnto aduantage, vnto more aduantage, and vnto most aduantage.
                                                        A Q V I-

A QVILONIVS. It wilbe hard, I can tell you, vnto a word of so diuers relations, to make any one description, that may hit iust with them all; and therfore without searching any further, we will admit this last togeather with the former.   SVBSOLANVS. So that heerby already we may begin (me thinkes) to difcouer that of Profit there be two forts, the one called Vtility , and the other Gaine.   AQVILONIVS. We may fo. SVBSOLANVS.   But may we not likewife fay , that of Vtility there be three forts; one ry fing of things, another of habits , and the third of men ?   A QVI-LONIVS. And this also.   SVBSOLANVS. I he Vtility rifing of things either fenfeleffe , vegetatiue or fenfitiue , may we not fay it to be double, to wit either of fuch things as be not defired for themfelues , but for fome other Vtility that is to rife of them (as when a man taketh a loathfome medicine to recouer his health therby :) or elfe of fuch other things as be defired both for themfelues, and alfo for fome other Vtility that is to grow of them, as when a man taketh a deleſtable medicine both becaufe it pleafeth his taft, and is alfo profitable for his health ? A QVILONIVS. This also doth content me ?   SVB-SOLANVS. The Vtility rifing of habits , may we not fay it alfo to be double , to wit, either Speculatiue (as the V-tility that rifeth of knowledg (be it Naturall , Diuine, or Mathematicall) or elfe practicall , as the Vtility to rife of ciuill , domefticall , or politicall skill ?   AQVILO-NIVS This may alfo be admitted.   SVBSOLANVS. And the Vtility rifing of men , may we not fay it to be ei-ther fatall (but yet accompanied with voluntary feeking, as the fauour of Princes , marriage , friendfhip , and the like :) or Naturall , as the Sonne to inherite vnto his Fa-ther , and the Brother to his Brother , or the Nephew to his Vncle; or Morall, as when one receaueth vtility of another, so farre as either decency or neighbourhood doth require: or Legall, as when one man receaueth vtility of another, so farre as the Law doth bynd him therunto, and no more, as to keep the peace, to render his due, and the like: or else Spirituall, as when one receaueth a benefit of another, not corporally, but for the benefit of his soule, as the Parishioner by his Curate, who also on the other side may receaue Tythes of his Parishioners for his Seruice in the Church. A Q V I L O N I V S. All this may be also admitted. S V B S O L A N V S. So now to speake of that second sort of Profit which is called Gaine, may we not consequently say, that of Gayning there be likewise three sorts; one to be made by Chaunce, another to be made by Lucke; and the third to be made by Industry? A Q V I L O N I V S. It doth not mislike me. S V B S O - L A N V S. The Gaine to be made by Chaunce, which a man doth vnwittingly meet withall, may we not say it to be triple, to wit, either by the way of fynding (as a man to light vpon a lost purse) or else by the way of encountring (as a man to meet in an Inne with a merchant who is contented to beare his charges out of *Italy* into *England*) or otherwise by the way of escaping (as a man to be deliuered out of the hands of theeus by the comming that way of other passingers?) A Q V I L O N I V S. All as yet goeth well. S V B S O L A N V S. The Gaine to be made by Lucke, which a man doth get wittingly, may we not say it to be also triple; namely either by the way of gaming (as to wyn a great summe of money, either at Dice or Cardes) or else by the way of venturing (as to become rich by far iourneys at sea) or otherwise by the way of experimenting (as to multiply wealth, by making of things, either commodious extractions, or commodious

compo-

compoſitions ?) AQVILONIVS. It may be allowed well inough. SVBSOLANVS. And now
as touching the gayne to be made of Induſtrie, may we
not ſay it to be double ; to wit, either by way of faction,
and force, or elſe by way of action, and agility? A-
QVILONIVS. I ſee no cauſe to the contrary. SVB-
SOLANVS The gaine to be made be Faction and force,
may we not ſay it to be quadruple, to wit, either vnarti-
ficially (as a man to get his liuing by poitage, or by any
other meere labour of the body)or e ſe artificially (as by
fiſhing, by fowling, and the like) or otherwiſe husband-
ly (to wit by tilling, by graſing, or by breding of cattell)
or elſe mechanically or manually (as by being a Carpen-
ter,a Shwoomaker,or a Taylour?) AQVILONIVS.
Nothing of this may be well denyed. SVBSOLA-
NVS. And ſo likewiſe the gaine to be made by Action
and Agility, may we not ſay it to be double, namely either Mercantile or elſe Mercenary? AQVILO-
NIVS. Me thinkes we may ſay ſo. SVB‘OLA-
NVS. The Mercantile gayne, may we not ſay it to be
quadruple, namely either by buying or ſelling or elſe by
commutation of one thing for another of diuers kindes,
or otherwiſe by vſury, or elſe by exchange of money for
money? AQVILONIVS. You ſay herein very
well. SVBSOLANVS. The Mercantile gaine to be
made by the way of buying and ſelling, may we not ſay it
to be alſo quardruple, to wit, either of Landes or poſſeſ-
fions, or elſe by cattell and other victualls, or otherwiſe
of furniture of houſhould or building, or elſe of any o-
ther wares whatſoeuer, either in Great or by Retaile?
AQVILONIVS. I admit it to be ſo. SVBSO-
LANVS. The Mercantile gaine to be made by the way
of comutation of one thing for another of diuers kinds,

may

may we not fay, that this fort of getting, is leffe in vfe
now adayes, fince money hath byn inuented, then heretofore it hath byn, when *Iacob* (as we read in *Iofue,cap.24.*)
emit à plÿs Emor Patris, Sichem agrum pro centum nouelles oui-
bus, & fuit in poffeßionem filiorum Iofeph?   A Q V I L O-
N I V S. This as you fay, is now out of vfe.   S V B S O-
L A N V S. The Mercantile gaine to be made by the way of
vfury, may we not fay it to be difallowed firft by the difcipline of the Philofophers, according as we read in *Ari-*
ftotle (Polit.lib. 1.cap. 6.) next by the Law of *Meyfes*, as
we read in *Leuit.(cap. 25.) Pecuniam tuam non dabis ad vfu-*
ram : and laftly by the Law of our Sauiour Chrift, who
faith (*Luc.cap. 6.) Si mutuum dederitis his à quibus fperatis*
accipere,quæ gratia eft vobis? nam & peccatores peccatoribus foe-
nerantur vt recipiant æqualia.   A Q V I L O N I V S.
This cannot be denyed.   S V B S O L A N V S. The
Mercantile Gayne to be made by the way of exchange, is
in fome cafes allowable (as when the Gaine is no more thē
the difference of the value of the money in the place wherunto it is exchanged, for the value of the money in the
place where the contract is made, adding only therunto all
ordinary charges duely occurring :) & in fome other cafes
it is difallowed, as when the Gaine is greater then the faid
difference of the value of the money, and the ordinary
charges occurring; and this alfo either by occafion of the
fraud of the giuer of the bill of exchange, or by the neceffity of the taker.   A Q V I L O N I V S. There can
be nothing more true.   S V B S O L A N V S. Now to
come on the other fide to the Mercenary kind of gayning,
may we not likewife fay it to be double, namely either
lawfull, or elfe vnlawfull?   A Q V I L O N I V S. Togeather with the reft, let this be alfo admitted.   S V B-
S O L A N V S. The lawfull Mercenary Gaine is alfo double,

to wit, either by the way of warre, or elfe by the way of peace. AQVILONIVS. I find nothing to be laid againft it. SVBSOLANVS. The Mercenary lawfull Gaine to be made by the way of warre, may we not fay it to be likewife double, namely either by Sea (as by receauing the ftipend of a Pilot, of a marriner, of a Gunner and fuch like : or elfe by Land, as by receauing the ftipend of a Captayne. of a fouldier, of an enginer, or fuch other? AQVILONIVS. As you do fay, fo do I affirme it. SVBSOLANVS. The lawfull Mercenary Gaine to be made by the way of peace, may we not fay it to be alfo double; to wit. either feruile (as by receauing the ftipend of a domefticall Officer, or of an ordinary feruant;) or elfe more free, as by receauing the ftipend of a teacher of any Art, the ftipend of a Lawier, or the ftipend of a Phifitian : the which neuertheles being better confidered, may be faid to be improper kindes of gayning, according to the opinion of the Philofopher (in the firft of his *Politiques*, the fixt Chapter, becaufe the proper gaine which commeth of teaching, is the Art learned, & the proper gaine of the Law is the counfell giuen, and of Phificke the health receaued ; and fo likewife in other things that be more Mechanicall, as the proper gaine to be made of a payre of fhooes, is the fauing of the feet by the wearing therof; and the price for which they be fould is the improper gaine, as rifing fecondarily therof, and not princially. AQVILONIVS. This fubtile confideration neuer entred into my head before, albeit I confeffe that it carrieth with it fufficient fhew of reafon. SVBSOLANVS. And now to come on the other fide, vnto vnlawfull Mercenary wayes of gayning, may we not likewife fay them to be double, namely either fecretly difhoneft, or apparently difhoneft? AQVI-
LONIVS.

L O N I V S. I haue looked for this all this while. S v B-
s o L A N v s. Of which two points, becaufe they may
grow to be more copious then the reft before haue by n, it
fhallbe good that we fpeake of them a part by themfelues.
A Q_V I L O N I V S. You may giue vnto them what fcope
you will, for I find my felfe well inough difpofed to fay
my part therin, as well as you.   S v B S O L A N v S.
To begin then with the fecret difhoneft Mercenary Gaine,
or to fay better, Honeft in apparence, though not indeed;
may we not reduce it vnto thefe heads, namely either vn'o
cloked Iniuftice, or vnto diffembled Carnality, or vnto
fmooth flattery, or elfe vnto cunning Cheating?   A-
Q_V I L O N I V S. Me thinkes you haue put in inough, as
being afraid, belike, to leaue out any thing.   S v B-
s o L A N v s. Of that fecret difhoneft Gaine which is wont
to rife by cloked Iniuftice, we fhall not need I fup, ofe to
fay heere any more then hath been fpoken therof already.
A Q_V I L O N I V S I am alfo of the fame mynd.   S v B-
s o L A N v s. So that to fpeake in order next of that otl er
fecret difhoneft Gaine, which is wont to rife by diffembl d
Carnality, may we not fay it to be double, to wit eith r
when fome one is but a mediator for another, or elfe a fol-
licitor for himfelfe?   A Q_V I L O N I V S. The firft of
thefe two, may be well inough omitted, as not being worthy to be treated of heere.   S v B S O L A N v S. As
touching then the fecond, may we not fay it to be three
wayes miferable? One in refpeɑt of the filthines therof,
another for the pleafure taken therein, and the third for
the Gaine it felfe, wherby this Carnall man is tied the rather therunto: whereas others, fuch as purfue the like folly with their owne expences and loffe, do therby deliuer
themfelues the fooner from their noyfome and loathfome
feruitude; and therfore we fee commonly that a Mercenary

ry Fornicator who followeth that filthy trade, either for
supplying of his owne need, or els for defire of fuperfluity,
cannot find in his hart to leaue off, till either his carnality
do firft leaue him, or he leaue himfelfe for altogeather,
with euident danger of eternall perdition. In whome is
verified the faying of the Prophet *Ofee*, fpeaking of fornicators (*cap.5.*) *They* (faith he) *will not haue in their thoughts
any will to returne to God againe*. Therfore fuch Carnall
men, whether they be mercenary or no (I meane, whe-
therfoeuer they feeke their pleafure, or their gaine) may
do well euer to remember not only the prohibition therof, but alfo the punifhment ordained for it in Holy Scriptures, as in *Leuit.* 19. *Si mœchatus quis fuerit cum vxore alterius, & adulterium perpetraucrit cum vxore proximi fui, morte
moriantur & mœchus & adultera*. And againe (Deut. 13.)
Non erit meretrix de fliabus Ifraël, nec fcortator de filijs Ifraël;
which is alfo confirmed by the Law of Grace, with a precept of greater purity and perfection (*Matth.* 5.) *Audiftis
quia dictum est antiquis, Non mœchaberis; ego autem dico vobis,
quia omnis qui viderit mulierem ad concupifcendam eam, iam
mœchatus est in corde fuo*. And againe (*Heb* 13.) *Fornicatores
enim & adulteros iudicabit Deus*. And the rather alfo becaufe
their vice and finne, as faith S. *Ambrofe* (*lib.* 1 . *de Abraham*) *etiam feris ac barbaris deteftabile eft*. A Q V I L O-
N I V S. For fo much hereof as concerneth the mercenary
ftipend of fornicators or adulterers, this which you haue
faid, doth indeed pertaine to me, who am a defender of
Profit: but for the reft (I meane the delights taken therin) your difcourfe toucheth *Fauonius*, more then me, for
that he is a fpeciall fauourer of Pleafure.

    ¶ Heere *Fauonius*, though he did not repyne to be
thought a friend to Pleafure in generall, yet taking it to
be fome reproach vnto himfelfe, to be interlaced in the

H

reckoning

reckoning of fo dilhoneft a caule , intruded himfelfe into
the purfuite of the other branches of *Subfolanus* laft par-
tion , faying fome what angerly to *Aquilonius* .   F A -
v o n i v s. Whether I be a fauourer of Pleafure or no , I
take you to be one of thofe , who for Mercenary Gaine
would make no fcruple at all to calumniate one that is abfent , to the fmooth flattering of another that is prefent ,
A QV I L O N I V s. As touching the calumniation we be
not yet come fo farre forward , though perhapps we may
be ere it be long ; but for the flattery whenfoeuer it procureth any gaine , I am no leffe then you haue fuppofed
me to be , and the rather for that in no place where I haue
trauelled, I haue euer hitherto found the hart of any man
fo hard,that was not greatly to be mollified with the hearing of his owne praife. For that as verity caufeth hatred,
fo adulation doth ingender loue, according to the old
Pouerbe: *Obfequium amicos,veritas odium parit* .   F A V O-
n i v s. That is with thofe who loue themfelues too much,
wherby they thinke they be not flattered but duely commended , though perhaps in truth they little deferue it :
wheras fuch others as know themfelues aright,albeit they
may be naturally defirous to heare their owne praife ; yet
will they be warv not to fuffer themfelues to be fcorned ,
or mocked with falfe adulation , like as was *Efopes* Crow,
which by the flattery of the Fox,let fall the meate fhe held
in her mouth .   A QV I L O N I V s. Herein confifteth
the praife of this Art , to be able to worke fuch miracles.
F A V O N I V S. Then you accompt flattery I perceaue
to be an Art .   A Q V I L O N I V S. Not only an Art,
but an Art of Arts , which goeth beyond all other Artes ,
F A V O N I v s. Let me aske you then this queftion,Whe-
ther he who flatters , doth vfe to fpeake as he thinketh?
A QV I L O N I V S. Such a one as doth fo ; may be rather
                                                           a true

a true praiſer, then a flatterer. FAVONIVS. So
that a flatterer ſpeaketh one thing and thinketh another.
AQVILONIVS. If he ſhould do otherwiſe, it were
then no Art at all, but a ſilly plaine kind of dealing. FA-
VONIVS. Then he who will play the Flatterer cūning-
ly, muſt firſt learne to be a falſe diſſembler. AQVI-
LONIVS. If you haue no worſe to ſay againſt him then
that, he will do well inough. FAVONIVS. So
as you take it, that to diſſemble is a very tolerable thing.
AQVILONIVS. I make no queſtion of it. FA-
VONIVS. Then I pray you tell me, Whether he who
vttereth with his tongue that which his inward diſſimulation hath contriued, may not be called a Lyar? A-
QVILONIVS. I am ſorry that word hath eſcaped
your mouth, becauſe albeit he may be ſo called, yet doth
he lye in a moſt pleaſing manner, and nothing at all ma-
liciouſly. FAVONIVS. But do you meane that
the ſame pleaſing Lye, ſhould be made for the benefit of
the party flattered, or els of the good of the Fatterer himſelfe? AQVILONIVS. You might thinke the
Flatterer a foole to do it, if it were not principally for his
owne benefit. FAVONIVS. Then his owne ſelfe-
loue is the principall cauſe of his flattery, therby to make
his aduantage of the party flattered. AQVILO-
NIVS. For whoſe loue els may he haue more cauſe to do
it? FAVONIVS. In ſo much, as by his flattering
he not only deceaueth treacherouſly the party flattered,
but ſeeketh to infect him alſo with the ſame vice of ſelfe-
loue, wherwith he himſelfe is already infected: and this
to the end to be able ſo to lead him vp and downe by the
Noſe, as we ſee Bearewardes, with a ring to lead their
Beares; and therfore we may well ſay, that as flattery
beginneth with diſſimulation and lying, ſo alſo it endeth

H 2   with

with treachery and deceyte .   AQVILONIVS. I
will not deny it , neyther do I miſlike it , if it be for his
profit and gaine .   FAVONIVS. Belike then (to
come now vnto the laſt part of *Subſolanus* his former diui-
ſion) you will not ſtick to admit alſo this Flatterer of ours,
to play the cũning Cheater for his greater gaine .   A-
QVILONIVS. Such kind of cũning cheating it may be,
as I will not ſtick to admit it in him indeed .   FAVO-
NIVS. As for example, What ſay you vnto one , who
hauing a Gould Chaine , cauſed a counterfaite one to be
made very like it, and offered the better chaine to be ſould
to a Goldſmith , vpon whome (after he had touched ,
and waighed it , yea and bargained alſo for it) he dexte-
rouſly ſhifted the coũterfaite Chaine inſteed of the other ?
AQVILONIVS. I do not directly allow of this , becauſe
he was ſo wealthy as to haue a gould chayne to ſell , and
therfore was not yet brought vnto ſuch neceſſity , as to
be permitted the acting of ſuch a fraud .   FAVO-
NIVS. Let me then propound vnto you this other caſe ,
of one who pretended in the time of Lent to haue loſt a
Budget with a hundred Crownes of money in it , and of
another his companion, who by accord betwixt them, was
to faygne to haue found it , ſo he who loſt it hauing commended the matter to be inquired of in the Pulpit by the
publick Preacher of the Towne , the other diſcouered to
him in ſecret the finding therof , but yet, with ſuch a pro-
teſtation of his owne pouerty , as the Preacher for the pitty he tooke of ſo conſcionable a man , got him by collection, that Lent , little leſſe then an hundred Crownes, the
which ſumme he, and his Companion deuyded betwixt
them ?   AQVILONIVS. Of the inuention it ſelfe
I allow well inough , but not of the baſe kind of begging .
FAVONIVS. What ſay you then by one , who binding
himſelfe

himfelf by obligatiō to repay a borrowed fumme of money, caft vpon the fame obligation fuch a duft, as eat out
all the letters,& fo fhifted of the payment by that kind of
fraud ?   AQVILONIVS. This inuention I like not at al,
becaufe another may vfe it againſt me that hath but once
heard of it,as well as I againſt him.   FAVONIVS.
Well then, I will propound vnto you yet this other , of
one who taking with him his Neighbour , did hide vnder
the ground an hundred Crownes , which money his neighbour hauing need of , conuayed fecretly from thence,
leauing in the place a bagg of ftones ?   AQVILO-
NIVS. It may be he had an intention to vfe the money
a whyle, and to returne it to the fame place againe. FA-
VONIVS. He retorned it indeed ,though he had no
fuch intention when he tooke it: for the owner therof hauing miffed it, and fufpecting that his neighbour had
taken it , told him that the day following he would hide
another hundred Crownes in the fame place : wherupon
his neighbour thinking to get the fame alfo, carried backe
the firſt hundred Crownes , and therby loft the fame.
AQVILONIVS. The more I reflect on the matter, the
more I difallow it , becaufe he betrayed the confidence
which was repofed in him , without any conſtraint of
neceffity.   FAVONIVS. What fay you then to
two companions , who carryed a hundred Crownes to
a rich old Vfurer to keep, taking an obligation of him ,
that he fhould not deliuer it vnto either of them , vnleffe
they came both togeather for it : after which it paffed not
long but that one of them , by the confent of his fellow
put on a fute of mourning apparrell , and pretending to
the Vfurer that his companion was dead ,got the hundred Crownes out of his handes : and fhortly after , the
other appearing,he obtayned fentence againſt the Vfurer

H 3   by

by vertue of his said obligation , for another hundred
Crownes .   A Q V I L O N I V S . To haue serued an
old Vsurer such a trick , it misliketh me nothing at all.
F A V O N I V S . But yet the Vsurer bethinking him better
of the matter , caused the sentence to be reuoked againe
by alledging to the Iudge the words of his obligation, that
he was not bound to repay the money , vnlesse both of
them togeather came for it , wherwith the sute ended , for
such reason as you may coniecture .   A Q V I L O-
N I V S . I am sory it tooke no better effect , for that the
shift (if it had byn in a time of necessity) was both good
and clenly .   F A V O N I V S . But what do you say
the while vnto the other sort of cunning Cheatinges ,
which be commonly vsed at all kinds of gaming : I meane
either in the act it selfe, or the circumstances , as by Charmes, Falsifications, Butty-playing,& the like ?   A Q V I-
L O N I V S . As though vnto all kind of gaming there hath
not alwayes byn annexed a certayne aduantagious liberty
of playing, which you make so much the worse , by com-
prizing it vnder the title of cunning Cheating : for though
true it be , that it hath in it some cunning , yet it is too
Courtly a practise, to be called Cheating .

 ¶ Heere *Subsolanus* being desirous to returne againe
vnto his vnfinished distribution , began to say vnto *Aquilonius* .   S V B S O L A N V S . Hauing treated hitherto
sufficiently of that kind of vnlawfull Mercenary Gaine ,
which is but secretly dishonest ; there resteth yet to speake
of that other part which is dishonest more apparantly , the
which we may reduce vnto these eight heades following ;
to wit , vnto publike proceedings, which be either fraudulent, or violent , or disloyall , or reproachfull , or cruell, or
inhumane , or scurrilous , or iniust .   A Q V I L O-
N I V S . A faire rablement of memorable particularities ,
                                                                and

and well picked out.   Svbsolanvs. That publike
difhoneſt Mercenary gaine, which is wont to riſe of publike fraud, may we not ſay it to be either by deceipt of
words, and that either with oathes, or without oathes,
or els by fraudulent deceipt in actions, as for example by
the way of buying or ſelling?   Aqvilonivs. Such
proceedings as theſe be ſeene indeed ſometimes to occur.
Svbsolanvs. That other difhoneſt Mercenary gaine
which is to be gotten by any publike violence, may we
not ſay it to be either, when it is done vnder the colour of
ſport, or els when it is done in plaine earneſt, as to rob
on the high way, to breake into houſes, and the like?
Aqvilonivs. It muſt be a great & vrgent neceſſity,
that ſhould driue men vnto theſe extremityes.   Svbsolanvs. The third difhoneſt Mercenary gaine which
is wont to riſe of publike diſloyalty, may we not ſay it to
be either by way of treachery, or els of treaſon?   A-
qvilonivs. Such things no doubt, be aduentured
vpon ſometimes for deſire of Profit.   Svbsolanvs. The fourth difhoneſt Mercenary gaine which is to
be gotten with the blot of publike reproach, may we not
ſay it to be either with ſhame of body, wherof there want
not examples, or els with ſhame of mynd, as to beare falſe
witnes, and the like?   Aqvilonivs. All is according as it is taken.   Svbsolanvs. The
fifth difhoneſt Mercenary gaine which is wont to riſe of
ſome publike cruelty, may we not ſay it to be either by the
way of flafhing (wherof the markes are rife inough ech-
where to be ſeen) or els by the way of mayming men in
their lymmes?   Aqvilonivs. You will ſcarce
leaue place anon for any diſorder at all to be any where
committed.   Svbsolanvs. The ſixt difhoneſt
Mercenary gaine which is to be gotten by any publick In-
                                    humanity,

humanity, may we not fay it to be either by the way of in-
faming men, or elfe by doing them fome other difcourtefy?
A Q V I L O N I V s. A very narrow fearcher into matters
you fhew your felfe to be .   S V B S O L A N V s. The
feauenth difhoneft Mercenary gaine, which is wont to rife
of publick Scurrility, may we not fay it to be either by the
way of vncleane fpeaking , or els by the way of more impudent iefting?   A Q V I L O N I V s. Now me thinks
you ftoop very low , to take exception to fuch ordinary
imperfections.   S V B S O L A N V s. And laftly the
eight difhoneft Mercenary gaine, which is to be gotten by
publike Iniuftice , may we not fay it to be, either publike
betwixt party and party , or els publike by the way of office?   A Q V I L O N I V s. By hemming in things thus
togeather after this manner, you may fay what you will.
S V B S O L A N V s. Now then it feemeth that it is already
high time to determine with all the old Moralifts, that nothing can be gainefull which is not iuft and honeft, wherof the reafon fhall euidently appeare hereafter , efpecially
in the end of this dayes Conference, when I fhall confider
of the Profit, or Difprofit that the Soule reapeth by fraudulent gaine; and therfore in the meane time, relying v-
pon the knowne , and excellent Axiome of *Cicero* in his *Offices* (to wit, *Nihil vtile quod non fit honeftum*) I affirme, that
no Gaine which is fraudulent , can be truly profitable, as
to fell Land which is litigious to one that knoweth it not ,
which is an act that repugneth with Iuftice , according as
doth all other fraudulent buying & felling , for the which
Claudius was taxed amongft the *Romans* , about a houfe
which he fould to *Calphurnius* .   A Q V I L O N I V s.
If we meafure Iuftice ftill fo ftrictly, we fhall make a faire
hand ere long .   S V B S O L A N V s. May we not alfo
fay , that no Gaine which is gotten with furious violence

can

can be truely profitable: As to extort any thing by force,
vnder the colour of sport or earneſt, according as thoſe
good fellowes be wont to do, who purchaſe their reuenewes by the high wayes; for which kind of faultes were
infamous amongſt the *Romans*, both *Bargulus* of *Illyria*,
and *Viriatus* of *Portugall*? AQVILONIVS. You
need not to haue ſought ſo far for examples, ſince our
owne Country doth yield vs inough of them. SVB-
SOLANVS. May we not likewiſe ſay, that no kind of
Gaine which groweth of diſloyalty, can be truly profitable: As to betray any other for his owne preferment;
as *Marius* the *Roman* betryed *Metellus* to get the Conſul-
ſhip from him? AQVILONIVS. It may be, that
at that time, there were as many in *Rome*, that did commend him, as diſcommend him for it. SVBSOLA-
NVS. May we not further ſay, that no Gaine which is
gotten with reproach or ſhame can be truly profitable:
As to falſify Deedes, and ſuch like, nor yet to be conſenting vnto any ſuch acts; for the which were taxed the two
great *Romans M. Craſſus*, and *Q. Hortenſius* to haue fauoured for their owne gaine, the falſified Teſtament of *L. Mi-
nutius* brought them out of *Greece*? AQVILO-
NIVS. To beare any blame with ſuch kind of perſonages
as theſe, would rather ſeeme to be a reputation then a reproach. SVBSOLANVS. May we not ſay with-
all, that no Gaine which is polluted with cruelty can be
truly profitable. as to be conſenting to the ſhedding of
bloud, or to the mayming of any man; as the *Athenians*
were taxed for cutting off the thumbes of the *Ægineti*,
leſt they ſhould be offenſiue to their Citty, by rowing in
their owne Gallyes? AQVILONIVS As I re-
member, ſome one of the Kings of *France*, had deſigned
to do the like vnto all ſuch Engliſh priſoners as he ſhould

I   happen

happen to take in the warres, to hynder therby their Archery. Svbsolanvs. May we not say moreouer, that no Gaine which is gotten with Inhumanity can be truly profitable; as to defame any man by word or writing, or to vse any other kind of discourtesy, as in *Rome* first *Petronius*, and after him *Rapius* were generally reproued for their inhumane prohibiting of strangers from their Cittyes, except such as would compound with them for their Licences? Aqvilonivs. To make good this, I could the sooner condescend, for somewhat I haue suffered my selfe in that kind. Svbsolanvs. May we not say as yet, that no Gaine which is gotten by scurrility can be truly profitable, or els by vndecent Iesting; for which vices was infamous amongst the *Grecians A istippus*, and amongst the *Romans, Sarmentus*, as also *Texius*? Aqvilonivs. Of all the rest these kind of Companions do least content me. Svbsolanvs. May we not say in like manner, that no Gaine which is gotten with publike Iniustice, can be truly profitable, whether so it be betwixt party and party, or els by the way of office; in which kind be condemned the *Athenians* for their vniust banishing their iustest sort of Cittizens? Aqvilonivs. As touching the Iniustice of Officers & Magistrates there hath inough byn said already, and for that other Iniustice betwixt party & party, we haue yet time inough to speake therof. Svbsolanvs. Then you will make a difference, I perceaue, betwixt the Iniustice of Magistrates, and the Iniustice of priuate men; as if priuate men were priuiledged herein more then Magistrates? Aqvilonivs. You say very well, for so indeed they seeme to be, by reason of the common vse and custome amongst men, which maketh priuate mens Iniustice, fraudes, and deceipts in priuate

matters

matters to be either generally approued , or at least lesse
condemned , then the Iniustice of publike Magistrates in
publike affaires ; and therfore according to the common
practise of the world , to what end doth any man set vp a
trade , but to exercise Iniustice ? or buy any pelting office,
but to gaine his liuing by Iniustice ? or fetch commodityes from forraine Countryes, but with subtile accompts
to deceiue others by Iniustice ; since seldome times it is
seene , that any of these do rise from little vnto much ,
without hauing first comitted many & many Iniustices ?
S v b s o l a n v s . Wherupon it would follow according to your opinion , that to learne also to do Iniustice
in this sort , were a profitable thing .   A q v i l o-
n i v s . A profitable thing . you may be sure .   S v b-
s o l a n v s . But may we likewise say it is honest ?   A-
q v i l o n i v s . Vnto him at leastwise (as hath been
said) that can do it couertly, by knowing very well with
what counterfait holines towards God , and what faigned
sincerity towards the world , to get not only wealth by
doing such Iniustice , but also the fame and reputation to
be the honestest man in his Parish .   S v b s o l a-
n v s . Then so much the more as these kind of men be iniust , so much the more they come to be exalted .   A-
q v i l o n i v s . If it were not so , how could so many
poore beginners rise daily , as we see, to be Magistrates in
the Cittyes where they dwell ?   S v b s o l a n v s .
Then so much also the more , may euery one of these be
said to be iust and honest , as he is vnindifferent and par-
tiall .   A q v i l o n i v s . Not only to be honest and
iust , but also to be graue and constant in his proceedings;
and all this by the credit of his Wealth , which according
to the opinion of the Philosopher , *Is a signe of eternall Glory*, as the only thing at this day , that doth gouerne the

whole world, hauing force to throw vnto the ground, not only the power of the Lawes, but the ſtrength of Armes, and the skill of Art, and Wit of man in all things. S v B- s o L A N v s. So that vnto one who hath little or nothing to begin withall, his neceſſity, you thinke, may permit him to deceiue any man by Iniuſtice? A Q V I L O N I V S. You ſay well; the Profit that may riſe of this Iniuſtice, ought not to be ſo culpable in him, as the like vniuſt profit, that may riſe vnto a rich Magiſtrate. S v B S O- L A N v s. Then ſomewhat, belike, you haue yet more at large to ſay, touching Profit in this lower degree, not in Magiſtrates as before, but in ſuch others, as being but poorely borne, haue no way els to liue, but by their owne exerciſe only? A Q V I L O N I V S. Vpon what other pillar els may we better lay the foundation of ſuch a poore mans Profit? S v B S O L A N v s. Will you therfore that we accompt all ſort of Mercenary gaine, which is the reward of Exerciſe, to be good and lawfull? A Q V I- L O N I V S. At leaſtwiſe ſtill vnto a poore and needy man, as I haue ſaid before. S v B S O L A N v s. But how far do you accompt this word *Exerciſe* to be extended? and vnto what? A Q V I L O N I V S. Vnto all ſorts of induſtryes, as well of the mynd, as the body. S v B- s o L A N v s. And all this you will haue vs hold to be lawfull vnto the ſupply of Pouerty? A Q V I L O N I V S. I hitherto ſee no cauſe to the contrary; and the rather alſo, for that according to *Heſiodus*, not Exerciſe, but Idlenes is ſaid to be Villany. S v B S O L A N v s. So that all gainefull Exerciſes you will haue to be lawfull ſtill to a poore man, whether they be of the mynd or body? A- Q V I L O N I V S. I haue alleadged you my authority, confined alſo, as ſome ſay, by *Socrates*, though *Xenophon* perhaps deny it. S v B S O L A N v s. As for example,

it

it may be lawful for him then to make his gaine by Craft,
becaufe it is an Exercife of the mynd, and alfo by Fraud
becaufe it is an Exercife of the body .   A QVILO-
NIVS. You haue not hard me to fay fo as yet .   SVB-
SOLANVS. Then fome exercifes belike may be gainefull, which are not lawfull .   A QVILONIVS.
The cenfure of the Law is one thing, and the vulgar opinion of men another, who do many times admit by cuftome fome things to be laudable, which be not ftrictly
lawfull .   SVBSOLANVS. You meane, perhaps,
that to vfe falfe weights may by the common cuftome
therof be laudable, though not lawfull .   A QVI-
LONIVS. You choofe out ftill the hardeft examples
that may be .   SVBSOLANVS. So that fome exercifes alfo may be gainefull, which be neither lawfull nor
laudable .   A QVILONIVS. It is inough for my
purpofe, if vnto the help of a poore man, they be but only
tolerable .   SVBSOLANVS. You thinke it then
belike a tolerable kind of counterfait gaine, to falfify one
thing for another?   A QVILONIVS. If fo it may
be done in fuch a place, at fuch a time, and by fuch a
poore perfon, as cannot well otherwife liue, what letteth,
I pray you, that it may not be accompted tolerable?
SVBSOLANVS. So as befides the pouerty of the perfon, there muft alfo concur the conuenience of time and
place, to make an euill gaine tolerable?   A QVILO-
NIVS. I put in inough to auoid the rather your exceptions againft it .   SVBSOLANVS. Then fome kind
of gaines may be tolerable in one place, and time, that
may not be tolerable in another?   A QVILONIVS.
I will not greatly ftand with you herein .   SVBSO-
LANVS. And where the exercife is not tolerable, there
the gaine which rifeth therof is not in any wife to be per-

mitted.

mitted.   A QVILONIVS. Hee as yet no great difficulty, why not to allow it.   SVBSOLANVS.
So that one, and the fame gaine may, by the diuerfity of
the time and place, be both tolerable, and not tolerable.
A QVILONIVS. Why not I pray you, as well as one
and the fame gaine, yea at one and the fame time, be both
profitable, and vnprofitable?   SVBSOLANVS.
You will make me, I hope, to vnderftand your mynd a
little better herein.   A QVILONIVS. As for example, to haue gained in the time of war a fierce & bold
horfe, is it not profitable? and yet if his fiercenes & boldnes be fuch as his Maifter cánot vfe him, then that which
is profitable, is alfo vnprofitable to him.   SVB-
SOLANVS. So as by this accompt it would feeme, that
euery thing which is contrary to profit, is vnprofitable.
A QVILONIVS. It foundeth fo of it felfe apparently
inough, if I had not confeffed it already.   SVBSO-
LANVS. Health, Liberty, and Wealth, be they not profitable things?   A QVILONIVS. Profitable I
graunt them to be.   SVBSOLANVS. Then all
that which is contrary to any of thefe is vnprofitable.
A QVILONIVS. How can it otherwife be, by the alleaged rule of contraryes?   SVBSOLANVS. As for
example, the hauing of a rich wife is vnprofitable, becaufe it may be an impediment to health; the ftudy of letters is vnprofitable, becaufe it may be a hinderance to
liberty; and the eating of meate is vnprofitable, becaufe
it is a confuming of wealth.   A QVILONIVS.
You be a merry companion, I fee, to deale with all, that
haue reduced this your difputation of Profit, vnto fo bafe
and vile a conceit in the end, as if beggary were a thing
to be iefted at.

¶   Heere *Fauonius* feing *Subfolanus* entred into a cogitation

tation with himselfe, what anſwere to make hereunto, began before him, to ſay vnto *Aquilonius*. F A V O-N I V S. I am nothing at all of your opinion, that Need may ſerue to excuſe any bad kind of getting. A Q V I-L O N I V S. Nor am I any thing at all of your opinion, for though bad getting, when ſo it is knowne to the world, may be ſomewhat reproachfull, yet pouerty I take to be a greater reproach, becauſe it cannot ſo well be hid. F A-V O N I V S. To hide honeſt pouerty there is no need, for that it bringeth with it no ſhame at all, and conſequently no reproach, as you ſuppoſe it to do; for though at the firſt, it may ſomewhat grieue the mynd with care and ſolliciitude, yet after it is once receiued without reſiſtance, and made familiar, it is facile to beare, and confortable by keeping men ſober, modeſt, continent, and alſo ſecure not only from infirmityes, but likewiſe from the malice of others. For wheras the rich man, if ſo he ſpend not all, is commonly ſaid to be couetous; the poore man we ſee, though his cupidity be neuer ſo great, is alwayes held to be of a free condition full of tranquillity, and repoſe. A-Q V I L O N I V S. What repoſe can there be in pouerty, when neither the mynd, nor the body receiueth thereby any contentment, but are ſtill tormented both the one and the other with the defects which pouerty draweth after it? F A V O N I V S. If Pouerty bring with it any defects, they be of leſſe moment by much, then thoſe that do accompany wealth, the which, by the Philoſopher, be ſaid in his *Ethicks*, to be theſe: firſt Pride, in making men vainely to thinke, that togeather with their riches they haue all other benefits, as well of the mynd, as of the body, and that men may any way poſſeſſe any thing. Secondly Prodigality, cauſing men therby to become ſuperfluous, not only for ſatisfying their ſumptuous deſires, but alſo to

make

make fhew and oftentation of their profperous fortune.
Laftly, it is accompained with Arrogancy, making men
ftill to thinke, that other do admire, and alfo affect that
which they do poffeffe ; whereby fuppofing with their
wealth to make good all their faults, they become to be fo
iniurious to their Neighbours, that the Philofopher concludeth them in the end, to be in little better cafe then for-
tunate Madmen.   A Q V I L O N I V S. As mad as
you make them to be, yet are they able well inough to defend, and fupport themfelues, which the poorer fort are no
way able to do, by reafon that their pouerty doth fo much
oppreffe them.   F A V O N I V S. It is rather the iniurious cruelty of the rich, that doth oppreffe the poore
more then their owne pouerty, the which cannot be burdenfome as you fuppofe, chiefly vnto one who is contented to liue according to the rules of Nature, but only when
it is accompanied rather with fuperfluous thoughts, then
with due feare of neceffary wants.   A Q V I L O N I V S.
You fpeake fo generally againft the cruelty of rich men,
without any diftinction made of their degrees and voca-
tions, as if he who getteth his riches well, and he who getteth it euilly, were both of one Predicament.   F A V O-
N I V S. The rich man fpoken of in the Scripture (*Luc.*
cap. 6.) you do not find, that he was condemned, becaufe
he got his goods euilly, fince the *Euangeli*ʃ doth not fay,
that either he was an Vfurer, or that he poffeffed his wealth
with an euill confcience, but that he vfed it not well, nor
with that charity as he ought to haue done.   A Q V I-
L O N I V S. So that riches you meane cannot be good vnto any, but vnto good men only.   F A V O N I V S.
Nor alwayes vnto good men neither, becaufe we fee by
experience, that vnto fome good men riches do them
hurt, by inciting them to Vice, and drawing them from
Vertue,

Vertue, though the riches themſelues be neither vertuous, nor vicious ; and therfore not euill things only , but things which be indifferent, and which in apparence be good , may alſo do harme , and ſometimes more harme then the things themſelues which be apparantly euill . And hereof it commeth , that a man may more eaſily let other mens goods alone, then vſe his owne well, becauſe on the one he knoweth that he cannot intrude without offence , but with the other he thinketh he may be more bold , to do with it what he will , without rendring any accompt for the ſame . And therfore it is no ſafety for a man to loue his owne riches too well , though they be ne-uer ſo iuſtly gotten, leaſt thereby he be induced , not only to be couetous of that he hath,but to loue thoſe other alſo which may be gotten with fraude , becauſe his too much feruent loue and deſire therof may blind his iudgment ſo much therin , as to make him thinke , at leaſt , that to be lawfull which is not . AQVILONIVS. Then if riches may be hurtfull vnto good men , as well as vnto euill men , vnto what end hath Nature prouided them ? FAVONIVS. She hath prouided them to this end , for men to take therof ſo much only as is ſufficient to prouide for their ſtates , and profeſſions without ſuperfluity : for as the Moone doth neuer eclipſe , but when ſhe is at the Full : ſo the mynd is neuer ſo much obſcured , as it is with the ſuperfluity of riches . And againe , as the Moone is then furtheſt off from the Sunne which giueth it light when it is at the Full; ſo a man when he is fulleſt of riches, is furtheſt off from that equity and iuſtice, which ought to giue him light in all his proceedings : and therefore he might do well herein to imitate that wary Fly,which put-teth not her feet into the great maſſe of Hony , but only taketh with her tongue, ſo much therof as ſerueth her

K turne

turne and no more, leaſt by doing otherwiſe ſhe might remayne taken and drowned therein . A Q V I L O-
N I V S. So that by this accompt the more that rich men
haue, ſo much the leſſe liberty they poſſeſſe. F A V O-
N I V S. Therof you may be ſure, ſince gold and ſiluer was
neuer made to loade men withall, as captiues thereunto,
but to loade mules and horſes therwith, which be captiues
by Nature, and neuertheles do not take vpon them more
then their forces be able to beare; wheras the couetous rich
man neuer thinketh he hath inough on his back, till he fall
to the ground with it, nor then neither vntill he hath taken
vpon him ſo much, as he is ouerwhelmed & quelled downe
vnder it. And is not this, thinke you, a thraldome and vtter loſſe of Liberty? A Q V I L O N I V S. You ſay
well at leaſt wiſe, for ſo much credit as there needeth to be
giuen to ſuch fabulous ſimilitudes; but the poorer ſort the
while being oppreſſed with their pouerty indeed, do looſe
therby their liberty for alltogeather, not fabulouſly, as you
reſemble the rich to do, but viſibly and palpably, to the
ſight and feeling of all men . F A V O N I V S. And
yet for al this many poore men we haue hard of, not only
amongſt Chriſtians, but amongſt the Pagan Philoſophers
themſelues, who notwithſtanding their pouerty haue voluntarily and freely neglected and contemned riches. As
for example, *Anacharſes* refuſed the treaſure ſent him by
Creſus: alſo *Anacreontes* refuſed the treaſure ſent him by
Policrates; and *Albionus* refuſed the treaſure ſent him by
Antigonus, beſides many more of that profeſſion, too long
to be here recited . A Q V I L O N I V S. I hold them
all to haue byn vnwiſe, or, to ſay better, for ſtarke fooles ;
becauſe, if ſo they had no need of it, they might haue giuen
it to others, who were in neceſſity, but by doing of neither, they did not therby make known themſelues ſo much

for

for contemners of riches, as for fishers after vayne glory:
the which passion being of the two the more deare vnto
them , therfore to buy them fame , they forsooke to take
money ; like as those good drinkers do , who sell their
wheate to buy them mault , not because they hate bread ,
but because of the two, they loue their drinke better.
FAVONIVS. Perhaps in pouerty there be yet some greater contentments then you be aware of , els what should
haue caused the great Conquerour of the world to say ,
that if he were not *Alexander* , he would wish to be *Diog .-
nes* , who was of all other the poorest Philosopher of his
time , or that was euer after him .   AQVILONIVS.
You haue lighted vpon a notable couple of fishers after
glory, and very well matched them togeather , the one by
the way of too much riches , and the other by the way of
too little sustenance , yea lesse then would serue his need,
or the decency of his profession .   FAVONIVS.
And yet not only *Alexander* himselfe , but many others
also did hold him to be the happiest man of that age.   A-
QVILONIVS. Excesse of passion is the cause of many
extrauagancies , and therfore *Diogene* yielded lesse to the
care of his need , then vnto the care of his said excessiue
vayne glorious passion .   FAVONIVS. And I am
of another opinion , to wit, that Passion is more flexible
then Need , the which is reputed not to be subiect vnto
any Law at all; wheras the other we see is restrayned
many wayes , as by penaltyes , by subordination , and
sometimes also by gratuity , all which in their kinds do
not a little bridle mens extrauagant passions.   AQVI-
LONIVS. I do not seeke to enter so deeply into the
search of such Quiddityes , but this I know by experience now adayes , that not the learnedst Philosophers but
the richest Worldlings be accompted, not only for the
K 2

happiest

happieft creatures, but alfo for the wifeft men .

¶   Heere *Subfolanus*, as one that could forbeare no longer to heare *Aquilonius* fo far out of the way, preuenting *Fauonius* his anfwere, began thus to fay vnto him . S V B S O L A N V S. Where, I pray you , was that couetous Wifdome , yon fpeake of, at the very firft beginning of things , when there was not yet in the world any kind of money , or riches to be found at all , but that ech where one commodity was changed for another ? Belike the men of thofe dayes , if wifedome , as you fay, had chiefly confifted in riches , were all fooles, and yet fome Wifemen haue faid , That happy , and moft happy were they , who liued in that fo fimple and honeft an age , while no vanityes were as yet difcouered amongft men , nor any difordinate appetites obfcured the light of the vnderftanding , with the temptations of the fraile and deceiuable fenfes ; and while there were as yet no weapons , nor warres , nor locks , nor doores, no robbing , nor ftealing, nor any violent temptations vnto any kind of wickednes. For though women and men did conuerfe togeather no leffe then they do now , yet the women were modeft and fhamefaft , and the men myld , and both of them continent , being accuftomed to mortify and fuppreffe the difobedience of the flefh , partly with abftinence , and partly with affiduous labour, fo as they felt no great motiues vnto finne: I meane that innocent and pacificall age , when no Mettall was as yet digged out of the earth , nor no oxe , nor horfe emploied to till the ground , but that euery one liued of that which the earth it felfe of it owne accord brought forth , without the help of any induftry or art; for fo God of his bounty had ordayned , that all thofe things , wherof man had need, as flefh, fruites, and the like, fhould be prouided for him , & produced for his vfe aboue the gound, hyding

and

and burying all thofe other things which were fuperfluous (as gold , filuer , and the reft) within the bowells
of the earth it felfe , to the end he fhould neither loue them
nor defire them , nor be tempted to vfe them , in refpe&
of the great harme he might receiue by them. Befides that,
no timbred Oake , nor Firre , nor Pyne had then byn framed into fhips , to furrow the windy feas , either for curi-
ofity to paffe from one Country to another , or els to fetch
home the variety of forrayne vnknowne delicacyes : the
which art of nauigating , whofoeuer firft found out (were
it either the *Sorians* , or the *Phenicians* , or els *Iafon* of *Ar-
gos* and his Confederates) certaine it is , that no other
occafion moued them therunto , but meere auarice only,
wherof hath enfued both rapines , violences , deaths , ruines and great difperfions of people. For if Nauigation had
neuer been found out , the King of *Colchos* had neuer byn
depriued of his golden Fleece , togeather with the death
of his Sonne , & the rapine of his daughter ; nor the Citty of *Troy* had neuer by the Greeks byn deftroyed , togeather with *Priamus* the King therof , and all his pofterity ;
nor *Greece* it felfe had neuer byn fo defolated , as it was ,
by the great nauy of *Xerxes* King of *Afia* . Moreouer in
that age no paper , nor pen was yet in vfe , wherewith to
write any Statutes , or Decrees , vntill the time that *Minos*
gaue Lawes to the *Candians* , *Lucurgus* to the *Lacedemonians* , *Solon* to the *Athenians* , *Trifmegiftus* to the *Thebans* ,
Phido to the *Corinthians* , *Caronda* to the *Carthaginians* , *R-
mulus* and *Numa Pompilius* to the *Romans* : for before thofe
times men liued vnder thofe happy , and pleafant confti-
tutions , which Nature her felfe had planted in their
breafts , full of fincerity , full of meekenes , and full of all
other pacificall confolation , as well mentall , as corporal.
Therfore now to anfwere to your former allegation ,

K 3   that

that rich men are the wifeit men , fhould thefe other men who were fo happy for all things els, be therfore faid to be fooles, becaule they chiefly wanted the vfe of money , and therby the delire to poſſeſſe the fame too greedily , as you would haue that wife man of yours to do ?   A Q V I-
L O N I V S. Whatſoeuer in thofe dayes they of whom you fpeake either might,or might not haue byn faid to be, I wil not much ftand vpon ; but this I will ftill affirme , that if now in this age of ours fuch poore playne dealing men , were liuing, neither would their fincerity, nor their meek-nes , nor their pacificall fpirits be able to get them fo much reputation of wit, as their rude pouerty would condemne them for fooles ; whiles fuffering thereby a number of worldly greiuances , they could neither be gratefull to themſelues , nor yet acceptable vnto others. For if fuch a poore man fhould now , but open his mouth to fpeake , euery body ftraight would be ready to laugh at him , and to aske , Who is this ? according to that in *Ecclef.* 13.
S V B S O L A N V S. Thofe worldly grieuances which po-uerty you fay bringeth with it ,do rather proceed of cupi-dity then of any neceſſary need , for that the body may be fuftayned with a little , and therfore I fee no reafon why men with fo much ftudy and care fhould feeke to feed, and nourifh the fame, or to adorne, and couer it fo fumptuouſ-ly as they do , fpending therein their riches fuperfluouſly, and with very little praife at all , if not rather with rebuke and fhame , fince they may otherwife fo eafily find , not only wherewith to feed, but alfo wherewith to veft , with-out feeking as they do for the fpices, and filkes of forrayne Countryes ; for that chiefly vnto thefe ends , we fee , is the faid cupidity of their riches conuerted, if not vnto auarice, the which of the two is the worft : for though the fame , after a fort , may be coloured with the care to be had of pofterity,

fterity , yet in the meane feafon , none are fo miferable as
they who defire ouermuch , fince therby they are ready
to fuffer a thoufand indignityes, & a thoufand difgraces,
if not alfo perills for the fatisfying of their vnfatiable defires, and many times alfo vnto their owne ruyne , as happened vnto *Crefus* the King of *Lydia*, and vnto *Craffus* the
Roman , the one ouercome by *Cyrus* for his wealth already gotten , and the other put to death by the *Parthians* in
feeking to get more then he had: fo as the Rich man fometimes mounteth , fometimes fincketh , fometimes commaundeth, fometimes ferueth , fometimes is fplendidous,
fometimes obfcure , fometimes threatneth , fometimes
intreateth , and all this for the refpect of things which be
vile; and therfore how much more ftable and fecure art
thou on the other fide (ô gentle Pouerty !) thou , I fay ,
who when thou obferueft the Lawes of Nature , doeft
fubdue all paynfull induftry , doeft ouercome all mortall
honour and doeft contemne the vayne difcourfes of men,
not caring for the heat of the fummer , nor much efteeming the cold of the winter, but contented to repaire the
one with the fhaddow of the leaued trees , and to withftand the other with the help of the cheap vntawed skins
of beafts, wherby in that homely weed thou fhunneft the
temptations of all idle loue , of all vaine lafciuioufnes, &
of all fhamefull luft , as alfo all the enuy of men , all the
daunger of theeues , and all the difturbance of broken
fleeps : wherfore to thee be the eternall praife of all in-
geniofity , of all inuentions , and of all arts , as vnto the
egregious Mother of all ftudy , of all fpeculation , and of
all operation : whofe vertues (to conclude) be many ,
whofe refuges more , and whofe benefits be infinite.   A-
QVILONIVS . Thefe be Sophifticall fictions , rather
then reafons , all of them found out by the art and malig-
nity

nity of such, as vnder a certaine kind of Philosophicall authority, do attend to inuent those abstracted arguments,
therby to giue credit and reputation to the beggarly and
bare state of their owne base fortune, because they are not
able to attayne vnto more; and therfore annexing Pride
vnto Beggary, do wax bold therby, to make an exteriour
shew of competency with the rich, while interiourly yet
they be glad, when they can, but to finger only some frag-
ments of their felicity and aboundance, vnder pretence
sometimes to buy them bookes, and other like necessaryes,
though they bestow it after, more lasciuiously then they
would willingly be knowne to do; and therefore there is
no heed to be taken at all vnto their publike words, and
sayings, but rather to their hidden thoughts, and secret
workings, contrary to that which they preach and teach
vnto others openly, making them belieue in shew that
their owne state is better, then the state of the rich, though
they thinke it to be otherwise, & would be glad to change
with them. Which kind of proceeding *Pliny* writing to his
friend *Fabatus*, doth say, That there is nothing more perillous then to thinke, that the state of one man is better then
another, because hereby they who find themselues to be in
the worst, neuer leaue to contend, if not also to conspire,
ag inst the fame of those others whom they suppose to be
in better state then they. And hence it commeth, that the
poore do inueigh so much against the rich, not for that
they would not be rich themselues, but as I haue said before, because they are not able to reach to any more, then
their beggarly fortune hath allotted them .   S v b s o-
l a n v s. What more in this world should either they, or
any other need to seeke for, then a quiet and pacificall
mynd, well contented with whatsoeuer God sendeth, be
it either Pouerty, or what other thing els; since with this
only

only confolation , a man is happy inough ; though he be
otherwife neuer fo poore ; and without this , he is nothing happy , though his riches be neuer fo great : So that
euery ftate is good , and euery ftate is euill , not fo much
in refpect of it felfe , as in refpect of the circumftances it
bringeth with it . For who will deny , that the ftate of a
rich man may not be good , if fo it be vfed with temperance ; or that the ftate of a poore man may not be euill ,
if fo it be not fupported with patience , fince not the fufferance of any aduerfity doth make a man happy and bleffed , but the pacificall mynd wherewith he tolerateth the
fame; and therfore euery one ought to conforme himfelfe
not vnto that ftate which he may thinke of in his mynd
(becaufe worldly men do moft of all inclyne vnto that
which their couetoufnes doth make them defire) but vnto that ftate and degree , whether fo it be rich or poore,
which God for the more fafety of his foule hath put him
into . For fo we fee all other things els conferue the ftates
which God firft gaue them , without repining thereat at
all ; as the Heauens , the Starres , the Aire , the Fire , the
Water, the Earth, and all forts of beafts, of fifhes , and of
plants , and all other earthly creatures, only man excepted , who by his fall into finne, is neuer contented with
his ftate, but is alwayes defirous of change : the Coun-
try-man would be a Cittizen , the Cittizen would be a
Souldier, the Souldier would be a Merchant, and the
Merchant would be a Gentleman ; and which is moft of
all ftrange , the poore man would leaue his quiet , his careleffe , and his vnpenfiue ftate , to change with the rich
man for his , who neither day nor night , nor fleeping ,
nor waking doth poffeffe either of body , or mynd any
fweet repofe .   A Q V I L O N I V S . It is a very hard
thing to be able to perfwade men with reafons , vnto that
                                L   which

which they feele to be otherwife in themfelues by experience ; for who may repofe more quietly then may the rich,
that haue all their neceffaryes prouided for to their hands ,
and alfo their labourfome Offices executed by others ? or
if by chance they breake any fleep , it is , you may be fure ,
in thinking of golden employments , or els touching ex-
ployts of Policy and Preferment : fo that, the not fleeping
of the rich , is more comfortable far , then is the vnquiet
and halfe ftarued fleep of the poore , in the next degree vnto death it felfe . And therfore , as it is more then neceffary for a poore man , both for his fleeping and waking , to
feeke to better his ftate , by the getting of riches to releiue
his penury , and to comfort his faid vnquiet repofe ; fo is it
no leffe neceffary for a rich man to conferue and increafe
his wealth already poffeffed , without being too careleffe ,
or too negligent therof , at euery fmattering Booke-mans
perfwafion; for like as ftrength was ordained to withftand
violences, and not that the ftrong fhould fillily fuffer themfelues to be ouerlaid ; and as health was ordayned to make
men able to follow their affaires , and not that the health-
full fhould retiredly ruft away in idlenes:fo riches were alfo ordayned to help to prouide for neceffaryes , & not that
the rich fhould either foolifhly forfake , or confume their
wealth lauifhly. For what praife could it be either to *Lucius
Mummius* the Roman Captayne (who fubdued *Corinth*)
to haue died fo poore , by neglecting his owne ftate , as
his Souldiers were driuen to make a common gathering
for his buriall? Or vnto *Paulus Æmilius* (who fubdued *Ma-
cedon*) to haue left his daughters fo poore , by the like occafion , that the Common Wealth was faine to giue them
their marriage money ? Or els vnto the younger *Africanus*
(who deftroyed *Carthage*) to haue neglected fo much the
care of his family , as his Daughters were fayne to begge
for

for their dowryes? Thefe be the braue examples of the
negle⳾ors and defpifers of riches, to haue greatly dam-
nified, if not vtterly vndone, their pofterity thereby;
contrary vnto that which we read of *Pallas*, of *Callistus*,
and of *Narciffus*, the infranchifed flaues to *Claudius* the
Emperour, who left behind them diuers millions of
Crownes; as alfo amongft the Philofophers, we read of
Cicero, of *Terentius Varro*, and of *Seneca* to haue rifen from
little to be men of great riches : and likewife amongft the
fouldiers we read of *Caius Marius*, *Lucius Sylla*, and of
Ventidius Baffus, who by their owne induftryes rofe vp
vnto infinite wealth, and their pofterity after them vnto
great fame and glory; where on the other fide, what in
this world can be more reproachfull then pouerty, or a
greater enemy vnto all kind of vertue, either in women
or men ? As for example, in women what more vnfaith-
full a Guardian may there be found of their chaftity (and
confequently of all that is good in them) then is want
and neceffity, when as the vnmarried be eafily drawne
thereby vnto all forts of lafciuioufnes, for fupply of their
need, and the married be drawne no leffe to make like ha-
uock of their honefty ? And in the fame fort touching the
ftate of men, what fo much doth abafe them, or maketh
abie⳾ and vile their mynds, not only in their owne conceits, but alfo in the opinion of others, as doth the burden of Pouerty : for (fo faith the Wife man, *Ecclef. cap. 9.*)
That the wifedome of the poore is defpifed. And againe (Ecclef. cap 40) *That it were better to be dead, then to liue in
want and need*; adding withall in his Prouerbes; *That all
the dayes of a poore mans life, be nothing els but mifery*. Befides
that, what alfo may be vnto gratuity a greater enemy
then the fame? What vnto fhamefaftnes, *Cùm non bene
conueniunt, nec in vna fede morantur pudor & egeftas?* And
L 2   what

what vnto the obferuation of all forts of Laws, both humane, and diuine, vnto the which neceffity beareth no refpect at all ? So that not without caufe is Pouerty called the greateft enemy vnto man, the companion vnto all kind of Vice, and of all other euills the extreameft, yea worfe then either fickenes, or imprifonment : for that vnto him who is wealthy, there be remedyes inough to be applyed for the one, and confolations inough to be found for the other; and therfore though you in words do feeme to fauour pouerty neuer fo much, yet I fuppofe for the putting of it in practife, you will ftriue againft it, no leffe then any other.   Svbsolanvs. To ftriue againft Pouerty, we are not exprefly commaunded, further then neceffity requireth, nor yet prohibited, fo long as men get riches without the violating of Iuftice, the which is vnderftood to be violated, not only by fraude, or force, as hath byn faid before; but partly by not reftoring that which is borrowed, and partly by not rendring at the day that which is hired, and likewife by not abftayning to weare out things left vs in cuftody and truft. And as none of thefe iniuftices are to be vfed for the reliefe of pouerty, fo alfo much leffe for the increafe of wealth, fince the fuperfluity therof is not, as you fuppofe, a fhunner of vice, but an enemy to vertue, as hath byn told you already, making men fo idle, fo flouthfull, and fo lafciuious, as they become altogeather effeminate, neither giuen to the practife of Armes, nor yet to the ftudy of letters. And therfore *Democritus* iudged the aboundance of riches to be foolifh, *Heraclitus* iudged it to be miferable, and *Crates* iudged it to be friuolous and burdenfome, for which refpect he threw his Wealth into the fea; though no kind of wealth be fo burdenfome as that, which being wrongfully gotten, doth

feldome

feldome tymes defcend vnto the third generation, & therfore the burden of honeft pouerty cannot be fo heauy to
beare by much, as the burden of a rich mans culpable cen-
fcience. For what els doth take away either the innocency
from the body, or the life from the foule, but the infection
of finne? So that finne alone is more hurtfull vnto man
then can be the hurt of all the world befides, or of Hell it
felfe. For what draue the Angells out of Heauen (*Ifa. 14.*)
and Adam out of Paradife (*Genef. 3.*) or the great Floud
into the world (*Gen. 8.*) but finne? Or what els ouerthrew
the great Tower of *Babylon* (*Gen. 11.*) or deftroyed *Ama-
lec*, and the Gyants (*Exod. 17.*) or caufed to be cut in
peeces the great army of *Senacherib* (4. *Reg. 19.*) but finne?
not to fpeake of the burning of fiue Cittyes (*Gen. 19.*) or
of the perfecuting of *Ægipt* with the feauen plagues (*Gen.
41.*) or of the drowning of *Pharao* in the red fea (*Exod. 14.*)
And finally (to omit all other examples ancient and moderne) what are all the miferyes, calamityes, & afflictions
that fall vpon men, but punifhments for finne? And therfore feeing that aboundance of riches is a fpeciall motiue,
and caufe of finne (as I haue declared before) it is euident
that rich men are in a dangerous ftate; in which refpect
our Sauiour himfelfe affirmeth, That it is as hard for a rich
man to enter into Heauen, as a Camel to paffe through a
needles eye: wheras poore men on the other fide, are in
farre greater fecurity, if they be good men withall: for
they do ftill receaue comfort from God in all their diftref-
fes be they neuer fo great, and do neuer want neceffaryes.
For fo God releiued the pouerty of *Agar* by an Angell (*Gen.
16.*) the diftreffe of *Dauid* and his people in the defert,
(2. *Reg. 17.*) the mifery of *Noemi* by *Ruth* the wife of
Booz. (*Ruth. 2.*) and the pouerty of *Elias* by an Angell
(3. *Reg. 29.*) befides the like done vpon diuers occafions

to the Apoftles themſelues (*Act.* 5. 1 2. 27.) and to innumerable other good men in all ages , wherof infinit examples might be alledged.Furthermore the poore man who
being confident of Gods mercifull prouidence , is contented with that which God giueth him , wanteth nothing ,
hauing all that he will haue , becauſe in not willing that
which is fuperfluous , he hath whatſoeuer he deſireth, and
therfore he alone may be ſaid to be poore, who is not contented with that which he hath, and deſireth ſuperfluityes.
And on the other ſide , only he may be ſaid to be rich, who
hath no need nor want of any thing , more then is requiſite , and who deſireth not that which he hath not , but
only ſo much as he muſt needs vſe , and may alſo conueniently haue : ſo as it is not the aboundance of wealth that
maketh a man rich, but the contented mynd ; nor the want
of wealth that maketh a poore man , but the mynd afflicted for that which is wanting . And therfore to be rich
with deſire of increaſe , is to be poore, and to be poore
without deſire of more , is to be rich : the which is another
accompt then the world doth vſe to make either of the one
or the other , reputing him to be poore who hath but little,
though he be content therewith , and him to be rich who
hath a great deale , though he liue beſides it , and neuer
thinkes he hath inough. And theſe kind of rich men be
inferiour far vnto that other ſort of poore men, both in life,
in death , and alſo after death : in life , I meane , becauſe
the poore man enioyeth more his liberty ; both to go where
he will , and to ſpeake what he will , without any great
heed taken vnto him ; alſo ſuffereth more eaſily miſeryes ,
as one who is more accuſtomed to beare them , and taketh
more pleaſure in any recreation , as one not ſo wonted to
haue them . Likewiſe the rich man is inferiour to the
poore man in reſpect of his death, becauſe no body conſpi-
reth

reth or defireth his end , for that nothing is to fall vnto them by the fame ; neither hath he himfelfe when he departeth any burden to difquiet his mynd, for that he hath not any accompts with the world to make, neither is he fo loath to leaue the world , as the rich man is, to whom not only the houre of death , but alfo the very remembrance therof is moft bitter , as teftifieth the holy Scripture, faying ; *O mors, quàm amara eſt memoria tui homini habenti pacem in ſubſtantijs ſuis !* Moreouer to fhew that the rich man is likewife inferiour to the poore man after his death , there fhall need heere no other proofe , then that which Chrift himfelfe hath faid therof (*Luc . 6.*) *Bleſſed are you that be poore , for yours is the Kingdome of heauen .* And againe ; *Miſerable are you rich men , who in your riches haue all your conſolation .* So that the rich man hath his glory here on earth and the poore man hath his in heauen ; and therfore God ordayned in the old Law (*Deuter. 10.*) *That the Leuites who were choſen for the Altar, and for his owne ſeruice , ſhould haue no poſſeſsions :* and in the new Law the Apoftle teftifieth (*1. Cor. 1.*) that *Pauperes elegit Deus ad hereditatem regni cæle is :* yea our Sauiour Chrift did not only liue in pouerty himfelfe , and choofe poore difciples , but alfo did aduife and counfell a young rich man, to fell all that he had , and giue it to the poore : So that pouerty, although it be moft where abhorred, yet is it a great, and an ineftimable treafure, in refpect both of the world to come, and alfo of this life , as being the mother of tranquillity , the excluder of difquietnes , the Port of contentment and reft , a fufferance without loffe, a paffion without ftrife , and the high way to eternall happines in heauen , fo that it be fought and willingly fuffered for the loue of God . A-QVILONIVS. And yet for all this we fee few rich men that do abandone their wealth, to make themfelues poore,

which

which is a great figne that there is fomething in pouerty more contrary to nature, then there is in riches.

¶ Heere *Fauonius* mifliking the obftinacy of *Aquilonius*, faid thus vnto him.   FAVONIVS. He who fpeaketh againft pouerty, fpeaketh againft riches: for firft, men were poore before they were rich, and fo labouring by little and little againft their faid pouerty, haue become to be rich in the end.   AQVILONIVS. Then according to this reafon, we might likewife fay, that he who fpeaketh againft Difprofit, fpeaketh againft Profit; albeit before, we haue faid them to be contraryes.   FAVONIVS. As contrary as they are, it cannot be denyed, but that Difprofit goeth before Profit, and fpending before getting; the Plowman muft fpend in tilling his ground, before he can reape any fruit; the Artizan muft lay out in buying of wares to worke vpon, before he can receiue any gaine; and the Merchant at fea muft put in venter to loofe all, before he can come to fee his owne againe. Alfo the Suitor at Law fpendeth much in following of his fuite, before he can come to haue any iudgment on his fide; the cūning Courtier giueth firft many Prefents, before he can get any reward in recompence; and the buyer of Land layeth out more money in one hower, then he is to fee againe in twenty yeares after. Likewife the makers of paper muft buy many rags, before their paper can be made; the Printers of bookes muft buy paper, before their books can be fold; and the ftudents of Sciences muft buy many bookes, before they can make any profit of their ftudyes; wherby it appeareth that Difprofit many times is the beginner of Profit.   AQVILONIVS. So as by this meanes you will inferre, that if you take away pouerty, you take away riches; and if you take away Difprofit, you take away Profit.   FAVONIVS. You

fay

say well, since for as much as belongeth to the first part
of your proposition, I do aske you, What delight a rich
man might hope to find in his riches, if so there were no
poore man to do his labours for him ? As for example, to
till his ground, to keep his horses, to go to the market, to
dresse his meat, to fetch home his wood, to playster his
walls, and the like; all which seruile offices, and many
other worse then these, if he should be driuen to do them
himselfe, his wealth might lye by him, and stand him in
little steed : so as though by taking away pouerty, you do
not actually take away the meanes vnto the getting, and
increasing of riches (which may sometimes be otherwise also obtayned, then by industrious pouerty) yet in
effect you should bring therby the rich man to be (for
want of Drudges to serue him) in little better case then
the poore man himselfe; which poore man, by doing but
only those labours for his owne proper vse, which he is
now hired to do for the rich man, and the rich man therby forced to do those labours for himselfe, which now
the poore man doth for him for his money, he would be
of the two, in worse case, by being lesse able then the rich
man to take such paynes; and therfore the poore man, if
he will, may better liue like a poore man, without the
help of the rich man, then the rich man may liue like a
rich man, without the help of the poore man.   A-
QVILONIVS. I thinke you two haue conspired togeather to sort out betwixt you all the subtiltyes, that may
be found in the fauour of pouerty, which yet when you
haue all done, is like inough (according to the Prouerbe)
betwixt two stooles to fall to the bare ground; where
barely also it may be like to lye, and that for a good while,
I suppose, ere either of you both will stoope to take it vp.
But what on the other side haue you yet to say, touching

our mentioned difprofitable Profit? Belike you meane to
reduce alfo the fame vnto fuch a iefting reckoning, as *Sub-
folinus*, a little before, brought the like propofition. FA-
VONIVS. You fhall fee that, ere it belong, by my manner of proceeding; wherin I haue likewife to aske you,
Whether al that wealth which is extant now in the world,
be not ech where already poffeffed? AQVILO-
NIVS. It can not be denyed, but that it is. FA-
VONIVS. Then whofoeuer will go about to make any
increafe of Profit, muft feeke to drawe to himfelfe fome
part of that wealth of the world which others do yet poffeffe. AQVILONIVS. If your meaning be of
money, either gold, or filuer, he muft do fo perforce.
FAVONIVS. So as he who hath money muft firft diminifh therof, before he, who hath no money, or els but little
money, can be able to increafe the fame. AQVILO-
NIVS. Good reafon it is, that it fhould be fo. FA-
VONIVS. Then the difprofit of the one muft precede
the Profit of the other, and fo by confequence, if you take
away the difprofit, you take away the Profit, as hath byn
faid before. AQVILONIVS. You deceiue your
felfe herein, and that not a little, fince it is not like, that
he who hath wealth, will fo diminifh himfelfe of his hauing, without fome recompence from him who hath to
participate therof, either by his feruice, or by his worke, or
els by fome other recompence, whereby his Difprofit one
way is to be reftored him againe, by his Profit fome other
way. FAVONIVS. But what do you fay moreo-
uer vnto this other point vnthought of, which yet remayneth behind: May not that which a rich man doth take to
be for his Profit, fall out otherwife to be Difprofitable vnto him? AQVILONIVS. You may do well to
explane your felfe fomewhat better, and then will I an-
                                                        fwere

{were you.　　Favonivs. As for example, If a rich Vſurer ſhould haue need of a poore Brokers ſeruice, to help to put out his money to vſury, giuing him for euery hundred ſo put forth a competent reward, and that the Broker being bribed on the other ſide, ſhould cauſe him to lend his money to one who hath no meanes to repay it; Heere I would know of you, by what kind of Profit, the Vſurer hath to repayre the domage of his Diſprofit?　Aqvilonivs. By ſeeking his remedy of the Broker: or if he be not able to make it him good, then to ſtand to his owne loſſe.　　Favonivs. So that in this caſe, his Profit like inough may be turned to Diſprofit.　Aqvilonivs. It cannot be auoyded, but that ſometimes ſuch caſualtyes will happen.　　Favonivs. But what if the Broker himſelfe ſhould looſe hereby the credit of his office for euer after; would not this be likewiſe vnto him a greater Diſprofit, then the Profit of his bribe receiued for doing that treachery?　Aqvilonivs· A bird in the hand, I can tell you, is better then two in the buſh; and therfore it is not good for ſuch a poore man, to leaue the certainty, for the incertainty, left his pouerty might wholy oppreſſe him, while his ſaid credit is yet but a growing.　　Favonivs. Then in a poore man I perceiue you accompt Treachery not to be Diſhoneſty.　　Aqvilonivs. Leſſe diſhoneſty in him by much, you may be ſure, then if it were in a rich man.　Favonivs. So as we may now ſay by this accompt of yours, that there be two ſorts of honeſties; one for rich men, & another for poore men.　Aqvilonivs. You might long ſince haue vnderſtood my meaning herein, without theſe replications.　　Favonivs. As for example, you meane that the rich mans honeſty muſt be tyed, at left, vnto all

　the

the ſtriƈteſt rules therof that may be, as well concerning
the habits of the mynd, as the vertues of the body, the one
to be limited with ſincerity, and the other with equity.
A QVILONIVS. It quadreth very well with his condition.   FAVONIVS. But the poore mans honeſty
you ſay, muſt be permitted to haue a larger ſcope, chiefly
in reſpeƈt of his neceſſity.   AQVILONIVS. It is
a thing, I can tell you, to be had in conſideration. FA-
VONIVS. So that, if I ſhould praƈtiſe with ſuch a needy
poore fellow, I muſt allow him the liberty to deceiue me,
if he can.   AQVILONIVS. Such publique allow-
ance therof is not neceſſary, but only a kind of ſilent toleration, in reſpeƈt of his vrgent need.   FAVONIVS.
As much to ſay, as that I muſt allow him the name of an
honeſt man, but yet not truſt him any more, then if he
were a very Knaue.   AQVILONIVs. Faire words,
I pray you, ſince Nature you know is of her ſelfe fraile,
and this world of ours more corrupted thē euer, according
to *Subſolanus* his aſſertion a little before.   FAVO-
NIVS. Will it not then be neceſſary for theſe reſpeƈts to
ſeeke to diſtinguiſh ſomewhat further, whom you take to
be a poore man, and whom not, to the end we may deale
with him accordingly?   AQVILONIVS. A poore
man, I take him to be, according to the limitation of the
Ciuill Law, whoſe wealth doth not paſſe the value of fifty Crownes.   FAVONIVS. Then if any neceſſity of myne ſhould conſtrayne me to vſe the help of a new
ſet vp Notary, not knowne to me before, I muſt firſt aske
him, whether his wealth do amount to fifty Crownes, before I do aduenture to vtter vnto him the ſecrets of my intention, to the end to know what kind of honeſty I may
looke for at his hands, either the ſtriƈt, or els the more
ample.   AQVILONIVS. You ſeeme, me thinkes,
inclined

inclined rather to quarrell, then to conclude, by picking thefe exceptions fo impertinent to the purpofe.

¶ Heere *Subfolanus* being defirous to draw this que-ftion to an end, began againe to fay to *Aquilonius*. S v b - s o L A N v s. Me thinkes it would now be requifite, fee-ing nothing can be profitable, as hath been faid before, that is not iuft, to add therunto this other affertion, that nothing can be iuft, which is not honeft ; for that no iu-ftice can ftand without honefty, nor no honefty with-out iuftice, nor no Profit without both : and therfore like as Honefty in a Magiftrate, is to be called Iuftice, fo Iuftice in a poore man is to be accounted Honefty, and both honefty and iuftice as well in the poore man, as in the Magiftrate, are to be called Vertues, becaufe he who is not vertuous can neither be iuft, nor yet honeft; wher-upon it followeth, that the ground of all lawfull Profit, muft firft proceed from Vertue, as from the originall of all morall goodnes, fince he who is vertuous, hath all-wayes a fcruple to get any thing indirectly, left he fhould be vrged to make reftitution therof againe with fhame ; for he who doth not this, deceiueth many others, and himfelfe alfo, vnto his owne vtter perdition in the end, as fhall appeare further hereafter. So that vertue, iuftice, honefty, and lawfull Profit go allwayes linked infepara-bly togeather ; the Profit being directed by iuftice, and honefty, and both thefe by vertue. Furthermore what fufficient excufe or pretence can there be for fraudulent dealing, when Nature her felfe hath prouided fufficient and lawfull meanes for the reliefe of pouerty, to wit, ho-neft induftry, and frugall parfimony, two fuch princi-pall, and alfo familiar kinds of helps, as few men be de-barred from them, at leaft wife, for the fupply of fo much as is needfull. For firft, as touching honeft induftry, it is

M 3   to

to be noted, that no man by nature hath more burden laid
vpon him, then of one mouth to feed, and of one backe
to cloath; vnto the fupply wherof, fhe hauing giuen him
two leggs, and alfo two hands, the number of Puruey-
ours, is double to the number of confumers : befides that,
fhe hath alfo giuen him agility of wit to teach him, and
ftrength of body to enable him, and freenes of will to put
him forward vnto the lawfull applying his faid leggs and
hands, for the fuftenance of his whole body. And as concerning his frugall parfimony to fpare and lay vp of that,
which he hath lawfully gotten, his owne reafon, befides
the inftinct of nature, ought not a little to mooue him therunto, fince dayly there may happen vnto him, not only
vnlooked for loffes, but alfo ficknes which may hinder his
induftry, if not age it felfe, which is not apt to worke any
more; and therfore the remedy vnto all thefe cafualtyes,
is that frugall parfimony fpoken of before, the which may
be called a fure and fauourable Hofpitall, if not rather a
Sanctuary to keep men from penury, and imprifonment,
far more fure then heretofore were either the publike Hofpitall of *Cadmus* in *Thebes*, or the famous Temple of *Diana*
in *Ephefus*; for if men would be content to leaue off all
defrauding, and liue frugally, that is to fay, with only fo
much as were neceffary, we fhould fee as few beggers, or
as few prifoners for debt, as we fee at this day either *Cen-
taures*, or *Gorgons*.   A QVILONIVS. Thefe rules
of yours againft fraude, and deceiuing, and in the fauour
of lawfull getting, were, I confeffe, to be confidered, if
euery man would be content to obferue them alike, as wel,
I meane, the contented poore man with his owne eftate,
as he who afpireth vnto higher fortune : but fince it is impoffible to bring it to paffe, but that deceiuers of men, for
their owne gaine, will ftill be found, I hold it therefore
a kind

a kind of worldly wifedome, rather to deceiue then to be deceiued; fo long as it is warily done, either for the fupply of need, or els, as hath byn faid, vnto the increafe of degree, for that euery man will not be content to liue alwayes in low eftate, as you by your former propofitions would fuppofe.   Svbsolanvs. Though he be neuer fo defirous to increafe his degree aboue the ranke of thofe of whome we haue laftly fpoken, yet to promote that defire of his, he muft not go about to deceiue others, vnder pretence of not being deceiued, fince hereby it might follow, that he may fo deceiue thofe who had no intention at all to deceiue him: befides that, if you will allow profitable deceiuing to be fuch a badge of a worldly wife man, you take thereby away from his wifedome, all the reputation of that vertue, iuftice, and honefty which we haue already fpoken of, and fo thereby do make no difference betwixt good men, and euill men. Aqvilonivs I would not you fhould take me for fuch a confounder of thefe things fo togeather, but that ftill, I make this difference betwixt them ; to wit, that thefe men for the moft part, whom you do accompt to be good, are ech where feene to be poore, needy, miferable, full of aduerfityes, full of wants, full of affliction, and full of all perfecution, becaufe either they cannot flatter, or not tolerate the lightnes of mens conditions, or not forbeare to fpeake of their faults too freely; wheras contrarywife, thofe other whom for following their gaine you accompt to be euill, are feene to be rich, iocund, exalted, loaden with rewards, with followers, and with all other felicityes of this world : in fo much as throughout all the places, where I do paffe, I heare in effect no other talke, then whofe is this fumptuous Pallace of fuch a Ribald? whofe is that other of fuch an Vfurer? whofe is that

great

great Kingdome of fuch an Vfurper? that other great dominion of fuch a Murderer? this wonderfull wealth of
fuch a Traytor? of fuch a Pander? or of fuch a Flatterer?
what fay you to this? Were it not better to be one of thefe
euill men, then one of your good men? Therfore fee, I
pray you, now whether I know or not, how to diftinguifh betwixt them, and that in fuch manner, that a man
of little skill may be able therof welnigh to make his election. So as to conclude, none but fuch as either haue not
the fortune, or not the wit to attayne to thefe benefits, are
driuen to fhrowd their bafer condition (and that poffibly
more for fhame then for loue) vnder the pofitiue titles of
honefty, and goodnes.   S v b s o l a n v s . In this
former accompt of yours, do you make your faid fraudulent rich man to confift of body only, or of both body and
foule?   A q v i l o n i v s . The care of his foule be
it vnto himfelfe, or to him that hath the charge therof, for
that point dependeth vpon another accompt.   S v b-
s o l a n v s . But yet let me aske you, whether your recited benefits, happening to fuch an euill man, be beneficiall alfo for his foule, or but for his body only?   A-
q v i l o n i v s. Belike you take me for the Curate of the
Parifh where I dwell, but you deceiue your felfe therin,
let euery man render accompt of his owne charge, for I
fpeake like one of myne owne profeffion.   S v b s o-
l a n v s. Yet this enfueth therof, that put the cafe, it were
neuer fo good for the body to be fraudulently rich, yet if
it be euill for the foule, the one halfe at the leaft of all your
euill mans felicityes, is loft by the affliction which the fame
may heap vpon the foule, of which point I will treat particularly in the conclufion of this dayes Conference; and
now in the meane tyme, we will confider whether all that
you haue faid be true in refpect of the body alone. Therfore

I would

I would know , whether he that feemeth vnto you for his wealth to be fo happy abroad , may not be full of other miferyes, and infelicityes at home ?   AQVI-LONIVS . It cannot be denied , but that fome difcontentments he may poffibly haue .   SVBSOLANVS. Thofe fome belike you meane to be either thefe , or fuch like ; As for example , to be afflicted with an vnruly , or difloyall wife , a difgracious or vnthrifty heire , a defamed or difhoneft generation of daughters , or which is a more noyfome euill, an vnplacable nature of his owne, either ftirred vp with drinke , whereby he allwayes rayleth , or ouerheated with choller , whereby continually he ftriketh , or els oppreffed with fufpition , whereby he neuer leaueth to torment both himfelfe and others , and fo enioyeth no pleafure or contentment of any thing he poffeffeth ; or if any little contentment he find , it is poffibly more when he is abroad , then in his owne houfe , albeit abroad alfo the reproachfull encounters of his externall difhoneft proceedings , cannot but much diminifh the fame , not fuffering fuch a polluted perfon to looke vpon good men with a right eye , nor to talke with them willingly , but cafting downe his head to fly and fhunne their company, for feare leaft any thing might efcape his mouth to his owne condemnation ; the which vigilancy of his, yet ferueth him to little purpofe , for that in his very fleep he many tymes bewrayeth his fouleft faults , the which is an vfuall punifhment that followeth ech where a guilty confcience , declaring thereby what a terrour it is to liue in fuch a ftate , as neither waking nor fleeping, he taketh any quiet confolation or repofe , but is alwayes tormented with the terrour of his owne wickedneffe. But admit that his impudency may fomewhat ouercome this defect , and that either in fenfuality of life , or fcurrilous

N   actions ,

actions , or other corrupt behauiour , he may happen to
find any more contentment abroad then at home ; yet is it
ſtill accompanied with little reputation , and alſo in effect
no more pleaſure then the wicked poorer ſort of men doe
likewiſe find ; and ſo his eſtate, by this accompt, is but little
better then the eſtate of him that poſſeſſeth much leſſe , if
it be not rather much worſe , by how much the care of
keeping his ill gotten wealth tormenteth him more . And
therfore let the euill rich man either ſtay at home, or go a-
broad where he will , let him gather wealth , or purchaſe
reuenewes , let him build very ſtately , or feed very deli-
cately, yea let him fill his Wardrobe with rich apparell, his
chambers with precious ornaments , his cheſts with plate,
his compt-bookes with debts , his ſtable with horſes , and
his houſe with neuer ſo many ſeruants ; yet ſhall he neuer
be able to rid his heart of griefe , his breaſt of feare, his cogitations of ſhame, his conferences of reproach, his ſolita-
rines of diſtractions , nor his conſcience of continuall biting remorſe, then the which there can be no greater ſignes
and tokens to be had of a moſt lamentable and miſerable
ſtate : the which is ſo much alſo the fuller of torment , and
affliction, by reaſon of his alwayes moſt vnſatiable and
greedy mynd of hauing and getting , neuer contented or
ſatisfied with that he poſſeſſeth , but the more he heapeth
and hoardeth vp, the more he ſtill deſireth : and all this vnto his greater affliction , ſeruitude , and ſlauery , by making thereby himſelfe more thrall then before, either vnto
the tempeſtuous variety of fickle fortune, or of filthy vice,
if not of both , the which may be ſaid to ſtriue , as it were,
whether ſhall be able to torment him moſt, or to make him
moſt miſerable , by reaſon of his bondage and ſubiection
alike vnto either ; albeit fortune without vice , cannot afflict much , be ſhe neuer of her ſelfe ſo contrary : but where
they

they accord to affault on both fides togeather, there is
no vnhappines of ftate to be compared vnto it, notwithftanding that the party to the fhew of the world do ftill
maintaine a ftately port, and be continually accompted
by the vulgar fort, to be the happieft man of his nation.
And therfore I may conclude, that as the Scorpion hath
in her the remedy of her owne poyfon; fo the euill man
carrieth alwayes with him the punifhment of his owne
wickednes, the which doth neuer leaue to torment and
afflict his mynd, both fleeping and waking, according as
it happened to *Appollidorus*, to *Hyparchus*, to *Paufanius*, and
many others whome *Plutarch* mentioneth. For where
there concurre togeather (as with the rich peruerfer fort
of men it is commonly feene to do) defire of vnlawfull
gaine, of vnlawfull pleafure, of implacable hatred, and
of vnlawfull reuenge; there without doubt concurreth a
great deale of hidden infelicity: & which is worft of all,
when the peruerfe rich man hapneth by any mutation of
fortune, to want of his accuftomed wealth, for the fupplying of his frequent iniquityes, then his vnruly defires
neuer leaue to exclaime and cry out vpon him, till they
bring him in the end to commit fome fouler outrages,
then euer before; as for example to fteale, to take by
force, yea and to violate the very Temples themfelues,
or otherwife to be tormented ftill with inceffant ftimu-
lations and dolours. Iudge therfore now vnto what
a happy and pleafant end your forfaid deceiuer of
men, for his owne commodity, may be like to come before he dye, befides all his other perturbations and afflictions fpoken of before, being counter-poyfes fufficient to weigh downe all the fuppofed and miftaken felicity, which you haue already attributed vnto him.
A Q V I L O N I V S. Becaufe I careflefly condefcended

vnto

vnto you, vpon your owne meele interrogation, that
fome difcontentments might happen indeed vnto fuch
a rich man, therfore belike you will cunningly threaten
it vpon me, as though I had in my meaning the Cata-
logue of all thefe Rabblements you haue heere repeated,
which, I affure you, I neuer fo much as dreamed of;
albeit in the meane while, by your heaping of things
in fuch manner togeather, you haue in words at leaft-
wife, gotten fome colourable fhew of refuting wholy my
former affertion : but fticke you a Gods name to the
words, and let me fticke to the matter, till we come to
difcouer betwixt your followers and myne in this doctrine,
whether fhall haue more neceffity, or need of ech others
help in the end.　　Svbsolanvs. Belike then,
honeft and vpright proceeding will not be able of it felfe
to gaine a man his bread, but that he muft be driuen to
feeke for his fuftenance, at the hands of the worfe, and
wickeder fort of men.　　Aqvilonivs. It
commeth many times, we fee, fo to paffe, for all that
you hold it fo ftrange a thing, contrary to that which
affirmeth therof the wife *Simonides*, who being asked
once, Whether Vertue or Riches were of more reputation,
made anfwere, that the Vertuous did more frequent the
doores of the rich, then the rich of the vertuous. Befides
that we fee, that the vertuous themfelues do not fticke to
giue to the rich the titles of all the vertues in the world,
yea and beare them all refpect, reuerence, and honour,
without reprouing them of any their vices, be they neuer
fo great, no not of their extorfions, which you do fo much
fpeake againft.　　Svbsolanvs. Howfoeuer
fome that are counted vertuous may flatter wicked rich
men, in fuch manner as you haue faid, yet men of folid
vertue do it not. But tell me, I pray you, be there no good
men,

men, that ariue to aboundance of wealth, and other
worldly benefits by good and lawfull meanes; as well
as thefe wicked men do by their euill meanes?   A-
QVILONIVS. Some few there may be, but not many.   SVBSOLANVS. And on the other fide,
thinke you, that there be no euill men, that for all their
vnrighteous dealing, do liue in want and mifery, and
feeke for fuftenance at good mens hands?   A-
QVILONIVS. Only fome fuch perhaps, as either know
not the way how to couer their iniquityes, or els fpend
more lauifhly then they fhould.   SVBSOLA-
NVS. Then it is not you fay impoffible, but that fome
good men may by their goodnes attayne vnto riches,
and that fome euill men notwithftanding all their frauds
may remayne ftill poore?   AQVILONIVS. My
meaning is not to ftand with you greatly herein.   SVB-
SOLANVS. But do you not alfo meane, that as to a-
bound in worldly commodityes is a good thing, fo on
the other fide to be an euill man, is an euill thing?   A-
QVILONIVS. It were a great errour to thinke otherwife.   SVBSOLANVS. Then where an euill
man becommeth to poffeffe aboundance of wealth, will
you not likewife graunt, that there an euill thing, and
a good thing come to be annexed togeather?   A-
QVILONIVS. You fay well, for it cannot be denyed.
SVBSOLANVS. But when in like manner a good
man poffeffeth aboundance of wealth, be there not two
good things annexed then togeather?   AQVILO-
NIVS. Of this there is alfo no doubt at all.   SVB-
SOLANVS. Moreouer, is the good faid to be good, becaufe it is good, or becaufe it is not euill?   AQVI-
LONIVS. Becaufe it is good.   SVBSOLANVS.
Then the good rich man, that poffeffeth two goods, is
he

he not better, then the euill rich man, who poffeffeth but one good? AQVILONIVS. Thefe fophiftications of yours, I cannot well deny, and yet they do not greatly pleafe me. SVBSOLANVS. And better then the euill poore man, that poffeffeth no good thing? AQVILONIVS. Let this alfo be graunted, to get me once out of this Labyrnith. SVBSOLANVS. But the number you will ftill fay of the good rich men, is fewer then of the euill rich men? AQVILONIVS. Of this you may reft vndoubtedly fure. SVBSOLANVS. And the number alfo of the euill rich men, fewer then of the euill poore men? AQVILONIVS. Without comparifon. SVBSOLANVS. So as it is more like, that an euill man may not become rich, then rich? AQVILONIVS. I told you the occafion before, in refpect of his vnskilfullnes, or lauifhnes, or fome other like peruerfity. SVBSOLANVS. But when fuch an euill man happeneth, by any fuch occafion, not to become rich, is he not in a very bad cafe, whiles both he is a bad man, and alfo a beggar: whereas a good man, though he be not rich, yet becaufe of his goodnes, is he not ftill in good cafe? AQVILONIVS. By your leaue not fo, for it is an euill thing vnto him to want riches. SVBSOLANVS. You would then inferre hereby, that a good man is not a good man? AQVILONIVS. Not fo neither, but that he may be in a euill cafe, in refpect of fome wants he may haue of things neceffary. SVBSOLANVS. You meane, I perceiue, becaufe he miffeth wealth to comfort him, and follace him in his goodnes? AQVILONIVS. That is my meaning indeed. SVBSOLANVS. Then wealth being annexed to the ftate of a good poore man, will make him, you imagine, more good?

good ?   A Q V I L O N I V S .   I haue affirmed in
effect fo much before .   S V B S O L A N V S . I fuppofe you meane it , becaufe being a good man , it is to be
thought he will apply it well .   A Q V I L O N I V S .
You fay rightly .   S V B S O L A N V S . But if wealth
fhould be annexed to the ftate of an euill poore man ,
would it not alfo make him better ?   A Q V I L O -
N I V S . Who doubteth therof ?   S V B S O L A N V S .
You meane it (perhaps) becaufe it is to be fuppofed ,
that being an euill man, he will apply it alfo well .   A -
Q V I L O N I V S . You make a follace , I perceiue, to ieft
at your friends .   S V B S O L A N V S . If then an
euill man may apply his wealth euilly , it would feeme
that wealth of it felfe is not abfolutly good .   A -
Q V I L O N I V S .   How can it but be abfolutly good ,
when as it is one of the principall inftruments vnto the
exercife of vertue , as of Magnificence , Liberality , Be-
neficence , and the like ?   S V B S O L A N V S .   So
is it likewife one of the principall inftruments vnto the
exercife of Vice , as of Arrogancy , Infolency , Reuenge ,
and the reft .   A Q V I L O N I V S .   Thefe effects
you fpeake of , do not confift in the Wealth , but in the
euill man , that doth euilly vfe it .   S V B S O L A -
N V S .   But if the wealth it felfe were truly , and abfo-
lutely good , it would make him the better that poffeffeth
it ; but this (according vnto *Seneca*) it doth not , who
fayth , What auayleth vnto a Foole his wealth , fince
he becommeth thereby no whit the wifer , nor the better ?   A Q V I L O N I V S .   If it make him not the
better , it may yet fuffice , that it maketh him not the
worfe .   S V B S O L A N V S .   If you will beleeue
the Philofopher in his Rhetoricke , it maketh him alfo
the worfe , feeing that it maketh men Proud , Iniuri-

ous ,

ous, and Intemperate. A QVILONIVS. He doth not meane, that it maketh all men ſo, but ſome men only : for if they be inclined vnto .Vice, it may make them more vicious ; as on the other ſide, if they be inclyned vnto Vertue, it may make them more vertuous : and therfore it is to be accompted among thoſe externall good things, which help vnto humane felicity. SVB-SOLANVS. There can be nothing more repugnant vnto reaſon, then to make Wealth a part of humane felicity; ſince on the other ſide, the ſame is rather held to be either an inſtrument, or a member of Iniquity. For ſo ſaith the Philoſopher in the Booke before mentioned, That rich men for the moſt part, are either Vnrighteous, or the Heires vnto thoſe that haue been Vnrighteous, as vnto ſome Extortioner, Deceiuer, Periurer, or the like. So as, if Wealth could make men happy, we might then conclude, that humane felicity were nothing els but the reward of Iniquity. A QVILONIVS. If Wealth may not make men happy, you may be ſure, that Pouerty may do it much leſſe; for if happines conſiſted in Pouerty, then might we likewiſe ſay, that Felicity were nothing els, but the reward of a diſcontented and diſquiet mynd, becauſe pouerty is accompanied with nothing more. SVBSOLANVS. If we will belieue *Arceſilaus*, it is accompanied rather with Humility with Induſtry, and aboue all with Security; for that the rich, and not the poore be the Preyes vnto Pilferers, Robbers, and Manquellers. And to the end you may know, what Pouerty is accompanied with true Humility, you are to vnderſtand, that of Pouertyes there be two ſorts, the one, as I may ſay Vnuoluntary, being incurred, and ſuffered againſt a mans will; and the other Voluntary, being choſen and vndertaken of a mans owne

owne free election: of which the firſt is yrkſome and grieuous , yea many times vitious and ſinfull , being accompanied which Enuy, vnlawfull Deſire of other mens goods , Fraud , and Deceipt , Pilfering , and Robbing , and ſometymes it cauſeth Murders and all kind of Miſchiefs , and therfore is hatefull both to God and Man . The ſecond may be deuided into two ſorts ; of the which the one may be termed Morall , and the other Religious, or Euangelicall . The Morall was practiſed by many of the old Philoſophers, who freely abandoned their wealth , and choſe to liue in pouerty , to auoyd the danger , and diſquiet of mynd , which commonly followeth Riches , as hath byn ſufficiently ſignified before . The Religious , or Euangelicall Pouerty being that only which is choſen and ſuffered for the pure Loue of God , was taught and practiſed by Chriſt our Sauiour himſelfe , and his Apoſtles , and hath him alwayes , and is ſtill profeſſed and practiſed in his Church by many of his ſeruants . And this ſort of Pouerty is that which is accompanyed with true Humility , Peace , Contentment , and heauenly Conſolations ; and the Poore of this ſort are thoſe whome our Sauiour called *Bleſſed*, and to whome he promiſed a hundred fold in this life , and the Kingdome of Heauen in the next . A Q V I L O N . If all men ſhould be poore , ſuch a Society would be like a body that were all head , or all legges , the which would not only be vnſeruiceable , but alſo deformed and therfore Nature hauing ordained ſome men to be poore, & ſome to be rich, it cannot well be ſaid that Wealth of it ſelfe is euill; or if by chance, it may ſeeme at any time to be euill, this is to be attributed ſtill vnto the euill mynd of him that euilly applyeth it , rather then to any thing els . S V B S O L A . Then if an euill man may apply his Wealth euilly, the euil applying therof may make an euill man the worſe . A Q V I L O N . As touching this,

O

I will

I will not greatly ftand with you . S v B S O L A . So that
Wealth by the fame reafon may hurt a good man alfo, if he
fhould happen to apply it euilly .   A q v i l o . Like inough it may .   S v B s o L A . Therefore when God retay-
neth a good man from waxing rich,it is not a figne of any
hate he beareth him,but only that for his more good he pre-
ferueth him from a temptation,to become the worfe .   A-
q v i l o . It may welnigh be fo; but what of al this?   Svb-
s o l a . And fo on the other fide , when God doth fuffer
an euill man by any vnlawfull meanes to become very
wealthy , it is not a figne of any loue he beareth him , but
that only for his greater confufion , he meaneth to let him
runne the more irrecuperably vnto his owne perdition .
A q v i l o n . Thefe melancholy notes of yours, do rather
diftemper then any whit tune me .   S v B s o L A . That is
becaufe you be already out of tune , & yet are loath to perceiue it; but hearken to this other point which may happen
to pleafe you better,That when God doth finally fuffer any
good man by his owne good meanes, and induftry, to become rich, it is a great figne that he giues him riches for
his greater good, becaufe he forefeeth that by applying of
them well , he is to wynne great merit thereby .   A q v i-
l o n . It pleafeth me indeed fo well,as I can be content to
leaue off with the loffe,and to talke of this matter no more,
becaufe the further we go, the worfe we agree .   S v B-
s o l a . Neuertheles before we end, I will by your leaue
(according to my promife made you heretofore) debate
with you , how all this your former doctrine , and difcourfe ftandeth with diuine Authority:which being performed , I hope you will reft fully fatisfied . And therfore for as much as the diuers kinds of vnlawfull gaine
(which you haue approued partly in priuate , and partly
in publike perfons)may be all reduced , as I may fay,
to one Predicament of Fraud, or Deceyt practifed in diuers

uers manners ; we are to ponder and waygh the fame in,
the iuſt and equall ballance, as well of the Law of Nature
imprinted in euery mans hart, as alſo of the diuine Law
written in the Holy Scriptures. Firſt then for the Law of
Nature; Can any man be ſo voyd of naturall Reaſon as
to doubt, whether all fraudulent Gaine be not flatly for-
biddē by the Law of Nature, which teacheth this knowne
principle, *Quod tibi fieri non vis, alteri ne feceris?* Therfore if
no man would be content to be deceaued by other men, it
followeth, that whoſoeuer ſeeketh to gaine by deceauing
others, tranſgreſſeth the Law of Nature. Beſides that,
man being ordeyned and borne not for himſelfe alone,
but to liue in community and ciuill ſociety ; it is euident
that nothing is more contrary to the Common Wealth
then Deceyt and Fraud, which being admitted would
deſtroy all Traffique, and Commerce, and all Truſt and
Confidence amongſt men, without the which there can
be no Iuſtice, *wherof Fidelity* (as *Cicero* ſayth very well in
his *Offices lib*. 1.) *is the foundation*, and conſequently there
could be no Common Wealth. In which reſpect *Cicero*
alſo ſaith in the ſame place, That nothing doth more
firmely vnite, and hold togeather the Common Wealth,
then Fidelity, which therfore *Valerius Maximus* (*lib*. 6.
cap. 6.) calleth *Venerabile Numen &c*. a Venerable and
Diuine Power, and the moſt ſure Pledge of humane ſe-
curity. And the *Romans* eſteemed it ſo much, that in
the honour of it they buylt a Temple, wherein all Leagues, and important Couenants were publikely made
and ſworne, and he that afterwards did breake them,
was deteſted of all men. Alſo man being made to the I-
mage of God, who is Verity and Truth it ſelfe, ought
alwayes to conſerue in himſelfe the ſimilitude and likenes of God, which likenes by fraud and deceyt he vtterly looſeth, becomming the true Image of the Diuell,

who

who is worthily called *Diabolus*, that is to fay, *A Deceyuer*, being, as our Sauiour tearmeth him (*Ioan*. 8 .) *Mendax*, *& pater eius*, a Lyar and the father of Lyes . And therefore no meruaile, that the written Law of God doth fo much condemne deceytfull and fraudulent dealing, that it accompanieth and compareth the fraudulent man with the Bloud-fucker, detefting them both: *Virum fanguinum*, *& dolofum* (fayth the Pfalmift) *abhominatur Dominus*. And therfore God alfo threatneth to punifh them both alike with vntimely death . *Viri fanguinum & dolofi* (faith the fame Pfalmift, *Pfal*. 54.) *non dimidiabunt dies fuos*. And how deteftable alfo in the fight of God is all deceyt and the Deceyuer, the Holy Ghoft fignifieth, and inculcateth very often els where in the Holy Scripture . faying (*Prou*. 1 .) *Euery Deceyuer is abhominable before God*. And againe (*cap*. 8.) *I deteft the double-tongued man*. And (*cap*. 20.) fpeaking of a common coofenage generally vfed alfo in thefe our dayes by falfe weyghts and meafures, he fayth: Weyght and Weyght, Meafure and Meafure is deteftable in the fight of God . Likewife the Prophet *Micheas* threatneth the Iewes with deftruction for their frauds, and deceyts (*cap*. 6.) *As yet* (faith he) *there is fire in the houfe of the impious, treafures of iniquity, and a leffer meafure full of wrath : why fhall I iuftify an impious ballance, and the deceytfull weyght of the bagge, by which their rich men were replenifhed with iniquity, and the Inhabitants therein fpake lyes ; and their tongue was fraudulent in their mouths, and therfore I began to ftryke thee with perdition for thy finnes*. Thus fayd Almighty God by the mouth of his Prophet. And the like, yea a more terrible threat of eternall perdition, is denounced by the Pfalmift to a deceytfull tongue . Thou haft loued (fayth he, *Pfal*. 51.) all words of precipitation, a deceytfull tongue ; therefore God will deftroy thee eternally : he will pluck thee vp, and re-

moue

moue thee out of thy Tabernacle, and roote thee out of
the Land of the liuing. Loe then how hatefull to Almighty God is all deceitfull and fraudulent dealing, be
it by word, or act. And this being true in priuate perfons,
what fhall we thinke of fraud and deceit in Magiftrates,
Iudges, and publike Perfons? How abhominable is the
fame to God and Man, and pernicious not only to the Cōmon Wealths which they gouerne, but alfo to themfelues
through the feuerity of Gods Iuftice and Iudgements v-
pon them? In which refpect King *Iofaphat* hauing conftituted and ordayned Iudges in the Cittyes of *Iuda*, faid
vnto them (*2.Par.19.*) *Videte quid faciatis &c.* Looke well
what you do, for you do not exercife the Iudgement of
Man, but of God, and whatfoeuer you fhall Iudge, fhall
redound to your felues. So he. And the hurt that redoundeth to the Common wealth, by the iniuftice of the Magiftrates, doth not confift only in the iniuryes done to the
members therof, but alfo in the punifhment that God inflicteth many times vpon the whole State for the finnes
of the Heads, when the fame are not punifhed and reformed in the offenders; fuch being the feuerity of Gods Iuftice, that when the Magiftrats are either themfelues corrupt, or els negligent in punifhing the faults of others, he
cōmonly impofeth fome generall penalty vpon the whole
common Wealth, and many times deftroyeth the fame, or
transferreth the gouerment therof to ftranges, as the holy Ghoft fignifieth in *Ecclefiaticus* (*Cap.10.*) faying: *Regnum à Gente in Gentem tranfertur &c.* A Kingdome is tranf-
ferred from Nation to Nation for Iniuftice, and Iniuries,
and Calumniations, and diuers Deceits. So as if we duly
confider the enormity of Fraudes, Deceits, and of all kind
of Iniuftice, efpecially in Magiftrates, in whome the fame
commonly paffeth without any humane punifhment, we
fhall eafily conclude the Fraudulent to be not only trea-

O 3   cherous

cherous to priuate men whome they deceaue and abufe,
but alfo trayterous to the common Wealth, by reafon of
the diuine Punifhment which they draw vpon the fame;
befides the eternall damnation which they purchafe to
themfelues for their owne offence therein if they do not
repent, and do fufficient fatisfaction for it in this life;
which Satisfaction neuerthelefle cannot be done in matters of Iniuftice and Iniuryes without reftitution of ill
gotten goods, honour, and fame, according to the moft
Chriftian and knowne axiome of *S. Auguftine : Non dimit-
titur peccatum, nifi reftituatur ablatum* . In which refped the
Publican *Zachaus* , being by our Sauiour conuerted, and
illuminated with the light of his Grace, did not content
himfeife to make a bare reftitution of the iuft valew only
what he had wrongfully and fraudulently got, but promifed to reftore the quadruple, that is to fay, foure times
fo much as he had guilfully & vnlawfully gained of any
man; alluding perhaps to the Law of *Moyfes* (*Exod.* 22.)
where it was ordeyned, That in cafes of Theft fometimes
the double, fometimes the quadruple, yea & otherwhiles
fiue times fo much as was ftolne fhould be reftored . In
which refped King *Dauid* fwore to *Nathan* (2. *Reg.* 12.)
that the rich man who had wrongfully taken a fheep from
a poore man, fhould not only dye for it, but alfo reftore
the quadruple, for fo indeed it was ordained in the Law.
Now then this being fo, it is to be confidered, what he
gayneth that enricheth himfelfe by Fraud and Deceyt,
feeing that he loofeth not only his reputation (if it be
knowne) but alfo his foule(how fecietly foeuer he do it)
in cafe he do not repent, and make Reftitution of his vnlawfull gaine,fo farre as his ability will extend.Therfore,
as I asked you before , whether you made accompt that
your fraudulent rich man fhould confift of body only, or
both of body and foule ; fo now I add thereto another demand

mand, to wit, whether you will haue him to be a beast, or
a man? for if you accompt him for a man, that is to say , a
reasonable creature , we must exact of him to do the office of a man, and not of a beast, to which purpose the Psalmist saith, *Nolite fieri sicut equus & mulus, quibus non est intel-*
lectus; that is to say , be not lead, or moued chiefly by
sense and pleasure, & by the apprehension only of present
obiects, as horses, mules, and other beasts are, but by reason , and the due consideration of future things , and of
the end of euery thing , and especially of that which belongeth to the eternall good of the soule, without which
consideration no man either is, or can be worthily accounted a man, and much lesse a wise man, for as the Wiseman
saith (*Ecclef. 37*) *Est sapiens animæ suæ sapiens*; and therfore
Moyses , bewayling the folly of the Iewes, in that behalfe,
calleth them, a people without wit and prudence, saying
(*Deut. 32*) *Gens absque consilio est, atque prudentia ; vtinam*
saperent, & intelligerent, ac nouissima prouiderent : & the Psalmist speaking of such rich worldlings, as you haue hitherto so highly commended, compareth them to brute beasts
(*Psal. 48.*) *Homo* (saith he) *cùm in honore esset, non intellexit*;
comparatus est iumentis insipientibus, & similis factus est illis .
And little better accompt made the Philosophers and wise
Paynims of such as prefer honour, riches, and worldly co-
modityes before Vertue. In which respect *Aristotle* compareth them to children , who esteeme their Puppies more
then gold : and *Seneca* saith (*Ep. 96.*) that they are far more
foolish then children , playing the fooles notably , not as
children do in tryfles, & matters of no moment or danger,
but in things of great wayght and consideration, so as, saith
he, *verius , catulíque insaniunt*, they are more truly & costly mad . Therfore now to conclude , concerning all that
Profit and Gaine which you haue hitherto placed in fraudulent meanes, it is most euident, that being preiudiciall
and

and hurtful to the foule, it cannot be accounted either gainfull, or any way profitable, but moft noyfome and pernicious according to our Sauiours expreffe teftimony, faying: *Quid prodeft homini, fi vniuerfum mundum lucretur, anima verò fua detrimentum patiatur?* wherupon it alfo followeth, that the Philofophers Axiome is true, to wit, *That nothing is profitable which is not honeft* (wherof I promifed you before to giue you now a fpeciall reafon.) For feeing that all Difhonefty whatfoeuer is hurtfull to the foule, it cannot poffibly be profitable, no more then a pleafant ftong wine can be holfome in a hoat burning Feuer, which albeit for the prefent feemeth to refrefh and comfort the fick man, yet afterwards turneth to his great domage: and euen fo fareth it with all euill gotten gaine, which, though at firft, and for a while contenteth the couetous mynd of the getter, yet in the end breedeth his euerlafting torment, if, as I haue faid before, he doth not fatisfy Gods Iuftice by repentance, and reftitution to his power. Therfore confider now with your felfe, what reafon you haue had in your former affertions, either to condemne good men fo much as you haue done, for their Pouerty arifing by honeft Syncerity, or to extoll bad men fo much aboue meafure, for their riches growing by their fraudulent Practifes, and other reproachfull Iniquityes. The which is as much as occurreth heere to be faid, concerning the whole fcope of vnlawfull Profit, generally confidered.

The end of the firft Booke.

THOMAS FITZHERBERT
A Defence of the Catholyke Cause
1602

A DEFENCE OF
THE CATHOLYKE CAVSE,

CONTAYNING A TREATISE IN CON-
FVTATION OF SVNDRY VNTRVTHES AND
slanders, published by the heretykes, as wel in infamous lybels
as otherwyse, against all english Catholyks in general, & some
in particular, not only concerning matter of state, but also
matter of religion: by occasion whereof diuers poynts
of the Catholyke faith now in controuersy,
are debated and discussed.

Written by T. F.

WITH

AN APOLOGY, OR DEFENCE, OF HIS
INNOCENCY IN A FAYNED CONSPIRACY
against her Maiesties person, for the which one Edward Squyre was wrongfully condemned and executed in Nouember in the yeare of our Lord
1598. wherewith the author and other Catholykes were also
falsly charged. Written by him the yeare folowing, and
not published vntil now, for the reasons declared
in the preface of this Treatyse.

Psalm. 118.

Redime me à calumnijs hominum, vt custodiam mandata
tua.

Redeeme me o Lord from the slanders of men, that I may
keep thy commandements.

Imprinted with licence 1602.

THE VNTRVTHES

AND SLANDERS CONCER-
ning matter of ftate, & fome particular per-
fons, confuted in this Treatife, and in
the Apology following.

The *fecond, touching the Catholyke Kinges late* **2.**
attempt in Ireland, which the Englifh Catholykes,
are alfo falfly fuppofed to haue procured. Treatyfe.
Chap. 1.

The third, *concerning Sir VVilliam Stanley & his deliuering Da-* **3.**
uenter to the king Catholjke. Treaſe. Chap. 1.

The fourth, *touching father Parfons, & his great labours in Gods* **4.**
Churche perueifly interpreted, & fhamefully flãdred by the here-
tykes. Treatife. Chap. 2.

The fifth, *an impudent & malitious vntruth auouched by O. E.* **5.**
in his late challenge, to wit, that no Catholykes are put to death in
England for religion, but for treafon, and attempts againft the ſtate.
Treatife. Chap. 3. Apology. Chap. 10. 22. & 23.

The fixt, *the improbable & abfurd fixtion of Squyres confpiracy* **6.**
againft her Maiefties perfon imputed to father Richard walpole of the
holy Society of Iefus, as principal contriuer, & to father Creswel of
the fame Society,& to the author of this Treatife as abetters. Apology.
Chap. 1. 2. 6. 7. 8. 9. 20. & 21.

The feuenth, *a flanderous vntruth publifhed as wel in thefe later as* **7.**
fome former libels, concerning VVilliams, York, & Patrick Cullen,
executed at London fome yeares paſt, and falfly fuppofed to be em-
ployed by the Englifh Catholykes then at Bruffels againft her Maiefties
perfon. Apology. Chap. 15.

‡ 2   The

8.   *The 8. an impertinent vntruth publyshed in a pamphlet concer-*
ning the fayned conspiracy of Edward Squyre, wherein it is affirmed
that there is great moderation, & lenity vsed in causes of religion.
Apology. Chap. 22. & 23.

9.   *The 9. a foolish inuectiue of the author of thesayd pamphlet*
against the Iesuits. Apology. Chap. 24.

VNTRVTHES AND SLAN-
DERS CONCERNING MAT-
TER OF RELIGION DISCOVE-
red & confuted vpon diuers occasions,
in this Treatise, & the Apology
following.

1.   A *False & impudent assertion of a shameles minister, who*
being present at the death of two martyrs at Lincolne, in the
yeare 1600. affirmed publikly that England receiued the protestants
religion, when it was first conuerted to the Christian faith, vnder the
Popes Eleutherius and Gregory the first. Treatise. Chap. 4. 5 & 6.

2.   *An other slanderous vntruth of the heretykes charging Catholykes*
with Idolatry, in the reuerend vse of holy Images. Treat. Chap. 11.
& 12.

2.   *The lyke slanderous & impudent vntruth touching the Catholikes*
opinion of merits of woorkes, published lately in a pamphlet concer-
ning the conuiction of my lord of Essex. Treat. Chap. 19.

4.   *A ridiculous miracle fayned by the author of the pamphlet aboue*
said, that concerned Squyres fayned conspiracy. Apolog. Chap. 25.

The table of the chapters followeth in the end of the Treatise.

THE

THE PREFACE,

VVHEREIN THE AVTOR

DECLARETH HIS INTENTION

IN THIS TREATISE, AND THE CAVSE
Why he wrote the same, and why the Apology concerning Edward
Squyre being written three yeres since, was not published vn-
til now.

T is now more then three yeres, gentle rea- Edvvard
der, since that one Edward Squyre, hauing bin Squyre exe-
sometyme prisoner in Spayne, and escaping cuted for a
thence into England, was condemned and exe- spiracy, and
cuted for a fayned conspiracy against her Ma- the author
iestyes person, wherto my self & some others of this trea-
were charged to be priuy; & for as much as it therevvith.
seemed to mee that this fraudulent manner of
our aduersaries proceeding against Catholykes, by way of slanders and diffamations, authorised with shew of publik Iustice, and The reasons
continued now many yeres, did beginne to redound not only to that moued
the vndeserued disgrace, & discredit of particular men wrongfully to vvryte an
accused, but also to the dishonour of our whole cause, I thought it Apology in
coueniét to write an Apology in my deféce, & to dedicate thesame his ovvne
to the Lords of her Maiesties priuy counsel, as wel to cleare my defence.
self to their honours of the cryme falsly imputed vnto mee, as also to discouer vnto them the treacherous dealing of such as abuse
her Maiesties autority and theirs in this behalf, to the spilling of
much innocent blood, with no smalle blemish to her Maiesties go-
üernment, and the assured exposition of the whole state, to the
wrath of God, if it be not remedied in tyme.

This Apology being written by me in Spayne, and made ready The Apolo-
for the print (now almost 3. yeres past) it seemed good as wel to gy stayd fró
me as the print, in

A

hope of some
toleration of
Catholyke
religion in
England.
me as to other of my friends, to stay the impression of it, vntil we should see the issue of the treaty of peace betwyxt England and Spayne then expected, with no smalle hope conceaued of many, that liberty of conscience, or at least some toleration of religion might ensue therof to the Catholikes of Englād, & therfore seeing my principal intention was no other, but with the occasion of my owne purgation to seek remedy of the wrongs donne vnto vs, by discouering to the lords of the councel the vnchristian and pernicious proceeding of our cheef persecutors, it seemed to mee that yf the desyred effects of toleration, and consequently our remedy did follow of the treaty, the labour & charges of printing my Apology should be needlesse.

Hope of toleration frustrate.
And although after many moneths expectation, and the meeting of the commissioners at Bullen, there appeared no lykelyhood at all, eyther of peace betwyxt the two kingdomes, or toleration of Catholyke religion in Englād (in which respect it seemed conuenient to some that my apology should be published) yet for as much, as so long tyme was then ouer past, that the matter of Squyre seemed to bee forgot, and that therfore the defence of my innocency might eyther be to litle purpose, or at least seeme out of season, I resolued to suppresse the same, and the rather for that I vnderstood that howsoeuer some simple men might be deceaued in Squyres cause, yet the wysest considering the weaknes, and inualydity of the proofes, and his denial of the fact at his death, did take it for an inuention, and a stratageme of state, conforme to dyuers other of like quality, which many wyse men amongst the protestātes themselues haue noted heretofore.

Squyres matter seemed to be forgot.
Squyres matter held by the wyse for a stratagem of state.

Squyres matter lately reuyued by 3. lybels, and much vrged against Catholyks.
The authors determinatiō to set out his Apology.
O. E.
In his nevv challeng to N.D. Chap 5
But now comming hether to Rome, and seing the matter reuiued and mightyly vrged to the preiudice of all Catholykes, by 2. seueral lybels composed lately in England, the one by an heretical minister ashamed of his name, and therfore Sutly shrowding it vnder a fals Visar of O. E. and the other written very lately by a puritan, as it seemeth, calling himself Thomas Diggs, I haue determined to set out my apology for the ful satisfaction of all indifferent men in this poynt; wherto I am moued the rather, for that I haue also sufficiently treated therin some othet matters handled by O. E. who laboureth to proue that all the persecution which Catholykes haue hetherto suffred, is iustly to be ascribed to their treasonable attēpts, besydes that he is not ashamed to affirme,

affirme, that none haue bé put to death in all her maiestyés raigne for matter of religion, which impudent assertion of his, I haue so sufficiently confuted in my sayd apology, as no more needeth to be sayd in that matter.

Neuertheles vpon this new occasion giuen by him, I haue thought good to prefix this treatise to thesaid Apology to giue thee good reader some more particular satisfaction concerning this point, and first to answere sincerely and truly vpon my owne knowlege an other slanderous and malitious conceit of his touching the il affection as he supposeth of diuers principal Catholykes to their country, and therefore for as much as I intend also, vpon occasions that may be offred, to debate and discusse in this treatise some pointes of Catholyke religion now in controuersy, and withal to cleare our doctrine in those pointes from certaine malitious slanders of our aduersaries, I haue thought good to entytle the whole, *A defence of the Catholyke cause*. Wherein I make no doubt but that thow wilt easely note (good reader) amongst many other thinges, the inconsideration of our aduersaries in that they are not content only to wrong vs in our goodes and persons, by extreme iniustice vsed towards vs, but also to wound vs so deeply in our fame by their calumniatious and slanderous lybels, and reportes, that they force vs much against our willes to lay open to the world their shameful and vnchristian proceedings, in defence of our owne innocencie, and for the honor of our cause, which not only all lawes of God nature and nations do allow and permit, but also conscience vrgeth and byndeth vs vnto in this case. For although priuate men may somtymes with great merit suffer themselues to be slaundered without contradiction, when no furder detrimét ensueth thereof, then the losse of their owne fame or their particular hurt, yet when the same is joyned, with other mennes harme or with a publyke damage, espetialy of religion, they cannot without offence to God neglect or omit their owne iust defence. Therefore I hope no man wil blame mee or other Catholykes in lyke case for offring iust purgation of our selues and our cause though it bee with the reproch of them that slander vs, *vt obstruatur os loquentium iniqua*, that the mouthes of calumniators may bee stopped.

And whereas thesame may seeme to redound to some disgrace or dishonor of the state by reason of the publyke authority & pretence of her maiesties seruice, wherewith our aduersaries do comonly

monly couer and colour all their malitious actions, I purpose for
my parte, to vse in this my defence, such due respect to the state &
to the supreme gouernours thereof (I meane her Maiestie and the
honorable Lordes of her counsel) that I hope to auoyd all iust
cause of offence, and giue ample testimony of the loyalty of a
moste dutiful subiect discouering to her Maiestie and their honors
by way of humble complaint, the great abuse offred by our
aduersaries, no lesse to them, then to vs, as wil more
particularly appeere in my Apologie directed
and dedicated to the Lordes of the
councel.

AN AN-

AN ANSWER TO
TVVO MALITIOVS
SLANDERS CONCERNING
*the conqueſt of England, falſly ſuppoſed to be pretended
and ſolicited by the Catholykes, and touching the late
enterpriſe of the king of Spayne in Ireland. Alſo concerning Sir VVilliam Stanley.*

CHAP. I.

MONGST many malitious
ſlanders, wherwith O. E. and
other heretyks ſeek to make
vs and our cauſe odious to all
men, one of the principaleſt
is, that wee deſyre and con-
ſpyre the cōqueſt of our countrey by the king of Spayne,
wherewith they charge not
only F. Parſons and the Ie-
ſuytes, but alſo other Engliſh
Catholykes that haue ſerued and ſerue the Catholyke
king, in which reſpect I cannot forbeare to teſtify the
truth of my knowledge in this poynt, hauing had ſufficiēt
meanes and occaſion to vnderſtand what hath ben treated
with the Catholike kings of Spayne by any of our nation
ſince the yeare of our Lord 1589. at what tyme I paſſed
from the court of France (by reaſon of the troubles there)
to the ſeruice of their Catholike Maieſties, whome I haue
ſerued euer ſince, and for ſome yeres together in the court

The autor
anſwereth
and confu-
teth this ſlā-
der vpon his
ovvne knovv
ledge.

A 3   of Spayne,

of Spayne, vntil now of late, that I retyred my felfe from thence to Rome, to fatisfy my priuate deuotiõ, by dedicating the reft of my declyning dayes, to the feruice of God in an ecclefiaftical funétion.

The autors proteftation vpon his cõ-fcience.

Therfore I here proteft vpon my confcience, not only in my owne behalf, but alfo in the behalf of F.Parfons, and the Englifh Catholykes that ferue his Catholyke Maiefty, that our dealings haue bin fo contrary to that which is imputed ynto vs, that we haue donne farre better offices for our country in this poynt, then the malice of our aduerfaries fuffereth them to fuppofe. For hauing wel confidered that the breach of amity betwyxt her Maieftie and the Catholike king, growing dayly by fundry aéts of hoftility on both parts, to an implacable quarrel,might moue him to feek the conqueft of our country (wherof his puiffant preparations in the yere 88.gaue no fmalle fufpition to the world) and not hauing any hope to be able to difwade his Maieftie from feeking fome fharp reuenge of the attempts made againft him by fea and land (wherto not only reafon of ftate, but alfo refpeét of his reputation and honour feemed to oblige him) wee determined to do our yttermoft endeuour fo to temper and qualify the fame, as it might not turne to any conqueft of our country. To

The ende-nour of Syr Fran. Engle-feld, F. Par-fons,F. Cref-vvel and of the autor to diuert the Catholik king from the conqueft of Engl. which purpofe fir Francis Englefield, whylft he liued,Father Parfons, Fa. Crefwel , and my felf, haue at dyuers tymes reprefented to his Maᵗⁱᵉ. of glorious memory,many important reafons to perfwade him, that it was not conuenient for him to feek the conqueft of England,nor probable eyther that he could conquer it, or yet if he were able to do it that he could long keep it in fubieétion ; and this wee haue vrged fo oft and with fuch pregnãt reafons, as wel to his Maᵘⁱᵉ. that now is,as to his father of glorious memory, that I verely beleeue , that if they euer had any inclination or refolutiõ to feek the conqueft of England, wee haue donne fufficient diligence to diuert them from all cogitation therof.

But

But whatfoeuer may be thought of their maiefties intentions in this behalf (which is not my intention here to defend nor treat of, but to fignify what hath ben our treaties or dealings with them) fure I am, that their Maties. haue vpō dyuers occafions affured vs, that their meaning was no other, but only to feek reparation of wrongs dōne vnto them, with the aduancement of Catholyke religion, howfoeuer the quarrel fhould end, eyther by extremity of warre, or compofition of peace, for though the profecutiō of the warre fhould proue more profperous vnto them then wee imagined it could do, yea and that the crowne of England might therby fall to their difpofition, yet they affirmed that theyr intentiō was no other, then to reftore and affure Catholyke religion there, by eftablifhing a Catholyke king, with whome they might reuew, and perpetually hold the ancient leagues fo long continued in tymes paft betwyxt the two kingdomes of England and Caftile to the mutual benefit of both. And if it fhould fo fal out that they fhould grow to treatyes, of peace (which was moft lykely would be the conclufion of this warre, fooner or later) they promifed to make inftance to her Maieftie eyther for liberty of cōfciéce for Catholikes, or at leaft for relaxfatiō of penal lawes & eafe of the prefent perfecutiō.

The Catho-lyk kings anfwer concerning his intention.

Reftitution of Catholyk religion in England.

Eafe of perfecution by treaty of peace.

Now then; this being the refolution of their maiefties (as they fignified vnto vs) confifting on two poynts, the one, no doubt in their owne opinions vncertayne, and in ours altogeather vnprobable, if not vnpofsible (as before I haue declared) and the other, moft lykely in tyme to enfew, efpecially confidering the frequent ouertures thefe later yeres to a treaty of peace, and the continual reports of her Maiefties propenfion, nor only therto, but alfo to giue fome toleration to Catholikes; any indifferent man may iudge, which of thefe two poynts wee were more lyke to expeєt and folicit, though wee fhould be as il affected and vnnatural to our country, as our aduerfaries imagine, who meafuring our charity and zeale in religion, by

The reafons vvhy the Catholyks rather expeєted remedy by peace then by warre.

Frequent ouertures to treatyie of peace thefe later yeres. Impofsibilites of conqueft. Her maiefties propenfiō to peace, and to

their

geue toleta-
tion to Ca-
tholyks. their owne fury, and malice againſt vs, perſuade themſelues, that becauſe they would if they were in our caſe,
The hereiyks
meaſure Ca-
tholyks by
themſelues. wiſh and procure by all meanes poſsible our vtter ouerthrow & ruin, wee therfore do the lyke by them; whereas wee following the doctrine and example of our Sa-
The charity
of Catholyks
tovvards
their ene-
mies. uiour and his ſaynts, in forgeuing our enemies, and hartely wiſhing the conuerſion of ſinners, do dayly and inſtant-
ly pray to almighty God for them, that it may pleaſe him
of his infinit mercy to forgiue and illuminate them.

The Catho-
lyks deſyre
reſtitution
of religiõ by
ſvveet mea-
ues.　　　And although we deſyre nothing more in our countrey, then the extirpation of hereſy and the reſtitution of
the Catholyk fayth, yet wee wiſh that it may pleaſe God
to woork it by ſuch ſweet meanes, that not only our mo-
narky may ſtil retayne the former liberty, dignity and honour that heatherto it hath had, but alſo that no mannes
finger may ſo much as ake for the ſame;

　　　And whoſoeuer doth note and regard with an indifferent eye, the proceeding of ſuch Catholykes as haue laboured moſt in our cauſe, and eſpecially of him whome
The erection
of Semina-
ryes tendeth
not to force
of armes. our enemies do moſte maligne, and calumniate at this
day (I meane the proceeding of father Parſons in the
erection and careful mayntenance of Seminaryes) & doth
further conſider the fruits therof, and the progreſſe of
Catholike religion in England of late yeres, he can neither
think, that the fathers intentions tend to force of armes or
The ſvvoord
needles
vvhere the
vvoord pre-
uayleth. violence of cõqueſt, nor yet that our cauſe is in ſuch deſperat tearmes, that wee neede to vſe the ſwoord ſeing the
force of the woord, and apoſtolical preaching wᵒorketh
Hereſy dayly
decaying. ſo good effect, that wee may wel hope, that hereſy decaying dayly as it doth, wil fall of it ſelf within a whyle,
The vvyſe
gouernours
can not but
note Gods
handivvork,
in the pro-
greſſe of Ca-
tholykreligiõ
in England. and that in the meane tyme, our wyſe gouernours noting
the ſpecial woork & hand of God therin, & how litle humain policy or rigour preuayleth againſt true religion, wil
not only moderate the rigorous cours hetherto held with
Catholikes, but alſo willingly receaue the light of truth, for
the which wee dayly pray to almighty God, & dayly wil.
　　　　　　　　　　　　　　　　　　　　　　　　　This

This then is the conqueſt that wee deſyre and expect vvhat conqueſt the Ca-
tholyks de-
ſyre in Eng-
land. in England, to wit, a conqueſt of ſoules to God, with the ſuppreſsion of hereſy, & iniquity, to the end, that the force of truth and piety may ſo captiuate and ſubdue the harts of all our countrymen, that they may be freed from the bondage of the deuil, wherin they liue, and that the Catholyke Churche and our country withall may floriſh, in the old manner, to the glory of God, & ſaluation of infinit ſoules that dayly periſh, and thus much for this poynt.

Now foraſmuch as I vnderſtād that rumours are ſpred abroad and a conceyt or ſuſpition bred thereby, in the heades of many, that the engliſh Catholykes haue alſo ſolicited the Catholyke king to the late enterpriſe of Ireland, I think good alſo to ſay ſomewhat concerning that point, that I verely think no Engliſh Catholyke was acquainted therewith otherwiſe thē by comō fame or opinion, ſeeing that neither F. Creſwel nor my ſelf (both reſiding at the Neyther F.
Parſ. at Rome
nor any En-
gliſhman in
Spayn made
priuy thereto. ſame tyme in the courte of Spaine) nor Sir William Stanley who was alſo come thether vpon occaſion of buſynes, were made priuy thereof, which I aſcrybe partly to the prudent manner of proceeding of thoſe councelers, who The prudent
manner of
proceeding
of the coun-
cel of Spayn. neuer impart any matter of importance to any whoſoeuer, except to ſuch, as are neceſſarily to be employed therin; & partly to the circumſpection that the Iriſh vſe in their The circumſpection of
the Yriſh. treaties in that court, who conſidering that their affayres, do no way perteyn to vs, are wont not only curiouſly to conceale theſame from vs, but alſo to deſyre the Kings miniſters not to communicate them with vs.

Of which ſmalle correſpondence betwyxt vs and them vvitnes
maye be takē
of Hugh Buy
agent of late.
for Odonel
in Spayn, and
novv in her
maieſtyes ſer
uice. in matters that concerne their country, there may now be ſufficient teſtimony taken of Hugh Buy, who hauing ben one of the moſt principal agents for Oneal & Odonel in the court of Spayne, and moſt gratful there (as appeared by the reward giuen him at his departure thens) paſſed neuertheleſſe ſhortly after his returne to Ireland to the ſeruice of her Maᵗ ͤ and therfore may teſtify, if he be demaunded,

B   ded,

ded, whether he treated with any Englishman in Spayne, or was willing wee should be trusted with his affayres, sure I am, & I think he wil witnes it, that during the tyme of his negotiatiõ there, which was some moneths, we neuer conferred togeather, nor so much as saluted one another.

And veryly for our further purgation of all suspition in this matter, I may wel say, that if we had ben as badly affected in that cause as is conceaued, and had ben consulted withall, or list to haue intruded our selues to speak our

Not lykly that Syr VVilliam Stanley could aproue the plot that was executed. opinions, wee could neuer haue aproued the plot that was executed, which any man may beleeue at least of Sr. William Stanley, as wel for the particular experience he hath of Ireland, and Irish warres, as also for his wisdome, & exact skil in military discipline, and all martial affayres,

The ridiculous folly of a lybeller, in obiecting to sir VVilliam Stanley his deliuering of Deuenter to the true ovvner. wherin, as it is wel knowne, he is inferior to few men liuing, & seing the occasion is offred to speak of him, I wil ad a woord or two cõcerning him, & his deliuering Dauéter to the Catholyke king, for that thesame is opprobriously carped at in a late pamphlet of a puritan cauling himself Thomas Digges, who as it seemeth hath so litle cõscience and knowledge of a Christian mannes obligation, that he cannot distinguish betwixt trechery and discharge of duty, it beeing euident in conscience, and true diuinity, that Sir William was bound vnder payne of damnable sinne, to deliuer it to the King who was the true owner therof, & from whome it was wrongfully detayned by his rebels;

Syr VVilliãs generosity & sincerity in rendring Dauenter. besydes that, his manner of doing it was such as argueth no lesse his generosity, then his sincerytie, seeing he made no compofition for money or other reward, as many others in lyke occasions haue donne, but rendred it simply without all respect of lucre and gayne, for the only discharge of his conscience, being then at liberty to serue where he would, to which purpose my Lord of Leister his general, had giuen him an ample pasport, which he hath yet to shew.

But herein I meane not further to enlarge my self, seeing
my late

my late Lord Cardinal of happy memorie sufficiently defended and iuftified S^r. Williams action in this behalf with
a learned and graue treatife of his, at thefame tyme, only
I wil fay of his perfon for the particular knowlege I
haue of him, that the honorable cours of lyf he hath led
euer fince hee became a Catholyke, & feruant to the king,
doth make him no leffe recomendable for true Chriftian
pietie and vertue then for wifdome & valour, in fo much
that hee is woorthely held of all ftrangers for the honor
of our nation, and the true mirour of a Chriftian foldier,
and as for his affection to his country I do proteft I am
wel affured, that no man wyfheth more honor & happy-
neffe thereto or is more alienat from all defyre of conqueft
thereof then hee, though our aduerfaries wil nedes imagin
otherwife of him, and all others that either ferue the Catholyke king or receaue any benefit of him, wherby thow
maift perceaue (good reader) how lamentable our cafe is,
feeing that wee are neither fuffred to enioy the comfort &
benefit of our religion country and freindes at home, nor
yet permitted without fufpition and flander of ill affection
to the ftate, to fuftaine our lyues abroad with the liberalitie
of him that only hath the meanes & the wil withal, to re-
lieue vs, as hee releeueth & entertaineth in lyke forte no
fmalle number of ftrangers of all nations, without any bad
conftructions made of him, or them for thefame. But whether it be reafon that to auoyd the vncharitable conceyts of
our aduerfaries & to fatisfy their defire of our ruyn, wee
fuffer our felues to perifh rather the to receaue relief of the
Catholyke king, I leaue it to the iudgmet of any indifferet
& vnpafsionate man and fo wil proceed to fay fomwhat
in particular of F. Parfons againft whome O. E. doth fpit
foorth or rather vomit fo much venim and poyfon, as he
fheweth euidetly what fpirit poffeffeth him, & giueth notable teftimony to F. P. his rare vertues, & great merits.

A DEFENCE

CONCERNING FATHER

Parsons in particular, and that the extreame
malice that the heretykes beare him, is
an euident argument of his
great vertue.

CHAP. II.

The hatred of heretyks, is a notable testimony of F. Parsons his great vertue.

WERE it possible that father Parsons should be so extreamly maligned, hated and calumniated, as he is, by heretykes, yf he were not a great seruant of God and guyded by his spirit? for was there euer any gteat

The greatest saynts of God alvvayes calumniated.

saynt in Gods Churche who laboured more then others, eyther to confound heresy, or to reforme corrupt manners, that felt not in his fame the cruel sting of the slanderous tongues of heretykes, and of other instruments

As the church vvas planted so it must be restored.

Ioan. 7 & 10.
Luc. 23.
Act. 6. 14. 17.
21. 24. 23.

of the deuil? for as the Churche was planted so it must be restored; and therfore as the scriptures do signify; the persecution that our Sauiour him self, and all his Apostles and disciples suffred by slanderous tongues, in the fyrst planting and buylding of the Churche, so also the ecclesiastical histories do witnes the lyke of other seruants of God, who endeuored afterwards to repayre the same, when it was

Gods seruãts so cunningly calumniated by euil men, that good men sometymes held them suspected.

decayed in some places by heresy and sinne, and that many of them besydes the punishmẽts inflicted vpon their persons, were so craftely calumniated by heretykes, that they sustayned much suspition and obloquy not only of many weak and bad Catholykes, but also otherwhyles of some good men; God suffring it for his greater glory and their more merit, whose innocency he euer cleared in the end, to the confusion of his enemies and theirs; A few examples may suffise, for that the matter is cleare enough of it self.

No man that hath red the ecclesiastical histories can be ignorant of the continual and violent persecutions that

saynt

faynt Athanafius fuffred in this kynd, who being the cheef
champion of Gods Churche againft the Arrian heretykes, was by the falfiy accufed of a rape, of burning houfes,
of breaking chalices, of extorfion, of wiche-craft, murders,
yea and treafons; as wel agaynft the Catholyke Emperour
Conftantine the great (who by that meanes was alienated
from him, and moued to banifh him) as alfo againft the
Arrian Emperour Conftantius, to whome he therfore
wrote an Apology of his innocencie.

S. Bafil for his great learning & rare vertue furnamed
the great, being alfo a notable impugner of all the heretykes of his tyme, was impugned & flandered by the with
fuch arte and cunning, that the very monkes of his owne
inftitution and rule were incenfed againft him, in fo
much that after he had fuffred it, as he fayth, 3. yeares together, and fuppreffed the forrow of his hart with filence, he was forced to write an Apology in his owne defence, as alfo many other famous & learned mé did for him
at the fame tyme, and fuch was the diligence and craft of
the heretykes, and fuch the credulity of many Catholykes,
that he complayned pitifully therof, geuing to vnderftand,
that not only all his actions, but alfo euery word he fpoke,
was watched, calumniated and wrefted to a wrong fence,
and that he found himfelf in fuch cafe that he knew not
who to truft.

S. Hierome one of the lights of the latin Churche, & the
fcourge of the heretykes of his age, hauing written a notable worke againft Iouinian the heretyk in defence of vir-
ginity, was flandred to haue defaced matrimony, through
the fubtilty of one of Iouinians fect that counterfeyted him
felf a Catholyke, and enuyed greatly S. Hieroms great credit, and the matter was fo clamoroufly profecuted againft
him in Rome, that many good Catholykes were alienated
frō him & his friéds, in which refpect he was fayne to wryte
an Apology in defence of his book. And at another tyme
being him-felf in Rome, and writing againft fome vices

of the

S. Athanafius
extremly ca-
lumniated.

Baron anno
316. & 339.
335.

Theodoret.
lib. 1. cap. 30.
Socrat. lib. 1.
cap. 21.
Epiph. hær.
68.

Athan. Apo-
log. ad Con-
ftant.

Baron. anno
363. & 371.

S. Bafil.

Bafil. Ep. 73.
& epift. 79.

Bafil. ad Eu-
ftachium
epift.

S. Hierome.

Baron. To.
anno 390.

Baron. anno
185. of the clergy though in general tearmes, he receiued such a
violent impugnation and persecution of all the bad priests
in the cittie, that he was forced to depart thence; which ne-
Hieron. epist.
s. ad Deme-
tria. uerthelesse, how little it impayred his credit in the end, he
signified 30. yeres after in an epistle to Demetrias, wherin
he maketh mention of thesaid treatise that caused all that
broyle against him, and addeth further *quid profuit, armasse
exercitum reclamantium, & vulnus conscientiæ dolore monstrasse, liber
manet & homines perierunt, that is to say, what did it auayle them, to
arme an army of clamarous men against me, and to bewray the wound
of their owne conscience by their greef, the book is yet extant, but the
men ar dead and gon,* thus farre saint Hierome; wherby he
The good
vvoorks of
good men re
mayn hono-
rable, vvhyles
their persecu
tours perish
vvith igno-
miny. signifieth, that although good men for good workes suffer
somtymes great persecutions, yet the good woorkes remayne, and not only the persecution passeth away, but also
the persecutors themselues perish and come to nought,
which by the way I wish the heretyks Fa. Parsons aduersaries to note; for let them rayle vpon him, slander him, and
cry our against him neuer so much, the memory and monuments that he shal leaue behynd him of his great seruice
to God & his Churche, wil remayne honorable to all posterity, when their clamours, and slanders shal vanish away
lyke smoke, and they themselues shalbe eyther cleane forgot, or els remayne ignominious for their heresy and the
persecution of him, and other good men.

S. Chrisosto-
me so calum
niated that
he vvas tvvys
banished by
Catholyk
Bishops. S. Chrisostome Bishop of Constantinople the ornament
of the east Churche, who made cōtinual warre against paganisme, heresy & vyce, as wel by the example of his saintly
lyfe, as by the force of his eloquence, and deuyne preaching
was so exagitat by the calumnious, and contumelious tongues of heretykes, and all sorts of wicked men, that he was
Baron. anno
407. expelled twyse, from his bishopryk, by Catholyke Bishops,
being falsly accused of treasons and many heynous matters,
and dyed at length in banishment; which shortly after God
did punish notorioufly in all his aduersaryes, and calumniatours, and in some of them (as Palladius noteth) by losse of
their

their fpeech & horrible paynes in their tongues, in regard, no dout of their contumelious fpeches and flanders geuen out againft him, and within a few yeres after his death, his innocency was made fo manifeft to all men, that his memory was celebrated in the Churche & he ferued for a great faint of God, as he hath ben euer fince. I omit to fpeak particularly of S. Hilary, S. Ambrofe, S. Auguftin* S. Gregory Nazianzen and dyuers other notable antagonifts of the heretykes of their tymes, all of thē notably calūniated by their aduerfaries, whome I fay, I wil omit for breuityes fake, & conclude with S. Ciril Bifhop of Alexandria, the hammer of the Neftoriā herefy; who in his epiftle to the clergy of Cōftantinople fignifieth that Neftorius the heretyke, did fend abroad certeyn wicked aud loft companions, to defame him euery where, as now the heretykes of England deale with father Parfons whom they feek to difgrace and defame by their fpyes, that they fend throughout Chriftendome, whereof the experience hath ben feen thefe yeares paft not only in other places, but alfo in the very Seminaries of his owne erectiō in Spayne, where haue ben difcouered within thefe 2. or 3. yeres dyuers fpyes fent from England, who counterfeiting great holynes and zeale in religion, endeuored nothing els, but to alienate the ftudents from the Iefuits their fuperiours, and particulerly from Fa. Parfons, filling their eares with fuch monftrous lyes, that if God of his goodnes had not fooner difcouered it, one of thofe Seminaries had ben put in as great combuftion, as was the Englifh colledge at Rome fome yeres agoe But S. Ciril who receiued lyke meafure at heretikes hāds, as Fa. Parfons now doth, fhal anfwere for both, who in certeyn letters of his to Neftorius him felf faith thus. *They caft a brode againft me reportes no leffe mad, then malitious fome fay I haue iniurioufly opreft the poort and blynd; others fay I drew a fword vpon my owne mother; and others, that I ftole gold with the healp of a mayd feruant; and fome agayne fay, that I haue ben always fufpected of fuch wickednes, as a mā would be loth fhould be foūd in his greateft enemy.*

But of

Baron. anno 427.

Baron. anno 369.

Idem an.387.

Aug.contra Iulianū lib. 6 cap.12.&

Baron. anno 426.

*Greg. Nazian oratione ad 150. Epifc. & in vita fua.

Item epift.81 editio nouæ.

Ciril.epift. 7. & 14.

Baron.anno 429.

S.Ciril flandered by mē fent abrode of purpofe to defame him.

Spyes fent abroad to defame F. Parfons.

Spyes difcouerēd in the feminaries of Spayne.

Baron. eod. an. & Ciryl. epift.8.

S.Cirils anfvver to Neftorius applyed to F.Parf.

A DEFENCE

*But of these fellowes, and such lyke I make smalle account, least I may
seeme to extend the measure of my weaknes aboue my maister and lord,
yea aboue all my predicessors, for whatsoeuer cours of lyfe a man holdeth ; it is skant possible for him to escape the sharp teeth of malitious
& wicked backbyters. But they hauing their mouths ful of slanaer, &
maledittion shal one day answere for it before the Iudge of all, and
I in the meane tyme, wil discharge my part, and do that which
becommeth mee, to wit, admonish thee, Nestorius, of thy duty as
my brother in our lord, &c.* Thus sayd S. Ciril to the heretyk
Nestorius ; and so wil I say in father Parsons behalf, to
the heretykes his aduersaries, to wit; that hee litle regardeth their rayling, considering he cannot look to be
more free from that kynd of persecution then his maister
Christ, and other seruants of God, that haue laboured in
the Churche before him, and that therfore leauing them to
answere for it, before the iust and rigorous Iudge, he wil
in the meane whyle, proceed to do his duty towards God

F Parsons re- and them, as heatherto he hath donne, repaying their ma-
payeth the
malice of his lice with charity, their fury with patience, their rayling
enemies with prayers to God for them, their slanderous pamphlets
vvith chari- and libels, with learned and godly bookes, and their em-
ty. ploying of spyes abroad to defame him, with sending in
priests from his Seminaries to conuert them, and to saue
Hiero. epist. their soules, which is all the hurt he wisheth them, for all
77. the rancour and malice they beare him, and the iniury they
Miserable to
do iniury but do him, for the which he thinketh they rather deserue pitty
not to suffer then hatred, for that as saynt Hierome sayth, *apud Christianos*
it.
Of F. Parf.his *non qui patitur, sed qui facit iniuriam miser est,* that is to say, *not*
great, & pro- *he which suffreth the iniury, but he which doth it is miserable.*
fitable la-
bours in gods And now to say somewhat particularly though very
Church. breefly of his labours in Gods Churche, which makes him
His notable hateful to the diuel and all heretyks ; yf wee consider the
books.
Soules gay- same, and the fruits therof, as the soules he gayned to God
ned to God whyles he was in England; the notable bookes he hath
by him in written ; the foure notable Seminaries which he hath
England. erected; (wherof 3. do stil florish in Spayne, and Flanders,
besydes

befydes two refidences for priefts in S.Lucar, and Lifbon) the important releef of two thowfand crownes rent, that he procured at one tyme for the Seminary at Doway, erected by my Lord Cardinal ; the pacification of the fcandalous tumults in the Englifh Colledge at Rome, attépted by diuers in vayne, and referued, as it fhould feeme, by almighty God to him, for the teftimony of his wifdome and vertue; the prefent gouernment of the fayd Colledge in fuch tráquility, vnity & loue, fuch æcconomy & difcipline, and fuch exercyfe of all vertue and learning, that it ferueth for an example & fpectacle to all Rome (fo that all our Seminaries which are now the honour and hope of our afflicted Churche, and in tyme wilbe the bane of herefy in England, haue either ben erected, or releeued & repayred, or otherwyfe exceedingly benefited by him) and yf wee confider withall, the great care and paynes he hath taken in all this ; the many long and tedious iourneys to ftrange and remote countryes ; the difficulties he hath paft by contradiction, and oppofition fomtymes of great parfonages; and the prudence longaminity and patience he hath fhewed in all ; and if wee ad therto his religious lyfe, fo examplar for all kynd of vertue, that thofe which maligne him moft, can fynd nothing iuftly to reprehend therin, and therfore to haue fomewhat to fay againft him, are fayne either to inuét manifeft lyes, fuch as here I haue touched, or els to calumniate his good woorkes with vayne furmifes, vnchaꝛitable fufpitions, and fals interpretations, from which kynd of calumniatió neither the innocency of Gods faints, nor yet the perfection of our Sauiour himfelf could be free; laftly if with all this, wee confider concurrence and manifeft afsiftance of almighty God to his endeuours in the progreffe of Catholyke religion in England, aduanced notably as all men fee, no leffe by his bookes and other labours then by his Seminaries, wee may euidently conclude three things, the firft that God hauing of his infinit mercy and prouidence determined to repayre the wracked walles of our

4. Notable Seminaries erected, and 2. refidences for priefts.

1000. Crovvnes rent procured for the Seminary of Dovvay.

The tumults of the Englifh in Rome pacified.

His vvyfe & examplar gouernment of the Englifh colledge at Rome.

All our Seminaries eyther erected, or re leeued, or exceedingly benefyted by him.

His lyfe fo religious, that his greateft enemies, can iuftly reprehéd nothing therein.

F. Parfons charged for lack of better matter vvith the actions of his very enemyes.

His good vvoorks calumniated, & il interpreted as our Saui ours vvere.

Gods manifeft concurréce vvith his labours in the progres of Cathol. religion.

Three conclutions dravvn of the premisses

of our Hierusalem, hath raysed him for a special meanes, and instrument therof, geuing him for that end, extraordinary graces and biefsings, as wel of credit with Princes abroad, as also of singuler zeale, prudence, fortitude, longanimity, patience, and other vertues requisit to so heroycal and excellent a woork, and no maruel, seeing that for the buylding of his material tabernacle he bestowed vpon some of his people extraordinary gyfts of caruing, grauing, and woorking in wood or metal all kynd of woork, wherof they had no skil before.

I.

God hath rayled F. Parsons for a special inftru ment to repayre his Church in England.

Exod. 31. 35. 36.

The second coclusion of thefe premiffes, is, that it is not posible, but that he beeing employed by almighty God in the seruice of his Churche, so particulerly, and with such fruit as wee see, shalbe impugned calumniated & persecuted by Gods enemies; for the deuil seking by all meanes to ouerthrow the Churche of God employeth all his instruments, and difchargeth the rage of his fury cheefly against those that are the cheef pillers and vpholders thereof.

2.

It is not pofsible but that F. pars. being employed, by almighty God shalbe impugned by the deuil, and all his inftruments.

The third & last poynt is, that yf he stil continue to the end, and cosummate his cours, according to his beginning and proceedings hetherto, as by Gods grace he wil, he shal not only gayne an eternal crowne of glory in heauen, but also leaue to all posterity an euerlasting fame of his Apostolical labours, and much the rather, for the contradiction, hatred and persecution that he receiueth at the hands of Gods enemies, which already maketh him famous throughout Christendome, and wil euer remayn for an euident argument of his great vertue and merits.

3.

His Apoftolical labours fhalbe the more glorious to all pofterity for the great cotradiction he receaueth of Gods enemies.

Thus much I haue thought good to touch breefly and truly here, to serue for a counterpeyse to the multitude of malitious flanders that O. E. heapeth vpon him in his two lybels, the particular answere whereof, I leaue to one that hath vndertaken the same, meaning only for my part to examin here a litle furder how truly he auoucheth, that none are put to death in England for religion,

The autor proceedeth to the difcouery of the impudency of O. E. affirming that

which

which befydes former examples and many reafons ai-
leadged in my Apology, almoft euery mannes experience in England may conuince for a notable vntruthe
by the martirdome of thofe, which haue fuffred in diuers
parts, within thefe 3. yeres fince the Apology was
written.

none are put
to death in
Engl for
religion.

EXAMPLES OF DIVERS

*Catholykes executed fince the Apology was written
for thefame caufes that the martirs were put to
death in the primatiue Churche, and of the
great iniuftice donne to two Priefts
condemned at Lincolne by
Iudge Glanduyle.*

CHAP. III.

I Appeale to the remembrance of al thofe that were
prefent at the araignment of M. Rigby a lay Gentleman in the yere 1600. whether there was any thing
concerning matter of ftate or the leaft fufpition thereof
layd to his charge, who being no way accufed or called
in queftion for any matter whatfoeuer, but comming to
the fefsions at Newgate of meere charity to excufe the
aparance of a Catholyke gentlewoman that was fick, was
examined of his religion, and condemned within a few
dayes after; for being a reconcyled Catholyk, wherof
neuertheles he might haue ben difcharged yf he would
haue confented but only to haue gon to the Churche,
which was offred him, both before the Iury gaue their
verdit; and alfo after.

Further-more what matter of ftate was fo much as ob-

M. Iohn
Righby exe-
cuted in the
yere 1600.

ieȼted

M.Palafer.
M.Talbot.
M.Ihon.
Norton.
iected to M.Palafer the prieſt, or to M. Talbot, and to M. Iohn Norton, condemned and executed theſame yeare at Durham, the firſt only for being a prieſt, and the other two for hauing bē acquaynted with him, & not detecting him, or to a vertuous wydow the laſt yere at York, for harboring a prieſt called M. Chriſtopher Whartō, who was exe-

Mrs Lyne.
cuted alſo with her, or to Mrs lyne the laſt yere at London for hauing receiued prieſts, againſt whome no matter of ſtate, but only their religion and prieſthood was proued,

M.Ihon Pibuſh.
M.Mark Barkvvorth.
M.Robert Nutter.
M.Edvvard Thvving.
M.Thurſtan Hunt.
M.Middletō.
M.Harriſon, & a lay man.
which was alſo moſt euident in M. Iohn Pibuſh, M. Mark Barkwoorth at London the laſt yere, & M. Robert Nutter, M. Edward Thwing M. Thurſtan Hunt, & M. Midleton, at Lācaſter, as alſo in the caſe of M.Filcock, & now this yeare M. Harriſon at York, all of them martyred only for beeing Catholyke Prieſts, and a lay man for hauing receiued the foreſaid N. Harriſon into his houſe.

Catholyke
Prieſts tray-
tors novv in
no other
ſort, then
vvere the
Chriſtian
Prieſts in the
primatiue
Churche.
Therfore can O.E. or any man be ſo impudent to ſay that theſe lay men & women dyed not for religion, or that the prieſts for whoſe cauſe they were condemned, or the other here mentioned were traytors in any other ſorte or ſence then were the prieſts of the primatiue Churche, accounted in lyke manner rebels and traytors only for doing the function of chriſtian Catholyke Prieſts, as appeareth in the ſtory of the bleſſed S. Alban the protomartyr of Bri-

Beda hiſtor.
Eccleſ.lib. 1.
S.Alban our
firſt marty.,
chargedvvith
receauing a
trayterous
Prieſt.
tany, who was charged by the Iudge to haue receiued into his houſe & conueyghed away rebellem & ſacrilegum ſacerdotem, a trayterous and ſacrilegious Prieſt, for that he put on the Prieſts apparel, and ſo offred himſelf to be taken by the ſearchers, that the Prieſt might eſcape; for the which, and for the conſtant profeſsion of the Chriſtian

S.Alban
martyred
about the
yere of our
Lord, 300.
An example
for Catho-
lyks.
faith he receiued a glorious crowne of martyrdome; wherin may be noted by the way how it pleaſed almighty God of his diuine prouidence, to geue vs in our firſt martyr ſuch a notable example of Chriſtian fortitude & charity, in harboring a perſecuted Prieſt, and ſauing his lyfe with the loſſe of his owne, to the end that in the lyke

caſes,

caſes, and occaſions (which now dayly occur) no terrour of temporal lawes, nor pretence of treaſons may withold vs from vſing the lyke charity towards the Prieſts of God; wherto our Sauiour Chriſt alſo inuiteth and incowrageth vs with promiſe of great reward ſaying *he which receiueth a Prophet in the name of a prophet, ſhal haue the reward of a Prophet, and he which receiues a iuſt man, in the name of a iuſt man, ſhal haue the reward of a iuſt man.* Matth. 10.

But yf we cóſider the proceedings of the perſecutors in thoſe dayes, wee ſhal ſynd that the Chriſtiás were not only perſecuted as traytors, and in theſame manner, but alſo for theſame poynts of religion that wee are perſecuted now, wherof I wil breefly repreſent vnto thee (good reader) an euident example, to the end thou mayſt the better iudge whether wee dy for religion or no, or whether there be any difference betwyxt the martirdome of the old Chriſtians, and of the Catholykes at this day. *Chriſtians martyred in the primatiue Churche by paynims, for the ſame points of religion, that Catholyks are perſecuted novv. Baron. To. 2. anno 303. Surius 11. Februa.*

Wee read in the ancient and Publyk records of the acts of the proconſuls of Africk vnder Dioclefian, and Maximian Emperours (vnder whome ſaynt Alban was martyred) that they made an edict wherin amongſt other things they forbad vpon payne of death the bleſſed ſacrifice of the maſſe which is called *Dominicum* in theſayd records, & therfore *dominicum agere* or *celebrare* is vnderſtood there to celebrate maſſe; and if our aduerſaries maruel what warrant I haue ſo to expound it, they ſhal vnderſtád, that this woord Maſſe in Engliſh, & *Miſſa* in Latin, vſed by ancient councels and Fathers aboue 1200. yeares agoe, and deriued of the hebrew woord *miſſah* (which ſignifyeth a voluntary ſacrifice or oblation) hath dyuers other names in the ancient Fathers as in the greekes *liturgia tremenda miſteria*, and *ſacrificium tremendum,* and in the Latins *ſolemnia, ablatio per ſacerdotem, cena Domini* and to omit diuers other more ordinary, *Dominicum* as appeareth in ſaynt Cyprian, who ſpeaking of the ſacrifice offred at the altar in remembrance and repreſentation of the paſſion of Chriſt (which wee cal the ſacri- *The ſacrifice of the Maſſe forbidden vpon payne of death by Dioclefian. Concil. Roman. ſnb Silueſtro 1. Con. Catth. 2. can. 3. Leo Mag. Epiſt. 81. Aug. ſer. 91. de tempore. Ambroſ. li. 5. epiſt. 33. Liturg. Dionyſ & Baſil. & Chryſoſt. Tertul. lib. 2. ad vxorem, li. de Caſtita. li. de oratione.*

Cypria. 63.

Ibidem.

sacrifice of the masse) tearmeth it sometymes, *sacrificium quod Christus obtulit* sometymes *ipsum nostræ redemptionis Sacramentum, &c.* somtymes only *Dominicum,* saying, *nunquid post cænam dominicum cel. bramus?* that is to say, *do wee offer the sacrifice of the body of our Lord, or do wee say masse after supper?* and this is euident by all his discours in that Epistle, where he treateth principally of the blessed sacrifice; and saith that Christ is *huius sacrificij autor, & doctor, the Autor, and teacher of this sacrifice,* and that the Priest representing the person of Christ doth offer *sacrificium verum & plenum, a true and ful sacrifice.*

Christians martyred vnder Dioclesian for hearing masse.

This then being presuposed, it is to be vnderstood that certayne deuout Christians in Afrik being secretly assembled at masse, were taken and brought before the proconsul *Anulinus* who examining them began with fayre woords to persuade them to haue care of their liues, and to obey the commandment of the Emperours, they answered *spem salutemq, Christianorum Dominicū esse, that the masse is the hope and saluation of Christians,* and that therfore they could not forgoe it; vpon which confession they were condemned to death; & amōgst the rest there was one *Emeritus* in whose house masse had bē celebrated, to whome the Proconsul sayd, *was the assembly made in thy house, contrary to the commandement of the Emperours?* he answered,yea; why didst thou,sayd the Proconsul, suffer it? I could quoth he,do no lesse,for that they are my brethren; yea;but thow oughtst to haue hindred it, sayd the Proconsul; I could not sayd the other, for wee that be Christians, *sine Dominico esse non possumus,* cannot be without masse; as though, sayd the Proconsul; thou art not bound to obey the edict of the Emperours, God, sayd the martyr, is greater then the Emperours, and ought more to be obeyed,where vpon he was condemned,and executed as the rest; here now I aske our aduersaries whether these men were put to death for religion, or no, and whether it fareth not euen so with vs at this day,as then it did with them.

The answere of the martyrs concerning the necessity of masse.

For

For although the maſſe be not now made treaſon but a mony matter, yet by a certayne conſequent, it is drawen within the compaſſe of treaſon, for it cannot be celebrated without a prieſt; the receiuing of whome is treaſon, I meane a Seminary Prieſt, there being now ſo few other in England (yf ther bee any at all) that the Catholykes muſt eyther receiue them with daunger of their liues, or lack the neceſſary food of their ſoules, which they hold more deare then lyfe, as the old Chriſtians alſo did. *To heare maſſe in England is treaſon by conſequence.*

But let vs compare breefly the proceedings of the perſecutors in thoſe tymes and theſe. In the examination of thoſe Chriſtians the old perſecutors would not content themſelues with theyr confeſſion, that they were Chriſtians, & ſo put them to death for their religion, but ſought to bring them within the compaſſe of their ſtatute; *wee aſke yow not, ſay they, whether yow bee Chriſtians, but whether yow haue hard maſſe contrary to the comaundment of the Emperours,* the lyke is donne now with vs, for it ſuffiſeth not our perſecutors that wee confeſſe our religion (as that wee are Catholykes) but they examine vs whether wee haue heard maſſe, whether we haue ben reconcyled by a Prieſt, or whether the Queene bee ſupreme head of the Churche, and ſuch lyke, therby to draw vs within the compaſſe of the lawes, that they may put vs to death vnder colour of treaſon. *A compariſon of the proceedings of the old perſecutours, vvith thoſe of this tyme in Engl.*

Furthermore the old Chriſtians ſayd for their iuſt defence, that they being Chriſtians, could not be without maſſe, and we now ſay the ſame, & that wee cannot forgo abſolution of our ſinnes, nor other ſpiritual comforts to be receiued at the hands of Prieſts only; to this, our perſecutors reply as the others did, that it is againſt the lawes and ſtatutes of her Maieſty, we anſwere with the old Chriſtias, God is aboue all Kings, and his law aboue all lawes: *Et oportet magis obedire Deo quam hominibus, we muſt rather obey God then men;* neuertheleſſe we are condemned for diſobedience to the lawes, as the old Chriſtians were; and dyed they *The anſwer of the old martyrs conform to ours novv. Act. cap. 5.*

The old martyrs vvere condemned for disobedience to the temporal lavves, as Catholyks are novv.

Treason pretended but religion condemned as vvel in the old martyrs as in ours novv.

they for religion and not wee? were they martyrs and not wee? were their enemies persecuters of Gods Churche & not ours? the cause is one, & the self same, the proceedings lyke, no difference in the issue; breach of lawes and treason is pretended, but religion condemned, and therfore as the whole Churche hath hetherto held, and honored those old Christians for glorious martyrs, so doth it now at this day and euer wil etteeme these other for no lesse, as I haue shewed in my Apology more at large, and therfore I wil proceed to speak a woord or two of the great iniustice donne since my Apology was writte, to two priests called *M. Hunt, and M. Sprat*, condemned, and executed at Lincolne in the yeare 1600.

Notable iniustice donne to M. Hunt, and M. Sprat condemned at Lincolne anno 1600.

These two being taken in a search and confessing themselues only to be Catholykes, were first imprisoned, and then shortly after indited for hauing conspyred, and practised the death of her Maiesty mooued her subiects to rebelion, withdrawne them from theyr natural and due obedience, and from the religion now established in England to the Roman fayth, and finally for hauing mayntayned the autority of the Pope, of all which poynts, no one touching matter of state was proued against them, no witnesse being produced, nor so much as the least presumptio of any attempt or cospiracy against her maiestyes person or state, or that they had persuaded any man to the Catholyk religion, or sayd any thing in fauour of the Popes autority more then that which they answered to the captious question of the Queenes supremacy, demaunded of them there, after their apprehension; lastly, it was not so much as proued that they were Priests, which though they denied not, yet they did not confesse, but put it to tryal, vrging to haue it proued by witnesses, or other sufficient arguments; whereas there was none at all but light presumtios therof, as that there was found in their males, two breuiaries (which many lay men vse as wel as Priests) and a few relicks and some holy oyle (which they might
haue

haue carried for other mennes vſe & not their owne) ſo that
to conclude, of all thoſe great treaſons whereof they were
indited, there was no one proued, except the matter of the
Queenes ſupremacy, which is a meere poynt of religion, as
I am ſure the puritans in England, and all other heretykes
abroad wil witneſſe with vs, who impugne theſame as wel
as wee ; and yet neither by the verdit of the Iury nor yet by
the ſentēce of the Iudge, were they cleared of any one point,
but condemned for all, as though they had bin guilty of all,
and ſo in truth, executed for matter of religion, though
ſlandred with matter of ſtate, whereby their martyrdome
was far more glorious, the malice of our aduerſaries more
manifeſt, the iniury donne vnto them vnexcuſable, the
ſinne of the Iudges, and Iury moſt execrable, which ſufficiently appeared by the iuſtice of God extended vpon Iudge
Glanduile who had ſhewed an extraordinary malice and Iudge Glan-
fury agaynſt them, and was therfore (as wel may bee pre- duile puni-
ſumed) within a few dayes after ſtrooken by the hand of ſhed exem-
God, in ſuch miraculous māner, as the reſt may take exam- plarly by al-
ple therby yf their harts be not indurat. mighty God.

    And beſydes theſe late martyrs before rehearſed, M. Tich-
borne, M. Fr. Page, and M. R. Watkinſon, were arraigned &
condemned at London, for beeing made Prieſtes beyond
the ſeas, and coming into England, contrary to the ſtatute, &
were executed at Tiburne the 20. of April this preſent yeare
1602. beeing there not ſuffred to declare the truth of their
cauſe and ſuffrance. And this was donne euen at ſuch tyme;
as hope was both giuen and conceaued of a more mylder
cours of proceeding towards Catholykes ; then heretofore.

    It is moſte grieuous to conſider how M. Tichborne by
one of his owne cote was betrayed, and apprehended : almighty God vouchſafe to reſtore to that wretched man
ſo great grace as he fel from ; in the dooing of that acte.

    M. Page and M. Watkinſon were apprehended in the
tyme of the ſeſsions, the one by a wicked woman ; ſubor-
                        D   ned

ned to diſſemble religion for ſuch purpoſes : the other by
one Bomer, who hauing late before playd the diſſembling
hypocrite & ſpy at Doway, returned into England there to
become the diſciple of his maſter Iudas.

At the ſame ſeſsions was condemned for fellony, and
alſo executed, one Iames Ducket, a Catholyke lay man, and
another lay man with him, about a treatiſe written by a
martyr diuers yeares ſince, concerning the cauſe of Catholyke ſufferers.

OF THE IMPVDENCIE OF

a miniſter, who being preſent at the death of two mar-
tyrs aforeſayd, affirmed publykly that our country was
conuerted by ſaynt Auguſtin the monke, to the
proteſtants religion, by occaſion whereof
the truth of the poynt is eui-
dently declared.

CHAP. IIII.

Allen the
miniſter.

I Can not omit to ſay ſomewhat here of the notable impudency of a fooliſh miniſter, who being preſent at the
death of the two martyrs at Lincolne aforenamed, and
hearing one of the declare vnto the people his innocecy,
proteſting amongſt other things that he dyed only for the
profeſsion of the Catholyke fayth, to the which our country
was conuerted from paganiſme, in the tyme of Pope Gregory the great, was not aſhamed to ſay publykly that the
religion now taught, & preached there, is the ſame wherto
England was firſt conuerted.

And although I hold not this miniſter for a man of that
woorth that he may merit my labour or any mans els ſe-
riouſly to confute his ydle babling, yet for as much as the
ſame

fame hath bin oft publifhed, and preached by many others, and many ignorant abufed therby, and feing the narration of our firſt conuerſion may no leſſe profit and edify the vnlearned reader, with the teſtimony of the truth, then content and delyte him, for the pleaſure of the hiſtory, I wil breefly treat, firſt of the conuerſion of the Saxons or Engliſh in the tyme of King Edelbert, and after of the conuerſion of the Britains in the tyme of King Lucius, & euidently proue that our Catholyke faith was preached and planted in our country at both tymes, and that our Kings and country continued euer after the latter conuerſion in the obedience of the Church of Rome vntil the tyme of K. Henry the eyght.

It appeareth by our chronicles, and hiſtories, that in the yere of our Lord 582. (according to S. Bedes computation) S. Gregory ſurnamed the great, the firſt of that name, ſent into England, ſaynt Auguſtin a monke with diuers others of his profeſsion, to preach the Chriſtian, fayth, to the Engliſh, and that they came thither, bearing a ſiluer croſſe, for their banner, and the Image of our Lord and ſauiour (as ſaynt Bede ſaith) paynted in a table, and hauing leaue of King Edelbert to preach to his ſubiects, began firſt the exercyſe of Chriſtian Catholyk religion in the citty of Canterbury in an ancient Chutch which they found there dedicated to S. Martin, from the tyme that the Romans liued there, in which Church; *ipſi primo* (ſayth ſaynt Bede) *conuenire Pſallere, orare miſſas facere, predicare & baptizare cœperunt, they firſt began to aſſemble themſelues, to ſing, to pray, to ſay maſſe, to preach, and baptiſe,* vntil the King being conuerted they had leaue to buyld ſome Churches, and to make others of the temples of the Idols; which ſaint Gregory ordayned ſhuld be donne with caſting holy water therin, buylding altars, and placing relikes of ſaynts, commaunding further that feaſts ſhould be celebrated in the dayes of the dedication of the ſayd Churches, & in the natiuity of the martyrs, whoſe relykes ſhould be kept there; beſyds that he appoynted ſaynt

Augu-

Beda hiſt. Angl. li. 1. ca. 23.

Lib. 1. ca. 26.

Ibid. ca. 29.

D 2

Augustin to be Metropolitan of England, and sent him holy vessels, and vestiments for altars and Priests, and relyckes of the Apostels, and martyrs, and granted him the vse of the pal, *ad sola missarum solemnia agenda, only for the celebration of solemne masses,* and further gaue him order to ordayne 12. Bishops vnder him self, and to make another Metropolitan at Yorke, who when those parts should be couerted, should haue as many vnder him, and be himself after saynt Augustins dayes, dependant only vpon the sea Apostolyk, and receiue the Pal from the same, furthermore saynt Augustin caused King Edelbert to buyld a Church from the ground in honour of the blessed Apostles S. Peter, & S. Paule, and a monastery not farre from Canturbury, whereof the first Abbot called Peter, was of so holy a lyfe that after his death, it was testified from heauen by a continual light that appeared ouer his tombe. Also King Edelbert caused S. Paules Church to be buylt in London, and another in Rochester dedicated to S. Andrew the Apostle.

Hereto may be added the exercise of the Popes autority, not only in the dayes of King Edelbert, but also after, in the raygne of other Christian Kings vntil the tyme that saynt Bede ended his history.

Pope Boniface sent the Pal to Iustus, fourth Archbishop of Canturbury after saynt Augustin. Honorius the Pope sent also the Pal to Honorius that succeded Iustus, and to Paulinus Archbishop of York; ordayning (at the request of King Edwin and his wyfe) that the longer liuer of them should consecrate a successor to the other that should dy first, to excuse so long a Iourney as to Rome.

The two Kings Oswy, and Egbert, the one of Northumberland, and the other of Kent, sent Wigard to Rome to be made Primat, when both the seas of Canturbury, and Yorke, were vacant; and Wigard dying there, Pope Vitalianus made Theodore a grecian, primat in his steede, Wilfrid Byshop of Yorke being twys vniustly expelled from his Bishoprik appealed both tymes to Rome, first to Pope Agatho,

---

Marginal notes (left column):

Cap. 29.

Cap. 33.

Lib. 2. cap. 3.

Lib. 1 cap 8.

Lib 2. cap. 17. & 18.

Li. 3 ca. 29.

Lib. 4. cap. 1.

Lib. 5. ca. 20.

Agatho, and after to Pope Iohn, and being cleared by their sentences was restored to his Bishoprik: and heerto I wil ad a woord or two concerning the exceeding great zeale and deuotion of the Saxon Kinges to the sea Apostolyke in those dayes. King Oswy determined to goe to Rome in Pilgri- Lib.cap.5. mage and had donne it yf death had not preuented him. Lib 5.cap.7. King Ceadwald wết thether to be baptysed, & dyed there.

King Hun his successor; after he had raygned 37. yeares Ibibem. wết thether also in Pilgrimage as many (sayth saynt Bede) in those dayes both of the layty and clergy, as wel women as men, were wont to doe; King Coenred did the lyke, Lib.5 cap.20. & had in his company the sonne of Sigher King of the east Saxons, and both of them entred into religion in Rome about the yeare of our Lord 709. not past 22. yeares before S. Bede ended his history, which was almost 900. yeres a goe; wherto may be added out of later historiographers the lyke examples of the extraordinary deuotion and obe-dience of our English Kings vnto the sea Apostolyke in euery age vntil after the conquest.

King Inas shortly after S. Bedes tyme about the yeare of Polid lib.4. our Lord 740. went to Rome, and made his Kingdome hist. Angl. tributary to the Pope, ordayning the Peter pence, the lyke did also afterwards Offa the King of the Mercians in the yeare of our Lord. 775.

Etheluolph King of England went to Rome in Pilgri-mage about the yeare of our Lord 847. and made that part of England which his father Egbert had conquered tribu-tary also to the Bishop of Rome.

King Edward being threatned with excommunication Polid.lib.6. by Pope Iohn the teth for that he was carelesse to prouide the English Church of Bishops, caused Pleimund the Bishop of Canterbury to make many, and after to goe to Rome to purge him selfe of his negligence about the yeare of our Lord 900.

King Edgar obtayned of Pope Iohn the 13. with li- Ibidem cence, to giue certayne liuings of secular Priests to

Monkes

Monkes about the yeare of our Lord. 965.

Polid. lib 7. Canutus King of England went to Rome in Pilgrimage about the yeare of our Lord 1024.

Alred in vita
S. Eduuardi. S. Edward King of England hauing made a vow to goe to Rome procured the same to be commuted by Pope Leo the nynth into the buylding of a monastery of S. Peter, he also confirmed the payment of the yearly tribute to the sea Apostolyke, about the yeare of our Lord 1060. which was not past 5. yeares before the conquest, after the which there were no lesse notable examples of this matter.

Gulielmus
Neubrice. li.
2. ca. 25. & 34. King Henry the second who by Pope Adrian was first intituled Lord of Ireland sent legats to Rome to craue pardon of Pope Alexander for the murder committed by his occasion vpon saint Thomas of Canterbury, where vpon two Cardinals were sent into England, before whome the King lyke a publike penitent, & a priuat person submitted himselfe to the Ecclesiastical discipline in a publik assembly of the cleargy and nobility.

When King Richard the first was kept prisoner by Frederick the Emperour his mother wrote to Celestinus Petrus ble-
senfis epist.
144. the Pope calling him *the successor of Peter, and the Vicar of Christ, quem Dominus constituit super gentes & regno in omni plenitudine potestatis, whome our Lord had placed ouer nations and Kingdomes in all fulnesse of power*, and willed him to vse the spiritual sword against the Emperour, as Alexander his predecessor had donne against Frederick his Father whome he did excommunicate.

Polid vergil
lib. 15. King Iohn being excommunicated by the Pope was not absolued before he tooke his crowne off frō his owne head, and deliuered it to Pandulfus the Popes legat, promising for himselfe and his heyres, that they should neuer receiue it afterwards but from the Bishop of Rome.

I omit others of later tyme, seing no mā I think doubteth, but that all the successors of King Iohn liued in the communion and obedience of the Roman Church, paying the old
yearely

yearely tribute called the Peter péce, vntil the tyme of King Polid. lib. 17.
Henry the 8. her maiestyes father, who being maried to
his brother Arthurs widdow by dispésation of the sea Apostolyke, continued many yeares after in the obedience therof, and in defence of the autority of the sayd sea, wrote a
learned book agaynst Luther, for the which ; the honorable
title of defender of the fayth was giuen him by Pope Leo,
which tytle her maiesty also vseth at this day, so that no
man can deny that our country was conuerted by S. Gregory to the Roman fayth, or that it hath continued therin
vntil K. Henries tyme; except he haue a brazen face and a
seared conscience, or els be ignorant of all antiquity.

But to returne to S. Augustin, and those first two hundreth yeres compryfed in the history of S. Bede, yf wee consider the notable miracles wherwith it pleased God to confirme this our Catholyke religion in those dayes for his
owne glory, and the conuersion of the panims, no man can
dout that it is the true fayth, except he be more faythlesse &
incredul. us then those infidels that were conuerted therby.

Saynt Bede signifieth that S. Augustin wrought so many
miracles (whereof he declareth some) that S. Gregory wrote Lib. 3. ca. 2.
vnto him to admonish him not to be proud therof, he also quest. 10. 11. 12. 13.
declareth very many famous miracles donne by a crosse Lib. 3 cap 2.
erected by King Oswald, and after by his relickes as wel in
Ireland and Germany, as England, and by the relickes of
faynt Eartongatha daughter to the King of Kent, and her
cosen Edelburg both virgins and nunnes, & of S. Edel-
dreda the Queene, that dyed a virgin in a monastery, whose
body was taken vp whole & vncorrupt after many yeares, Lib. 4. ca. 10.
at the discouery whereof diuels were expelled, and many
disseasses cured. Also he recounteth the lyke notable mira-
cles of S. Chad, S. Cutbert, S. Ædelwald, and faynt Iohn a Lib. 5. ca. 1. 2. 3. 4. 5. 6.
Bishop which they did whyles they were yet liuing, and lib. 3. cap. 15.
others donne by holy oyle, & by the blessed sacrifice of the
masse, all which for breuities sake I omit, remitting our aduersaries to the autor in the places aleaged in the margent.

OF

OF THE FIRST CON-
*version of our country whyles it was called Britany in
the tyme of King Lucius, with euident proofes
that our Catholyke fayth was
then preached & plan-
ted there.*

CHAP. V.

BVᴛ for as much as our country hath ben twyse cō-uerted from paganisme, first in the tyme of the Bri-tains, and after in the tyme of the Saxons or English, they wil say perhaps that although we proue, that the second tyme our Catholyke religion was planted and esta-blished there, when many errors (as they would haue the world to thinke) were crept into the Church, yet at the first conuersion in King Lucius dayes, their religion was taught and deliuered to the Britains, which some of their croniclers are not ashamed to intimat to their readers, and namely Holinshed who (yf my memory fayle me not, for I haue not his book here) maketh Eleutherius the Pope write a letter to King Lucius more lyke a minister of En-gland, then a Bishop of Rome.

Therefore I wil take a litle paynes to examine this poynt, & wil make it manifest that our Catholyke religion which saint Augustin planted amongst the English, was de-liuered 400. yeres before to King Lucius and the Britains by Fugatius and Damianus, or as some say Donatianus, sent into Britany by Pope Eleutherius in the yeare of our Lord 182.

And although no ancient historiographer or writer (for ought I haue seene) do signify particularly, what poynts of religion were preached to King Lucius at his conuersion, partly for that matters of so great antiquity are but very breefly

*Polid.lib.1.
Platina in
Eleuther
Beda hist.
Angl.lib.1.
cap.4.*

breefly and obscurely handled, and partly because in those dayes (when there was no other but our Catholyke religiō vniuersally professed, & this of the protestants not so much as dreamt of,) it was needlesse to signify the poynts or articles therof, for that it could not be immagined to be any other but the Roman fayth ; yet in the discourse of the tymes and ages next ensewing the conuersion of King Lucius (whyles the fayth which he receiued remayned pure, and vncorrupt) the cleare light of truth doth sufficiently shew it selfe, through the clouds of the obscure brenity wherewith the matters of those tymes are treated.

To this purpose it is to be vnderstood, that as our famous countryman S. Bede testifieth, the fayth preached to King Lucius and the Britains remayned in integrity and purity, vntil the tyme of the Arrians, which was for the space of almost 200. yeares, and although he signify that from that tyme forward, the people of Britany weare geuen to noueltyes, and harkened to euery new doctrine, yet it is euident in him that neyther the Arrian heresy nor yet the Pelagian afterwards, took any root there, or could infect the whole body of the Britain Church, but only troobled the peace thereof, for a short tyme, in so much, that it should seeme, the first was rooted out by the industry, of the good Pastors and Bishops of Britany, whereof some were present at the great councel of Sardica held against the Arrians shortly after that of Nice (in which respect S. Hilary doth worthely prayse the Britain Bishops, for that they wholy reiected the Arrian heresy) and the later, I meane the heresy of Pelagius, which saynt Bede sayth the britains would *nullatenus suscipere, in no sort receiue*, was suppressed by S. German, and saint Lupus, two Bishops of France who at the request of the Britains came into Britany and confounded the Pelagians in open disputation ; whereby the people were so incensed against the said heretykes that they could hardly hold theire hands from them, and in conclusion banished those that would not yeld to the true Catholyke faith, and

Lib. 1. hist. ecclef. ca. 17.

Athan. Apolog. 2. contra arrianos.

Hilari epist. ad Epistolos· &c.

Lib. 1. cap 17.

Ibid. cap. 21.

E here

here vpon ensewed such peace and tranquility in the britan Church, that for a long tyme after (as saynt Bede testifieth) the fayth remayned there *intemerata* vncorrupt, wherby it appeareth that after the expulsion of the Pelagians (which was about the yeare of our Lord 450.) the Church of Britany reteyned the same fayth that it receiued at the first conuersion, and therfore yf we fynd the vse and practise of our religion vntil these tymes it may serue for a testimony that the same was deliuered to King Lucius.

First we read that presently after the persecution of Dioclesian wherin our protomartyr saynt Alban with some others was put to death about the yeare of our Lord 286. the Christians that had liued before in woods and caues, not only repayred the Churches which the persecuters had destroyed, but also made new in honour of the martyrs, celebrated festiual dayes, and buylt amongst others a most sumptuous Church in honour of S. Alban, where many miracles were wount to be donne continually vntil the tyme of S. Bede (as he himselfe witnesseth,) & afterwards, when the Pelagian heresy had somwhat infected the country, saynt German going thether out of France to confound the Pelagians, at the request of the Britans themselues as I haue declared before appeased a great storme at sea, with casting therein a little water in the name of the Trinity) which no dout was holy water) and being arriued there, he restored sight vnto a noble mans daughter applying vnto her eyes certayne relyckes which he caryed about him, &c. after hauing confuted the Pelagians, and reduced all to the purity of fayth, (as saynt Bede sayth,) meaning therby the fayth first preached to King Lucius he went to the toomb of S. Alban to geue thankes to God *per ipsum* by him (sayth saynt Bede) that is to say by his meanes or meditatiō; & causing the sayd tōbe to be opened he placed very honorably therin certayne relickes of the Apostles, & dyuers other martyrs, & going to the place where the blood of the blessed martyr was shed he took away with him some of the dust which was stil bloody.

Cap. 7. & 8.

Beda Eccl. hist. lib. 1. cap. 17.

Further

Furthermore it hapned after, in the tyme that the Britans kept their lent a litle before the feast of the resurrect on of our Lord, that they were molested by the Picts and Saxós, whyles faynt German was yet there; and therefore they craued the help of his prayers, and direction, difpayring altogeather of theyr owne forces, and he vndertaking the conduct of them ordayned that when they fhould come to ioyne battayle all the army of the Britains fhould cry out a loud three tymes *Alleluya*, which they did, and therewith they put their enemyes to flight, and gayned a notable victory. This being donne, and the affayres of the Iland both fpiritual, and temporal wel compofed, faynt Bede fayth the holy Bifhops had a profperous returne, partly by their owne merits, & partly by the intercefsion of bleffed faynt Alban, whereby he geueth to vnderftand that fuch was their opinion according to the great deuotion they had fhewed before to the bleffed martyr.

It is alfo to be gathered playnly out of S. Bede that there were monafteries of Monkes and religious men in Britany before this tyme, for fpeaking of the rebellion of Conftantinus againft Honorius which was in the yeare of our Lord 407. he fayth that hauing proclaymed himfelfe Emperour he made his fonne Conftance *Cæfarem ex monacho*, Cæfar of a monk.

Here I wifh thee to note, Good reader that faynt Bede in his breefe introduction to his Ecclefiaftical hiftory (where he intended to treat fpecially of the fecond conuerfion of our country in the tyme of the Saxons) toucheth the 400. yeares before, from the tyme of King Lucius; fo breefely, that he paffeth with filence about 350. yeres therof at one tyme and other, noting only fome things by the way, afwel concerning the temporal, as fpiritual affayres, in diuers tymes & ages to make fome conexion of his hiftory from the beginning.

Therfore I leaue it to thy confideration what teftimony and euidence we fhould haue found of our Catholyke religion,

Ibid. ca. 18.

Lib.1.ca.11

ligion, yf he had treated those matters particularly, and at large, seing in the course of so few yeres as he runneth ouer, and in to few leaues, & lynes or a part only of his first book, (which is also very breefe,) wee fynd the practyse of so many poynts of our religion, testified and confirmed, as buylding of Churches in the honour of martyres, the reuerend vse of saynts relyckes, and greate miracles donne by the same, the intercession of saynts for vs, and the custome to prayse and geue God thankes by them ; also monastical lyfe which includeth vowes of religion and chastity, the vse of hollywater, the custome which in our Church is yet most frequent, of *Alleluya* whereby it may be gathered that the seruice of the Church (out of the which the same, no dout was then taken) was not in the vulgar tongue, finally the keeping of lent, easter and others feastes, wherby playnly appeareth the vse & force of traditiō in the Church of God, without the testimony of expresse scripture, and all this we see was vsed in the Church of Britanny, when the fayth deliuered to King Lúcius was yet in purity, which proueth euidently, that he was conuerted to the same Catholyke religion that saynt Augustine planted after-wards a mongst the English Saxons, which wee that be Catholykes professe vntil this day.

THE SAME IS CON-
firmed and proued out of Gildas.

CHAP. VI.

THIS may easely be confirmed out of Gildas the britan surnamed the sage, who wrote shortly after the Saxons came into Britany almost 200. yeares before S. Bede, in whose treatyse of the distruction of Britany, and in his reprehension of the Ecclesiastical men

of those

of thofe dayes, it is euident ynough, what religion was profeffed from Lucius tyme vntil his, for firft fpeaking of the
perfecution vnder Diocierian, he fayth that *electi facerdotes
gregis domini, the chofen Priefts of our Lords flock were killed*, meaning fuch priefts as did offer facrifice vpon the altar, for fo he
fufficiently interpreteth him felfe, when he reprehendeth
the negligece of the Britain Priefts of his dayes, whome he
calleth *facerdotes raro facrificantes, ac raro puro corde inter altaria*   Gildas in ca-
ftantes, Priefts facrifiing fildome, and feldome comming to the Altar   ftigatio in
with a pure harte, and tearmeth the Altars *venerabiles aras and*   ecclef.ordi-
facrofancta altaria, fedem Cæleftis facrificij, the reuerend and holly   nem.
altars, and the feat of the heauenly facrifue, and calleth that which   Gildas Ibid.
is offred therein *facrofancta Chrifti facrificia, the holly facrifices of*   Et de excidio
Chrift, and further geueth to vnderftand that the hands of   Britaniæ.
the Prieftes were confecrated at thofe dayes, as yet they are
in the Catholyke Church, when holy orders are geuen,
wherby wee may playnly fee that the Priefts of our primatiue Church in England, and their function (confifting
principally, in offring to almighty God facrifice vpon the
Altar) is all one with ours. Furthermore treating of the
martirdome of S. Alban and his fellowes, he fayth *that yf God*   Ibidem.
had not permitted for che great finnes of the Britains, that the barba-
rous nations which were entred (he meaneth the Picts and
Saxons) *did deprive the People of the toombs of faynt Alban, and of*
the other martyrs, and of the place of their martyrdomes, the fame
might ftryk vnto them a feruor of deuotion, and deuine charity, infi-
nuating therby the great confolation, and fpiritual benefite
that the Chriftians were wont to receiue by the vifitation
of thofe holy places; Alfo he fayth, that before ful 10.
yeares paft after that perfecution, the Chriftians *repayred the*   Ibidem.
old Churches diftroyed by the perfecutors, and buylt new in honour of
the martyrs, and kept feftiual and holy dayes, laftly he playnly
fignifieth that the Chriftians vfed in his tyme to make vowes of chaftity and that their were monafteries wherin
religious and monaftical life was exercyfed, for he maketh
mention of an holy Abot called *Amphibalus*, and moft   Ibidem.

E 3   bitterly

bitterly reprehendeth two wicked Princes *Cuneglasus*, and
Maglocunus, the first for marying a widdow that had vowed
perpetual chastity, and the other for that being become a
monke he returned to the world and maryed, hauing a former wyfe then liuing; wherein he also geueth to vnderstãd
that it was not then lawful for him *post monachi votum irritum
after the breach of his monastical vow* to returne to his owne
wyfe, and much lesse to mary another.

Ibidem.

To this purpose also, it may be obserued in Gildas as
before I noted in saynt Bede, that vntil the tyme of the
Arrians there entred no infectiõ of heresy into Britany, &
therfory hauing signifyed the sincerity and zeale of the
Christians after saynt Albans death, in buylding Churches
of martyrs, keping feastiual dayes and doing other workes
of deuotion, as I declared before, he addeth, *mansit hæc Christi
capitis membrorum consonantia suauis donec Arriana perfidia, &c,
this sweet consonance or agreement of the members of Christ the head
remayned vntil the Arrian heresy spread her poyson there*; and although he insinuat, as saynt Bede also doth, that afterwards
the people became new fangled, and embraced other heresyes (meaning no dout the Pelagian heresy (which as I
haue shewed before out of S. Bede was quickly extinguished there) yet afterwards he signifieth playnly that neither
the Arrian, nor Pelagian nor any other heresy took root in
Britany, and that the Churche was cleare therof after the
cõming in of the Saxons, about the tyme of his byrth, which

Ibidem.

was in the yere of our Lord 594. for speaking of the tyme,
and of the ouerthrow geuen by Ambrosius Aurelianus to

Polido. verg.
hist. Angl.
lib. 5.

the Saxons and Picts, and of the great slaughter of them
shortly after, at blackamore in York-shire (which as Poli-
dore supposeth is called in Gildas mons Badonicus (he sayth
that the people hauing noted the punishment of God vpon
them for their sinnes, and his mercy in giuing them after-

Gildas de
excidio Bri-
taniæ.

wards so greate victories, *ob hoc reges, publici, priuati, sacerdotes,
ecclesiastici suum quique ordinem seruauerunt, for this cause* (saith
hee) *the Kings, and others as wel publik, as priuat persons, Priests,
and eccle-*

and ecclesiastical men did every one their dutyes, and although he declare presently after that by the extreame negligence of their Kings and gouernours ecclesiastical and temporal, which immediatly succeded, greate corruption was entred at the same tyme that he wrote, yet it is euident ynough in him that it was not corruption of fayth but of manners, as pryd, ambition, dissolutiō of lyfe, drōkenesse, lying, periury, tyranny in the Kings, simony & couetousnesse in the clergy, sildome sacrifices, breach of vowes of chastity, and of mo-niastical lyfe, profaning of altars, and such lyke, for the which he threatneth, and as it were prophesyeth, the vtter destru-ction of Britany, which shortly after followed; so that amongst other things which he was persuaded brought the plague of God vpon our country, we see he taxed certayne customes peculiar to our aduersaries, and the proper fruits of their religion tending only to the ouerthrow of ours, & therfore, it playnly appeareth that ours was then in vre, and receiued detriment by those who (though they were not protestants in profession) yet were protestants in humour and condition, I meane profaners of Altars and holy things, breakers of vowes, of chastity, and Apostatats from reli-gious, and monastical lyfe; such as Luther and many of his followers haue ben since.

And now to come to later tymes after Gildas, yf we consider the relicks of Christian religion which saynt Au-gustine found in Britany, & amongst other things, the great monastery of Bangor, wherein were aboue two thowsand monks, it wilbe manifest that the ancient religion of the Britains was our Catholike fayth, for although in the space of a hundreth seuenty and three yeres, that passed from the comming in of the Saxons vntil their conuersion, the Britain Church was not only much decayed, but also had receiued some aspersion of erronious and euil customes, yet in fayth and opinion they diffred not from S. Augustine, in so much that he offred to hold communion with them, if they would concurre with him in three things only, the first in

Beda hist. Angl. lib. 2. cap. 2.

the

the tyme of celebrating the feaſt of eaſter, the ſecond in the manner of adminiſtring the ſacrament of Baptiſme, and the third in preaching the faith to the Saxons; all which the monkes of Bangor refuſed, vpon no better reaſon, then for that S. Auguſtine did not ryſe to them when they came to the ſynod, condemning him therefore to be a proud man, notwithſtanding that he had reſtored a blynd man to ſight by his prayers in the preſence of all the Biſhops and clergy of Britany, who vndertooke to do the lyke in confirmation of their cuſtomes, but could not performe it.

Lib.2.cap.2. Therfore as ſaynt Bede reporteth, S. Auguſtine did foretel to the ſayd Monkes of Bangor, that ſeing they would not haue peace with their brethren, they ſhould haue warre with their enemies, and yf they would not preach vnto the Engliſh nation the way of lyfe, they ſhould by their hands receiue reuenge of death, which after was truly fulfilled; for Ibidem. Edelfrid a pagan King of Northumberlād killed a thouſand & two hundred Monkes of that monaſtery at one tyme by the iuſt iudgement of God (as ſaynt Bede ſayth) for their obſtinacy.

Thus much for this matter, wherby thou mayſt ſee, good reader that ſaynt Auguſtine found in wales amongſt the Britains the ſame religion & faith in ſubſtance that he then preached to the Engliſh or Saxons, and which we Catholykes ſtil profeſſe, which being conſidered, with that which I haue proued before concerning the continual practiſe therof in the primatiue Church of Britany, whyles the ſame was in purity and integrity, no man that hath common ſence, can dout that the ſame fayth was deliuered by Pope Eleutherius to King Lucius, and generally profeſſed throughout Chriſtendom at thoſe dayes, in which reſpect Tertul.li. ad- we fynd honorable mention, and teſtimony of the faith of uerſus Iu- the Britains, in the Fathers both Greekes, and Latins from deos,Origen. the tyme of their conuerſion, as in Tertulian in K. Lucius in Ezech. hom.4. & in tyme, and in Origen preſently after, in S. Athanaſius, and S. hom.6.in luc. Hilarius in the tyme of the Arrians, of which two the firſt Athanaſ.2. teſti-

teſtifieth that the Biſhops of Britany came to the councel of Sardica, and the other commendeth the Britan Church for reiecting the Arrian hereſy (as I haue noted before) alſo in S. Chriſoſtome, and ſaynt Hierom who commendeth the deuotion of the Britans that came to Bethlem in pilgrimage in his dayes, about the ſame tyme that the Saxons entred into Britany.

Apolog.
Hilar. lib. de
ſinodis Chri-
ſoſt. hom. 18.
in Matth.
Hieron ad
marcel vt
migret. ad
Bethleem.

CERTAINE POINTS OF CON-
trouerſy are diſcuſſed, wherby it is prooued that King
Lucius receiued our Catholyke fayth, and firſt
of the Popes ſupremacy in Eccle-
ſiaſtical cauſes.

CHAP. VII.

BVt to the end that this vndouted truth may be cleared of all dout, I wil ioyne Iſſue with our aduerſaries, vpon ſome two or three poynts now in controuerſy betwyxt vs, and them, and breefly proue, that the doctrin that we teach concerning the ſame, was publykly held for truth throughout Chriſtendome in King Lucius dayes, and that therfore he could receiue no other then the ſame from the Church of Rome, and this I vndertake the more willingly, for that albeit all matters of controuerſy haue ben very learnedly and ſufficiently handled, yea and whole volumes written of them, by our Engliſh Catholykes in the beginning of her maieſtyes raygne, yet by reaſon of the ſtrayt prohibition of theſayd bookes, there are an infinit number in England, eſpecially of the younger ſort, that neuer ſaw the ſame, to whome I deſyre to giue in this treatyſe at leaſt ſome litle taſt, of the truth of our Catholyke religion, ſo farre as my determined breuity wil permit.

F   Fyrſt

First who can with any reason deny that the Popes supremacy (the confession whereof is now made treason in England) was in King Lucius dayes acknowledged generally of all men? for what moued him being so farre from Rome, to seeke to receiue the faith of Christ from thence but that he desyred to haue it from the fountayne & head? were there not Christians at the same tyme in England, as there had ben from the tyme of Ioseph of Arimathia, by some of whome it is lyke he was conuerted, and might haue ben Baptysed? or yf there were no Christians there that might satisfy his deuotion and desyre in that behalfe, was there not at the same tyme very learned Bishops in France by whome he might haue receiued satisfaction without sending so farre as to Rome? what then moued him therto, but that he vnderstood that the admission of all Christs sheep into his fold the Church, belonged principally to the successor of S. Peter, to whome our sauiour particularly commended the feeding of his flock? which faynt Bede insinuateth sufficiently saying that King Lucius beseeched Eleutherius by his letters *that he might be made a Christian per eius mandatum, by his commandement.*

Neither can there any other probable reason be geuen why a few yeres after Donaldus King of Scots sent to Pope victor the next successor of Eleutherius to receiue of him the Christian fayth, which at the same tyme florished not only in France, as before I haue sayd, but also in England from whence he might haue had Bishops, and Priests, to instruct and baptise him and his people.

But for the more manifest proof of this poynt let vs heare what S. Ireneus (who florished at the same tyme in France) teacheth concerning the autority of the sea Apostolike gouerned then by Eleutherius, from whome K. Lucius receiued the fayth.

VVhen we shew, sayth he, the tradition of the greatest and most Aunciẽt Church, knowen to all men, founded & constitute at Rome, by the two most glorious Apostles Peter, & Paule & that the same tradi-

tion

Margin notes:

Polido. lib.1. hist. Angl.

Ioan 21. Beda hist. Angl. lib.1.ca 4.

Hector Boethius hist. Scot.lib.6.

Ireneus lib.3. cap 3.

tion receiued from the sayd Apostles is deriued euen to this our tyme by the succession of Bishops, we confound all those that any way eyther by an ouerweening of their owne wits, or by vayne glory, or by blyndnesse, and euil opinion are led away with fals conceyts ; for euery Churche, that is to say, the faythful which are euery where must needs haue recours to this Church & agree therewith propter potentiorē principalitatem, *for the greater, or more mighty principality of the same, wherein the tradition of the Apostles hath ben alwayes conserued by them which are euery where abroad,* and a litle after, hauing declared the succession of the Bishops of Rome from saynt Peter to Eleutherius who he sayth was the twelfth) he addeth ; *by this ordination and succession, the tradition which is in the Church from the Apostles, and the preaching of the truth is come euen to vs,* & hec est plenissima ostēlio *& this is a most ful & euident demonstration that the fayth which hath ben conserued in the Churche from the Apostles, vntil now, is that one true fayth which geueth lyfe.*

Thus farre S. Ireneus ; out of whose words may be gathered three things very imporrant, and manifest against our aduersaries ; The first, the force of traditiō in the Churche of God, & that the same alone being duly proued is sufficient to conuince all heretykes that teach any thing contrary therto. The second that the continual succession of the Bishops of Rome in one seat and doctrin is an infalible argument of the truth. The which also Tertulian in the same tyme not only obserued but also prescrybed for a rule against all heretykes in his book of Prescriptions. To which purpose S. Augustin sayth, *the succession of Priests from the seat of Peter the Apostle to whome our Lord recōmended his sheep to be fed, holdeth me in the Catholyke Church,* and in another place *number the Priests, euen from the very seat of Peter, and in that order of fathers, see who succeded one an other ; that is the rock, which the proud gats of hel do not ouercome*; Optatus Mileuitanus, in lyke sort vrgeth this succession of the Roman Bishops against the Donatists, reckoning vp all the Bishops from S. Peter to Siricius, with whome he sayth all the world did commu-

F 2   nicat,

Margin notes:
Tertul. lib. de prescrip.
Ang. contra epist. Manichæi quam vocat Fundamenti.
Aug. in Psalmo contra partē Donati.
Optatus Mileuita. lib. 2. contra parmenio.

nicat, and there-vpon concludeth ; *therfore yow*, sayth he, *that challege to your selues a holy Churche, tel vs the beginning of your chayre.*

Thus reasoned these fathers against heretykes aboue 1200. yeres ago as also did S. Ireneus before, in K. Lucius tyme, and thesame say wee now with no lesse reason against the heretykes of our tyme ; we shew them our doctrin conserued in a perpetual succession of Bishops, from the Apostles vntil this day, we demaund the lyke of them, and seing they cannot shew it we conclude with S. Irenæus that they remayne confounded, and that they are to be re-giftred in the number of those *that eyther by an ouerweening of their owne wits, or by vayne glory, or by blyndnes and passion are led away with fals conceits.*

Irenæus li. 3. cap. 3.

The third poynt, that I wish to be noted in the words of S. Irenæus, is the supreme dignity of the Roman Churche aboue all other, seing that he cauleth it the greatest & most ancient (not in respect of tyme, for the Churches of Hierusalem and Antioch were before it) but for autority and therfor vrgeth it as a matter of necesfity, & duty, *that all other Churches whatsoeuer and all faythful people throughout the world ought to haue recours therto, and agree therwith,* propter potentiore principalitaté *for the greater and more powreful principality, and autority therof,* which autority is founded vpon no other ground then vpon the institution of our Sauiour himselfe who gaue the gouerment of his Church to S. Peter the Apostle, not only for him selfe but also for his successors, which. I wil prooue heare, with as conuenient breuity, as the importance of the matter wil permit.

Irenæus Ibidem.

THAT

THAT OVR SAVIOVR
made S. Peter supreme head of his Churche.

CHAP. VIII.

THE supreme autority of S. Peter ouer the Churche of God, is to be proued directly out of the holy scriptures, by many places, and arguments, but 3. shal suffice for breuityes sake.

The first place is in S. Mathew where our sauiour pro- Math.16. mised to S. Peter to buyld his Church vpon him, saying *Tu es Petrus & super hanc Petram ædificabo Ecclesiam meam,* that is to say *thou art Peter, or a rock, and vpon this rock I wil buyld my Churche,* signifying by this allegory that he made him the foundation or head of his Church; for the head is to the body, & the gouernour to the common welth, as the foundation is to the buylding, that is to say the principal part, the stay, strength and assurance therof; and this appeareth more playnly in the Siriac tongue in which saynt Mathew wrote his gospel, where there is no difference betwyxt *Petrus* & *Petra,* Peter and a rook. For in steede of *thou art Peter,* &c. the Siriac hath, thow art a rock, and vpon this rock I wil buyld my Churche.

For this cause (as [a] S. Ciril, S. [b] Chrisostome, S. [c] Hilary and others do note) the name of S. Peter being first Simon was changed by our Sauiour who sayd vnto him *tu vocaberis cephas,* thou shalt bee called Cephas, which the Euangelist expoundeth saying, *quod interpretatur* πετρος, which is interpreted a rock, or stone, for so signifieth πετρος in the greeke; and therfore Cirillus Bishop of Alexandria saith vpon those words, now our sauiour Christ *fortelleth that his name shalbe no more Simon, but* πετρος *that is to say a rock, signifieng aptly by the very word it selfe, that he would buyld his Churche vpon him as vpon a most sure rock and stone,* whereto S.
Hilary

a Ciril lib. 2. cap.2.Ioan.
b Chrisost. in cap.16.mat.
c Hilar. in ca. 16.mat. leo. epist.89 ad epistolos.
Viennensis ecclesi.Ambros. serm de obitu Theodosij in fine.

Hilary agreeth expounding the same woords and speaking to S. Peter thus O happy foundation, of the Churche by imposition, of thy new name, in this respect S. Peter is called in the greeke text sometymes κηφας by making a greek word or the Siriac; and sometymes πετρος becaue they are synonima, and do both of them signify a rock.

Therfore I cannot omit to discouer vnto thee here(good reader) a suttle shift of our aduersaries in translating those words of our sauiour, *Tu es Petrus & super hanc Petram*, for although they censure, and controle, all the translations that the Catholyke Church vseth, and professe to translate the scriptures immediatly out of the hebrew, yet in translating this place, they follow the latin, becaue the hebrew is far more cleare againft them in this controuersy for the better vnderstanding whereof, it is to be considered that all the ambiguity & dout therin ryseth of the difference that may be noted in the greeke, Latin and English translations, not only of them all from the Siriac or Hebrew, but also of one from another; for that euery translator obseruing the dialect or propriety of his owne tongue, hath some variety from the rest, and the English most of all; for although in the greeke & Latin & all other languages deriued of them, the name of Peter and a rock or stone is eyther all one (as πετρος in the greeke) or els haue great affinity and a manifest allusion the one to the other, (as in Latin Petrus and Petra, in Italian Pietro & Pietra in the Spanish Pedro and Piedra, in the portugues Pedro & Pedra, and in the french, Pierre for both, (though ther be difference in the gender) yet in our English tongue, Peter neither signifieth a rock nor a stone, neyther yet hath any alusion, nor affinity therwith, in which respect our English translation much lesse expresseth the force and true sence of our sauiours words in the hebrew, then eyther the greeke or the Latin; of both which I wil treate a litle for the better explication of this question, and first of the greeke.

Albeit πετρα in greek is more commonly vsed for a rock
then

then πετρος yet becaufe πετρος is of the mafculine-gender, & hath alfo the fame fignification, yt feemed more fit to be applyed to the name of a man then πετρα, whervpon yt followed that when not only faynt Peter was commonly cauled Πετρος of the greekes, (to expreffe therby in their language the Syriac woord Cephas) but alfo many others had take vnto them that name for the honour they bore to S. Peter, the word πετρος came to haue two fignifications, the one a rock or ftone, and the other the name of a man which wee cal Peter, and therfore he that tranflated S. Mathewes gofpel into the greeke out of the Siriac or hebrew, vfed both the words πετρος & πετρα in tranflating, thow art a rock and vpon this rok I wil buyld my Church ; for in the firft place he hath πετρος, and in the fecond πετρα to denote in the firft, as wel the trew fignificatio of Cephas, that is to fay a rock, as alfo the name by the which S. Peter was beft knowen to the greekes, and to expreffe in the later the allegory of a rock, according to the very words of our fauiour, left perhaps otherwyfe the readers attending more to the name, then to the fignification therof, fhould not perceiue the force of our fauiours allegory, who to fignify the ftrength and ftabilitie of his Churche gaue the name of a rock to faynt Peter, vpon whome he meant to buyld the fame, and therfore, I fay, the greeke tranflator elegantly vfeth both πετρος and πετρα, explicating the firft by the later, and exprefsing the allegory in both.

And as for the Latin tranflation it is manifeft that it followeth the greek, and not the hebrew, nor Siriac, and that therfore, for πετρος it hath Petrus, partly for the allufion that Petrus hath both to πετρος in greeke & alfo to Petra in Latin (both which fignify a rock) and partly for that, from the tyme that faynt Peter was knowne by the name of πετρος to the Romans, Petrus (which is deriued of πετρος, by turning os into vs, to make it a Latin word) was no leffe vfed for his name and other mens amogft them then Πετρος amongft the greekes. And although now in common vfe Petrus doth
signify

signify nothing els but Peter, in which respect it may seeme that the Latyn translator rather expresseth the bare name of a mā, then the true sence or signification of πετρος or Cephas neuerthelesse the circumstances being considered, yt is euident that Petrus or Peter in the scripture, doth not only signify the name of a man, but also a rock.

To which purpose there is to be noted a great difference in Petrus, when it is spoken of the Apostle S. Peter, & when it is spoken of any other man; as for example, Cook is a name now common to many of good cauling, though perhaps at first it grew to be a name, from some one that by reason of his office was commonly cauled Cook, and therfore though now in such as haue no such office, yt signifieth nothing but a bare name, yet in him that was first cauled so, it signified rather his office then his name; and in lyke māner, though Petrus now haue no other signification but the proper name of a man, as Thomas or Iohn and the lyke, yet in S. Peter the Apostle, who was the first that was cauled so, it signified the office and quality, which Christ gaue him when he made him a rock to buyld his Church vpon, and cauled him *Cephas* to signify the same; the which word *Cephas* is interpreted *Petrus*, in our Latin translation and

Ioan. 1.

Peter in English for where as the Euangelist himselfe expoundeth *Cephas* by the word πετρος in greeke saying, *quod interpretatur Petrus* that is to say *which is interpreted a rock*, the Latin translator saith, *quod interpretatur Petrus which is interpreted Peter* meaning therby also a rock, or a man that meta-

Matth. 16.

phorically was a rock, for other wyse he geueth not the true sence of *Cephas*, nor of πετρος.

Agayne in this sentence *tu es Petrus & super hanc Petram, thow art Peter and vpon this rock, &c.* these words *super hanc Petram* do playnly expound *Petrus* to signify a rock; for that the pronoun *this* can not haue so proper relation to any other word, as to the next antecedent, which *is Petrus*, so that

Math. 16.

the sence must needs be thus, *thou art a rock, and vpon this rock I wil buyld my Church.*

Here

Here also may be considered the correspondence that the words of our sauiour to S. Peter, haue with S. Peters words to him, for when our sauiour asked his Apostles, *quem me esse dicitis, who say you that I am,* he asked not what they called his name, but what they sayd was his quality, & dignity; and therfore saynt Peter answered not, thou art Iesus, (which was the name that was geuen him at his circumsision) but, thou art *Messias,* that is to say, the anoynted, or as we commonly say, *Christ, the sonne of the liuing God*; which our sauiour recompensed; not by telling him his name, which was Simon, but by giuing him another name, and such a one as signified the office, qualitie and dignitie that he bestowed vpon him; and therfore he sayd vnto him, thou art *Cephas,* or *Petrus,* that is to say, *a rock* or *Peter,* and vpon this rock I wil buyld my Churche, which saynt Leo, expresly noteth saying in the person of Christ to S. Peter thus, *as my father hath made knowen vnto thee my diuinity euen so I make knowne to thee thy excellency, that thou art Peter that is to say a rock, &c.* and S. Hierome expounding the same words of our sauiour and speaking also in his person, sayth thus, *because thow Symon hast sayd to mee thou art Christ the sonne of God, I also say to thee, not with a vayne or Idle speeche, that hath no operation or effect, but quia meum dixisse fecisse est, because my saying is a doing, or a making, therfore I say vnto thee thow art Peter for a rock, and vpon this rock I wil buyld my Churche,* thus farre S. Hierom, signifieng that Christ both made him a rock, and cauled him a rock; which yet he declareth more playnly in that which he addeth immediatly, *as Christ,* sayth he, *being himselfe the light granted to his disciples that they should be cauled the light of the world, ita Simoni qui credebat in Petram Christum, petri largitus est nomen, so to Simon who beleued in Christ the rock, he gaue the name of a rock* (for yf we expound not *Petri,* so, the similitude is to no purpose and therfore it followeth immediatly,) *and according to the metaphor of a rock it is truly sayd to him, I wil buyld my Churche vpon thee* here yow see S. Hierome vnderstandeth *Petrum* & *Petram* that is to say

Leo Serm. 3. in anniuers pontificatus.

Hieron. in cap. 16. Matth.

G   *Peter*

Ambrof. fer. 2. de facct. *Peter* & *a rock* to be all one ; and fo doth S. Ambrofe expounding *tu es Petrus, thow art Peter ; he is cauled* (faith he) *a r.ck, becaufe he firft layd the foundation of fayth amongft the gentils, and lyke an vnmoueable ftone, doth hold vp or fufteyn the frame and weight of the whole Chriftian woork.*

Bafil. in homil. de pæ- nitcn. This may be confirmed out of faynt Bafil who fayth, *Petrus dixerat tu es filius dei viui & vicißim audierat fe eße Petram, Peter fayd thou art the fonne of God, and heard agayne, that he him felfe was a rock,* which according to our Latin and Englifh tranflation of the fcripture, is not trew, if Petrus and Peter do not fignify a rock, and thus wee fee that *Petrus* being fpoken in the fcriptures of S. Peter, and efpecially in thofe words of our fauiour, *Tu es Petrus,* doth fignify a rock, noleffe then πετρος in the greeke or *cepha* in the Hebrew, which in our Latin tranflatio is interpreted *Petrus,* & in our Englifh Peter. In this refpect Tertulian in K. Lucius tyme cauleth

Tertul. lib. de præfcrip. S.Peter *ædificandæ ecclefia Petram, the rock where vpon the Church was to be buylt,* & Origen in the fame age (for he was borne about the tyme of King Lucius his conuerfion or within

Origen. ho- mil. S. in Exodum. fyue or fix yeres after) tearmeth him *magnū illud ecclefia fundamentum & Petram folidißimam fuper quam Chriftus fundauit Ecclefiam,* that is to fay, *the great foundation of the Churche, and the moft folid or ftedfaft rock where-vpon Chrift founded his Churche,* & S.Cypriā (who florifhed alfo within 40. or 50. yeres after the conuerfion of K.Lucius) hauing rehearfed thefe words

Cyprian. lib. de vnita Ecclefiæ. of our fauiour, thow art Peter, &c. concludeth thus *fuper illum vnum adificat ecclefiam fuam, & illis pafcendas mandat oues fuas* that is to fay, *vpon him being one he buyldeth his Churche, and to him he commendeth his fheep to be fed,* and after declaring the caufe therof, and the reafon why our fauiour made him cheefe, or head of his Apoftles, (though they were otherwyfe equal with him in honour and power of the

Cypria. Ibid. Apoftlefhip, yet fayth he, *to manifeft vnity he cōftituted one chayre, and fo difpofed by his autority that vnity fhould haue beginning from one,* and a litle after *Primatus Petro datur vt vna Ecclefia Chrifti, & Cathedra vna monftretur, the fupremacy is geuen to Peter, that the Churche*

Churche of Chrift may be fhewed to be one and one chayre, wherby he fignifieth that our fauiour to conferue vnity, afwel amongft his Apoftles, as alfo in his whole Church, and to auoyd the occafion of fchifme, which ordinarily ryfeth of pluralitie of heads, ordeyned and appoynted one head ouer all, to wit S. Peter, the which reafon ys alfo obferued by Optatus Miliuitanus, and other moft learned, and auncient fathers, who acknowledge neuerthelefle an equalitie of Apoftolical autoritie, in all the Apoftles; which I note here the rather for that our aduerfaries are wont to obiect the fame agaynft the fupremacy of S. Peter, as though the one did contradict or ouerthrowe the other, whereas they may learne of faynt Hierome, that *although all the Apoftles re-ceiued the Keyes of the Kingdome of heauen, yea and that the ftrength of the Churche was eftablifhed vpon them,* equaly that is to fay, afwel vpon one of them, as vpon an other, though not in lyke degree vpon euery one, *yet* fayth he, *one was chofen amongft twelue to the end that a head being appoynted all occafion of fchifme may be taken away,* and S. Leo the great fayth, *amongft the moft blefled Apoftles, there was, in fimilitudine honoris, difcretio quædam poteftatis, a certayne diftinction or difference of power, in the lykenes or equalitie of honour, & although the election of them all, was a lyke, yet it was graunted to one vt cæteris præmineret, that is to fay, that he fhould haue autoritie ouer the reft,* whereof he yeildeth a reafon, in an other place, *to the end,* fayth he, *that from him* (he meaneth S. Peter) *as from a certayne head our Lord might power his giftes vpon the whole body; and that whofoeuer fhould be fo bold as to depart from the folidity of Peter, he might vnderftand him felfe to be no way partaker of the deuine miftery* vpon thefe reafons, I fay & vpon the warrant of our fauiours owne woords the moft learned fathers of the Church, both Greekes, and La-tins do acknowledge, thefame to be buylt vpon S. Peter, & confequetly teach him to be head of the Churche, as of the Greekes, Origen, S. Athanafius, S. Epiphanius, S. Bafil fur-named the great, S. Gregorius Nazianzen, S. Cirillus, S. Chrifoftome, Pfellus alledged by Theodoretus, and Theo-phila-

Optat. lib. 2. cont: a Par-menio.

Hieron. con-tra. Iouinianū

Leo epift 8. 4. ad Anaftaf. cap. 11.

Epift. 8. 9 ad Epifc. vien.

Origen. in ca. 6. ad Roma. Athan. epift. ad felicem. Epiph in An-corato Bafil. lib. 2. in eu-nom. Greg.

philactus, and of the Latins S. Ambrose, S. Augustin, Maximus, S. Leo the great, S. Hilary, and to omit dyuers others the great general councel of Chalcedon held by 630. Fathers Latins, and Greekes aboue 1100. yeres agoe, in which councel S. Peter is cauled *Petra & crepido Ecclesia the rock & toppe of the Churche.*

Yet I think no man can be so simple as to ymagin that these Fathers affirming the Church to be buylt vpon S. Peter, denied our sauiour Christ to be the first, & principal foundation therof; of whome the blessed Apostle worthely sayth, *that no man can lay any other foundation, then that which is layed already; Iesus Christ;* which place, our aduersaries are wont to obiect against this our Catholyk doctrin; whereas they may learne not only in the Fathers, but also in the scriptures themselues that there are dyuers foundations of the Churche, though some be more principal then other, & our sauiour Christ the first and cheefe ground-work of the whole buylding; as also in a Kingdome, or common welth, there are diuers heads, though subordinate one to an other, & all subiect to one head, all which may be called foundations in the polityke buylding, because the same leaneth and resteth vpon them, and is sustayned by them, though not by all alyke or in equal degree. To this purpose wee read in the Apocalipse that *the walles of the citty,* that is to say the Church, are sayd to haue *twelue foundations, & in them the names of the 12. Apostles of the lambe;* and agayne in saynt Paule to the Ephesians, *you are,* sayth he, *Citizens of saynts, & domesticals of God, buylt vpon the foundations of the Apostles, and Prophets.*

Therfore S. Augustyn sayth that our sauiour may as wel be cauled *fundamentum, fundamentorum,* the foundatio of foundations, a *Pastor Pastorū, & Sanctus Sanctorū,* the shepherd of sheperds, or holly of hollies; the reason wherof S. Basil geueth notably for the explication of this matter. *Though Peter,* sayth he, *be a rock, yet he is not a rock as Christ is, for Christ is the true vnmouable rock of himselfe, Peter is vnmouable by Christ the rock,*

rock, for Iesus doth communicat & imparte his dignityes, not depri- *aing himselfe of them, but retaining them himselfe, & yet bestowing them vpon others ; he is the light, & yet he sayth you are the light he is the Priest & yet he maketh Priests, he is the rock, and made a rock,* thus far saynt Bafil. Thefame teacheth S. Leo very elegantly explicating the words of our fauiour. *Tu es Petrus,* and speaking in our fauiours perfon thus. *Thow art Peter, that is to say, although I am the inuiolable rock, the corner stone Which vniteth both fyds of the buylding, & the foundation, befyds the Which no mã can lay any other, yet thow art alfo a rock, becaufe thow art confolidat & hardened by my strength, to the end that thofe things Which ar proper vnto me by my owne power, may be to the cõmon with mee by participation.*

Basili. ho. de Pænit.

Leo Serm. 2. in anniuerf. pontificatus fui.

Hereby it appeareth that although our fauiour Chrift be the cheefe and principal foundation, that is to fay the head of his churche, yet by buylding the fame vpon S. Peter, he made him alfo the foundation or head therof, next after himfelfe, and as there are dyuers other heads vnder S. Peter, who in refpect of theyr fubiects may be truly cauled, & are heads, and yet in refpect of S. Peter are fubiects, euen fo, S. Peter, in refpect of all the whole church, may properly be cauled, and truly is the head therof, though he be fubordinat & fubiect to Chrift, as all the reft are both to Chrift and him; and therfore S. Leo in the place aforefayd, fayth that *there ar in the people of God many priests, and many Pastors, all whome Peter doth properly gouerne though Christ do principally gouerne therin.*

Leo. Ibid.

Thus much for the firft proofe wherein I haue ben more large, then I determined, and therefore I wilbe breefer in the other two.

The fecond place wherevpon I ground the fupremacy of S. Peter, is the words of our fauiour following the former in S. Mathew videlicet. *I wil geeue thee the keyes of the kingdome of heauen, and whatfoeuer thou shalt bynd vpon earth, it shalbe bound alfo in heauen, and whatfoeuer thou shalt loofe vpon earth, it shalbe loofed alfo in heauen;* By the keyes is fignified

Matth. 16.

G 3　preemipreheminent power, and authority, wherevpon grew the commō cuſtume of deliuering to princes the keyes of tow-nes, and fortreſſes, when the people therin yeild, and ſubmit themſelues to their abſolute wil, & power; and in the ſcrip-tures, the woord *clauis* that is to ſay, a key is often vſed in the ſame ſence; as in the Apocalipſe, to ſignify the prehemi-nent authority of our ſauiour it is ſayd of him, *habet clauem Dauid, he hath the key of Dauid*, and the Prophet Iſayas ſpea-king of the ſupreme eccleſiaſtical power of a high Prieſt in the old law, I *wil geue*, ſayth he, *the key of Dauid vpon his ſhoulder*; and therfore although ſome of the doctors ſay ſometymes, that all the Apoſtles receiued the keyes, (ha-uing reſpect to ſome effects thereof) yet it is manifeſt that they receiued not the ſame in ſuch ample manner, and with ſuch prerogatiue as S. Peter, to which purpoſe it is to be no-ted, that albeit our ſauiour gaue to all his Apoſtles, autho-rity to remit and retayne ſinnes, yet he made no mention of geuing the keyes to any but to S. Peter, in which reſpect, *Optatus Mileuitanus* ſayth, *ſolus Petrus claues accepit, only Peter re-ceiued the keyes*; and Origen vpon the ſame words of our ſa-uiour doth note, that becauſe it behoued that P. Seter ſhould haue *aliquid maius ſome what more* then the other Apoſtles, therfore Chriſt ſayd vnto him, I *wil geue thee the keyes of the kingdome of heauen*, and Origen addeth further, that there was no ſmalle differéce betwyxt the Apoſtles commiſsion to bynd and looſe, and the commiſsion of S. Peter which he affirmeth to be more ample, becauſe (ſayth he) *non erant in tanta perfectione ſicut Petrus*, they were not in ſuch perfec-tion as Peter, and therfore S. Leo ſayth, that the authority or power to bynd and looſe, was geuen *Petro præ cæteris to Peter aboue the reſt* of the Apoſtles; and the reaſon is, for that he being their head, and they ſubordinat to him, he recei-ued the ſame for him ſelfe and them, and they held it as from him, & vnder him, though they had it alſo, by Chriſts commiſsió as wel as hee which S. Auguſtin teacheth clear-ly, when he ſayth, that the keyes of the kingdome of hea-uen were

(marginal notes:)

Apocal. 3.
Iſay. 22.

Optat. lib. 1.
contra par-
men.

Origen. tract.
6. in Matth.

Leo epiſt. 29.
ad Epiſcopos
viennen.

Aug. tract.
24. in euan-
gel. Ioan.

uen were geuen to S. Peter, becaufe he reprefented the whole church,of which reprefentatiõ he yeildeth the reafon adding immediatly, *Propter apoftolatus fui primatum*, or as he fayth in an other place, *propter primatum quem in difcipulis habuit, by reafon of the fupremacy he had ouer the reft of the Apoftles* geuing to vnderftand therby, that the keyes being geuen to S. Peter as head of the Apoftles, and confequently as head of the Church,they were geuen alfo to the Apoftles, and to the whole Church,for what is geuen to the king as king, the fame is geuen to the common wealth, and from him or by him,as head therof, is communicated, & imparted to the whole body. For this caufe S. Chrifoftome treating of the promis that our fauiour made to S. Peter to buyld his Churche vpõ him, and to geue him the keyes of the kingdome of heauen, affirmeth that he made him head or gouuernour of the whole world. Thus much for the fecond proof. *Chrifoft. ho. 55. in Matth.*

The third, and laft fhalbe, the commifsion and charge that our fauiour gaue particularly to S. Peter to feed his fheep, wherby he made him general Paftor ouer his whole flock,whereof *Eufebius Emiffenus* fayth thus, *firft Chrift comitted vnto him his lambs, & then his fheepe, becaufe he made him not only a paftor or fhepherd, but alfo the paftor of Paftors; Therefore Peter feedeth the lambes, & he feedeth the fheepe, he feedeth the young ones,& their dammes, he gouerneth the fubiects, & their prelats, fo that he is Paftor of all; for befydes lambes & fheepe there is nothing in the Church.* *Eufe. Emiffe hom.de natiuit. Ioannis euangel.*

This is more euident in the Greeke wherein the gofpel of S. Ihon was written, then in our latin tranflation, for where as we haue 3. tymes *pafce* that is to fay feed, the greeke hath in the fecond place ποίμαινε which doth not only fignify to *feed,* but alfo to *gouerne* and *rule* wherby the Euangelift fignifyed that Chrift gaue to S. Peter commifsion, not only to feed his flock with preaching and teaching,but alfo to exercyfe all paftoral authority ouer them, that is to fay to rule and gouern them, in which fence the

Greeke

Matth.2.
Mich.5.
Apocal.19
Pſalm.2.

Iſay.44.

Aug.in cap.
21.Ioan.

Theophil in
ca.21. Ioan.

Chriſoſt. lib.
2.de ſacer-
dotio.

Hom.8.7.in
Ioan.

Hom.1.de
pænit.

Leo Epiſc.
89 ad Epiſ-
copos vien-
nenſ.

Greeke word ποιμαινειν is often vſed in the holy Scriptures, as in S.Mathew and Micheas the Prophet, where it is ſayd of Bethlem; *there ſhal come foorth of thee a captayne that ſhal gouern my people Iſrael,* and in the Apocalipſe, *he ſhal rule them in an yron rod,* and againe in the Pſalm, *thow ſhalt gouerne or rule theym in a rod of yron,* in which places as alſo in dyuers others of the ſcripture to lyke purpoſe, the greeke hath ποιμαινει and ποιμανεις and in the ſame ſence our lord ſaith in the Prophet that the great Monark Cirus ſhould be his Paſtor becauſe he ſhould gouern and rule his people, and Homer oftentymes cauleth king Agamemnon ποιμενα λαχον the king or Paſtor of this people (for the word ποιμενευς ſignifieth both) and therfore S. Auguſtin expounding thoſe words *feede my ſheep,* ſayth that Chriſt recommended his ſheepe to S·Peter *paſcendas, id eſt docendas regendaſque, to be fed, that is to ſay to be taught and gouerned;* Theophilactus alſo vpō the ſame place witneſſeth that Chriſt gaue to S. Peter *præfecturam onium totius mundi, the gouernment of the ſheepe of the whole world;* and S.Chriſoſtome treating of thoſe words of our ſauiour ſayth, that he would haue S.Peter to *be endewed with authority,* and *farre to excel the other Apoſtles,* and agayne expounding the ſame words otherwhere, he ſayth that Chriſt ſpake vnto him only, becauſe he was *the mouth & head of the Apoſtles,* and committed vnto him *curam fratrum ſuorum, the charge of his brethren,* and a litle after; that Chriſt *gaue him the charge of the whole world,* which he alſo affirmeth in an other place of the vniuerſal Churche, ſaying, *that the ſupremacy and gouernment of the Churche throughout the whole world was geuen him by Chriſt.*

I wil conclude with S. Leo, *whereas, ſaith he, the power of bynding and looſing was geuen to Peter aboue the reſt of the Apoſtles; the care & charge of feeding the ſheepe of Chriſt was more ſpecially committed to him; to whome whoſoeuer ſhal thinck the principality* or ſupremacy *is to be denied, he cannot by any meanes diminiſh his dignity, but being puſt vp with the ſpirit of his owne pryde, he caſts him ſelfe head-long to hel.*

Thus

Thus thow feeft, good reader, that our doctrin of the
fupremacy of S.Peter, is no nouelty of our inuention, but
the vniform and conftant opinion, of the moft learned and
ancient Fathers of the Churche grounded vpon the fcriptures, in which refpect we fynd in all thefayd auncient Doctors moft eminent and excellent tytles of fuperioritie, and
prærogatiue attributed to S.Peter, who in S.Hilary is
cauled *the bleſſed porter of heauen*, in S.Auguftin *the firſt or cheef
of the Apoſtles* in Eufebius *the greateſt of the Apoſtles*, and *maiſter
of the warfare of God*, in Epiphanius *the captayn of the Diſciples*,
in S.Ciril *Prince and head of the Apoſtles*, in S.Ambrofe *the Vicar that Chriſt left vs of hiſ loue*, and to omit others for breuityes fake, in S.Chryfoftome, *the toppe or head of the congregá-
tion of the Apoſtles*, *an vnconſumable rock, the vmoueable top of the
buylding*, and laftly †*the paſtor and head of the Churche*.

Hilar. in cap.
16. Matth.

Aug. tract.
56. in Ioan.

Eufeb lib. 2.
hift. cap. 14.

Epipha. hæ-
retic. 51.

Ciril. fib. 12.
in Io. ca. 64.

Ambrof in
ca. vltimum
Lucæ.

Chrifoft. ho.
87. in Ioan.

* Hom. 9.
de pænitent.

Homil. 55. in
Matth. & ho.
87. in Ioan.

THAT THE SVCCESSORS OF
*S.Peeter, to wit, the Biſhops of Rome, ſucceed him
in the ſupremacy of the Churche.*

CHAP. IX.

AND for as much as it is euident that our fauiour
Chrift gaue not this authority to S.Peeter for his
owne particular benefit, but for the general good of
his Churche, nor for his owne dayes only, but
during the tyme of the Churche militát, to the end, that ſo
long as their fhould be any fheep in his fold, fo long ther
fhould be an vniuerfal Paftor to feed and gouerne them,
and that his Churche which is a vifible body, might haue
continually a vifible head, no leſſe now in the new law, thé
heretofore in the old, which was a figure of the new, and
had a continual fucceffion of Bifhops from Aaron, therfore
I fay, all the ancient fathers worthely acknowledged this
our fauiours inftitution, and this autority of an vniuerfal

H
Paftor,

Chrisost. li. 2. de sacerd. Paftor, not only in S. Peter but alfo in his fucceffors, where vpon S. Chrifoftome faith *that Chrift committed the care of his* Epift. ad Eu-tich. *fheep, tum Petro, tum Petri fuccefforibus both to Peeter, and to Pe. ters* Leo mag. fer. 2 in anni. affum. *fucceffors,* and Petrus Bifhop of Rauena in his epiftle to Eu-tyches, *bleffed Peeter* fayth he, *liues & gouerns ftil in his owne feat,* and Leo magnus afirmeth *that Peeter continueth, and liueth, in* Concil. chal-ced. act. *his fucceffors,* and therfore the great councel of Chalcedon abouefayd hauing heard the epiftle of the fayd Leo con-demning the herefy of Eutyches fayd *Petrus per Leonem locutus eft, Peter hath fpoken by the mouth of Leo.*

In this refpect alfo the bleffed martyr S. Cyprian (who Cypri epift. 55. as I fayd before wrote foone after the conuerfion of K. Lucius) cauleth the Roman Church *Cathedrā Petri, ecclefiam principalē, vnde vnitas facerdotalis exorta eft, the chayre of Peeter, the principal or cheef Churche from whence fpringeth all Prieftly vnity,* fignifieng therby that as the vnity of the natural body con-fifteth in that dyuers members being combyned vnder one head, do all receiue from the fame the influence of one lyfe, fo alfo the vnity of the miftical body of Chrift confifteth, in that diuers Churches being conioyned, vnder one head, which is the Roman Churche, or chayre of Peter, do all receiue from the fame the influence of one fpirit and do-ctrin which he declareth playnly in his book of the vnity of the Churche, where he fayth, *euē as there are many beames of the Sunne, and one light, many bowes of one tree, and yet one ftrength founded in one root & many brookes flowing from one fountayne, & a vnity therof conferued in the fpring, euen fo the Churche of our Lord, cafting foorth her light euery where ftretcheth her beames, through out the world & yet the light is one, fhee extends her bowes ouer the whole earth, & fpreads her flowing riuers farre & neare, and yet there is one head, one beginning, and one fruitful, and plentiful mother.* Thus far this famous martyr who fpeaking alfo other where of Peters chayre, declareth the miferable ftate of thofe that are deuided & feperated from the fame, which I wifh our aduerfaryes diligently to note, *there is* fayth he *one God, one Chrift, one Churche, one chayre founded vpon Peeter by our*
Lord

Lords woords, an other Altar cãnot be erected nor a new priesthood ordayned whosoeuer gathereth any where els scattreth & it is counterfeyt, wicked, and sacrilegious, whatsoeuer humain fury doth institute, & ordayne to violate the ordenance of God, and agayne to the same purpose, *he which holdeth not sayth he this vnity of the Churche doth he beleeue that he holds the fayth of the churche? he which forsakes the chayre of Peeter where vpon the churche was founded, can he hope to be in the churche?* Finally this blessed martyr writting to S. Cornelius the Pope, calleth the Roman Church *Matricem, & radicem catholicæ Ecclesiæ, the mother & root, of the Catholyke Churche,* which he wisheth all men to acknowledge and hold most firmly, and transferring the same presently after to the person of Cornelius, he sayth that he would haue all *his collegues retayne & hold* stedfastly his communion, *that is as much to say,* sayth he, *as to hold the vnity, & charity of the Catholyke church,* geuing to vnderstand that he which doth not communicate with the bishop of Rome, the chayre of Peter, the fountayne of vnity, the root and mother of the Catholyke Churche he is not a member of the same, nor gathereth with Christ but scattreth.

Cypria.li.de vnit.ecclesi

Epist. ad Cornel. 45.

Ibidem.

The very same in substãce the famous Doctor S. Hierom teacheth as wel of S. Peeter, as of his chayre, and successors; of S. Peeter he sayth, tHat he was therfore *chosen of our sauiour, one only amongst twelue, that a head being appoynted all occasions of schisme & diuision might be taken away:* and of his chayre, and successors, he sayth, to S. Damasus the Pope, *qui cathedræ Petri iungitur, meus est, he which is ioyned to the chayre of Peter, he is myne,* and agayne to him in an other Epistle, *I,* sayth he, *following no cheef but Christ am lincked in communiõ with thy beatitude, that is to say with the chayre of Peter, vpon that rock the Churche was buylt, whosoeuer eateth the lambe out of this house is profane, if any man be not in the arke of Noe he shal perish in the flud,* and a litle after, *I know not Vitalis, I refuse Meletius, I know not Paulinus, whosoeuer doth not gather with thee scattreth, he which is not of Christ is of Antichrist,* thus far S. Hierome of the supremacy of Peeters chayre, and particularly of Pope Damasus, of

Hieron. aduersus Iouinia.

Epist. 52. ad Damasum.

Epist. 57. ad eundem.

whome

H 2

Ambro. in 1.
epift.ad Ti-
moth.ca. 3.
ᵃ Epiph. hæ-
retic 68.
ᵇ Athan. 2.
Apolog. & in
epift. ad fe-
lior.
ᶜ Bafilius
epift. 52.ad
Athanaf.
ᵈ Greg. Naz.
in carmine
de vita fua.
ᵉ Chrif. epift.
1.& 2.ad In-
nocentium.
ᶠ Ciril.epift.
10 ad neftor.
& epift.11.ad
cler. & pop.
conftant.&
epift 18. ad
celeftinum.
ᵍ Theodor.in
epift.ad leon.
ʰ Sozom.li. 3
hift.ca.7.
ⁱ Optat.lib. 2.
cont parin.
ᵏ Ambrof. de
obitu fatiri.
ˡ Aug.epift.
162.& 92 ad
In.
ᵐ Prof.lib.de
ingratis.
ⁿ Vict. lib 2.
de peruand.
ᵒ Vincen.in
fuo commēt.
ᵖ Caffiodo.li.
11.Epift. 2 ad
Ioan. Papam.
Concil. chal.
act. 3.
Epift. concil.
chalced.ad
Leonem.
Lib. 3.cap. 9.

whome S. Ambrofe in the fame tyme acknowledged no leffe; faying, *Ecclefia domus Dei dicitur cuius rector hodie eft Damafus, the Churche is cauled the houfe of God, the gouernour whereof at this day is Damafus,* with thefe all other Doctors of the Churche; Greekes and Latins agree, concerning the fupremacy of the bifhops of Rome; as ᵃEpiphanius, ᵇAthanafius, ᶜBafilius, ᵈGregorius Nazianzenus, ᵉChryfoftomus, ᶠCyrillus, ᵍTheodoretus, ʰSozomenus, ⁱOptatus, ᵏAmbrofius, ˡAuguftinus, ᵐProfper, ⁿVictor Vticenfis, ᵒVincentius Lirinenfis, and ᵖCafsiodorus, all which did wryte aboue 1000. yeres ago and playnly acknowledged the fupremacy of the bifhop of Rome as appeareth in the places aleaged in the margent, wherto I remit our aduerfaries; to auoyd prolixitie, concluding with the great councel of Chalcedon abouefayd, wherein Pope Leo was cauled *vniuerfal Bifhop,* dyuers tymes, befyds that in an epiftle written to him by the whole councel it is playnly fignified that *the Vineyard of our Lord* that is to fay the Churche; was committed to his charge and cuftody.

To returne therfore to S. Ireneus in the tyme of King Lucius thou feeft good reader how true is that, which he fayth of the necefsitie and obligation that all faythful people haue to agree with the Roman Churche, *propter potentiorē principalitatem,* for the mightier, or more powerful principalitie therof, that is to fay, for the fupreme dignity it hath ouer all other churches, as the mother ouer her children, the head ouer the body, and the fpring and root of vnity.

THAT

THAT THE BISHOPS OF

*Rome exercyfed fupreme authoritie and iurifdiction
in the tyme of king Lucius.*

CHAP. X.

NOw then let vs confider how the byfhops of Rome did exercyfe this theyr authority before,and in the tyme of K.Lucius,and neare vnto the fame, the which may appeare partly by the appellatiõs out of all parts to the fea Apoftolyke, and the reftitution, or depofition of bifhops by the fayd fea, and partly by the decrees made by thefame for the whole Churche, and the cenfures layd vpon fuch as would not receiue and obey them.

Wee read in Tertulian (who liued in king Lucius tyme) that Montanus Prifca and Maximilla fals prophets in Phrigia,being excomunicat and expelled by their bifhops, came to Rome to be reftored by Pope Victor, whome they had almoft circumuented, hauing abtayned of him letters to the churches of Afia for their reftitution, which letters neuerthelefle Pope Victor reuoked by the aduife of Praxeas,who difcouered to him their trechery; wherof Tertulian complayneth bitterly, being then become an obftinate Montanift , faying that otherwyfe Pope Victor had reftored Mõtanus, and geuen peace to the churches of Afia , lo then how great was the authoritie of the bifhops of Rome in forayn & remote parts, by the teftimony of Tertulian who was then an heretyke and a great enemy to the Roman Churche.

S.Cyprian about 250. yeares after Chrift teftifyeth that Fortunatus,and Felix being depofed in Afrike by him; appealed to Pope Cornelius, and that Bafilides in lyke manner,being depofed in Spayne appealed to Pope Steuen who fucceded Cornelius, and although S. Cyprian fhew that Bafilides being iuftly condemned did vniuftly appeale and

Epiph.hærcf. 42.

Tertulian. li. aduerfus Praxeam.

Cipr.lib. 1. epift. 3.

Cipr.lib. 1. epiftol. 4.

deceiue

deceiue the Pope by fals suggeſtion & that therfore his appellation could not auayle him, yet he confeſſeth that the Pope receiued the appellation, wherein he ſayth he was not to be blamed,but Baſilides for deceauing him, ſo that wee ſee the cuſtome of appealing to the biſhop of Rome out of al partes,is moſt ancient,whereof I wil alſo alleadge ſome other examples of later tymes, though aboue 1000. yeres agoe.

S. Theodor. hiſt. Eccleſ. lib.7.cap.4.

Athanaſius being depoſed by the Arrians in Greece, appealed vnto Iulius the firſt,biſhop of Rome,and by him was reſtored 1300. yeres agoe and the eccleſiaſtical hiſtories do witneſſe, that not only he, but alſo Paulus byſhop of Conſtantinople, Marcellus byſhop of Ancira, and Aſclepa byſhop of Gaza, and Lucianus of Hadrianopolis were all at Rome at one tyme iniuſtly expelled from their biſhoprikes, and that Pope Iulius *diſcuſſing the crymes obiected to euery*

Tripart hiſt. lib.4.cap. 15.

*one of them,*tanquam omnium curam gerens propter propriæ ſedis dignitatem, *as one that had care of them all for the dignity of his owne ſea, reſtored euery one of them to their Churches*, & wrote to the Byſhops of the eaſt blaming them for the wrong they had donne them, and threatning them that he would not ſuffer it, if they proceeded to do the lyke hereafter.

Epiſt Ioan. Chriſoſt.ad Innocen.

Liberatus in breuiario. cap. 12.

Theod. epiſt. ad Leonem.

Greg.lib.2. cap.6.

S.Chryſoſtome byſhop of Conſtantinople, appealed to Pope Innocentius the firſt, and Flauianus byſhop of the ſame citty, and Theodoretus byſhop of Cyrus appealed in the ſame age, to Pope Leo, who reſtored Theodoretus as teſtifieth the great general councel of Calcedon, ſaying *reſtituit ei Epiſcopatum Sᵐᵘˢ. Archiepiſcopus Leo.* The moſt holy Archbiſhop Leo,reſtored to him his biſhoprik. And S.Gregory the great byſhop of Rome,did excommunicate a byſhop of Greece called Iohn for that he had preſumed to Iudge an other byſhop that had appealed to the ſea Apoſtolyke.

Concil.Sardicen.can. 4. & 7.

Laſtly this cuſtome of appealing to the Biſhop of Rome was confirmed by two ſeueral cannons, in the ſecond great general councel held at Sardica, in the tyme of Athana-

Athanasius the great, whereat were present some byshops of Britany, and this shal suffise for the appellatio of byshops to Rome, and their restitution.

Now to speak a word or two of the deposition of Byshops wee fynd an euident example therof, within 40. or 50. yeares after the conuersion of K. Lucius, for S. Cyprian wrote to Steuen the Pope to desyre him to excomunicat & depose Marcian the Bishop of Arles in France, and to sub- *Cypri lib. 3. epist. 13.* stitute an other in his place by vertue of his letters to the people there, & further desyred him to aduertyse him who should succede him, that he & the Bishops of Africk might know to whome to direct their letters, so that wee see the authority and custome in the Church of Rome to depose forraine Bishops, is no new thing, nor a iurisdiction vsurped in later tymes by fauour of Christian Emperours, seing in the great persecutions in the primitiue Churche, when none were more persecuted by the Emperours then the Popes them selues, (who vntil this tyme were almost all martired) they exercysed this authority, as their successors haue done euer since, indifferetly without exception vpon all Bishops whosoeuer, yea vpon the 4. principal patriarkes of Constantinople Alexandria, Antioch, and Hierusalem, in so much that Nicolaus the first Pope of that name writing *Nicol. epist. ad Michael.* to Michael Emperour of Constantinople about a 1000. yeres ago reckoneth 8. Patriarchs of that Churche deposed by Bishops of Rome before his tyme, and Flauianus Pa- *Theodoretus lib 5. hist. cap. 23.* triarch of Antioch was deposed by Pope Damasus 1200. yeares ago and although the Emperour Theodosius labored to restore him yet he commaunded him to go to Rome to answere for him selfe, and both S. Chrysostome *Socrat. lib. 5. hist. cap. 15.* Bishop of Constantinople, and also Theophilus Bishop of *Sozomen li. 8. cap. 3.* Alexandria were intercessors for him to the Pope; to con- *Theodot. lib. 5. cap. 23.* clude; he could not hold his Bishoprik in peace, vntil the Pope being pacified, was contet therwith, and promised to receaue his legats, & therfore Flauianus presently sent him many Byshops, and some of the cheef of the Clergy of
Antioch.

Tomo 2.con-
cil.in actis
Syxti.
Antioch. Alſo Pope Sixtus the 3. depoſed Polichronius
Biſhop of Hieruſalem.

I omit later examples wherof there are many, to ſay
ſomewhat of the general decrees of Popes made before, or
in the dayes of K. Lucius.

Tertulia lib.
de pudicitia.
Wee read in Tertullian (who as I ſayd before floriſhed
in King Lucius tyme) that the Biſhops of Rome made decrees agaynſt the hereſyes of Montanus and his followers,
and although Tertulian was then an egregious Montaniſt
himſelfe, and an enemy to the Roman Church (which had
condemned his hereſyes) neuertheleſſe in that which he
wryteth agaynſt one of the ſayd edicts, he ſufficiently
ſheweth what was the authority of the Byſhops of Rome
in thoſe dayes, recyting the edict in this manner, *Pontifex
Maximus, Episcopus Episcoporum dicit, &c.* that is to ſay, *the
cheef or greateſt Biſhop, the Biſhop of Biſhops doth ſay, &c.* wherby it appeareth what was the title of the Biſhop of Rome at
thoſe dayes, for although it ſhould be true, that Tertulian
being then an heretyk and condemned by the Biſhop of
Rome, vſed thoſe words of *Pontifex Maximus, Episcopus Episcoporum,* ironice, yet is it manifeſt, that he did it eyther for that
ſuch were the tytles of the edict, (which was moſt probable,) or els, becauſe he was generally ſo called at that
tyme, by all thoſe that held communion with him.

Platina in
vita pij. de
conſecra. di-
ſtict, 3. ca. 21.
& li. 1. cōcil.
But before this tyme; Pius the firſt Pope of that name
about 160. yeres after Chriſt made an edict about the keeping of Eaſter which was after confirmed by Pope Victor, & the Churches of Aſia were excomunicated by him
for not receiuing the ſame.

But to the end good reader thou mayſt the better vnderſtand how this matter paſſed, and euidently ſee the ſupreme autoritie of the Biſhops of Rome in thoſe dayes, it is
to be conſidered; that there hauing been from the tyme of
the Apoſtles a different manner of keeping Eaſter in the
Churche of Rome, and the Churches of the leſſer Aſia (the
Romans keeping it alwayes vpon the ſunday, according
to the

to the tradition of the Apoſtles, S.Peter, and ſaynt Paule; & they of Aſia obſeruing the tyme and cuſtome of the Iewes, pretending the example and tradition of S.Iohn the Euangeliſt)Pius the firſt of that name, Biſhop of Rome, deſyring to reduce all the Churche to vniformity, made a decree that the feaſt of Eaſter ſhould be celebrated only vpō ſunday, but for that the Churches of Aſia made great dificulty to leaue their tradition, as wel Pius, as Anicetus, Soter, and Eleutherius forbore, (for peace and quietneſſe ſake) to compel them by Eccleſiaſtical cenſures to the obſeruation therof; but afterwards Viɛtor who ſucceeded Eleutherius, noting that not only thoſe which inclyned to keep the ceremonies of the old law, were much confirmed therby in their opinion, but alſo ſome in Rome namely one Blaſtus ſought to introduce that cuſtome there, and Iudayſme withall, cauled a councel of the Biſhops of Italy neere adioyning, and not only cauſed other councels to be aſſembled in France, but alſo directed his commaundements to the Biſhops of the eaſt, to do the lyke namely to Theophilus Biſhop of Cæſarea, as that S.Bede reporteth in theſe words, *victor the Pope Biſhop of the citty of Rome dixerit authoritatem*, that is to ſay *directed a commaundement to Theophilus, Byſhop of Cæſarea and Palaſtina that it ſhould be determined how the eaſter ſhould be celebrated there, where our Lord the ſauiour of the world conuerſed. Therfore percepta autoritate, the authority or commaundement being receiued, Theophilus aſſembled Biſhops not only out of his owne prouince but alſo out of diuers other cuntryes, and when they were come togeather in great numbers. Theophilus, protulit autoritatem ad ſe miſſam Papæ Victoris, Theophilus ſhewed the autority or commaundment that Pope Victor had ſent him, & declared quid ſibi operis fuiſſet iniunctum, what was enioyned him to do, &c.* herein by the way I wiſh to be noted how the Biſhop of Rome in thoſe dayes (that is to ſay in the tyme of Lucius) exerciſed his autority in calling of councels, both of the Byſhops of the Latin or weſt Church, & alſo of the eaſt, ſeing Theophilus Byſhop of Palæſtina aſſembled the prelats not only of his

Euſeb. lib. 5. cap. 24.

Tertul de præſcrip. cap. 53. & Euſebius hiſt. ecclef. lib 5. cap. 14.

Beda. de Æquinoɛt. vernali.

I   owne

owne prouince, but also of diuers other by vertue of the
commission geuen him by Pope Victor.

But to proceed, yt being determined by all thofe coūcels
that the teaft of Eafter fhould be kept on the funday according to the cuftome of the Romā Churche, Victor the
Pope renewed the decree of Pius his predeceffor and denounced excomunication againft all the Churches of Afia
that would not cōforme them-felues therto, which though
fome holy and learned Bifhops, & amongft other Irenæus
thought to bee rigoroufly done, and not with fuch confideratiō, as it feemed to them the peace of the Church required, yet none of them, nor any of the fchifmatykes themfelues, took any exception to his autority, as though he had
donne more then he might do, which no dout they would
haue done yf he had exceeded the limits of his power therfore Eufebius fayth, that Irenæus *did admonifh him that he*
would not cut off from the body of the whole Church, fo many Churches
for obferuing a tradition vfed amongft them according to an old cu-
ftome, and Nicephorus, teftifieth that they aduifed him *vt be-*
nignius ftatueret, that fhould determine therof with more benignity
and myldnes, wherin wee fee Pope Victors authoritie, and
power to excommunicat all other Bifhops; fufficiently acknowledged, though there was queftion of the iuftneffe of
the caufe, and conueniency of the fact neuertheleffe yt appeared afterwards by the determination of the whole
Churche of God, yea & of the greateft part of the Afian
Churches themfelues, that Victor had reafon in that which
he did; for as Nicephorus teftifieth, not only Afia did at
légth yeild therin, but alfo *vbique terrarum in orbe decretum eft,*
it was decreed through out the world that the feaft of Eafter
fhould be celebrated vpō the funday, in fo much that thofe
which would not yeild therto were held for heretykes, &
cauled *quarta decimani* for fo they are accounted and termed
by Nicephorus faynt Auguftin, Epiphanius Philaftrius and
the councels of Antioch and Laodicea; and to conclude
this poynt, yt fhal not be impertinent to the matter in hād,

to con-

Margin notes:
Eufeb.lib.5.
hift.cap.24.

Eufeb.Ibid.

Nicepho. lib.
4.cap.38.

Lib.4 cap.39.
Niceph. Ibid.

Aug. hær. 29.
Epiph.hær.
50.concil.
Antioch. cap.
1.Laodicenū
cap 7.

Philaſtrius in Catalogo hære.

to conſider how this controuerſy about the keep:ng of eaſter, ended many yeares after in Eng.and, betwyxt the Engliſh Byſhops mayntayning the cuſtome of Rome, and the Scottiſh that were Schiſmatykes and obſerued the cuſtome of Aſia which venerable Bede recounteth, ſaying; that Biſhop Colman, with his Scotiſh clergy , being aſſembled in Northumberland, with Agilbert Biſhop of the eaſt Saxons, & his Prieſts Wilfred and Agathon in the preſence of King Oſwy , after long debating the matter on both ſydes, Wilfred anſwered to Colman(who relyed vpon the autority of Anatholius,and Columba his predeceſſors) although,quoth he, Columba was a holy man, yet could he not be perferred before Peter the moſt bleſſed Prince of the Apoſtles, to whome our Lord ſayd, *thou art Peter, and vpon this rock I wil buyld my Churche, & hel gates ſhal not preuayle againſt it, and to thee I wil geue the Keyes of the Kingdome of heauen,* when Wilfrid had ſayd this; King Oſwy, who had ben brought vp by the Scots, and infected with their ſchiſme, aſked Colman wheather he could proue that ſo great autority was geuen to Columba, and Colman anſwered no, and do you on both ſyds, ſayth the King, grant without controuerſy, that this was ſayd principally to Peter, and that the Keyes of the Kingdome of heauen were geuen him by our Lord, and both parts anſwered yea; nay then, quoth the King merily, I aſſure yow, I wil not in any thing contradict that porter, but as farre as my knowledge and power ſhal extend, I wil obey his commaundments leaſt perhaps, when I ſhal come to heauen, and haue him my enemy that keepeth the keyes, no man wil open me the gates; The King hauing ſayd thus all that were preſent both litle and great (ſayth ſaynt Bede) allowed therof, and yeilded to receiue the Catholyke cuſtome of keeping Eaſter on the ſunday. Thus wee ſee this great controuerſy ended alſo in England neere a thouſand yeres agoe,by the autority of the ſea Apoſtolyke, ſo that to returne to Pope Victor, wee may truly ſay he had the victory, or rather that ſaynt

Beda in hiſt. Eccleſ. Angl. lib. 3. cap. 2.

Matth. 16.

I 2   Peter

Peeter by him, and his fucceffors vanquifhed all fuch as op-
pofed themfelues to this traditiō of the Roman Churche.

Seing then in the tyme of K. Lucius, the Bifhops of
Rome both claymed and exercifed fupreme authority ouer
all other Bifhops, making general edicts, condemning heretykes, depofing and reftoring Bifhops, cauling councels,
and excommunicating whole prouinces and countryes, I
appeale to thee gentle reader, whether he was not then
generally held for fupreme head of the Church, & whether
it is lykly, that when Eleutherius the Pope made King
Lucius a Chriftian, he made him a proteftāt, that is to fay,
an enemy to the fea Apoftolyk, a perfecuter of Priefts, and of
all fuch as defend the dignity, and autoritie, of faynt Peeter
his predeceffor, from whome he claymed, and held the fupremacy, of the Churche, which now all proteftants deny
to his fucceffors.

And agayne, feeing I haue proued that the autority of the
fea Apoftolyke is not grounded vpon any humain tradition
but vpon the inftitution of our fauiour himfelfe, who left
his flock and fheep to faynt Peeter to be fed, and buylt his
Churche vpon him, as vpon a fure rock, promifing that hel
gates fhould not preuayle againft it, ordayning for the
auoyding of Schifme & diuifion one head, from the which
the dyuers and manyfold members of his Churche might
receiue the influence of one doctrin and fpirit, what fhal
wee fay of them, that are not of this fold, that do not communicat with this head, that are not planted vpō this root
of vnity, nor buylt vpon this rock; that agaynft the chayre
of Peeter fet vp a chayre of peftiléce, can they be the fheep
of Chrift, or members of his miftical body? or receiue the
influence of his fpirit? it is no maruel, yf they be caryed
away with euery blaft of new doctrin, torne and rent
with euery fchifme, and caft at length vpon the rockes of
herefy or atheifme; haue wee not then fufficient reafon to
giue lands, lyues, or what honour, pleafure, or comodity
foeuer the world yeildeth, rather then to be driuen from
                                                        this

Ioan. 21.
Matth. 16.

this safe harbor of truth, and ancor of vnity, into the seas of schisme and heresy, to the assured shipwrack of our soules? and when wee spend our blood for this cause, do we not dy for religion, yea for a most important point of religion, though it be made treason? wherof wee may truly saye with the blessed martyr Sir Thomas More that it is a treason without sinne, for the which a mã may be hanged and haue no harme, dy and liue for euer, seeme to some a traytor; and be a glorious martyr.

THE MATTER OF HOLY

Images is debated, and the vse therof proued to haue ben in the Churche of God euer since our Sauiours tyme.

CHAP. XI.

BVt let vs examine a poynt or two more of religion wherein our aduersaries dissent from vs, that wee may see wheather K. Lucius were more lyke to learne their doctrin concerning the same or ours, and for that they think they haue a maruelous aduãtage of vs in the matter of Images, and relykes of saints, wherein they charge vs with flat Idolatrie, and breach of the commaundment of God, I wil say somwhat therof.

And fyrst I cannot but maruel at their grosnesse, that cannot distinguish betwiyt an Idol and an Image, wherof they may learne the difference in Origen and Theodoretus, expoũding these words of the cõmaundmẽt, *non facies tibi Idolũ, thou shalt not make to thy self any Idol*, (for the septuaginta whose translation they follow, for sculptile haue εἰδωλον, that is to say an Idol) wherevpon they say, that an Idol is a fals similitude representing a thing which is not, & that a similitude, or Image, is a representation of a thing which truly is, to which purpose also S. Paule sayth, *Idolum*

Orige. hom. 8. in Exodũ.
Theodoret. quæst. 38. in Exodum.
Exod. 20.

nihil

Leuit.19.26.
Num 23.
Ozea 6.
nibil eſt in mundo , an Idol is nothing in the World, for that Idols
repreſent no truth,but mere fictions vanityes, and lyes,and
therfore ar cauled in the Hebrew text of the holy ſcriptures *Elilim* and *Auanim* wheron it followeth , that all Images
or other creatures held or adored for Gods, wh:ch they
neither are,nor yet poſsibly can bee, are truly and properly
Idols,wheras other Images, that repreſent a truth can not
ſo bee cauled, and this difference is euident in the holy
ſcriptures, which neuer atribute the name of Idol to the
true Image of any thing, but to the fals gods of the gentils,
and vſeth the name of *Image,*for the ſimilitud of that,which
is truly the thing that it is thought to be, or hath the true
proprietyes that by the Image are repreſented, & ſo Chriſt

Sap.7.
Coloſſen.1.
Hebr.1.
is cauled the Image of his father , and Salomon is ſayd to
haue made in the temple Images of Lions,Oxen,Flowers,
yea and of the Cherubins, who (though they were Angels

3.Reg.7.
and Spirits) were neuertheleſſe pourtrayed lyke men , (to
expreſſe the forme, wherein they appeared to Moyſes on

Conc.Nicæ.
2.Act 4.
the mountayne) and with wings to ſhew the celerity of
their motion, ſo that the repreſentation made therby, was
true, as of a true apparition,and a true propriety in the An-
gelical nature;

Herevpon it foloweth , that Images which are not honored for Gods,but ordayned for the honor of Chriſt, and
his ſaynts (who are truly that which they are repreſented
to be) are no Idols, and therfore our aduerſaries are eyther
very ignorant, or malicious, when they confound theſe
woords in ſuch ſort as to cal Images Idols, and to tranſlate
Idolum in the ſcripture *an Image* as they commonly do very
abſurdly,and ſometymes ridiculouſly, as in S. Paule where
he ſpeaketh of *couetouſnes* ſaying, it is ειδωλολατρια, that is to
ſay, *Idolatry,* or *the ſeruice of Idols* , and in an other place;

Coloſſen.3.
Epheſ 5.
that the couetous man is ειδωλολατρης, *an Idolater* or *a Woer-
ſhipper of Idols* (meaning therby that couetous men make
theyr money, and their riches their Gods) they tranſlate it,
couetouſnes *is the ſeruice of Images,* and the coueteous man is
a Woor-

a worshipper of Images, as though there were no other Idolatry, but that which may be donne to Images, or that Image and Idole were all one, or that it could be sayd with any propriety, or reason, that a couetous man makes his money an Image, as it may be properly sayd, that he makes it an Idol, becaufe he makes yt his God, which yt neither is, nor can be, in which refpect it may wel be cauled an Idol.

Furdermore they bewray in themfelues either great fimplicity or peruers malice, in that they permit no honour nor reuerence to be donne to the Image of Chrift, & his faynts; for doth not reafon and common experience teach vs that the *honour or reuerence donne to the Image paffeth from thence to the Prototipon,* that is to fay, to the thing or perfon it reprefenteth? he which crowneth (fayth S. Ambrofe) *the image of the emperour, crowneth the Emperour, and he which contemnes his image feemeth to do iniury to his perfon.* when the people of Antiochia caft downe the image of the Empreffe, wyfe to Theodofius the Emperour, he took it for fo great an affront to her and him felfe, that he had lyke to haue deftroyed the whole citty in reuenge thereof; and S. Chryfoftome complayneth greeuoufly of the indignity donne to the Emperour therin. The lyke was iudged in England of the violéce dône by Hacket to the Queenes picture, which was iuftly held for a difloyal act agaynft her Mageftyes perfon: And who knoweth not that he which ftandeth bare headed in the prefence cháber before the Queenes chayre and cloth of ftate doth honour the Queene therein.

Alfo it was the cuftome in tymes paft to adore the images of the Roman Emperours, which the Chriftians refufed not to do, in which refpect Iulian the Apoftata, thinking either to draw them to adore his fals Gods, or els to haue fome pretence to punifh them for contempt of his perfon, placed his owne image amongft the images of falfe Gods, (as I haue noted in my Apology vpon an other occafion) wherupon S. Gregory Nazianzen fayth, that the fimple Chriftians who did not fal into account of the deceat,

Bafil.lib.de fpiritu fancto. ca.18. & Aug. lib 3. de doct. Chriftiana. cap.9.

Ambro.ferm. 10. in Pfal.118

Theodore.li. 5.hift. cap.19.

Chrifoft. orati.2 & 3. ad popu. Antio.

Gregor. Naz. orat. 1. in Iul. Item Paulus Diaconus in vita Iulianus.

ceat,were to be excufed of ignorance,for that they thought they adored no more but the Emperours image; if therfore it be lawful to adore the image of an Emperour or earthly king for that he is the image of almighty God, I meane, if it bee lawful to adore the image of Gods image,how much more is it lawful to do reuerence to the image of God him felfe, I meane of Chrift God and man?

And fure I am that many in England which wil not haue, nor reuerence; the image of our fauiour for feare of committing idolatry, wil make no bones at all, to keep fome picture or remembrance of their Maiftres to kiffe it, and to vfe other tokens of affection and refpect towards it, to fhew therby their good wil to her.

And how many are there in England that condemne catholykes for keeping images and pictures to moue them to deuotion, and yet make no fcruple to keep lafciuious pictures to prouoke themfelues to luft? wherby they might fee by their owne experience, if they were not wilfully blynd, what is the effect of good and deuout pictures in wel difpofed mynds, and what it would bee in themfel-ues if they were as fpiritual, and feruerous in the loue of God, as they are carnal and fyry in fenfual appetyt; for who douteth that deuout reprefentatiõs do as eafely moue pious and godly minds to holy cogitations, and affections, as lafciuious obiects do kindle carnal mynds to concu-pifcence and luft? and therfor S. Gregory Niffen fayth, that he neuer beheld the picture of Abraham facrififing his fonne Ifaac, but hee was moued to teares,and yet it is likely that he had often read the ftory therof, without any fuch effect,as Bafilius byfhop of Ancyra noted very wel in the 7. general councel of Nice, when the fame was alea-ged there out of S.Gregory aboue 800. yeres agoe,where-vpõ Theodorus byfhop of Catane alfo inferred,in the fame councel, that much more may the ftory of our fauiours pafsion reprefented by picture woorke the lyke effect in deuout perfons that behold the fame. Wherof I think
good

Greg.Niff.in orat. de dei-tate filij & fpiritus Sãcti, allega.in con-cil.

Cõcil. Nicen. 2.

Ibidem.

good to declare here a manifest example of my owne knowledge.

It chaced in the house of a Catholyke where. I was, that a young mayd of 15. or 16. yeres of age, (who had ben alwayes brought vp amongsts protestates) comming thether, and seeing a picture of Christ crusified demaunded whose picture it was, and being told that it was the picture of our sauiour Christ, wherby she might see what he suffred for vs, she was moued with such compassion that after she had stedfastly beheld it a whyle, she burst out first into sighes, & after into teares, saying that shee had often heard of it, but neuer seene it before, adding further our Lord helpe vs if he suffred all this for vs.

Wherby it may appeare, how true is that, which saynt Gregory the greate sayth of Images, to wit, that they are the bookes of the ignorant, who are many tymes more moued with pictures, then with preaching, and vnderstand that which is taught the much better, when it is by Images or pictures represented to their eyes; for as the Poet sayth. ^{Greg.lib. 9. epist. ad Serenum episcopum Massili.epis.9.}

Segnius irritant animos immissa per auros
   Quam quæ sunt oculis commissa fidelibus.   ^{Horat. de arte poetica.}

That is to say; those things that are conceaued by hearing do lesse moue the mynds of men, then such thinges as are committed to the sight.

This the deuil knoweth so wel, as to hinder the same & all other good effects of holy Images, and deuout pictures, yea and to exterminat, as much as in him lyeth, all external monuments, and memories of the lyfe and passion of our sauiour, and his saynts, and so by degrees to root out all Christian religion, he hath stirred vp in all ages his instruments and seruants to make warre against holy Images vnder colour of zeale to Gods honour and glory.

To this purpose it may be noted, that the first and cheef impugners of the lawful vse of Images, for some hundreth yeares togeather, were eyther Iewes, or magicians or ma-

K   nifest

nifeſt heretikes, or otherwyſe knowen for moſt wicked men. The firſt wherof was a perſian cauled *Xenatas* about 500.yeres after Chriſt, whome Nicephorus cauleth *the ſeruant of Satan*, ſaying that he made himſelfe a Biſhop, before he was baptiſed, and that *he was the firſt that taught that the Image of Chriſt, and of his ſaynts ought not to be woorſhiped*, and almoſt 200.yeres after, in the yere of our Lord 676. the Iewes impugned the vſe of Images in their Talmud; and about the yere of our Lord 700. a Iew perſuaded a Mahometan King in Arabia to burne all the Images in the Churches of the Chriſtians, and ſhortly after Leo Iſaurus the Emperour did the lyke by perſuaſion of a Iew, whoſe example his ſonne Leo Copronimus followed, being a magician, and a neſtorian heretyk, and about the yere 800. Leo Armenius the Emperour and his ſucceſſors Michael Balbus and Theophilus, (all three moſt wicked men, & the laſt addicted both to iudaiſme, and necromancy) made a new warre againſt Images, which the wycleſiſts alſo did 500. yeares after, and now of late the Lutherans, and Caluiniſts; whereas all thoſe that defended the vſe of Images againſt Leo, and thoſe other Emperours, were moſt holy, and learned men, as Gregorius and Hadrianus Biſhops of Rome in thoſe dayes, and Germanus, and Tharaſius Biſhops of Conſtantinople, S. Iohn Damaſcen, Methodius, Leontius, Ionas Aurelianenſis, Paulus Diaconus, and diuers others, all of them men of ſinguler learning, and vertue, by the teſtimony of all autors, both Greeks & Latins.

Niceph.li.16. cap.27.

Con.Nicen. z.act.5.

Cedren Zonaras, Nicet. in vita leon. Iſau.

Ijdem in vitis horum Imperat.

THE

THE COMMANDEMENT OF
*God touching images explicated, and the practise
of the Churche declared.*

CHAP. XII.

BVT our aduerfaries obiect againſt vs the commãde- Exod 20.
ment of God, to wit, thou ſhalt not make to thy ſelfe
any grauen Image, nor any ſimilitude of any thing,
&c. wherto I anſwere yf they take the bare letter
without the true ſence and circumſtances, no man may
make any Image whatſoeuer, nor ſo much as any lykneſſe
of any thing in heauen or earth, but yf wee conſider the circumſtances, the end, and reaſon of the commaundement, it
maketh nothing at all againſt vs, for it is manifeſt that the
ſcope, and end therof is only to forbid Idolatry and the making of Idols, that is to ſay ſuch Images only as are made
with intent to adore them for Gods, and therfore (as Ter-
tulian noteth expreſly,) it preſently followeth, *non adorabis* Tertul. lib.2.
ea neque coles; thou ſhalt not adore, nor worſhip them, which yet contra Mar-
appeareth more playnly in Leuiticus, where theſame pro- cionem.
hibition being renewed, the intent or end is expreſly added,
ad adorandum according to the Septuaginta or as S. Hierome Leuit. 26.
tranſlateth it *vt adoretis* that is to ſay, *to the end to do godly ho-*
nor therto; ſo that, where that end or intent is not, the making or vſe of an Image, is not forbidden for that it is no
Idole; and therfore the Septuaginta in ſteede of *Sculptile*
haue *Idolum,* for that a graué Image is not to be vnderſtood
to be forbidden, by that commandment, but when it is an
Idole; which interpretatiõ of the Septuaginta, both Origin,
and Theodoret do follow in that place, as I haue noted
before; beſydes that, almighty God commaunded afterwards, the brazen Serpent to be ſet vp in the wildernes, & Num 21.
alſo Cherubins in the téple, where the Iewes were wount Exod. 25.
to adore; the which had ben contrary to his owne com-

maundement, yf he had abſolutly forbidden the making of Images, or hauing them in temples and Churches; yea & wee may playnly gather out of ſaynt Hierome, that there was woorſhip and reuerence donne to the Cherubins, for

Hieron. epiſt. ad marcellā.

he ſayth, that the *Sancta Sanctorum* was woorſhiped of the Iewes, becauſe the Cherubins, & the Arke, and the Manna were there; to which purpoſe ſaynt Auſtugin geueth a

Aug. lib. 3. de Doctri. Chriſt. cap. 9.

general rule in his book of Chriſtian doctrin, ſaying that all profitable ſignes, inſtituted by almighty God, ought to be reuerenced and woorſhipped, for that the honor donne to them doth paſſe to that which they repreſent; & in his

Aug. lib. 3. de Trinit. ca. 10.

book of the bleſſed Trinity ſpeaking of ſignes that being dedicated to ſome religious vſe deſerue veneratiō, he putteth for example the brazen Serpent ſet vp in the wilderneſſe,

4 Reg. 18.

which neuertheles was afterwards worthely deſtroyed by K. Ezechias, when the Iewes committed Idolatry therto, & who douteth but that the holy ſcriptures, & holy veſſels or any other thing dedicated to the ſeruice of God, is to be vſed with reuerēce & reſpect, & that God is honored therby? So that neither the making of Images, ordayned for Gods honor & ſeruice, nor yet the reuerend vſe therof, was forbidden by that comandemēt, but only the abuſe, which was Idolatry, and therfore our aduerſaries do ſhamefully abuſe

Lib. 2. contra Marcio.

the people, and impudently bely vs, when they ſay wee make Idols of the Images of Chriſt, and his ſaynts; & ſhew themſelues very groſſe in that they ſeeke to aboliſh altogeather the vſe of Images, or pictures, becauſe ſome abuſe perhaps is, or may be incident therto; for there is nothing in the world ſo neceſſary, ſo excelent, or holy, but yf it be vſed, it is or may be abuſed, the remedy wherof, is not to take away wholy the vſe of the thing, but to correct the abuſe, as; not to forbid wyne to all men, becauſe ſome are drunk therwith, but to teach drunkards to vſe it with moderation, and hereof the Churche hath ſuch care in the matter of Images, that the people are ſufficiently inſtructed of the vſe therof by their curats, paſtors and preachers, in

fo much

ſo much that no Catholyke man, nor yet any chyld I dare ſay, that hath but learned his Catechiſme is ignorant that the image of Chriſt, is no more Chriſt himſelfe then the Image of the Queene, is the Queene, and that the honor donne therto, reſteth not in the Image, but redoundeth to Chriſt who is repreſented therby, and therfore is no more Idolatry, then the reuerence donne to the Queenes picture or cloth of eſtate is treaſon.

To come then to the practyſe of the Churche, the vſe of images was not only alowed, but alſo ordayned by a cannon of the Apoſtles, wherin they decreed that the image of our Sauiour Ieſus Chriſt God and man, and of his ſaynts, ſhould be made by the hands of men and erected againſt Idols, and Iewes for the confuſion of both;

So farre were they from thinking the vſe of Images, to be Idolatry, that they ordayned the ſame, for confuſion and ouerthrow of Idols, and Idolaters, and it is not to be douted, that the Apoſtles made ſuch a decree for the vſe of Images, ſeeing the ſeuenth general councel of Nice maketh mention therof, relying vpon the authority of ſaynt Baſil, affirming that it was ordayned by the Apoſtles that Images ſhould be erected and honored; beſyds that Pamphilus the martyr doth teſtify, that he found in Origens library the decrees of the Apoſtles made at Antioch, amongſt the which; is this; the which may alſo bee confirmed by the vſe and practyſe of the Churche of God, ſince the tyme of Chriſt, and his Apoſtles. Sinod. Nice. 2.act.1.

Baſil.epiſt.ad Iulian. in actis.2.Nicœ. cōcilij act. 2.

Vide Turrianum canonibus apoſtolicis. cap. 25.

Wee read that Nicodemus that came to Chriſt by night made an Image of him crucified, and that before his death he gaue it to Gamaliel who deliuered it to Iames byſhop of Hieruſalem, and he to Simeon, and Simeon to Zacheus, and Zacheus to his ſucceſſors, and that ſo it paſſed from one to an other, vntil the Chriſtians were forced to remoue from thence to Beritus a citty of Siria where afterwards the Iewes finding it, vſed it moſt opprobriouſly, & pearced it with a lance, out of the which iſſued great aboundance Athanaſius lib.de paſſione Imaginis domini

Idem. Ibib.

K 3   of blood

of blood that did many miracles, and this was so notorious, that the blood was sent to dyuers parts, and a feast celebrated in Greece in memory therof in the moneth of Nouember; this story was read in the second councel of Nice,
Eusebius lib. and approued by 350.byshops aboue 800. yeres agoe.Euse-
y.hist.ca 14. bius witnesseth that the woman which was cured by our
sauiour of a flux of blood, did set vp in the citty of Cæsarea
in memory of the benefit, a brazen Image of our Sauiour,
and that there grew an herb at the foot therof, which
when it once touched the hem of his garment,had the ver-
Ibidem. tue to cure all disseases, and this Image Eusebius sayth he
Sozomen. li. saw himselfe in his tyme, and the ecclesiastical histories
5 hist ca. 20. written after, do signify that it remayned there vntill Iulian
the Apostata caused it to be taken doune, and his owne
Image to be set vp in the place, which was shrotly after
ouerthrowen,and burnt with fyre from heauen, wherin it
is to be noted, that almighty God did not only confirme
the vse of Images by the continual miracles of the hearb,
Euseb. lib.7. but also in destroying the Image of Iulian,set vp in the place
cap.14. of his, shewed his indignation towards all such as contemne his Image, or do any iniury therto. Eusebius also
sayth that he had seene ancient Images of S.Peter, & saynt
a Lib. 4. hist. Paule kept by the Christians in his tyme. [a]Euagrius, [b]Ni-
cap.26.
b Lib. 2. hist. cephorus,and [c]S.Iohn Damascen do declare, that amongst
cap. 7. other auncient monuments of the City of Edessa, therwas
c Lib.4 de a long tyme kept a true portrait of our sauiour Christ
fide orthod.
cap.17. which he himselfe sent to Abgarus king of that citty; and
Leo a reader of Constantinople affirmed before the whole
councel of Nice aforesayd, that he had seene it, and Eua-
In meno- grius,and Theophanes recount great miracles donne ther-
logio græco- by, in so much that the Greekes celebrated a solemne feast
rum.
Lib 2.hist. therof in September,as appeareth in the menologio, or ka-
cap.43. lib.6 lender of the Greekes; Nicephorus also sayth, that the holy
cap 16.lib.
14.cap. 2. Euangelist S. Luke did draw the true pourtraicts of our
blessed Lady,and the Apostle S. Peter, which was kept at
Constantinople in the tyme of Theodosius the Emperour,

Tertul-

Tertullian maketh mention of the picture of our sauiour in the forme of the good sheepheard carying a sheepe vpon his back, ordinarily paynted vpon the chalices that were vsed in the Churche in his tyme, which was in the raygne of king Lucius, so that there is no dout but the vse of Images, and pictures hath ben receiued in the Church of God, euer since the Apostels tyme, although by reason of the great persecutions vnder the Pagan Emperours they could neither be so frequent, nor publyk as after they began to bee in the tyme of Constantine the great, who buylding gorgious temples adorned the same, not only with the signe of the crosse, but also with the Images of our sauiour, and of the twelue Apostels, of Angels, and of S. Iohn Baptist.

Tertul. li. de pudicitia.

Damasus in pontificali de sancto Siluestro.

S. Augustin noteth that the paynims might see our sauiour Christ paynted with S. Peter and S. Paule in many places. S. Hierome comendeth the feruor and deuotion of Paula, that went vp the mountayne of Caluary, and prostrayting her selfe before the Crosse, adored it as though she had seene our sauiour hanging theron, S. Chrysostome in his liturgy, which Erasmus translated, signifieth that the priest going foorth with the gospel in his hand, and a candel caried before him vsed to bow downe his head, to do reuerence to an Image of Christ.

De consensu euang. lib. 1. cap. 10.

Hieron. in epitaph paulæ. Christost in Liturgia.

S. Basil, S. Gregory Nissen, Euodius, Prudentius, and S. Paulinus do make honorable mention of the Images of S. Barlaam, S. Theodorus, S. Steeuen, S. Cassian, S. Martin in Churches in their tyme, which was 1200. yeres agoe: and yf good reader, I should alledge the testimonies of all the fathers, that from the tyme of Constantine did witnes, & approue the publyk vse of Images in the Churche, I should write a whole volume of this matter, and therfore it may suffyse the to vnderstand that although some auncient Fathers as S. Ireneus, Epiphanius and S. Augustin do reproue somtymes the abuse of some Images, as that the heretykes called Gnostici, and others of the sect of Simon placed the images of Christ, and of S. Peter, and S. Paule with other of

Basil. in S. Barlaam.
Greg. Nis. orat. in Theodorum.
Euodius di. miraculis S. Stepha. pruden. in him.
Pauli Epist. 12. ad senerum.
Irenæ lib. 1. cap. 24. Epipha. hær. 27.
August. ad quoduult. hær. 7.

Pitha-

Pithagoras, Homer, Ariſtotle, Helen, Minerua, and ſuch lyke, and adored them as Gods with ſacriſices, and incenſe after the manner of the gentils, yet they neuer diſalowed the lawful vſe therof, and therfore thoſe, that haue at any tyme reiected the ſame haue ben alwayes noted, and abhorred of all as heretykes, and called Iconomachi, or Iconoclaſtæ, againſt whome was aſſembled 800. yeres agoe the ſeuenth great general Councel at Nice where they were condemned for heretykes, and woors then Samaritans; by 350. Biſhops.

Ioã. Damaſc. de hæreſ. in fine.

Syno. Nicæn. 2. act 5. in ſine.

OF THE RELICKS
of Saynts.

CHAP. XIII.

Marc. 6.

NOw to ſay ſomewhat of holy relicks; There is no dout but the vſe thereof proceeded of the examples in H. Scripture of the great miracles done by the touching of Chriſts garment by the handkerchef and gyrdle of S. Paule, by the ſhadow of S. Peter, and in the old Teſtament by the body of Elizeus, wherewith a dead man was reuiued, by all which the firſt Chriſtians were induced to reuerence and honour euery thing that pertayned to the ſeruants of God, and to expect conſolation therby, wherfore when S. Peter, and S. Paule ſuffred at Rome, the Chriſtians of the eaſt, came thether, to haue theyr relycks as belonging to them by right, for that they were their cuntrymen, when S. Ignatius, who was thyrd byſhop of Antioch after S. Peter was martyred at Rome, the Chriſtiãs caryed his relickes with great ſolemnity to Antioch, and as S. Chryſoſtome teſtifieth many miracles were donne by the ſame. At the martyrdome of S. Policarp byſhop of Smyrna who alſo liued in the Apoſtles tyme, & was put to death not aboue 12. yeres before king Lucius receiued the

Marc. 6.

Act. 16.
Act. 5.
4. Regum. 13.

Gregor. lib. 3. ep. 30.

Chryſoſt. ſerm. de S. Ignatio, to. 5.

fayth

fayth) the Chriſtians of his dioceſſe that were preſent, gathered vp his relikes, & vſed them with great reuerēce, as
they themſelues witneſſed in an epiſtle which Euſebius re- Euſeb lib.4.
cyteth at large, wherin amongſt other things they ſay thus. hiſt.cap.1.
Afterwards hauing gathered out of the aſhes his bones „
more worthy then precious ſtones, and more pure then „
gold, we placed them in a place ſeemely, and fit for them, „
where aſſembling our ſelues ſometymes, wee may by the „
help of our Lord, celebrat the day of his martyrdome, as „
of his natiuity, with great ioy and exultation, thus farre „
the Chriſtiās of the Churche of. Smyrna S. Cipriā, beſydes Ep. 34.
the yerely celebration of martyrs feaſts, maketh often
mention of oblations, and ſacrifices offred in memory of
them, ſo doth alſo Tertullian, ſo that by theſe teſtimonies
it appeareth, that in the tyme not only of King Lucius but
alſo of the Apoſtles, and their Diſciples the relikes of Gods
ſeruants were kept, and highly honored, and feaſts of their
martyrdome celebrated, vnder tytle of their natiuityes, as
ſtil it is vſed in our Cathol. Churche, and no maruel, ſeing
the Chriſtians at that tyme vſed to creep and kiſſe their
chaynes, whyles they were yet liuing in priſon, as Ter- Lib. ad vxo-
tullian witneſſeth, and yf we cōſider the vniforme conſent rem.
of all fathers in all ages, concerning this poynt, wee may
wel wounder at the malice of our aduerſaries that do deny
it, eſpecially ſeing in the primatiue Church it was ſo euident that the very paynims knew it, and therfore were
wont to caſt the aſhes, & bones of the martyrs into riuers,
or otherwyſe to make them a way, to the end the Chriſtians ſhould not recouer them, and Eunapius Sardiānus of Eunap. in vi-
Alexandria a paynim writteth that the Chriſtians in his ta philoſo.
tyme honored their martyrs being dead, kneeling and pro-
ſtrating them ſelues before their tombs, and making them
their Embaſſadours to deliuer their prayers to God.

But to returne to the fathers of the Churche, S. Auguſtin De ciuit. Dei
to confound the gentils reherſeth many miracles donne by lib.22.cap. 8.
the very flowers that had but only touched the relicaries
                L   where

Greg. Niff.
orat.in laudē
magni Theo
doti.
where the relickes of faynts were kept S. Gregory Niſſen
fayth that the Chriſtians that came to the tombs of faynts,
did take it for a great fauour that they might be ſuffred to
cary away ſome of the duſt that was about the ſame. S.

Aug de ci-
uit. Dei.li. 22
cap.8.
Auguſtin alſo telleth that the ſonne of one Irenaus was reſtored to lyfe, being anoynted only with the oyle of a lamp
that did hang before the tomb of a martyr ; in lyke manner

Theodor in
hiſt. Sanct.
Patrum.c.22.
in Iacobo.
Venantius
For·u. in vi-
ta S.Marrini,
lib.4.
Paulus Dia.
co.de geſt.
longob.lib.2
cap 9.
*Gregor.Na-
zianz. in Iu-
lian.orat. 1.
Theodoret, Venantius, Fortunatus, & Paulus Diaconus, recount wonderful miracles donne by the oyle of lamps that
burned by martyrs tombs, yea *S. Gregory Nazianzen fayth
of his owne knowledge, that not only a litle duſt, or bone of
the martyrs but alſo the very remembrance of them ſup-
plyeth ſometymes the want of their whole bodyes, and
concludeth with this exclamation , *O rem prodigioſam, ſa-
lutem aſſert ſola recordatio*, o prodigious thing the only remembrance of them giueth health, and in his oration in
prayſe of S. Ciprian he calleth to witneſſe many that knew
by their owne tryal, and experience , what great vertue &
power was in this very duſt & aſhes to expel diuels to cure

Ambr. ferm.
93.de lanctis
Nazario &
celſo.
Ambroſ.ep.
85.de inuēt.
corporum
Sanct.
Geruaſij &
Protaſij ad
ſororem.
Auguſt. lib.
confeſſio.9.
cap.7.
diſeaſes, and for the foreknowing of things to come; S.
Ambroſe aſketh why faythful men ſhould not honour relickes of ſaynts, which the very diuels reuerence, and feare,
who alſo ſignifieth that he had a reuelation from almighty
God of the place where the bodyes of S. Geruas, and Pro-
taſe were buryed in Millan, wher-vpon he took them vp
with great ſolemnity, as S. Augſtin alſo witneſſeth; who
was preſent, and reporteth a great miracle of a blynd man
that recouered his ſight at the ſame tyme, and diuels expeld
by the merits of thoſe bleſſed martyrs.

Chryfoſt.in
demonſtra .
quod Chri-
ſtus ſit Deus.
S. Chriſoſtome proueth againſt the Painims, by the honour donne to ſaynts relicks, that Chriſt is God, to whoſe
power and omnipotency he ſayth, it is to be aſcrybed; that
his diſciples, and ſeruants (who whyles they were liuing
did ſeeme moſt contemtible) became after they were dead
more venerable then Kings, in ſo much that at Rome and
Conſtantinople Kings and praſidents (ſayth he) runne to
the

the tombe of a fisher, and take it for a great fauour that their
bodyes may be buried, not hard by the Apostles bodyes,
but without the circuit of their tombs, and be made as it
were porters of Fishermen. Furthermore in his book
against the gentils, where he discourseth at large of the lyfe
& death of S. Babilas the martyr he signifieth that his body
being placed in the suburbs of Antioch neare to a temple
where there was an Oracle of Apollo, it put the diuel to
silence, and when Iulian the Apostata thought by the remoue of it to remedy thesame, the Temple, and Idole were
presently after destroyed with fire from heauen, wherwith
as saynt Chrisostome testifieth Iulian and all the gentils
were wounderfully confounded; and so may our heretykes be in lyke manner, seing that they not only impugne
with them this euident argument of the diuinity of Christ,
but also hold that for Idolatry which maistreth the diuel,
ouerthroweth Idols and confoundeth Idolaters.

I omit infinit others for breuities sake, & conclude with
saynt Hierome who declareth the custome of the whole   Hieron. ad-
Churche of God both in his tyme, and longe before, therby   uer. vigilant.
to confute Vigilantius the heretyke that taught the same
doctrine in this behalfe that our heretykes teach at this
day; whofoeuer sayth he adored martyrs? *Who euer taught
men to be God? yt greueth vigilantius to see the relickes of martyrs
couered with costly and precious veyles belyke Constantin the Emperour committed sacrilege When he tranflated, to Constantinople the
holly relyckes of saynt Andrew, S. Luke, S. Timothe, Wherat the diuels
roare, and now also Arcadius, the Emperour belyke committeth sacri-
ledge Who after so long tyme hath tranflated the bones of Samuel the
Prophet into Thracia, and all the Bishops that caryed the ashes lapt
in silk, and in a vessel of gold are to be condemned for fooles and sacrilegious persons, yea then the faythful people of all Churches are
fooles also for going to receiue the same, With no lesse Ioy then if they
had seene the Prophet a liue, in so much that frō Palestina to Calcedon
ther Was all the Way swarmes of people that With one voyce sounded
forth the prayse of Christ, lastly so shal Wee say that the Bishop of*

Rome doth il when he offreth sacrifice to our Lord ouer S. Peter, and saynt Paules venerable bones (as wee tearme them though thou caulest them vile dust) and when he taketh their tombs for the altars of Christ; lo here (good reader) the vse of Images and relykes, and the honor due to them approued by the Fathers of all ages, confirmed by the custome of all Christian nations, ratyfied by miracles, acknowledged by infidels, and Paynims, confessed by diuels, and yet denied and deryded by the heretyks of this tyme, are they not then more obstinat and malicious then heathens, yea then diuels themselues?

THAT OVR DOCTRIN

concerning the sacrifice of the Masse was generally receiued, and beleued, in the tyme of king Lucius, & first that it was foretold & prophecyed by Malachias.

CHAP. XIIII.

BVT I wil passe to an-other importāt poynt, I mean the sacrifice of the Masse, to see whether our doctrin concerning the same or theirs was deliuered by our sauiour to the Apostles and taught in king Lucius tyme or no.

The sacrifice of the Masse consisting in the oblation of the blessed body and blood of our sauiour Iesus Christ, was prophesyed by Malachias, præfigured by the sacrifice of Melchisedeth, instituted and offred by our sauiour at his last supper, deliuered by him to his Apostles, practysed by them and by the Churche of God euer since.

Malach. 1.　　Malachias the Prophet foretelling the reiection of the Iewes, and the election of the gentils, signifieth withall the translation of the Iewes law and priesthood into a new law, and a new priesthood, and compareth or rather opposeth the priests of the one, to the priests of the other,

sacrifice

facrifice to facrifice, place to place, altar to altar, and a poluted bread which they were wōt to offer only in Hieiufalem, to a cleane oblatiō which fhould be offred to God amongft the Gentils euery where throughout the whole world, faying to the priefts of the Iewes in the perfon of God, that feing they difpyfed his name, and offred vpon his altars a polluted bread, and blynd and lame facrifices, *non eft mihi voluntas in vobis, &c.* fayth hee, *my wil is no longer to be* Malach ca.1. *ferued of you, neyther wil I accept any more facrifice at your hands, for my name is great amongft the Gentils euen from the eaft to the weft, & there is a cleane oblation offred to my name in euery place, &c.* Thus farre the Prophet, who cannot be vnderftood to fpeake of any other facrifice then of the Maffe, which being nothing els but the oblation of the bleffed body and blood of our fauiour Iefus Chrift in forme of bread and wyne, is a moft pure and cleane oblation, and cannot be polluted by the wickednes of the priefts, as the bread offred in the old law was wont to be ; to which purpofe it may be noted that the Prophet fpeaking of dyuers kinds of facrifices, fome confifting of beafts or catel (which he fignifyed by the words blynd and lame) and other in bread, he attributeth the word polluted or defiled to the bread only, not without miftery, to oppofe therto the cleane facrifice of the gentils in forme of bread, cauling it a cleane oblation, and putting the fpecial force of the antithefis betwyxt the figure, and the verity, for that the *fhew bread* or *bread of propofition* (being Hieron. in as S. Hierome fayth the bread which the priefts polluted) Malach.1. was a proper figure of the holy euchariſt, as he alfo tefti- Hieron. ibid. fyeth.

Furdermore this facrifice cannot be vnderftood of the facrifice of our fauiour vpon the croffe, which was offred only once, and in one place, and not amongft the gentils; neither yet of fpiritual facrifices, as of thankes geuing, prayer, fafting, and other good workes, which are improperly cauled facrifices, and therfore it is to be noted that whenfoeuer this woord facrifyce is improperly taken in the scripture some other woord is alwayes ioyned thereto, to signify the same, as *hostia laudis, sacrificium iustitiæ. Sacrificium cordis contriti, the host or sacrifice of prayse, the sacrifice of iustice, the sacrifice of a contrit hart,* and on the other syde whensoeuer it is alone without any woord adioyned, to restrayne or diminish the sence (as it is in this prophesy) it signifyeth a true and proper sacrifice;

Psalm.115.
Psalm 4.
Psalm.50.

This difference may wel be noted, where it is said, *misericordiam volui, non sacrificium,* I wil haue mercy and not sacrifice, and agayne *obedientia est melior quam victima,* obedience is better then sacrifice, in which sentences sacrifyce properly taken, is opposed to mercy and obedience, which also may improperly be cauled sacrifices, as wel as thankes geuing, prayse of God or any other good worke whatsoeuer.

Ofee.6.
1.Reg.11.

Agayne the prophet speaketh heere of a sacrifice or oblation which should be but one, cauling it a cleane oblation, but the spiritual sacrifices are as many as there are good woorkes of the faythful.

Also he speaketh of a sacrifice proper to the new law, and to the gentils, & such a one as should succeede the sacrifices of the Iewes, and be offred in steede therof; but spiritual sacrifices haue ben in all tymes, and common both to Iewes and gentils;

But howsoeuer other men may vnderstand this prophesy our aduersaryes cannot with any reason expound it, of the good woorks of Christians, seeing they teach that the best woorkes of the iustest men are polluted, and vncleane, sinful and damnable, which therfore cannot, according to their doctrin, be that sacrifice which almighty God himselfe cauled by the mouth of his prophet, a cleane oblation.

Lastly the most learned and auncient fathers of the Churche do vniformly expound this prophesy of the sacrifice of the masse; as S.Iustin the learned Philosopher and famous martyr, within 150. yeres after Christ, sayth that, *of the sacrifices of the gentils that are offred in euery place, videlicet,*

Iustin.in dialo.cum Triphō.

the

the bread and cup of the Eucharist, Malachias the Prophet euen then spoke and foretold that Wee should glorify his name therby.

Ireneus also hauing declared in what manner our sauiour did institute the blessed Sacramét of the Eucharist at
his last supper, and that the Churche receyuing thesame of
the Aposties offreth it to God throughout the world, addeth, *de quo & in duodecim prophetis Malachias sic præsignificauit
non est mihi voluntas in vobis, &c.* that is to say, *Wherof Malachias
one of the twelue prophets did signify before hand,* speaking to the
Iewes in this manner, *my wil is no longer to be serued by
you, &c.*

Irenæ. lib. 4. cap. 32. item c. 33. & 34.

S. Chrysostome hauing alledged the same Prophesy
concludeth. *Behold,* sayth he, *how clearly and playnly he hath interpreted the mistical table, which is the vnbloody host.*

Chrysost. hom. in psal. 95.

He that listeth to see more testimonyes of the fathers let
him read Tertulian, S. Ciprian, S. Hierome, S. Augustin,
S. Ciril, Eusebius, Theodoretus, and S. Ihon Damascen in
the places alledged in the margent.

Tertul. li. 3. contra mar-
tio in fine. Cypria. lib. 1. contra Iu-
dæos, cap. 16 Hieron. in

Zachar. cap. 2. Aug. lib. 1. contra aduersar. leg & prophet cap. 2. Ciril. li. de adorat.
Euseb. lib. 1. de preparat. euangel. Theodoret super. Malach. 1. Damascen. lib. 4. de
orthodoxa fide.

THAT

THAT NOT ONLY THE SA-

*crifice of Melchisedech but also the sacrifices of the old law,
were figures of the sacrifice of the masse & are changed into the same, and by the way is declared the necessity of sacrifice, as wel for
common welth, as for religion.*

CHAP. XV.

NOw to speake of the sacrifice of Melchisedech I think our aduersaries wil not deny that our sauiour was and is a Priest according to the order of Melchisedech, and that he shalbe so for euer as the Prophet Dauid testifieth of him, saying, *tu es sacerdos in eternū secundum ordinem Melchisedech, thou art a Priest for euer according to the order of Melchisedech,* the which saynt Paule also sheweth amply in his epistle to the Hebrews ; the which being granted, two things do euidently follow thereon.

The first is, that for as much as priesthood and sacrifice ar correlatiues, and cannot be the one without the other; in which respect saynt Paule sayth that a Priest or Bishop is

Hebr. 5. & 8. ordeyned *vt offerat dona & sacrificia, to offer gifts and sacrifices,* & agayne that our sauiour being a Priest *must needs haue some-what to offer ,* and seing his sacrifice vpon the crosse was offred by him but once, neither can euer be reiterat in that manner, and therfore cannot be that continual sacrifice which must needs correspond to his eternal priesthood, & bee continually offred in his Church, I conclude that besydes his sacrifice vpon the crosse, he did institut and leaue behind him some other, to be offred dayly, not only for remission of dayly sinnes, but also for a most deuine act of religion wherby all faythful people may dayly do to almighty God the due worship & seruice they owe him, the which kind of worship by publik sacrifice, was not only vsed in the law of Moyses, but also in the law of nature, & is so due to God

from

from man, and proceedeth so intrinsecally from the very grounds and principles of nature it selfe, that their can be no perfect religion nor good common welth without it.

For as for religion whereas the special office and end therof is to acknowledge by external acts the seruice and subiection wee owe to our Lord and creator, and the dominion he hath ouer vs, it is manifest that no external act of religion doth so fully and conueniently expresse and signify the same as sacrifice, wherby wee gratefully offer to almighty God his owne creatures, not only rendring him part of his owne gifts, and yeilding him thankes therfore, but also destroying them in his honour, to testify as wel that he is souuerayn Lord of lyfe and death, as that we hold our beeing and all wee haue of him, and depend wholy of his wil and prouidence, yea and that we owe our owne lyfe to him in sacrifice and doe as it were redeeme the same with the death or destruction of an other crea- Euseb. de ture; in signification wherof, he which in the old law did præp. euang. present to the priest any beast to be sacrifised, did hold him lib. 1. cap. 1o. by the head, wheron the priest did also lay his hands, to shew that it was offred as a price *pro capite*, for the head or lyfe of him, that made the oblation.

Therfore for as much as this kynd of worship is the greatest & most proper testimony we can externaly yeild, of vassellage and seruitude to our creator, it cannot without preiudice of his right be comunicated to any creature whatsoeuer, in which respect it is cauled by the deuynes Aug. li. cōtra *latria* as due to God alone and for that cause not only the aduersar. le- deuil (that seeketh to robbe almighty God of his glory) gis. but also such men as haue made themselues to be held for Gods, haue euer affected this kynd of woorship as the highest and most due to diuinity. Seeing then sacrifice is most essential to religion, and a most proper and principal act therof, it followeth that there can be no perfect religion without priesthood and sacrifice for which cause

M   S.Paul

S.Paule speaking of the tranflation of the law maketh it to depend wholy vpon the tranflation of the priefthood, faying that *the priefthood being tranflated there muft needs be withal, a tranflation of the law.* And Daniel the Prophet defcribing the religion of the Iewes falne to defolation, fayd, that they had neither facrifice, oblation nor incence amongft them.

Hebr. 7.
Daniel ca. 3.

And now to fpeake a word or two, by the way, of common welth, where as nothing is more natural to man-kynd then the fame (to the which all men are by a general inftinct of nature fo inclyned, that ther was neuer found any people fo barbarous but they liued in fociety) it is to be noted, that it hath neuer ben read nor heard of that any common welth hath ben without facrifice, whervpon Plutarch fayth, that though a man may happely fynd fome cittyes without wals, without fcooles, without learning, without theaters, without money, yet no man euer faw citty without temples wherin facrifice might be offred to God; And Ariftotle fpeaking of things precifely neceffary for common welth, ordeyneth that *fpecial care be had of fa-crifice to the Gods.* Wherof two reafons may be geuen, the one for that nothing is more truly political, nor tendeth more directly to the eftablifhment of common welth then publik facrifice, wherby not only a league of frindfhip and ciuil vnity is made amongft men by the participation & communion of the thing that is facrififed, but alfo their paffeth, as it were, a couenant betwyxt God and them, wherby they become his particuler people, and he their God and protector, without whofe particuler prouidence and protection no common welth can eyther profper or ftand. The other reafon is for that facrifice being as before I haue declared moft neceffary to religion, is confequently neceffary for common welth, wherof the true & natural end is religion, God hauing ordeyned man and all humain things, principally for his owne feruice and therfore the very heathen Philofophers, namely Plato and all his fol-

Plutarch ad-uers Colote epicureum.

Arift. lib. 7. politic.

lowers,

lowers, make the end of common welth to be nothing els
but a religious wifdome, confifting in the knowledge, loue
and feruice of God; and Ariftotle placeth it in contemplation of deuine things, wherto he alfo fpecially requyreth
the knowledge, loue, and feruice of God, which is nothing
els but religion; in which refpect he geueth the cheef pre-
eminence and dignity amongft the magiftrats to priefts,
whofe fpecial function and office is to offer facrifice. The
which is alfo confirmed by the cuftome of all good comon
welths, as the ancient kingdomes of the Ægyptians, and
Romans, wherein the kings themfelues were priefts, and
offred facrifice; as alfo the cheefe magiftrats amongft the
Gretians were wont to do, and in the common welth of
the Romans after the fupprefsion of their kings, yea and
when they florifhed moft, the office of priefts was fo pre-
eminent, that the cheefe bifhops commanded and contro-
led the confuls, and as Cicero fayth, *præfuerunt tum religioni-
bus deorum, tum fumma reip.* that is to fay, *had the cheefe authority not only in matters concerning religion but alfo in the common
welth.*

Seeing then religion is naturally the end of common
welth, and facrifice a moft neceffary and principal act of
religion, it followeth that facrifice is no leffe natural and
effential to common welth then to Religion.

But to leaue the confideration of common welth apart,
and to conclude with religion and facrifice, I fay that for
as much as they are both moft natural to man, and that
the woorkes and effects of grace do not ouerthrow, but
nobilitate and perfect the good inclinations and woorkes
of nature, yt muft needs follow that our fauiour by the law
of grace, did no more depriue man of publike facrifice
then of religion, but that as he left him a moft perfect and
deuine Religion, farre excelling that which he had before
eyther in the law of nature, or in the law of Moyfes, fo he
left him alfo a moft deuine facrifice, wherby he might dayly
pay the tribute of nature in a farre more excellent manner

M 2   then

Plato. Plotinus. Iamblicus. Ariftot. Polit. lib. 7. & Ethic. lib. 10. cap. 8. & lib. 8. ca. 14. & 12 Ariftot. li. 7. politic. Plato. Plutarc. in vitis Romul. numæ. & Tulli holift. Idem in problem. Valerius li. 1. ca. 1. Lucius florus in epito. lib. 47. Cicero. oratio. pro domo fua.

then he did in eyther of the former states.

This is no lesse plainly, then learnedly taught by saynt Clement, S. Peters disciple and successor, who in his book of Apostolical constitucions declaring that our Sauiour did not by the law of grace abrogate the law of nature, nor take away so much as any natural inclination in man, but confirme and perfect the first, and moderate the later, he sheweth withall, what was fulfilled and what was chāged in the law of Moyses, and amongst other things that he sayth were changed, he nameth baptisme priesthood and sacrifice, saying that in steed of dayly baptismes our sauiour ordayned only one, and for bloody sacrifice he instituted

Clemen.
Apostolica-
rum con-
stitut.lib.6.
cap.2. 3.

rationale in cruentum , & misticum sacrificium quod in mortem domini per symbola corporis & sanguinis sui celebratur, that is to say *a reasonable vnbloody & mistical sacrifice, the which is celebrated by the sacraments or signes of his body and blood in representation of his death* ; Thus sayth saint Clement of the proper sacrifice of the new law, that is to say the masse, as it is euident by his

Irenæus li. 4.
cap. 34.

owne words ; which saint Ireneus confirmeth, signifying that as there were *oblations* in the old law, so there are *oblations* in the new law, and *sacrificia in populo, sacrificia in Ecclesia, sacrifices amongst the people of the Iewes, and sacrifices in the Churche*; in so much that he teacheth, that sacrifices were not reiected by mutatiō of the law, but changed: whereto he addeth also this differēce, that sacrifice is now offred by vs, not as it was by the Iewes, that is to say as by bond men, but by free men, because our sauiour hath deliuered vs from the bondage of the law, and thus sayth this ancient father of the sacrifice of the holy eucharist or masse, which a litle before he cauleth the *new oblation of the new testament* applying therto the prophesy of Malachy, as I haue noted in the last chapter.

To this purpose it is also to be noted that the most ancient and learned fathers do teach that the sacrifices of the old lawe (as wel bloody as vnbloody) were figures of this sacrifice, the which they affirme not only of the ᵇ bread

of proof propofition, and the flowre which was offred for them that were cleanfed from leprofy,but alfo of the facrifice of the Pafchal lambe; and faynt Auguftin teacheth expref- fely that all the facrifices of the old law were no ieffe figu- res of this facrifice of the Churche, then of the facrifice of of the croffe, faying that *fingulare facrificium* &c. *the finguler* or moft excellét *facrifice,* which *fpiritual Ifrael* that is to fay, the Churche,doth offer euery where according to the **order** of Melchifedech, was fignified *by the fhadowes of facrifices Wherin the people of the Iewes did ferue,*and agayne in the fame place,he fayth *that omnia genera priorum facrificiorum,all kinds of former facrifices,* were fhadowes of the facrifice of the Churche.Whereof the reafon maybe gathered out of him felfe; to wit becaufe this facrifice of the Churche is the felfe fame, that was offred vpon the croffe, that is to fay, our fauiour him felfe, whome all the facrifices of the old law did properly prefigure;the which reafon S.Auguft.feemeth himfelf to yeild,faying that our fauiour fent thofe whome he healed of their leprofy to the Priefts of the old law to offer facrifice, becaufe the facrifice which was to be cele- brated in the Churche, in fteede of all the facrifices of the old law, was not then inftituted, and geuing as it were, a further reafon therof, he fayth, *quia illis omnibus ipfe prænun- ciabatur,becaufe he him felfe was fore fhewed or fignified by them all* as though he fhould fay, that for as much as our fauiour who was prefigured by all the facrifices of the old law, was to bee offred in the facrifice of the Churche, or new law , therfore thefayd facrifice of the Churche was alfo prefigured by all thofe former facrifices,& to be offred in fteede of them ; which otherwhere he teacheth expreffely in thefe woords *the table* (fayth he) *which the prieft of the new teftament,* that is to fay our fauiour Chrift *doth exhibit is of his owne body and blood; for that is the facrifice, which fucceedeth all the facrifices of the old law, that were offred in fhadow or figure of that which was to come,* and a litle after ; *in fteede of all thofe facrifices his body is offred, and miniftred to the communicants,* thus

M 3   farre

b Hieron.in ca.1.Malach.
c Iuftin. in dial.
d Origen in in 26.Mat.
Tertul lib.4. contra Mar- cion.Cipria. lib.de vnit. ecclefiæ Am- brof. in 1. ca. Luc.
e Aug lib.1. contra ad- uerfar.leg. & prophet. cap. 18.& 19.

Auguft. de baptifmo có- tra Dona- tiftas lib.3. cap.19.

Auguft.de ciuit Deilib. 17.cap.20.

farre faynt Auguſtin, to whome I wil ad twoo or three other of the moſt famous fathers of the churche S. Leo ſurnamed the great, ſayth, *now that the varietyes of carnal & fleſhly ſacrifices do ceaſſe, thy body and blood*, o Lord, doth ſupply, for all the differences of hoſts and ſacrifices in the old law; And S.

Chriſoſtome hauing mentioned particulerly the many and

diuers ſacrifices of the old law, addeth, *all which the grace of the new teſtament doth comprehend in one ſacrifice ordeyning one, & the ſame a true hoſt*; in which woords ſaynt Chriſoſtome meaneth the ſacrifice of the Euchariſt, which he cauleth a litle before the *miſtical table a pure and vnbloody hoſt, a heauenly & moſt reuerend ſacrifice* which alſo he confirmeth otherwhere

ſaying that Chriſt did *change the ſacrifices of the old law, and in ſteede therof commanded himſelfe to be offred*, in the euchariſt.

Laſtly S. Cyprian ſpeaking of the fleſh of our ſauiour left to his Churche for a ſacrifice, ſayth, that it was ſo to be prepared that it might continually be offred, leaſt yf it were conſumed (as other fleſh is, that is bought in the market and eaten) it could not ſuffice for all the chriſtian world to ſerue them for an hoſt or ſacrifice of chriſtian religion in ſo much that he affirmeth that *yf it were conſumed, it ſemed ther could be no more religion* ſignifying therby not only the neceſſary concurrence of religion and ſacrifice, whereof I haue ſpoken before, but alſo that the ſacrifice of the maſſe is the proper ſacrifice of the new teſtament, and that the eternity of the ſaid teſtament dependeth vpon the eternity of this ſacrifice, which is the firſt point that (as I vndertook to proue,) doth neceſſarily follow of the eternal prieſthood of Chriſt according to the order of Melchiſedech.

The ſecōd poynt which I gather of Chriſts Prieſt-hood is, that ſeeing he fulfilled the figures of all the bloody ſacrifices oftred by the Prieſts of the order of Aaron (of which order he himſelfe was not) it were abſurd to ſay, that he fulfilled not the ſpecial & proper ſacrifice of Melchiſedech of whoſe order he was.

The proper ſacrifice of Melchiſedech conſiſted in bread

and

and wyne as it appeareth in genesis ; where it is sayd that when Melchisedech went to meete Abraham *protulit* (or as saynt Cyprian also readeth it) *obtulit panē & vinum he brought forth or offred bread and wyne*, and to shew the reason therof it followeth immediatly, *erat enim sacerdos Dei altißimi for he was the Priest of the highest God*, wherby it is signified that bread and wyne were the proper obiects wherein he exer-cised his priestly function and the only matter of his sa-crifice. Ciprian. li.z. epist. z. ad Cecilium.

But for as much as the vnderstanding of this scripture, is much controuersed betwyxt vs and our aduersaries, who deny that Melchisedechs sacrifice consisted of bread and wyne, (which they say he brought forth only to releeue Abraham, and his company, and not to offer to God in sa-crifice) I remit me to the opinion or rather to the vniforme cōsent of the most anciēt & learned fathers of the Churche, who do not only vnderstand this scripture as wee do, but also teach that Christ fulfilled this figure of Melchisedechs sacrifice; at his last super.

Clemens Alexandrinus doth signify that Melchisedech did with some particuler ceremonies consecrat, or dedicat the bread and wyne whiche he gaue to Abraham; for he sayth that he gaue him *panem & vinum , sanctificatam nutri-mentū in typum eucharistiæ, a sanctified or consecrated meate; in figure of the eucharist.* Clem. Alex. lib. 4. Stro-mat.

S. Cyprian sayth, *we see the Sacrament or mistery of our Lords sacrifice præfigured in the priesthood of Melchisedech as the deuine scripture testifieth saying, Melchisedech King of Salem brought foorth bread and wyne, for he was the Priest of the highest God, and blessed Abraham*, & a litle after, he sayth, that our sauiours order of Priesthood was deriued of Melchisedechs sacrifice, for that our sauiour *offred sacrifice to God his Father, and offred the same that Melchisedech offred, to wit bread and wyne, that is to say his body and blood.* Ciprian. li.z. epist. z. ad cæcilium.

S. Augustin speaking of the oblation of Melchisedech whenhe went to meet Abraham. *There appeered first sayth he,*

the

the sacrifice that now is offred to God by Christians throughout the world.

S. Hierome to Marcella sayth *thou shalt fynd in genesis Mel-chisedech King of Salem who euen then offred bread and wyne in figure of Christ, and did dedicate the mistery of Christians consisting in the body and blood of our sauiour.* Thus sayth S. Hierome who teacheth also the same expressely in his epistle to Euagrius, confirming it with the testimony and autority of Hipolitus the ancient martyr, Ireneus, Eusebius Cæsariensis, Eusebius Emissenus, Apollinarius, and Eustathius Byshops of Antioch.

Theodoretus declareth euidently that Melchisedech *brought foorth bread and wyne* both *to God* for sacrifice and also *to Abraham,* for that he fore-saw in Abrahams seede, that is to say in Christ, a true paterne or example of his priesthood, and furder he sayth that Christ fulfilling the figure began to exercise the function of the priesthood of Melchisedech in his last supper; and if I should alleadge all the places of the Fathers that confirme the same I should be too tædious, and therfore I remit those that desyre to see more, to these that follow, vz. Eusebius, S. Ambrose, S. Hierome, S. Aug. S. Chrisostome Primasius, S. Athanasius, Photius Oecumenius, S. Iohn Damascen, Arnobius, and Cassiodorus, and to the most of those that haue written vpon the 109. Psalme.

5. ad Hæbræ. Damascen. lib. 4. de orthod. cap. 14. Arnob. & Cassiodo. in Psalm. 109.

THAT

THAT OVR SAVIOVR

Christ instituted and offred at his last super the sacrifice of his blessed body, and blood, proued by his owne woords, & by the expositions of the Fathers, with a declaration how he is sacrificed in the masse, and lastly that he gaue commission and power to his disciples, to offer his body and blood in sacrifice, that is to say, to say masse.

CHAP. XVI.

IT appeareth by the premisses that the sacrifice of the Churche that is to say the masse was prophesied and foretold by the Prophet Malachias, and prefigured not only by the sacrifice of Melchisedech consisting in bread and wyne, but also by all the sacrifices of the old law, yea & that our sauiour at his last super did exercise his Priestly function according to the order of Melchisedech in instituting and offering the same when he sacrifised his blessed body and blood in formes of bread and wyne, which I wil confirme in this chapter by the words of our sauiour himselfe which he vsed in the institution and oblation therof, saying ; *this is my body which is geuen for you,* and *this is my blood which is or shalbe shed for you, &c.* Luc. 22.
Matth.26.

Wherein it is to be noted, that not only the liturgies of the Apostles and of saynt Basil, saynt Chrisostome, & saynt Ambrose (which last is stil vsed in Milan euer since S. Ambrose his tyme) but also saynt Paule, and all the 3. euangelists that report the words of our sauiour, doe as wel in the Greeke text, as in the Siriac & Caldie, speak all in the present tése, saying *datur, frágitur traditur, fúditur pro vobis & in remissioné peccatorũ,* that is to say, *is geuē, broken, deliuered, & shed, for you, and for the remißion of sinnes,* signifiing that the same was then presently donne in that vnbloody sacrifice, & not that it should be done only afterwards in the sacrifice vpon the crosse, though if wee haue also respect therto, yea and

Liturgia Iacobi. Clemés lib.8.constit. cap.17.
Liturgiæ Basilij Chrisost. & Ambros.
1.Cor. 11.
Matth.26.
Mar.14.
Luc. 22.

N   to the

to the facrifice of the maſſe dayly to be offred in the Churche, it might truly be ſpoken in the future tenſe as our Latin tranſlation of ſaynt Luke hath of the chalice *effundetur* *it ſhalbe ſhed,* though before ſpeaking of the body it hath *datur, it is geuen,* where it is alſo further to be noted, that in the Greeke text of ſaynt Luke, this woord *effunditur* or or rather effuſum eſt, *is ſhed,* hath playne relation to the blood in the chalice, and not to the blood that was to be ſhed on the croſſe for that the woord εκχυνομενον which ſignifieth effuſum is ſpoken of ποτηριον that is to ſay *the cup,* & therfore the text is τουτο το ποτηριον η καινη διαθηκη εν τω αιματι μου το υπερ ημων εκχυνομενον that is to ſay, *this is the cup, the new teſtament in my blood which cup is ſhed for you,* wherby the figure of metonomia, the cup is vſed for the blood in the cup, wherto S. Auguſtin alludeth ſpeaking of the effuſion of our ſauiours blood vpon the altar ; *the body of our Lord* ſaith he *is offred vpon the altar, and therefore the innocents that were killed do woorthely demand reuenge of their blood vnder the altar, vbi ſanguis Chriſti effunditur pro peccatoribus, where the blood of Chriſt is ſhed for ſinners.*

The lyke may alſo be noted of our ſauiours woords concerning his body, as S. Paule reporteth them in the Greek, in which tongue he wrote, where, in ſteede of *this is my body which ſhalbe geuen for you* (as we haue it in the Latin) we read *this is my body* το υπερ ημων κλωμενον *which is broken for you,* which ſaynt Chriſoſtome expounding of our ſauiours body in the Sacrament ſayth, *he is broken for all a lyke, and is made a body for all a lyke;* and furder declareth playnly in an other place, that this cannot be vnderſtood of his body on the croſſe ; for expounding theſe woords of S. Paule in the chapter before, vz. *panis quem frangimus, the bread which wee breake,* he ſayth: *this wee may ſee fulfilled in the euchariſt, & not on the croſſe, but the contrary , for it was ſaid, a bone of him ſhal not bee broken, but that which he ſuffred not vpon the croſſe, he ſuffreth for thee in the oblation, and is content to be broken that he may fil all men.* Thus farre ſaynt Chriſoſtome who is not ſo groſly

to be

Luc. 22.

Aug. ſerm. 4. de innocent.

1. Cor. 11.

Chriſoſt. hom. 1. Cor. 11.

Idem hom. in 1 Cor. 10.

to be vnderstood, as though he should meane that our sauiours bones which were not broken on the crosse, are
broken in the eucharist, with the hurt and greefe of his
person, but that his exceeding bounty towards man is such,
that he is content, not only to take vpon him a sacramental
forme of bread, but also to be handled, broken, and eaten to
the end he may be distributed & made meate to feede and
fil all men, yet so neuertheles that though it may be said as
S. Chrisostome sayth, that he suffreth fraction or breaking
in the Sacrament when it is broken (by reason of his real &
true presence therein) yet he suffreth it without hurt or
diuision of his person, by reason of his impassibilitie and
omnipotency, being whole & perfect in euery part therof
though it be deuided and broken into neuer so many.

This is the meaning of this learned Father, who notably confirmeth therby our doctrin, not only concerning
the verity of Chrifts body in the sacrament, but also concerning our sauiours sacrifice therof at his last super, seeing
his exposition of our sauiours woords admitteth no relation to his sacrifice vpon the crosse, wherupon it followeth
that his body, which as he sayd him selfe *was geuen & broken
for his Disciples*, and his blood which he sayd was *shed for
many, aud for remißion of sinnes*, was then presently geuen and
shed by him, that is to say offred by him in sacrifice.

This is notably confirmed by an other circumstance
that is to be considered in the woords of our Sauiour concerning the promulgatiō of his new law or manifestation
of his new testament in the institution of the Sacrament of
the Eucharist, for as the old testament was dedicated by
the blood of a sacrifice, not to come but then offred to God
when it was promulgat (with the which blood Moyses
sprinkled the people, saying *this is the blood of the testament* Exod.24.
that God hath sent vnto you) so the new Testament was also Hebr.9.
dedicated by the blood of a sacrifice, not to be offred only
after-wards vpon the crosse but then also presently offred
by our sauiour, who therefore alluded euidently to the de-

dication

dication of the old law, and to the verywoords of Moyses, saying *this is my blood of the new Testament*; sanctifying his Churche farre more inwardly and effectually with the blood of his owne sacrifised body; when he gaue it to his Apostoles to drink, then Moyses sanctified the people of the Iewes when he sprinkled them exteriorly with the blood of a sacrificed beast, and therfore saynt Ireneus calleth the Sacrament of the Eucharist *nouam oblationem noui Testamenti the new oblation of the new Testament*, and S. Augustin cauleth it *Sacrificium noui Testamenti, the sacrifice of the new Testament,* and in an other place defyneth it to be a *ryte* or ceremony *commanded by almighty God in the manifestation of the new Testament,*pertayning to the wourship which is due to God alone and called latria, *quo sibi sacrificari precepit, with which ryte or ceremony he commanded sacrifice to be donne to himself,*and S. Chrisostome expounding these woords of our sauiour in saynt Paul. *Hic calix nouum Testamentum est in sanguine meo,this cup is the new Testament in my blood,* compareth euidently the cup of the old Testament with the cup of the new, blood with blood, and sacrifice with sacrifice, saying *the cup of the old Testament was certayne licors, and the blood of brute beasts, for after they had sacrificed* in the old law, *they took the blood in a cup and offred it, and therfore becaufe* Christ *in steede of the blood of brute beasts introduced or brought in his owne blood, hee reneved the memory of the old sacrifice,&c.*

Thus far S.Chrisostome of the woords of our sauiour; and then prosecuting the interpretatio of S.Pauls discours therevpon, he addeth that Saynt Paule represented to the Corinthians our sauiours actio at his super to the end they might be so affected, as though they where sitting at the same table with him *& ab ipso Christo accipientes hoc sacrificium, and as though they receiued this sacrifice of Christ himselfe,* declaring euidently that the sacrifice where with our sauiour did dedicat his testament according to the figure in the old law, was not only offred one the crosse but also at his super; whereof the reason is euident; for at his supper he was a

publyk

publik perfon, a maifter of a family, free and at his owne
liberty to make and publifh his lawes, to affemble his
friends, and witneffes of his wil, and thofe whome he
meant to make his heyres, his vicars, and fubftituts; all
which he did; whereas vpon the croffe, he reprefented no Hæbt. 9.
publik perfon, no maifter of a family, no law maker, nor fo
much as a free man, but feemed the moft abiect and miferable man in the world, forfaken of all men, and therefore
S. Paule teacheth not that he did make, inftitut or publifh
his Teftament vpon the croffe, but that he confirmed it
there by his death, and that from thens forward it tooke
effect, as men ar wont before they dye to make their Teftaments, which when they are dead beginne to be of
force.

And for the furder explication of this queftion it is to
bee confidered, that although the facrifice of the Croffe
was a moft abfolute and perfect cofummation of all facrifices whatfoeuer, and a ful redemption and fatisfaction for
the finnes of the world, yet neuertheleffe it cannot be fayd
properly to haue diftinguifhed the old teftament from the
new, for that it was as I may tearme it, a certayne common and tranfcendent good; indifferent to both ftates and
teftaments, whereto all facrifices as wel of the law of nature and the law of Moyfes, had a relation, as now alfo the
facrifice of the Churche hath in the law of grace, yet with
this difference, as S. Auguftin noteth, that the facrifice of Aug lib. 20.
the croffe was prefigured and promifed to come by the contra faufti
many and fundry facrifices of the old law, and now is re- fide ad Pe-
prefented as paft, by our one and only facrifice of the new trum cap. 19.
law; which facrifice, though it be thefame that our fauiour
offred at his laft fupper, yet it hath a different refpect to the
facrifice of the croffe, for that ours reprefenteth thefame
as already paft, and our fauiours facrifice in his laft fupper,
going before the other vpon the croffe, did not only reprefent thefame to come, but alfo was as it were a preamble
thereto, where in as venerable Bede our cuntryman fayth,

he began by pafsion, for that, as Rupertus affirmeth, *in an-gustia passionis agoniȝans , being already in the Agony and anguish of his passion, he offred himselfe with his owne hands to God his father,* and as Isichius teftifieth, *preuenting his enemies, first sacrifised himselfe in his mististical supper, and after on the Crosse,* wherof S. Leo alfo fayth, that he preuented his death by a voluntary oblation of himfelfe in the Sacrament, and S. Gregorius Niffenus explicating this matter diuinly, fayth thus: *Remember* fayth he *the woords of our Lord to wit, no man shal take my lyfe from me, but I my selfe will geue it, &c. For he which doth geue al things of his owne power and authority doth not expect necessity by treason, nor the violent fury of the Iewes, nor the vniust iudgement of Pilat, that their wickednes, & malice shuld be the beginning of our saluation, but by a secret & ineffable manner of sacrifice, he doth preoccupat or preuent the violence of men by his owne disposition offring himselfe an oblation or sacrifice for vs; being both the priest & the lambe which taketh away the sinnes of the world. But perhaps thou wilt say vnto me when chanced this? euen then when he gaue to his familiar friends his body to be eaten, & his blood to be dronke; for a man cannot eat the sheep, but the slaughter must go before, Therefore when he gaue his body to his disciples to be eaten he did playnly demonstrat and shew, that the lamb was already immolated & sacrificed, for the body of the host whyles it is liuing is not fit to be eaten.* Thus farre this famous Græcian, brother to faynt Bafil, whofe doctrin cócerning the facrifice of our fauiours body before it be eaten, is moft confonant to our fauiours owne woords, not only when he inftituted the holy eucharift (whereof I haue fpoken already) but alfo before, when he promifed it, for that whé foeuer he fpoke therof, he reprefented the fame to the vnderftanding of the hearers, as a body facrificed & dead, not fpeaking of his whole perfon, or of himfelfe as liuing, but of his flefh, of his body, of his blood, *as, my flesh is truly meate, and my blood is truly drink, and the bread which. I wil geue is my flesh, this is my body, this is my blood,* or if he fpoke of himfelfe, or of his perfon, it was with an addition to fhew that he was to be eaten, as when *he*

Beda.
Rupert lib. 2.
in Exodum.

Ifichius in
Leuit. cap. 4.

Leo fermo. 7.
de paffione.

Greg. Niffen.
orat. 4 de re-
furrectione.

Ioan 6.
Matth.

said

fayd he which eateth me lueth for me, which kynd of fpeeche Ioan 6.
made fome of his difciples forfake him, faying it was *durus
fermo, a hard fpeeche*, conceauing therby that they were to
eate him dead, as other flefh bought in the fhambles, wheras
he fpoke in that manner to fignify that he fhuld be facrificed before he fhould be eate, and therefore he euer fpoke of
himfelfe, as already killed and dead, for that no creature
whyles he is liuing, is in cafe to be eaten, as S. Gregory Greg. Niffen.
Niffen doth note very wel, in the place before alledged, in orat. 1. de re-
which refpect Pafchafius alfo fayth, that *our Lord is killed to* furrect.
the end wee may eate him, and Ifichius; that Chrift *killed himfelfe* corpore &
when he fupped with his difciples, not becaufe he is truly mini cap.18.
killed, or doth truly dy; but becaufe he dyeth miftically, that Ifichi.lib. 2.
is to fay, for that his death is miftically and truly reprefen- in leuit. ca. 8.
ted, by the feparation of his blood from his body vnder fe-
ueral and dyuers formes of bread and wyne; for although
by reafon of his immortality, and impafsibilytie he cannot
dy, neyther yet be fo deuided, but that he remayneth
whole vnder both kynds, yet, for as much as the forme of
wyne rather reprefenteth his blood, then his body, and the
forme of bread, rather his body, the his blood (according to
the very woords of our fauiour, faying of the one kynd, *this
is my body*, and of the other, *this is my blood*) it followeth I
fay, that by reafon of this feparation, wrought by the force
of the woordes of confecration he is exhibited in the Sacrament as dead, and fo dyeth in miftery, as wel to reprefent
his death vpon the croffe, as alfo to offer himfelfe in facrifice to his father, for the which it is not of necefsity that
he truly and realy dy, but it fuffifeth that he dy in fome
fort, that is to fay miftically, for although all liuing
creatures that are facrificed are offred to God with the
loffe of their lyues, and fo are made true facrifices, yet
in fuch other creatures, as are not fubiect to death, it fufficeth that they be offred to almighty God, and receiue withall fome notable mutation, or change, to make the action
to be facrifical, and different from a fimple oblation, for
                                                    when

when any thing is offred to God, and remayneth ftil in his owne kynd, forme, and nature, it is called an oblation, & fo the firft fruits, the tythes, the firft begotten, or borne, of liuing creatures, yea and religious perfons, as leuits, and others in the old law were only offred to God, for that they were no way changed, wheras al things facrifyfed were eyther wholy deftroyed or confumed by fwoord, or fyre, or els at leaft receiued by the actiõ of the prieft, fome notable mutation.

Therfore feeing our fauiour being now eternal, immortal, and impafsible is not fubiect to death, nor to any deftruction or mutation by loffe of his lyfe, it fufficeth to make him a true facrifice that he be offred to God with fuch mutation or change, as may ftand with his prefent ftate, and condition; as wee fee he is offred in this facrifice, wherein, the felfe fame body that was borne of the bleffed virgin Mary, and is now in heauen glorified with the proper forme and lineaments of a natural body, is by the omnipotency of our fauiours woords pronounced by the prieft, reprefented vpon the altar as dead, and in formes of bread and wyne, his body to be handled, broken, eaten, and his blood to be dronke, or fhed, as the body or blood of any other liuing creature that is killed in facrifice, wherby he is alfo in fome fort cõfumed, for that his body being eaten and his blood dronke he loofeth the forme, and peculiar mãner of beeing that he hath in the facrament; which beeing deuynes caul Sacramental : in refpect of all which admirable mutations, S. Auguftin doth notably and truly apply to our fauiour in this facrifice the hiftory of King Dauid, when he changed his countenance (as the fcripture fayth) before Abimelech or king Achis (for they are both one) which he fayth, was verifyed in our fauiour Chrift, when he changed his countenance in the priefthood, and facrifice of Melchifedech geuing his body and blood to be eaten and dronk.

There was, fayth he, *a facrifice of the Iewes in beafts, according to the*

Aug. in præ-
fat. Pfalm. 33.
v. lib. Regum
cap. 21.

to the order of Aaron, and that in mistery, and there was not then the sacrifice of the body and blood of our Lord, which the faithful know, and is dispersed throughout the world, and a litle after shewing how Melchisedech brought forth bread and wyne when he blessed Abraham, he teacheth that it was a figure of this sacrifice, & then prosecuting the history how Dauid be ng taken for a mad man, went from Abimelech (which signifieth regnum Patris, that is to say, as he expoundeth it, the people of the Iewes,) he applyeth also the same to our Sauiour, saying that whē he told the Iewes that his flesh was meat, & his blood drinke, they took him for a mad man, and abandoned him, wherevpon he also forsook them, & changing his countenance in the sacrifice of Melchisedech, (that is to say, leauing all the sacrifices of the order of Aarō, and as it were disguysing him-selfe vnder the formes of bread and wyne, which was the sacrifice of Melchisedech) he passed from the Iewes to the Gentils.

This is the effect of S. Augustinus discours in that place concerning the mutation or change incident to our Sauiours person in the sacrament of the Eucharist, and requisit to the sacrifice whereof I treat, wherby it hath the nature of a true sacrifice, as I haue declared before, which being considered, with the circumstances of our sauiours owne woords, as wel in the promise as in the institution thereof, all signifying that his flesh, his body, aud his blood was to be eaten & dronk, as of a creature killed in sacrifice, yea & that the same was then presently geuen or offred by him to his Father for his disciples (who represented the whole Churche) and for remission of sinnes; besyds his manifest allusion to the promulgation of the old Testament, dedicated with the blood of a present sacrifice, and lastly the consent of the learned Fathers of the Churche confirming our Catholyke doctrin in this behalfe, no reasonable man can dout but that our Sauiour at his last super did ordeyn the Sacrament of the Eucharist to serue vs not only for a food and spiritual meate, but also for a sacrifice offring the

O   same

same him-felfe firft to his Father, and then geuing com-
miſsiō and power to his Diſcples to do that which he did,
to wit to offer and ſacrifice the ſame, ſaying *hoc facite in meam*
commemoratione, that is to ſay, *do, make, or ſacrifice this in remem-*
brance of me, for this woord *facite* as wel in the Syriac Hebrew and Greek as in the Latyn, ſignifieth to ſacrifice, no
leſſe then to do or make as in Leuiticus, *faciet vnum pro pec-*
cato, he ſhal ſacrifice one (of the turtle doues) *for remiſſiō of ſinne,*
and in the book of Kings, *faciam bovem alterum, I wil ſacrifice*
the other oxe, & the lyke may be ſeene in diuers other places
of the holy ſcriptures, where the Hebrew & Greek woord
which doth properly ſignify *facere* muſt needs be vnderſtood to do ſacrifice, in which ſence *facere* is alſo vſed
amongſt the Latins, *as cum faciam vitula pro frugibus, &c.* When
I ſhal ſacrifice a calfe for my corne, &c, alſo in Plautus, *faciam tibi*
fideliam mulſi plenam, I wil ſacrifice vnto the a pot ful of ſweete wyne,
and agayne in Cicero. Iunoni omnes conſules facere neceſſe eſt, all the
conſuls muſt needs ſacrifice, to Iuno. But howſoeuer it is, it litle
importeth for the matter in queſtiō whether *facere* do properly ſignify to ſacrifice or no ſeing it is euident that all the
doctors of the Churche do vnderſtād that Chriſt cōmaun-
ding his Apoſtles to do that which he did, commaunded
them to ſacrifice, S.Denis who was conuerted by S.Paul at
Athens, declaring the practiſe of the Churche in his tyme,
ſayth that the Biſhop in the tyme of the holy myſteries, ex-
cuſeth himſelf to almighty God, for that he is ſo bold to
ſacrifice the hoſt that geueth health or ſaluation, aleadging
for his excuſe our Sauiours commandment to wit, hoc facite, do this in my remembrance.

S.Clement in his Apoſtolical conſtitutions ſpeaking to
Prieſts in the name of the Apoſtles, ſayth, *ſuſcitato Domino*
offerte ſacrificium veſtrum de quo vobis pracepit per nos, hoc facite in
meam commemorationem, on eaſter day, When, our Lord is riſen, offer
your ſacrifice, *as he commaunded yow by vs,* ſaying, do this in my remembrance.

Martialis who alſo conuerſed with the Apoſtles, ſayth
that,

that the Chriſtians offred the body and blood of our Sa- Martial.ad Burdegal.
uiour Ieſus Chriſt to lyfe euerlaſting, becauſe *he commaunded*
them to do it in remembrance of him.

Iuſtin the Philoſopher, and Martyr within 140. yeares Iuſtin. in dialog. cum Tripho.
after Chriſt ſayth, that God, who receiueth ſacrifice at the
hands of none but of Prieſts, did foretel by his Prophet, that
thoſe ſacrifices ſhould be grateful to him which Ieſus Chriſt
commaunded to be offred in the Euchariſt.

S. Cyprian ſayth ; *our Lord and God Ieſus Chriſte, is the cheeſe* Cyprian. epiſt 63.ad Cæcilium.
Prieſt, and offred firſt ſacrifice to God the Father and commaunded
that the ſame ſhould be donne in his remembrance S. Chryſoſtome Chriſ hom. 17.in epiſt ad Hebræ.
teaching that the ſacrifice which is dayly offred in the
Churche, ys alwayes one and the ſelf ſame ſacrifice, be it
offred neuer ſo oft, addeth, *that Which We do, is donne in reme-* Aug.lib. 20. contra fauſtũ cap.21 Am-
brance of that Which Was donne by our Sauiour, for he ſayd, do this broſ in c. 10. epiſt. ad He-
in remembrance of me. I omit for breuityes ſake, S. Auguſtin, bræ.Prima-
S. Ambroſe, Primaſius Biſhop of vtica, S. Iſidore, Haymo ſius in ca 10. ad Hebræ.
and diuers others that teſtify in lyke manner, that our Sa- Iſidor lib de
uiour, ſaying to his Apoſtles do this, gaue them cõmiſſion vocatio gen-
and power to ſacrifice, and thus much for the inſtitution of tium.cap 26.
the maſſe by our Sauiour. Haymo in ca. 5.epiſt. ad Hebræ.

O 2   THAT

THAT THE APOSTLES

practysed the commission geuen them by our Sauiours sacrificing or saying Masse them selues, and leauing the vse and practyse therof vnto the Churche, and that the ancient Fathers not only in King Lucius tyme, but also for the first 500. yeares after Christ, teach it to be a true sacrifice, and propitiatory for the liuing and for the dead.

CHAP. XVII.

NOW then to speake breefly of the practyse of the Apostles, and of Gods Churche euer since, It being manifest by that which I haue sayd already, that our Sauiour himselfe did not only institute & offer the sacrifice of his body, and blood at his last super, but also gaue commission and power to his disciples to do that, which he did, it cannot be douted, but that they executed this power and commission, and did not only consecrate and make the body of our sauiour, as he did, but also sacrificed the same.

Therefore whereas we read in the Acts of the Apostles that they vsed to assemble themselues together *ad frangendum panem, to break bread,* it is doutles to be vnderstood, that they offred this sacrifice informe of bread, according to the commission & cōmaundmēt of our Sauiour, & that thesame was the publike ministery wherein the scripture sayth they were occupied, when they were commanded by the holy ghost to segregat Paul and Barnabas, whereof it is sayd, *ministrātibus illis Domino & ieiunantibus, &c. whyles they were ministring to our Lord and fasting &c.* which being in the Greeke λει τουργȣντων δε αντων τω κυριω doth signify the ministery of sacrifice, in which sence λει τουργεω λει τȣργος, and λει τȣργια are taken in the scripture when they are vsed absolutely, and spoken of any publyke and holy ministery

wherof

Actor.20.

Actor.13.

wherof wee haue examples as wel in the epiftle to the Hebrewes in dyuers places, as alfo in the gofpel of S. Luke,
author of the Acts of the Apoftles, who fpeaking of Zacharias the prieft, and of his miniftery or office, which was
to offer facrifice calleth it λει τυργια and therfore *Erafmus* (of
whofe iudgement in iyke cafes our aduerfaries are wont
to make no fmale account) had great reafon to tranflate
the forefayd woords λει τυργουντων δε αυτων, &c. *facrificantibus
illis Domino, &c. as they were facrifycing to our Lord, &c.* and fo
common was this fence & vnderftanding of λειτυργια for facrifice that the grecians haue no other proper woord for
the facrifice of the Maffe.

Furdermore that the miniftery of the Apoftles in brea- 1.Cor.10.
king bread, was a facrifice, it appeareth euidetly by S. Paule,
who to withdraw the Corinthians from facrificing to
Idols, did reprefent vnto them the facrifice which he and
the Apoftles did vfe to offer in the breaking of bread, making a playne antithefis betwyxt the one facrifice and the
other, and comparing the bread which they brake as wel
with the lawful facrifices of the Iewes, as alfo with the vn-
lawful facrifices of the gentils. Of the firft he fayth. *Behold
Ifrael according to the flefo are not thofe which eate of the facrifices* 1.Cor.10.
partakers of the Altar? and agayne fpeaking of the other, *flie,*
fayth he, *from tho woorfhip*, that is to fay, the facrifices of
Idols, and yeilding a reafon, therof, *the cup,* fayth he, *which
wee bleffe, is it not a communication of the blood of our Lord; & the
bread which wee breake, is it not a participation of our Lords body,*
and after more playnly, *thofe things which the gentils do facrifice, they facrifice to deuils, and not to God, I wold not haue yow to be
partakers with deuils, yow cannot drinke the cup of our Lord, and the
cup of deuils, yow cannot be partakers of the table of our Lord, and
the table of deuils, &c.* Thus farre the Apoftle who as yow
fee euidently compareth or rather oppofeth cup to cup,
table to table, Altar to Altar, facrifice to facrifice, and therfore faynt Ambrofe vnderftandeth in this place *the table* Ambrof in
of our Lord to be the Altar, faying, he which is partaker of the table 1. ad cor. 10.
of Deuils,

O 3

of Deuils, *mensa Domini id est altari obstrepit,* doth oppose himselfe against *the table of our Lord, that is to say the Altar,* and saynt

Hilar. in psal. 65.

Hilary expoundeth it to be *mensam sacrificiorum the table of sacrifices.* Also S. Chrisostome vpon these woords *Calix benedictionis the cup of blessing,* and the rest that followeth in the

Chrisost. ho. 24. in 10. cap. 1. epist. ad Cor.

text, sayth in the person of Christ, *if thou desyre blood, sayth he, do not sprinkle the Altar of Idols with the bleod of bruit beasts, but my altar with my blood,* S. Augustin in lyke sort interpreteth

Aug. lib. contra aduers. leg. & Prophet.

this place of the sacrifice of the Churche, saying that S. Paul teacheth the Corinthians, *ad quod sacrificiū debeant pertinere, to what sacrifice they ought to belong,* and Haymo, who wrote about 800. yeres agoe, sayth that *calix benedictionis, the cup of*

Haymo in epist. ad Corinth.

blessing, which S. Paule speaketh of, is that cup which is blessed *a sacerdoribus in Altari, of priests in the altar,* so that if wee consider the circumstances of S. Paules woords with the interpretation of these learned Fathers, it can not be denyed, but that he and the other Apostles in the ceremony of breaking bread, did not only administer the Sacrament of the eucharist to the people (as our aduersaries would haue it) but also offer sacrifice. Which may sufficiently be côfirmed, as wel by the liturgy or masse of S. Iames the Apostle, yet extant, agreeing with ours for as much as concernet the substance of the sacrifice, as also by a constitution of the Apostles mentioned by S. Clement, saynt Peters disciple;

Clem. lib. 2. constit. ca 63.

wherein; they decreed, that nothing should be offred *super Altare, vpon the Altar,* more then our Lord had commaunded: and speaking furder in the same decree of the sunday he signifyeth that they exercysed that day, 3. seueral acts of religion, that is to say. *euangelij prædicationem, oblationem sacrificij, & sacri cibi dispensationem; the preaching of the gospel, oblation of sacrifice, and the distribution of the holy meate,* that is to say the holy eucharist; wherby it is euident that the publyke ministery of the Apostles, consisted not only in preaching and ministring the Sacrament of the eucharist, but also in oblation of sacrifice ; here to I may ad the testimony of saynt Andrew the Apostle. Who being vrged by Egeas the pro-

consul

consul to sacrifice to the fals Gods, answered that he *sacrifi-* Epist. Ec-clesiæ Achaiæ
ced dayly and distributed to the people, the flesh of the immaculat
lambe, as witnesseth the Epistle of the churches of Achaia
declaring the story of his passion; besyds that Epiphanius a
most auncient Father of the Churche doth testify that all
the Apostles did sacrifice, who writing against the sect of Epiphanius hæres. 79.
heretykes called Colliridians and reprehending them
woorthely for hauing certayne women priests that offred
sacrifice to our lady (which could not be offred to any but
to God alone) sayth, it was neuer heard of since the world
beganne that any woman did sacrifice, neither our first
mother Eua, nor any of the holy women in the old Testament, no nor the virgin Mary her selfe, nor the 4. daughters of Philip the deacon though they were prophetesses,
and then, hauing named Zacharias father to saynt Iohn for
one that offred sacrifice in the old law, he addeth, that all
the 12. Apostles (whome he nameth particulerly) did sacrifice; whereof it were a sufficient argument, though
there were no other, that those Fathers who partly liued
with them and receiued of them the Christian fayth, and
partly succeeded them immediatly, do signify not only the
vse of the sacrifice in the Churche in theyr tyme, but also
their constant and most reuerend opinion thereof, as it
may appeare sufficiently by that which I haue already Clemés. li. 5. constit. c. 20.
aleadged out of S. Clement, S. Denis, S. Martial, S. Iustin,
and S. Ireneus, all which do vniformely teach that Christ Dionisius Ec-clesiæ Hie-rarch cap. 3.
deliuered this sacrifice to his Apostles, and the last of them Martial.
to wit S. Ireneus scholer to S. Policarp who was scholer epist. ad Bur-degal. Iustin.
to S. Iohn the Euangelist, sayth, *that the Churche receiuing it of* Dial. cum
the Apostels did offer it throughout the world, in his tyme, which Tripho.
as I haue sayd before was in the tyme of K. Lucius and Irineus. li. 4. aduers. hæres.
therfore I shal not neede to enlarge my selfe furder in this ca. 32. & 34.
matter to produce the testimonies of the later fathers partly because I haue already accomplished my principal intention in this treatyse, which is to proue that king Lucius
could receaue from the Churche of Rome, no other but
                                                              our

our Catholyke Roman fayth as wel in this poynt of the
facrifice of the Maſſe as in all other which wee profeſſe,
and partly becauſe in handling and explicating the prophe-
cies, and figures of the old teſtament, and the actions and
woords of our Sauiour, and of his Apoſtles concerning the
inſtitution vſe and practyſe of this ſacrifice, I haue already
aleadged ſo many playne and euident teſtimonies of the
fathers, that it is needles to aleadge any more. Seeing it is
moſt manyfeſt therby that all thoſe of the firſt 500. yeares
both taught our doctrin in this poynt, and vnderſtood the
ſcriptures concerning the ſame as wee doe, and that they
ſpeake not of this ſacrifice (as our aduerſaries wil needs
vnderſtand them) as of an improper ſacrifice, but in ſuch
ſort, that they euidently ſhew their opinions, of the propriety, verity, and excellent dignity therof: and therſore in
S. Denis ſcholer to S. Paule; it is called; τελε τῶν τελετη, which
Budæus tranſlateth *ſacrificium ſacrificiorum, the ſacrifice of ſa-*
crifices. In S. Cyprian, *verum & plenum ſacrificium, a true and ful*
ſacrifice, which he ſayth, *the prieſt doth offer in the perſon of Chriſt*
to God the Father. In S. Chriſoſtome, *ſacrificium tremendum &*
horroris plenum cæleſte ſummóque venerandum ſacrificium, a dreadful
ſacrifice & ful of horror, a heauenly & moſt reuerend ſacrifice. In
S. Auguſtin, *ſingulare ſummum & veriſſimum ſacrificium, cui*
omnia falſa ſacrificia ceſſerunt, the ſinguler, and the moſt higheſt, and
moſt true ſacrifice, wherto all the *falſe ſacrifices of the gentils haue*
geuen place. In Euſebius, *ſacrificium Deo plenum*, a ſacrifice ful
of God. In S. Iohn Damaſcen *tremendum, vitale ſacrificium, a*
dreadful ſacrifice and geuing lyfe. In Theodoretus, *ſacrificationem*
agni dominici, the ſacrificing of the lambe of God, and in the firſt
general councel of Nice held by aboue 300. Fathers, *ſuum in*
ſacra menſa agnum illum Dei tollentem peccata mundi, incruente a
ſacerdotibus immolatum, the lambe of God placed vpon the holy table,
the which lambe taketh away the ſinnes of the world, and is vn-
bloodily ſacrificed by the prieſts, wherto may iuſtly be added
the doctrin of all the Fathers, that this ſacrifice is propitiatory for the liuing, and for the dead, grounded no dout
vpon

Cyprian.
epiſt. lib. 2.
epiſt. 3. vel
epiſt. 63 ad
Cæcil.
Chriſoſt. ho.
60. ad popul.
& ho. in
pſal. 95.
Aug. lib. 10.
de ciuit. cap.
20. & lib. de
ſpiritum &
litera. ca. 11.

In tomo con-
cil lib. 3. de
conſtir. Ni-
cæn. conc.
conſtit. 6.

vpon the woords of our sauiour himselfe in his first institution, and oblation therof, when he said to his Apostles
representing the whole Church *this is my body which is geuen
pro vobis* for you, that is to say, for remission of your sinnes
and more playnly, in oblation of the cup, *this is my blood which
is shed pro vobis,* or as saynt Math. sayth *pro multis in remissione*   Matth. ca. 26.
peccatorum, for you & for many to the remission of sinnes. for this
cause saynt Iames the *Apostle* in his liturgy saith *offerimus tibi
wee offer to thee* o Lord *the vnbloody sacrifice for our sinnes, and the
ignorance of the people,* and saynt Martial the most ancient   Martial ad
martyr who as I haue sayd liued with the Apostles, affir-   Burdegalens.
meth that by the remedy of this sacrifice lyfe is to be geuen
vs, & death to be eschewed, and S. Denis a foresaid cauleth   Dionis. lib. de
it *salutarem hostiam, the host or sacrifice that geueth health or salua-*   Ecclesiast.
                                                                Hierar. cap. 3.
tion, S. Athanasius sayth that the oblation of the vnbloody   S. Athanas.
host is *propitiatio, a propitiation* or remission of sinnes. Origin   allegat. a Da-
                                                                masceno. in
cauleth it *the only commemoration which makes God mercyful*   serm. pro de-
to men.   functis.
                                                                Origen hom.
    S. Cyprian termeth it *medicamentum & holocaustum ad sa-*   13. in Leuit.
nandas infirmitates, & purgandas iniquitates, a medicin & burnt sa-   Cyprian de
crifice for the healing of infirmityes and the purging of sinnes.   cœn. Domini

    S. Ambrose speaking of the Eucharist sayth that Christ   Ambros. lib.
offreth him selfe therin quasi sacerdos, vt peccata nostra dimittat, as   de offic. cap.
a Priest that he may forgeue our sinnes.   48.

    S. Augustin considering that all the sacrifices of the old   August. in
law were figures of this sacrifice, (as he often affirmeth,) &   Leuit qu. 57.
that amongst infinit others, there were some that were
called hostiæ pro peccato, sacrifices for remission of sinne.
By the sacrifices saith he, *that were offred for sinnes, this one of ours, is
signified wherein is true remission of sinne,* and to ad somewhat   Iacobus in
more hereto concerning the custome of Gods Churche to   sua liturg.
offer this sacrifice also as propitiatory for the dead S. Iames
the Apostle in his liturgy prayeth to almighty God that the
sacrifice may be acceptable vnto him for remission of the
peoples sinnes and for the repose of the soules of the dead,   Clement.
also saynt Clement teacheth for a constitution of the   const. Apost.
                                                                lib. 6.
    P   Apostles

Chrif.hom.
3. in epift. ad
Philip. Item
hom 41 in
epift 1. ad
Corinth.
Idem hom.
69 ad popul.
antioch
Greg niffen
allegatus a
Ioan Damaf-
ceno in ora-
tione pro de-
functis.

Ioan. Damaf-
ceno in ora
tione pro de-
functis.

Tertulli li.de
caftita.
Item lib. de
monogam.li.
de corona
militis.

Cypri.epift.
66.

Catech. 5.
miftago-

Aug de ver-
bi, Apofto-
li, ferm. 22.
vel fe. ūdum
alios 34.

Cap. 12.

Apoftles to offer the holy Eucharift in Churches, and Churchyards for the dead. S. Chrifoftome alfo often affirmeth it for a decree of the Apofties to offer facrifice for the dead, faying ; *it was not rafhly decreed by the Apoftles that in the moft dreadful myfteries there fhould be commemoration made of the dead, for when the people, & clergy ftand with their hands lifted vp to heauen, & the reuerend facrifice fet vpon the Altar, how is it poffible that praying for them, wee fhould not pacify the wrath of God towards them.* S. Gregory Niffen in lyke manner proueth the vtility and profit therof, by the authority of the Difciples of Chrift that taught & deliuered the cuftome to the Churche as witnefeth faynt Iohn Damafcen, who affirming it to be an Apoftical tradition, confirmeth the fame with the teftimonies of S. Athanafius, and faynt Gregory Niffen.

Tertullian often maketh mention of oblations offred for the dead yerely in their anniuerfaries, aleadging it amongft dyuers other for an ancient cuftome, and vnwritten tradition of the Churche.

S. Cyprian alfo mentioneth a conftitution made before his tyme that for fuch as make Priefts their executors or tutors to their Children, no oblation or facrifice fhould be offred after their death, which ftatute he ordayned fhould be executed vpon one called victor that had offended againft the fame.

S. Cyril Byfhop of Hierufalem, hauing fpoken of other parts of the facrifice of the maffe, fayth ; *then wee pray for all thofe that are dead, beleeuing that their foules, for whome the prayer of the dreadful facrifice is offred receiue very great help therby.*

S. Auguftin fayth that according to the tradition of the ancient fathers the whole Church vfeth to pray, and offer the facrifice of the bleffed body and blood of Chrift for thofe that are dead, and that it is not to be douted but that they are helped thereby, and in his book of confefsions he fignifieth, *that the facrifice of our redemption,* that is to fay the bleffed body and blood of our Sauiour was offred for his mothers foule when fhee was dead.

S. Gregory

S. Gregory the great to declare the excellent effect of the sacrifice of the masse, offred for the dead, telleth of one that being taken prisoner in the warre, and thought to be dead was deliuered on certayne dayes of the weeke of his chaynes, and fetters, which fel from him so oft as his wyfe caused the sacrifice of the masse to bee offred for his soule, and of this S. Gregory taketh witnes of many of his auditors whome (as he sayth) he presumed did know the same. *Homil. 37. in euangelia.*

The lyke also in euery respect recounteth venerable Bede our countryman in the story of England (which he wrote about 800. yeares agoe) of one Imma seruant to King Elbuin, which Imma being prisoner in the hands of his enemies and chayned, could not be tyed so fast, but that his chaynes fel of once a day, at a certayne hower, when his brother, called Iunna an Abbot, sayd masse for him, thinking he had ben slayne, and this sayth saynt Bede he thought good to put into his history, for that he took it for most certayne, hauing vnderstood it of credible persons that had heard the party tel it to whome yt happened. *Beda Eccles. hist. Angl. li. 4. cap. 22.*

To conclude, this custome of offring the blessed sacrifice of the masse for the dead, was inuyolably kept in the Churche of God, euen from the Apostles tyme without contradition, vntil Aerius an Arrian heretyke impugned the same & all prayer for the dead about 360. yeres after Christ, for the which he is put in the Catologue of heretykes by saynt Augustin, & S. Epiphanius, as our aduersaryes deserue also to be for teaching and defending the same hæresy. *Aug. hær. 53. Epipha. hære. 75.*

AN

AN ANSVVERE TO THE

obiections of our aduersaries out of S. Paules epistle to the Hebrewes, with a declaration that the heretykes of this tyme, who abolish the sacrifice of the Masse, haue not the new Testament of Christ, and that they are most pernitious enemies to humain kynd.

CHAP. XVIII.

BV T now our aduersaries against vs, or rather against these expresse scriptures and Fathers, obiect some texts and arguments of S. Paule to the Hebrewes, by the which he conuinceth the ignorance, and error of the Iewes who conceaued that their was no other redemption then that which was obtayned by their sacrifices of beasts or of fruits of the earth, *obseruantes*, sayth S. Augustin, *signa pro rebus ipsis nescientes quo referrentur, taking the figures or signes of things, for the thinges themselues not knowing whither they were to be referred,* and therfore S. Paul proueth that this absolut perfection which they ascrybed to their sacrifices, could not be found in the priesthood & sacrifices according to the order of Aaron but in the sacrifice & priesthood according to the order of Melchisedech, which he declareth by euident arguments grounded vpon the vnity and excellency as wel of the priest, and host or sacrifice, as of the act of oblation, shewing the infirmity of the priests by their mortality, plurality and continual necessity to offer dayly, first for their owne sinnes, and after for other mennes, whereas in the other of Melchisedech, he sayth, there was a priest, that is to say our Sauiour Christ, who had an eternal priesthood, and therfore needed no successor, and being vnpolluted and without sinne had no neede to offer sacrifice for himselfe, and so was more fit and worthy to obtayne pardon for the sinnes of the people; and as for the hosts or sacrifices he sheweth also the infirmity

thereof,

thereof, for that they were but only of brute beafts, and in that refpect could not be of that infinit valew, that was requifit for an abfolute and general redemption, whereas the facrifice in the priefthood of Melchifedech was of infinit price, being the body of our Sauiour offred voluntarily by himfelfe, who was both the facrifice, & the prieft. Laftly he proueth alfo the infufficiency of the facri- Cap. x. fices, by the continual and dayly oblation therof, for that fayth he, yf they could haue made perfect fuch as offred them, *ceßaßent offerri, there would haue ben an end of offring them,* for *vbi eft peccatorum remißio, iam nõ eft oblatio pro peccatis, where there is remißion of finnes, there needeth no oblation for finne.* But our Sauiour by his facrifice vpon the croffe, *vnica oblatione consummauit in æternum fanctificatos, did consummat* or make per- Cap. 7. fect *for euer, all thofe that are fanctified with one only oblation,* for otherwyfe, fayth he, he muft haue fuffred oftentymes, which as wel for the excellent dignity of the prieft, as for the infinit valew of the hoft, was needles.

Thus argued S. Paule againft the Iewes, which our ad-uerfaries do abfurdly wreft againft the facrifice of the Maffe, faying that the fame is wholy ouerthrowen by the fame argumèts, not only in refpect of the multitude of our priefts, but alfo for our dayly oblations, and becaufe wee attribut remifsion of finne thereto, which they fay, S. Paule afcribeth only to the facrifice of the croffe. For the ful an-fwere and fatisfaction of this cauil, it is to be vnderftood, firft that S. Paule doth not impugne by thefe arguments any facrifice whatfoeuer, but only the facrifices of the the priefthood of Aaron, neither yet he impugneth thofe in fuch fence that he denyeth them to be true facrifices, but only proueth by the infirmity thereof, and of the priefts that offred them, that they could not fuffice for the perfect fanctification, and iuftification of man, nor for the general redemption of the world, to which purpofe he fayth of Heb. cap. 7. the priefthood of Aaron, *if there were,* fayth he, *confumation* or perfection *by the leuitical prieft-hood, what needed there to ryfe*

a prieft

a priest according to the order of Melchisedech, and agayne, *the law could bring nothing to perfection, but was an introduction to a better hope, &c.* and speaking of the sacrifice of our Sauiour vpon the crosse, he fayth that *he entred once into the holyes, hauing found æternal redemption, not by the blood* of goats or calues, but by his owne blood, and agayne *with one oblation he did consummat for euer all those that are sanctified ;* by all which he geueth to vnderstand that where as mankynd was by the falle of our Father Adam made a bondman and slaue of sinne, and subiect to the penalty of eternal danation he therefore needed some effectual meanes as wel to redeeme, and free him from this penalty, as also to cleare him from sinne, to sanctify him and iustify him (all which he comprehendeth in the woord consummation) and this I say, he sheweth, could not be performed by the blood of goats and calues, but by the blood of a sacrifice of infinit price and valew, that is to say of Iesus Christ God and man, who therfore he fayth, not only purchased for man euerlasting redemption from damnation, but also did consummat or make perfect for euer all those that that are sanctified, that is to say he purchased perfection of grace, sanctification and iustification, for all those that euer were iust from the beginning of the world ; or euer shalbe to the end thereof, and therefore what benefit soeuer any of the faythful receiued in this kynd eyther by any sacrifice or by any good woorke in the law of nature, or in the law of Moyses S. Paule attributeth the same to the merit of Chrifts sacrifice vpon the crosse, for that none were euer iustifyed before Christ, but *perfidem futuræ passionis, sicut nos per fidem præterita,* by the fayth, sayth saint Augustin, of his passion to come as wee are iustifyed by the fayth of his passion past, in which respect the scripture sayth *agnus occisus est ab origine mūdi, the labe was killed from the beginning of the world,* that is to say, the death of the lambe, which was Christ, hath alwayes had his operation and effect from the beginning of the woorld : so that S. Paules doctrin is no other but that the redemption, iustification,

Ibidem.
Hebr.ca 9.
Hebr.10.

Aug.li.confessio.10.cap. 43.
Apoc.13.

fication, and faluation of man, cannot be afcribed to the
merit of any facrifice or of all the facrifices of the old law,
but to the merit of the facrifice of our Sauiour vpon the
croffe, once offred for all, to the which all other facrifices
haue relation, it being abfolute of it felfe, and depending of
no other.

But what proueth this againft the Catholyks concerning the facrifice of the maffe? doth it proue that it is no
facrifice? or that it is not propitiatory for finne? nothing
leffe; for yf the facrifices of the priefthood according to the
order of Aarō, reprefenting the facrifice of the croffe, were
true facrifices, though they were but of brute beafts, why
may not our facrifice according to the order of Melchifedech be alfo a true facrifice? being not only a far more
excellent reprefentation, of the facrifice of the croffe then
the others were, but alfo the very fame in fubftáce, to wit,
the bleffed body of our Sauiour him-felfe, and therefore of
infinit pryce, and valew, though neuertheles it was not ordayned for the redemptiō of the world, (as was the bloody
oblation of the fame body vpon the croffe,) but for an vnbloody reprefentation of that bloody facrifice, yea and for a
perticular application, of the benefit thereof, to all thofe
that fhould worthely offer it or participat of it.

For it is to be confidered that the facrifice of the croffe Aug. fer
profper. in
libel artic.
was as S. Auguftin calleth it a general cup, or vniuerfal
medicin, propofed to all the world in common, but not falfo impofi,
artic.1.
applyed to any in particuler, the application whereof was
left by almighty God to fuch other meanes as it pleafed
him to ordayne for that purpofe, no les now in the new
law, then he did before in the old, as wee fee by effect not
only in this facrifice, but alfo in the facraments of baptifme
and pennance, in fayth, prayer, fafting, almes, and other
good woorks, all which are meanes to apply the fruits of
our Sauiours pafsiō vnto vs (as our aduerfaries do not deny
of there fpecial faith, without the which they do not think
that the pafsion of Chrift is beneficial to any,) for otherwyfe.

wyfe it would follow, that all men fhould be faued a lyke, becaufe Chrift dyed for all a lyke.

If therefore there be facraments, and other meanes to apply the fruit of our fauiours pafsion vnto vs, without preiudice to the honour therof, why may there not be alfo a facrifice to that end, efpecially fuch a facrifice as this, which as I haue fayd is not only a moft liuely reprefentation of the other vpon the croffe, but alfo the very fame in fubftance, though different in the manner of the oblation ; and agayn feing the fruit of our Sauiours facrifice vpon the croffe hath had his cours, effect, and operation from the beginning of the world, as I fignified before and yet neuertheles there was both in the law of nature and in the law of Moyfes *hoftia pro peccato, facrifice for finne.* Why may there not now alfo be a facrifice for remifsion of finnes, efpecially feing our dayly finnes, do no leffe require now a dayly remifsiõ then did the finnes of thofe that were vnder the law of Moyfes.

This faynt Paule feemeth to infinuate fufficiently in thofe very woords which our aduerfaries do moft vrge Hebr. cap. 8. agaynft this poynt, to wit, *where there is, remifsion of finnes ther no oblation or facrifice for finne is needful,* where vpon I fay it followeth, that where there is not remifsion of finne, there needeth facrifice for finne.

Therefore to anfwere our aduerfaries, and to explicat this text I fay that S. Paule fpeaketh of fuch remifsion of finne, as was purchafed for mankynd in general by the general redemption of all, and not of the particuler application therof to any, and therefore in that fence he fayth, that the general ranfome for finne being payed, and remiffion therof being in general procured by the facrifice of the croffe, it were needles that eyther the fame or any fuch general facrifice, fhould be offred agayne ; But feing the particuler application therof is needful for the remifsion of finne, no leffe now, then it was in the old law, yt foloweth that fome facrifice is now as needful as then it was, where
vpon

vpon Primasius S. Augustins scoller expounding this same
epistle of saynt Paule to the Hebrewes, sayth ; *our Priests do*
offer sacrifice dayly because wee need dayly to be clensed, and for as
much as Christ cannot dy, he therfore gaue vs the Sacrament of his
body and blood, to the end that as his passion was the redemption and
saluation of the world that is to say of all men in general, *so also*
this oblation may be a redemption and clensing to all those that offer it
in verity, thus sayth he ; geuing to vnderstand that the benefit of our redemption and remission of sinne purchased
for all men in general by the sacrifice of the crosse, is by
this other sacrifice particulerly applyed to euery one that
woorthely offreth thesame, so that the dayly iteratiõ therof is nolesse needful, then conforme to the doctrin of S.
Paule, who denieth not the sacrifices of the old law to be
true sacrifices because they were dayly offred, but to be, as I
may tearme it, that redemptory & absolut sacrifice, which
was to be offred but once ; wherevpõ it followeth that the
obiections of our aduersaries out of S. Paule as wel concerning the multiplicity and succession of our Priests, as the
multitude and iteration of masses, are most absurd and friuolous, for though wee should grant it to bee true (as it is
most fals) that eyther wee haue such a succession or multiplicity of Priests or such variety of hosts and sacrifices in
our masse as was in the old law, yet S. Paules argument
would proue no more against vs, then it did against the
Iewes, I meane it would not follow theron, that the masse
is no sacrifice, no more then it followeth of the same argument, that the sacrifices of the Iewes were not true sacrifices, which S. Paule neuer denied, but it would follow that
the masse should not be that absolut and independant sacrifice which was to redeeme the woorld, the which wee
deny not and therfore this their obiection out of saynt
Paule proueth nothing but their owne blyndnes, or malice
that do not or wil not vnderstand eyther him, or vs, in this
matter.

But to satisfy this poynt more fully, it is to be considered
that the

Primatius in
epist. ad
Hæbræ.

Q

that the multitude of our Priefts doth no more contradict the vnity of Chrifts prieft-hood, then the multitude of Doctors & Paftors in the Churche, (by whome he feedeth & teacheth the fame)doth contradict the vnity of his Paftoral office and dignity, In which refpect faynt Paule fayth *pro* *Chrifto legatione fungimur tanquam Deo exhortante per nos, that is to fay Wee are Embaffadours or delegats of Chrift ; for God, as it were doth exhort by vs.*

2. Corinth. cap. 5.

To which purpofe it is to be vnderftood, that our Priefts are not abfolute of themfelues, and indepédant, as were the Priefts in the old law, who fucceeded one an other in equal power and dignity, (I meane the high Priefts of whome only S. Paule fpeaketh) for though Aaron was the firft, yet euery fucceffor of his was as abfolute as he, and not depédant of him, in which fence faynt Paule calleth them many, becaufe being euery one an abfolute head of himfelfe, fucceding one an other, they grew in tyme, to a great multitude of heads to whome he therfore oppofeth the vnity of Melchifedechs prieft-hood confifting in the one and only perfon of Chrift, whofe fubftitutes and minifters our Priefts are (and not his fucceffors)offring facrifice, and executing their function in his name and as S. Cyprian fayth *vice illius, as his Vicars.* And although Chrift as head, cheefe Prieft, and general Paftor of his Churche, doth concurre particularly with his members and minifters in the execution of their Prieftly and Paftoral charge, yet he doth it in nothing fo particularly and properly as in this facrifice by reafon of his true and real prefence therein, being not only offred by the Prieft but alfo voluntarily offring himfelfe to his Father, *offertur vt homo,* fayth faynt Ambros, *quafi recipiens pafsionem, & offert fe ipfe quafi facerdos, he is offred as man, and as receiuing or fuffring his pafsion, and he offreth him-felfe as Prieft,* in which refpect he is both Prieft and facrifice as wel now on the altar, as he was in his pafsion vpon the croffe, though for our greater comfort he vfeth alfo therein the interuention and miniftery of Priefts, who being nothing

Cypri. epift. 43. ad cæcilium.

Ambrof. li. 1. de officijs. ca. 42.

els but

els but his inftruments, and exercyfing all one Prieftly function, vnder him their head, do all pertayne to that one
æternal Prieft-hood of Chrift according to the order of
Melchifedech, which as Lactantius fayth, muft of necefsity
be in the Churche. *Iefus Chrift* fayth he, *being a Prieft did make* Lactant lib.
4 inftit. c 14.
for him felfe a great æternal temple, that is to fay the Churche,
in quo templo æternum facerdotium habeat neceffe eft fecundum or-
dinem Melchifedech, in which temple he muft needs haue an æternal
Prieft-hood according to the order of Melchifedech, fo that the vnity
of Chrifts prieft-hood is not impeached by the multitude of
his minifters, no more then the vnity of a Kings monarchy
by the multitude of his inferiour officers by whome he gouerneth.

And as for the multitude of maffes which our aduerfaries
carp at, as reiected by S. Paule the Fathers of the Churche
fhal anfwer for vs, S. Chrifoftome expoüding this epiftle of
S. Paule anfwereth this very fame obiection that our ad-
uerfaries make agaynft vs; *This facrifice* fayth he *is an example* Chrif. ho 17.
in epift ad
Hebræ.
of that facrifice vpon the croffe, for wee alwayes offer the very felf
fame thing, not now one lambe and another to morrow, but the very
fame ; therefore this is one facrifice; for otherwyfe becaufe it is offred
in many places, there fhould be many Chrifts, thus farre faynt
Chryfoftome.

The very fame argument and reafon, and the very lyke
woords vfeth faynt Ambrofe to proue the vnity of this fa-
crifice and concludeth, *non enim aliud facrificium, ficut pontifex* Ambrof. in
epiftol. ad
Hæbræ.
veteris legis fed idipfum femper offerimus, we offer not an other or dif-
ferent facrifice as did the Bifhop of the old law, but wee alwayes offer
the felf fame. Alfo Primafius, *the diuinity* fayth he, *of the fonne of*
God, which is euery where, doth caufe that they be not many facrifices
but one, though they be offred by many, & it caufeth in lyke man- Primafius in
9. ad Hæbræ.
ner that *it is that body which was conceaued in the virgins wombe*
and not many bodyes, as alfo that it is but one facrifice, and not dyuers,
as were the facrifices of the Iewes, Thus fayth he.

We read the very fame in fubftance, in Theopilac-
tus, Oecumenius Sedulius, Haymo and others that haue
written

Theophilas
Oecumen.
Sedulius
Haymo, in c.
10 epist. ad
Hebiz.

written vpon faynt Paules epiftle to the Hebrewes, of
whome the meaneft may in any indifferent mannes iudgement, counteruayl all the fectaryes of this tyme, who framing new fantafies of their owne braynes, or reuiuing old
herefyes, are forced for the mayntenance therof, to wring
and wreft the holy fcriptures from the meaning of the
holy ghoft to their priuat fence, and to côdemne the iudgement of all the anciét fathers of the Churche; who liuing in
fuch tymes as thefe matters were not in controuerfy, can
not be fufpected of parciality, and much leffe of ignorance
of the fcriptures, feing their learned commentaries and ex-
pofitions thereof geue fufficient teftimony of their continual trauails & labours therin, befydes that their moft vertuous lyues led in continual prayer, penance and religious
difcipline (for the which the Chriftian world admireth,
and honoreth them as great feruants of God and faynts,)
is a fufficient argumét, that God rather afsifted them with
his fpirit in the vnderftáding of the fcripture, then Martin
Luther, Zwinglius, Beza, Caluin and fuch other flagitious,
and wicked apoftatats, whofe vicious and leud lyues
(whereof the world is yet a witnes) do manifeftly declare, with what kynd of fpirit, they were poffeffed.

Therefore he that would leaue the general confent of al
the ancient fathers, to follow the phantaftical or rather
phrenetical opinions of thefe new fangled fellowes, deferu-
eth to be deceiued, and can haue no excufe of wilful
blyndnes eyther before God or the world.

But now to conclude this queftion concerning the facrifice of the Maffe I draw out of all the premiffes 4. con-
clufions.

The firft is that, which at the firft I vndertook to proue,
to wit, that the oblation of the bleffed body and blood of
our Sauiour Iefus Chrift (which wee caul the Maffe) ys
the proper facrifice of the new teftament, prophefied by
Malachias, prefigured by the facrifice of Melchifedech,
promifed, inftituted and offred, by our Sauiour, practifed
by his

by his Apostles, and by the Churche euer since.

The second is, that it is propitiatory not only for the liuing but also for the dead.

The third, that the heretykes of this tyme that contradict & abolish thesame, hold not the law of the new Testament instituted by Christ, seing they haue not the proper priesthood and sacrifice therof, without the which the sayd law and Testament cannot be, S. Paule teaching such a necessary concurrence of the one with the other, that he affirmeth, that *the priesthood being translated the law must also of necessity be translated* as I haue shewed before, therfore seeing they haue not this priesthood and sacrifice, it followith they haue not the law and Testament of Christ, which can not be without thesame. `Hebr.7.`

The fourth poynt that followeth of the premisses, is that they are most pernicious enemies of humainkind, seing they labour to depriue vs, of the most souerain remedy that God of his infinit goodnes hath left vs for the reparation of our dayly wracks by sinne, and for the consolation both of the quick and the dead; for which cause the old Christians in the persecutions vnder Dioclesian, being persecuted for hearing masse, as wee are now (as I haue shewed in the beginning of this treatise) answered the tyrants that the masse was *spes salusque Christianorum, the hope and health, or saluation of Christians*, and that therfore they could not forgo it, the reason wherof I haue declared before, to wit, for that therby are aplyed vnto vs the fruits of our Sauiours passion which is not only represented, but also dayly renewed in the sacrifice of the masse as witnesseth saynt Gregory; *so often*, sayth he, *as wee offer the host of his passion, so often wee renew his passion*, and as saynt Cyprian sayth, *passio Domini est sacrificium quod offerimus, the sacrifice which wee offer is the passion of our Lord*. Lastly; Martialis the most ancient martir and Disciple of Christ sayth, *that which the Iewes did sacrifice vpon the Altar of the crosse, wee do propose on the sanctified altar for our saluation, knowing that by that only remedy lyfe is to be geuen vs,* `Baron. an. 303. Surius. 11. Februar.` `Greg. hom. 37. in euagel.` `Epist. 63. ad cæcilium.` `Epist. ad Burdegalen.`

and death

and death to be eschewed, thus far the blessed martyr. This
remedy I say the heretykes of these our dayes doe seek by
their pestilent doctrin to take from vs, yea and do in deed
depryue vs of it in our country, not only by their doctrine,
but also by rigorous and violent lawes, resembling therin
as wel the old persecutors of Gods Churche that did the
lyke, as also Antichrist that is to come, who as Daniel the
Prophet fortelleth shal take a way *iuge sacrificium, the cõtinual*
sacrifice of the Churche, which is the sacrifice of the masse) and
the ancient Byshop and martyr Hypolitus doth testify in
his book of the consummation of the world, that in the
tyme of Antichrist, *Churches shalbe lyke cottages, and that the*
precious body and blood of Christ shal not be in those dayes, the liturgy
shalbe taken a way, the singing of the Psalmes shal ceasse and the
reading of the scripture shal not be heard, thus farre saynt Hipolitus, that wrote within 250. yeares after Christ.

Seing then the Caluinists, and Lutherans abolish the sacrifice of the masse, yea and bring christian religion to a
very desolation and ruine, ouerthrowing altars, churches,
monasteries, images, relickes of saynts, the signe of the
crosse, sacraments, ceremonies and all external memories,
and monuments of christianity, and in steed of the blessed
body and blood of our sauiour, bring into the churche nothing but a bare signe therof, what els are they but true figures, or the forerunners of Antichrist, that shal set vp the
abomination of desolation in the temple of God, as sayth the Prophet, that is to say, shal bring an abominable desolation
vpon the Churche and true religion of Christ ?

Dan. 9.

Hipol. in
orat. de con-
sum. mundi

Danielis c. 9.

OVR

OVR DOCTRIN OF THE

*merits of woorkes and Iuſtification , is proued and
cleared, from the ſlanders of our aduerſaries, commonly
publyſhed in their Sermons, and lately inſinuated in a
book ſet forth, concerning the conuiction of my Lord of
Eſſex.*

CAP. XIX.

FOR as much as my intention in this treatiſe was to
detect and confute, certayn ſlanderous lyes of our aduerſaryes, ſpread abroad agaynſt vs in ſome of theyr
late bookes and lybels, no leſſe touching matter of
religion, then matter of ſtate, I can not forbeare to diſcouer
vnto thee here good reader, their notable impudency in
charging vs to be enemies of the Paſsion of Chriſt, and to
euacuate the merits therof, by aſcribing our ſaluatiō to our
owne workes, which they are wount to publiſh in their
ſermons, and common table talke, and haue of late inſinuated in a pamphlet concerning the conuiction of my
Lord of Eſſex, wherein treating of Sir Chriſtofer Blunt,
that he proteſted to dy a Catholyke, ſome fooliſh miniſter
(I think) foyſted in an aparentheſis, ſignifying that he dyed
not ſuch a Catholyk, but that he hoped to be ſaued by the
merits of Chriſts paſsion, not aſcribing his ſaluation to his
owne workes ; as though other Catholykes that teach
merits of workes, did not hope to be ſaued by the paſsion of
Chriſt, wherin I know not whether I ſhould wounder
more at their ignorance, or their malice ; their ignorance if
they know not what we hold , and their malice if they
know it, and yet ſlander vs.

For who knoweth not, that wee acknowledge the bleſſed paſsion of our Sauiour to be the root and ground of
our redemption, and reconciliation to God, and the fountayne from whence floweth all our iuſtification , and
ſalua-

1.Petri c 1
Ep ad Rom.
cap.5.

A&.4.
Pſalm.125.

Ioan.3.

Ep. ad Hebr.
5.
Ep. ad Rom.
cap.2.

Ep.Iacob c.1

Matth.cap.7.

ſaluation, ſaying with S.Peter that *we are redeemed with the precious blood of Chriſt the immaculat lambe*, and with S.Paule that *wee are iuſtified in his blood, & ſhalbe ſaued from wrath by him*, and that *there is no other name wherein wee can be ſaued, but the name of* IESVS; neuertheleſſe wee know withall that though his paſsion, be moſt meritorious, & the redemption that wee haue therby moſt copious, yet it was his wil that wee ſhuld doe ſomewhat of our parts, to haue the benefit therof, which our aduerſaries cannot but grant, confeſsing as they doe, that to be partakers therof they muſt be baptyſed, they muſt beleeue, they muſt repēt after they haue ſinned, & ſeeing vpon the warrāt of the holy ſcriptures they ad all this to the paſsion of Chriſt, without derogation to the dignity therof, what reaſon haue they to blame vs, if vpon the ſame warrant we ad another condition no leſſe expreſſe in ſcripture then any of the reſt, ſeeing our ſauiour himſelfe ſayth, *if thou wilt enter into lyfe keepe the commaundments*, to which purpoſe S.Paule alſo ſayth, *omnibus obtemperantibus ſibi factus eſt cauſa ſalutis*, that is to ſay, *he was made a cauſe of ſaluation to all ſuch as obey him*, and in another place, *the dooers of the law ſhalbe iuſtified before God, and not the hearers only*, and S.Iames, *wee think a man to be iuſtified by workes, and not by faith only*, and our Sauiour himſelfe; *not euery one*, ſayth he, *that ſayth to mee Lord, Lord, ſhal enter into the kingdome of heauen, but he which doth the wil of my Father*, by all which wee ſee that good workes are neceſſary to ſaluation, and muſt concurre therto, with the merits of Chriſts paſsion, which being the root & fountayne of all mannes merit, giueth as it were lyfe and force, both to fayth, and alſo to the good workes of faythful men to make them meritorious before God, wherin three things are to be noted, for the better explication of this matter.

The firſt is; that there is two manners of iuſtification, the one, the iuſtification of the wicked man be he infidel or chriſtian in mortal ſinne, the other the iuſtification of the iuſt man, or an increaſe of Iuſtice; the firſt proceedeth merely

rely of the grace of God without merit of workes, for that it is not in the power of nature being auerted and alienat from God to conuert it selfe vnto him, without his grace & vocation, & therfore S. Paule worthely excludeth frō the first iustificatiō both of the Iewes, & the gentils all merit of man. The second, which is the iustification of the iust man, or encrease of Iustice, is procured by good woorkes proceeding of Gods grace, without the which their can be no iustification, and therfore the Catholikes do teach not only the precedence of Gods grace before euery good woork, according to that of the prophet *misericordia eius praueniet me, his mercy shal preuent or goe before me,* but also the concurrence therof, according as S. Paule sayth, *non ego sed gratia Dei mecum, not I but the grace of God with me,* and as our Sauiour sayth, *sine me nihil potestis facere, without me you can do nothing,* and agayne S. Paule, *omnia possum in eo qui me comfortat, I can do all things in him that strengthneth or comforteth me;*

Of the first iustification S. Paule sayth in diuers places that wee are *iustified gratis, freely or for nothing, by the grace of God, by fayth, and not by woorkes,* as meritorious, and of the second he sayth (speaking of the effect of almes) yt shal multiply your seed, and shal augment the increase of the fruit of your iustice; and saynt Iames, *a man sayth he is iustified by woorkes and not by fayth only,* and saynt Iohn, *he which doth iustice is iust,* and in the Apocalipse, *he which is iust let him be iustifyed still,* and of both these iustifications, sayth the autor of the imperfect woorke vpon S. Mathew, *the first iustice is to know God the Father, and Christ his sonne, and the last iustice is to do good woorkes,* finally S. Augustin witnesseth, that for as much as there were some that taught in the very tyme of the Apostles that fayth withour woorkes might suffise to saluation, (which errour he sayth did grow of the corrupt, & il vnderstanding of saynt Paules Epistles,) S. Peter, S. Iohn, S. Iames, and S. Iude did expressely direct their intentions in their Epistles to proue the necessity of good workes,

R   and Iu-

Marginal notes:
Roman. 2. 3. 5.
Psalmo. 58.
1. Cor. ca 15.
Ioan. 15.
ad Philip 4.
Roman. 2. 3. 5.
2. Cor. cap. 9.
Epist. Iacob cap. 2.
Autor operis imperfecti Matth.
Aug. de fide & openbus cap 14.

and iuſtification therby , and thus much for the firſt poynt.

2.

The ſecond poynt that I wiſh to be noted is, that where woorkes are at any tyme excluded in the ſcriptures, Fathers, or councels from iuſtification, it is always to be vnderſtood eyther of woorkes done by the only force of nature before fayth, or of woorkes of the law of Moyſes, proceeding only of the force of the law, or of woorkes of the faythful not proceeding of Gods grace.

3.

The third poynt is, that all the reaſon of merit in mānes fayth, or woorkes proceedeth of two grounds, the one the grace of God, which moueth & enableth a man therto; the other the promiſſe of almighty God to reward theſame in both which the merits of Chriſts paſsion are euer preſupoſed to be the firſt foundation of all the buylding;

Math. 10.
& Marc 9. with which preſuppoſition our Sauiour ſayth, *he which geues but a cup of cold water in my name ſhal not looſe his reward,*
Matth. 5.
& Luc 6. and agayne to his Diſciples *your reward is copious in heauen,* & ſpeaking of the Iudgement at the later day, he playnly aſcribeth the reward of lyfe euerlaſting to workes, ſaying,
Math. 25. *come yee bleſſed of my Father and poſſeſſe the Kingdome prepared for you for when I was hungry you gaue me to eate, when I was naked*
Apoc. 22.
Rom. 2. *you clothed me, &c.* And therefore S. Iohn, and S. Paule ſay, *God wil render vnto euery one according to his workes,* to this purpoſe alſo the Prophet Dauid ſayth, *I enclyned my hart, o Lord,*
Epiſt 2. ad
Timoth. c. 4. *to do thy iuſtifications for reward,* and S. Paule I haue ſayth he fought a good fyght, I haue kept my fayth, I haue conſummated or ended my courſe, & now there is layed vp for me the croune of iuſtice, which our Lord the iuſt Iudge wil render me in that day; vpon theſe words of S. Paule
Oecumeni in
ea verba ep.
2. ad timoth.
cap. 4. OEcumenius ſayth, *conſider that he craues it as due when he ſayth reddet mihi & non dabit, he wil render it vnto me, and not he wil giue it me, which he alſo ſignifieth in that he cauleth him the iuſt iudge:*
Theophilac.
in 2. Timoth.
cap. 4. Theophilactus alſo ſayth theſame, vpon theſame words, and concludeth thus, *the croune is a debt by reaſon of the iuſtice of the iudge,* S. Auguſtin aleadging theſame place of
S. Paule

S. Paule in his book of grace and free wil, sayth, *he* Aug. de gra.
now rehearseth merita sua bona, his good deserts or merits, that & libero ar-
he which after his il deserts got grace, may after *his good* bi, cap 6.
merits get the croune, &c. but let vs heare concerning this
matter of merit, some two or 3. about king Lucius Igat epist. ad
tyme, S. Ignatius disciple to saynt Iohn the Euangelist, Roman.
sayth in his epistle to the Romans, being condemned to
be deuowred of wild beasts, *suffer me to be the food or meat*
of beasts that I may promereri Deum, gayn, or as a man may say
earne almighty God. Tertullian sayth, *how ar their many mansions* Tertul in
in the Fathers house, but according to the variety of mens merits, and scorpiaco.
Clemens Alexandrinus ; *there are* sayth he *many mansions ac-* Clemens
cording to the worthinesse and merits of those which beleeue, and Alex. 6. stro-
origen teacheth, *that God doth not giue according to nature, but* Orige l b. 2.
according to merits, S. Cyprian sayth, *that a penitent man, prome-* in epist. ad
retur Dominum, obsequijs suis & operibus iustis, doth deserue, or as I Roman.
sayd before *earne* our Lord with his obedience and iust Cyprian.
weorkes, and in his book of the vnity of the Churche, spea- epist. 14 ad
king of them that hauing donne great miracles in the 3. epist. 18.
name of Christ, shalbe reiected of him at the day of Iudg- S. Augustin
ment, he sayth, *iustice or righteousnes is needful, vt promerere quis* geueth also
possit Deum iudicem, that a man may gayne God the iudge, which reirpretation
in the words next folowing he expoundeth, saying *preceptis* of multæ,
eius & monitis obtemperandum est vt merita nostra accipiant mer- tractatu 6.7.
cedem, wee must obey his precepts and admonitions that our merits in euang. Io.
may receiue reward, thereto I wil ad S. Augustin explicating Cyprian. lib.
notably this questiō according to our Catholyk fayth euer Ecclesiæ.
taught in the Churche of God, *when grace,* sayth he, *is geuen* Aug. de gra-
then begin also our good merits by the meanes of that grace, for yf arbitrio ca 6.
grace be taken away man doth presently fal head-long by his owne
free wil, therfore when a man beginneth to haue good merits, he
ought not to atribute them vnto himselfe, but to God, to whome it is
sayd in the Psalme, o Lord be my healper, and do not forsake me, &c.
Thus farre S. Augustin but to auoyd the multitude of allegations, which might be infinit to this purpose, I wil conclude with the secōd councel of Aurange celebrated 1200.

Conf. Auta-
ficanum, fe-
cundum,
Cano.18.
yeres agoe, *reward* fayth the councel, *is due to good workes, yf*
they bee donne, but grace which is not due, or giuen by defert, doth goe
before, that they may be donne.

Thus thow feeft good reader the doctrin of Catholykes
concerning merit of good woorkes, conforme to the fcriptures and fathers, and no way preiuditial to the dignity &
honour of our Sauiours pafsion, but moft honorable to the
fame, feing wee teach that all good merits receiue their
vigour and force from the merits therof, he hauing therby
obtayned for vs of his father, not only remifsion of finne,
but alfo grace to doe works acceptable to him and meritorious of eternal faluation, which woorkes though they
be ours in refpect of the concurrence of our free wil yet
for as much as they be his gifts in that they proceede of his
grace they deferue the reward that he hath promifed for
the fame, & therfore refpecting any woorks of man what-
Roman. 8.
foeuer as of them-felues, wee fay with faynt Paule, that
the pafsions or fuffrings of this lyfe are not worthy of the future glory
that fhalbe reueyled in vs, but confidering the fame as the gyfts
2. Corin 4.
of God, and ennobled with his grace, wee fay alfo with
him; that *the fhort and light tribulation which wee fuffer here,*
doth woorke an eternal weyght of glory in vs.

Therfore I wil end with S. Auguftin, faying that *when*
Aug. ep. 105.
ad fixiu pres
byterum.
God doth croune our merits, he doth croune his owne gyfts, feing
then, this is the vniforme doctrin of all Catholykes,
wherin do we derogate any thing from the pafsion of
Chrift, or arrogat to our felues, or our owne woorkes more
then the feripture doth giue vs warrant for.

THAT

THAT OVR ADVERSARIES

*who affirme that we derogat from the merits of Chrifts
pafsion do themfelues wholy euacuat, and fruftrat the
fame, by their moft wicked, and abfurd doctrin of imputatiue iuftice, and dyuers other poynts confuted in this
chapter.*

CAP. XX.

BVT now let vs examine the opinion of thefe fellowes, that feeme to be fo ielous of the honour of
Chrift and of his pafsion, and I dout not wee fhal
fynd that they do vtterly obfcure and fruftrat the
fame, for where as our Sauiour Chrift *gaue himfelfe to death,*   Tit. 2.
as S.Paule fayth, *to the end he might redeeme vs from iniquity, and
make vs cleane from finne, and a people acceptable to himfelfe, and
followers of good woorkes,* they teach expreffely that he hath
performed nothing of all this. For though they grant that
he redeemed vs from death, and by his pafsion purchafed
vs lyfe euerlafting, yet they confeffe not, that he redeemed
or made vs cleane from finne (as we fee S.Paule teacheth)   Caluinus lib.
but playnly affirme the contrary, faying, that original finne   2. inftit.ca.1.
is not taken away by baptifme, nor any other finne after   Lutherus lib.
baptifme remitted, but couered, and not imputed; in fo   de libertate
much that they teach further as a neceffary confequent   Chriftia. & in
therof, that the workes of the moft iuft man, are not only   affectione
infected with finne, but alfo finnes of themfelues, defer-   art. 2. 31 32.
 uing eternal damnation & that therfore there is no righ-   & 16. con-
teoufnes or iuftice really in man, but only in Chrift, and   teffio Au-
imputed to man; whervpon it muft needs follow, that   gufta.artic 6.
the fall of Adam our father, was of more force to make vs   Caluin.lib.3.
finners, then the pafsion of our Sauiour to free vs from   inftir.cap. 11.
finne, and to make vs iuft, which is no leffe dishonorable   Luther. ad c.
to Chrift then contrary to expreffe fcripture, where S.   2.ad Galat.
Paule faith, that *as by the difobedience of one* (Adam) *many were*   Rom.5.

made sinners, so by the obedience of one (Christ) many were made
iust; if then we were truly sinners by Adam, wee are also
truly iust by Christ, or els our help is not equiualent to our
harme, nor our remedy to our disease, nor our rising to our
falle, nor our gayne to our losse, nor consequently Christ to
Adam, which were impiety to thinke, and blasphemy to
say, and yet so must our aduersaries be forced to say if
they wil defend their opinion; but for as much as not only
this their absurd doctrin of imputatiue iustice, but also diuers other execrable errours, or rather damnable heresies
spring all out of one root, that is to say the foresayd opinion that original sinne is not cleane remitted, and taken
away by baptisme, I wil by the confutation therof ouerthrow all the rest that depend theron, and shew withall
the dishonour they doe to Christ, and his merits which
they seeme somuch to esteeme.

    Let vs then consider the effects of baptisme in the rege-
nerat, which to spake generally are two, the one the remission of sinnes, and the other a regeneration, or renouation of the inward man, of the first the Prophet Ezechiel
sayth, *I wil power vpon you a cleane water, and you shalbe cleansed
from all your filth, or corruption,* in which sence the Apostle cauleth it; *the water of lyfe* wherwith Christ *sanctifyeth and maketh cleane his Churche,* and speaking of the baptised that had
ben fornicators, and Idolaters, *these yow were* sayth he, *but now
yow are washed, yow are sanctified, yow are iustified,* by which
text S. Chrisostom, and S. Hierome proue that all sinnes are
forgeuen in baptisme, & the reason is, for that by the vertue
therof the ful merits of Christs death and passion, are communicated vnto vs, in which respect, saynt Paule sayth that
all that are baptised in Christe, are baptysed in his death, and that
wee are therby *buryed with him to death* of sinne, wherof S.
Augustin sayth *as in Christ there was a true death, so there is in vs a
true remißion of sinne,* which cannot be denyed, except wee
wil deny the vertue and force of the blessed blood, and
death of Christ which hath his operation therby, wherof
                             the Apo-

Ezechiel.
cap. 36.
ad Ephes. 5.
ad titum. 3.
1. Cor. 6.
Chrisf. in
hom. ad bap.
Hier. in epist.
ad oceanum.
Rom. 6.
Colossen. 1.

Aug. in Eu-
chiri cap. 52.

the Apostle sayth, *he reconcyled vs by his death, that he might make* Colos. 1.
vs holy, and immaculat, and irreprehensible before him, and in an ^ad Habr. 9.
other place making a comparison betwyxt the effects of
the sacrifices of Christ vpon the crosse, and the sacrifices of
the old law, he sayth, *but how much more shal the blood of Christ*
make cleane our conscience from dead woorkes (that is to say from
sinne) *to serue the liuing God:* to this purpose sayth saynt Iohn,
sanguis Iesu Christi emundat nos ab omni peccato, the blood of Iesu
Christ doth make vs cleane from all sinne, in which respect our 1.Ioan.1.
Sauiour Christ is truly cauled the *lamb of God which taketh*
away the sinnes of the world.

Therfore saynt Chrisostome sayth that a man newly Ioan. 1 in
baptysed is *mundior solis radijs, cleaner then the beames of the sunne,* homil ad
and compareth the sinne of the baptised to a sparke of fyre,
faling into the mayne sea, wherein it is presently extin-
guished, S. Basil cauleth it a *remission of debt,* and the death of Basil. in ex-
sinne. S. Gregory Nazianzen tearmeth it *peccati diluuium the* Baptis.
deluge wherein sin is drowned, (and lastly not to be tedious,
with many allegations, in a matter where in all learned
fathers doe vniformly agree) S. Augustin sayth *baptisme* Angl. lib. 3.
washeth away all sinnes, yea all whatsoeuer, of deeds, thoughts, contra duas
words, of original sinne, or other committed ignorantly or wittingly, epist. pelagia-
and in an other place, he sayth, yt doth *auferre crimina, non* Lib. 1. contra
radere, take sinnes cleane away, and not shaue them only. easdem epist.

What then shal wee say of Luther, and his felloowes cap. 13.
that deny such a manifest principle of Christian religion,
affirming that original sinne is not taken away by baptisme, but that it remayneth & infecteth all menes workes
can any thing be sayd more to the derogation of Christs
merits, on which they wil seeme sometymes wholy to
rely? can their other heresyes concerning the necesity of
sinne, the impossibility to keepe the commandments, the
sinful or stayned righteousnes of the iustest man, or yet
their imputatiue iustice, all grounded and necessarily depending vpon the rotten foundation of this pestilent opinion, can they I say, be lyke to stand when their foundation
fayleth,

fayleth, as yow fee? but this wil be more euident, yf we cōſider the other effect of Baptiſme, which is regeneration, or renouation of the ſoule, wherof the Prophet ſayth, *I wil geue yow a new hart and a* new ſpirit, in which reſpect the Apoſtle cauleth Baptiſme *lauacrum regenerationis, and renouationis, the water of regeneration, and renouation,* for that as our Sauiour himſelf ſignified a man is *borne a new by water, & the holy ghoſt,* & becometh as ſaynt Paule ſayth *noua creatura a new creature* by grace of *the holy ſpirit which is aboundantly poured vpon him,* to which purpoſe the Apoſtle ſayth that *charity is diffuſed in our harts, by the holy ghoſt which is giuen vs,* and that *Chriſt dwelleth in our harts,* and that *wee liue for iuſtification, for that the ſpirit of God dwelleth in vs,* all which proue a real and inhærent iuſtice in vs, and not a iuſtice in Chriſt, imputed only to vs, this the Apoſtle ſignifyeth by the ſimilitude of Baptiſme with the death & reſurrection of Chriſt ſaying that *wee are buryed with him by baptiſme to the end that as Chriſt did riſe from death, ſo wee may walke in newnes of lyfe,* vpon which words, S. Auguſtin ſayth, *as in Chriſt there was a true reſurrection, ſo in vs there is a true iuſtification,* and S. Chriſoſtome proueth theſame by the woords of S. Paule, (where he ſayth, *you are waſhed, you are ſanctified, you are iuſtified) be ſheweth* ſayth he, *that you are not only made cleane, but alſo that you are made holy and iuſt,* to which purpoſe he noteth that it is cauled *lauacrum regenerationis,* and not *remiſſionis or purificationis, the water of regeneration,* and not *of remiſſion or purification,* for ſayth he, *it doth not ſimply remit ſinnes, but makes, vs as though wee were of a heauenly generation,* which Clemens Alexandrinus confirmeth ſaying *being baptiſed we are illuminated, being illuminated we are adopted to be the childrē of God, being adopted wee are made perfect, being perfited wee are made immortal, according to that of the Pſalmiſt, I ſay you are all Gods, and the children of the higheſt.* Theſame alſo in effect ſayth S. Gregory Nazianzen *Baptiſme* ſayth he, *giuing help to our firſt natiuity, of old makes new, and of human deuine,* all which doth playnly proue that which we teach, with ſaynt Auguſtin, who

Ezechi. 36.
Tit. 3.
Ioan 3.
Galat 6.
Tit. 3.
Roma. 5.
Act 15.
Rom. 8.
Rom. 6.
Aug. in Enchiri cap. 52.
2. Cor 6.
Chryſoſt. hom. ad Bap. Titul. 3.
Clem. Alex. lib. 1. pædag. cap. 6.
Pſalm. 81.
in o. at. in ſanctum baptiſma.
De peccatorum meritis & remiſſione cap. 9. lib. 1.

who fayth *the grace of Chriſt doth woorke inwardly our illumi-nation, and iuſtification,*neuertheles wee deny not that the iu-ſtice wherwith wee are made iuſt, is the iuſtice of God by whoſe grace we haue it, but we deny that it is not ours, & really in vs, when he hath of his great mercy and liberality geuen it vs, ſo that we ſay it is both his and ours, his, becauſe he giues it, & ours, becauſe wee haue it by his gift. Therfore ſaynt Auguſtin ſayth,*let no Chriſtian man feare to ſay* De ſpiritu & *that we are made iuſt, not by our ſelues but by the grace of God, wor-* littera ca. 19. *king the ſame in vs.* In this ſence Elizabeth and Zacharias ^{Luc.1.} were called iuſt in the ſcripture, of whome wee read *that* Luc.1. *ambo erant iuſti, they were both iuſt,* not before men only, but *ante Deum before God* and not becauſe Iuſtice was imputed to them, but becauſe they did walke *in omnibus mandatis & Iu-ſtiſicationibus Domini ſine querela, in all the commaudments & Iuſti-ſications of our Lord without blame,* in this ſence alſo it is ſaid Rom.2. in the ſcripture, *the doers of the law are iuſtified before God, not the hearers only,* which ſaynt Iohn confirmeth, forewarning as it were and arming vs, againſt theſe ſeducers, (for ſo he tearmeth all thoſe which teach that a man is not iuſt by 1.Ioan.3. really doing the acts, or works, of iuſtice,) *let no man ſayth he ſeduce yow, he which doth Iuſtice or righteouſnes ys iuſt, as God is iuſt, he which doth ſinne, is of the diuel, to this end apeared the ſonne of God, that he might diſſolue the workes of the deuil:* thus farre S. Iohn. Tit. 2.

If then the comming of our Sauiour, and his ſuffring Rom.6. was *to diſſolue the woorkes of the diuel,* which is ſinne, and (as yt Ezech.36. is ſigniﬁed in inﬁnit other places of ſcripture,) to redeeme vs from iniquity, *to deliuer vs from the ſeruitude of ſinne, to renew vs in ſpirit, to make vs new creatures, to cleanſe vs, to ſanctify vs, to iu-ſtify vs,* that is to ſay to make vs iuſt, yea *to make vs immaculat,* Tit.3 coloſ.1. *and irreprehēſible,* to make vs his ^a tēples his ^b friends, his ^c childrē, 4 1.Cor.3. how is this performed, yf notwithſtanding the merits of ^b Ioan. 15. his paſsion applyed vnto vs by Baptiſme, and other meanes, ^c Rom. 8. wee are only reputed to be iuſt, and not ſo in deed, but re-mayne ſtil ſoyled with ſinne, bondmen of iniquity, and 1.Ioan.3.

S   children

children of the diuel (as S. Iohn fayth we are if wee be in finne) how can we fay that Chrift conquered the deuil and finne, and deliuered vs from the feruitude and bondage of them both if we remayn flaues of both ? for being bondmen of finne, as Luther makes vs, wee are alfo flaues of the diuel by confequent, and can it be any derogation to the merits of our Sauiours pafsion, to fay that he made vs (who were before thralles & captiues to both the deuil and finne) able to vanquifh, and conquer them both ? nay is it not far more glorious to him to conquer them dayly in vs and by vs, then if he had only once conquered them for vs ? for by making fuch weak ones, as wee, tread them vnder our feet, his conqueft and triumph is farre more glorious, his mercy to vs more manifeft, his enemies & ours more con-

1. Cor. cap. 5. founded, and wee infinitly more obliged, and therefore wee may fay with faint Paule, *Deo gratias qui dedit nobis victoriam, God be thanked which gaue vs victory*, but how by our felues no; *per Dominum Iefum Chriftum, by our Lord Iefus Chrift*.

Thus thou feeft good reader how confonet to the fcriptures how glorious to our Sauiour, & how comfortable to vs is our doctrin concerning iuftification, and merits of workes, & on the other fyde how erronious, and iniurious to his pafsion is the opinion of our aduerfaries who to the end they may with better colour and more boldly bark againft good woorkes, and the merit therof, feeme to haue in fingular eftimation the merits of his pafsion; But where the ful force and true effect therof is to be fhewed to Gods greater glory, to the confufion of our enemy the diuel, and our fingular comfort, there they hold it to be of no force or valew, yea rather they make it a cloke to couer finne then a meanes to cleanfe it, and to take it away, and fo they eftablifh in the kingdome of Chrift, the tyrannie of the diuel, whofe inftruments and proctors they fhew themfelues to be, woorking in mennes myndes by their doctrin, that which the diuel doth woork by temptation, that is

to fay

to fay difcouraging all men from doing wel, and from keeping the commandments, by teaching thefame to be needielfe, impofsible, and of no merit, wherby they giue ful fcope to fenfuality, and finne, and carry men after them headlong to hel as I could make it moft euident yf I lift to profecute this poynt, which my purpofed breuity wil not permit.

THE CONCLVSION CON-

uincing by the premiffes, that our Catholyk doctrin, was deliuered to King Lucius, by Pope Eleutherius, and is the vndouted truth, that Chrift left to his Church, with a note of the notable impudency of our Englifh minifters.

CHAP. XXI.

NOW to returne to King Lucius and to conclude, I dout not good reader but thow haft perceiued by thefe few poynts which I haue handled, what hath alwayes bin the doctrin of the Churche of God concerning thefame, and that therfore King Lucius could receiue no other frõ the Catholyke Romã Churche by the which he was conuerted to the Chriftian fayth, and yf I thought it needful to rip vp euery other particuler point controuerfed betwyxt our aduerfaries and vs, I could eafely fhew the fame in euery one.

But what needeth it ? feing they cannot proue that any Pope, I wil not fay from S. Eleutherius to S. Gregory, but from S. Peter to Clement the eight that now gouerneth the Churche, hath taught, and decreed any different doctrin from his predeceffors, whereas on the other fyde wee fhew euidently that in a perpetual fuccefsion of our

S 2   Roman

Roman Bishops, there hath ben also a continual succession of one, & the selfe same doctrin, where vpon it followeth infalibly that King Ethelbert, and the English could not receiue from S. Gregory the Pope an' other fayth then King Lucius and the britans receiued from saynt Eleutherius, and that wee which now hold communion with the Roman Churche teache no other doctrin then that which was taught by them to our ancestors, and hath succesiuely come from S. Peter, & consequently from our Sauiour Christ.

Therefore thou mayst wel wonder, good reader, at the impudency of our English ministers, that are not a shamed to preache & teache the contrary, wherby thow mayst also see how lamentable is the case of our poor country wherein such haue the charge, and cure of soules, as haue not so much as common honesty to say the truth in matters as cleare as the Sunne, and teach such a religion as for lack of better reasons, and arguments, they are forst to mayntayne it with manifest lyes, slanders, yea and murders of innocent men, whome they execute for fayned crymes vnder colour of matter of state, acknowledging therby sufficiently the truth of our Catholyk fayth seing they are ashamed to auow that they troouble any man for it, whyles they confesse that they punish and put to death heretykes, namely the Anabaptists, directly for their religion, and their impudency is so much the more notorious, for that their publyk proceedings in the dayly execution of penal and capital lawes, touching only matter of religion, doth contradict and conuince their sayings and writings, wherein they affirme that they put none to death for religion.

But for as much as I haue treated this matter at large in diuers partes of my Apology, besydes that I vnderstand that some others also entend to treate thereof in the answere of a ridiculous challenge; made by O. E.

fraught

fraught with moſt abſurd paradoxes, as wel concerning
this poynt, as others touching our Catholyke fayth, I
remit thee, good reader, therto, and ſo conclude this
treatys, beſeeching almighty God to geue our aduerſaries the light of his grace, and vs in the meane tyme pacience and conſtancy, and to thee indifferency to
iudge of maters ſo much importing the eternal good and ſaluation of thy ſoule,
which I hartely wiſh no leſſe
then my owne.

F I N I S.

A TABLE OF
THE CHAPTERS.
OF THIS TREA-
T I S E.

THE preface, wherein are declared the cauſes of
the long delay of printing the Apology, and withall
is noted the impudency of a late wryter in England
diſguyſing his name with the letters O. E. who anſweth
the fiction of Squyres employment for a truth and affirmeth that none are put to death in England for religion.
An Anſwere to two malitious ſlanders, auowched in
the foreſayd libels concerning the conqueſt of England,
falſly ſuppoſed to be pretended, & ſollicited, by the Catho-

S 3   lyks, &

That

Of this treatyse.

it to

A Table of the Chapters.

AN APOLOGY

OF T. F. IN DEFENCE

OF HIM-SELF AND OTHER

CATHOLYKS, FALSLY CHARGED WITH A
fayned conspiracy agaynst her Maiesties person, for the
which one Edward Squyre was wrong-fully condemned
and executed in the yeare of our Lord 1598. wherein are
discouered the wicked, and malicious practises of some inferior persons to whose examination the causes of Catholykes are commonly committed, and their iniurious
manner of proceding, not only against thesayd Squyre
but also agaynst many Catholykes that haue ben
vniustly condemned for lyke fayned con-
spiracies, against her maiesty
and the state.

VVritten in the yeare of our Lord 1599. *and dedicated to
the right honorable the Lords of her mayesties priuie
councel.*

Ecclesiast. cap. 3. 5. 16.
Vidi sub sole in loco iudicij iniquitatem, & in loco iustitiæ impietatem.

*I haue seene vnder the Sunne iniquity in place of iudgement, and im-
piety in place of iustice.*

Imprinted with licence 1602.

AN ADVERTIS-
MENT TO THE
READER ABOVT A FOR-
MER ANSWERE OF M.
M. Ar.

Fter I had set downe to my self this defence or Apologie in the forme that here it goeth, there came to my hādes a certayne breif pamphlet writen in Rome by M. Mar. Ar. presentlie vpon the execution of Squier in England, which confutation thoughe for the substance of the matter it seemed to me very sufficient to giue any man satisfaction by shewing the whole matter of Squyers accusatiō, condēnation, and execution to be a very fiction and deuised for certayne endes which there are touched; yet thought I not amisse to let this Apologie passe also as it was made, partly for that it conteyneth my owne particuler defence which the other toucheth not, but handleth the whole action in general, and partly also for that the māner of both our proceedings is different, he shewing the whole subiect and argument to be a fayned thing, and I that albeit some occasion had byn geuen of suspition yet the forme of proceeding against Squyer & the rest to be vniust & against all reason, equitie, law, and conscience.

M. Mar. Ar. to proue his intent layeth downe the historical narration of all the whole matter and men touched in thesame, to wit how Squver and Rolles were taken vpon the sea and brought prisoners to Siuil, and had their liberty there by Father Parsons meanes, and how afterwards geuing newe occasion of offence in matters of religiō they were taken agayne at S. Lucars, & brought back to Siuil, and there agayne after certayne monethes imprisonment, deliuered out of prison & put in different Monasteryes for to be instructed, whence they fled away to the sea syde, and

excu-

excufed their flight afterwards by letters to Father Walpoole that was moft in daunger by that flight which letters are yet extant.

It fheweth alfo the improbability of the deuife, to wit, that Father Walpoole (being the man he is) fhould euer haue thought of fuch a fond way of fending poyfon into England by fuch a fellow as Squyer was, fufpected ftil to be a diffembled proteftant, as afterwards he proued, and that thing could not be wrought, nor the poyfon caryed fo farre but that Rolles his compagnion muft know fomewhat thereof, who being at that prefent in the Towre of London, and neither brought foorth, nor mentioned, nor yet made partaker of the fact, was a token that matters went not wel, nor were directly handled.

Befides this that book declareth by many examples the practifes of Proteftants in thefe our dayes for making Catholykes odious, efpecially Iefuites of which order Father Walpoole is, who was fayned to be the contriuer of this confpiracy which is fhewed to be as farre from the condition of the man, as the matter it felf is from all probability of truth, to wit, any fuch poyfon to be made, bought and fold in Siuil proued by the death of a dog, fent into England by fea in bladders of leather, poured vpon the Quenes Sadle, as alfo vpon the chayre of the Earle of Effex without hurt to the fitter or ryder, the matter difcouered by one Stanley, that neyther fawe Squyer in Spayne, nor fpoke with him, and it was denyed by Squyer firft at the barre, and after at his death, and fince his death called in dowt by Stanley his firft detector, (as by fome hath byn written from the place where he abydeth) the force alfo of that poyfon (yf any fuch had byn) is declared by reafons and authoritie both of phyfick and Philofophie that it could not worke any fuch effect as was ymagined, or pretended, & confequentlie that thofe applaufes & congratulations both by woords, fighs, & teares which a company of flatterers fhewed foorth at Squyers arraynment and condemnation for her Maᵗⁱᵉˢ fo miraculous efcape was moft ridiculous and vayne.

This is the fumme & effect of that anfwere as breifly fet downe, as I can gather it, and it maketh the fiction moft euident to all fuch as without partiality wil read it, though I heare fay that it may chance come out agayne more ample in a fecod edition, with many Autentical letters, as wel of the citty of Siuil, as of the courte of Inquifitio in that place, to fhew the manner of Squyers and Rolles running

running away from thofe partes with fome other circumſtances to improue the probabilitie of the deuiſed ſlander in England, which letters and inſtruments I thought not good to inſert heere to my Apologie but to leaue thē to M. Mar. Ar. now at his returne hither from Rome to ad to his former Anſwere if ſo he ſhal think good, for that he maketh mention thereof in theſame, and as for this my defence (gentle reader I ſhal not need to aduiſe thee of the ſubſtance, manner, method, or argument therof, for that the breife chapters enſuing wil ſufficiently ſet foorth the ſame, only I would admoniſh thee to conſider maturely with thy ſelf how rhow mayeſt be vſed in matters of Religion which do moſt import thy ſoule and ſaluation, when in matters of faĉt and open aĉtion thow ſhalt fynd thy ſelf ſo egregiouſly abuſed.

A 3   TO

TO THE RIGHT HO-
NORABLE THE LORDES
OF HER MA^ties. PRYVIE
councel.

Ight honorable *vnderstanding*
by common fame, confirmed by
letters from Italy, Flanders,
and France, *that one Edward*
Squire, was lately condemned,
and executed in England, *for*
hauing attempted to poyson the
Queenes Ma^ie. and my Lord
of Essex by the instigation as
was surmised of one Father VValpoole *a Iesuite in Siuil, with*
the priuity & consent of Father Creswel and my selfe, here
in Madrid, *I was (I assure your Lordships) at the first brute*
amased and much afflicted to heare that these good men so
farre of in my conscience from such cogitations, and my self
no lesse, were slaundered with matter so haynous, & odious,
and although I had recours presentlie to the brazen wall of
<blockquote>
Horat. lib. 1.
epist. ad Me-
cœn.
</blockquote>
our owne innocency (as the Poet speaketh) and the comfort
of a good conscience which our Sauiour geueth his seruãts in
like cases, saying to his Apostles, happie are yow when men
<blockquote>
Matth. 5.
</blockquote>
shall rayle vpon you, and persecute you, and speake all euil
of you, belying you for my sake, reioyce and be glad, for your
reward is copious in heauen, although I say I rested cõforted
with this consideration, & so resolued my self to patience,
& silence, yet waying afterwards, that as the Latyn prouerb
sayth, Qui tacet, consentire videtur, he that holds his peace
seemes

seemes to confent, & that my fylence might not onlie turne
to my further condēnation in this matter, but alfo to the preiudice of all the good Catholyks of England, againft whome
every fuppofed fault of any one or two (be it neuer fo falfe) is
commonlie wrefted to the reproche & condemnation of all; I
could not forbeare to offer to all indifferēt men this neceffarie
defence and Apology of my innocencie in this affayre, as alfo
to addreffe the fame to your Lordfhips hands efpecially for
2. caufes which heer I wil expreffe.

The one was for that it is not only conuenient in refpeƈt
of your place & dignitie, as alfo of the duety I owe & beare
you, but alfo importeth for the preuētion of the inconueniēce
aforefaid, that I feek to fatisfie your honours, before all others
in whofe hands principally refteth the fatisfaƈtion of her
Matie. & the moderation of the rigour, or iniuƈt perfecution
& vexation which vpon this falfe conceyt may otherwayes
be vfed againft the innocents Catholyks of England, which
haue neyther parte nor fault therin.

The other is for that perfuading my felfe, that fo fond a
fiƈtion, or rather fo foule & vnchriftian a praƈtyfe tēding to
the fpilling of guyltleffe blood in this aƈte, & to the flaunder
of innocent people both at home & abroad, could not proceed
from the body of a councel confifting of men fo honnorable
graue, & wife, as your Lordfhips are prefumed to be, but rather frō fome inferiour perfons of leffe confideratiō, & more
defyrous of garboyles to whofe examinations fuch caufes cōmonly are committed, who may haue abufed perhaps your
Lordfhips in this behalf dazling your eyes with pretence of
daungers to her Ma^{eits} perfon : in confideration whereof I
thought my felfe bound as wel in confcience as duety to your
Lordfhips to difcouer vnto you not onely the trecherous
deuifes,

deuifes, & dryfts of thofe that contryued this infamous tragedy, but alfo the difhonour daunger and ineuitable dom-
mages that muft needes redound to her Ma.tie. to your honours, and to the whole ftate in tyme, if fuch proceedings be
permitted, in which refpect if thofe ancient fenators & go-
uernors among the Romans being heathens, did think it
conuenient euen for honour of theyr common wealth to
chaften oftentymes moft fharpely, & examplarly certayne
newe deuifers of publyk fhifies, deceyptes, & difhonorable
trecheryes vfed by the though it were againft their enemyes,
and in farre countreys, and to the common publiq̧ benefit
of theyr ftate as they pretended, whereof many examples may
be read in Liuy, Halicarnaffeus & others, & S. Auguftine
in his book of the city of God, thinketh that God gaue them
fo florifhing a Monarchie ouer the world for this honorable kynd of proceeding in moral iuftice, how much more
ought Chriftian councelours deteft and punifh fuch bafe &
vile proceedings or rather malitious and diabolical as this
is whereof now I am to treate, vfed againft the blood of Chriftian fubiectes at home in your owne fights, to no publique
benefit, but rather to publique infamy, and fhame among
all nations where it fhalbe knowne, wherefore this
a matter fo worthie & neceffary for your L.
to know & remedy, I hope you wil take
it wel that it cometh dedicated
to your felues.

THE

THE AVTORS PROTE-

*ſtation of his innocency with the confutation of the
fiction by the improbability of the end
that was ſuppoſed to moue
Squyre thereunto.*

CHAP. I.

FIRST then for as much as my innocēcy
in this matter, is beſt knowne and moſt
cleare vnto my ſelfe, by the teſtimony of
my owne cōſcience which is to me *mille
teſtes*, as the law ſayth, no one but a thouſand witneſſes, and would be no leſſe
cleare to your Lordſhips, yf my hart
were knowne as wel to you, as it is to God and my ſelfe, **I**
think yt conuenient for the firſt poynt of my diſcharge to
caul him to witnes that is the ſearcher of hartes & raynes: Pſalm. 7.
which manner of purgation though it may argue weaknes
or want of credit in him that vſeth it, (for as S. Chryſo- Chryſoſt.
ſtome ſayth, an othe is a geuing of ſurety where mans acta Apoſtol.
manners haue no credit) neuertheleſſe it is ſo conforme to
all lawes humayne and deuine, and ſo confirmed by cuſtome of all countreys, and common wealthes, that it
cannot iuſtlie be refuſed when the party is neyther infamous for falſhood, nor conuict by euident teſtimonyes; of
the cryme obiected to the contrarie, in which reſpect S.
Paule ſayth an othe is the end of euery controuerſie for Heb. 6.
the confirmation of the truth. Therfore I do here caul
almightie God his Angels and Sayntes to witneſſe that
I am ſo farre from being guilty of this matter which
I am charged with, that I neuer ſaw in my lyfe for ought
I know, the ſayd Edward Squyre, nor euer had any correſpondence or dealing with him by letters, or any other

B meanes,

meanes, neyther yet euer conſpired my ſelf, or was any
way priuie to any other mānes conſpiracy of the death of
her Maᵗⁱᵉ or of my Lord of Eſſex, & this I affirme in ſuch
ſort, as yf it be not true in all and in euery part, I renounce
all the benefit I expect of my Sauiour Ieſus Chriſt, which
I would not do for all the good in the world, as your
Lordſhips may beleeue of me, yf it pleaſe yow to conſider
that for the only reſpect not to offend God, and my conſcience, I left all the peaſures and commodityes of my
owne countrey, to lead this baniſhed lyfe for many yeares,
not hauing bene any way charged whileſt I was in Englād with matter of ſtate, or any other greater cryme, then
that I would not go to your Churches, and prayers, perſuading my ſelfe as ſtyl I do, that I ſhould offend God dam-
nably therin.

If therfore I haue bene & am contented to looſe all that
a man can looſe, lyfe excepted, rather then to do an act offenſiue to God and my conſcience, I hope no charitable
man can conceiue of me that I would now without all
compulſion, hope of gayne or feare of loſſe, aduiſedly for-
ſweare my ſelf & with a wilful and damnable periury
fruſtrate and looſe all that fruit of my former ſufferings.

Neuertheleſſe yf any man be ſo paſsionate and vncharitable, that he wil not be ſatisfied with this my proteſtatiõ,
and ſolemne othe, let him way wel the matter it ſelf with
all the circumſtances, & then I doubt not but he wil eaſely
ſee the wrong donne both to Squyre and vs, that are conioyned and mentioned in his accuſation.

Firſt therfore for this purpoſe it is to be conſidered
what was Squyres end therein, ſeing as the Philoſopher
ſayth, the end is the firſt thing in intention, though the laſt
in execution, & in a matter of ſo great weight & daunger
as this, there muſt needes be ſome great conſideration that
moued him therto, which the contriuers of this tragedy
knew ſo wel that for the better colouring of the deuiſe,
they forged the moſt forcible motiue and higheſt end that

Vvhat Squire vvas, and vvhat his end might be

may

may be, which is zeale of religion, and hope of æternal reward, induced perhaps therto by the late example yet fresh
in memorie of the last King of Fraunce, killed by a fryer,
moued with meere zeale without all hope of téporal gayne,
or pofsibility to escape ; therfore they fayd that Squyre by
F. Walpooles perfuafions entended the death of her Ma^{ue.}
and my L. of Effex, to the end to do a meritorious act, and
to gayne euerlafting glorie, but the vanity of this fiction is
eu:dent, feing it is manifeit, that he was a proteftant as he
fhewed playnely at his death, when yt was no tyme to
diffemble, where-vpon I inferre that feing his religion
taught him that there is no merit in workes, and much
leffe in fuch workes, how could he imagyn that the killing
of her Ma^{ue.} fhould be meritorious, or any way grateful to
God, fhe being the principal piller of his religion by whofe
death the fame fhould be endangered, and the Catholyke
fayth lyke to be furthered, or at the leaft he muft needs
imagyn that F. Walpoole had no other end therin but the
furtherance of his religion, yf he moued him to any fuch
matter, could he then be fo contrary to him-felf, as for zeal
of religion or hope of merit to feek the ouerthrow of his
owne religion ? this is incredible, abfurd, and impofsible ;
Seing then it is cleare that he could haue no fuch motiue
or end as was fuppofed, and vrged in his accufation, what
may be thought of the whole matter buylt vpon fo weak
& fals a ground, but that the foundation fayling the whole
buylding muft needes fal withal? for the further proof
wherof, and our ful purgation, though it might fuffife
without further difcourfe that Squyre at his death cleared
both himfelf and vs, yet to the end that the impiety, &
malice of our aduerfaryes may be withal fo euident that
they fhal haue no colour, or pretence to haue proceeded
according to *allegata & probata*, (which in fome cafes may
excuffe a iudge from all offence, though he condemne an
innocent man) I wil particularly examine the groundes
where-vpon he was condemned.

B 2   THE

THE EXAMINATION OF THE

grounds wher-vpon Squyre was condemned,
and how vncertayne is the tryal of
truthe by torment.

CHAP. II.

ALTHOVGH I haue litle vnderstanding of our
englifh common lawes, whereof I neuer had further knowledge, then that which I got by the experience of fome fewe cafes that I faw tryed at
the common Afsizes, and in the Kings bench (which alfo
by my long abfence from England, I haue in part forgoten)
and therfore cannot proue by the words, and texts therof,
nor by book cafes that Squyre was wrongfully condened,
yet yf I proue the fame by the approued lawes of other
countreys, yea and by reafon and confcience which are the
grounds of all good lawes, yt muft needs follow , that
eyther he was condemned flatly againft our englifh lawes
alfo, or els that thefame are repugnant to confcience and
reafon, which were as great an inconueniece as the other,
and fuch as I am fure no common Lawyer of England wil
grant, neyther is it to be fuppofed.

Now then to come to the examination of this matter, yf
it be true that is heer reported, (as it is lyke to be, for that
we heare yt vniformely from dyuers partes) that Squyre
was condemned without any witneffes prefented at his arraynment, vpon fome light prefumptions and his owne
confefsion extorted by torment, as he fayd him-felfe at the
barre, and alfo at his death, it is cleare that he was wrongfully condemned , for that no law can allow that fuch a
confefsion fhould fuffife for the condemnation of any man,
without fome other euident proofes ; yt being manifeft,
that the innocet may be forft by tormet as foone to accufe
himfelf falfly as the nocent truely to confeffe his fault;
which the cyuil law propofeth to all Iudges carefully to be
consi-

considered, saying that Iudgment by torment is deceytful, for that often the innocent are compelled thereby to confesse faults which they neuer committed; and S. Augustin wisely noting the inconuenience of such tryals, lamentably bewayleth the practise thereof, and the infirmity of mânes Iudgement in this manner, in these wordes.

Lib.1. §.qu. ff de quæst.

When a man (sayth he) is tormented in his owne cause to try whether he be culpable or no, many tymes the innocent suffreth most certayne paynes for an vncertayne fault, not because any cryme of his is knowne, but because his innocency is vnknowne, so that the ignorance of the iudge causeth the calamity of the innocent, and that which is more intollerable, yea &to be lamented with fountaynes of teares, we see that whiles the Iudge tormenteth the accused, least he should kyl an innocent, it happeneth by the miserie of humayn ignorance, that he falleth into the inconuenience that he seeketh to auoyd, and ignorantly killeth a guyltles man, whom he tormented to know whether he was guylty or no, for the accused rather chusing to dy then to indure the torment, doth many tymes accuse himself of that which he neuer did; Thus much S. Augustyn in this discourse.

Aug. 19. de ciuit. dei c. 6

Hereof also Valerius Maximus geueth a notable exâple in a seruant of Marcus Agrius, who being accused to haue kylled a seruant of Titus Fanius, did for feare of torment most constantly affirme that he had donne it, though after he was executed the partie whom he confessed to haue killed returned home safe, wherto I might ad many examples of lyke matters that fal out in dayly experience, but that I wil not be tedious to your Lordships, and therfor I wil only touch breifly by the way one that concerneth my self, not vnlike to this of Squyres which happened in the yeare of our Lord 1 5 9 5. at my being with the Dukes grace of Feria in Bruxels, where I was through the rigorous, yf not malitious proceedings of a certayne Iudge, brought to be accused by two seuerall persons, not only to

Lib. 8.cap. 4.

The Auctor in danger by false accusation vpon torments.

haue

haue intelligence which S^r. Robert Cecyl (whofe honour knoweth how innocent I am therof) but a fo to haue confpired togither with them the burning of the Kings munition at Machlyn, though afterwards, through the goodnes of almighty God, and the particuler fauour of the Dukes grace (to whom I am therfore to acknowledge an æternal obligation) I was fully cleared therof; for the proceffe being at the Dukes requeft reueiwed by the priuie councel, & the proceedings of the Iudge throughly examined, it appeared that he had not only geuen two torments to eyther of the prifoners without iuft caufe, and fo forft them to accufe both me and them felues wrongfully, but alfo côfronted them togither in fuch fort, that the one inftructed the other what he fhould fay, yea and that he razed their depofitions that were different, and made them agree by his owne arte, wherto the prifoners confented alfo for feare of new torments, chufing rather to dy then to indure the fame, and determining to difcharge theyr confciences at their deathes, as wel for their owne purgation as myne, and this appearing to be true by the examination not only of the prifoners them-felues, but alfo of the Iudges clark, & the Iaylor (befydes that it was euidêt, that there had beene no munition at Machlyn to burne of 25. yeares before) the prifoners were quit of that matter by fentence, and I for that I was neuer in the hands of the Iuftice, was only declared to be cleare and innocent by teftimony giuen me vnder the hands of the priuie councel, and the Iudge was alfo forft to reftore my honour, and to do me fuch reparation of the wrong, as I refted fatisfied.

And I doubt not but yf I had as potent a patron & frend in England at this prefent as I had at Bruxels, who might procure the proceedings of this matter of Squyre to be fifted, & examined to the bottome as hee did the other, there would be found no leffe indirect dealing in this, then there was in that if not much worfe, & more cunningly hâdled, as after wil in parte appeare.

OF THE

OF THE CRVELTY OF
*the Rackmaiſters in England, and of the
manner of their exami-
nations.*

CHAP. III.

BVt to the end your Lordſhips may the better conceyue how Squyre was circumuented, and forced to
accuſe both him-ſelf & F. Walpoole may it pleaſe
yow to enter into the conſideration of ſome of the
barbarous vſage & tyranie that the Rackmaiſters, tormen-
tours, and inferiour officers; and examiners by whoſe
hands he paſſed haue vſed in the cauſes of Catholykes for
many yeares, and dayly do vſe obſeruing no order of
Iuſtice, nor forme of law, neyther in examining nor
tormenting; for they examin men, not only of their owne
works words and thoughtes, yea and what they would
do or ſay in ſuch and ſuch caſes, (a thing neuer practiſed
eyther amongſt Chryſtians or heathens) but alſo of other
men by name, and with ſuch particularities as they teach
them when they are in torment, what they would haue
them ſay of them-ſelues, and others, for their owne eaſe,
againſt all conſcience, and law, which law ſayth, he
which examineth in tormét ought not to aſke particulerly
whether Lucius Titius did the murder but generally who
did it, for otherwayes he playeth the parte of an inſtructor,
and not of an examiner.

Lib. 1. §. qui
qu. ff. de qu.

Furthermore they ſeek many tymes by ſubtyle, and
captious queſtions to entangle at vnawars ſome ſimple
Catholykes, that know not the particuler penalties of the
lawes, nor the daungers therof, and after they cauſe them,
to be executed thervpon, wherof I could alleadge many
exáples, but one ſhal ſuffiſe which of my owne knowledge
I can affirme to be true.

M.Fleet-

M. Fleetwood not many yeares ſince Recorder of
London, examining M. Iohn Nelſon Prieſt, aſked him
many queſtions, as yt were by the way of conference,
concerning Schiſme and the definition thereof, and who
were to be called Schiſmatikes, and ſo drew him by litle &
litle frō one poynt to an other ſo farre that at laſt he made
him by neceſſarie conſequences confeſſe, that the Queene
was a Schiſmatike, and when the poore man ſaw by the
triumph that he made therat and by the diligent wryting
of the clarke that he was fallen into the ſnare of ſome penal
law, he proteſted that he knew not whether he had offended any law or no, and that willingly he would not
haue donne it, yf he had knowne it, but notwith-ſtanding
the ſeruāt of God was after indyted ther-vpon, araygned,
and executed, and when preſentlie after theſame day one
M. Metam a learned and graue Prieſt being conuented before the commiſſioners and demaunded by the Recorder
of theſame matters, and in theſame ſubtyle manner, refuſed to anſwere to ſuch bloody queſtions (not to geue
him and the reſt occaſion of ſo great a ſinne, as to ſpil his
blood) the Recorder fel into an extreame great rage, and
reuiled him ſhamefully, reproching him with tymiditie,
and cowardiſe, the lyke whereof I think was neuer hard
nor red of in any Chriſtian, no nor heathē cōmon wealth,
as that thoſe which ſhould be the miniſters of Iuſtice,
guardians and defenders of the Lawes and meanes to
keep men from tranſgreſsion thereof, ſhould procure
them to be tranſgreſſours, and be offended with men, becauſe they wil not offend : yea and vſe theſayd Lawes,
not as lanternes, or guydes, to lead and direct men to do
their duety, but as ſtumbling blockes to ouerthrow them,
as ſnares to entangle them, and as knyues to cut theyr
throtes, and neyther giue them leaue to ſpeak, nor to
think, nor to hold their peace, which poynt Tyberius
Cæſar though otherwiſe tyrannical, did miſlike, ſaying
(as Suetonius reporteth of him) that in a free common
wealth,

wealth, the tongue and thought ought to be free, which libertie of fpeach neuerthelefſe we craue not,but only that it might be lawful for to think what we lift (not matters of treafon or confpiracy againſt the Prince or ftate as fyco-phants do bable) but matters of our fayth and confcience fuch as all Englifh-men from the tyme that we were made Chriftians haue thought and profeffed vntil thefe our dayes, and all Catholykes befydes throughout the world do ftil think, and this with all dutie and loue to their temporal Princes,at leaft mee thinks yt were reafon that we ſhould haue leaue to be filent, and not to offend the lawes by forced fpeach when we neyther meane nor lift to do it,for as the traigical poet fayth.

> *Though nothing els permitted be,let filence breed no blame,*
> *For no man craues of any King,leſſe fauour then the ſame.*

To conclude this poynt of their examinations I cannot perfuade my felfe that our lawes can allow them, feeing the Imperial Lawes do ordayne exemplar punifhment againſt fuch magiftrates as ſhal make any malitious or captious interrogatories, as appeareth by a law of Adrian the Emperour, which fayth. *Si quid maligne interrogaſſe,&c.* yf it fhal be proued that they haue examined any mali-cioufly or captioufly. Let them be punifhed in example of all others to the end that the lyke be not committed hereafter.

Seneca in Oedip.

Marcianus ſ. C. L. Diuus Adrianus, 6. ff. de cufto-dia,& exhi-birione reoꝝ

C   OF THE

OF THE TORMENTORS

and their manner of proceeding against law and conscience.

CHAP. IIII.

SEEING such are their examinatiõs, what maruail is yt though their torments be no lesse exorbitãt, which they giue commonly to Catholykes without accuser or witnes, and without measure or certayne number, as of late yeares to omit other examples was euident in two rare gentlemen Priests and religious-learned fathers Southwel and Walpoole whom they tormented, the one 10. and the other 14. tymes, though they had neither accuser nor witnes, nor iust presumption of other matter against them then their religion for the which only they were after condemned, and executed, whereas by the ciuil law a man cannot be tormented except their be proofes against him [a] *Luce clariora*, as Baldus sayth, clearer then the Sunne it self, & testified at least by one witnes [b] *omni exceptione maior* (against whome no exception can be take) that eyther hath seene the cryme cõmitted, or otherwayes vnderstood it, as certaynly as though he had seene it, in which torment also a certayne moderation is præscribed, which is not lawful for the Iudge to exceed, as it shal not be reiterated [c] but when new proofes are presented, (and as some lawyers say more pregnant then the first) and that the partie tormented be neyther [d] killed nor lamed therwith, neyther yet that any other kynd of torture be vsed then ordinarie in so much that the [e] Doctors do marueloufly enueigh against such Iudges as inuent newe manners of torments calling them [f] *carnifices* and not *Iudices*, hangmen, and not Iudges. Likewise the Canonists do teach, that it is a mortal sinne for a Iudge to geue torment without sufficient witnesse and euidence, or to ex-

ceed

P. Southwel.
F. vvalpoole.

[a] Baldus cõf. 259. verba in quisitionis ver 7. ratio lib. 1.
[b] Bart. l. ma rit. in principio ff de q. l. confessio extra iudi.
[c] Alex. con. 5. num. 4. lib 1. Albert in rubr C de q num. 8.
[d] Barol in l. quæstionis mo.iun. n. 1. ff. de qu & in lege coin ff. ad l corn.
[e] Brun de iu dicio & tortura f. 65. post, num 6
[f] siluest. verbo Tortura.

ceed the number of meafure præfcribed by the law, fo
that it dependeth not vpon the wil of the Iudge, nor yet is
it the lawful power of a Prince to difpéce therewith, or to
command it to be downe in other manner as fome very
learned Cyuilians haue fignified vnto kings and princes in
fome cafes and occafions, as them-felues haue written,
therfore the ciuil lawe worthelie ordayneth, a *pænam ca-*
pitis, payne of death againft the Iudges which geue torment without fufficient proofes, and appoynteth other
greiuous punifhments for them that obferue not the præ-
fcript and ordináce of the law in geuing thefame, wherein
I report my felfe to the Doctors of the Arches, and M. of
the chancery that are Ciuilians and canonifts who cänot
be ignorant of their lawes in this point.

Afflict, and
gram mat.
voto 10 nu.
13. \ voto
32.num.9.

a Mars in l.
queftionis
modum nu.
73 ff de qu.
& in l. 1.
prærerea nu.
7.in fin. ff.ad
leg cornel.de
ficariis.

Wherby your lordfhip may vnderftand what they deferue that torment the Catholyks vpó their owne braynes,
and bare fufpitions, without any proof, or witnes in the
world, & that with fuch extremety as they lame fome, and
kil others, and with fuch deuilifh deuifes as amongft Chriftians hath not bene hard of whereof I could alleadge fome
lamentable examples of Prieftes hanged vp by rhe mébers,
or priuy partes, as of M. Tho. Pormort and M. George
Beefley but efpecialy of M. Francis Dikenfon of whofe torments I think good to relate fome perticulers omitting
to auoyd prolixitie, the ftories of the others.

It is not many yeares fince thefaid M. Francis Dikenfon
Prieft was taken and committed to prifon by one of the
perfecutors, who feing him to be a very proper yong man
in the flower of his age, and imagining that he might
quickly ouerthrow him by the finne of the flefh, found
meanes to haue a woman conueyed to his bed, who being
repelled by him, and the enemy feing that the practife
took no effect, but came to be knowne not oniy to all
thofe that were in prifon, but alfo to many others abroad
to the commendation of the Priefts chaftitie, and honour
of the Catholyke Religion, he was fo incefed againft him,

M.Fra.Di-
kenfon.

C 2   that

that he caufed him to be háged vp, firlt by the priuie partes
(which he made to be pearfed in diuers places with whote
yrons) and after by the hands vntil he was half dead, and
then called in many to fee his fayd priuie partes, inflamed
and rankled) with the burning of the whote yrons, faying
vnto them after they were gone foorth agayne, behold
this chafte Prieft, how he hath dreffed and fpoyled himfelfe with naughty women, and not content therewith
caufed him alfo to be araygned, and executed for being a
Prieft, without hauing any other matter againft him;
which kynd of cruelty tending to the ouerthrow both of
foule, body, honour, and all, can hardly be matched I
think with any example of the old heathen perfecutours
of the primitiue Churche.

   This I haue thought good to reprefent to your Lordfhips, as wel that it may pleafe yow of your wifedomes &
piety to haue an eye hereafter vnto fuch proceedings, as
alfo that your honours may conceyue what fuch merciles
men as thefe, might make fo weak a man as Squyre was
to fay, or do, to the preiudice of himfelf and others, and
yf neuerthelesse they haue wrought the lyke effect (God
be thanked) but in very fewe of that great numbers of
Catholykes that haue paft their handes in this our perfecution, it is not to be afcribed to any other thing els, but to
the miraculous afsiftance that God for his owne glorie
hath geuen and geueth to thefe witneffes of his truth, no
leffe then he did in tymes paft to the ancient martyrs.

THAT

THAT THE COMMON
*lawes of England do not admit torment in tryal
of cryminal caufes, for the condemnation
of the delinquent.*

CHAP. V.

BVt now to proceed with the matter of Squyre; our lawmakers wyfely confidering the great incōueniences that grow of the fecret tryal of caufes by torment, the danger of errour, the corruption of iuftice, the circumuention of the party accufed, the flaunder and calumniation of the innocent, and laftlie the fmal ground that is to be made vpon a confefsion wrong out by the rack, not only ordayned the publike tryal, which we haue in vfe, but alfo excluded all torment from the fame, admitting onely the teftimony of lawful and fufficient witneffes, which being had the partie is condemned in our law, though he neuer confeffe the cryme, fo that the confefsion being not material or neceffarie for condemnation (as in other countreys it is) torment which ferueth only to extort the fame, is fuperfluous, for where the effect is not neceffarie, the caufe is alfo needles.

And yf our law forbiddeth not, or perhaps ordayneth the vfe of torment in matters of confpiracy againft the Prince and ftate, it is to be vnderftood, that it is not to the end to force the partie to confeffe for his condemnation, but for the bolting out of the bottome and circumftances of the matter, & to know all the confæderates for the præuention of the dauger which may enfewe to the common welth, for otherwyes I muft needes fay, that our lawe fhould be contrary to it felfe, and that the daunger of errour, and of corruption of Iuftice, which our lawmakers fought to preuent by our publyke tryal, fhould be nothing at all remedied therby.

For

For what doth it profit the prifoner to be brought in publykly to heare his iudgment read in the hearing of all, to haue the witneffes confronted w.th him, to be tryed by a verdit of 12. fubftantial men, and to haue fo many caufes of exceptions alowed him againft the fayd witneffes, and Iurie (as in the practife of our lawe is feene) what doth all this I fay auayle him, if the rackmaifter may haue the fingring of him firft, and force him by torture to accufe him-felfe, and that the fame accufation fhal fuffife to preiudice all the priuiledges that our law alloweth him?

Againe why are the iurors brought to the barre, but to fee the witneffes depofed, to heare their euidence, and the anfwere of the party ther-vnto, and to vnderftand the whole groundes of the matter for the ful fatisfaction of their confciences, and to the end they may geue a true verdit.

Edvvard Squyres araignment. But in this cafe of Squyre what cleare euidence was produced? what witneffes were depofed? what warrant had the Iury for their confciences, who hearing by his owne report, that he had beene forced by torments to accufe him-felf, condemned him neuertheleffe vpon his owne confefsion, firft extorted in the Tower by torture and by him ratified afterward at the bar for feare of new torments (as afterward fhalbe declared) befides fome friuolous and vaine arguments vrged by M. Atturney and other lawyers whofe occupatiou is, to amplifie, and exaggerate euery trifle, to make mountaynes of molehils and with their retoryke (fuch as it is) to perfuade ignorant mé, that thee moone is made of greene cheefe? Truly eyther this is farre from the wifedome pyetie and intention of our lawmakers, and from the courfe of our lawes, or els we haue the moft rigorous and abfurd lawes in the world.

But feing the groundes of Squyres condemnation confifted principally in two poynts, the one his owne confef-

confefsion vpon torment, and the other the prefump-
ptions vrged by the lawyers which did feeme to fortifie the fame, I wil br.efly treat of eyther of them a
part, therby to fhewe what may be iudged therby of
their validitie, And firft of the prefumpt.ons.

OF THE PRESVMPTIONS
*vrged by the lawyers againft Squyre, and firft of
the depofition of Iohn Stallage
alias Stanley.*

C H A P. VI.

TH E R E was red to the Iury the depofition of one
Iohn Stallage alias Stanley who lately before was
come from Spayne, and had affirmed that one day
in my lodging in Madrid I enueighed againft
Squyre with great pafsion, and othes, faying that he had
deceyued vs in not performing his promife, and that I
feared we fhould be vtterly difcredited with the King
therby. Wherto I anfwere that I proteft before God, and
vpon my faluation, that I neuer faid any fuch thing to
Stanley in my lyfe, neyther is there any man (I fuppofe)
that knoweth him and me, and both our qualities, behaui-
ours and conditions, wil thinke it probable that I would
vfe fuch wordes before him if there had byn caufe, or that
fo eafely, and eagerlie I would fal to fweareing vpon the
fuddayne, which hath byn fo farre of from all the reft of
my former lyfe, as my acquaintance wil beare me witneffe.
But to the end it may appeare to your honours what a
fubftantial witnes he was, I craue your pacience, whyles I
difcourfe of the fufficiency firft of the man, and then of the
matter by him alledged.

For the firft I affure your Lordfhips that if his honeftie
were

were to be tried by a Iurie of his contrymen in Spayne, I
meane eyther his fellow prifoners in Siuil, or the Catholykes in Madrid, he would foone be fet after Squyre, for that
no man here hath other opinion of him, then that he is a
notable drunkard, a common lyer, a pilfering, cofening, and
cogging compagnion, yea and (as he himfelf hath made
no bones to boaft) a purfecatcher vpon the high-way, & as
I haue credibly hard a commō horfe-ftealer, for the which,
& fuch other vertues of his I vnderftand he hath fcowred
fundry geoles in England, and fhould haue flowred the
gallowes long ere this, yf he had had his right, and of thefe
his good conditions, fufficient teftimony may be had, not
only by the Englifhmen ftil in prifon at Siuil, but alfo by
thofe that efcaped hence, and are in England, who cannot
but teftifie the fame, yf they be put to their othes.

And as for his behauiour heer, I affure your Lordfhips,
that within a fewe dayes after he was fet at libertie, and
that we had noted his demeanour, we were both weary &
afhamed of him, for befydes his vyle and fcandalous lyfe, to
bad to be told, he would fometymes be in fuch defperate
moodes that he would blafpheeme God, faying that he
could not forgeue his finnes, and fometymes threaten to
make himfelf away, becaufe he was not regarded and
rewarded according to his expectation, though much
better then his lewd conditions deferued, and to giue
your Lordfhips fome particuler examples of his trecherie,
yea and his periurie (which for the mater in hand is moft
to be confidered) your honours fhal vnderftand that firft
he betrayed his owne fellow prifoners in Siuil reuealing
certayne treatyes and practifes they had in hand for their
libertie, and other purpofes, and caufed fome letters they
had written to fome of your Lorfhips to be taken; Secōdly
he difcouered an Englifh fhip that aryued there, not for any
zeale to this Kings feruice, but in hope to get a third parte
of the goods, & laftly accufed a frenchman called Thomas
Dobret to be an Englifh man, my Lord of Effex his feruāt,
and his

and his ſpy, which neuertheleſſe preſently vpon his eſcape from hence he reuoked by certayne letters that he
wrote from S. Iohn de Luys aſwel to one of the Iudges
criminal of Madrid, as to Father Creſwel and me wherein
he defyed, and reuyled vs with very vnſeemly ſpeach, blaſ-
pheming againſt our Religion and proteſting that all he
had donne as wel in Dobrets mater, as otherwyes was
only to get his libertie, and that Dobret was no Engliſh-
man, but a frenchman, for ought he knew, and ſo by his
owne confeſsion acknowledged himſelf to be periured,
as may wel be ſuppoſed, ſeeing he had giuen his teſtimony
before againſt Dobret by oth and this the Engliſh marchâts
at S. Ihon de Luys who ſent vs his letters open can teſtifie,
ſo that according to the rule of the law (*qui ſemel eſt ma-*
lus, ſemper malus eſſe preſumitur) he which is once euil, is
alwayes preſumed to be ſo in the ſame kynd, it may be wel
inferred, that ſeing he made no conſcience heer to calumniate and accuſe others falſely therby to get his owne libertie, he would make as litle ſcruple there to coyne ſome
matter of Squyre and vs, to curry fauour with your Lordſhips, & with the ſhewe of ſome plauſible ſeruice, to coun-
terpeyſe the offences he had committed heer againſt your
ſtate, yf the ſame ſhould chaûce to come to your Lordſhips,
eares, and thus much for the man, now to the matter.

Firſt that which Stanley affirmed that he heard of me in
Madrid was not perticuler concerning Squyres employ
to kil her Ma^{iie} (for the which he was condemned) but
general concerning ſome ſeruice to be donne by him,
which might haue beene vnderſtood (if I had ſpoken it as
I neuer did) of ſome other matter of leſſe importance, and
daunger to the ſtate, then the Queenes death, in ſo much
that howſoeuer it might ſerue to induce ſome light pre-
ſumption, it could be no euidence ſufficient to condemne
Squyre, neyther yet to geue him torment other circumſtances being conſidered as after ſhal be proued.

Secondly this Stanley teſtified nothing vpon his owne

D know-

L ſi cui ff. de
accuſat Bart.
in l. Caſsius
de Sena.

vs heer which cannot ſuffiſe in law to condemne any
man, eſpecially in this caſe, ſeing it was acknowledged by
M. Atturney that we of whome he was ſuppoſed to haue
heard it, had ſuborned him to ouerthrow Squyre, and beſydes to do ſome great miſcheif in England vnder colour
to accuſe Squyre of that matter, ſo that both he and we are
ſuppoſed to haue conſpired to betray Squyre. Whervpon
may be inferred two things very euident the one, that
Stanley being Squyres accuſer he could be no witneſſe
againſt him, for that in law they are to be a diſtinct perſons.
The other that though he were not his accuſer, but witneſſe, yet might not his accuſation or teſtimony be of any
force againſt him for that yf it be true (as law determineth)
that a mortal enemie to any man cannot be his b accuſer
nor a c lawful witneſſe againſt him (becauſe the law pre-
ſumeth that whatſoeuer he pretendeth he is not moued
therby by zeale of Iuſtice, but by deſire of reuenge) what
ſhal we ſay of Stanley of whome it was preſumed, by the
lawyers thē-ſelues that neyther zeale of Iuſtice, nor loue
of his countrey, nor cōſideration of his duety to her Maᵗⁱᵉ·
nor any other good reſpect moued him to accuſe Squyre,
or to be witnes againſt him, but (as in Iudgement it was
auowed and ſuppoſed) that he was ſuborned, and ſent in
by vs heer of purpoſe to cut Squyres throte, and vnder
colour therof to do alſo ſome other notable miſcheif
wher-vpon in lyke manner it may be no leſſe probably cō-
iectured, that yf we heer made no conſcience to employ
Stanley, to two miſcheuous and pernicious purpoſes at
once making the one a colour for the other, we would
make as litle ſcruple, for the better compaſſing of our de-
ſignments, to bely Squyre alſo vnto him and ſo his teſtimonie ſhould be falſe, which although it be farre from our
cuſtomes and conſciences, yet I ſay it might haue ſeemed
probable ynough to thoſe that would not ſtick to vſe the
lyke practiſes towards vs, yea & haue donne many tymes,

as wel

L. teſtium &
ibi gloſſa c.
de teſtibus in
c. tam lieteris
cap. licet ex
quadam de
teſtibus.

a L. Actor. c.
de probatio-
nibus.
b Angel. de
malef. in ver-
bo, & ad quæ
relam. poſt
num. 36.
c Aret in c.
cum, oporteat
nu. 19. text in
c. per tuas de
ſimonia.
Eart. in l. 1. ff.
de quæſt.

as wel by counterfet letters fent to fome principal men of our nation, in fuch fort as they might be intercepted, conteyning thankes for feruices donne, as alfo by woords caft out at home of fome of vs in the prefence of fuch as were lyke to blow it abroad to our difgrace, by which meanes a very honeft and wyfe gentleman, and confident feruant of the Kinges was cauled in queftiõ of late yeares by fome aduerfaries of his, who accufed him to haue intelligence with the ftate of England for that a councelour now dead had fayd of him in the prefence of fome principal Catholykes that he was an honeft man, and a frend to his countrey, but the commiffioners that were deputed for the hearing and examining of the matter on this fyde the feas, had neyther fo litle law or confcience or fo fmal iudgement in difcouering trecherous deuifes as to fuffer the partie to be fo much as apprehended vpon fuch an accufation. Practifes of Englifh perfecutors againft Catholyks abroade.

Therefore to conclude if fuch a teftimonie as this of Stanley be held good in our law, (as it is in no law els of the world) fuch a gappe is layd open to calumniatours, as no man in England can make account that this head is fure vpon his fhoulders.

But put the cafe that Stanley had beene both a lawful witneffe, and his teftimonie neuer fo much to the purpofe, yet he could not by any law, eyther humayn, or ᵃ diuine be fufficient to condemne Squyre being alone, and that no mã els witneffed thefame particularitie that he did, as had beene requifitie to proue it iuridically, in a matter of lyfe and death, wherein as the law fayth, *vox vnius vox uullius*, the faying of one, is the faying of none, and our Saiuour fayth *in ore duorum aut trium teftium ftet omne verbum*, let euery matter be decyded by the witneffe of two or three witneffes. ᵃ Deut. c. 17, Mars conf. 1 n. 2 5. Siluest verbo teftis, quæft. 5. Matt. 18.

And although in fome cafes our lawes admit one only witnes, yet the fame cannot be with any reafon or confcience practifed, but when the iurers themfelues haue fo

fuffi-

fufficient knowlege of the matter, that they need not any further teftimony for which purpofe our law ordayneth (yf I be not deceaued)that the Iury fhalbe impaneled in the fame county where the acte was donne,to the end that the iurers, may haue (eyther all or fome of them at leaft) fome perticular vnderftanding thereof. But in fuch cafes as this of Squyre(whereof the iury could haue no knowlege but by the euidence and proofes produced)our lawes cannot fo far difagree from all other lawes humain and diuine, as to códemne a man to death vpon the teftimony of one alone, though it bee neuer fo direct and pertinent to the purpofe and much les when it is fo indirect weak and impertinent as was this teftimony of Stanley.

Furthermore feeing that Stanley was not depofed in the prefence of the prifoner, nor of the Iury but only his depofition red,how did the Iurie know for the fatisfaction and difcharge of their confciences, whether he had geuen his teftimony voluntarily or by violence, and whether he would ftand vnto it to Squyres face or no, which they were bound to confider, yea and to be affured of yt before they fhould find him guyltie vpon his euidence, for no doubt to thofe ends the law ordayneth the publike prefentation and depofition of the witneffes before the Iurie & the prifoner, for what might be thought, but if Stanley had fayd any fuch thing, yet that he had reuoked it agayne, and would not ftand vnto it, or that there was fome other iugling in the matter feing he being then liuing,and in the

Bart. in l. fin. ff. de quæft. pariorum poft innocé. tiam in cap bonæ.

tower was not brought to the court to be depofed there & confronted with the prifoner as reafon and the cuftome of our law requireth, wherto the ciuil law is alfo cóforme which ordayneth that the witneffes examined *in fumaria*

Gloffa fingul in l pactum inter hæredem.ff.de pactis.

informatione be produced agayne *in plenario indicio*, or els that their teftimony is nothing worth, and this is thought fo neceffarie in all caufes criminal that it cánot be difpéced with no not with the confent of the delinquent himfelfe, who cánot in fuch cafes renounce his owne iuft defences.

Therfore

Therfore to conclude seeing that Stanley was subiect to all exceptions aswel for his lewd conditions, and suspition of subornatiō against Squyre as also for beeing but a single witnesse, and his euidence not of knowledge but of hearesay, not particular concerning the killing of the Queene nor giuen in publyke, and in presence of the Iury but in priuate, there were so many detects therin, that yf the Iurie found Squyre guyltie therevpon, I must needs say they were worthy to weare papers for their paynes and may perchaunce weare fierbrands els where if they repent not, for spilling Christian blood so wilfullie.

OF THE TESTIMONIE
geuen by a priuie councelor.

CHAP. VII.

IT is further reported heere that a priuie councelor being present at Squyres arayguemēt did witnesse that he had seene a letter which had passed betweene me, & a kinsman of myne at Rome wherein we aduertised one the other, that although Squyre had not yet performed that which he promised, yet he continued his determination to do it when oportunity should serue.

Hereto for answere I do first make the same asseueration as before vpon my Saluation, that there neuer passed any letter betweene my kinsman and me concerning Squyre in any sence or to any purpose whatsoeuer, and that I think in my conscience my said kinsman neuer hard tel of him, nor so much as dreamed of him, or any matter of his in his lyfe except now by this occasion of his execution written from England.

Secondly I say that persuading my selfe that so great a councelor would not so litle respect his honour, and con-

science

ſcience as to forge of his owne head a matter ſo falſe and
odious as this, and to affirme it in ſuch an honorable and
publyke aſſembly to the preiudice of any mannes lyfe and
fame if he had ſeene no ſuch letter in deed I muſt needes
think that he was abuſed by ſome of his intelligencers or
inferiour informers, who to make a ſhewe of their double
diligence in ſuch affayres did counterfet theſayd letter in
my name or my coſens.

But howſoeuer that was, in this teſtimonie two thinges
are to be conſidered, the one, the eſtate and qualitie of his
perſon, the other the weight and valewe of the matter,
which being weighed ioyntly may ſeeme not a litle to preiudice this cauſe, but conſidered a parte do nothing at all
hurte the ſame.

Cicero orat.
pro muræna. For the firſt I ſay as Cicero ſaid in the lyke caſe in defence of Muræna when Cato was the accuſer, that the di-
gnitie, autoritie, and other partes that God hath giuen to
that our engliſh Cato for a publike good, ought not to turne
to the damage of any particuler man, further then the matter meriteth, but rather to his benefit, to which purpoſe
Cicero recouteth, that when the famous Scipio Africanus
accuſed Lucius Cotta, the great credit, and authoritie of
the accuſer was ſo far from hurting the defendant that it
greatly profited him; for ſayth he the wyſe and prudent
Iudges would not ſuffer any man ſo to faul in Iudgement
that he might ſeeme to be ouerthrowne principally by the
power of his aduerſarie, and Valerius Maximus telleth of
Valerius
Max. lib. 8.
cap. 5. Quintus Pompeius Aufidius, that being accuſed of extor-
ſion, and much preſſed with the teſtimonies of Luciu Q.
Metellus, and of Caius and Q. Cepio, men of ſoueraigne dignitie in that common wealth he was neuertheleſſe abſol-
ued, leaſt (ſayth he) it might ſeeme that he was oppreſt by
the might of ſo potent enemies. Such was the honorable
proceeding of the ancient Romans, who thought it no
reaſo, that a witnes or accuſer ſhould bring into Iudgemet
ouer great power or more authoritie then ordinarie, or
ouermuch

ouermuch fauour, and credit, which ought to be employed to the defence of the innocent, to the help of the poore & impotent, & to the comfort of the afflicted, rather then to the daunger ; diftreffe, and diftruction of fubiects.

This I am bold to intimate to your Lordfhips, not to blame the aforefaid wife and woorthy councelor (to whome I beare all due reuerence and refpect) but to the end it may appeere that yf his autoritie & dignitie, moued the Iury more then the weight of the matter which hee teftified, as yt is lykely it did, it neither ought fo to haue donne, neyther was it I am fure any parte of his honours meaning or defire that it fhould do, and thus much for his perfon.

As for the matter which he teftified ; I fhal not need to fpend many wordes therin, for that I am perfuaded his honour did not fpeake as a witneffe, but by the way of difcourfe, feing that fo farre as I vnderftand, he was not depofed and fworne, neyther yet the letter brought foorth and red in the court, nor proued to be a true and no coun-terfeit letter, which I verely beleeue his honour wil not for all the good in the world, affirme vpon his credit, & much leffe vpon his oth, as it had beene neceffarie eyther he or fome other fhould haue donne to make thefame forcible in law, wherof I faw once the experience in an action of *fcandalum magnatum*, in the Kinges bench, where a letter of the plaintiffes being prefented by the defendant, I re-member M. Atkinfon who pleaded for the playntife, reie-cted it as not written by him, wher-vpon the defendant was forced to produce a councelour at Law for witneffe who vpon his oth affirmed that the letter was of the plain-tifes hand, and fealed with his owne feale.

And yf this were needful in a ciuil action yt muft needs be much more in a caufe criminal & capital wherein moft ᵃ euident, and pregnant proofes are required, efpecially in our law, wherin the Iuries that are to Iudge thereof are ignorant men, in which refpect they had need to haue the

ᵃ L. fciant cuncti c de probatio. Boffius titulo de conuictis. num.9.

matter

the matter as cleare as the sunne, for otherwyes our tryal were the most absurd and barbarous tryal in the world, and therfore whensoeuer yt is obiected by the Ciuilians against our law, that simple Idiotes haue in their handes the Iudgment of our causes, and (as Anacharsis merilie said to Solon of the populer state of the Athenians) that wyse men propound, and plead cases, and fooles decyde them, when this I say is obiected our common Lawyers answere, that our Iurers are not to Iudge de Iure, but de facto, not of matter of Lawes, or right it self, but of matter of fact only that is to say, not of intricate, and ambiguous pointes but of playne and euident matters, as of actes donne, which neuerthelesse yf they be to be proued by presumptions, coniectures, and doubtful euidences, ignorant men wil assone be deceyued therin as in matter of lawe, wher-vpon I inferre, that yf in the ciuil, and all other good approued Lawes, (wherin Learned and wise men are to Iudge of the euidence) yt is required, that the same be most manifest, and testified, by eye witnesses, or others that haue as certayne knowledge therof as eye witnesses, and this especiallie in matters of lyfe, and death; much more is it needful in our Law, wherin ignorant and simple men are to determine the cause, and yf we do not say that this was the intention of our Lawmakers, that ordayned our Iuries, we cannot with reason defend eyther them or their lawes in this behalf, nor excuse them from exceeding great absurdities, and iniurious proceeding.

Plutar. in Solons lyfe.

THAT

THAT THE EVIDENCE
againſt Squyre was not ſufficient in Law to geue him tor-
ment, & that therfore his confeſſion extorted therby was
voyd in Law, and his condemnation vniuſt.

CHAP. VIII.

BVT ſome perhaps wil ſay that although theſe two
teſtimonies of the priuie councelour, and of Stanley
were not ſufficient in Law to condemne Squyre yet
they ſuffiſed to geue ſuſpition of the matter, and to
make him apprehended examined and tormented, wher-
vpon enſewed his confeſsion which being ratified after by
himſelf at the barre, was a ſufficient warrant to the iurie
to fynd him guilty, and to the Iudges to pronounce ſentence againſt him of death, as they did.

    For ſatisfaction of this poynt I wil brieflie prooue, firſt
that this euidence was not ſufficient to geue Squyre torment ; ſecondly that his confeſsion vpon torment was
voyd in Law and laſtlie that his ratification therof at the
barre could not reualidate the ſame, and although for this
purpoſe I muſt ayd my ſelfe of the Ciuil law as hitherto I
haue donne, for lack of knowledge & bookes of our owne
lawes, yet I am wel aſſured, no wyſe and learned common
lawyer can reiect the reaſons alleadged by the ciuil law, as
wel for that they are grounded on equitie and conſcience
(in which reſpect they are receyued and confirmed in lyke
manner by the Eccleſiaſtical, and canon lawes of Chriſtendome) as alſo for that our law, ſo farre admitteth the ciuil
law, that in many caſes yt remitteth vs vnto the deciſion
thereof, as we may ſee in matters of teſtaments, and ma-
riages, and in diuers caſes of the chancerie, for which purpoſe do ſerue our Arches, Admiraltie, and M. of the chancery, and this muſt needs haue place, much more in this
caſe then in many others, for that the tryal by torment

L. ſi cui ff. de
accuſat Bart.
in l. Caſsius
de Sena.

E   properly

properly belongeth to the ciuil law, and not to ours, which law of ours abhorring (as it seemeth) the crueltie, and rigour of torture doth exclude it from the tryal of cōmon causes (as before I haue sayd) and therfore if in any case it boroweth the vse therof, of the ciuil law, it must eyther vse it with the same circumstances, and conditions, or els with more moderation seing it tendeth more to mercie & pittie then the other doth.

Now then to the matter, though the ciuil law vseth torment in tryal of criminal causes, to force the partie to confesse the cryme yf he wil not voluntarily do yt, neuerthelesse yt ordeyneth that it shal be geuen with such circumspection, and consideration, as yf the forme and circumstances of the law be trulie obserued there is litle daunger or none at all of doing wrong to the party.

L. 1. ff. de qu.

First yt commandeth that the iudge begin not with torment neyther proceed hastely therto, but with mature consideration aswel of the qualitie and credit of the partie, as of the lykelihood and truth of the cryme obiected.

Bald. conf. 259. verba in questionis ver septima satio lib. 1.

Secondlie that the euidence and proofes produced be most manifest as in the 4. Chapter of this treatise I haue sufficiently proued.

Bartol. l. Maritus ff de qu l. cōfesio extraiudicialis.

Thirdlie that the witnesses shal be such as no lawful exception can be taken against them.

Bart. in l. qui fine nu. 6. ff. de quæst.

And although the Iudge may geue torment with one lawful witnesse that produceth indicium indubitatum as the lawyers tearme it, an vndoubted and cleare euidéce (as for example when there is an eye witnesse against whom no exception can be taken, for so sayth Bartol) yet when the sayd euidence is not so manifest two witnesses at least are required and the same to be contestes, that is to say, affirming one and the selfsame thing.

Bart. ibid. nu. 7. Innocēt c. sicut extra de Symon glos. singul. in l. sin. verbo vel inditijs c. familiæ hercifcum, recepta a Bartolo Baldo & Saliceto.

This being true; it appeareth that Squyre was tormented against all law, for that the matter and euidence that was brought against him was neyther cleare, nor yet
testified

testified by lawful and sufficiēt witnesse; for as for Stáley besydes that he was subiect to many exceptions aswei of suspition of subornation, as also for being his accuser, in which respect he could not be a witnesse, his euidence was lykewise in it self so defectious that yt could be of no moment or consideration in the world as I haue proued in the 6. Chapter.

And as for the letter which the priuie councelor testified he had seene, it was not proued to be a true and no counterfeyt letter, and therfore no such cleare euidence as law requireth to the geuing of torment, besydes that yf his honour wil be taken for a witnes yet he was not contestis with Stanley for that they did not testifie both of them one and the self same thing as is needful when the euidence is so weake as this, neyther did that letter mention any perticuler act but imployment of Squyre in general, & for generalities no particuler man can be punished as sayth the law.

Therfore I conclude that he being tormented vniustlie, and against law the confession so extorted could not be of force to condemne him, though he ratified the same afterwards publykly at the barre; for all ciuil lawyers do agree, that yf the euidence be not sufficient to the geuing of torment, yea and also sufficiently proued (in such manner as before I haue declared) then the confession extorted therby is a *nulla*, that is to say, to be accompted none at all, though the partie should ratifie it a thousand tymes after (for so they write) yea and further, that although after such ratification, there should be presented sufficient proofes (wherby yt should be manifest that the confession was true) yet yt could not be therby reualidate and made good in law for his condemnation, though it were in cases of assassinat treason or any other lyke haynous cryme whatsoeuer, and this being true in the ciuil law, it cannot be contradicted by ours, which is more fauorable to lyfe, and admitteth no torture in tryal of causes for condemnation, nor relyeth so

a Glos. vnica in l. qu. habendæ ff. de quæ st.
Foller. in pract. crim. to. 307. nu. 1.
Maif. conf. 95. num. 10.
Alex in l. qui in aliena 6. celus nu. 12.
b Grammat. cont 37 nu. 6 & 7
c Barr. in l. maritus n 2. ff. de qu l rem Iulius (larus in practica crim quæst. 5). num. 14.

much

much vpon confession of the partie extorted by torment, as vpon sufficient euidence of lawful witnesse, which in this case of Squyre was none at all; in which respect the Iudges and Iurie hearing him say, that he had beene tormeted, and seing the euidence and witnes insufficient for the geuing of torment, ought to haue held his confession, and the ratification therof suspected, and so to haue at least suspended their iudgment vntil better proofes had beene produced; presuming that for as much as he might assure himselfe, that all the benefit he should reape by the reuocation of his sayd confession, would be but new torments worse then death, he resolued himself to ratifie the same and at his death to discharge his conscience, and to cleare himself, as those which accused me at Bruxels determined to do, and as infinite others haue donne in lyke cases. And that this was also his resolution it appeared manifestly at his death, at what tyme he vtterly denyed not only the fact, and all intention therof, but also that he had bene employed to any such end by any man, accusing his owne frayltie in that he had for torment belyed himself; which being considered with the weaknes of the euidence, doth no lesse manifest his innocencie and ours, then discouer the impietie of those that enueygled him to bely and slaunder himselfe & others, wherof I wil speake more hereafter.

A N

AN EXPOSTVLATION
*which M. Cook her Maiesties
Atturney.*

CHAP. IX.

FOR as much, as I vnderstand that **M. Cook** her Maties Atturney was a principal actor in the tragedy of Squyre, and played the part as wel of a kynd, as of a kindly cook, in seasoning such an vnsauory matter with salt teares, and of a notable calumniatour, in belying and slandering me with father Walpole and others, charging me not only with discouering the matter to Stanley (whereof I haue spoken before) but also with imparting it to the King my maister of glorious memory, making his Matie therby an abettour of that imaginary conspiracy, I cannot forbeare to answere him breefly thereto, and to debate the matter with himself.

There fore, good M. Cook, how simple soeuer yow conceiue me to bee, yet I would haue yow to vnderstand, that I haue not got so litle experience, and skil of Kings humors, in these 15. or 16. yeares that I haue haunted their courts, and serued some of them, that if I should haue employed Squyre or any man els, to kil her Matie I would haue acquaynted any king or soۀerayne Prince therewith, whereby they might take me for a Queene or King killer; for howsoeuer the act might turne to their benefits, or be to their lykings, I ame sure they would say with Augustus Cæsar, I loue the treason but I hate the traytour, besvdes that I am not ignorant that they hold it for a necessary poynt of state, to mayntayne the soueraigne maiesty of Princes as sacred and inuiolable, yea though yt be of their very enemies, & therefore whē Darius was querthrowne by Alexander the greate, and trayterously killed afterwards by a subiect of his owne called Bessus, he recommended

Plutar. in the lyfe of Romulus.

E 3   the

the reuenge thereof to no other, but to Alexander himfelf, faying that yt was not his particular but the common caule of Kings, and a matter of neceffary example,
which fhould be both difhonorable and daungerous, for
him to negleĉt, in which refpeĉt Alexander afterwards
reuenged the fame, not efteeming (fayth the ftory) Darius
to be fo much his enemy, as he that flew him.

This confideration might haue fuffifed (I affure yow M.
Cook) to with hold me from acquaynting his Ma ᵗᵉ with
the matter, yf there had ben any fuch, but much more his
Maᵗⁱᵉˢ great vertue, piety and Iuftice, fo knowen to all the
Chriftian world (howfoeuer yow and your fellowes in
your hemifphere are ignorant thereof) that I know not
who durft haue prefumed fo much as to intimat any
fuch matter to him, whofe royal harte (the very harbour
of honour and true magnanimity) was no more compatible with murders & mifchiefs, the your bafe mynd is capable of Kingly conceits.

This fhal fuffife for anfwere to your difcours of my imparting the matter to the King, feing there was no other
ground thereof, but your owne imagination, which was
no leffe Idle, then your head was addle all that day, being
the morow after your mariage, as I vnderftand, when yow
were not as yet come to your felf, hauing left, as yt fhould
feeme, not only your hart, but alfo your wits at home with
my lady your wyfe, as yt may wel appeare by the aboundance of teares yow fhed in your pittiful pleading, where
of I cannot but fay as Catulus fayd to a bad oratour that
hauing employed all his eloquence to moue his audience to
pitty, afked him his opinion thereof, whereto he anfwered;
in truth (quoth he) yow mooued much pitty, for there was
no man there, that thought not both yow & your oration
much to be pittied, and fo Sir I may fay of yow, that no
dout yow mooued all wyfe men that were prefent to
pitty yow, and to hold yow eyther for the fimpleft, or
els the moft malitious man that euer occupied your place,

the fim-

the fimpleſt if your teares were from the hart, & the moſt malitious yf they were fayned.

For though yow had ben a man of farre leſſe vnderſtanding in the lawes of England then one that ſhould deſerue to be the Queenes Atturney, and had not ben employed in the examinatiō of the cauſe (as by all lykelyhood yow were) yet yow could not but note ſuch weakenes & inſufficiency of the euidence, ſuch wreſting of law, and conſequentiy ſo litle appearence of truth, and leſſe of her Maᵗⁱᵉˢ daunger, that yow could haue no cauſe of teares, except yt were to bewayle the lamentable caſe of the poore priſoner, yea and your owne, for being in great part guilty of his blood, which if yow ſaw not, but weapt in good earneſt for pitty of her Maᵗⁱᵉ your law ſerued yow for litle, and your wits for leſſe, and I dare ſay there were ſome on the bench that laught wel in their ſleeues to ſee your ſimplicity, and thought yow were more fit, (as good a cook as yow are) to be a turne ſpit in the Queenes kiching then her atturney in the kings benche.

But yf yow ſaw the poore mannes inocency & yet could ſhed teares lyke the crocodil to his diſtruction your malice ſurpaſſed all that euer I heard of. And truly the beſt that your beſt friends can conceiue thereof, is that it proceeded from ſome natural infirmity of a moyſt and Ide brayne and therefore I would aduiſe my lady your wyfe, hereafter to keep yow at home, (ſeing yow haue ſuch a childſſh trick when yow come abroad, to cry for nothing) or els to ſend with yow a nours with an aple to ſtil yow when yow cry, for otherwyſe verely yow wil ſhame your ſelf, and your friends, and ſo I leaue yow vntil yow geue me furder occaſion, which if yow do, yow may aſſure your ſelf that I wil follow the councel of Salomon and anſwere a fool according to his fooliſhnes, leaſt by other mennes ſilence he may think himſelf to be wyſe.

OF THE

OF THE LIKE SLAVNDERS

rayſed diuers tymes heretofore againſt Catholykes, and of the concurrence of calumniation and perſecution.

CHAP. X.

YOVR lordſhips haue ſeene vpon what ſmal ground or rather none at all Squyre was condemned, and we heere ſlaundered, wherby yow may iudge how Iuſtice is adminiſtred now in your Realme, by thoſe that are or ſhould be the Miniſters therof for the better declaration wherof, and the further iuſtification as wel of vs heere for this matter, as alſo of all Catholykes for the lyke ſlaunders rayſed againſt them diuers tymes heretofore both at home and abroad, I wil be ſo bould as to repreſent vnto your Lordſhips ſundry manifeſt wronges, and open iniuſtices donne vnto vs in this kynd, for yf this had beene the firſt we ſhould haue had leſſe cauſe to complayne, & this might haue paſſed the better vncōtrold, as many others of lyke ſort haue donne, but ſeing this māner of proceeding againſt vs is now ſo vſual in England that it is growne to a common practiſe, (and therby much guyltles blood ſhed many innocent men ſlaundered, many weake ſcandalized, the ſimple abuſed, and deceyued, the true cauſe of our ſuffring obſcured, and our religion defamed) no reaſonable man can blame me (I hope) if vpon ſo iuſt an occaſion, as the defence of my brethren, our common cauſe, and my ſelfe, (that am more perticularly intereſſed in this matter then many others) I lance a litle this long feſtring ſore, to the end that the malignitie therof being diſcouered, it may receyue ſome cure and remedie through your Lordſhips wiſedomes, whome yt importeth, and in whoſe hands yt reſteth to remedie the ſame.

For this purpoſe may it pleaſe yow to conſider that ther
is ſuch

is such a symphathy betwixt persecution & calumniation
as they are euer lightly found to concurre and go accom-
pagned, for besyds that calumniation is of it self a kynd of
persecution, we neuer read that Gods Churche was euer
persecuted, but his seruants were calumniated & slaundred
in which respect our Sauiour forewarning his Apostles, &
Disciples of the persecutions that they were to suffer, ar-
meth them no lesse against slaunderous, and calumnious
tongues, then against other furious assaultes of his & their
enemies, saying, happy are yow when men shal rayle vpon   Matth. 5.
yow, and persecute yow, & speak all euil of yow, belying
yow for my sake ; and after exhorting them to pray for
their persecutours insinuateth also the concurrence of calumniatours, saying pray for them, that persecute and ca-   Ibidem.
lumniate yow; and S. Paule speaking of persecution raysed   1. Cor. cap 4.
against him, & the rest of the Apostles sayth, we are cursed
and we blesse, we are persecuted, and we indure yt, we are
blasphemed and wee beseech.

This wil be also more manifest yf we consider the na-   The deuils name & nature and propertie of the cheife persecutour of Gods   ture.
Churche, whose armes, and instruments all other persecutours are, I meane the deuil himselfe, who being (as the
Scripture sayth) a lyer, and the father of lyes, yea and a
slaunderer (in which respect he is called Diabolus which
signyfieth nothing els in the greeke tongue but a calumniatour) can no more forbeare to lye, and slaunder, then the
dog to bark, when he is augrie, or the snake to hisse, and
therfore whesoeuer by Gods permission he maketh warre
against the Churche he employeth his instruments no lesse
to slaunder and calumniate Gods seruants, then corporally to afflict and persecute them.

Hereof the experience hath beene seene, in all the persecutions, aswel of our Sauiour himself, as of his Apostles, &
infinite other Martyrs whensoeuer the Churche hath
beene persecuted, eyther by Infidels or heretyks ; our Sauiour was slaudered to be a seducer of the people, to woork   Ioan. 7. & 10.

F   by the

Io.7 & 19.
Luc.23.

Act.14 17.
21.24 25.

Actor. 6.

by the deuil, to be enemie to Cæsar, to hinder the paying of his tribute, and laftly to make himſelf a King, S. Paule was falſly charged with prophaning the Temple, with ſowing ſedition, ſtirring vp the people to rebellion, and many other ſuch lyke odious and greiuous matters, S. Stephen the firſt Martyr was ſtoned to death vpon the teſtimonie of falſe witneſſes, that were ſuborned to accuſe him of blaſphemy againſt God and Moyſes ; In lyke ſort in the perſecutions vnder Nero, Dioclefian, Antonius & others the Chryſtians were put to death vnder colour that they had ſet a fyre the citie of Rome, killed & ſacrifiſed children eaten mánes fleſh & ſtirred vp the people to ſeditiō againſt the Emperours, and their Gods and religion.

Tacit. lib.15.
Tertul.in .
Apol.Iuſtin
Apol.:.ad
Antonin.
Euſeb.lib. 5.
cap.1. & 4.

Hiſt.Trip. li.
6 c.27. Ruf.
lib 10.Victor
de perſec
Vandal.

The Arrian heretikes in Greece accuſed S. Athanaſius to be a whore maiſter a witche, and a traytour : The Vandales that were alſo Arrians in Africk kylled the Catholykes there vnder pretence that they had ſecret intelligence with the Romans againſt their ſtate and gouermét, as we are now : and laſtly the Empereſſe Theodora, wyfe to Iuſtiniā the Emperour did cruelly perſecute S.Siluerius Pope of Rome and all his cleargie, obiecting falſlie againſt them that they had written to the Gothes to inuite them to inuade the Roman Empyre, and other lyke calumniations wherby to ſpil their blood with leſſe admiratiō, and repugnance of the common people.

Paul.Diac.
lib.16.

Orat. in laudem cæſarij fratris.

In all which it is to be noted, that (as S. Gregorie Nazianzen ſayd of Iulian the Apoſtata, when he perſecuted the Chriſtians) the enemies of Gods Churche endeuoured by all ſubtyle & crafty meanes, to procure that they which ſuffred for Chriſts cauſe ſhould be puniſhed as wicked and facinorous men yea and to make them and their religion more odious to all, they ſlaundered them commonly with matters perniçious, and daungerous to all as with treaſon againſt the Prince and State, ſo that whileſt they were puniſhed as publyke enemies & neyther fauoured nor pittied by any, their perſecutors had free ſcope to diſcharge all
their

their furie vpon them without contradiction.

This hauing beene alwayes the custome and practise of the enemies of the Christian, and Catholyke fayth, which we professe, yt is no marueil though those which impugne the same in England in these our dayes (prouoked or rather possessed by the same spirit of lyes, and calumniations, that their prædecessours were) do hold the same course that they haue donne partly slaundering vs with such deuised matter as this of Squyre, which neuer had essence or being *in rerum natura*, but only in imagination and fiction of the deuisers, and partly ordayning lawes and statutes, wherby some principal points of Catholyke Religion, or els some necessarie consequence, exercise and issue therof being made treason many may be intrapped within some shew of offence against these lawes and statutes, wherupon agayne yt enseweth that the common people (who hold for Gospel all that our English parlament enacteth, and haue not the capacitie to discerne betwixt a true and a fayned treason) hearing that the Catholykes are alwayes put to death as traytours (whome they vnderstand to be none but such as commit some heynous crymes against the Prince or state) are brought to imagyn that all Catholyks are perturbers, and enemies of the common wealth, and that their religion is not the common, and general religion of Christendome or that ancient fayth in which all their forefathers liued, and dyed, and our Realme florished so many hundred yeares together, but rather some particuler, and pestilent opinion of some sect sprong vp of late, that cannot stand with the safety of Kinges, and Princes, nor with the quietnes of their states.

And verely I dare say that such of the common sorte as are not aboue 40. yeares of age, and neuer saw Catholyke tymes in England and haue heard of so many executions of trayterous papists, as we are tearmed, do think Papistery to be nothing els, but a very compact of treason, or perhaps vnderstand that Papist, and

The falshood of the English persecutors.

F 2   traytour

traytour are but different wordes, that fignifie one and the felfe fame thing, fo that although all perfecutours haue fought to couer their perfecutions with the cloke of treafon, I thinke none haue wrought yt fo cunninglie as ours haue donne by meanes of thefe lawes feconded with fuch flaunders as this of Squyre againft Father Walpoole and mee and others heer, of which kynd, there haue beene fo many, and of fuch diuers fortes in fundry partes of England thefe later yeares, as neyther I, nor perhaps any one particuler man can take vpon him to difcouer the fame, and therfore I wil only touch with conuenient breuitie a few, which eyther are with in the compaffe of my owne knowledge and remembrance, or haue come to my vnderftanding by vndoubted, and affured meanes, and may be proued by fufficient witneffes that were prefent thereat, yf need require, and libertie graunted to make the proof.

OF THE MOST NOTORIOVS

iniuftice committed in the condemnation of Father Edmond Campion of the Societye of Iefus, and of eleuen other learned and godly Priefts for a fayned confpiracy againft her Matie and the ftate in the yeare 1581.

CHAP. XI.

I AM fure there are many yet liuing that were prefent at the araygnment of that worthy man, Father Campion of the Societye of Iefus, & of eleuē venerable Priefts with him, and do remember the notorious iniuftice donne vnto them in fight of all the world, who were indyted and condemned in the yeare of our Lord 1581. For a certayne confpiracie made at Rome & Rhemes in Frãce to difpoffeffe her Matie of the crowne

by in-

by inuafion of the realme with the helpe of forrayne
Princes, the wh ch confpiracy was fuppofed to be held
in the moneth of May of the precedent yeare to wit the 22.
of her Ma.ᵗⁱᵉˢ. Raigne at Rome and Rhemes, for proof
wherof firſt ſpake the Queenes foliciter and Atturney with
other of the Queenes councel who began to dilate the
matter with large difcourfes (as the old Roman oratours
were wont to do when they ment to draw out the day and
leaue no tyme to their aduerfaries) handling thefes only,&
not hypothefes, to wit general propofitions and comon
places of the greiuoufneile of treafon, of the peril of Kingdomes where traytours liue and do cloke their intenfions
with fhew of Religion, of the great importáce of the faftie
of her Ma.ᵗⁱᵉˢ. perfon and the daungers fhe had paffed, and
how much fhe was maligned by Catholykes both at home
and abroad and other lyke ſtuffe.

Then came they to declare how many wayes rebellions
and tumultes had byn attempted by fuch kynd of people, as
the excommunication of Pius Quintus, the hanging vp of
it by M.Felton, the ryfing in the North by the Earles of
Northumberland and Weſtmerland, the late attempts of
Doctor Sanders and others in Ireland, and when no end
was made in amplifying & exaggerating of thefe matters,
the prifoners often tymes defyred that they would come to
the perticuler poynts of the inditement and proue fome
perticularities againſt any one of them of whom fome faid
that nothing was alleadged but original finne, & the factes
of others, fome that they were very children when moſt of
the matters alleadged did happen, fome that they were of
farre different places, ſtates and conditions.

And when thefe accufers or rather declamers went ſtil
forward to vrge the infurrections of other Catholykes
againſt thefe that were prefent F. Campion among
other thinges fayd, Sir, fuppofing that diuers men Catholyke in Religion hauing for the fayd Religion, or
other caufes taken fometymes armes (as of Proteſtants

F 3   alfo

alfo I thinke, no man can deny yt that confidereth what hath paffed in our dayes in Germanie, Fraunce, Flaunders and Scotland) yet what is this to any of vs heere at the barre, though we be of thefame Religion, this doth not proue vs to be of the fame action; yf a fheep were ftolne and a whole familie called in queftion for the fame were it a good manner of proceeding for the accufers to fay your great grand fathers and fathers, and fifters and kynsfolke loued all mutton, ergo yow haue ftolne the fheep, if yow wil proue any thing againft vs, M. Attorney and Solicitor yow muft leaue your ranging fpeech & come to fay thow Campion or thow Sherwyn, or thow fuch a one, haft done, or dealt, or committed this act.

This fayd that feruant of God, and to all indifferent men that were prefent his demaund feemed moft iuft and reafonable, but yet would yt not be hard for a great while, at laft notwithftanding were brought in certayne witneffes whofe names were Slead, Cradock, Munday, & Eliot. The firft had bene a feruing man in Rome and fayd he had heard by common report that fome ftyrres were lyke to be fhortlie in England; Cradock had byn a broken Merchant about Italie, and imprifoned in Rome for a fpie and teftified of one that to comfort him in prifon fhould fay, he was happie that he was foorth of England, feing yt was lyke that great troubles would enfewe there; Munday was a player of commedies, and had byn fome fewe dayes in Roome, and could fay litle or nothing at all; Eliot was a feruingman who hauing byn a Catholyke before, but now in danger for ftealing away a yong gentlewoman out of M. Ropers houfe, and for fufpition of a robery for which he and his frends were boûd to appeare at the next affyfes) to get himfelf free, betrayed firft his beft and greateft frend M. Payne a Prieft, and afterward took F. Campion and now came into iudgment, not to accufe any particuler man prefent of any matter of weight but to make them odious by relating a certayne

fiction

fiction of his owne againft M. Payne abfent but in the
tower whom he accufed to haue told him of a deuife
that had byn thought of to kyl her Matie in tyme of progreffe or hunting with fiftie armed men, which the other
after vpon his death took to be moft falfe.

Now then all thefe witneffes being brought in, and
faying no more in effect them heer hath byn layd downe
how infufficient there depofitions were to condemne any
one of this companie, and much leffe all and euery one of
them together I referre me to the iudgement of any man
that hath but common fence, for albeit we graunt that
thefe witneffes were all honeft men, (as it is euident they
were lewd and infamous fellowes) what proued they
againft F. Campion or any of the refte there araygned?
what particularities brought they of the confpiracie, and
pretended inuafion as with what forces yt fhould be done,
what forreyn Princes had ben treated with all, and how
or by whome the matter had beene negociated, & by what
meanes they at Rome conferred with them at Rhemes and
how it came to paffe that the confpiracie came to be held
by fo many feueral perfons, and in fuch diftant places at
one tyme, as in the end of one moneth of May? no doubt
for the condemnation of the prifoners, yt had beene requifite that yf not all, at leaft fome of thefe particulars
fhould haue beene proued, eyther againft them all or at
leaft againft fome one of them as yt is euident yt was not,
for though we fhould graunt that fome bodie had told
Slead, or Cradock in Rome that there would be great
ftyrres in England fhortlie, what did that touch F. Campion in particular or any of the reft?

And wheras one fayd that he had heard alfo at Rhemes
of fome fuch ftyrres lyke to enfew, what proued this againft
any of thofe that came from Rome, or yet againft thofe
that were come from Rhemes diuers yeares or monethes
before or els afterward feing that there was at that tyme
neare hand 200. Englifh at Rhemes of whom it could
not be

not be with any reafon prefumed that they were all priuie of the confpiracie, yf there had byn any fuch, and yf only fome were priuie therof how did it appeare that thofe which were araygned were of that number feing the witneffes did not particulerlie charge any of them therewith?

Laftly he which teftified that M. Payne the Prieft, told him of a confpiracy of fome Catholykes to kyl the Queene in a progreffe what proued he againft any of them at the barre, feing that M. Payne was none of their companie, and the matter altogither differét from the other where vpon they were indited.

Was this then fuch playne and fufficient euidence as is neceffarie in law for condemnation of a man in matter of lyfe and death, which euidence as before I haue fhewed in Squyres cafe, ought to be as cleare as the Súne, not general but particuler, not of hearefay, but of affured, and certayne knowledge and teftified by witneffes, auouching one and the felf fame particulers.

But what need I labour to ouerthrow their teftimonies by law feing it was cleare to all them, that were prefent at their araignméts or deathes, that they were neyther all knowne one to an other, neyther yet to the witneffes themfelues, before they were brought to the barre and that fome of them were in England and fome in other places, at the fame tyme that they were fuppofed to haue cófpired at Rome and Rhemes as diuers of them affirmed, and was by the othe of M. Thomas Lancafter manifeftly proued of M. Colington the Prieft, who was quit thervpon, and the lyke was alfo auouched of an other of them by one M. William Nicolfon who being prefent and moued in confcience to teftifie a truth, called to the Iudges from the place where he ftood, and offred to depofe that he knew that one of the prifoners (whofe name I haue forgot) was otherwhere then was fayd in his inditemét, at the fame tyme that the cryme was fuppofed to be committed,

mitted,which offer of his,ferued to no other purpofe then
to bring himfelfe in the bryres, for being examined what
he was, and found to be a Prieft he was prefently fent to
prifon.

Alfo M. Thomas Ford, and M. Iohn Shert two of the
Priefts that were condemned, protefted not only at the
barre, but alfo at ther deathes that they were in England
at that tyme, and fome yeares before that the confpiracie
was fuppofed to be made at Rome and Rhemes, which M.
Ford fayd he could proue by 500. witneffes , but that he
feared to bring his frends in trouble thereby, wherto M.
Shert alfo added that Munday his accufer had publikly cō-
feffed , that he had neuer feene him eyther at Rome, or
Rhemes, which Munday being præfent could not deny;
and M. Robert Iohnfon an other of the fame company
executed next after M. Shert hauing protefted his innocencie as all the reft had donne before,alleadged for proof
therof, that he had neuer in his lyfe feene fome of thofe
that were condemned as his complices, vntil he came to
the barre,and Munday the principal accufer of him,and of
the others,being commanded by the officers to charge him
with the cryme to his face, confeffed openly that he had
neuer knowne or feene him beyond the feas.

Laftly M. Luke Kyrbie who as before is mentioned
was particulerly accufed by one of the witneffes to haue
told him , that there would be ftirres fhortly in England,
did not only by probable arguments ouerthrow his teftimonie at the tyme of his death,but alfo perfuaded him ear-
neftlie to repentance for his fals accufation,by the example
of Iohn Nicols (one that had alfo falfly accufed him and
the reft) who being moued with remorfe of confcience,
came to him fome dayes before to the prifon in the towre,
and in the præfence of 4. witneffes (wherof one was his
keeper)reuoked all that he had fayd, and written againft
them; and this I fay, M. Kyrbie did not only proteft at his
death, but alfo found meanes to write a few dayes before

G   to a

to a frend of his, which letter is yet extant, wherin he alfo declareth, that Nicols fayd vnto him at the fame tyme, that Müday & Sled (who were two other of their accufers) were forced to accufe them by the importunitie of others, and that he could difcouer notable villanies of them; which he fayd he would do and in difcharge of his confcience geue to vnderftand to Syr Francis Wallingham, and Sr. Owen Hopton, how vniuftly they were all condemned.

Thus your Lordfhips haue heard what fubftantial witneffes thefe were, and how friuolous, impertinent yea and flatly fals were there depofitions, which the Iurie and udges, acknowledged fufficiently, when they did quit M. Colington, vpon the othe of M. Thomas Lancafter, wherby alfo they conuinced themfelues of notable iniuftice in condemning the reft, for yf the teftimony of the witneffes deferued to be reieóted in Collingtons caufe, (who was accufed ioyntly with the others, and as deeplie as they) it ought not to haue beene admitted againft any of

Alex.in l ſi ex falſis nu. 13.c de tran- fact.& conſ. 27.nu.3. li.2. quem refert Decius conſ. 105.& Crotta in verbo Iuramentum eſt quid Alciat. lib. 1.§. ſed & ſi mihi num.43 ff.de verborum oblig Iulius clarus in pra-&ica crim. q. 53.§.8.

them it being a rule & maxime in Law that *Iuramentum eſt indiuiſible*, an oth cannot be deuided, fo as one part may be true and the other falfe, and therfore being difproued in part is to be reieóted in the whole, as all Ciuilians do vniformely affirme.

And truly my Lords the iniuftice was fo notorius to all men of Iudgment, that afsifted at the araygnment, yea and to the Iurie themfelues, that one of them, being after afked by a familier frend of his with what confcience he could condemne them vpon that euidence, anfwered he could do no leffe, for otherwayes he fhould not haue beene taken for a frend to Cæfar. Iudge Wray alfo that was the cheife, and gaue fentence the firft day, being called vpon the next to go and fit vpon the reft (for they were deuided into two dayes) was heard to fay to the other officers when he went out of his owne houfe, that except matters paffed in better order, and more fubftantially then the day before, all of them would be fhamed about that matter. And I proteft

that

that a gentleman of Lincolns Inne a ſtudent of the law, &
a familiar frend of myne (though an earneſt proteſtant)
hauing beene at the araygnment told me the day after in
fleetſtreet that the euidence againſt Cápion was ſo weake,
that vntil he heard the iurie geue their verdit, he could
not perſuade himſelfe, that they would or could fynd him
guiltie, and when I aſked him how it could ſtand with conſcience to condemne innocent men, content your ſelf;
quoth he, it was neceſſary for the ſtate, wherto what I
replyed ſhal not be needful to ſignifie in this place, but
what a ſtate that may be, and how likely to ſtand, that needeth to be vpholden with the blood of innocents, I wil
declare in parte hereafter.

And for concluſion of this matter I remit it to the Iudgment of any indifferent and vnpaſsionate man, whether it
be liklie, that ſo many could be guiltie of ſuch a conſpiracie, and paſſe ſuch cruel torture, as all of them did, and
yet not any one of them eyther for rigour of torment or
for conſcience ſake confeſſe it ſooner or later, which none
of them euer did, but ſtood all to the denial of yt, to their
deathes, and then alſo took yt vpon their ſaluations, that
they were innocent, alleadging and vrging diuers arguments, and reaſons for the proof therof wherin I appeale
to ſome of your Lordſhips that were preſent at the execution of ſome of them, yf not of all; and ſeemed to be not a
litle edified with the ſincere pietie, deuotion, and feruent
deſyre, they ſhewed to ſaue their ſoules, which could not
be compatible which fals proteſtations, or rather damnable periurie as theirs muſt needs be, if they were any
way guyltie.

And I doubt not but all ſuch as were there, do alſo remember what dutiful affection they ſhewed towards
her Maᵗⁱᵉˢ· perſon in particular for whom they prayed
moſt earneſtlie, and when ſome of curioſitie, or rather
of a præiudicate opinion of their diſloyaltie, demanded of
them for what Queene they prayed, ſuſpecting they had

*Their dea-
thes & pro-
teſtations.*

ment the Queene of Scotland, they anſwerẹd for our ſo-

ueraigne Ladie Elizabeth Queene of England which was
a ſufficient teſtimony of their loyal hartes, free from
all thoſe treaſonable intenſions, and practiſes wherwith
they were charged.

This then being conſidered, and the inſufficiency of
the euydence before declared, no man can be ſo wilfully blynd as not to ſee their innocencie and the open
iniurie donne vnto them, the lyke wherof I think hath
not beene red nor heard of amongſt Chriſtians; as that
ſo many, and ſo worthy men ſhould be condemned altogither, and as a man may ſay in groſſe, for matters
that could not be proued, no nor iuſtly preſumed of
any one of them all, but ſo barbarous a thing is he-
reſie that where yt beareth ſway, yt baniſheth not only
true Religion, but alſo all pietie, iuſtice conſcience,
and ſhame, wherof yf the iudges, Iurie, and lawyers,
that handled and determined this cauſe had had any
feeling at all, that tribunal which hath hertofore beene
a mirrour of Iuſtice, could not haue beene ſtayned
and infamed with ſuch an execrable murder of ſo many
innocent men, amongſt whome where ſome, whoſe rare
and ſinguler partes, their very enimies could not but
acknowledge, and all Chriſtendome admired: but let vs
ſee ſome others.

OF THE

OF THE LIKE INIVSTICE
vfed againft M. Payne a Prieft, for a furmifed conspiracie againft her Ma-iesties perfon.

CHAP. XII.

IN the yeare of our Lord 1 5 8 2. a vertuous Prieft called M. Iohn Payne, hauing beene prifoner in the Tower fome tyme was tranfported from thence into Effex to be arayned for confpiring the death of her Ma.ie· and was there condemned for the fame partly vpon certayne weake, and friuolous prefumptions, but cheiflie vpon the teftimonie of one falfe witnes, and betrayer of him, named George Eliot.

The præfumptions were thefe, the firft that aboue fiue yeares before he had bene in Fraunce and Flanders, the fecond that he was made Prieft by the Bifhop of Cambray, and that he had geuen oth of obedience vnto the Pope. The third, that in Flanders he had fpoken with traytors, as the Earle of Weftmerland, Doctor Allen and Doctor Briftow.

The witnes teftified that M. Payne had fayd to him fome yeares before, that many plots had beene layd, & attempts made for the reformation of Religion in England, though none had fucceeded, and that which feemed to him the beft and moft lykly, was one that my Lord of Weftmerland, and the Doctors Allen, and Briftow had tould him that is to fay to kil the Queene and fome of her Councel, with 50. armed men, as fhe fhould go her progreffe, and prefently to declare the Queene of Scotland for Queene of England, adding further that it was no more offence to kil her Ma.ie· then to kil a cock, or a hen,

To all

To all this he anſwered ſo ſufficiently, as I ſhal not

neede to trouble my ſelf further then to make relation
therof, for firſt to the preſumptions he ſayd, that of his
paſsing to Flanders, his taking orders of the Biſhop of
Cambray, and his ſpeaking with D. Allen, and Doctor
Br ſtow, there could be iuſtly preſumed no further
matter againſt him then that he was a Catholyke Prieſt,
for that many did the ſame, without any intention or
imagination of treaſon againſt her Ma.tie with the which
thoſe things had no affinitie, and as for my Lord of Weſtmerland he proteſted, he had neuer ſpoken with him in
his lyfe.

To the teſtimony of the witnes he anſwered, firſt that
he excepted againſt him as his betrayer & moꝛtal enemie,
becauſe theſaid witneſſe knew that he ſuſpected him for a
murder that had beene committed; Secondlie he ſayd he
could proue that he was infamous for roberies and other
crymes, and particulerly for deceyuing & coſining a Ladie
(whom he named) of a certayne ſumme of money, laſtly he
vrged vnto the Iurie a moſt eſſential point to be conſidered as that he was but a ſingle witnes, and therfore could
not ſuffiſe in law to condemne him, all which auayld him
nothing, for notwithſtanding, the Iurie would needs fynd
him guiltie, and when the Iudge aſked him what he could
ſay further why he ſhould not haue ſentence of death, he
inſiſted much vpon the point a foreſaid, ſaying it was
againſt all law humayne and deuine to condemne him or
any man els, vpon the teſtimonie of one infamous witnes,
wherto the Iudge made no other anſwere, then that the
Iurie knew whether he was guiltie or no, and when he
replied, that they were ſimple & ignorant men, & neyther
knew what was treaſon nor law, and in feare of peril yf
they ſhould quit him, and therfore deſired him to inſtruct
them therin, he anſwered nothing but præſentlie proceeded to ſentence and condemned him to death, according to which ſentence he was after executed, and at his
death

death being importuned by my Lord Riche and others at the place of execution to confeſſe his treaſon, he prayed to almighty God that he might neuer be pertaker of his glorie, yf he had euer ſo much as imagined any ſuch matter againſt her Maᵗⁱᵉ· as was layd to his charge, and ſo he prayed my Lord Riche to ſignifie vnto her, beſeechingGod to preſerue her in all felicitie ſpiritual, and temporal to his moſt glorie and to her owne beſt good euery way, and ſo dyed forgeuing all, and praying for all as a bleſſed innocent man ſhould do.

OF THE LYKE VNIVST CON-
demnation of M. Iames Fen, and M. George
Haddock Prieſts vpon the lyke falſe
pretences.

CHAP. XIII.

IN the yeare of our Lord 1 5 8 4. 2. Prieſts called M. Iames Fen, and M. George Haddock were condēned at Lōdon for cōſpiring the death, of her Maᵗⁱᵉ· ioyntly togither at Rome, wheras M. Fen proteſted at the barre vpon the Saluation of his ſoule that he had neuer ſeene the other Prieſt that was ſayd to be his confederate, before they were brought thither to be araygned, and that he was neuer in Rome in his lyfe, nor nearer therto then Rhemes in France for ought he knew, and further offred to proue by ſufficient witneſſes that he was in England, yea and alſo in priſon at the very ſame tyme that this conſpiracy was ſuppoſed to be made in Rome, which when he preſſed much as matter ſufficient to cleare him, the iudge anſwered, that although there might be errour in the places, and circumſtances yet it was manifeſt that he was a traytour and therfore ſhould dy for the ſame as afterwards
                                                    he did

he did togither with the other Prieſt, who took it both of them vpon their deathes, that they were innocent of all that matter that they were condemned for, and particulerly M. Fen hauing recommended his ſoule to almightie God, did alſo beſeech him to keep and preſerue her Maᵗⁱᵉ· proteſting that he had euer borne ſuch a loyal affection towards her, that he would not haue donne her any hurt for all the world, no not in the leaſt heaire of her head, though he had had neuer ſo much power and oportunity to do the ſame.

Hereby your Lordſhips may ſee what equitie and iniuſtice is vſed towards Catholykes, in whoſe cauſes euery vayne ſuſpition is taken for a vehemēt præſumption, euery præſumption for a proof, euery witnes for lawful, how inſufficiēt ſoeuer he be, no anſwere though neuer ſo much to the purpoſe admitted, no indifferency vſed, no Law obſerued, wherto I wil ad that when it hath beene in ſome caſes euidētly proued that the witneſſes were ſuborned, & hyred for money, their teſtimonies notwithſtanding haue beene held for good and the priſoners haue byn condemned thervpon, as was manifeſt in the cauſe of two Catholykes condemned in Wales, vpon the ſtatute of perſuading others to Catholyke religion, which though yt was not matter of conſpiracie againſt her Maᵗⁱᵉ· and the ſtate, yet it may ſerue for an example of the iniuſtice vſed againſt Catholykes, and ſo wil I touch yt in the chapter folowing.

OF TVVO

OF TVVO CATHOLIKES

*in wales condemned vpon the testimonie of wit-
nesses suborned, and hyred for
money.*

CHAP. XIIII,

TWO substantial men the one cauled Ihon Hewes & the other Richard White, hauing beene many mes most cruelly tormented, and examined by S^r. George Bróley, & others his afsistants in the Marches of Wales, & cófessed nothing wher-vpon hold might be taken to execute any of the captious lawes vpon them, were neuerthelesse designed to the slaughter, and for that purpose 3. witnesses were suborned to accuse them, that they had persuaded some to be Catholykes: the prisoners being araygned thervpon, excepted against the witnesses, that one of them had beene nayled on the pillorie for periurie in the same shyre as it was notoriouslie knowne to all men, and that aswel hee as the rest were hyred to testifie against them, the iudges answered to the first exception, that though the partie had beene periured in one case yet he might say true in an other, and then did put the prisoners to the proof of the subornation for which purpose, they auowed that a gentleman of good estimation, who was then in the same towne could testifie it, and therfor desyred he might be called, the gentleman was sent for, and being deposed, witnessed, that one Peter Roden told him that Gronow, (for so was one of the witnesses cauled) and his compagnions had receyued 15. shillings a peece to geue testimonie against the prisoners, and that he was also offred so much himself, and had refusedit. The iudges knowing belyke that this was true, & fearing that it would be made too manifest; would

H not

not fend for Peter Roden, but reiected the teftimony of the Gentleman as improbable, faying what fhould any man gayne by the death of thefe men, that he fhould fuborne witneffes againft them? and fo without further tryal of the truth therof, bad the Iurie go togither, who hauing fome fcruple to condemne them vpon the teftimonie of fuch infamous, and fuborned witneffes could not agree thervpon, vntil two of them had beene to conferre with Sᵗ. George Bromley, by whom as it fhould feeme, their confciences were fo wel fatisfyed, that they found them guiltie, where-vpon they were condemned, and the one of them called Richard White executed at wrexam where he had beene long tyme before prifoner.

OF VVILLIAMS YORKE, AND

Patrick Cullen executed alfo for fayned confpira-cies againft her Maᵗⁱᵉˢ perfon.

C H A P. XV.

BVᵗ to returne to fayned confpiracies againft her Maᵗⁱᵉ I omit diuers for lack of perfect knowledge of the particularities, and wil fpeake only of fome publifhed 4. or 5. yeares agoe in a pamphlet printed in diuers languages, as in Englifh, Frēch, and Duitch, cō-cerning a confpiracy of Doctor Lopez, and two other portuguefes, in which pamphlet two Englifhmen called Williams, and Yorke, and Patrick Cullen an Irifhman, were charged to haue confpired the death of her Maᵗⁱᵉ by the inftigation of the banifhed Englifh Catholykes at Bruffels.

And for as much as the pamphleter would feeme to iuftifie the condemnation, and execution, of thefayd two
Englifh-

Eng ithmen , & the Irithman by their owne confefsions,
I wu but defyre your Lordthips for the difcouery of that
fiction, only to confider the circumftances thereof, not
meaning to medle with the matter of Doctor Lopez and
his fellowes, becaufe no Englith Catholyke was charged
therewith.

The pamphleter fayth they confeffed that the Englith
Catholykes at Bruffels held certayne councels amongft
them-felues, where at were prefent two Doctors of diuinity, a Iefuit, 5. or 6. gentiemen and others, all which
are named in the pamphlet, who he fayth confpired altogeather the death of her Mayeftie, and perfuaded Williãs,
and Yorke to vndertake the execution thereof, with the
promife of fort e thoufand crounes, & that for the greater
fatisfaction, and fafter binding of them, father Holt the
Iefuit took the blefled Sacramét (which he had brought
to the councel) kiffed yt, and gaue yt vnto them, fwearing
vpon the fame , that he would pay them the fayd fome,
when they fhould haue effected that which they had
promifed.

For the examinatiõ of this fuppofed cõfefsion, I would
wifh to be confidered , what likelyhood or probability Abfurd improbilities
there is, that thofe two foldiers Williams, & Yorke, both
of them young men (whereof the firft was held but for a
cold and weake Catholyk, and the later fufpected to be a
proteftant , as in deede he was, & then newly come from
England, without any recommendation, or teftimony of
his affection to Catholyke religion, or of his good behauiour) could winne fo much credit fo quickly , amongft
fuch principal Catholykes, as to be admitted to their
councels (yf they had held any) and to bee made partakers of fo high a fecret, efpecially feing that the Catholykes
on this fyde the fea are not ignorant, that fpyes are dayly
fent from England , to difcouer what paffeth amongft
them, in which refpect they are fo farre from trufting in
weighty affayres thofe they know not , as they hold fuf-

H 2   pected

pected thofe of their owne religio,that come from thence
and bring not fufficient recommendation, what fhew
otherwyfe foeuer they make of zeale to the Catholyke
fayth;

Is it then credible that fo many graue perfonages, Doctors,Priefts,and gentlemen,all of them wyfe, and men of
experience would recommend fuch a matter,as the killing
of her Ma.ie to men vnknowen vnto them, fufpected, yea
and mercenary, (feing as the pamphlet fayth they ment to
do yt for hyre) did they not know (feing all the world
knoweth yt) that no man can attempt fuch a matter
without loofing his owne lyfe, or putting the fame in euident daunger,whether hee hit or miffe (whereof the late
examples, afwel of thofe that killed the Prince of Orange,
and the laft King of France, as of thofe that haue fayled to
kil him that now raygneth do geeue fufficient teftimony)
in which refpect neither thofe two that were fuppofed to
vndertake this act for recompence,could haue any probable
hope euer to enioy the reward promifed, neyther thofe
Priefts and gentlemen could perfuade themfelues, with
any reafon, that thefe or any others that fhould promife
to doe the fame for any fuch confideration of reward
would euer execute it.

Furdermore is yt probable, that thofe two which
fhould doe the feat, would confent that a matter fo daungerous for them fhould be communicated to fo many,or
that the principal of the fayd fuppofed councelers, being
men of greate confideration & dayly practifed in affayres
would condifcend to treate fuch a matter in a councel of
men fo different in quality, and humours, as it is wel
knowne they were,that the pamphlet nameth; feing fome
of them for caufes not vnknowne, I am fure,to the pamphleter, did fcars communicate togeather in matters of
common conuerfation, and much les in matters of fuch
importance,yea and that fome others of them were held
fufpected,of moft of that company, to haue fecret intelligence

ligence with fome councellours in Englád, for the which
they were afterwards cauled in queſtion? and therefore it
were an abſurd thing to think that ſo many ſo diuerſly
diſpoſed, and affeƈted, and ſome of them ſuſpeƈted of the
reſt, ſhould treat togeather a matter of ſo great ſecreſie,
weight, and daunger, as the killing of her Mayeſty, beſyds
that, it is euident (and vpon my knowledge I affirme it)
that of thoſe which were named to be of this immaginary
councel at Bruſſels, ſome did reſyde ordinarily in Antwerp, ſome at S. Omers, and ſome at Maſtrich, yea and
were in the ſayd places of their ordinary reſidence, at the
ſame tyme that the pamphleter ſayth they held theſe coūcels at Bruſſels, which being knowne in Flanders to be
moſt true did ſerue notably for the deteƈtion of this ſlaū-
derous fiƈtion among the wyſer ſort of thoſe of that country, which did read the pamphlet in french, or duitch, who
wondred no leſſe at the autors impudency in this behalf; then they laughed alſo hartely at his folly, when
they noted the ridiculous ieſt of fa. Holts carying the
bleſſed Sacrament to the ſuppoſed councel, his kiſsing it,
& ſwearing vpon it, when he did miniſter it, to Williams,
and Yorke; which are things ſo farre from the cuſtome
and vſe of the Catholyke Churche, as euery child on this
ſyde the ſea, knoweth it to be an impudent and groſſe
lye;
    And where as the pamphleter relyeth wholy vpon
their confeſsions for the iuſtification of their condemnation, yt is moſt certayne that howſoeuer they might be
forced by torment ſecretly to confeſſe thoſe particulers,
or otherwyſe falſly to accuſe themſelues, as Squyre was,
yet Williams at his death vtterly denyed the ſame, and as
for York yt was euident ynough, that he dyed diſtraƈted
of his ſences, and was not in caſe to deny or confeſſe, any
thing at that tyme, as all thoſe that were preſent at their
deaths maye wel remember.
    And as for Patrick Cullen, (of whome I wil ſpeak a

woord

Patrik Cul'en at his death. woord or two) yt is manifeſt that he neuer confeſſed eyther publikly or priuatly that he was any way employed
againſt her Ma.ᵗⁱᵉˢ perſon, which at his death M. Topliſſ
acknowledged ſufficiently, when he ſayd vnto him, yt is
now no more tyme (Cullen) to diſguiſe the matter, ſeing
thou muſt dy, and therefore confeſſe thy treaſon,and aſke
her Maᵗⁱᵉ forgiuenes, whereto he anſwered *that he called
God to witnes that he was neuer employed againſt her Maⁱᵉ nor
came into England which any ſuch intention,* and yet the pamphleter affirmeth that he was alſo condemned vpon his
owne confeſsion, though he lay downe no particularties,
nor circumſtances therof, in which reſpect it needeth no
furder anſwere and therefore to conclude ; yt reſteth only
that I here proteſt, as I do before God, that I being at
Bruſſels at the ſame tyme that theſe men were executed,
and the pamphlet publiſhed,ſome of the principal of thoſe
gentlemen that were ſlandered with theſe matters, did
ſweare vnto me,and take it moſt deepely vpon the charge
of their ſoules, that they neuer had any acquaintance, or
conference, with Williams and York,in their liues, nor
euer knew them otherwyſe then by ſight, & that there
was neuer held amongſt them any ſuch councels , or aſ-
ſemblies,nor any of thoſe 3. anie way employed againſt
her Maᵗⁱᵉ perſon for ought they knew, which as I take
my ſelfe in conſcience bound to beleeue, (knowing the
greate integrity and vertue of the parties, as I do) ſo I
haue thought good vpon this occaſion to teſtify it vnto
your Lordſhips, and to all others that ſhal read this Apology, for your more aboundant ſatisfaction in this behalf.

OF THE

OF THE ENDS THAT OVR

Aduerſaryes haue or may haue in ſlaundering Catho-
lykes with ſuch treaſonable attemptes, & firſt of the end
that they haue common with all perſecutors of Gods
Churche and how much they faile of their purpoſe
therin.

CHAP. XVI.

IT appeareth (my Lords) by theſe examples that the
ſlaundering of Catholykes with treaſonable attempts
in our coûtry is no new practiſe, but an old for many
yeares, and ſo oft reiterate, that it is now growne to be
ſtale and a common cuſtome, or rather held for a ſpecial
and neceſſarie point of ſtate, but with what benefit to
the ſtate, it ſhal be diſcuſſed after when I ſhal haue brieflie
declared the ends that the Autors of theſe calumniations
haue or may haue therin, the which may be conſidered,
eyther as common to all the enemies of Catholyke religiõ,
or els as particuler to theſe our Aduerſaries now a dayes,
of the firſt I haue ſpoken before diſcourſing of the con-
currêce of caꞱumniation and perſecution, where I proued
that it hath beene alwayes the cuſtome of the perſecutours of Catholykes to ſeek by imputation of fals crymes
to obſcure the true cauſe of their ſufferings, and conſequently the glorie of their martyrdomes, wherin neuertheleſſe how much they haue fayled of their purpoſe (I
meane as wel theſe of our tyme, as thoſe other their præ-
deceſſours) it is euident by common experience, ſeing almightie God hath in all ages ſo diſpoſed, and daylie doth
for his owne glorie, that the cleare light of truth, and innocencie hath diſperſed the clouds of calumniation in
ſuch ſort that his ſeruants haue triumphed ouer all the
malice of men, and remayned no leſſe glorious with a
double

double crowne of martyrdome then their enemies ignominious and odious for there double perfecution.

The glory of martyrs op-
preffed by calumniatio. For the proof hereof let vs look back to former tymes,
& fee what the perfecutors of Gods Churche, haue gayned
by the lyke deuifes; haue they therby any iote obfcured
the glorie of Gods feruants, who are efteemed, honoured,
and ferued through-out the Chriftian world for glorious
Martyrs, and faynts of God, and receyue more honour, &
glorie in one feftiual day of theirs, then all the Monarks
of the world in all the feafts of their lyfe? Are not the Altars & Temples buylded to God in their memories more
triumphant then the thrones, and trophæs of all earthly
Kings? doth any Princes power extend it felfe fo farre
as theirs, whofe dominion reacheth from the eaft to the
weft, frō the one Pole to the other, whofe fubiects, feruāts,
and fupplyants, are not only the common people but
Princes and potentates, Kings & Emperours, that crouch
kneele and prefent their petitions, at their toombes and
monuments, or wherfoeuer ther is any litle memory of
them? Are all the royal robes, crownes and diademes of
Emperours and Kings fo much efteemed, and reuerenced
in their owne Kingdomes as is throughout Chriftendome the leaft rag, or relyke of any one of them, wherto
we fee Almightie God geueth no leffe vertue and power
oftentymes when it is for his glorie, and their manifeftation, to cure the ficke, to heale the lame, to rayfe the dead,
to caft out Deuils, then he gaue to the hemme of our Sauiours garment, to the hand kerchefs that touched S. Paules
body, to the fhadow of S. Peter? This hath alwayes
beene fo notorious in Gods Churche, that S. Chrifoftome
fpeaking of the great miracles done by the body and relykes of the bleffed martyr faint Babilas, maketh the fame
a manifeft argument againft the Paynims to proue that
Chrift is God, which I wifh by the way, that our Proteftants in England may note for their confufion, feing that
denying the vertue of faynts Reliks they do paganize with
them,

Matth. 9.
Act. 19.
Act 5.

Tom. 5. con-
tra Gent.
quid Chriftus
fit Deus in
vita Babilæ.

them, and do deny therby an euident argument of Chrifts diuinitie, but to proceed.

On the other fyde what honour haue their calumnia-tours, and perfecutours purchafed to themfelues? are not their very names odious and execrable to all pofteritie, & as the memory of the other is æternized with immortal glorie, is not theirs buryed in æternal infamie? To this purpofe fayth the book of wifedome that the wicked fhal Sap. cap. 4. fee the end of the iuft man, and fhal not vnderftand what God hath determined of him, and why our Lord did humble him, they fhal fee him, and contemne him; but our Lord fhal deride them, for they fhal fal afterwards without honour, & fhal euer be amōgft the dead in fhame and infamie.

Hereby may our aduerfaries partly iudge what they fhal gayne in the end by murdering fo many Catholyks as they do, vnder colour of treafons, and enormious crymes; but for their further fatisfaction in this point let them look abroad into Chriftendome, and fee what acount is alreadie made of their fuppofed traytors I meane fuch as die directlie for religion made lately treafon, who of all Chriftian Catholyke people in the world are held for no leffe glorious martyrs, thē thofe of the primitiue Churche as appeareth not only by the publike teftimonie of the moft famous wryters of this age, but alfo by the deuotion that all Catholyks, yea and the greateft Princes, and po-tentates of Chriftendome do beare to the leaft relyke of any one of them, which they think themfelues happie to haue, & keep with all due refpect, and reuerence, befydes that it hath pleafed almightie God to glorifie his name already with diuers notable miracles donne by the fame, which hereafter wil be knowne with fufficient teftimony of the truth therof, and as for their martyrdomes I haue no doubt but as alreadie they are knowne, ac-knowledged and honoured by all true Catholykes fo in tyme alfo conuenient they wil be approued by the

I   Autho-

authoritie of the whole Churche, whiles in the meane tyme the memory of their perfecutors fhal be damned, eyther to the deep pit of obliuion or els to euerlafting ignominie as they may fee it hath alreadie happened to their prædeceffours, and thus much for the end common to all perfecutours.

OF OTHER ENDS PARTI-
culer to our Englifh aduerfaries and of their difloyaltie therin towards her **Mayeſtie.**

CHAP. XVII.

TH E other ends particuler to our home aduerfa-ries at this day may be thought to be partlie pub-lyke, and for the common good (as they in the depth of their wifedome, or rather in the height of their follie do imagin) and partlie for their owne parti-cular profit or emolument.

The publyke are thefe, firft to incenfe the Queenes Matie againft vs to the end fhe may geue them leaue to exercife freelie all crueltie vpon vs, wherby they hope in tyme to deftroy vs, and to extinguifh the memorie of Ca-tholyke religion, wherin I wifh them by the way to note, how farre they are deceyued of their expectation, & how almightie God doth daylie infatuate, and fruftrate their councels, and turne them to their owne confufion, feing that notwithftanding all their rigour, there are at this day many more recufants in England, and fincere Ca-tholyks that wil geue their liues for their Religion then ther were when the perfecution firft began ; fo that we fee how true it is which Tertulian fayth *Sanguis Marty-rum femen Ecclefia*, the blood of Martyrs is the feed of the Churche : But to proceede.

The

The fecond is to irritate alfo her Ma.tie againft the King Catholyke who is therfore cômóly made an abettor of all thofe fayned confpiracies, leaft otherwayes fhe being of her owne incl.nat.on defirous of peace, might come to fome côpolit.on with him,&fo Chriftendome be brought to repofe,which thefe mé imagin would in tyme grow to be daungerous to their gofpei, or rather to their particular ftates & commodities which they may be prefumed to efteeme more then any ghofpel, but how this piece of pollicie ftandeth with true reafon of ftate I wil fignifie hereafter.

Thirdly it is not vnlikely,that the deuifers of thefe fayned confpiracies feeing themfelues employed by your Lordfhips otherwhyles in fome matters of ftate, take themfeiues for fo great ftatifts,that they make no doubt to extend their care further then your Lordfhips meane they fhould do, to wit to the whole ftate and gouernment yea to the perfon of her Ma.tie though litle to her good or comfort holding it a high point of policy, and neceffary for the comon welth, that her Ma.tie be kept (as a man may fay) in aw with theafe bugbeares of imaginary at-tempts againft her perfon, to the end fhee may bee the more plyable and eafy to be gouerned,for as the poet faith, *res eft imperiofa timor,*feare is an imperious thing.

Martial lib. 2, Epigram.

Furthermore the end which they may haue for their owne particular commoditie is to make themfelues and their feruices more gratful to her Ma.tie and to your Lord-fhips by their pretended difcouerie of fo many daungerous treafons againft her Ma.tie and the ftate.

Whereto I wil ad that it alfo importeth your honours to confider whether any of thofe that are taken to be the cheife difcouerers of thefe fuppofed treafons, may be thought to fauour the title of any particuler pretender to the crowne after her Ma.tie for in fuch cafe they may perhaps vfe this artifice to fhadow fome defignemét of their owne,no leffe daungerous to her Ma.tie perfon then this

which they feigne and lay to our charge, to the end they
may the more affuredlie and fecurely execute the fame,&
that afterwards the fufpition and blame therof may reft
vpon vs, which we read was the practife of Seianus in the
tyme of Tiberius the Emperour, who afpiring to the Empyre, and determining to make away Agripina that was a
great mote in his eye, firft fuborned fome to put into her
head that the Emperour meant to poyfon her, and after
made rumors to be fpred all ouer Rome that fome had
confpired her death.

I fay not this my Lords to charge any man particularly
(for I know not who they are, that are the forgers of thefe
falfe coynes) but becaufe I fee that the lyke practifes haue
beene vfed to the deftruction of Princes, and may with
reafon think, that thofe which haue fo litle confcience to
procure the fpilling of fo much innocent blood by fuch
damnable deuifes as thefe, wil make leffe fcruple to break
all lawes humayn and diuine when there is queftion of a
crowne, I therfore infinuate this to your honours as
matter worthy of your confideration, efpecially feing it
cannot be thought that they beare any good, and loyal affection to her Matie. knowing that fhe cannot but be much
afflicted with the vehement apprehenfion of thefe fuppofed treafons, and yet neuer ceafing to torment her therwith, framing dayly new fantafies of fayned feares, as
though heauen and earth had confpired againft her, the
concept wherof (accompagnied with other cares incident
to the gouernment of fuch a potent ftate) might fuffife to
procure the vntymely death of the moft couragious prince
that liueth, and what it may woork in her Matie no leffe
timorous of nature by reafon of her fexe, then decaying
now in bodilie vigeur, by reafon of her declining yeares,
any man may eafely iudge.

THAT

THAT THESE PROCEE-
dings of our aduersaries which they hold for po-
lityke are against all pollicy, and true
reason of state.

CHAP. XVIII.

BVT put the case that her Ma.^{tie·} be so inuincible of courage, that there is no feare of any such effect to follow, yet let it be considered whether in other respects it stand with true reason of state to incence her Ma.^{tie·} against her subiects by lyes and slaunders, and them against her, by insupportable wrongs and cruelties, which were no dout the next way to put all in combustion, yf the Catholykes loyalty, obedience, and patience, were not such, as God be thanked yt is, and I hope euer wilbe, such I say, as neuer hath ben red nor heard of in any people so opprest, so long tyme together, so many in number, so honorable in quality, and condition, and so frended abroad as they might bee (in respect of their religion) yf they would seek the remedy that other discontented people haue sought in former tymes, whereby the state of England hath ben changed, and turned vpsyde downe, twyse or thryse already since the conquest; for how were the two Kings Richard the 2. & 3. dispossessed of their crownes, and lyues but by their owne subiects malcontent, succored with smale forces from abroad? & yet no such cause geuen them as is to vs, who are esteemed for no better then *opprobrium hominum & abiectio plebis,* the skorne of men, and outcasts of the people, & as saynt Paule sayth *peripsema mūdi, the very scūme of the world,* contēned trodē 1.Cor.4.13. vnder foot, & derided of all men depriued of all priuiledge of natural subiects, of honnors & dignities, lādes, & lyues, for no greater offences, then our auncient, & the yniuersal

fayth

fayth of Chriſtendome, made treaſon, yea for fayned
crymes neuer meant nor dreamt of.

To this purpoſe it is to be conſidered,that no force,nor
power is ſo great (as Cicero ſayth) that can reſiſt the
hatred of a multitude,neyther any empyre ſo potent, that

Cice. offic.

can long ſtand by rigour,oppreſsion, and cruelty,& there-

Ariſt. epoiit.
lib. 5.

fore amongſt the cauſes of the ouerthrow of empyres,
and Kingdomes, Ariſtotle worthely reckoneth hatred,
and feare of the ſubieċts ; exemplyfying theſame with the
ſmale continuance of all the tyranical ſtates, that had ben

Cicer epiſt.
ad Attidum.

in his tyme,or before ; and Cæſar confeſsing that he neuer
knew any cruel man, that could long conſerue him-ſelf
and his ſtate,but only Sylla (which yet was not long) he
wyſely added, that he would not follow his example ;
wherein he had great reaſon, for one ſwallow as they
ſay, makes no ſommer, neyther can the example of a few
which eſcape, counteruayle a common experience, that
teacheth what euident daungers do accompany cruelty,&
oppreſsion,which no humain power nor pollicy cá make
ſecure, as it is euident enough to all wyſe men that wil
conſider how litle ſecuritie Kings, and Princes, that haue
incurred the hatred of their people, haue found in the remedyes, and defences, that humain pollicy hath inuented ;
I meane in their treaſures,fortreſſes, gards, armies, multitude of ſpyes, wiſdome and vigilance of councellours,and
ſuch lyke ; for haue not a number of them notwithſtanding all this,ben by their ſubieċts chaſtiſed, and reformed,
depoſed, expelled, impriſoned, killed and thoſe that haue
eſcaped beſt, haue they not commonly liued a miſerable
lyfe,affliċted and tormented with continual feares, ielou-
ſyes,and ſuſpitions of their beſt friends ? for as Seneca

Senee.

ſayth, *he that is feared of many muſt needs feare many* what did

Suetoa.

all the welth, power, and force of the Roman empyre
auayle the Emperour Claudius,poyſoned by his taſter,and
Nero ſo purſued by the people, that he was forſt to cut his
owne throte,or Domitian killed by his chamberlaynes,or

Como-

Comodus murdred by his concubyn, Phocas by one of his ~Sex Aurel~ *vict.* cheefeſt fauorits, or Caligula, Pertinax, Caracalla, Helio- ~Capitolin~ gabalus, Pupienus, Balbinus, Philippe, Galien, Seuerus, ~Lamprid.~ ~Eurrop.~ Macrinus, Aurelianus, Maximinus, Probus, with diuers others, ſome of them ſlayn by their owne gards, and ſome by their ſouldiars; to whome wee may ad the laſt King of France, killed by one alone, in the midſt of his puiſant army, when he thought himſelfe moſt potent and ſecure.

Whereby it euidently appeareth how vnſure, daungerous and pernicious are the pollicies of our aduerſaries, who following the abſurd and peſtilent doctrin of Machiauel think they can aſſure her Maties· eſtat by rigour cruelty and iniuſtice wheareas both reaſon & experience teacheth *that mercy and truth* (as Salomon ſayth) *do preſerue the Prince and that his crowne, and throne is fortified with clemency,* to which purpoſe alſo Seneca ſayth, *the loue of ſubiects* ~Pro.20,~ *is to the Prince a caſtel inexpugnable, and clemency a ſufficient gard* ~Seneca lib. 1~ *though he be alone in the midſt of the market-place,* ſo that theſe ~de elemen.~ ~cap.19.~ moſt cruel and bloody deuiſes of our perſecutours, are not only impious, but alſo fooliſh in that very point wherein they wil haue them ſeeme moſt wyſe.

But yf it be conſidered how they riuet this peece of pollicy with an other point of ſtate, and what may by lykelihood enſew thereof, yt may be thought their meaning is no other but to put fyre to gunpowder and to ſet all on a flame and themſelues alſo to burne therewith, or to rūne away by the light for vſing the matter towards vs as they doe, procuring ſo much as in them lyeth, to alienat vs from our natural obedience to her Matie· and to dryue vs to ſome deſperat courſe (which neuertheleſſe I hope they ſhal neuer be able to doe) a man would think they would at leaſt ſeek to put her maieſty in peace with her neighbours abroad.

But they are ſo farre from the ſame, that they doe not only incite her Matie· dayly againſt the moſt potent Prince of Europ,

of Europ, by flaundring him vnto her, with practifes
againft her perfon and lyfe, but alfo do feek to kindle
him againft her by infamous libels publifhed in diuers
languages, and ftuffed with lyes and flaunders, with iniurious and difhonorable fpeeches aga nit his perfon to
make him an enemy irreconciliable ; for who knoweth
not that iniurious woords offend much more many
tymes then deeds (as Plutark wel noteth) efpecially againft
Princes that moft of all efteeme their honours ? for fo
long as their contentions ar only for ampiifying their dominions, or meerly for matter of ftate, the enmity commonly endeth with the occafion of the quarrel, and the
dammages are by reftitution or recompence eafely repayred (whereby wee fee that thofe Princes which haue
had the greateft differences and warres betweene them
felues do many tymes after become the greateft confederats and frends) but perfonal iniuries efpecially touching honour and reputation, as they proceed from an
exceffyue hatred in them that offer them, fo are they
not eafely pardoned, neyther yet amongft Princes repa-
rable by any reftitution.

What then is the meaning of thefe make-bates ? wil
they oblige her Ma.ᵗⁱᵉ· to a perpetual warre not with fome
petty Prince or poore potentat, but with the moft potét,
rich, and mighty Monark of Europe? and vpon what confidence ? is yt the welth and force of England? the ftrength
of allyes, and confederats ? or yet the good fucceffe of
thefe late warres, which mooues them therto? who
knoweth not that in power & welth her maiefty (though
fhe be moft puiffant and rich) yet is farre inferiour to
him ? in which refpect that which Plutark noteth of
Cleomenes, King of Lacedemony, and Antigonus the
great King of Macedony, may wel be fayd in this
cafe.

It feemed (fayth hee) to proceed of great wifdome, valour, and
prowes that Cleomenes could with the forces of one only ftate mayn-

*Plutar.in the
lyfe of Ti-
moleon.*

*In the lyfe of
Agis & Cleo-
menas.*

tayne warre againſt the power and treaſure of the Kingdome of Ma-
cedony, and all the people of Peloponeſe and not only defend his owne,
but alſo take places and townes of his enemies. But he which firſt ſaid
that money is the ſinowes of warre had great reaſon, for euen as
amongſt wraſtlers thoſe which haue ſtrong bodies by nature, and
hardened by continual exerciſe do alwayes in tyme ouertrhow them
which haue nothing but art and agilitie, euen ſo Antigonus who had
the power and welth of a great and rich Kingdome to ſuſtayne the
expences of the warre, at length weried and ouerlayd Cleomenes that
had no ſuch meanes to beare the charges therof, thus ſayth Plutark in ſubſtance, of theſe two Kinges; and ſo may wee
ſay of her maieſty and the King Catholyke, that by all lyk-
lyhood the multitude of his Kingdomes, the welth & infinit number of his ſubiects, the aboundance of his treaſures that fiow from his Indies, and the ſtrength of his
armies and garriſons continually kept in pay, cannot but
weare out in tyme, the power and wealth of England,
though it were much greater and richer then it is, eſpecialy yf eyther any breach ſhould fal out betwyxt the
french and vs, or any ciuil warres amongſt them, or a new
ſtorme aryſe from any other part, in which caſes how
England would be able to weald with ſo potent an
enemy as is his maieſty, I leaue to your lordſhips wiſe
conſideration.

But perhaps theſe men preſume vpon her Maties. league and amity with forrayn Princes and States, let them
therefore conſider what aſſurance is therein, ſeing experience teacheth that the amity of Princes neuer laſteth
longer then fortune fauoreth or conſideration of profit
concurreth, beſ des that infinit occaſions of Ielouſies, and
vnexpected quarrels fall out dayly amõgſt Princes which
break the ſureſt leagues, and make the beſt friends the
greateſt enemies.

What reſteth then to make theſe brewbates ſo confi-
dent? is it her Maties. good ſucceſſe? but of all other reaſons that ought leaſt to mooue them, for he is not wyſe

(ſayd

(fayd Iafon to Epaminondas) that feares not the euents of warre, which are fo variable as neyther force nor pollicy, nor fkil of art military nor any humain meanes can affure; whereof wee neede not to feek examples abroad, feeing wee hane enough at home, yf wee but confider the varietie and counterchange of good & bad fucceffe in the warres betwyxt King Henry the fixt and King Edward the fourth and the great victories, and dominions which our Kinges her Maᵗⁱᵉˢ predeceffors had in France fome yeares togeather, and that at laft they loft againft all that they had got there; fuch is the inconftancy of humain affayres, ftable in nothing but in inftability, and therefore after a glowing Sunne of profperity all wyfe men feare a fharp fhower of aduerfity knowing that

Prouerb. cap. 14. *extrema gaudij luctus occupat,* which a poet of our tyme wel expreffed in this diftich.

Mirrour of Magift.

When hope and hap, when health and welth are higheft,
Then woe and wrack, difeafe and need are nigheft.

In which refpect, that is no fmalle point of wifdome in any profperous and victorious Prince euer to feare the after clap, and to bee fuch an enemy as he may after be a friend and fo to make warre as he exclude not himfelf from poffibility of peace yf his former fortune fayle him, yea and during the courfe of his profperity to harken to any reafonable compofition, rather then to ftand to the hazards of future euents, which many great Princes and famous Captaynes not obferuing, haue obfcured all their former glory with final difgrace, and made themfelues lamentable examples of humain infelicity.

Plutark in the lyfe of Paulus Aemilius. Perfeus King of Macedony puffed vp with pride for diuers victories that he had got againft the Romans, prouoked them fo long with continual iniuries that at length Paulus Æmilius conquered his country, & caried him and all his children prifoners to Rome in triumphe.

And

And Charles the laſt Duke of Burgundy, being growne ſo hauty and inſolent with his great power, proſperitie, excellent wit and courage, that he would not harken to the moſt reaſonable offers, and humble ſutes of the Swiſſers (with whome he was at variance) loſt two battayles vnto them at Granſon and Morat, and his credit, and friends with all, where vpon enſued his other diſgraces, and finally the ruin of him and his ſtate. Philip: •emin.

This (my good Lords) I ſay to ſhew the inconſideration of our aduerſaries who promiſing themſelues (as it ſeemeth) a perpetuity of her Maties lyfe and proſperity, think it good pollicy to kindle the coales of theſe preſent warres, betwyxt her and the King Catholyke, with abuſe and iniury of them both (as before hath ben declared) ſeeking to make an immortal hatred betwyxt them, and a quarrel irreconciliable, and yet are withall ſo vnaduiſed at home, as to procure (as much as in them lyeth) to alienat from her Matie the harts of her owne ſubiects, by moſt exorbitant cruelties, and open iniuries, drawing her and the whole eſtate thereby into euident daungers both domeſtical and forrayn, which daungers if they ſhould concurre to the effects that may be feared, though their owne ruines alſo would be included therein, yet were that but a ſmalle ſatisfaction, or recompence, for the loſſe of ſo many other better then them ſelues.

K 2   OF

OF TVVO OTHER INEVI-

table dammages, that must needs enfew to her Ma.tie & her whole ftate by the effufion of inno-cent blood with an intimation of fome part of the remedy.

CHAP. XIX.

BVt albeit there were no occafion of feare, eyther at home or abroad as God be thanked at home there is litle (though no God a mercy to thefe bufy fellowes) yet what greater indignity or iniury can be offred to her maiefty by her fubiects then to abufe her royal name and authoritie, to the murdering of fo many innocents as by thefe deuifes are put to death in England, where-vpon do follow two ineuitable dam-mages to her maiefty, and her realme, the one the infamy that her maiefties gouernmēt doth incurre in all the Chri-ftian world, as is manifeft to all thofe that trauel ouer other countries, or read the bookes and hiftories that dayly are written therof by ftrangers in all languages, which no trackt of tyme fhal be able to abolifh.

The other is the vengance of almighty God due by his iuftice to all fuch notable wrongs donne by publyk authority of her Ma.tie. and her lawes, the which what yt may bring vpon her and the realme in tyme, any man that beleueth there is a God, and iuft Iudge of humain actions, cannot but feare, feing not only the holy Scrip-tures, but alfo prophane hiftories do yeeld innumerable examples of Gods wrath extended vpon realmes and ftates for iniuftices committed therein; *Kingdomes are tranf-ferred, fayth the fcripture, from nation to nation, for iniuftices, in-iuries, contumelies, and diuers deceits*; and amongft all iniuftices there is none that more offendeth God, the the effufion of

Ecclefiaftic. cap. 10.

innọ-

innocent blood, and therefore the Prophet exclaymeth in *Ezech.24.*
the perfon of God, *wo be to the bloody cittie whereof I wil*
make a great heap, as of a pile of wood to burn; and the fame
Prophet threatning the deftruction of Hierufalem, and *Ezech.22.*
declaring the caufes thereof reconeth for one of the *Ibid.*
principal, *the fhedding of innocent blood, her Princes* (fayth he)
were lyke woulues rauening for their pray, to fhed blood, & agayne *Ibid.*
their were calumniatours and flanderers in her, to fhed blood. lyke
wyfe, afterwards in the fame place our lord fpeaketh to
Hierufalem, faying, *they haue receiued gifts and rewards in thee*
to fpil blood, behold my wrath is kindled againft thee for thy coue-
toufnes, and the blood that hath beene fhed in thee, and therefore
I wil difpers thee into diuers nations, and fcatter thee into diuers
countries, &c.

Alfo when the King and people of Iuda, and Hieru- *4.Reg. ca.24.*
falem were led into captiuite by Nabucodonozor the
fcripture fayth exprefly that it was donne for *the blood*
which Manaffes had fhed, when he filled Hierufalem with the blood
of innocents, and therefore God would not bee appeafed.

In lyke manner our Sauiour himfelf prophefing of the
deftruction of Hierufalem by the Romans afcribed the *Matth.23.*
fame principally to the fpilling of innocent blood, not
only of his owne but alfo of the prophets, that he had fent
and was to fend, Hierufalem (fayth he) *which kils the*
Prophets, and ftoneft them which are fent to thee, behold your hows
fhal bee left defert, &c.

Hereof many notable examples occurre in prophane *Iuft. lib.23.*
hiftories, but 2. or 3. fhal fuffife for breuities fake.

Iuftin telleth of the people of Epiras feuerely punifhed
and almoft deftroyed, with dearth, famin, warre, and
ficknes by Gods iuft Iudgement for the cruel flaughter of
Laodomia daughter of Alexander their King.

No leffe notable and manifeft was Gods iuft iudge- *Plutark in his*
ment vpon the Lacedemonians for a horible murder and *treatife inti-*
rape comitted by two of their cittizens vpon the two *tuled nara-*
daughters of Scedafus, who demaunding Iuftice moft in- *tonie.*

ſtantly of the King councel, and people, and being denied it of them all, craued it at Gods hands with infinit imprecations, and maledictions againſt their ſtate, and ſo killed himſelf alſo vpon his daughters tombe, where vpon enſewed (as Diodorus, Siculus, & Plutark doo note) the memorable ouerthrow geuen to the Lacedemonians by Epimanondas, hard by the tombe of the two maydens in the playne of Leuctra where the offence was comitted in which deffeit they loſt not only their hole armie, but alſo the empire of Greece, which they had before in their hands many yeares.

Diod ſicul lib. 15. ca 14.

Such is the ſtyle of Gods Iuſtice, to puniſh iniuſtice, not only in them that commit it, but alſo in thoſe that permit and ſuffer it, yea and in reſpect of the ſympathy and communication which is in the body politike no leſſe then in the body natural (where in the detrimét of the leaſt méber redoundeth to the hurt of the whole) he imputeth ſome tymes the fault of one to all, & ſometymes for the peoples offences he puniſheth the Prince (in which reſpect Salomon ſayth the ſinnes of the people make many Princes) and ſometymes for the Princes faults he puniſheth the people, and otherwhyles for the ſinnes of eyther he deſtroyeth both.

Prouerb. cap. 28.

When Acham had ſtolne part of the ſpoyle of Hierico contrary to the commaundement of God, 3000. of the children of Iſrael were ouerthrowne by them of Hay, for his offence, which our lord imputed to them all, ſaying, *Iſrael hath ſinned and tranſgreſſed my commaundement, &c.*

Ioſue cap 7.

2. Reg. ca 24. Ibid.

For the ſinne of Dauid in numbring the people, 70000. of his ſubiects periſhed, and for the peoples offences God permitted him to ſinne.

2. Paralip. cap. 2. 3.
4. Reg. ca. 24.
1. Reg. ca. 12.

For King Achaz cauſe, ſayth the ſcripture, God did humble the people of Iuda & after gaue them into captiuity for the ſinnes of their King Manaſſes.

Laſtly when Samuel had anoynted Saule for King he ſayd

said vnto the people yf yow perseuer in your wickednes, both yow and your King shal perish.

Herein neuertheles this difference may be noted, that when almighty God doth punish both he vseth more rigour towards the Princes and heads of the people, then towards the meaner sort.

Whereof the holy ghost declareth the reason in the book of wisdome where he speaketh to Kings,& Princes, in this manner ; *Audite reges,&c. hearken O kinges,and vnderstad,learne yow which are Iudges of the bounds of the earth in respect that power is geuen vnto yow from our lord, and strength from the highest, who wil examine your woorkes, and search your thoughts, and becauſe when yow were ministers of his kingdome, yow did not Iudge rightly nor keep the law of Iuſtice, nor walk in the way of God,he wil appeare vnto yow quickly, and horibly, for moſt rigorous Iudgment is donne vpon them that gouerne : with the poore and meane man mercy is vſed, but mighty men ſhal ſuffer torments mightily.* Sap 6.

This my lords I am bold to represent vnto your lordships that yow may see thereby the euident daunger that your whole estate may be brought into by the extreame wrongs that our persecutours do vs howsoeuer her Ma.tie and your Lordships may bee free from the same in wil or consent,as I make no dout but yow are.

For if the Prince and people are so conioyned & linked togeather with the communication of merit or demerit, that God doth commonly chastise, the one for the others fault, and for the offenses of eyther sometymes destroyeth both (as I haue before declared,) if the priuat theft of Acham could cause the puklik calamity of the children of Israel, that had no way consented thereto, what may be feared to ensew of so horible and publik a crime, of our persecutours, as the effusion of innocent blood, thirsted sought,and spilt, so oft, and by so many subtilities and deuiſes, by slaunders and fayned treasons, by extreame torments vniuſtly geuen, by periuries, by corruption of witnesses, A conſequēce to be conſidered. Ioſue.7.

neffes, Iuries, and Iudges (where by an infinit number of all forts are drawne to the partic pation of the offence) and all this vnder pretence of publyk autorit e of her maiefty, of her councel and her lawes, what may be feared (I fay) but that the finne s not priuat, and particuler, but pnblik and general, and that the whole ftate remayneth engaged for the payment of the penalty.

It refteth then my lords that of your wifdomes and piety yow procure fome redreffe of thefe inconueniences for auerfion of Gods wrath from yow & vs & the whole realme, and for preuention of the mifcheefe that other-wyfe muft needs enfue. And if it pleafe your lordfhips to geue me leaue to put yow in mynd of one neceffary meane thereof, and as I haue layd open the fore, fo to re-prefent alfo fome part of the falue, yt importeth much that for the expiation of fo great a finne, and fatisfaction of Gods Iuftice yow lay the penalty vpon the authors and inftruments of the iniuftice as appeareth by the example

Iofue cap. 7. of Achams theft, whereof our lord fayd to Iofue, *I wilbe no longer with yow vntil yow haue deftroyed him that is guilty of this*
Num. cap. 25. *cryme*, and when Phinees killed the Ifraelit which com-mitted fornication with the Madianit, he auerted the wrath of God from the children of Ifrael, as the fcriptnre teftifieth. Alfo when the people were punifhed with 3. yeares famin in Dauids tyme for the offence of Saule in killing the Gabaonits, the famin leffed when feuen of

2. Reg. ca. 21. Sauls offspring were deliuered to the Gabaonits, and by them crucified, the lyke reporteth Plutark of a moft fu-rious plague where with God punifhed the cities of

Plutar. in Rome and Laurentum for the murder of King Tatius in
Romulo. Rome, and of certayne Embaffadours of Laurentium, which plague fuddenly ceafed in both the cities when iuftice was donne vpon the murderers in both places.

I haue not fayd this with any defire of reuenge, or vn-charitable affection towards our aduerfaries, but in ref-pect of my duty to her Matie and your lordfhips, and for
the

the tender loue that I doe beare to my country, and vniuerſal good of all. For as for them (I meane our enemies)
I aſſure your Lordſhips I am ſo far from deſyring any
reuenge of them that I pitty their caſe, knowing that
except they repent, and do worthy pennance God wil
ſurely reuenge his owne cauſe and ours, vpon them, and
throw into the fyre, thoſe rods of his wrath, when he hath
worne them to the ſtumps; for ſuch is the cours of his
iuſtice, to chaſtiſe firſt his ſeruants and children by the miniſtery of wicked men (not moouing, but vſing their euil
wils, and malice for the execution of his holy wil) and
afterwards to puniſh them moſt ſeuerely for the ſame; &
therefore though he ordayned the deſtruction of the
Temple of Hieruſalem, and the captiuity of his people
for their ſinnes, yet afterwards he vtterly deſtroyed the 4. Reg. ca. 24.
Babilonians for hauing ben the meanes, and inſtruments
thereof, to which purpoſe, the Prophet ſayth, our Lord
ſtirred vp the Kings of the Medes to diſtroy Babilon, *for it* Hier. cap. 51.
is the reuenge of our Lord and the reuenge of his Temple, & agayne,
I wil render to Babilon (ſaith almighty God by the ſame Pro- Ibidem.
phet) *and to all the inhabitants of Caldea, all the euil that they haue*
donne in Sion. And after in theſame chapter, he comforteth
his people in captiuity, ſaying, *behold I wil make Babilon a* Ezech. 25.
deſert, &c and no maruel; ſeing he alſo deſtroyed the
Amonits, Moabits, and other their neighbours, for hauing
laughed, and ſkorned at their deſolation and captiuity;
ſuch is the loue which our Lord beareth to his ſeruãts, as
he reuengeth the leaſt iniury that is donne thẽ, of whome Matth. 10.
he hath ſuch particular care, as he nũbreth the very heares Luc. 10.
of their heads, as our Sauiour ſayth, & taketh all that is
donne to them, be it good or euil as donne to himſelf.

And now hauing layd before your lordſhips by way of
ſome degreſsion, theſe conſiderations (yet as annexed notwithſtanding & conioyned with Squires cauſe by cohe-
rence of the manner of proceeding (I ſhal returne to treate
ſome few lines more of a pamphlet ſet foorth for Squyres
condemnation after his execution.

L   O F

OF A CERTAYNE PAM-

phlet printed in England concerning the conspi-
racie of Squyre after his death, and first of two notable
lies which the Author therof auoweth vpon his owne
knowledge.

CHAP. XX.

Having determined to speake no more of
Squyres affayre but rather to haue ended with
this that hath beene said, I receyued from a frend
of myne a pamphlet printed in England by the
deputies of Christopher Barker the Queenes printer concerning the matter and offence of Squire, intituled, A letter
written out of England to an English gentleman remayning at Padua, conteyning a true report of a strange conspiracy &c. the which pamphlet doth geue me occasion
to enlarge my self somewhat further then I meant.

For although I hold thesame to be sufficiently answered as wel by that which I haue already discoursed in
this Apology, as also by the foresaid treatise lately published by our frend M. A. in confutation of the whole
fiction, besydes that the pamphlet it self hauing neyther
name of author nor priuiledge, nor licence for the printing
may seeme rather to be reiected as an infamous libel, then
held worthy of further answere; neuertheles considering
that the Author therof taketh vpon him such particuler
knowledge of all the proceedings in that matter, that he
seemeth to be no ordinary person, but rather some one that
had his hand in the pye, and agayne forasmuch as it may
be thought that the Queenes printers, neyther would nor
durst set foorth any such pamphlet touching her Ma.tie &
the state, withoue the warrant of some man in authoritie,
and lastly for that the Author therof amongst many fooles
bolts that be hath shot therein, seemeth to haue leuelled

one particularly at me , though he name me not, I haue
thought good briefly to touch some points therof.

To come then to the matter , his difcourfe confifteth Parts of the
of 3. partes: the firft, his declaration of Squyres confefsion, Pamphlet.
touching the particulers, as wel of the fuppofed confpiracy, as alfo of the execution therof: the fecod the maner
of the difcouery of it, the third this pamphletters coment
and cenfure vpon the fame, interpofed ,fomerymes by the
way of difcourfe.

In the firft I only wifh to be noted two notorious and
impudent lyes, within the compaffe of ten lynes auowed
by him vpon his owne knowledge. The one that Squyres
confefsion concerning the confpiracy was deliuered by
himfelf, without torture, or fhew of torture; the other
that it was in nô point retracted or difauowed, eyther at
his tryal, or at his death, whereas all thofe that were prefent thereat, are witneffes of the contrary, and amongft
many others fome of your Lordfhips that afsifted at his
tryal may wel remember I am fure that he vrged a long
tyme that his confefsion was extorted by torment, and although he confeffed the fact after vpon fome perfuafions
and expectation perhaps of pardon, yet at his death when
it imported him for his euerlafting good to difcharge his
confcience, he reuoked his faid confefsion, not only difa-
uowing the fact,and all intention therof, but alfo his fuppofed employment by Father Walpoole, and when the
fhyrif vrged him with his confefsion made at feueral
tymes, he anfwered in the hearing of all the afsiftants and
lookers on,that he would as wel haue faid any thing els in
the world at that tyme to deliuer himfelf from the torments which he endured, and being preffed to confeffe at
leaft his fubornation, and employment by the Iefuit (for
Father Walpoole was not otherwyes named there) he
flatlie denyed it,and gaue a fufficient reafon to cleare both
himfelf and the father, faying that he ranne away from
Seuil without the fathers knowledge, and that therfore it

L 2   might

might eafely be iudged that he was not fuborned nor fent by him.

And this I affirme as wel vpon diuers relations that I haue feene thereof in wryting, as alfo vpon the report of a credible perfon who was prefent at h s execution, with whom I haue fpoken here in Madrid, fo that I dare herin boldly appeale to the confciences not only of M. fhiriffe who was kindled with great choller againſt the poore man for denying it, but alfo of all the afsiſtants and beholders, who were much amazed to heare matter fo farre from their expectation, their vttered by him that dyed.

What then may I fay of the impudency of this man that maketh no bones to put in print, yea and to affirme vpon his knowledge fuch a notable ly, difprouable by the teſtimony of fo many hnndreths as were prefent at Squires death? wherto ferueth all his exaggeratiõs of the foulneſſe of the fact, his opprobrious fpeeches againſt Father Walpoole his deuifes of charmes, coniurations, enchantments, exorcifmes, cyrcles, & all his Sinons tale fo fmothely framed, but to bewray both his vanitie and malice, feing he taketh delight and glorie in the vayne oſtentation of his owne lying tongue to the ſlaũder both of the quick and the dead, and therfore let him confider what the pfalmiſt fayth to him, & fuch other calumniatours, Why doeſt thow glory in malice thow which art potent in iniquitie &c. thow haſt loued all woords of ruyne and deſtruction, thow which art a very tongue of tromperie, and deceit, & therfore God wil deſtroy the finally, and pluck the vp and remoue the from thy tabernacle, and thy root from the land of the liuing.

Pfalm. 51.

OF CER-

OF CERTAYNE ABSVRD

improbabilities in the same pamphlet touching the manner of the discouery of Squires supposed conspiracy.

CHAP. XXI.

AFterwards when he cometh to acquaint his Paduan frend with the manner how the matter was discouered he sayth thus, when tyme passed sayd he, and nothing came of it, they (he meaneth vs heere) made construction of it, that Squyre had byn false to them, one of the more passionate of them inueigheth bitterly against Squyre tels how he was trusted, and how he had vndonne the cause, and the better to be reuenged on him, is content that one (that they let slip hyther, as if he had fled from them) should geue information of this matter not with the circumstances, but generally against Squyre, partly to winne himself credit, and partly to wreak themselues on Squyre.

Thus farre this pamphleters wordes which being conferred with that which as before I haue signified, was vrged against Squyre at his araignment concerning the same matter, wil be the better vnderstood.

It was then declared (I meane at the barre) vnder the confession of Ihon Stallage, alias Stanley lately before fled frō hence , that I did one day in my owne lodging inueigh against Squyre with great passion and oth, saying that he had deceyued vs, and that we should be discredited with the King therby, and further that persuading our selues that Squyre had already reuealed the matter, we sent in Stanley to do some other great mischeef, with pretence to accuse Squyre therof, wherby it appeareth that the passionate man, who the pamphleter sayth reuealed it was my self, & that Stallage was not only he to whom I told
it, but

it, but alfo the man that we let flip to accufe Squyre to be
reuenged of him, which how improbable and abfurd it
is, I remit to the iudgement of any indifferent man that
knoweth him and vs, or hath but any fparck of prudence
to difcouer a cogging ly.

Great abfur-dities and improbabi-lities. For firft how is it credible that we had fo litle wit, and
difcours as (yf we had recommended any fuch matter to
Squyre) to affure our felues that he had beene fals vnto
vs & reuealed it only becaufe he had not executed it with
in leffe then a yeare? wherof there might be fo many
lawful impediments ymagined, as howfoeuer we might
fufpect him, yet could we haue no reafon fo fully to condemne him, that we fhould fend one our felues to difcouer
it, whervpon muft needs follow great inconuenience to
vs, whether he had detected yt himfelf or no; for yf he
had not, we fhould not only do wrong to him, but alfo to
our felues, yea and to all the Catholykes of England in mi-
niftring matter of a new and general perfecution; for if
our aduerfaries are fayne to inuent fuch lyke matters
many tymes to take occafion ther-vpon to perfecute vs
could we be ignorant that they would do it much more yf
they had fuch a iuft occafion miniftred by our felues,
wherby all Catholykes and we efpecially fhould be decried
euery where for manquellars, & princekillers, traytours,
and homicides, in all tribunals pulpits affemblies, books
and fermons, and many an innocent man fuffer for our
caufe, vpon this general condemnation.

Is it likely then, that we would take fuch a defperate
refolution, only vpon a bare fufpition? And put the cafe
that he had reuealed it, and that we had affured our felues
therof, could we haue any reafon in the world to geue
further light of the matter our felues, and fo to fortifie his
accufation of vs, which of it felf could not haue the credit, nor confequently be fo preiudicial to our common
caufe as when it fhould be feconded with a teftimony of
our owne?

But

But they say we are pasionate men, and especially I, and therfore were transported with desyre of reuenge, for so saith the pamphleter that to wreak our selues on Squyre we sent in Stallage to accuse him, because we were persuaded that he was fals to vs; let vs then examine this a litle, and see what cohærence there is therein.

I would, gladly know as wel of the Author of the pamphlet, as of M. Atturney and others that vrged this point against Squyre, and vs at the barre, what reuenge we could expect to haue of Squyre by reuealing that which we thought he himself had reuealed? were we so simple to think that we could hurt him therby? truly, though these fyne headés wil not allow vs so much wit as themselues, yet they do vs wrong to take from vs ordinary discourse and common sense, seing these are things so euident, that it rather may be wondred how their deep conceits could take them for probable, then imagined that we should commit so grosse errours, so that this deuise is sufficiently disproued by the absurdities therof.

But how simple soeuer these men take vs to be, it appeareth that the pamphleter was not wel in his wits, when he acknowledged that Stanley was suborned by vs to accuse Squyre, and that two letters which he preteded to haue stolne out of one of our studies, weere found to be counterfeit, yea and that thervpon it was collected that Squyre was an honest man (which in deed was the most direct construction that could be made theron) wherby the pamphleter notably discouereth the extreame iniustice donne to Squyre; for yf the subornation of Stanley was so manifest, that it serued for an argument of Squyres honestie, it is cleare that the torment geuen to him vpon Stanleys accusation was against all law and conscience, whervpon it also followeth that the torment being vniustly geuen, the confession extorted therby was vtterly voyd in law, and by consequence the condemnation grounded vpon the confession most vniust, and iniurious.

A notable folly of the pamphletes.

rious, as I haue fufficiently proued in the 8. chapter.

Furthermore whereas the Pamphleter confeffeth that Stanley had two counterfeit letters cocerning this matter, which he prætended to haue ftolne out of one of our ftudies, he geueth me no fmal occatio to think that the letter which the priuie councellor vrged againft Squyre at his araignment, as written betwixt my kinfman and me, was one of them whervpon for my part I wil make no further collection then that the pamphleter fheweth himfelfe to be a very fimple man in publifhing fuch thinges, as directly redound to the ouerthrow of the caufe which he vndertaketh to defend.

Wel to conclude this point for as much as it doth not appeare vpon what ground the pamphleter and his fellowes affirme that Stanley was fent into England, & fuborned by vs, whether vpon their owne imagination, or els vpon his confefsion ; I fay that their charitie towards vs, and their proceedings heretofore in lyke caufes being cofidered togither with Stanleys good confcience and conditions (wherof I haue fpoken amply before) it as litle importeth what they fay or imagin of vs, as what he hath confeffed or fhal confeffe except it be at the gallowes, which is now (as matters are handled in England) the only tribunal of truth, I meane the only place where truth is tryed, as may appeare by the late exaple of Squyre, fo that when I fhal vnderftand that Stanley is hanged alfo, and that at his death he hath ratified this, I fhal then fay that there is fome more probability therin, though fince the wryting of this it is fignified (as hath beene faid) that he denieth all agayne now in the towre.

And truly if our aduerfaryes did not perfuade thefelues that he would at his death cofeffe the truth as Squyre did, & fo marre all I doubt not but they would haue hanged him ere this, being the man he is and fo wel deferuing it, but now as the matter ftandeth, I think for auoyding the forefaid trial of Tyburne, he may rather feare a fig then a
halter,

Tyburne trieth truth.

halter feing thofe that haue him in their clouches,
cannot but conceyue that the truth of this matter may in
tyme come to be difcouered to their fhame, no leffe by his
lyfe then by his publyk death, fo that I think he may make
his wil, if he haue any thing to difpofe, though the hagman
is neuer lyke to haue his coat. Thus much to the text of the
páphlet, now to the gloffe, & for that hereafter I muft be a
litle more playne with the Author therof, then the refpect
and dutie, I owe to your Lordfhips would permit, If I
fhould côtinue my fpeach to yow, I wil by your Lordfhips
leaues addreffe the fame hence-forth to him and his
fellowes.

OF CERTAINE IMPERTI-
*nent and foolifh gloffes of the Author of the pamphlet,
and firft concerning the moderation and lenitie which
he fayth is vfed in caufes of Religion where it is not
mixt with matter of ftate.*

CHAP. XXII.

IN the third page yow appeale Sir Pamphleter to the
knowledge of your frend in Padua for the diftinction &
moderation of the proceeding in England in ecclefiaftical caufes with what lenitie and gentlenes it hath
beene caryed, except where it was mixed with matter of
ftate, for fuch are your owne wordes.

Hereto I anfwere that by your reftriction & exception
of ftate matters yow ouerthrow your general propofition
of clemency, and proue that ther is no moderation lenitie
nor gentlenes vfed at all, for where is not matter of ftate
mixed with religion now a dayes in England, are not fo
many effential poynts of Catholyke religion made treafon
as no man can do the duetie of a Catholyke, but he is *ipfo*

M   *facto*

facto a traytour , feing no man can be fo much as abfolued of his finnes, nor receyue any Sacrament of Gods Churche by the only true minifters thereof (I meane Prieftes) but he committeth treafon? befydes the other captious lawes about the Supremacie, the exacting of the oth, and the vrging of Catholykes to come to hæretical feruice, & communion, vnder colour of temporal obediece to the Prince, is not in all this, ftate mixt with religion, yea and to no other end then to perfecute vs vnder colour of treafon and matter of ftate, while ye perfecute religion, and for religion.

Was not this the very practife of Iulian the Apoftata who to couer his perfecution of Chriftians fometymes caufed his picture to be fet with Iupiter or other fals Gods and fometymes made himfelfe to be paynted with their enfeignes and refemblance, therby to make fuch mixture of religion, and matter of ftate, that thofe which fhould refufe to commit Idololatry might be punifhed vnder colour of contempt of his emperial perfon.

Sozom lib.5. cap.16. Nicepho lib.10. cap.23.

Sozom. Ibidem.

Hereof fayth Sozomenus , *Nam fic cogitabat, &c.* for fo Iulian thought that if he perfuaded the to that, he fhould more eafely bring them to his wil in other points of religion alfo, and if they refifted in this he might punifh them without mercie, as offenders againft both the common wealth and the Empyre.

Is not this now practifed in England in effect? for what other thing is it to annex the keyes of Peter with the Princes crowne, the deuine power with the humain, the fupremacy fpiritual with the gouernment temporal (dignities no leffe diftinct in nature, then incompatible in lay perfons, and efpecially in women fexe) what other thing is it, I fay, then to ioyne Iulian with Iupiter, and to paynt the Prince with the enfeignes and refemblance of deitie, and to what other end then vnder colour of treafon & matter of ftate to make away all thofe that fhal refufe to acknowledge this pretended ecclefiaftical fupremacy.

Such.

Such then is your mixture of religion with matter of state, as whiles yow pretend to punish none for Catholyke religion, yow persecute cruelly all Catholykes for no other true cause then religion, yea and as the pharises did, yow persecute and crucifie Christ agayne in his members, as an enemy to Cæsar, and for the same reason of state that they did cry to Pilate *si dimittis hunc non es amicus Cæsaris*, if yow let him scape yow are not Cæsars frend for that his fault is not religion but matter of state againſt Cæsar and agayne *si dimittimus hunc venient Romani , &c.* yf we diſmiſſe this man the Romans (togither with Spaniards) wil come and take from vs both our place and people, and wil conquer, ſpoyle & deſtroy vs, for which reſpect yow haue already killed ſome hundreths of Catholykes vpon lyke ſuſpitions and calumniations by vertue of your new ſtatutes, beſydes many murdred for fayned conſpiracies, and fals imputed crymes, and an exceeding multitude of others conſumed and waſted with impriſonment, others pyned away in baniſhment, others empoueriſhed & ruined with taxes, impoſitions, and penalties, and an infinite number dayly languiſhing in captiuity, penurie, and miſerie, for that they wil not yeeld as yow cal it temporal obedience in comming to your ſeruice, and communion, & yet forſooth yow trouble none for religion.

But yf it pleaſe yow and your frend in Padua that knoweth as yow ſay this matter ſo wel to conſider it a litle better, yow wil eaſely ſee that the diſtinction that yow and your fellowes make is confuſion, your moderation perſecution, your lenity ſeueritie, your ſhew and talk of mercy nothing els but a mere mockerie and playne coſinage of the ſimple reader, for to preache one thing and practiſe an other, is I trow the higheſt point of coſinage that may be.

But what maruaile is it if yow draw our religion to matter of ſtate ſeing your owne religion hath no other rule, nor ground but reaſon of ſtate, for albeit the ſubſtance

M 2   of reof religion, which now yow profeſſe different from ours, be patcht vp of old and new hereſies, eſpecially of theſe laſt of Luther, Zwinglius and Caluin, yet that which is properly yours, and the key and ſtay of all the reſt and maketh yow a bodie and part different from other Sectes of Lutheranes, Zwinglians, and Caluenſiſts, Puritanes, Brownifts, Anabaptiſts and the lyke, is the obedience that yow acknowledge in eccleſiaſtical cauſes to a lay head, which although it was firſt introduced into England by King Henry the 8. only vpon animoſitie againſt the ſea Apoſtolyke (becauſe the ſaid ſea would not allow his deuorce from Queene Catherine (which King in all other poynts deteſted your religion) yet being abolished by Queene Marie her Ma.ties ſyſter, and laſt prædeceſſour, it was returned agayne in the beginning of her Ma.ties raigne that now is, only vpon reaſon of ſtate as all the world knoweth, and ſo hath hyherto byn continued.

    For thoſe polityke ſtatiſtes of ours that had the vſe of her Ma.ties eares in the beginning, conſidering that the Queene of Scotland being then maried vnto the French King, pretended title vnto the crowne of England, and fearing that the ſea Apoſtolyk would fauour her pretence in reſpect of the mariage of her Ma.ties mother; yea and that the people would alſo incline that way, if they remayned ſtil in the obedience of the ſaid ſea, they had re-
3. Reg. ca. 12. courſe to Hieroboams pollicy and abuſing the facilitie of her Ma.ties good nature and yong yeares perſuaded her to change the religion then publikly profeſſed, and not only to baniſh the authority of the Pope, but alſo to follow her father, and brothers example in taking the title of eccleſiaſtical ſupremacy vpõ her ſelf, a thing abſurd, ridiculous, vnnatural, impoſsible, & therefore worthely reiected, im-
Luther Cal-uin Kẽnitius. pugned, and derided by Luther and Caluyn themſelues and by their folowers, and the Puritaines at this day in England, and all other ſectaries abroad, as a matter without all præſident or example in any Chriſtian common wealth
or colour

or colour of Scripture, except of some few texts that treat
of obedience to Princes in general no lesse to Heathen
Kings, then Christian, and therfore can not with any shew
of reason be vnderstood of their primacy in causes ecclesiastical.

Seing then your religion so far as it is distinct from
others, hath no other ground then reason of state, I doubt
not, but yf the matter were wel examined what God they
beleeued in, that persuaded her Ma.ue therto, or yow and
your fellowes that manitayne it vpon the same reason, and
by such vnchristian practises, as yow do, yow would be
found to be cópreheded in the third diuisió of varro, who
said that 3. kynds of men had three different kynds of
Gods, the Poëts one, the Philosophers an other, and statists
or Polityks a third & that euery one of them had a different
religion according to the difference of their Gods, as that
the religion of the Poets was fabulous, the other of the
Philosophers natural, the third of the Statists, polityke, and
accomodated to gouernment. ^{Aug.6 de ci-uitat. Dei c.5.}

And this is that which yow professe ; For the God yow
beleeue in is the Prince, your scriptures are the actes of
Parliament, your religion is to conserue the state *perfas &
nefas*, and therfore as all good Christians do measure the
reason of state by religion, which is the true rule, and the
end therof, and from the which it cannot in reason dissent
or disagre, so yow on the other syde reduce and frame religion to your fals reason of state, and by that meanes
peruert all the order both of nature and grace preferring
the body before the soule, temporal things before spiritual
humayn before deuine, earth before heauen the world
before God, and which is more yow subiect both earth,
heauen, body soule, the world, yea God and all, to the priuate pleasure, and profit of the Prince, as though he were
the end, the Lord, and God of all the world, and of nature
itself, wherypon ensew those monstrous pollicies which
wee see fraught with all frand, hipocrisy, periuries, slauders,

murders,

murders, and all kynd of cruelty, oppreſsion and impiety, which haue ruined infinite Kinges with their countries, & Kingdomes, and what they wil bring our poore country vnto in the end, tyme wil tel, wherto I remit me, for as the Italian prouerb ſayth, *La vita il fine, il di loda la ſera,* the end prayſeth the lyfe, and the euening the day.

OF THE TRVE CAVSES OF

more moderation vſed in the beginning then after-wards, & of the difference made by the Lawes, betwixt Seminarie, and Q. Mary prieſts.

CHAP. XXIII.

BVT to proceed in your obſeruations, you go for-ward to geue example that there is moderation vſed in eccleſiaſtical cauſes, where matter of ſtate is not mixt with religion, ſaying, for els I would gladly learne what ſhould make the difference betweene the tem-per of the lawes in the firſt yeare of the Queene, and in the 23. and 27. but that at the one tyme they were papiſts in conſcience, and at the other, they were growne papiſts in faction, or what ſhould make the difference at this day in law betwixt a Queene Marie prieſt, & a Seminary prieſt, ſaue that the one is a prieſt of ſuſpition, and the other a prieſt of ſedition.

Hereto I anſwere that becauſe you ſay you would gladly learne, and that I take yow to be of a good wit and docile, I wil take paynes to teach you this poynt that you ſay you would ſo fayne learne. Know you therfore that there were diuers cauſes of more moderation and lenity vſed for ſome yeares in the beginning then afterwards, & yet not thoſe which you ſpeak of and ſo you ſhew your

ſelf

felf eyther ignorant, or malitious in both.

The firft an ordinary rule of ftate which thofe great ftatifts that procured this change could not neglect I meane in cafe of innouation to vfe no fuddayne violence, but to proceed by degrees, efpecially in matter of religion, which is feldome changed without tumult and trouble, wherof they had feene the experience in the tymes of both the kings Henry and Edward, & therfore they had great reafon to water their wyne at the beginning, and to vfe moderation at leaft for fome yeares vntil the ftate and gouernment were fetled.

The fecond caufe was the doctrine of your owne gofpellers in Q. Maryes tyme, who becaufe fome of their folowers were burnt for herefy (according to the Canons and lawes of the Churche) cryed out that they were perfecuted, and publifhed in their bookes and fermons, that faith ought to be free, and not forced, & that therfore it was againft all confcience to punifh or trouble men for their religion, in which refpect the authors of the change, that ferued themfelues of them in the ecclefiaftical and paftoral dignityes, could not for fhame at the very firft, vfe the bloody proceeding which afterwards they did, though neuertheleffe they forbore not in the very beginning to imprifon, and otherwife to afflict, all Bifhops and cheif paftours; and fuch others as would not fubfcribe, & come to their Churches, for the which caufe I remember that befydes a great number of ecclefiaftical and temporal perfons, fome of my owne kindred and familie were called to London, and imprifoned in the fecond yeare of her Maiefties raigne, and fo remayned prifoners many yeares after.

The third caufe was the vayne hope that thofe polityks had that a religion fo fenfual, and ful of liberty as theirs, authorized with the power of the Prince, vpholden with lawes, promulgate with all artifice of writers preachers, and perfwaders, would eafely within a fewe yeares infinuate

nuate it felf into the hartes of all men, efpecially of the youth, wherby they made accompte, that the elder fort being worne out, there would be within a fewe yeares litle memorie or none at all left of Catholike religion; but when they faw after fome yeares experience, how much they were deceiued of their expectation, and that through the zealous endeauours of the learned Englifh Catholikes abroad, learned bookes written, Colledges & Seminaryes erected, priefts made and fent in, & therby infinite numbers reduced to the vnity of the Catholike Churche, not only of the fchifmatiks that fel at the firft, eyther by ignorance, or for feare, but alfo of the Proteftāts themfelues (and amongft them euen many minifters and principal preachers) and none fooner conuerted, or more zealoufly affected to Catholike religion, then the yongeft and fyneft wits, wherwith our new Seminaryes beganne to be peopled; when thofe ftatifts I fay, faw this, they thought it then tyme to beftyrre themfelues, and to perfecute in good earneft, and yet to do it in fuch fort, as they might, if it were pofsible, auoyd the name, & fufpition of perfecutors both at home and abroad, and therfore they vfed the fame pollicy that Iulian the Apoftata did, of

Orat. 3. in Iulianum & orat. 10. in laudem Cæfarij.

whom S. Gregory Nazianzenus writeth, that he profefsed not externally his impiety with the courage that other perfecutors his predeceffours were wont to do, neyther did he oppofe himfelf againft our faith lyke an Emperour that would gayne honour in fhewing his might and power by open oppreffion of the Catholyks, but made warre vpon them in a cowardly and bafe māner couering his perfecution with craftie, and fubtyle deuifes, enuying them, the name and glorie of Martyrdome that the fouldiours of Chrift had got in former perfecutions, and therfore he endeuored to vfe violence in fuch fort as it fhould not appeare, ordayning that the Chriftians which fuffred for Chrift fhould be put to death as malefactours, this affirmeth. S. Gregory Nazianzen of Iulian the apoftata

wherein

wherein yow may fee a true pattron of your owne proceedings, for to exemplify thefame with anfwere to the
queftion yow afke concerning the temper of the lawes
made in the 23. yere of her Ma⁽ᵗⁱᵉˢ⁾ raigne, what other caufe
had yow to make thofe lawes in that yeare, but that yow
knew that Father Campian and diuers Seminary Priefts
were come into Englâd lately before, & therfore to make
the world beleue that their comming was to no other
end but to fow fedition, and trouble the State, yow did
not only make thofe lawes, but alfo fhamfully murdered
thefame yeare thefaid famous man, and 11.godly innocent
Priefts with him for fayned confpiracies proued againft
no one of them,& difauowed by them all at their deathes,
which fufficient proof of their innocenty, as before I haue
declared at large in the 11.chapter, befydes many other
fince made away in lyke manner vpon lyke fals pretences,
and efpecially in the yeare 88. after the Kinges Armada
had paft through the channel, in which yeare yow executed aboue 40. Priefts,and Catholykes in diuers partes of
England, to make the world beleue that they had ntelli-
gence with the Spaniards or had procured the comming
of thefaid Armada, which could not bee proued, nor fo
much as iuftly fufpected of any one of them.

Moreouer I dare boldly affirme, neyther fhal yow euer
be able with truth to controle me, that wheras our Seminaries haue yeilded within thefe 30.yeares 5. or 6.hûdreth
Priefts that haue laboured in that vyneyard (wherof yow
haue put to death more then a hundreth)yow could neuer
iuftly charge any one of them with fedition or matter of
ftate except it were Ballard executed with Babington and
the reft, whom as I wil not excufe, (becaufe I know not
how farre he waded in thofe matters) fo wil I not condemne him, confidering the proceedings of yow and your
fellowes with Catholykes in lyke cafes, yet this I wilbe
bold to fay. that if he had any dealing therin, it was without the confent or knowledg of any of his fuperiours, yea

Of Ballard.

N   or of

or of any intrinsecal frend of theirs, wherof I could yeild a sufficient reason, if it were conuenient.

But let vs admit that he was as deep in those matters as any of the rest; haue yow therfore any reason to condemne all other Seminary Priests for his act, I do not blame yow heer for punishing any Catholyke that yow should fynd to be truly seditious, but I fynd it strange, & against all reason and iustice, that yow do not only punish vs for fayned crymes, but also impute the doings of one or of a few to all, which was alwayes in my tyme, and I think it stil, the absurd dealing of your lawyers in the araignment of Catholykes vrging against them the attemptes of Doctor Sanders in Ireland, and Feltons setting vp of the Bul, and such like, as though euery Catholyke were priuie to their doings, or thought himself bound in conscience to do as they did, which kynd of argument your lawyers would neuer vse, if they were not eyther most malitious or ignorant, or thought all their audience to be fooles: For what conclusion can be drawne from one or some particuler to a general, as to say, Eaton the preacher did pennance on the Pillery in cheapsyde and after at Paules Crosse for lying with his daughter, such a minister was hanged for a rape, such an other for sodomy, such a one for a murder; ergo, all ministers are murderers, sodomites, rauishers of women, and incestuous persons.

Would your ministers allow this conclusion, or els that lawes should be made against them all for the offence of some of them? and yet to say truly there haue beene so many examples of ministers conuict & executed for such crymes that yow might with more reason exterminate the whole ministery, as a very sink of sinne, then condemne all Catholykes as seditious, for Doctor Saders, and Feltons cause, or all Seminary Priests for Ballards.

But to conclude this point, it is euident ynough, that neyther Ballards offence (yf he committed any) nor theirs

that

that were executed with him could be any occasion of those rigorous lawes against Seminary Priests which were made some yeares before, when (as I haue said) yow had not any one example of a Seminary man, that had beene, or could be touched with any sedition, other then such as yow fayned of them your selues.

Furthermore what iust cause had yow to make the di-stinction in your lawes betwixt Queene Marie Priests, & Seminary Priests? haue yow found any more in the one then in the other, but only that yow know the old Priests of Queene Martyrs tyme were so spent and wasted already that ther was not left of them perhaps half a score in England (who also yow thought would be in a short tyme consumed) wheras of the others, yow saw a continual spring, that would flow perpetually, to the vndouted destruction of your heresy in tyme, if it were not stopped, in which respect, yow thought good to seeme to fauour the first, that yow might with more shew of reason persecute the later. *Q. Marie Priests.*

Neuerthelesse yow haue hanged some of those Q. Marie Priests as wel as the other, only for doing their function counting them therin no lesse seditious then the Seminary Priests, and yet yow say yow spare the one sort as only superstitious, and punish the other as seditious.

But such seditious and superstitious Priests as these are, were the very Apostles and Disciples of our Sauiour, for they absolued from sinne, as these do, they administred the Sacraments of Baptisme, of the Alter, extreeme vnction, & the rest as these do, they said masse (that is to say) they offred in sacrifise the blessed, bodie and blood of our Sauiour as these do, they did preach, and teach the Christian Catholyke doctrine as these do, finally they were persecuted & punished for sedition as these are. *2.Cor.2.* *Act.10.* *Act.2.&20.* *Iam 5.* *Act.14.* *Act.17.* *Act.24.*

Thus Sir yow may see yow had not those causes which yow pretend, to change the temper of your

lawes

lawes, nor to diftinguifh betwyxt Seminarie and Queene
Marie Priefts, neyther any reafon at all to cal them
eyther fuperftitious, or feditious. But let vs fee fome
more of your glofes.

THE CONFVTATION OF

*an inuectiue which the Author of the Pam-
phlet maketh againft the
Iefuits.*

CHAP. XXIIII.

IN your 10. and 11. page yow make a digrefsion to
treat of the ftrange myfteries as yow cal them of the Iefuits doctrin, how they mingle heauen and hel, and
lift vp the hands of the fubiects againft the anointed of
God, yow wonder that Princes do not concurre in fup-
prefsing them, who yow fay make traffyck of their facred
lyues; yow compare them to pirats that are publyke
enemies to humayne fociety, and to the Templars that
were all put downe throughout Chriftendome within
a few weekes, and laftly yow fynd it ftrange that the
Bifhop of Rome doth not purge out a leuen as yow
cal them, fo ftrange and odious.

Thefe in deed are very ftrange and odious fpeeches,
and no maruayle for there can be no more fympathy
betwixt the Iefuits and yow then betwixt good and bad,
light and darknes, Chrift and Belial; it is no maruaile,
that the theef hateth the gallowes, the dog the whip or
the woolf the maftif, that keepes the flock, neyther
that yow and all other heretyks maligne thofe, whofe
schooles are your fcourge, whofe bookes your bane,
whofe vertue is your confufion, whofe vigilance and
induftry is the gard of fimple foules againft the affaults

Of the Ie-
fuits,

of your

of your herefy and impiety, wherin the great goodnes of
God is to be noted who for euery difeafe prouideth a remedy, for euery poyfon an antidote, for euery harme a
help, fo it pleafed him of his diuine wifdome to prouide
againft a Symon Magus, a Saynt Peter ; againft an
Arrius, an Athanafius ; againft a Neftorius, a Cyril ;
againft a Vigilantius, a Hierome ; againft a Pelagius,
an Auguftinus; (who was borne in Africk thefame day,
that the other was borne in England) againft the heretyks
called Albigenfes, a Dominik and his holy order of the
fryer preachers; and laftly in this our age, againft a Martyn
Luther and his curfed crue of vitious Apoftates he rayfed
an Ignatius de Loyola with his blefled company, of vertuous, and Apoftolical priefts, commonly called Iefuites,
whom though the Deuil, and all his inftruments (I meane
you, and all other heretykes, apoftatates, and atheifts) haue
no leffe impugned then the catholike Churche it felfe,
which they defend, yet neuertheleffe theyr holy Societie
is through the prouidence of God propagate and fpred
throughout the Chriftian world from one pole to the
other; and therby the wrackes and ruynes of Chriftendome repayred, infidels conuerted, heretyks confounded,
youth inftructed, the weake edifyed, no leffe to the glory
of God, then to the confufion of his enimyes & theirs.

But to come to the particulers of your flaunderous digrefsion ; yow wonder that Princes do not concurre to
the fupprefsion of this fect, as yow cal it, that maketh a
traffick of their lyues ; & I wonder, yow are not afhamed
to buyld fuch a malitious flaunder vpon fo falfe a ground,
feing I haue euidently proued that this matter of Squyre
(whervpon yow runne all this defcant) is a meere fiction
a lewd, and a lowdly, improbale in it felf, proued by no
witnes, or euidence, extorted from him by torment; retracted and difauowed at his death, though yow fhamefully fay the contrarie: befydes that it is now aboue 20.
yeares fince the Iefuits firft entred England in which tyme
N 3   yow

yow haue rackt, and rent diuers of them (Father Southwel 10. tymes, Father Walpoole 14. Father Campion I know not how oft) and diuers others for their caule, and all to fynd out fome fuch matter, and yet yow neuer got fo much as any inkling of any, fo that this contumelious fpeech of yours, is but a vaine blaft, that (as a man may fay) fhakes no corne, nor cracks any mannes credit but your owne.

Furthermore how childifh and vayne is the comparifon yow make of them to pyrats, therby to conclude them to be publyke enemies of humayn fociety, meaning (by lyke) by humayne fociety your felues, whofe publyke enemies yow may in deed accompt them in refpect of your herefies, yet in that fence there is neyther truth nor propriety in your manner of fpeech, for though I allow yow to be humayn and earthly in the higheft degree, yet a true fociety yow cannot be called, being fo diffociate, and deuided in religion amongft your felues as yow are, except it be the fociety of Sampfons foxes whofe tayles were only tyed together and their heads feuered.

But if yow confider the infinit numbers and multitudes of thofe that from one end of the world to the other do loue at this day and reuerence the Iefuits (as fathers, that giue them fpiritual food as phifitions that cure the difeafes of their foules, and as pilots (not pyrats) that guyde them to the port of eternal faluation) you fhal eafely fee the vanity, and idlenes of your difcourfe, and eyther be forced to graunt that they are no enemyes to humain fociety, or els abfurdly fay, that all men befydes your felues are feazed with fuch a lethargy, or fenceleffe ftupidity that they cannot difcerne enemyes from frends.

Can any man that is not mad or drunken with herefy as you feeme to be, or ouercome with paffion perfwade himfelf that fo many wife pious, and polityk kinges, Princes, councels, magiftrates, and gouernours (whofe dominions extending from one pole to the other, do conteyne the nobleft, and worthyeft parts of humain fociety among Chri-

Chriftians) would be fo vnaduifed to receyue them into their kingdomes countryes, cityes, & courtes, fofter them, cherifh them, loue, reuerence and honour them as they do, if they were fuch publike enemyes to humaine focietie as you make them, or any way hurtful to their ftates, perilous to Princes liues, preiudicial to publike good, or rather if they were not moft neceflary, and beneficial to them all?

This is fo manifeft to men of difcourfe and reafon that I need not further to enlarge my felf therein, feing there is no man fo fimple that wil preferre the vayne and malitious conceit of a few poor fectary Caluinifts hated & contemned by all other fectes of the fame breed, before the iudgment and experience of all the reft of Chriftendome, whereof you are not woorthy to be counted the parings, neyther for your number nor for any other refpect whatfoeuer, and albeit I might fay much more in this behalf yet for that the matter is euident of it felf, and the innocency and honour of thefe feruants of God hath byn defended by many learned bookes in thefe our dayes againft the barkings of all fectaryes and other their enemyes, and emulatours which their vocation and vertues cannot but purchafe vnto them, I fhal leaue of to fpeake any more of this argument for the prefent, and fo pafle ouer to that which remayneth.

OF THE

OF THE HIPOCRISY OF

the author of the Pamphlet and his fellowes, and of
a ridiculous miracle fayned in her Maiesties
suppofed efcape.

CHAP. XXV.

IT refteth now only to fpeak a word or two of the rel.g.ous zeale, and deuotion towards God, which you fhew in your g'ofes wherin you interlace not only examples of fcripture, but alfo cófiderations of Gods extraordinary and vifible prouidence in the preferuation of her Maieftie from this great confpiracy, for the manifeftation of his owne g.ory, in fo much that you make it miraculous comparing her Maiefties fuppofed efcape to the fhaking of the viper from S. Paules hand without hurt, but in fuch ridiculous manner, as in truth it made me and others good fport when I red it, for though I haue heard many fond comparifons, and fimilitudes of ydle braynes in my dayes, yet neuer heard I fuch an other as this is, and that in print.

A ridiculous comparifon. You fay thus, & they are your owne wordes as they ly in the book, that as the viper was vpon S. Paules hand and fhaked of without hurt, fo this was donne in Iuly, in the heate of the yeare, when the pores and veynes were openeft, to receyue any maligne vapour, or tincture if her Maieftie by any accident had layd her hand vpon the place.

Of which wordes there can be no other fenfe gathered (in my opinion) then this that as S. Paule being bitten with the viper fhaked her from his hand, and had no hurt, fo if by chaunce her Maieftie had layed her hand vpon the poyfoned pomel of the Sadle in the moneth of Iuly when the pores and veynes are open fhe might haue byn poyfoned or receaue maligne vapors or tinctures. But good Syr

yow

yow might haue done wel to haue put this cōceit in ryme,
for so it would haue beene at least ryme without reason,
wheras now it is neyther ryme nor reason, yet if yow had
said that her Matie had toucht the poysoned place, as yow
signify the contrary (which marres the fashion both of
your comparison, and of your miracle) there had beene
some more similitude, and matter miraculous, but as yow
haue handled it there is neyther miracle nor meaning, so
farre as my reason reacheth, and consequently this very
first miracle that euer yow had for confirmation of your
Gospel in England is miscaried for lack of good handling.
But to leaue this to the laughter of all wyse men, I wil
proceed to some other considerations.

Who is he that seing so much mētion in your discourse
of God, of his mercy, of his prouidence ordinary, and extraordinary, and of his more then natural influence to the
preseruation of her Matie would not think yow to be a
very religious and deuout man, or could imagyn that yow
knew in your conscience, that all this matter of Squyre was
a fiction, as it is euident yow did? wherof I need to bring
no better proof then those two notable lyes before mentioned, which yow take vpon your owne conscience,
though not only your self, but also many hundreths that
were at Squyres death know the contrary; wherby it appeareth that all your shew of religion deuotion and zeale
tendeth to nothing els, but to set a glos vpon this your
counterfeit ware, to make it the more salable amongst the
common people; which exceedeth all impiety.

For what can be so execrable, or sacriligious, as to abuse
the sacred name of almighty God, the holy scriptures, and
shew of deuotion and religion to such a mischeuous end,
as to slaunder and calumniate, which any man that be-
lieueth there is a God would tremble to do. But such is
the custome of yow, and your compagnions to make a
maske and visard of religion to couer therwith your impious, and irreligious practises, persuading your selues, that

O   although

although fome of the wifeſt may difcouer your treacherie, yet yow ſhal cary away many of the multitude, which is the fruit yow expect of this and fuch other your infamous, and ſlaunderous libels, forgeting that of Cicero *nullum ſimulatum diuturnum*, no fayned, or difembled thing can long continue, wherof our Sauiour warneth vs fufficiently, ſaying, beware of the leuen of hipocrites; nothing is fecret, that ſhal not be reuealed, nothing is hid that ſhal not be knowne, for thoſe things which yow haue faid in the dark ſhal be fpoken in the light, and that which yow haue fpoké priuily in your chamber ſhalbe preached in the houſe tops.

So that yow Sr libeller, and your fellowes cannot look to delude the world alwayes as yow haue donne many yeares but that fooner or later God wil open the peoples eyes, and difcouer vnto them your hipocrify and difguifed impiety, yea and perhaps make them his inftruments to reuenge his caufe, and their owne vpon yow, wherein may bee fulfilled, that which Iobe faith of the hipocrite, *the heauês ſhal reueale his iniquitie, and the earth ſhal ryſe againſt him.*

Wel Sir, though much more matter woorthy to bee treated do offer it felf vnto mee at this prefent, by occafion of this your libel, yet not to ouerlode yow at once, nor to weery the reader, this ſhal fuffife for anſwere thereynto : only I wil aduertife yow of one thing, that although yow diſſemble your name (fearing belike that the notable vntruth auowed by yow might turne to your ſhame if yow ſhould be knowne) yet I am not ignorant who yow are, and haue forborne to name yow, only to requite your curtefy in ſparing to name mee in your faid libel, which at the bar other your fellow barriſters did not forbeare to do, fo that beeing now euery way out of your debt, as I take it, I take my leaue of yow, wiſhing yow as much grace as to my felf.

THE

THE CONCLVSION TO
the Lords of the Councel.

CHAP. XXVI.

MY very good Lords, although it is a cōmon saying, and commonly true, *that obsequium amicos, veritas adiū parit, flattery gets friends, & truth hatred,* in which respect I might wel feare that the playnesse which I haue vsed in this discours might be offesiue to your Lordships, yet framing in my self a farre other conceit, of your wisdomes, & iudgements then of the common sort of men (whose eares do itch rather after vanity, then verity, after pleasure rather then profit) I persuade my self that your Lordships are such friends and patrons of truth, that yow cannot mislike to heare it, when it is deliuered vpon so iust an occasion, as the defence of honour and innocency, & to so good an end as a publyk benefit, and therefore I hope that when your Lordships shal haue wel wayed the particulers represented heere to your consideration, I meane our innocency, the trechery of our aduersaries, the abuse offred therein to her Ma*tie* and your honours, the infamy that groweth thereby to your gouernment, the daungers both domestical, & forrayne, the offece to God in shedding innocent blood, and lastly the punishment due thereto from his iustice, your Lordships wil not only aproue my playnesse accompanied with reason, sincerity & truth, but also employ your wisdomes, charity, and autority, to the reparation of our wrongs, and releef of our miseries, whereof I say, I cannot but haue exceeding great hope, when I consider the great zeale your honours haue shewed to the mayntenance of iustice, in the punishment of such as yow haue vnderstood to haue abused your cōmissions towards Catholykes, in farre lesse matters then this which I haue touched in this Apology, whereof I haue knowen, and

heard

heard of diuers examples; as wel before I came out of England, as since, whereby it is euident, that these other extreame iniuries that our aduersaries day y do vnto vs, proceed meerly of their owne malice, and no way of your Lordships wil, comm fsion, or consent, and that for the remedy, there wanteth nothing, but that your honours may haue notice thereof, which I haue therefore presumed to geue yow in this Apology by the occasion of this my purgation, which I present vnto yow in all humility, beseeching your Lordships, for conclusion of this treatise, to consider from what root all these foule vnchristian practises of our aduersaries do spring, as that they are nothing els but the fruit of heresy, which hath no other period where to rest, but atheisme, or apostacy from Christ, as euidently appeareth by all the east parts of the world, which from lyke schisme, and heresy, are falne to flat infidelity; which if it please your Lordships wel to weigh, and the true remedy withall, which Machiauel (though in other things he be most absurd and impious) yet wysely teacheth in this case, to wit, to reduce a corrupted state of common wealth, to the point frō whence it first declined, I hope your honours wil see the necessity of the reduction of our realme to the ancient Catholyke religion, and to the vnity of the Catholyke body of Christendome; whereof it was many hundred yeares togeather a principal mēber, in all honour, and security, florishing in iustice, equity, and piety, whereas now by this disunion, and diuorce, from the said Catholyke body, and religion, it is not only exposed to many daungers, and much infamy, but is also replenished with iniustice and impiety, as appeareth by the ordinary, & dayly proceedings of our aduersaries against vs, declared sufficiently in this Apology, which I leaue to your honours wyse consideration, humbly beseeching almighty God to illuminat your Lordships, and her Mayesty also in this behaulf, which if it shal please his deuine Ma.tie to do, and with so great a grace, and blesing, as is the light of his Ca-

tholyke

tholyke fayth, to consummate and perfect those other rare gifts that he hath already bestowed vpon her Ma.ᵉⁱᵉ. (I meane her many princely partes, her power by sea, & land, her peace at home, her prosperity abroad, her long lyfe and raygne) shee wilbe one of the most fortunat, famous, & glorious Princes, that England or Christiandome hath had in many ages, and a most rare example of Gods inspeakable mercy to the endles comfort of all true Christians. From Madrid, the last of August. 1 5 9 9.

Your Lordships humble seruant
T. F.

THE TABLE OF
the Chapters.

Of

the end

Such fevv faultes as may haue efcaped
in the printing, it may pleafe the
courteous reader to pardon.

APPENDIX

the Apostle sayth, *he reconcyled vs by his death, that he might make* Colof. 1.
vs holy, and immaculat, and irreprehensible before him, and in an ^{ad Habr. 9.} ad Habr. 9.
other place making a comparison betwyxt the effects of
the sacrifices of Christ vpon the crosse, and the sacrifices of
the old law, he sayth, *but how much more shal the blood of Christ
make cleane our conscience from dead woorkes* (that is to say from
sinne) *to serue the liuing God:* to this purpose sayth saynt Iohn,
*sanguis Iesu Christi emundat nos ab omni peccato, the blood of Iesu
Christ doth make vs cleane from all sinne,* in which respect our 1. Ioan. 1.
Sauiour Christ is truly cauled the *lamb of God which taketh
away the sinnes of the world.*

Therfore saynt Chrisostome sayth that a man newly Ioan. 1 in
baptysed is *mundior solis radijs, cleaner then the beames of the sunne,* homil ad
Baptizan.
and compareth the sinne of the baptised to a sparke of fyre,
faling into the mayne sea, wherein it is presently extin-
guished, S. Basil cauleth it a *remission of debt,* and the death of Basil. in ex-
hortat. ad
sinne. S. Gregory Nazianzen tearmeth it *peccati diluuium the* Baptif.
deluge wherein sin is drowned, (and lastly not to be tedious,
with many allegations, in a matter where in all learned
fathers doe vniformly agree) S. Augustin sayth *baptisme* Angl. lib. 3.
washeth away all sinnes, yea all whatsoeuer, of deeds, thoughts, contra duas
words, of original sinne, or other committed ignorantly or wittingly, epist. pelagia-
norum ca 3.
and in an other place, he sayth, yt doth *auferre crimina, non* Lib. 1. contra
radere, take sinnes cleane away, and not shaue them only. eafdem epifc.

What then shal wee say of Luther, and his fellowes cap. 13.
that deny such a manifest principle of Christian religion,
affirming that original sinne is not taken away by baptisme, but that it remayneth & infecteth all menes workes
can any thing be sayd more to the derogation of Chrifts
merits, on which they wil seeme sometymes wholy to
rely? can their other heresyes concerning the necefsity of
sinne, the impossibility to keepe the commandments, the
sinful or stayned righteousnes of the iustest man, or yet
their imputatiue iustice, all grounded and necessarily depending vpon the rotten foundation of this pestilent opinion, can they I say, be lyke to stand when their foundation
fayleth,

fayleth, as yow fee? but this wil be more euident, yf we cōfider the other effect of Baptifme, which is regeneration, or renouation of the foule, wherof the Prophet fayth, *I wil geue yow a new hart and a* new fpirit, in which refpect the Apoftle cauleth Baptifme *lauacrum regenerationis, and renouationis, the water of regeneration, and renouation,* for that as our Sauiour himfelf fignified a man is *borne a new by water, & the holy ghoft,* & becometh as faynt Paule fayth *noua creatura a new creature* by grace of the holy fpirit *which is aboundantly poured vpon him,* to which purpofe the Apoftle fayth that *charity is diffufed in our harts, by the holy ghoft which is giuen vs,* and that *Chrift dwelleth in our harts,* and that *wee liue for iuftification, for that the fpirit of God dwelleth in vs,* all which proue a real and inhærent iuftice in vs, and not a iuftice in Chrift, imputed only to vs, this the Apoftle fignifyeth by the fimilitude of Baptifme with the death & refurrection of Chrift faying that *wee are buryed with him by baptifme to the end that as Chrift did rife from death, fo wee may walke in newnes of lyfe,* vpon which words, S. Auguftin fayth, *as in Chrift there was a true refurrection, fo in vs there is a true iuftification,* and S. Chrifoftome proueth thefame by the woords of S. Paule, (where he fayth, *you are wafhed, you are fanctified, you are iuftified*) *he fheweth* fayth he, *that you are not only made cleane, but alfo that you are made holy and iuft,* to which purpofe he noteth that it is cauled *lauacrum regenerationis,* and not *remiffionis* or *purificationis, the water of regeneration,* and not *of remiffion or purification,* for fayth he, *it doth not fimply remit finnes, but makes, vs as though wee were of a heauenly generation,* which Clemens Alexandrinus confirmeth faying *being baptifed we are illuminated, being illuminated we are adopted to be the childrē of God, being adopted wee are made perfect, being perfited wee are made immortal, according to that of the Pfalmift, I fay you are all Gods, and the children of the higheft.* Thefame alfo in effect fayth S. Gregory Nazianzen *Baptifme* fayth he, *giuing help to our firft natiuity, of old makes vs new, and of human deuine,* all which doth playnly proue that which we teach, with faynt Auguftin,

who

Ezechi. 36.

Tit. 3.

Ioan. 3.
Galat 6.

Tit. 3.
Roma. 5.
Act 15.
Rom. 8.

Rom. 6.

Aug. in Enchir. cap. 52.

1 Cor. 6.
Chryfoft.
hom. ad Bap.
Titul. 3.

Clem. Alex.
lib. 1. pædag.
cap. 6.
Pfalm. 81.
in o. at. in
fanctum baptifma.

De peccatorum meritis
& remiffione
cap. 9. lib. 1.

ENGLISH RECUSANT LITERATURE
1558–1640

Selected and Edited by
D. M. ROGERS

Volume 241

PHILIPS NUMAN
Miracles Lately Wrought
1606

PHILIPS NUMAN

Miracles Lately Wrought by the
Intercession of the Glorious Virgin
Marie at Mont-aigu

1606

The Scolar Press
1975

ISBN o 85967 231 x

Published and printed in Great Britain by
The Scolar Press Limited, 59-61 East Parade,
Ilkley, Yorkshire and
39 Great Russell Street,
London WC1

1853139

MIRACLES

LATELY VVROVGHT

BY THE INTERCESSION

OF THE GLORIOVS VIR-
gin Marie, at Mont-aigu , nere vnto Siché
in Brabant.

Gathered out of the publik inftruments, and
informations taken thereof. By authoritie of the Lord Archbifhop
of Maclin.

Tranflated out of the French copie into Englifh by M.
Robert Chambers Prieft, and confeffor of the Englifh
Religious Dames in the Citie of Bruxelles.

PRINTED,
At Antwarp, by Arnold Conings,
1 6 0 6.
Cum Priuilegio.

TO THE
MOST HIGHE
AND MIGHTIE PRINCE,
IAMES BY THE GRACE OF
GOD KING OF GREAT BRYTAINE,
France, and Ireland, Defender of the Faith.

I DOVBT not (Dread Soueraine) but that by some meanes the reporte of the st.aunge, and wunderfull things which lately haue happened in these Netherlands are come to your graces knowledge, where at all the world here stådeth so much amazed and astonished: but whether your Maiestie hath bene informed of al the particularities, I iustly doubt, because I can not by any waies vnderstand, that your Highnes is any whit moued therewith. *Aristotle* saieth. *Omnes homines naturaliter scire desiderant.* All men haue a natural desire to attaine to the true, & perfect knowledge of things: but the wiser, and learneder sorte are especially adicted there-vnto, principaly, when the object is admirable, of weight and importance : for then as it
A 2   yeeldeth

Meta:li.
I.tex. I.

yeeldeth vnto their spirits extraordinarie contentment and perfection, so to be ignorant thereof,
putteth them in hazard of error, notable domage,
and confusion. Whence hath proceeded the exquisit
diligence and curious inquisition, which we haue
seen vsed in this present matter, not onely by our
Prelates, Doctors, and Professors of learning, vnto
whom the direction of our soules in the way of God
doth chiefly appartaine, but also by the temporal Princes, Nobilitie, and men of ciuil pollicie, whose wisdome and due regard of their own credites, disdai-
ned, to permit them selues to be led by the noses,
to the future peril of their soules, together with the
present disparagement of their honours, and reputa-
tions. The which manner of these mennes proceding in this affaire, gaue me occasion to suspect, that
your Maiestie was not sufficiently informed hereof:
for other wise, it is not to be imagined (consideration
beeing had of the common and general opinion
which men here conceiue of your Graces singuler
prudence, and literature) that your Royal wisdom
would passe ouer these things as though your grace
had no apprehension or esteeme thereof, which of
very many are held as most pernicious, & abominable, in the sight both of God and man: and of innumerable others are reputed as most venerable, and
glorious demonstrations of our Lord his sweet loue
care & prouidence towardes his louing Spouse his
Church. which he vouchsafeth to adorne in this
honorable and admirable maner.

Vpon which coniecture my Gracious lord and
souueraine I haue aduentured to send vnto your
Princely view the authentical relation of diuers
things, which in these last yeares haue happened
amongst vs: a subiect vndoubtedly not vnwoorthy
                                                    your

your mature consideration, and exquisit iudgement.
And I haue laboured to translate it out of the Frech
copie, not that I thinck your Maiestie ignorant of
that language, but that by the way I might also sa-
tiffy the greedie desire of many your maiesties louing subiects, who haue altedie hard the bruit, but
yet haue not had the assured & certaine knowledge
of the matter. And I am the more bold to write vnto
your Maiestie of these things, considering what by
others hath bin done vnto great Emperours, and
kings in the like case. For I read that *Pontius* Diuers
Pilate wrote vnto *Tyberius Cæsar* touching the authors
miracles of our Lord and Sauiour. I note how the vvho
famous. *Nicephorus* dedicated his Ecclesiasticall hi- haue
storie to *Andronicus Paleologus* the Emperour, in which vvritten
historie, (amongst other things) sundrie worthie ces of
miracles are comprised. I synd that our renoumed miracles
countrieman *Venerable Bede* directed vnto King *Ceo-*
lulphe his miraculous historie of our English Saxons conuersion to the faith of Christ. I haue seen (to
omitt prolixitie in this matter) the book which the
Abbot & cōgregatiō of the moncks of Mōt *Serra-*
to, offred vnto the *French king* now liuing cōtayning
a narration of certaine miracles wrought at the said
mont *Serrato*. Againe I haue bin much hartned to
present this relatiō vnto your Maiestie, in regard of
the great opinion & esteeme the worthie, godly, and
Prudent Princes of these Contries haue of this matter, which they haue manifested by theyr often Pilgrimages to the place of *Montaigue*, where also by
their goodly, riche, and stately ornaments and oblations they haue giuen all the world to vnderstand
the high regard, and account they make hereof.
But chiefly I haue ben animated herevnto, for that
it is not vnknown, what extraordinarie pleasure
        A 3   and

and contentment, your Maieftie taketh to imploy your Roial labors in those things, that appertaine vnto God.

What things do more apertaine vnto God (Gracious Soueraine, then miracles::which is as much to say, as those workes which can be wrought onely by God, of which ranck these (whereof here relation is made)are beleeued to bee, as beeing femblable vnto those diuine operations, where by the Sauieur of the world did manifeft his Godhead to the world. For here your Grace may behould, how the blynd fee, the deaf heare, the lame walk, the deuils are expelled he leaporous are made cleane, and many other painful, deformed and defperate maladies are cured.

I know it would be a great miracle yf these works would be admitted of all men for miracles. Wherefore I am humbly to intreat your gracious patience, to perufe what here I haue fet down in an fwere of those obiections, whereby I find them ordinarilie to be oppugned. I feare that I fhal be deemed of many to be ouer prolix, but I befeech them to confider, that it is Gods caufe which I handle, and that I endeuour to informe my gracious Lord and Prince in fuch forte of the veritie hereof, that with greater light and affurance he might pronounce his expected royal fentence, to the glorie of God, his own honour, & ineftimable commoditie of many thoufands. And although I haue not here fo conuenient place to vtter the hundreth parte of those things which otherwife I wou'd, therfore I intend (by our Lords help) hereafter more to inlarge my felf herein as occafion fhal be offered

Who is he (gracious Soueraine) that hath but half an eye and feeth not of what confequence it is for any Societie of people to be affifted with the prefence of miracles? For where miracles are feen to fa-

uour

your the persons, or things that apperrain to their Congregation, who can deny but that God is wel pleased whith them, and wel allowreth of their rites, faith and profession? Miracles are works that surpasse the power of any creature *Benedictus Dominus Deus Israel, qui facit mirabilia solus. Blessed be the lord God of Israel vvho onely vvorketh maruelous things, or miracles,* as the Prophet sayeth. When therefore he vouchsafeth to work any miracle in the defence or honour of any person, or any point belonging to any Religion, or beleef, such a miracle is as it were his very woord, and soueraine diuine sentence, giue vpon the same, which none may deny, gainsay, or doubt of, without note of infidel'itie, & sacrilegious blasphemie. The holy Scriptures by the deuil himself, and many Heretickes both are, and haue bene fowly and wickedly cited, and interpreted: the testimonies of the auncient holy Fathers are by diuers sects diuersly abused: the old famous Martyrs, Confessors, and Virgins are chalenged of many, and as it were violently hailed into their Congregations, as yf they had bin of their churches, and professions: former general Councels, Canons of Popes, and decrees of Sinods are of sundrie factions alleaged as fauouring their sundrie inuentions: in fine, there is no proof vsd by the Catholicks, which the impugners of the Catholick Church draw not into their books, sermons, and disputations, but at miracks al parties must make a stand, and be silent; there, God him self alone must speak, and shewe himself, for such woorks are out of all the reach of any finite and created power, none beeing able to rule the chariot of this Sunne, but onely such Iosuaes, as vnto whome our Lord wil vouchsafe to graūt so great authoritie, and commaundrie. Which the wisdome of

Psal. 7ï.

vvhat authoritie miracleshaue to proue Religiō.

A 4   God

God our Sauiour Iesus Christ wel vnderstood, and
therfore he vsed this medium, proof and argument
for the authoritie, and veritie of his doctrine and in
condemnation of the Iewes incredulitie saying: *Si
opera non fecissem in ijs quæ nemo alius fecit, peccatum
non haberent.* Yf I had not done among them workes that no other man hath don, they should not
haue sinne. In like manner the same Lord beeing to
send his Apostles to instruct the world in a Religion which to the Iewes was scandalous, to the
Gentiles meere follie, & to all men passing the com-
passe of reason, he furnished them with the same meanes, whereby to make their hearers capable of their
doctrine, and to induce them to subiect their heads
and harts there-vnto. And by what eloquence or
forcible persuasion was this to be effectuated? Verily
by no other meanes, then that God himself should
affirme, and auerre their preaching by his miraculous
working, as it is said: *Conuocatis duodecim discipu-
lis suis, dedit illis potestatem spirituum immundorum, vt
eijcerent eos, & curarent omnem languorem & omnem
infirmitatem.* Hauing called his touelue disciples together, he gaue them pouver ouer vncleane spirits, that
they should cast them out, and should cure al diseases,
and al infirmities. Which vnspeakeable goodnes and
prouidence of God, if we wil duely consider, we may
euidently see his incomprehensible wisdome, & loue
towards vs his most vnworthie Creatures, in pro-
uiding for our instruction in his wayes such assured
meanes, whereby, to learne the truthe, and to auoid
al errour: that if al the world would haue layed
their heades together to inuent a way, they could not
haue found a more perspicuous, more profitable, or
more glorious then this, which he of his blessed mercie hath vouchesafed vnto vs, For God being the
truthe

Io. 15.

1.Cor. 1.

Mat 11.
marc. 3.
Luc. 9.

God can
not vvor
ke mira-
cles for

truthe it self, he cã not by his omnipotẽcie giue his **the**
testimonie to any error or falshood: & beeing very **proof of**
goodnesse it self, it is impossible that he wil permit **any fals**
vs to be seduced by any his extraordinarie supernatu- **religiõ.**
ral operations, neither can he or wil he yeeld any honor to that, which in it self is euil: For as truthe is
a thing perfectly good and the chyld of God, so
falshood is detestable and naught, and the wicked
impe of the deuil. Of which thing that renoumed &
famous champion of Gods Church Sainct *Augustin* **Aug. q.**
had a true and perfect conceipt, Who sayd: *Omnes* **114 de**
Philosophi, & sectarum inuentores, diuersis disputationi- **quæstio-**
bus inuicem se confuderunt.Nullus ad alterum transiens, **nibus no**
quia vnusquisque in quo imbutus fuerat,permanebat. Al **ui & ve-**
the Philosophers, and sectmaisters, cõfounded each other **teris te-**
by sundrie disputes. Neuer any one of them yeelding to **stamẽti,**
the other, for euery one held to that vvhich once he had
learned. Behold the ordinarie issue of al wranglings
and contentions, euen amongst the wittier and learneder sorte. But he proceedeth: *Hinc factum est vt*
Dei prouidentia (cuius sensus inuestigari non potest) præ-
dicationi suæ virtutem adiungeret , vt veritas predicatio-
nis virtutis testimonio probaretur:vt qui verbis contra-
dicerent,virtutibus non auderent. Hence it came to pas
that the prouidence of God , (whose sense no man
can fynd out)ioined power to his preaching, that the
truthe of his preaching might be prooued by the testimonie of his power: that if any would gainesay
his woords, they should not dare to contradict his
powerable woorkes. And that glorious doctor S.
Gregorie for his rare learning and wisdome surna- **Greg.**
med the great, speaking of the miracles of God and **hom.29**
his Saincts confirmeth the same saying. *Hi quam* **in Ezech**
vera de Deo dixerint, testantur miracula , quia talia per
illum non facerent,nisi vera de illo narrarent.Hovv tru-

by

ly these people haue spoken of God, their miracles beare
vvittnes, for they could neuer vvork such things by him,
if they had not spoken truly of him. Whereby we see
of what force & authoritie miracles are to persuade
men to accept of that doctrine, wh ch otherwise
by their reason they can not comprehend. And the
sayd holy Doctor proceedeth, adding an o her point
worthie the noting. *Si Igitur de fide tentamur, quam
ex illorum prædicatione concepimus, loquentium miracula conspicimus, & in fide quam ab eis accepimus confir-
mámur: quid ergo illorum miracula, nisi ipsa sunt nostra
prepugnacula?* If therfore vve be tempted about our
faith, vvich by their preaching vve haue learned, vve
behold the miracles of our Preachers, and thereby are
confirmed in the faith, vvich from them vve haue receiued therfore vvhat other things are their miracles but
that they are our fortresses.* Which conclusion seemeth
to be so iust, and founded in reason, that I thinck
there is none that dare so much as doubt of it, much
lesse deny it.

　　Yet I confesse though the deuil cannot make mē
to deny this euident principle, notwithstanding he
endeuoureth to make voyd the force and authoritie
thereof. For when he dare not coap with his armed
aduersarie, if he can persuade him to cast away his
weapons, he nothing doubteth but that then he shal
easelie subdue him. So I read that he dealt with a
certayn kynde of miscreāts called *vvaldenses* or Poor
men of Lions, who amongst diuers other their
lewd blasphemies and heresies, were persuaded to
auouche that God neuer wrought any miracles in his
Church: whereby the subtil enimie inducing them,
and others by them to dispoile the Church of her miracles, it was verie easie for him afterwards to make
men dispise, what-soeuer vpon the credit of miracles
　　　　　　　　　　　　　　　　　　　　the

Prateo-
lus de
vitis Hæ
ret. lib.
14 nũ.
13.

thesayd Churche might argue against them. Vnto which poor wittles people certaine others do neerly approache, who althongh they wil perhaps confesse al such miracles as are cōtained in the bookes of holy Scripture: Yet because they thinck that not long after the tyme that those bookes were written, either hel gates preuailed against the rock of the Church, or that the Citie builded vpon an hil, was ouer couered with some Aegyptian duskie darcknes, or els shut vp in some vnknowne caue and valley: consequētly they inferr that there neuer apeared miracles since that chāge. whereby they wil haue vs beleeue that either they haue quite perished, or els haue bene wrought in hugger mugger & in great secret. For as they know where smoke is there comonlie is some fier, and where they see a shadow they must confesse the presence of some bodie: so if they should graunt the perpetual course of miracles, they must also graunt the perpetuitie of that Church for which and in which they haue bin wrought. *(margin: Cōtaine to our sauioures promis and vvarrāt. Math 16 Math. 5.)*

In the discouerie of which their absurditie I might first alledge them the testimonie of their own Fox, who telleth vs of diuers miracles appertaining to his martyrs. . But they may answer me, that Fox is fabulous, I yeeld he is so, for that he is easilie prooued so to be, and I know it would be lost and lewd labor for any to endeuour to prooue the contrarie Yet would I learne what they repute those benedictions to be, which Sir Francis Hastings, and al most euery preacher and gospeller affirme that God hath heaped vpon our Realme, since the alteration of Religion was made therein Yf they be but the ordinarie mercies of God, as he maketh his Sunne to rise vpon the good and bad, and sendeth downe his rayne vpon the iust and vniust: then they make *(margin: Fox in his Actes & monumēts. In his vvatchevvord. Math. 5.)*

no more for their Gospel, then the like do for the
Turkes Alcoran: or els they can prooue vnto vs that
God hath supernaturally blessed them onely in regard of their Religion, thereby manifesting vnto
them and others, that England professeth his true
faith, and that his true worship onely florisheth,
therein: which when I see them do, then both I and
they must graunt them as many miracles, as they
can score vp their supernatural blessings, and consequently we both must conclude that miracles are
not yet decayed. But because I know the things
whereof they make this bragge are of the wiser sorte
esteemed presumptions, phantasies, inuentions, and
meer fopperie therfore I leaue it to each mannes wisdome to inferr hereof the continuance of miracles as
he pleaseth. And I wish them rather to peruse the
writings and volumes of those that haue set down
the infinit miracles which by diuers holy Persons &
in diuers holy places amongst Catholicks haue bene
wrought. To recite here the onely bare names of
those that haue most laudably emploied their labors
herein, would be an endles trauaile: where the should
I begin? how shal I proceed? and when shal I make
an end, if I would vndertake to reherse the sundrie
particularities touching this matter which in these
Authors I finde registred?

But I know as they blush not to deny so euident a truthe as is the continuance of miracles, so wil
they not be ashamed to contemne, disgrace, and scorne
al such as haue recorded them, nothing regarding the
opinion or esteeme, that either the Christian world
now hath, or euer had of their wisdome, sanctitie,
learning, sinceritie, and discretion. Yet if they wil
not credit those writers who haue penned the gestes
and miracles of particuler persons, & places, at leastwise

wise let them not disdaine the publick records, and
Cronicles of whole Kingdomes and nations: especiallie in such things as by the people of the said kingdomes and nations are generally held and confessed
toibe true; yea, which often tymes the Croniclers of
other Realmes and cōmon welthes do acknowledge
& auouche with them, without any differéce, doubt,
or contradiction.

In those publick monuments they may read how
the said dominions and countries receaued first their
Christianitie, & withall they shal finde, that miracles
were stil a principal motiue and instigation there-vnto. It is not vnknown how the faith of Christ was
preached in *Iurie*, how it was afterward spred through
Grece, *Italie*, *Spaine* and other Cuntries, where the
Apostles, and Disciples of *Christ* preached. I suppose
few wil deny but that they did worke miracles in all
places wheresoeuer they came to teach the Gospel for
so it is written: *Illi autem profecti prædicauerunt vbi-*
que: Domino cooperante, & sermonē confirmāte sequē-
tibᵒ signis, But they going forth preached euery vvhere,
our Lord vvorking vvithal, and confirming the vvord
vvith signes that follovved. Let them onely peruse the
later ages. and let them passe through them successiuely, by euery Nation as it was conuerted. And
if it please them they may begin with that people
which now we call French, and they shal see, that
the French men hold that they receiued their faith by
the preaching and miracles of *S. Remigius*, & others:
likewise we Englsh say that our conuersion was first
wrought by the endeuours and miracles of. *Sainct*
Augustin the monke, & of his fellowes. The Danes
and Suetians affirm that *S. Rhembertus* by p eaching,
and working of miracles made them Christians. The

Hincma-
rus in e-
ius vita.
Beda in
Hist. See
Boz:de
signis
Ecclesiæ.

People

H. 5. cap.
1. & 2.

People of *Bohemia* tel that they were conuerted by the miracles first of two Brethren called *Cirillus* and *Methodius*, & then of the holy Dutches *Ludmilla*, and of their king *Vencesaus*. The Sclauonians haue in their records that they were brought to the faith by the labors & miracles of *S. Bonifacius*. The Polonians with their Prince *Miesca* by meanes of a miracle were first baptized. The Hungarians by miracles, and the industrie of *Adalbertus* bishop of *Prage* and of their Prince *Geisa* became Christians. The Tartarias with their king *Cassanus* submitted them selues to the faith of Christ, being moued thereunto by a notable miracle. Almost in our age the *vvest Indies* began by the miracles of *Martinus Valentinus* and *Aloisius Bertrandus* to admitt the Christian beleef. And to conclude the *East India* by the miracles of *Consaluus Siluerius*, of the blessed *Francis Xauerius*, and of *Gasper* surnamed *Belga* al three of the Societie of the holy name of Iesus began lykewise to forsake their Paganisme, and to imbrace the doctrin of Christ Iesus.

What may any reasonably answer to this Historical demonstration and Chronical deduction of the perpetuitie and continuance of miracles? Wil this opposit people say for al this, that these heathens were neuer brought to make acceptance of Christ his Gospel by miracles, can they by any sufficient authors or conuenient proofs shew vs the contrarie? wil they flap vs in the mouthes that al these are fictions, and standing stil vpon their bare & incredulous denial, giue the ly to al the monuments, traditions and writers of al these kingdomes and Nations? Be it so if of force without any reason they wil haue it so, yet I wil demonstrate vnto thē (yf they wil not deny theyr own writes) that they must necessarilie graunt

so

so manie successiue miracles as there haue bin cuni-
tres and People who haue imbraced the faith without the motiue of external miracles.

For what can be more miraculous then to see so
many great & barbarous nations, with their Kings
and Nobles, settled in a Religion, by them selues and
all their aunceters, indeed whith great Honou:s,
riches pomp and preuileges, taught and magnified
by their own Priestes, whose credit and necessarie
maintenance depended thereon: by which their pa-
gā religion they were liceied to cōmitt almost what
soeuer their proude, vnbrideled licentious sensual
appetites could desire? What could be more miraculous I say, then to see these people at the bare preaching and asseueration of some Bishops or Priests,
(yea imagin & say of some superintendēts & ministers) who should teach them, that the God which
they ought to beleeue & adore, is three persons and
yet but one God: that one of these persons is both
man and God, two natures but one person: whose
mother both before his birth, in his birth, and after
his birth was alwayes a pure virgin, and an immacu-
late mayd: and that this God after he had for the
space of some yeares indured many miseries, indignitie, sclaunders, and persecutions of certaine men
that maligned him, was afterwards betraied to them
and atached by them, and after sundrie disgraces and
afflictiōs most cruelly and shamefully hanged, & put
to death. Yea supose that these preachers should haue
tould them, that this God in his life tyme wrought
manie miracles, and that after his death he did rise
againe to life, and ascended vp to heauen: whether
also these Pagans & Siluagioes should come, if they
would throw down their Goddes, destroy their
temples, forsake their Priestes, abhor their sacrifices

suffer

suffer their heades to be washed in the name of God,
for the remission of their sinnes, and withal if they
would imbrace chastitie, meekenes, patience, pennance, humilitie, and beleeue many things surpassing their vnderstanding and submit them selues to
diuers other things contrarie to their sence, yea alto
gether opposit to their pride, and libertie which before they enioyed. He that wil say that such people as
these were brought to this, without an exceeding
great miracle, yf not by many miracles, I wil not say
that he is a miracle, but surely I think your Royal
wisdome wil deeme and iudge him a wonderous
monster.

Furthermore I beseech your Maiestie to consider if a reprobate Iewe were to demande of these
negatiue people, whether they thought our Lord
God did more honour, or gaue more preuileges to
the new law, or to the old, that is, (as true
Christians would say) to the woork of Christ, or to
Alvvai- that of Moyses: to that which was in verie substáce
es mira- or to the figure thereof: to that which was the per-
cles in fection, or to that which was to be perfected? What
the ty answer I pray your Grace wil they shape him? A
me of shame on the if they would giue the sinagoge the
the ould vpper hand, and shoulder down the Gospel, for that
lavve. were a very vnciuil or rather vngodly trick of a Gospeller. And yet the Iewe wil demonstrate vnto thé,
how our Lord adorned and assisted his people and
auncestours with miracles, and powrable woikes
aboue the force of Nature al the tyme of Moyses,
of their Iudges, of their kings, of their Prophets
euen in the tyme of their captiuitie, in the tyme of
their Machabe's, yea and of our Sauiour Christ him
self, as is manifest by the perpetual miracle of the
Probatica Piscina. Yea what if the sayd Iewe standing

ding vpon the proof and prerogatiue of miracles
should therein preferre the state of tho'e that liued
onely vnder the law of Nature before vs that liue
in the law of grace: For he wil tel them of the miraculous sacrifice of *Abel*, of the translation of *Enoch* Miracles
of his perpetual miraculous conseruation in *Paradise* in the
euer since, of the cōming of al kyndes of liuing crea- first state
tures to *Noe* his Arik, of their more then admirable re.
manner of nuriture, agreement, and abode in the
same, of the waters of the vniuersal deluge, of the
confusion of tongues, of the destruction of *Sodom*
and *Gomorha*, of the preseruation of *Lot* with his
daughters, of the metamorphosis of his wyf into a
piller of sault, of the vocation of *Abraham*, of al his
visions, of the often aparitions of Angels both to
him and others, of the generation of *Isaac*, of his
miraculous deliuerie, of so many miracles wrought
in the behalf of *Iacob*, *Ioseph*, *Moyses*, and the people
of Israel both in Egipt, & when they were departed
thence, vntil the tyme that the law was deliuered
them. When the Iewe hath thus out-braued the
Church of Christ with their miracles, wil these people that can not disgest the perpetual course therof
amongst Christians, brook that the Church which
our lord & sauiour chose as his most louing spowse,
wherein he promised to abyde to the end of the
world, which he bought with his most precious
blood, and adorned with so great and most worthie
Sacramēts, should be destitute of such a grace, should
be bereaued of so necessarie a strength, should be depriued of so conuenient and needeful a glorie?

Yf they wil not be a shamed to play thus the base
craaens, and so much to disgrace the honor of the
Christian Religion, and the most honorable worke
of Christ Iesus, then I chalendge them to shewe vs
B   some

some auncient & authenticall Writers, Chronicles, Records, Doctors, or learned writers, that euer noted the tyme when God withdrew his powrable hand from these kinde of supernatural workes, or that euer they should end so long as his Church should last.

But they can neuer do it, as we on the other side are able to shewe them the perpetual course and succession of miracles in the Catholick Church, euen from the Apostles dayes to ours, as that learned and eloquent Father *Lewis Richeome* hath already done in his discourse of miracles, dedicated to the Frēch king now liuing: and I hope ere long they shal further perceaue by that huge and infinit masse of these matters, which the Reuerend, learned, and worthie Father *Giles Seondonck* Rector of our English Seminarie in Sainct Omers hath gathred together, and that onely of such things, as in this kynd haue happened in these two latter ages: which if the world shal once see him publish in that authentical manner as he intendeth, it wil not be a little astonished to thinck, that euer there should haue rifen amongst men men so brazē faced, or blockish ignorant, that either durst, or could make so shamefull a doubt, much lesse so desperate a denial of this euer flowing current of miracles.

Lowys Richeome au discours des miracles chap 36. num. 2.

But it maybe these good soules are thus scrupulous in acknowledging this current in regard of the word of God: for as they take themselues to be the onely champions and protectors of the word, so haue they solemnly and seriously told vs, that they wil neither teache, or learne, or beleeue any thing, which is not expressly, or by necessarie interpretation in the word. Be it so, let vs enter with them into the word. There we read that the power of working miracles was giuen to the first Pastors of the Church. I confesse it. Now let them shew me

by the

by the word, or any good glosse of the word, that this power was recalled, yea or that ener it was to be recalled. I fynd in the word and book of God, that when our Sauioure gaue power of working miracles vnto his Apostles, he gaue it vnto them together with their power of preaching, which power to preache he also gaue in them vnto al their successors, who neuer were to haue an end vntill the world did end: Euen so when our Sauiour gaue them authoritie to work miracles, vnder the like forme of words, it is not to be doubted but in them he indued their successours with thesame miraculous power, acording to the exigéce of his Church, which power should neuer expire, or els let them try the text shew vs the contrarie. Again I read that our Lord said: *Ecce ego vobiscum sum omnibus diebus vsque ad consummationem saculi.* Behold I am whith you al daies enen vnto the consummation of the world. VVhere our benigne Lord promiseth that his Apostles and disciples should continue to the end of the world &, he with them, not with them in their own persons, for they are dead and departed hence, therfore with them in their successors with whome also his perpetual fauourable assistance was to remain without any diminution or limitation, and that by them he would adorne and fortifie his Church with the self same power of miracles, wherewith at the beginning in his Apostles he established it. By which promise we may conceiue inestimable comfort, in beeng stil assured of his diuine presence amongst vs in al our losses and crosses, and therfore we can not imagin how it is likely that when the pagan persesutors, and Heretikes should oppose, charitie wax cold, faith be scarce found in the world, that then our most louing lord would walk vp & down ca e-

B 3   lesly

Math. 10
Marc. 6.
16.
Luc. 9.
10.

Ephes. 4.

Math. 28
Tvvo things promised by Christ that should perpetually remaine in his Churche

lefly in heauen, and feeme to haue little regard how
his honor fhould be abufed, his Church afflicted, his
louing frendes and children trodden vnder foot, and
the deuil with his followers to feduce the world
at his pleafure.

Yes forfooth fay they : *Antechrift* when he fhal
come he fhall doe ftrange wunders. And I tel them
that the Aegyptian magicians wrought ftrange
wonnders, and *Simon Magus* wrought ftrange
wonnders, did therfore *Moyfes* and *Aaron* work no
miracles? Did fainct *Peter* and the reft of the Apoftles
and Difciples no miracles? fhal *Enoch* and *Elias* haue
no hand in miracles? It is impious to fay or thinck,
that when *Antechrift* the man of finne, the chief of
al Heretikes and falfe prophets fhal feek to outface
the Church of Chrift with his diabolical woûders,
that then the true miracles of God fhal no where
apeare to confront his vngodly mallice. Our lord
hath alredie reuealed the contrarie, to witt, that euen
in the ruffe and pride of *Antechrift* his raigne, two
witneffes fhal be fent, who in miracles fhal fo put
down *Antechrift* and al his, that in their life tyme
they fhal plague the world at their pleafure, and after
their death fhal mount vp to heauen as conquerours
euen in the eyes of their verie enimies.

Yet perhaps our contradictors wil fay, that miracles are not now needful. It is quickly fayd. I
would to God the contrarie could not be fo eafilie &
perfpicuoufely prooued, yea demôftrated. Were miracles neceffarie to conuert Infidels, & to induce thê
to enter into the Church, and are they not neceffarie
to confonnd Heretikes, and to reduce them back
again to the Church which they haue forfaken? Is a
kings power and afsiftance onely to be requited in
conquering his forrein foes, and is it to be neglected in

Exod. 7.
8.
Act 8

Apoc.11

Apoc.11

ted in the repressing of the mutenous rebellion, &
intestin sedition of his own subiectes against him?
See the opinion of the Apostle Sainct *Paul*, who
persuading the Corinthians to giue credit vnto him,
& his doctrin, & to reiect those whome he termeth
false Apostles, craftie workers, transfigured into the
Apostles of Christ ; after he had recounted many
things that touched him self, after he had declared
vnto them his high reuelations, and visions, at last
he saieth. *Signa Apostolatus mei facta sunt super vos
in omni patientia: in signis & prodigiis & virtutibus.*
*The signes of my Apostleship haue ben don vpon you in
al patience, in signes and vvounders and mightie deedes.*
By the memorie of which miracles he endeuoured to
grace his doctrin and to confirm the faithful therein,
and perchaunce to recall those that might haue ben
seduced Did not almightie God shew straunge miracles and dreadful powrable workes against *Core,
Dathan,* and *Abiron,* who preached no new doctrin
but onely endeuoured to raise a schisme and faction
against those heades and rulers of Ecclesiastical causes, whom God had apointed? And to the end the
memorie of those miracles might not dy, he caused
the incensors of the seditious Schismatikes to be
beaten into plates, and so to be fastned to the vety
alter of God, to forewarn thereby their after co-
mers, and to deterre them from committing the like
sinne, least God should work again either corporalie,
or spiritually the like extermination and reuendge.
O Gracious Souueraine, who seeth not the Maho-
metaines in al the Turkes Empire, the Iewes in most
Cities and Cuntries? the infected Grecians in the
east Church? the Pollitick or Parlementarie Prote
stants in our own Cuntrie? diuers sortes of Lutherans in Denmarck, Saxonie, & other Prouinces in

B 3   Germanie

Marginal notes:
Miracles
are stil
necessa-
rie for
the
Church.
2. Cor.
12.

Num. 16

Diuers
cuntries
infected
vvith di-
uers fal-
ce sectes
& here-
sies.

Germanie, the Puritanes or rigid Caluinists in *Ge-neua*, *Scotland* and many partes of *France*, the *Zuinglians* in *Zuitzerland*? the Anabaptists in *Morauia*, *Holland*, and diuers other Prouinces of the low Cuntries? the Suenckfildians in *Suethland*?the Stancarians in the lesser *Poland*? the Osiandrins in *Prusfia* and in both thefe and diuers other Cuntries innumerable other fectes, not onely banded aga nst the Catholicks, but alfo bitterly bickering amongst the felues? Who readeth not their vehement inuectiues and moft feu re enacted lawes? who is he that can diffemble fo many blouddie battailes? fuch open Rebelllons? fuch burnings? fuch quarterings? fuch maffacrings? fuch effufion of Chriftian bloud? Yea of moft Chriftian Princes bloud? as the doleful and tragical endes o fdiuers your Maiefties neereft and deereft in bloud do wittnes & teftifie to al the world. Therfore can any iuftly fay that this world had euer more need that God fhould miraculoufely fhew himfelf where he refideth, and in what Congregation or Church his onely true fauing faith and worfhip is to be found, feing all thefe oppofitions and horrible hurliburlies ftil are, and euer erft were pretended to haue ben raifed for him, and for his onely caufe?

But wil any know why the fox wil eate no grapes? furely becaufe he can not get them; and wil they vnderftand why heretikes think miracles fuperfluous,& why they do not care for the?verelybecaufe they fee that neuer any falce fect or Herefie could euer haue the honor or comfort to haue any one miracle for the. Where as we Catholicks by the goodnes of God fo aboud with the,that except we wil denie our very fences, we can not fo much as doubt of them,& therfore(as it becometh reasonable & mo-

deft

deſt men) wee neceſſarilie acknowledge their beeing
and continuance , acording to that Philoſophical
axiome: *Ea ſunt, quæ negari ſine ſtultitia & pertinacia
non poſſunt. Thoſe things are, vvhich vvithout follie &
frovvard obſtinacie can not be denied to be.* For do not
we ſee the deuotion that Chriſtian people generaly
haue to *Sainct Sebaſtian* and *Sainct Roch* to be preſer-
ued from the plague? the vſual flocking of people to
the bodie of *Sainct Hubert* in the Cuntrie of *Liege* &
eſpecially of thoſe that are bitten with mad dogs? he
perpetual concours made to the ſhrine of *S. Marcou*
in *France*, by thoſe hat are attainted with the kings
euil, ſo comonly called for that the kings of *England*
and *France* your Maieſties moſt renowned & deuout
progenitours haue alwaies miraculouſely cure i that
diſeaſe Do we not alſo behold how men inuocate
Sainct Blaſius for the paine & ſwelling of the throat?
Sainct Eraſmus againſt the griefs of the bowels , and
inttalls? *Sainct Lawrence* againſt the daunger of fier?
Sainct Nicholas in the peril of ſhipwrack and drowning? *Sainct Anthonie* againſt the diſeaſe called the
wyldfier? *Sainct Apollonia* againſt the toothe ache?
Sainct Anthonie of Padua for the recouerie of things
loſt? and finally diuers other particuler Sainctes for
diuers other particuler helps and benefits, as our Engliſh in their battails call vpon *Sainct George* , the
Scotiſh nation and Burgundians vpon *S. Andrevv*,
the French vpon *Sainct Denis*, the Spaniards vpon
Sainct Iames, and I think there is not a kingdome or
Common welth, but they haue one ſainct or other
for their Protectour and defendour with almightie
God. Now who ſo wil ſay that theſe people Kingdoms and Nations haue done this without hauing
had or receiued any benefit by theſe Sainctes, beſides
that moſt immodeſtly they oppoſe them ſelues

Sainctes
called v-
pon for
the cu-
ring of
diuers
diſeaſes.

B 4   againſt

against the common voice & asseueration of al these
people Kingdoms and Nations, so they most ignorantly goe about to controule their long vsual and
assured experience, not aleaging any sollid thing to
the contrarie, but either Atheistical scoffs, or bare
doubtes, or wilful denials, or at the most, friuolous
and blynd coniectures, which wil neuer irooue,
much lesse satisfie any, that hath either witt,learning,
or care of his soule. And to conclude, do not we behold the most frequented pilgrimages from all the
coastes of the world for all kyndes of helps, to our
ladie of *Loretto* in *Italie?* to our ladie of *Mont serrato*,
and to the body of S. *Iames* in *Spaine?* to our ladie of
Mondouie in *Sauoie?* to our ladie of *Liesse* in *France?*

**Our la-
dies
vvorking
miracles
in diuers
cuntries.** and to be brief (for it would be an endles matter to
recount al these fountaines and heades of miracles)
I onely desire them to cast their eies vpon these *Netherlands* and amongst other places therein attentiuely and seriousely behold *Heuer, Halle,*& the place
called *Montague,*where they shal see how Almightie
God at the intercession of his most worthie and glorious Mother doth as it were powre down from
heauen whole showres and streames of heauenly
miracles, & so if they be not altogether starck stone
blynd they shal euidently see that miracles are not
yet ceased.

Yet say what we wil, or can say; I fynd by experience that there is nothing so cleere and manifest,
**Greate
obstina-
cie.** but if men list not to behold it they wil not onely
stil deny it, but wil frame to them selues (a meruelous thing) a quite contrarie conceit, and vnderstād
it in a quite opposit manner to the nature thereof like
to those absurd people vnto whome the Prophet
speaketh in such bitternes saying: *Va qui dicitis ma-*
Esai. 5. *lum bonum,& bonum malum: ponentes tenebras lucem,*
                                                    & lucem

& lucem tenebras: ponentes amarum in dulce, & dulce in amarum. Væ qui sapientes estis in oculis vestris, & coram vobismetipsis prudentes. VVo be to you that say euil is good, and good is euil : setting darcknes to be light , and light to be darcknes : putting that thing vvhich is bitter into that vvhich is svveet, & the svveet into that vvhich is bitter. VVo be to you that are vvise in your ovvn sight, and are prudent in your ovvn conceites. For these conceited wisards wil haue men persuaded that these workes of God are the operations of the deuil , that these miracles are tricks of sorcerie, that these euident demonstrations of our lord his supernatural power are secret collusions of infernal feyndes, that the benefits which haue descended down vpon vs from heauen, are certain pestilent pernicious contagions that are vamped out of the accursed dungeon and pitt of hel; whereby they affirme good to be badde, light to be darcknes , God to be the deuil. And whence cometh all this mistaking but because they account them selues more learned and wise , then all those of the Churche of God: because they preferre their own iudgement before the knowledge of all their learned vertuous & graue auncestours ; because they are of opinion that the wisdome of all ages, of al Pastors and Prelates, of al the vniuersities of the Christian world, of al the Prouincial National and general councelles, must stoop & adore their blynd-ouerweening capritches.

Itts a plagne that God sendeth vnto the prowd, to depriue them of the little light he hath giuen the, thereby to punnish their haughtie animositie, and to expose them to the scorne or rather pitie of al those that behould the, how they goe peaking alone with a self imagination and ad niration of their own subtilitie, or rather stupiditie. For so it fared with our first

A Punnishment that God inflicteth vpō those that are to

Parents,

much
côceiued
of th-ir
own iud-
gement.

Psal. 48.

Próu.18.
Math 9
Marc. 3.
How 'di-
uers mif-
creants
attribu-
ted Gods
mira·les
to the
deuil.
Linda-
nus du-
bit. dia-
log.2.
Acneid.
4.
Aug de
ciuit. l.
21.c.8.
4.Reg.
20.
Iofue 3.

Parents, who caft them felues and all their miferable pofteritie into incredible igno ance and darknes, onely for prefuming or endeuouring to attaine
to greater witt and knowledge, then God had be-
ftowed vpon them or thought fitt for them, in fo
much as the Prophet could fay of man. *Comparatus
eft Iumentis infipientibus & fimilis factus eft illis : He
became to be compaired to the foolifh beaftes and vuas
made like vnto them.* It is an old prouerb that Herefie and Frenzie alwaies goe together. For euery Heretike being naturally proud, will beleeue none but
himfelf, & therfore Antiquitie,Confent,and vniuer-
falitie (things of high regard to the ancient learned
holy Fathe·s)are by him conte nne·d as ftrawes,and
eft eemed as rediculous trifles, wherein they contrarie his phantafie,according to the faying of the wife
man: *Non recipit ftultus verba prudentia,nifi ea dixeris,
qua verfantur in corde eius. A fool receaueth not the
vuordes of vuifdome except you tel him thofe things that
are in his ovun hart.* Yea let God fpeak vnto him
by miracles from heauen, a'l fha'be efteemed witchcraft, and damnable deuilifh practizes. For fo the Ie-
wifh Scribes interpreted the workes of our Sauiour,
fo afterwards *Porphirius, Eunomius, Euftathius, Vigilantius* and other old condemned Apoftataes & Heretikes reported of the miracles of his Sainctes, and
martyrs. So feemed the heathen Poet *Virgil* (as fayeth
Sainct Auguftin) to haue interpreted the miracles
that were wrought amongft the auncient Ifraelites,
and in particuler the ftaying of the flood *Iordã* whyle
Iofue whith his people paffed drietoot through thefame, & the turning back of the Sun in his ordinatie,
courfe at the prayer of *Ifaie* the prophet.As though
thefe two great Sainctes could not but by the help
of forcerie. *Siftere aquã fluuijs, & vertere fydera retro.*

To ftay

To stay the running streames of riuers and to turn barkwardes the very starres of heaue. And now there is no sect, either by vs, or by any our aduersaries esteemed as erroneous, false, and deuilish, but it holdeth and beleeueth that the miracles of the Catholike Churche are superstitious, the works of Satan, and consequently to be abhorred and detested of euery one: Which is an euident proof of their puritie and excellencie. For moste or all of these sectes being of the deuil as both they & we suppose, I cannot imagin howe these people can reasonably thinck that the deuil wil band so earnestly against h m self, & that he wil either prouoke or permit his vassailes, by impugning our miracles to seek the overthrow of so principal a piller and supporte of his kingdom: supposing I say that our miracles are of him as these matters of miracles together whith other sectes would haue the world to beleeue. And that this difficultie may be the better cleered, I beseech them to peruse the huge list of these sayd different and opposit sectes, which they shal finde in *Lindanus*, *Hosius*, *Staphilus*, and *Prateolus*: where they shal fynd whith what swarmes of these Infidellities and Heresies the world is mightely pested at this day. There shal they behold the *Mahometanes*, *Ieuues*, *Lutherans*, *Caluinists*, *Zuinglians*, *Anabaptists*, *Trinitarians*, *Stancarians*, *Manivuiuers*, *Houulers*, *Helmaisters*, *Bysleepers*, *Signifiers*, *Figurers*, *Demoniacals*, to say nothing of the sundrie repugnant professions of faith lately sprung vp in our *Brytanie*, besides innumerable others els where, too too tedious and loathsom here to be recited: all which vndoubtedly proceeding from the deuil, as from the first parent and author of al infidellitie & dissensio: it seemeth a thing most strange, yea altogether vnintelligible, (if the enimie be able

The miracles of the Catholick Church can not be of the deuil.

able to performe such miracles which we affirm to be wrought in the Catholick Church) that either amongst all, or the most, or at least among some of these, he wil not shew what he is able to do in this kynd, for the establishing and gracing of their errors, or els by prophaning the credit and honour of miracles, that he wil not assist euery sect with his secret admirable working, thereby to bring the world in doubt what faith to imbrace, or els therby to dispaire euer to come to the knowledge of the only sauing truthe and religion.

Furthermore yf the deuil be able to work such miracles as these, it is strange that he would not there in haue concurred with *Nero, Simon Magus, Porphirius, Iulian the Apostata, and Mahomet* his most potent instruments, who wanted nether power nor mallice to haue exceedingly aduanced his partie. And surely by nothing more could they haue so born down the Gospel of Christ, then if they had ben able to haue performed those miracles (as vndoubtedly they greatly desired) which our Sauiour, his Apostles, and Martyrs wrought in such aboundance.

But because these wretches saw how no power either of their own or of their feyndish Gods could extend it self to such works, they were forced (thereby to shroud their own nakednes and turpitude) to condemne all these admirable effectes & operatios, saying they proceeded from witchcraft, sorcerie, and the arte Magick. Wherefore I would intreate the impugners of our Miracles to teach vs, by what good reason we or they may defend the puritie of the auncient miracles of Christ, of his Apostles and martyrs against theise their calumniatots; amongst whome some were so farr persuaded that Christ himself was a Magician, that they blushed not to affirme, that he

had

note this vvell.

had compiled a book of that accursed arte, and had dedicated the same to his two chiefe Apostles *Peter* and *Paul*. And this they did to disgrace and deface the miracles that were obiected against them by the Christians, in defence of their faith.

Aug. de consensu Euang. cap. 9. & 16.

But it is much to be feared that we shal haue little help of our aduersaries in this matter, but that they wil rather beare vp those Pagans, Iewes, and mahometanes by answering for them, and shewing that the miracles aleaged by our forefathers were tricks of magick, and sorcerie, for whatsoeuer they can inuent or imagin against these later miracles that are now wrought in the Catholick Churche, vndoubtedly a Pagan Turk or Iewe wil in like manner oppose against those former of the Primitiue Church, so that the argument of the old Doctors, Martyrs, Apostles, and of Christ himself, drawn from the authoritie of miracles shal be quite ouerthrown, and shal serue for no proof of the veritie of our Religion. It may be perhaps they wil confonnd the Turks, Iewes, and Gentiles with scirptures; and out of them they wil conuince that the miracles of the Primitiue Church must be beleeued I know not what these worthie Scripturians may more then miraculously wo ke with these miscreants when they shal once com ouer them with their Scriptures; especially with the Pagans, who hitherto haue made no more esteeme of the Bible, then of Aesops fables, or Ouids Metamorphosis. But this I dare say; if the Iewes and perhaps the Mahometanes once chace to buckle with thē in those parts of the holy Scripture which they admit, these goodly Bible-clarkes shal finde them to haue as hard heades, to be as peeuish stiffnecked, and as wel conceited of their own spirit in interpreting Gods book as the prowdest Gospeller

peller that dare once to coap with them. And therfore the wisdō of God who knew what would best conuince the pertinacitie of the Iewes, although he had aleaged sundrie Scriptures for his mission, yet did he rather cōdemne them as reprobate for not beleuing him in regard of his miracles, then in regard of the manifest places of scripturs so often by him produced for himself, & against them. And althogh he willed them to search the Scriptures, and to examin them about his mission and authoritie; that was because vpon former miracles they were wel persuaded of the veritie of the Scriptures; but when the Gentiles were to be conuerted, miracles were there Scriptures, and onely in them did they read that the Christian doctrin came from God. So that miracles are more euident proofes of a true religion thē are the Scripturs, especially considerng how Scriptures are so subiect to false misconstruing, & deuilish bad interpretation, as experience most manifestly demonstrateth. Whereby al the world may see and laugh at the absurditie of those that say, we know your miracles are not of God, and yf we demand, why so they wil answer because your doctrin which they approoue is not of God; and if we would know of them the reason of so resolute an assertion they wil tel vs because our Religion is not acording to the word of God. A reason forsooth that the Iewes, and Mahometans (as I said) may in like manner frame against our Christian faith, & all the Heretikes that either are, or haue bene, or ever hereafter shalbe may with as good proof aleage against whatsoeuer they shal not pleate to admitt, because it is not according to their glosse and interpretation of holy Scripture.

As the Catholick Church hath certain assured
good

Io. 15.

Io. 5.

meanes to attaine to the true intelligence of holy
Scripture thereby to auoid all danger of error and
Heresie, so hath it most euident notes whereby to
discerne false dealing from true miracles, that thereby
she may not be deceiued with witchcraft and forcerie, so that as vpon those groundes she buildeth her
assurance of her true vnderstanding of the word of
God, so by these marckes she cometh to the assured
knowledge of the powerable workes of God. For our   Hovv to
blessd Sauiour himself hath deliuered vnto her, one   knovve
moste cleere signe hereof, when he was forced to de-   true mi-
fend his miracles from the Iewish calumniation, by   racles
which they were attributed to the deuil. For he sayd   from the
Omne regnum diuisum cōtra se, desolabitur. Euery king-   vvorkes
dom diuided against it self, shalbe desolate. As yf he   of force-
                                                        rie.
sayd, the deuil wil not work any thing against him-   Math. 12
self, that thereby his kingdom may be destroyed. But
when we consider who they are, vpon whome
these miraculous benefits are bestowed, we synd
them to be those, that first prepare their way hereunto by true and zealous repentance of their sinnes, by
labouring to expel out of their soules whatsoeuer
may be displeasing to God, or any way pleasing to the
deuil; who endeuour to raise in them selues true loue
and affection towardes their maker, & perfct resig-
nation with al patience to his holy wil, desiring
nothing more then that the wil of God should be
fulfilled in them, to his greatest honor and glorie: All
which things (with many pointes besides that their
faith and religion teacheth them) beeing most acceptable vnto God and highly making for his honor, &
consequently most contrarie to the deuil, yf he should
second with his workes, and remunerat his enimies
with so singuler fauours as we see these deuo t people dayly blessed withal, what other thing doth he,
                                                        but

but thereby ruyn & subuert his infernal kingdome.
Likewise the Church discerneth true miracles from
witchcraft by an other sentence of our lord in the
same place. For he saith: *Qui non est mecum , contra
me est : & qui non congregat mecum, spargit. He that is
not vvith me,is against me : and he that gathereth not
vvith me,disperseth.* As if he would haue sayd : the
deuil who is mine enimie, and consequently is not
with me doth nothing but that which he knoweth
is most displeasing to me : and al his studie beeing
how he may disunite, whome I haue gathered together in true concord and charitie , the end of his
workes is to seuer soules from God by sinne , and to
break the mutual peace of my flock by sowing his
seed of contention and discord amongst them. For
as the workes of the deuil are to disturb al cocord in
faith and religion , and by leading men in-to sinne
to make them rebells & enimies to God his diuine
maiestie, so the miracles of God are wrought for the
producing and maintenance of vnitie in faith, & perfect vnion with almightie God in vnfained charitie,
which we see performed by these miracles , which
are onely wrought in the Catholick Church , which
Church in matter of beleef is and alwayes hath bens
perfectly vnited in it self,and whose doctrin allowerh
of no vice , but rather teacheth all vertue , and hath
the best yea the onely meanes to aduaunce mennes
soules to their spiritual and cheifest perfectio. Againe
the Church discouereth the coslusion of the deuil
from the working of God , by noting the meanes
that are vsed in the purchasing of these miracles,
which are nothing els , but most serious prayer vnto
almightie God, ioined with fasting,almes deedes,
honoring of God his mother, and his holy saincts
his deerest and most honorable frendes: Which honor

Margin note: The vvor-
kes of
God and
of the
deuil
haue co-
trarie
endes.

nor they doe to them, for the more honor and reuerence they beare to God himself: Which things in
holy scripture are singulerly commended, whereas
the contrarie are the euident workes of the deuil, &
whosoeuer is adicted to them, or impenitently per-
seuereth in them, (be he of what religion soeuer)
can neuer be made pertaker of God his sweetenes in
his necessities by these miracles. Moreouer, the Catholik Church seeth that these miracles are sub-
stancial woorkes, notably and perfectly profiting
the bodies and soules of those vnto whome they
are imparted: Whereas the workes of our hateful
enimie are rather hurteful and domageable to the
creatures of God, then any wayes confortable vnto
them in their miseres and afflictions. We likewise
note that these miracles are in themselues perfect,
and intiere; where as the workes of the deuil are
most commonly defectiue in many things. Also the
workes of the deuil are done for vaine or pernicious
endes, as that the workers (who are alwaies bad vngodly people) may be woundered at, or that they
may thereby obtain some gayne or filthy pleasure,
or wreak their hatred and reuenge against their enimies: they are commonly wrought by certain secret, absurd, ridiculous, superstitious prayers, charmes, signes, or circumstances: Which neuer do
accompaine the Catholik miracles. And finally
(for it is not necessarie to recounr al the differences) if euer God permitt the deuil to work any his
deceitful wounders in the behalf of any sect or heresie, they are soon bewraied, if they be duely examined, they vanish away at the presence either of faithful people, or of other true miracles, and they are
fully discried in that they oppugn the Religió that
hath bene alredy establhshed, and confirmed by infi-

nit most

hit most euident and assured miracles, by the confession of al antiquitie, by the consent of al nations, by
the censure of al General Councels, by the assertions
of al holy Fathers, of all Histories, of al Schooles, of
al vniuersities, by the triumphant deathes of innumerable Martyrs, by the profession of infinit Confessors, Virgins, Lay & Religious people, of al estates,
degrees, and ages.

As the old saying is true, that cunning hath no
enimie but the ignorant: so we daily euidently experience that the Catholik Church is by none more
oppugned then by those that are most ignorant of
her wayes and doctrin. Which thing the Apostle
S. Peter did foretel of the heretikes which were to
bad against the Church, whome he termeth *Irratio-*
nabilia pecora, naturaliter in captionem & in perniciem,
in his quæ ignorant blasphemantes. Vnreasonable beastes,
naturally tending to the snare, and into destruction, blas-
pheming in those things vvhich they knovve not. For
wee see none more forward to condemn the Catholik Religion then they, that onely vpon their own
conceited surmises, or vpon fraudulent falce reportes
of their own doctors & teachers impugne it. Which
their blynd furie as they exercise against euery point
of our faith, so perticulerly in this, that they are not
ashamed to assigne our miracles to superstition and
forcerie. Whetfore I pray them to tel me, who is he
that hath but onely read or hard the forme to make
his Sacramécal Cófession (a thing dayly yea allmost
howrely practized amongst Catholiks) but he hath
also learned amongst other things, that witchcraft,
forcerie, & all kyndes of superstition are accompted
for grieuous sinnes, as being directly against the
commaundement of almightie God? And those that
haue made more progresse in learning, if they haue
bene

Marginal notes:

VVho they are that most condemn the Catholik faith.

2.pet. 2.

Hovv hateful al-
so forcerie
and su-
perstitiō
is to ca-
tholiks.

bene but slenderly acquainted with Catholik writers, can not be ignorant what volumes haue bene
writte and diuulged in particuler against these vices,
as also to discouer their fraud mallice and impietie.
And as for the Canon, Imperial, & Ciuil lawes, how Ioan-
seuerely they haue bene and are enacted against these nés Azor
enormities, and how rigourousely executed in euery instit.
Catholik Cuntrie against the offendors, I am sure moral.
none but the deafe and blynd can be vnwitting lib. y.
thereof. Yea, what a particuler and zealous hatred cap.26.
Catholiks beare against al superstition, is manifest q.z.& z.
in that the children of the Catholik Church are by
their Pastors and Prelats strictly forbidden, somuch Regulæ
as to read, set, or retaine any books or treateses indicis
(though they do not beleeue them) of magick, sor- librorū
cerie, chyromancie, iudiciarie astrologie, or of any prohibi-
art what soeuer which includeth any expresse or torum
secret pact, couenant, interuention, or familiaritie Trid.
with the deuil. Moreouer, the bookes whose argu- Reg.8.
ments are otherwise good and lawful, yet if they & 9.
containe any thing that tendeth to superstition and
vaine obseruation are in like manner forbidden vnder Bulla Pij
paine of mortal sinne, and the persons culpable are to 4. ibidē,
be otherwise punished, as their Bishops shal thinck
expedient. Yet because there are many straunge and Thepru-
secret things that may be effectuated & wrought by dent dis-
natural power, without any concourse of the deuil, cretion
which to the expert in Physick & natural Phylo- of Ca-
phie are not vnknown: many things also that are tholiks
meere superstitious and diabolical, and many things
again that are diuine and supernatural: sundrie of our
Catholik writers haue worthely trauailed to discouer and cleere ech part, for the better direction
both of the spiritual and temporal magistrate herein: that these things might not ly so huddled vp in
confusion

confusion, that by their ignorance any inconueniéce or indignitie might happen: Where in amongst others the learned *Martin Delrius* hath in three cō- petent tomes or volumes shewed his exquisit dili- gence & skill. So that hereby all men may see how litle daunger there is to be feared that Catholik mi- racles haue any affinitie with superstition and sorce- rie, both through the vigilant diligence that Ca- tholiks haue to sift euery point and particuler cir- cumstance in them, as also in regard of the ingrafted hatred and disdaine that the Catholik Church bea- reth against the deuil, and al his execrable workes, as being contrarie to God, and all goodnes.

If these your pretended miracles (say our aduersaires) be not workes of sorcerie, then are they coosening tricks of your priestes & clergie men, who cunning- ly deceiue the world, for their own lucre and gayne. But this calumniation is soon wiped away, if they would consider, that many of these miracles are wrought vpon people that neuer were at the miracu- lous place: diuers vpon strangers who onely vowed or intended to goe thither, many vpō the poor who were not able to giue contentment to such inordi- nate auarice: many were donne in the veiw of hun- drethes that were present: they haue bene all most diligently and curiously examined by the Princes au- thoritie, and Ciuil Magistrates in many Cities, townes, and other places, who neuer hetherto could fynd the least suspicion in these matters of any such abhominable euil dealing. And the like may be answered to those, who so confidently aleadge, that these things were performed by way of Physick, & in particuler by the help of the Fhylosophers stone, (good lord what doe not men inuent when they would blynd themselues that they might not see the truthe)

Marginal notes:

Disqui- sitionū Magica- rum. Tomi tres Mar tini Del- si.

A calū- niation vvith the an svves.

Follie in incre- dulitie.

truthe) whereby they shew their stonie harts and heades.

Vpon these men I feare that Apostolical sentence wilbe verified if they do not repent them, *Reuelatur ira Dei de cælo, super omnem impietatem & iniustitiam hominum eorum qui veritatē Dei in iniustitia detinent.* The wrathe of God from heauen is reuealed vpon al impietie & iniustice of those men that deteine the veritie of God in iniustice. For how vniustly they haue sought to keep both from their owne and other mennes knowledge the truthe of God, your Royal wisdome may sufficiently perceiue, first in not crediting God his miracles, nor God, by his miracles, again, by wholy denying his miracles, afterward, Iudaically that is impiousely attributing them to the damned deuils of hel, and finally vncharitably and iniuriousely condemning those whose innocencie & sinceritie neither the dilligent and warie Catholik, nor the curious prying mallicious Heretike could euer yet iustly touche. Therfore I say vnto the with the Prophet *Hodie si vocem Domini audieritis, nolite obdurare corda vestra.* If you wil heare the voice of our Lord by miracles speaking & preaching vnto you, euē in our dayes, & proclaming where he doth reside, denouncing vnto you where you shal fynd him beware that you harden not your hartes, as those old exasperating people did, vnto whome our lord did sweare being moued with his iust anger and disdaine against their stubbernes and incredulitie, that they should neuer enter into his rest, that they should neuer haue parte of his eternal felicitie.

Which heauy and dreadful doome they may auoyd if laying asyde all animositie and priuate affection, they would meekely, that is, with Christian modestie, patience, and humilitie for Christ

C 3   his

his sake, and for their own soules saluation take the paines to vewe either with their corporal eies, or with the attentiue eies of their mynde what is donne in the mountaine of *Montaigue*. Where they may see a most famous and frequent Pilgrimage to a picture of the Mother of God, or to a place chosen out by her, wherein shee sheweth her gracious fauours to humble and distressed supplianis: where they shal behould troupes of penitent sinners prostrate before the feet of their confessors; and declaring vnto them their trespasses: where they eftsoones deuoutly adore and receiue the bodie of God in the forme of bread: where they are present at the continual celebration of Masses: where they hear perpetual and reuerent inuocation of our Ladie, & of other Sainctes: where they attentiuely harken to innumerable sermons and exhortations, persuading those things which either the Catholik Church commaundeth, or counseleth to be beleeued and imbraced, or inciting them to auoyd those things which thesaid Church either in faith or manners misliketh or condemneth. And while these things and many other such like, are in doing, they shal often tymes espie the power and sweet goodnes of God to discend vpon the holy assembly, whereby some that are blynd receiue their sight, some that are deaf recouer their hearing, some that are leaperous are clesed, some that are possessed with vncleane spirits are freed from their tyranie, others that are lame walk strong homeward, leauing their crutches and stiltes at the place for a memorie, and many other such supernatural miraculous operations to be their atchieued: where-by they may with vs iustly and with verie good consequence inferr, that holy Pilgrimages, honoring of holy Images, confession of our sinnes to the priest, acknowledging of

the

The assuredned of the Catholik doctrine.

the real presence of Christ his bodie in the blessed
Sacramēt, celebration of Masses, praying to sainctes,
yea (in brief) they may inferr the whole doctrin and
practis of the Catholik Apostolik and Romaine
Church to be grateful and highely pleasing vnto the
Maiestie of God: for otherwise if these things were
so wicked, blasphemous iniurious abhominable, an d
execrable vnto him, (as our aduersaries would persuade men) it is to be thought, that in his iust and
zealous indignation he would rather cause the earth
to swallow down euen into hel both the place and
people, then to permitt them to departe thence
fraught with such vnspeakable comforts and solaces
both of their bodies and soules, as we dayly perceaue
they doe.

So that hereby euery one may see, in what price
and esteeme the Catholik Church is to our Lord,
whose children he thus particulerly & onely blesseth,
and as it were vphouldeth in their faith with the hād
of his powrable celestial operatiōs, which he vouchsafeth to impart vnto them euē by the meanes of no
lesse then of his most louing and glorious Mother,
and for her glorie; a circumstance e xcludīng al cause
of doubt that the deuil should haue any claw in this
matter. For our lord hath said: *Inimicitias ponam inter
te & mulierem. I vvil put enmitie betvvixt thee and
the vvoman.* Whereby we may vnderstānd that as
the deuil wil neuer to his power permit her to be
honored, much lesse wil he worke wounders to procure or increase her honor. Neither wil this blessed
woman permitt her enimie euer to abuse her due
honor, or to circumuēt those that desire for her sun-
nes sake, and for her own sake, to serue & honour
her; but let him vse al the craft he can inuent, and al
the force he hath, yet shal our triumphant *Iudith* haue

Gen. 3

C 4   the

the perfect victorie ouer him. For, *Ipsa conteret caput tuum* She shal crush thy head vvicked and feendish serpent, saith our God. Great is the force vndoubtedly of the mother of God; who not onely was, and is able to combate with the deuil, but to crush him, & domineere ouer him, as oper a poor worme whose head is brused and squised to durt. Therfore it is no meruail if miracles are atchiued by her meanes, who was able to bring vnder her foot that feendish Leuia-

Iob 41. than, of whom our Lord saith: *Non est super terram potestas quæ comparetur ei, qui factus est vt nullum time-ret; There is no povver vpon earth that may be compared to him, vvho is so made that he might feare none*

Come, come and see how this miraculous mother of

The po-
vver of
our bles-
sed La-
dievvith
almigh-
tie God.
Ger. 1.

our God hath power to procure miracles to proceed from God at her word, as beeing the mother of the eternal word and therfore was she onely preuiledged to vse the most forceble word, that euer God vied towardes his creatures. For our lord said *Fiat*: & this his mother repeated thesaid *Fiat*. Fiat lux, said he, *Fiat firmamentum, Fiant luminaria, &c. Let the light be made, let the firmament be made, let the starres of*

Psal. 32. *heauen be made. Ipse dixit & facta sunt He said the vvord and they vvere made.* This holy virgin said to the Angel: *Fiat mihi secundum verbum tuum. Be it*

Lut. 1.
Io. 1.

donne to me acording to thy vvord. Et verbum caro fa-ctum est, & habitauit in nobis. And the vvord vvas made flesh, and dvvelt in vs. The word *Fiat* procee-ding out of the mouth of God, was the cause that the world was created: the word *Fiat* out of the mouth of this blessed virgin, was the cause that God himself was incarnate: By his *Fiat*, he made the world and man, by her Fiat, God entred into the world, and became man. Which being so great a miracle, the fruites whereof the faithful still reap

vpon

vpō earth, & the continuance whereof the Angels &
sainctes perpetually enioy in heauen, no marueil if
these miracles (which in this book are related) be
wrought in her faueur, & at her word, seing that in
dignitie & perfection they are infinitly inferiour to
those, which by her and for her, haue alredie bene
performed. And verily if we consider who this Virgin is, what is her degree and dignitie, we can not
much wounder at this her prerogatiue. For in one
word she is the mother of God, who did beare in her
sacred wombe the second person in Trinitie our lord
and Sauiour Iesus Christ the Souueraine King and
Iudge of Men & Angels. With whom this blessed
Virgin had not onely domestical familiaritie for
many yeares, but had motherly authoritie ouer him,   Luc. 2.
for he was obedient vnto her, yea subiect vnto her,   The
yea subiect to Ioseph for her sake, which truly was a   most mi-
power aboue all power, a miracle aboue all miracles,   raculou-
to haue in pious and reuerend subiection the high   se preui-
Maiestie of heauen, the author and supreme worker   lege of
of all miracles. Who had such admirable respect to   our B.
this his most honorable mother, that as in his life   Ladie.
tyme he alwaies yelded vnto her authoritie, so euen
at the instant of his death, while he was performing
that great and dreadful bloodie sacrifise on the altar
of the Crosse, euen in the very act of the reconciliation of mankynd to his heauenly Father, he could
not then neglect or be vnmyndeful of his most worthie mother, but must needes of his sonnely pietie
apoint his best beloued Apostle to be her carefull
sonne in his steed: wherfore now that this our Lord
is settled in his throne of maiestie, now that he rai-
gneth in his kingdom of glorie, where, (as he promised) he ministreth to his seruants, with what respect doth he behaue himself to his glorious best beloued

loued and best deseruing mother? let vs behold king *Salomon* in this point, who so honored his mother *Bersabee*, that he adored her, that on his right hand he placed a throne for her & spake these dutiful wordes vnto her. *Pete mater mea : neque enim fas est vt auer-*

3.Reg.2.

tam faciem tuam. Mother shevv your request : for it, is not lawful that I should turne your face from me. That is: that I should suffer you to depart discontented from me. Which *Salomō* did & said vndoubtedly in regard of the natural duty which he knew he did owe to his mother. For he had before his eies that commaundement of God. *Honora Patrem tuum, &*

Exod. 20

matrem tuam. Honor thy Father, and thy mother. This precept our Sauiour Iesus doth incomparably more respect and obserue, then *Salomon* either did or could:for that it was his own law, as also for that it is a law meerely natural, & consequently indispensable, the which God himself the Author of nature can no more violate, thē he can denie or hate himself, or be subiect to the deuil.

Let therfore no mā wunder (Gracious soueraine) that both your subiects at home, and all Catholik Princes, People, & common welthes abroad persuaded themselues, that the sayd Cathol·ks in our cuntrie should cease to be tossed with the furious waues of persecution, so soon as they saw your Maiestie to be settled at our sterne. For this their persuasiō grew not onely of that they had seen your Graces cariage alwaies to haue bene free from all rigor & seuerit·e; nor for that your royal clemencie alwayes hated the odious & infamous name of a persecutor, nor for that they knew you needed not to maintaine your iust and vndoubted rule by those meanes, which to your Predecessor seemed necessarie for hers, nor for that they thought your Princely wisdom would not

exasperate

exasperate and dishonor other Christian Princes and
People, by persecuting your subiectes, for being of
thesame faith and religion with them: nor for that
diuers your subiectes had reported this your myld
disposition and intention in euery forreine Princes
Court and Cuntrie, and which very many of them
affirmed to haue had it from your Graces self, nor for
that they held your Maiestie for wise and learned,
and that therfore the right of the Catholik cause
should be seriously and maturely examined, before it
should be condemned: nor for that they did thinck,
that your Royal wisdome would easilie see that by
persecution our faith hath been no whit diminished,
but rather admirably increaced: nor for many other
reasons which they deemed would withhould your
Grace from so disgracious, daungerous, hateful, and
vngodly a course: but they were especially moued
vnto this honorable and pious conceite of your Maiestie, for that they thought it would neuer enter into
your Princely breast, to arme your royal hand against
the professors of that faith, which all your Maiesties
most honorable Progenitors in England, France, and
Scotland euer most zelously and religiously imbraced, since fiist those Cuntries receiued their Christianitie: but especially in regard of your Graces most
famous & renoumed Mother, who (as all the world
knoweh, and to her honour protesteth) most zelou-
sely professed the same in her life, and heroically sealed this her profession with the effusion of her royal
blood at her sacred death. And their godly persuasion
was founded vpon this, that they held this pious precept to be deeply grauen in your royal hart: *Honora*   Eccl. 7.
patrē tuū, & gemitus matris tuæ ne obliuiscaris. Honour
your Father and forget not the sobs of your Mother. They
thought your Graces deerest mothers manifold sobs

                                                        teares,

teares, and direful groanes in bringing you foorth
into this world in her reſtles cares, cogitations, and
prayers to God for your preſeruation, in the ſundrie
vndutiful perilous inſurrections of her own ſub-
iectes againſt her, in her moſt coacted exile & expul-
ſion out of her owne kingdom, in her long reſtraint
and vniuſt captiuitie, and finally on the tragical ſcaf-
fo'd where the innocent Queene your graces kyn-
deſt Parent was bloudely depriued of her life : they
thought (I ſay) theſe forcible groanes and ſhowres
of teares of ſo deere a Mother would not onely haue
inclined her moſt beloued Chyld with all dutiful reuerence, but would euen naturally that is, moſt for-
cibly haue compelled him to reſpect her, and her
cauſe, that is, the Catholik cauſe, for which ſhe ſuſtained theſe calamities and indignities. And vndoubtedly all the world could not but haue iuſtly condemned that perſon as very iniurious to your
Maieſtie, who euer ſhould haue dared to haue had
as much as a thought that your Highnes would euer
(I do not ſay)commaund, but ſo much as permitt
that the Catholiks, your mothers chiefeſt if not her
onely frendes ſhould be any wayes moleſted, and
much leſſe indamaged, impoueriſhed, impriſoned,
condemned and put to death for the profeſſion of her
faith. For the world hath not yet forgotten, neither
can the memorie thereof euer decay, how that Catholiks haue bene hampered, tortured, ſpoiled of
their goodes, hanged, boweled and mangled, yea, forreine nations do ſtil behould the exile and pouertie
of diuers, who at this preſent remaine depriued of
their lands and liuelihoods, for hauing loued, honored, pitied, or affectionated the afflicted innocent
mother of King Iames our redoubted lord Whereby
the dutiful behauiour of that heathen Roman *Corio-*
lanus

Plutar-
chus.

Ianus cometh into mennes myndes, who was so natural as for his mothers sake to depose the seuere chastisment and reuenge which he had prepared against those that were so vnkynd and vngrateful towardes him : by which example they conclude, that your Maiestie being a Christian and the sonne of a most glorious Christian martyr can not but graunt vnto your Catholik subiects, the most zelous & sincere frends of you both, their long desired comfort , and the iust freedome from their vniust distresses and oppressions. But let others conceiue what they list of this old Pagan example : we rather think this Philosophical sentence shal haue more force in your graces hart: *Sequere Deum.Follow your God* sayd the wise man. Which that your maiestie may the better be animated vnto, here in this insuing relation is displaid the admirable honour which our God himself doth to his Mother, & to mortal people for her sake. Vnto whome he beareth so great reuerence, that not onely he heareth her for her frendes, but of his inestimable pietie is most gracious vnto her for his own verye enimies: as our famous learned and deuout Archbishop of Canturburie *Sainct Anselm* hath noted sayng: *O fœlix Maria sicut omnis peccator a te auersus & a te despectus necesse est vt intereat, ita omnis peccator ad te conuersus & a te respectus impossibile est vt pereat. O Happie Marie as euery sinner auerted from thee and dispised by thee must necessarilie dy: so euery sinner conuerted to thee and regarded by thee can not perish possibly.* O the rare preuilege wherewith by her Sone this Mother is thus honoured, wherein, if Christian people abroad may once chance to see your Maiestie to imitate the souueraigne King of æternal glorie to your Catholik subiectes at home, who (as all the world knoweth) were neuer enimies but most affe-

Ansel.i̅
Medit.

ctionat

tionate and loyal vnto your Royal Maiestie, as this
your Godly imitation wil be great solace vnto vs, so
wil it yeeld an vnspeakable contentment vnto thē,
and withal be most honorable to your Highnes, &
vnto Gods diuine Maiestie exceedingly gratefull.
And to the end in honoring your natural Mother,
your Grace may not feare to dishonour and displease
your æternal Father, behold his supernatural powrable workes in approbation of that faith in which
shē liued, and for which she dyed. For not beleeuing
the like workes our God held the Iewes inexcusable,
so in crediting these your Maiestie shal not need to
feare to displease, but rather to please him highly.
Who onely for the temporal and euerlasting benefit
of his creatures, and for the amplification of his own
Souerainne honour & glorie vouchsafed thē. I know
that they wil be vehemently cōtradicted & impugned, before they shal obtaine their due esteeme &
credit, and therfore I haue endeuoured to cleere the
chiefest difficulties which I perceiue to be ordinarilie
obiected against them. I graunt my discours hath
bene very prolix, your Maiestie seeth the matter is
important, & I was very desirous your Royal wisdom
might be exactly informed hereof. God graunt that
what I haue done may be iudged sufficient. Yf I shal
hereafter vnderstand that ought is wanting or omitted herein, it shal by the help of God be added & sup-
plied. Meane while cōmiting the whole to the sweet
disposition of Almightie God I do withal commēd
your Maiestie to his best guidance and protection.

Io. 15.

Io. 5.

Your Maiesties most humble Beades-man
Robert Chambers.

THE
TRANSLATOR TO
THE CHRISTIAN
Reader.

HERE is a certain foul fault (gentle Reader) for which we Catholikes are very ordinarilie and odiously reproched, which is, that we are passing light and exceedingly prone to beleeue euery fable: and vpon this blynd simplicitie easilie drawne into any superstition and error touching the worship of God. The reason whereof is held to be our ignorance in the word of God, and the litle sight we haue in the holy Bible: rather harkening to the traditions of men (as is the phrase) and to the voice of the Church, then in marcking what the writé woord teacheth vs. It is very certaine that Catholikes say with the Royal Prophet: *Quanta mandauit patribus nostris nota facere ea filijs suis? vt cognoscat generatio altera. Filij qui nascentur & exurgent & narrabunt filijs suis.* Hovv great

Psal. 77. vvhy traditions are hi-

ghly re-
garded
by Ca-
tholiks.

Mar. 16.

Deut. 3.

Math. 12

Aug. cō-
tra Epiſt.
funda-
menti.

great things did God commaūd our Forefathers to make them knowwn to their children, that an other generatiō may knowv them? The ſonnes that vvere to be borne & to riſe vp after them, they ſhal tel them againe to their children. As our bleſſed Sauiour did, when sending his Apoſtles to inſtruct the world, he bad them preache, that is, deliuer by word of mouth, or tradition his word, but he commaunded them not to write his word. And ſo from them (vpon the tradition of our Elders) we receiue what the Apoſtles haue ſayd or written to be Gods woord, although we fynd no ſuch declaratiō for neither their Epiſtles or Goſpels, in the book of his woord. Which thing we accompliſh according to the commaundement of Moyſes ſaying, *Interroga Patrem tuum, & annunciabit tibi: maiores tuos, & dicent tibi.* Aſk thy faꝛher and he vvil declare vnto thee: demaund of thyne aunceters and they vvil tel thee: which thing our Aduerſairies themſelues obſerue, in admitting vpon the credit of the Catholik church the bookes of holy Scripture: vpon which ground followeth how wee ought to ſubmit our ſences and iudgements to whatſoeuer the ſayd Catholik church ſhal teach vs: els blott that article out of the creed: *Credo Eccleſiam Catholicam* I beleeue the Catholik Churche: els let thoſe wordes of our bleſſed Sauiour be ſcraped out of the Goſpel, *Si Eccleſiam non audierit ſit tibi ſicut Ethnicus & Publicanus* yf he vvil not heare the Churche, let him be to thee as an Heathen and Publicane. and cōſequently let Sainct *Auguſtin* be hiſſed out

of

of his pulpit for saying: *Euangelio non crederem*
nisi me Ecclesiæ commoueret auctoritas. I vvould not
beleeue the Gospel, except the authoritie of the Church
moeued me therevnto. Yet for all this: I beseech
our Aduersaries, not to be so hastie in spen-
ding their sentences vpon vs, as if for these
causes we read not, we studie not, we searche
not the holy Scriptures. As if we haue not
millions of Sermons, treateses, and commentaries sounding the depth of holy Scriptures.
As if we haue not had hundrethes of Prouincial, National, & General Coūcells, wherin haue bene the learned Prelates of sundrie nations, sometimes to the number of
two hundreth seuentiefiue, sometimes of
two hundreth nyntiefiue, sometimes sf three
hundreth and eighteene sometimes of three
hundreth seuentiefix, sometimes of fix hundreth and thirtie, and sometimes of a thousand who by feruēt paryer, continual fasting,
eaget disputing and other learned conferences haue searched out the true sence
& meaning of holy Scripture, which if they
would wel marke, they should also wel perceiue, how without all iudgement they iudge
vs, & without vnderstanding our case they
blyndely condemne vs, and so they would
conclude: that if any point of the Catholik
doctrine seeme vnto them difficil & strauge:
it is for that they estraunge them-selues
from vs, and are altogether vnacquainted
with our groundes and reasons, and not that

we

(marginal notes:)
Hovv diligētly Catho-likes studie the holy scriptu-res.

Cōciliū Roma-num 2. Triden-tinum Nicenā 1. sardicēse

Calce-donēse.

Latera-nēnse. 2. id.

VVy the Catho-lick do-ctrein seemeth strange to Here-tickes.

D

we are so vngrounded and vnreasonable, as
they imagyn. I could exemplify this in all
the points of our faith, that are in cōtrouer-
sie betwixt vs and them, if this present treates
and discours would admitt so large a discours.
But because I know that kynd of proceeding wil here be thought altogether super-
fluous: therfore in briefe manner and for a
taste I wil explicate the state of the Catholik
doctrine touching onely such perticulers as
concerne the matter & subiect of this insuing
relation, which I wil shew how they stand
with the verdict of God his holy woord, &
first I wil begin with Pilgrimages.

It is a sure and certaine veritie which the
Catholik churche alwayes confesseth, that
God is in euery place: for so he himself hath
avouched, that he filleth both heauen and
earth, and therefore there is no place where
in he may not be honoured and called vpon.
Yet, as our lord hath sanctified some particuler
dayes for his seruice, so hath he made choice
of some perticuler places where in he would
be particulerly honoured For he cōmaunded
Abraham to offer his sonne *Isaac* vpon one
certaine determinate hil. *Iacob* had by vision
that the mount *Bethel* was a place of extraordinarie sanctitie, and for that cause he sayd,
*Quam terribilis est locus iste? non est hic aliud nisi do-
mus dei, & porta cæli*. How dread-ful is this
place? this place is nothing els but the hows
of God, and the gate of heauen. Which
assecueration

Hierem. 21.

Exod. 20

The vse of Pil-
grima-
ges proo
ued by
holy
scriptu-
re.

Gen. 22.

asseueration of the Patriarch, our Lord did so
much approoue, that he took to himself the
title of that place saying to the sayd, *Iacob* Gen. 31
Ego sum Deus Bethel, I am the God of Bethel. So Horeb
was called the mountaine of God, which our
Lord esteemed so holy, that he caused *Moyses* Exod. 3.
his especial seruant to put of his shooes in
honour and reuerence thereof. Finally our Det. 12.
Lord made choice of one particuler place, in
which only, he would haue his people to offer
sacrifise vnto him : where when *Salomon* had 3. Reg. 8
erected his Téple he beseeched God not onely
to bestow certaine perticuler preuileges and
miraculous fauours vpon such as prayed there
in, and vpon such straungers as came from
farr Cuntries in pilgrimage thither, but vpon
all such as should in their prayers turn their
faces towards the holy place, when vpő other
iust impediments they could not performe
their deuotions in the holy Temple it self.
Which măner of worshipping God (by pilgrimages) ended not after-wards, for that
our Sauiour fore-told the Samaritane that :
Veniet hora quando neqʒ in monte hoc, neqʒ in Hiero-
solymis adorabitis Patrem. The houver shal come vvhē
neither in this hyl, nor in Ierusalem You shal adore the Io. 4.
Father. Which was sayd because the Hebrues
were to be expelled out of these places, where
by their sacrifices (meant by the word adoration) should cease, and should not be tyed any
longer to one place as they were before, but
that his sōueraine worship and adoration

should

should be more frequent, so that no place should be depriued of the same.

True, Yea most true was that prediction, that the Father of heauen should neither be in the former sort adored either in *Garizim* or in *Hierusalem*, yet were it very fond to inferre thervpon: that he should haue no external worship, or churches, or places for the administratio of his diuine Sacramentes in all the world besydes: or that the auncient laudable vse of Pilgrimages should be abrogated for the tyme to come. For we read the cotrarie: how our Lord would haue his Apostles goe from *Hierusalem* in Pilgrimage into *Galile*, there to see him after his Resurrection. We read that he led them out of *Hierusalem* into *Bethania* to the mount *Oliuet* there to be present at his glorious Ascension. We read that he commauded them to *Hierusale*, there to receaue the holy Ghoste. Moreouer we read that *Sainct Paul* made a log Pilgrimage vnto *Hierusalem* to keep there his *Pentecost* or whitsontyd. And I dare say that no Scripturist can shew me by any plaine Scripture either of Christ or of his Apostles, that the vse of deuout Pilgrimages were or euer should be prohibited to Christians.

Neither doth it any whit alter the case in that these Pilgrimages or iourneys & walkes of deuotio are made to certaine places, where the Saincts of God are honoured. For as they are not Saincts but principally by the mercie and grace of God; so what honour is exibited vnto them, is in regard that they are the honorable

M.4.28.

Luc. 24.
Act.21.

Act. 20.

Sainctes are to be honoured.

nerable frendes of God, and consequently it
hath his principal reference to God. Who although he say that he wil not giue his honour
to any other, yet hath he promised to honour
his Saincts & true seruants. Therfore there
is no reason that any man should be scrupulous to say & auouche with the Prophet *Dauid*,
Mihi autem nimis honorati sunt am ici tui Deus, Thy
frendes o God are exceedingly honoured of me. Neither
need any feare to adore and worship them, as
Abraham and diuers other diuine illuminated
Saincts did his holy Angels and frendes. For
although *Sainct Peter* would not permitt *Corne-*
lius the Centutio to adore him, and although
the Angel refused the adoration of *Sainct Iohn*
Yet may we not argue that therfore the foresayd Saincts or Angels, or holy deuout people
did err, sinne and offend, either in admitting,
or yeelding the foresayd honors and adora-
tions: nor that they consequently (who shal
follow their deuotions to-wards God his
Sainctes) are in any sorte to be reprehended
for the same.

Isa. 48.
Ioh. 12.
Psal. 138.
Gen. 18.
Iosue 5,
4 Reg. 1.
4. Reg. 2.
Iudi. 13.
Act. 10.
Apoc. 19
& 22.

As for the refusal of *S. Peter*, it is euident,
that he would not be adored as a God, and
therfore he told his *Catechumenus*, that he was
a man. And as for *Sainct Iohn* I dare be so bold
as to thinck, that he was not so grosse, as to
offer twice to comit Idolatrie, or to offer that
reuerence which was vnfitting for the Angel,
or displeasing to Almightie God: for to impute
so heynous an offence vnto him, proceedeth

D 3 of

Aec 8.
Aug. q.
6. in Ge.
5. Greg.
Lib 27.
Moral.
Cap. 11.
& hom.
8. in E-
uāg Bed
An et
Rupert.
in 19. A-
poc.

Math. 22

of too too muddie a conceit, of so high, so wise, so illuminated a Prophet, Apostle, & the eagle of all the Euangelists. Vnderstand therfore that in that contention in humilitie betwixt those two holy frendes, is shrined vp a further mysterie : and by the double deuotion of this belooued of our Lord, cōclude that Angels and Sainets (who as our Sauiour sayeth shal be in heauen like to Angels) may be worthely honoured, worshiped, and adored. Honoured, worshiped and adored I say, not with that soueraine honour, worship, and adoration, which is onely due to the supreme Maiestie of God : but in a farre inferior manner, according to their excellencie and dignitie wherewith God hath indued them. For the giftes of God as beeing of God, are worthie to be honoured & regarded & the persons also vnto whome he cōferreth them.

VVat
honour
is due to
Sainctes
Exod. 20
pron. 23.
1. Pet. 2.
Leui. 32.

vvhe-
ther vve
may
prayto
sainets

I know the modester sorte of our contradictors (seeing that we are commaunded to honour our Parents, our Princes, onr Elders and betters) wil easily graunt that the Sainets of God should haue their place of honour, as beeing in greater heigth, glorie, and dignitie aboue the rest: but to pray vnto them, that they thinck very vnmeet and inconuenient. Which inconuenience I could neuer hetherto see, although I haue read diuers things obiected against suche prayers. What? do they thinck that the Sainets beeing now ioyned with God, wil not pray for vs, who so charitably
tably

tably prayed for their frendes, and enimies
whyle they liued in this worldly banishement
See the contrarie practised by *Onias* & *Hieremie* 2. Mach. 15.
after their deathes: consider, what the Se-
niors and the Angel did in the the Apocalips? Apoc. 5.
and note how *Sainct Peter* promised thesame, & 8.
after his departure out of this lyfe. Is it that 2. P. 8.
the prayers of Sainctes are of no valew in heauen, which were of that miraculous efficacie
whyle they liued here on earth? Is it for that
God regardeth not his Sainctes when they are
once dead? Who told *Isaac* after his blessed Gen. 26.
Fathers deceasse that. *Benedicentur in semine tuo
omnes Gentes terra, eo quod obedierit Abraham voci
mea, & custodierit precepta & mandata mea, & cere-
monias legesq́ seruauerit.* All the nations of the earth
shal be blessed in thy seed, for so much as Abrahā obeyed
my voice and kept my preceptes and comaundementes, &
obserued my ceremonies and lavves. Is it for that God
can not, wil not, or doth not let them vnderstand our prayers and necessities? O then the
ignorance of *Iacob*, who blessing the sonues of
Ioseph prayed vnto his good Angel, who hard Gen. 48.
him not, saying, *Angelus qui eruit me de cunctis
malis benedicat pueris istis.* The Angel that hath deliuered me from all my daungers blesse these boyes. Ah what
ment the Angel *Raphael* to tel old *Tobie* that Tob. 12.
though he stood before the throne of God,
yet did he offer the holy mannes prayers tea-
tes and good workes to his diuinie Miaestie?
Is it for that their prayers should derogate
from Christs mediatio? And why should that
happen vnto them more now that they are
                                                with

with God, then when they liued here amongst mortal men? Yea, I say whosoeuer thincketh that the mediation of Christ and of his Saintes for vs are of one natute, and condition, is exttemely ignorant of the Catholik doctrine, & of the meaning of holy Scripture touching this point, and consequently very Iniurious to the honour and dignitie of our blessed Redeemer: Who is not our mediator by praying for vs, as his Saincts do, but by his ful satissaction for our sinne, to his fathers Iustice, and by the meanes of his most sacred death & passion. Is it finally for that God louerh vs more then his Saincts, knoweth better then they our necessities? or for that he inuiteth vs to come vnto him? and for that it is needles to take a longer way when the shorter is more speedie & profitable? why then should we pray for our selues? or one for another, being so sinful wretches, & clogged with innumerable imperfections, & not rather vse the assistance of Gods blessed frendes, who might offer vp vnto him the prayers of our vnworthines, & with their most honourable & pleasing intercession, grace and succour vs before the feareful throne of his dread Maiestie?

Hovv-our sauiour is our mediator and herehis Sainctes.

By this euery one may see, how Catholiks in honouring Gods Saincts, thereby more honour God himself: and in praying vnto them practife more their humiltie towardes him: of whome the Psalmist singeth: *Respexit in orationem humilium. Our lord hath regarded the prayer of humble men.* And

Psal. 101

And in this forte, I befeech them to vnderstand, (yf so they please) that we Catholikes
are very far from either iuiurying or disho-
nouring God, or his Sainêts, in that we make
& honour their pictures and images, thereby
the more to expresse, and professe the honour
and reuerence we beare vnto our God, & to
his happie heauely frendes. We know that
those that sclauder vs for dooing these things,
can kneel before the Councel table , & stand
reuerently vncouered before his Maiesties
thaire of eftate, without any fear of treason, or
lese Maiestie. We blame them not, we thinck
they haue reason for this their dooing, In the
name of God, let them haue also a charitable
conceipt of Catholikes actions , and learne
to vnderstand the motiues & groundes thereof. Then shal they fee that we make no more
of an image, then of an image : which is, a representation of the thing or person ; whose
image it is: & whe we honour it, we honour
either at the sight thereof the person of honour whome it representeth, or we honour it
for that it is an honorable representation of
such an honorable personage . And when
we reuerētly kneeling pray before it, we offer
our prayers to that person in heauen, whose
presence by the picture is the more setled &
imprinted in our myndes. There is scarce any
man so barbarous to be found , but taketh
pleasure to see the images of his Prince, Parē-
tes, and frendes to be regarded & vsed hono-

VVy Ca-
tholikẹ
honour
the Ima-
ges of
God &
his Sain-
êes.

D 5   rabiy

rably for their fakes: as on the contrarie it much molesteth and grieueth them, to see them disgraced, stabd, or troden vnder foot in demonstration of the hatred that is borne to the persons whose images they are. Yea such actions seeme to offend them asmuch, (if not more) as any iniurious and contumelious wordes vttered against them. Our Contrie afoordeth vs herein a most memorable example, to witt in the araignemét of that phanatical wretch *vuilliam Hacket* who although he had most blasphemoufly termed him-self Iefus Chrift: Yet (as *Iohn Stovv* writeth) was he by two inditemétes foúd giltie, & acordingly condemned and executed, for hauing spoken diuers most falce & traiterous wordes against her Maieftie; (he sayeth nothing out of the sayd iditemés of his most detestable blasphemie & treasó against God) & for hauing razed and defaced her Maiefties armes, as also a certain picture of the Queenes Maieftie, and did malicioufly, and traiterousely thruft an iron inftrument into that part of thesayd picture, that did represét the breaft & hart of the Queenes Maieftie. Which things seemed so heyuous, that the iudges thought it more meet to condemne and execute him as a traitourto the Prince, then as an abhóminable accurfed violatour of the moft soueraine Maieftie of the high king of heauen. And so he was. Whereby it appeareth how they thought her Maieftie iniuried and difgraced,

by

Stovv in his Annales.
Anno 33 Reg. Eliza.

by the iniurie & disgrace which thesaid caitif offered vnto her armes and image. Vpon which consideration I would aske, what punishmét they haue merited, that haue so dispitefuly & barbarously thrown down mágled and trodden vnder their accursed sinful feet the Pictures of God himself, and of his blessed Mother, & of his holy Saincts? which outrage they committed, to shew them-selues contrarie to the Catholiks: Who, as for the loue, honour, and deuout memorie of God and his holy ones they set vp their Images in their Churches, Oratories, & other honorable places of their Cities and Cuntries: so these people being desirous to manifest the opposition of their myndes, to the intentions of the Catholiks, & to shew how they detested their meaning, they pulled them down, and by diuers infamous base dishonorable wayes consumed them, that thereby the world might see their hatred towards God, their contempt of his diuine Maiestie, and how they desired to raze out of the memories of men whatsoeuer by holy pictures were represented vnto them: Neither can they excuse this their impietie, by their old spurgalled allegations of the twentith of *Exodus* by the fifth of the first of *S. Iohn*, and such like places, by them-selues falcely and with most vngodly iniquitie corrupted. Putting into the text Images for Idols, as though they nothing differed. Which interpretatió yf we should admit, thé

VVhy Catholikes set vp the Images of God & his Saincts.

then, who soeuer retaineth the kinges picture
or armes, or the crosse of Christ in his coine,
whosoeuer hath his parentes or fredes pour-
traitures, whosoeuer hangeth vp in his howse
tapistrie wherein are figured men, beastes,
foules, fishes, trees or hearbes, whosoeuer
hath his armes of gentrie, or beareth his Mai-
sters cognisance, is made culpable of a most
hainous sinne against God, and is made giltie
of eternal damnation. Yet can their *Fox* set
them out the pictures of his Martyrs, and his
people may gaze vpon them. The images of
vviclef, Luther, Hus, Melancthon, Caluin, & of such
Apostata condemned companions may be painted, sold, & hanged vp in euery ones howse
to be tooted vpon. Yea in dishonour of the
Pope, Cardinalles, Bishops, Priestes, Monkes,
and Nunnes many ridiculous shapes may be
deuised to recreate and make merry our gos-
pelling brethren and sisters, without any peril of Idolatrie, or breache of Gods comaun-
dements, although their Minister crie to them
from the communion table, that thow shalt
not make to thy self any grauen image, nor
any likenes of that which is in heauen aboue,
nor in the earth beneath, nor in the waters
vnder the earth. Yet one sorte of images they
can allow to be made to them selues, which
they wil buy, set vp in their roomes and deceit
places of their howses, & there grauely glote
vpon them, because they thinck the persons
there pointed, to be lightes of the gospel,
chosen

See Fox
his boo-
kes of
Actes.

chosen trumpettes of the truth great frendes of the lord, & what not? The other sorte they can diuise, which wil also be sold, & bought, to iybe & scoff at, and that in contempt of the Prælates, and principal members of the Catholik Church, whome they hate and dispise with their hartes. In both these kyndes of pictures they can fynd a relation either in good or bad manner to the persons whome they represent, but the pictures of Christ and of his holy Sainhts, must needes be Idols: they can represent nothing that is good, or worthie veneration. So it is thar *Animalis homo*   1.Cor 2. *non percipit ea qua sunt spiritus Dei. The sensual man perceiueth not those things that are of the Spirit of God.* For if those people were in deed so spiritual, as they are often verie precise forsooth in their wordes, they would easilie discerne an Idol from an Image. For if they wil daigne to view what is set before the first commaundement, & what insueth, they shal fynd that our Lord beginneth with: *I am thy lord thy God &c*, Af-   Exo. 20. terwards, *Thou shalt haue no stränge Gods before me.* And after that: *Thou shalt not make to thy self any caruing* & And then addeth: *Thou shalt not adore them or vvorship them: I am the lord thy strong God &c.* Where they may see, that he forbiddeth to make vnto them-selues carued Gods, which are Idols. For he is the lord God. And that they should not yeeld diuine adoration and worship vnto them: which is Idolatrie.   Exod.25 For he sayth, I am the lord thy strong God. Els *Moysis*, and *Salomon* and God him self should

haue

haue violated this precept, in caufing two Angels to be made ouer the ark, the brafen ferpēt in the wildernes, to fore-fignifie as by a miftical image, Chrift vpō the croffe as our Sauiour himfelf expounded it: the two great *Cherubes* of oliue in the Holy of Holyes, with diuers other *Cherubines*. palme trees, & fundrie other pictures. And it were right impious to fay, that the holy Prophet *Ezechiel* cōmitted Idolatrie, for adoring God in the likenes and fimilitude of a man: or to blame God him-felf for that he wil haue man to be refpected becaufe he is his image. And therfore he threatneth to púnifh thofe perfons moft feuerely, that fhal vniuftly fhed the blood of Man, for that he is the image of God : as yf thereby he would forbid men to abufe, break, and confume his image : and here vpon conclude, the image of God is good, therfore it may be had, therfore it may be honoured for his fake.

The reafon of which doctrin (yf thou marke wel curteo⁹ reader) cōfifteth in thefe poincts ? Firft, to worfhip and honour God for himfelf, as being the Fountaine of all goodnes: then his faincts , for that he hath imparted and deriued vnto them the abundance of his vnfpeakeable graces and glorie: & fo the images of them both are to be worfhiped as their reprefentations, and for that they notably apertaine vnto them: and thus confequently Catholiks do very wel if for the honour of God and of his Saincts , they difcreetely and
orderly

Num.21
3.Reg.6
2.Par. 3.

Ezech.1.
3.

Gen.9.

The
ground
and rea-
fon of al
thefe
pointes.

orderly loue, and reuerence any thing that
concerneth them. Which honour and reuerence as they may professe with their mouthes, or by their wordes, so may they manifest thesame accordingly and in the same degree, by their outward gestures and actions.
For which cause they are much to be blamed
who blame the deuotions of Catholiks, for
honouring the Reliques of Saincts, or such
things as belong vnto them, or to their very
Images. As we see the good deuout Catholiks here, for the honour they beare to God,
to worship his worthie Mother and for her
worship, they reuerence her Image: & for the
reuerence of her Image, they beare also a reuerent esteeme of the very wood of the tree
wherein the said Image was placed. Acording
to that which is recorded in *Exodus:* where the *Exod. 3.*
Angel that apeared for God to Moyses in the
fiery bush, was for that cause honored with
the title of God: and for the sayd Angel his
more reuerence, *Moyses* was prohibited to ap-
roach neer vnto the bush wherein he appeered: & in regard of the bush, the very mou-
taine where it grew was accounted so holy,
that *Moyses* must put of his shooes, and walk
vpon it bare-foot for the honour there of.
And at other tymes, our lord would so honour
the cloak of *Elias*, the dead corps of *Eliseus*, the   *4 Reg. 2*
shadow of the body of *Sainct Peter*, the nap-   *4 Reg 13*
kins of *Sainct Paul*, and the like of other sain-   *Act. 5.*
ctes, that at their presence or bare touching   *Act. 19.*
he would woork most admirable miracles, &

bestow

beſtow moſt gratious benefites vpon his people, becauſe the ſayd things did belong vnto
his honorable Sainᵈts,

And this may ſuffice in brief to declare by
holy Scripture, the reaſon of the Catholike
Churches faith and praᵈtiſe, in theſe matters,
where-in the ignorant of the Catholike do-
ᵈtrin, or ſuch as by the ignorance or mallice
of others are ill perſuaded there-of, may be
offended, in reading this enſuing treates. As
for other things (which alſo vnto them may
ſeeme ſtrange) they ſhal (if they pleaſe to in-
quire) fynd them ſo plaine and euident in the
word of God, as none but they that are altogether ignorant of the word of God, or beleeue not the Scriptures can haue any ſcruple
therein. As, how gratefull a thing it is to God
diſcreetely & deuoutly to make vowes vnto
him, and for his honour to offer vnto him (for
the beautifing of ſuch places where he wil be
honoured) parte, of their wordly welth, iewels or ſuch things as by thē are held iu price.

For the firſt, we haue the counſel of the
Royal Prophet ſaying: *Vouete, & reddite Domino*
Deo veſtro: omnes qui in circuitu eius affertis munera.
Make vowues and fulfil them to your Lord God: all you
that round about him bring him your preſents. And
vpon the aſſurednes of this doᵈtrine theſame
Prophet ſayd. *Vota mea reddam in conſpeᵈtu timen-*
tium eum: I vvil render my vowues in the ſight of ſuch
as feare our lord.

And for the ſecond: we read how *Moyſes* by
the

To ma-
ke holy
and dif-
crete
vovve is
is very
accepta-
ble to
God.
Pſal. 75.

the commaundement of God perſuaded his Iſraelites, to ſhew their liberallitie in adorning of the Tabernacle. Wherein they were ſo zealous and forward, that *Moyſes* was conſtrained to reſtraine them by expreſſe commaundement and ſound of trumpet. And although ſome with the ſonne of *Iſcariot* crie out. *Vt quid perditio hæc? vvhat a loſſe is this, for it vvere better to giue it to the poor.* Yet the deuout Chriſtian ſhal haue Chriſt to beare him out, for powring with the deuout *Magdalen* his precious oyles vpon his ſacred head, and for making moderate and diſcreet largeſſe of his temporal goodes acording to his abilitie, in honorably ſetting forth the worſhip & places of worſhip of his God.

I do not think (louing Reader) but many oppoſitions wil be made both againſt theſe things which I haue here ſayd, as alſo againſt ſundrie other matters which are contayned in the hiſtorie following: for we haue to deal with an incredulous, prowd, contradicting generation. Thow maiſt wel iudge that al can not here be ſayd, that may be ſayd. Wherefore I aſſure thee, that if thow wilt but manifeſt thy difficulties to thoſe that are learned and inſtructed in the groundes of the Catholyk Religion, thou ſhalt fynd ful and perfect ſatisfaction, and thou ſhalt euidently ſee, that what ſoeuer is obiected againſt theſe matters, are but either meer doubtes, or ſtrained illations, or falſe and friuolous collections, or vnchari-

E   table

table railing or their own forged inuentions, or lying headles reportes, or vnciuil and vngodly scoffing and iesting, or such like trumperie.

Be thou therfore fully perswaded of this poinct : that as God is the truthe it self, and as the deuil is the father and author of lyes, so God wil not haue his cause defended and maintained, but by the onely truthe , and he detesteth whatsoeuer is taken out of his enimies shoppe. As God and the deuil can neuer agree, so truthe and lyes can neuer consorte together , and it is either great ignorance or impietie to thinck, that Gods cause either is, or euer can be driuen to so hard an exigent, that it must be supported and held vp by such broken stuffe. True it is, a ly may go masked vnder such a veil that it may be take for truth, by such as are not curious to note & marck the carsage thereof: but the nature of man beeing alwayes amourous of the truthe , and ielous that falshood should foiste her-self into the place of truthe , the wiser sorte are more daintie and nice to admitt any thing, vntil vpon serious examination they haue looked more diligently into matters: Where vpõ it happeneth, that tyme and diligence trying truthe , falshood is ferrited out to her more detestation, her authours greater shame , and the future safegard of those that were in peril to haue bene gulled by her. So that vpon this consideration thou maist confidently conclude,

The cause of God wvil nor be supported by lyes.

that if the Catholyk Religion were backed and
bolstred vp by such bad dealing, (as all heretikes lowdly but more lewdly auouche) it
had bene ruined long ere this. But we experience the contrarie to our comfort & astonishment: that so many heretikes hauing risen
in all the quarters and cuntries of the world,
who by open lying, cunning conueiance of
tongue, & tyrannical force, omitting nothing,
that might ouerthrow either all, or the greatest
parte of our holy beleef: although they haue
wrested many notable partes of *Europe* out of
the armes and bosome, of our deer Mother the
Catholyke Churche, yet hath she regained tre-
ble (at least) her losse in the *Indiaes*: and the
pointes also which they haue so long battred
at, haue bene the more learnedly, perspicuous-
ly & heroically defended, more feruently imbraced, and more zelously practised, then perhaps they euer were in former ages. And so it
cometh to passe, that we see now Sacramental
Confession more vsed, the holy Masse more
frequented, the blessed Sacrament more honoured, Reliques of Sainctes and their Images
more reuerenced, Pilgrimages more haunted,
the Popes pardons more desired, Religious
Congregations in greater number and better
order, the Churches precepts more obeyed,
yea and the Pope (against whome al Heretikes
chiefely shoot) more respected & reuerenced,
and his dignitie power and prerogatiues more
cōfessed by Kings, Princes, Prælates, the lear-

Note
this eui-
dent ex-
periéce.

E 2   ned

ned and common forte of all kingdoms, and
nations then euer before. Whyle the heretiks
who at the beginning were but in fewe sectes,
are now almost in euery kingdome and common wealth where they are permitted, rent &
torne in to so many different synagogues,
faithes, and professions, eche one writing,
wrangling, railing & raging against other, and
according to their power, one faction corporally punnishing and plaging the other, that
as we perceiue their sectes dayly to increace, so
we see the professors of ech sect to decrease,
and either to return again to the Catholike
Church, or to set abroache newe doctrines of
their owne, or finally to care for no Faith, no
Churche, no Religion, and no God at all.

And thus we see the old saying prooue true
that atheisme is the natural impe of heresie.
For men hauing entred thereby into a wrangling, contradictious, proud, selfliyking, froward, & mistrusting humor: they wil yeeld to
nothing, if they can any way shift it of: whereby
not onely faith in matters that are supernatural and surpassing our vnderstanding, but euen
humane or common credence, sence and iudgement, is as it were wholy extinguished, and
amongst men dayly more and more decayeth.
Who knoweth not that as too hastie creduli-
tie proceedeth of simplicitie and weakenes of
witt, so that it is a signe of a wicked vicious
mynd to be too difficile & restie in beleeuing:
for such persons beeing either suspicious of
                                                    other

other mennes honeftie and fidelitie, or knowing how prone they themfelues are to deceiue and circumuent others to their power,
they are very hardly induced to truft any. The
mean therfore is to be chofen, which is: there
to fubmitt our felues where reafon and fufficient authoritie may feeme iuftly to exact it of
vs. As (to exemplifie in the prefent matter of
thefe miracles here related) what greater reasó
fhould moue a reafonable man then to fee fo
many and fuch wounderful miracles dayly to
be wrought in things appertaining to matters
of faith and religion? Whereby, not onely the
people of the cuntrie, but ftrangers of forrein
nations, not onely perfons of the commõ forte
but the moft præcellent in dignitie and nobilitie, not onely thofe of the ordinary and
common intendement, but the moft learned
and inftructed in all kynd of literature and
knowledge, not onely priuate howfholds and
families, but the very Magiftrates and Commu-
nities of Cities and Prouinces are driuen into
vnfpeakeable admiration and aftonifhment.
Who after all the diligent fearche examination
and inquifition which either by witt, induftrie,
learning, authoritie, and confcience they were
able to vfe, they could neuer hitherto fynd the
leaft fufpition of any fraud or iniquitie: but
rather they are forted to confeffe the miraculous finger of God in ech thing, whereby it
pleafeth him in fuch admirable forte to honour
his mofte facred Mother, to cõfort his grieued

and

& afflicted childrē, to animate the more faithful, to cōfirm the feeble wauerers, & to reduce those that are in error vnder the gouernment and due obedience of the true paſtors of their ſoules.

Ioſue 5. When *Ioſue* in the field of *Iericko* beheld the Angel of God with his naked ſword in his hand, who declared vnto him that he was the Prince of the army of our Lord, vndoubtedly he was exceedingly glad of that viſion, to ſee that he, and his army had ſuch a guyd, and protector from heauen. As it is also reported of the people of God, that they were ſingulerly comforted & encouraged to fight againſt their enimies, after they had hard their *Iudas*

2 Mach. 15. *Machabeus* relate vnto thē his dreame, wherein he ſaw *Onias* the high prieſt and *Hieremie* the Prophet earneſtly praying for them, and that from *Hieremie* he had receiued a golden ſword

A cōfort for diſtreſſed Catholikes. with theſe wordes. *Take the holy ſvvord a gift ſent thee from God, in vvhich thou ſhalt abaſe and bring vnder the aduerſaries of my people of Iſrael.* In like manner what Catholikes are their, who amiddeſt ſo many aduerſaries of their faith and religion, ſtand enuironed and are on euery ſide battred with ſclaunders and calumniations, both againſt their faith and perſons, impouerſhed by the loſſe of their goods, diſgraced by depriuation of their dignities, reſtrained by impriſonments, toſſed by ielouſes, inquiries and ſearches, conſumed with inward & outward torments & moſt barbarous cruel bloudie

bloudie deathes, what Catholikes are there
(I say) who seeing the hand of God stretched
out by heauély signes to approoue & honour
the cause of these their suffrings, but must needes feel in them-selues an vnspeakeable ioy
and iubilation, and to be thereby exceedingly
inflamed to maintaine & confesse a cause, from
heauen so mightily and powrably defended,
not by the sword and presence onely of an Angel, not onely by the intercessions of an *Onias*
or of a *Hieremie*, but by the fauourable assiftáce
of the high Queen of Angels, prophets, and
Sainctes the most blessed Mother of our God
Christ Iesus? where, we behold not by the relation of others, but immediatly by our selues,
not in a dreame or obscure vision, but with
our corporal eies, not onely one goldé sword,
but so many works of heauenly power, as so
many swords to hewe down al such aduersaries as band them selues against God and his
holy Catholike Church. Which is a matter of
that consequence, that if our aduersaries either
by any of their Ministerie, or by any rite of
their religion could haue cured in this sorte
but one lame dog, it should haue rung farr &
neere, and wounderful trophese should haue
bene raised in memorie thereof.

Marck therfore (Catholik brother) and
with due gratitude behold how liberal God
hath bene to thee in these things, thereby to
solace thee in the throng of so many miseries
and contrarieties. Whilest the vngodly cried

E 4   vpon

vpon the Princes & Parlaments againſt poor
Catholiks: *Exinanite Exinanite vſque ad fundamen-*
tum in ea. Downe with the Papiſts, let vs root
them out let vs diſgrace them, begger them,
take their guydes and paſtors from the face of
the earth, that ſo no memorie may remaine
of them. Not-withſtanding behold (O Catholik) *Pro patribus tuis nati ſunt tibi filij.* When
thy old Paſtors began to be worne out, and
to be weeded away, a new offſpring aroſe, with
their learning to inſtruct thee, with their vertuous example to direct thee, with their dayly
prayers and ſacrifices to aſſiſt thee, with their
patience and indurance to confirm thee,
with their deathes & blood ſpilt to incourage
thee, and to gaine others, (euen of thyne aduerſaries) to confeſſe and imbrace the ſame
faith with thee. Is this to ſee how natural effects follow their natural cauſes? how ſclau-
ders defame, authoritie diſgraceth, lawes reſtraine, welth worketh, force keepeth downe,
pouertie deiecteth, torments terrifie, & death
conſumeth? No, but rather thou maiſt ſee the
old admirable ſignes renued again amongſt
vs.

The three children to walk ſinging at their
eaſe in the fierie fornace, *Ieſus* to heale the
blynd by daubing durt vpon his eies, cõtraries
to worke contraries, and that now again that
may be ſayd of thyne afflicted which the holy
Ghoſt once recorded of the bleſſed Apoſtles:
Ibant gaudentes a conſpectu concilij, quoniam digni ha-
bi ti

Pſal. 136

Pſal. 44.

Dan. 3.

Ioh. 9.

Act. 5.

biti sunt pro nomine Iesū contumeliam pati. They went reioycing from the sight of the councel, becaufe they were accounted worthie to suffer reproache for the name of *Iesus.* Verilie, these are moft admirable miracles: although there had bene amongft you no fick cured, no deuils expelled, no apparitions and ftraunge vifions feene, none of your inhumane and bloudie Perfecutors moft dreadefully by the reueging hand of God derriued of their vngodly and accurfed liues. At which moft admirable workes of God becaufe I know our aduerfaries wil either contemne, or afcribe to other fubtil-ties, or humaine cafuallities: therfore behold here before thyne eies, the miracles related in this book, and efteeme of them (as they are) moft admirable, moft knowne, moft ap-prooued.

What can the derider contradictor or perfe-cuter of our Catholik faith cauil againft thefe? what more cleer euidence can he require from heauen then thefe? would he haue the dread Maieftie of God to difcend and fit in the clowdes, and thence to commaund him fub-miffion and reuerence vnto thefe thinges? Veri-ly he fhal fee our lord defcend according as the Prophet *Zacharie* hath fore told faying: *Veniet Dominus Deus meus omnesφ, fancti cum eo. The lord my God fhal come and all the Sainctes vvith him.* There fhal he fee with our lord his euer bleffed Mo-ther, his Apoftles and Difciples. *Sainct Clement, Sainct Laurence, Sainct Nicholas, Sainct Martin, Sainct Gregorie*

Many miracles haue bin vvrought amongft Catholi-kes in England in the ti-me of their perfecu-tion as could be particu-lerly fet dovvn yf it might be vvith-out the peril of thofe to vvhom they ha-ue hap-pened.

Zach.14

Gregorie, surnamed Thaumaturgus, our S. Augustin, S.
Bennet , Sainct Basil, Sainct Francis, Sainct Bernard, S.
Edvvard, Sainct Levvis, Sainct Catherin, Sainct Cecilie,
Sainct Clare, Sainct Bregit, with millions more
all of one and our fayth: against whose mira-
cles let him then dispute, and to make his partie good against that glorious fellowship , let
him range himself with VViclef, Husse, Luther,
Caluin , Beze , Knox, Fox, Screek , Rotman, Hooper,
Couper , Knoblouch , Grumpeck, Klup, VVhitle, Bore,
Ioane Lashford, Alice Driuer, and such companiós:
& let his soule take her luck & lott with these
mates, Who as they cast themselues out of the
Communion of the former Saincts , abandoned their faith , and banded against that
Church in which they liued , and for which
many of them spilt their bloud , and wrought
such innumerable miracles. Let him then raile
against thē for beeing Massing Popes, Bishops,
Priests, Deacons, Abbottes, Mounkes, Nunnes.
No, no, if he do not before that tyme alter his
humor he shal vndoubtedly lifting vp his wret
ched eies towardes the Sainctes of the Catholyke Church, intune with his miserable con-
fortę that most heauie and doleful dump set
down by the wise-man in these wordes. Hi sunt
quos habuimus aliquando in derisum & in similitudinem
improperij. Nos insensati vitam illorum æstimabamus
insaniam, & finem illorum sine honore: Ecce quomodo
computati sunt inter filios Dei, & inter sanctos sors illorum est, &c. These are they vuhome sometymes vve had
in derision, & held like to infamie: VVe senceles people
did esteeme their lyfe madnes, and their end vvithout honour

Sap.5.

your : Behold hovv they are reckned amongst the sonnes of God, and theyr lott is amongest his holy ones: Therfore, vve haue erred feom the vvay of truthe, and the light of iustice hath not shyned vnto vs. VVhat hath our pride profited vs? or vvhat hath the glorie of our riches yeelded vs? All those things are vanished avvay like a shaddovv. &c. These and the like complaints shal they yell out who for their sinnes and want of true faith are in the day of our Lord to be bånished for euer frō his face, to the mansion of all calamities. *For, vvithout faith it is impossible to please God.* And there is but one true sauing faith, as there is but one God by whome we must be saued as the holy Apostle affirmeth. Therfore (louing reader) if thou thinckest in thy cōscience, & as thou wilt answere it before the dreadful iudgement seat of God, that thou hast found any where more solid and euident proofes for the true faith then are to be foūd in the Catholik, Apostolik, and Romane Churche, (as it is impossible) there hazard thou thy soule.

If not: then beware that our iust Lord at the vncertaine hower of thy most certaine death reuenge not himself on thy soule for thy contempt vsed towardes him, in respecting or preferring any worldly, carnal, transitorie bable of this life, before his souereigne Maiestie. Thou seest what admirable motiues he hath affoorded thee, whereby thou maist also perceiue how deerly he loueth thee & tendreth thy saluatiō, although he hath no need of thee. Shew thy self therfore gratefull

Heb. 11.
Eph. 4.

ful for this his grace, that after this lyfe
he may make thee alſo pertaker of his eternal
glorie: for which firſt he created thee, and
afterwardes moſt mercifully redeemed thee,
and vnto which now by theſe his diuine workes he moſt louingly
inuiteth thee.

THE

THE
PREFACE OF THE
AVTHOR.

 Ee giue thee here (louing Reader) a brief rebearfal of fuch thinges as concerne the place of Montaigue nere to the towne of Siché in the Duchie of Brabát: VVee haue alfo fet downe the miracles which haue hapned there of late, by the merits and interceffion of the glorious virgin Marie, Yet not all, but only thofe that are prooued and verified by publike wrytings and atteftations of Magiftrates, and other authenticall declarations: afwel to preuent therby the flaunders of herettikes, as alfo for the better information & fatiffactió of good Catholikes. As for the heretikes, they haue allwayes had an ancient cuftome with great vehemencie to calumniate and blame thofe things, in the Ca-tholike Romaine Church, which they in their fynagogs lift not to beleeue. And before thé

the

the Pharifies vfed the like, who afcribed the
miracles of our Sauiour and his difciples to the
power of the Diuell. This all fectaries that
haue bene fince the beginning in the Church haue
allwayes imitated, and the heretikes of our
dayes do ftill verie markablie practize, who beganne their herefies by vttering blafphemies
againft the Moother of God and his Sainctes.
And publikly not onlie in their talk, but alfo
in their writings, bragging them-felues to be
Image-breakers.

A certaine pamphlet in flemmifh came of late
to our handes printed and compofed (as it feemeth) by fome pernicious Caluinift of Holland
againft the honour donne to the Moother of God
at Mountaigue. In which pamphlet he writeth execrable blafphemies, he forgeth fables &
lyes againft thofe of the Church, he bafely fcof-
feth at the pietie of Princes & Lordes of the
Countrie, and at all fuch as loue and ferue the
glorious virgin. And finallie he endeuoreth by
lyes to deface and obfcure the honour donne to
God and his bleffed Mother. Howbeit this companion and all fuch like night-owles wil they
nil they, muft needes endure the moft cleare
light which our lord maketh dayly to blafe before
our eyes, to his owne and his Moothers glorie:
and through the euidence of theife miracles, they

muft

must ly trodden vnder the feet of this woman, together with the old serpent their head and captaine.

And in vaine shal their labor bee that endeuour to hinder the Sunne to giue his light vnto the earth, the will of our Lord beeing such as the truth shall clerelie be seene, and pierce through the most obscure and duskie clowdes of heresies, Farre more proffitable therefore and holesome would it be for them to open the windowes of their hartes and to let these diuine beames enter in. And what beames can be more cleere or of more force, then these so palpable arguments & euident demonstrations of the pure & sincere veritie. Doe not these (I beseeche you) so apparent miracles crie out the verie same that our Sauiour speaketh in the ghospel? If you beleeue not me, beleeue the woorks which I doe. And that which the Parents of the blynd man sayd. Enquire of him, he is of age, he will answere for him-self, he is thirtie yeares old.

These corrupters of the truth think to abuse the simple people, telling them that Catholikes woorship Idols, and that they honour the virgin Marie as if she were a goddesse, and adore Images: but this is an old song so often by them chaunted, so often disputed, and in such sorte refuted

futed as there is no Catholike of so sleder iudge-
ment who knoweth not the blessed virgin to
be honored as a Patronesse and Aduocate to her
Sonne and not as a Goddesse , and that the honor
donne to her Image hath relation to her person
and not to her Image. And morcouer that all
manner of adoration whether it be Latria,
Dulia, *or* Hyperdulia *must not be taken or*
vnderstood according to the outward woork &
apparence but according to the intention of the
partie from whome it proceedeth.

After an other sorte this may in like manner
be proffitable to Catholikes, forsomuch as there
are some amongst them who seeme to doubt of
these miracles, for diuersmen by a certaine kynd
of incredulitie, and others vpon a spirit of con-
tradiction either deny that these are miracles,
or they will not beleeue, that they haue vere-
ly bene wrought. Vnto these wee must say that
which our Sauiour sayd vnto Sainct Thomas,
Come and feele &c. *Yf they will not yeeld*
credit to that which wee set downe, let them
goe and see, and feele with their fingers, or else
enquire the veritie of those who haue bene cured,
for I am assured they shall fynd good store of
them. And if after this they will not yet beleeue,
assure your selues (as Aristotle *sayd of those*
that denyed the principles of sciences) that they
do it

do it for want of witte and iudgement, or els
it must be beaten into their braynes with beetles
or bastinadoes.

There are also others who take occasion to
doubt hereof, because many hauing bene miraculously cured, did not for all that obtaine their
health at an instant, or at the verie place, but by
litle and litle with some alteration of their bodies:
vnto whome wee may by good reason answere,
that to prooue a miracle it suffiseth that the operation and effect be aboue the course of nature,
and not by any naturall meanes or remedies: and
such are all those miracles which here in this historie wee haue sette downe.

Moreouer amongst these miracles some are
more perfit and notable then some others are: a-
mongst the more notable are esteemed those, when
the diseases are cured at the verie same instant,
whereof wee haue verie many, and yet the others
are not without miracle, although they haue hapned in successe of tyme, because they were
wrought aboue the course of nature.

For who is he that will or can deny that whē
our Lord cured the blynd man it was a true and
perfit miracle? who at the beginning saw men
walke like trees, yet no man doubteth that he
afterward receiued his perfit sight.

Neither is it any wayes repugnant to the na-

F   ture

ture of a miracle that at the tyme of their healing they feel a change or alteration either in their soules or in their bodies: for (not alleaging the other reasons which wee will set downe in the ensuing historie) who is he that knoweth if those whome our Lord & his saints miraculously cured did not feel the like also in them selues? No author nor wryter denieth or affirmeth that they were restored to their health without such alterations. And forsomuch as those miracles were wrought principallie for the confirmation of our faith, it suffised only to set downe the bare truth without further expressing the circumstances, or what other thinges els therin occurred. Our Lord recounted his miracles to the disciples of S. Iohn Baptist (who doubted whether he were the true Messias or no) without making any mention of the circustances or other qualities, saying: Go, tell vnto Iohn. The blynde see, the lame vvalk, the deaf heare, the leprous are made cleane, giuing vs therby to vnderstand that such cures (although he had sayd nothing) yeelded certaine & infallible proof that he was the true Messias. And whē wee heare, see, and feel the like to be donne by the merits & intercession of the glorious mother of God at the Mountaine of Mountaigue, who is hee that is so wilfully blynd as will not acknowlege the holy

Catholik

TO THE AVTHOR.

Catholike Romaine Church adorned and honored
with such signes & miracles, to be the only spouse
of Christ, the doue and beloued of our Lord, the
fortresse and piller of truthe, in whoms onlie true
and perfit miracles are to be found?

Awake therefore (O you misledde with heresies) open the eyes of your vnderstanding, and behold the light wherwith the God of mercies
vouchsafeth to lighten the darknes of your ini-
quities and ignorance: Yf he had not publikly
wrought these signes and miracles that none but
he is able to woork, perhaps this misguided people
might in some sorte be excused: but seeing they
haue had so great and manifest signes and testimonies, they shalbe inexcusable in that they do
not woork their owne conuersions.

And you faithful Catholikes who for the pro-
speritie of our enemies, or euill successe of the affaires of our religion, or for the abuses and imper-
fectiō in the life & māners of those of the Church
or layetie, are wont to stagger or be faint-harted,
confirme and settle your selues hereby: you are in
S. Peeters ship, wherin (notwithstanding all
waues & tempests) it pleaseth our lord to woork
his miracles.

And all you that by the miracles and intercession of the glorious virgin Marie most holie
Moother of God, haue receiued health or help,

F 2   forbeare

forbeare not to manifest the same to your superiours and others (sith it is much honorable to reueale the woorkes of God) whome wee exhort in our Lord that they giue aduertisement therof to the right Reuerend the lord Archbishop of Maclin, VVherby the name of God may be sanctified amongst vs, and that his mercie may be exalted and magnified in his Saincts. For how many soeuer his miracles are, so many exhortatiōs and sermons they be, and which more forciblie moue the hartes of men then the sermons of any be he neuer so excellent for his knowlege or eloquence. And for our part let vs endeuor to giue euerlasting praise to the mercie of God, who in this our miserable and afflicted state (as for the present is this of the low Countries) he vouchsafeth to send vs comfort by woorking so great and goodlie woorkes, yea such as wee think in that countrey neuer hapned the like.

Lt vs also praise the moother of God, and let vs so begge her protection as she rising once like an amiable Aurora, will disperse the darke obscuritie of our miseries, and as a most bright & faire Moone, will vouchsafe to yeeld light to those which ly in the dark night of errors and heresies, and as a cleare shyning Sunne would pearce with the beames of grace and vertue the hartes of the faithful people, which haue the

feare

feare of God: and finallie like a well marshalled
battaile driue all the heresies out of the woorld:
and by her holie protection defend these low
Countreis from all corporall and spiritual in-
uasions: by the power of him who doeth
her such honor both in heauen
and in earth,
Amen.

F 3   THE

THE
HISTORIE
OF THE MIRACLES
WROVGHT BY THE IN-
TERCESSION OF OVR
ble ffed Ladie, at a place called *Mount-*
aigue, in the duchie of *Brabant*.

HE holie fcripture ma-
keth mention of an Oke
behynd the towne of *Si-*
chem in *Paleſtine* vnder the
which *Iacob* buried the
Idols & the Iewels that
hanged at the eares of his people. And at
thefame Oke the Captaine *Iofue* renewed the couenant betwixt God and the
people of *Iſrael.* Verie fitlie ought wee to
fette furth the renowmed fame of the
Oke which ftandeth nere to our *Sichen*
in the Duchie of *Brabant*, at the which
Oke in a place vulgarly called *Scherpen-*
heuuel

heuuel and in French *Mountaigue* before
an Image of the Mother of God beeing
verie simple and of litle shew (as the
place it self is) it pleaseth his diuine maiestie to woork daylie many miracles, by
the glorie whereof it seemeth that his
desire and pleasure is that the heretikes
beeing curbed, and the Catholikes made
more submissiue the pride of heretikes
and the idolles of other vyces might here
ly buried: and that in this place he will
be appeased by the prayers of good and
godly Christiás : and that he will renew
his friendship and alliance with the people of these low Countreis, for wee
esteem the glorie of miracles to be accounted one of the most assured notes &
markes of the true Church, grounded
vpon the woords of our Sauiour in the
ghospell saying : *Such signes shall follow*
those that beleeue in me. They shal lay their han-
des vpon the diseased & they shal be healed, &c.
And the holie Apostle saith that vnto the
preaching and teaching of the way of saluation, our Lord added a testimonie of
his owne hand by signes, miracles, and
other supernaturall works of his power.
For euen as the miracles of our Lord serued

Marc. 16
Hebr. 2.

tied for proofes to make mé beleeue that he was the true Sauiour of the world according to that which he saith in the gholpell, euen ſo the true and vndoubted miracles which can not be wrought without the puiſſance of God, yeeld teſtimonie to his bodie, which is his holie Church. For which cauſe that moſt lerned Doctor S. *Auſtin* ſaith, that the Catholike Church obteined ſoueraigne authoritie, when heretikes were iudged and condemned by the maieſtie of miracles, And in an other place, that the authoritie of the Churche began by miracles, and by the ſame ſhe mainteyneth her force. And againe, the concord and vnion of all nations (ſaith he) together with the authoritie of miracles, holdeth mee in the holie Church. And *Richard de S. Victore* durſt cóſidétlie ſay, *Lord if this be erroneous which wee beleeue, it is by thy ſelf that wee are deceaued, for theſe thinges were eſtabliſhed and confirmed amongſt vs with ſuch ſignes and miracles as none but thou wert able to woork.*

Amongſt theſe miracles they are not the leaſt which his diuine goodnes vouchſafed to woork euen from the beginning of the Chriſtian cómon wealth, in di-

De vtilitate credendi cap. 17. eodem lib. cap. 16 & cótra op. funda. cap. 4.

lib. 1. de T.initate cap. 2.

in diuers places at the Images and for
the honor and woorſhip of the Mother
of God.

It is an vndoubted ancient tradition
that S. *Luke* painted an Image of our *Lady*,
the which wee haue by the teſtimony of
diuers credible writers and authors, as
of *Theodorus, Nicephorus, Metaphraſtes*, But
whether he painted more then one wee
are not aſſured, yet this is certaine, that
many Images were drawne according to
that which he had firſt painted, and were
afterwards ſent to diuers places, neither
ought it to be deemed impertinent that
ſome haue attributed them to S. *Luke*, for
ſomuch as they were perfit draughtes &
reſemblances of the originall firſt painted
by his owne hand. Of which Imagss that
was one, which S. *Gregorie* the firſt caried
in ſolemne proceſſion in *Rome*, whereby
the great infection of the plague ceaſed,
where with the ayre was corrupted, in
the yeare of our lord 509. And all the
people of *Rome* are of opinion that it is the
ſame Image which is now kept in the
Church of S. *Maria Maior*. Such alſo was
that, which (as they ſay) theſayd S. *Gre-*
gorie ſent to S. *Leander* Biſhop of *Seuil* in
Spaine,

lib. 14.
in vita
S. Luce.

Atil.
Seſtra:lib
de 7 vr-
bis Eccle
Baron in
Annal.

Gaſpar
varre-
rius in
chorogra
Hiſp.

Spaine, the which the Spaniardes honor and now call by the name of *Nueſtra Señora de Guadalupe*.

The Image that ſometime was honored in the Citie of *Conſtantinople* , (and in regard of the deuotion vſed therunto, the Mother of God now and then deliuered her ſeruants from the handēs of the Saraſins) is held by ſome to be that which the Empreſſe *Eudoxia* ſent to *Pulcheria* frō *Iheruſalem* to *Conſtantinople*, the which authors of good credit write , was afterwards tranſlated to *Venice* where at this preſent it remaineth. *Alphonſus de Vilegas* in his book intituled *Flos Sanctorum* teſtifieth by the authoritie of very many lerned men , that at this preſent there is in the Citie of *Saragoſa* in *Spayne* a Chappell built and an Image of our lady there placed by the handes of *S. Iames* the Apoſtle, and honored with many miracles, which the Spainardes call *Nueſtra Señra del pilar*. *Nauarrus* reherſeth by the teſtimony of *Oſorius* that in the Citie of *Calicut* in the *Indies* there is yet to be ſeene an Image of our Lady with her Chyld in her armes, the which they hold was there left by one of the three kinges, or by ſome principall

Sigonius in Hiſt. Ital.

Antoni⁹ Benter. in Chronico. Et Franciſ. Arias lib. de imit. virg. cap. 20.

cipall

cipall perſon of their trayne, who was at
the adoring of our Lord in *Bethleem*.

They who haue left vs written the hiſtorie & particularities of that puiſſant
kingdome of *China* lying in the vttermoſt
boundes of the eaſt, aſſure vs that they
found in the Citie of *Chinceo* a meruelous
ſumptuous temple, where the Inhabitants of the Countrey being Pagans, had
placed in a Chappell a hundreth and eleuen Idols; and beſides them three very
rich ſtatues. wherof the one had one bodie and three faces, beholding each the
other very attentiuely, the other was of
a woman bearing a Chyld in her armes:
the third of a man apparailed in ſuch ſort
as the Chriſtiàs paint the holie Apoſtles,
ſo that it ſeemeth the Image of the virgin *Marie* was there knowne and had in
honor.

The admirable and renowned hiſtorie of our Ladie of Laureto is famous
ouer al the world, wherin wee may ſee
how our Lord hath made choiſe of foure
diuers places wherunto he cauſed that
holie houſe wherin the diuine incarnation was wrought, to be tranſlated by the
miniſtery of **Angells**, wherof the fourth
place

(marginal notes:)

Ioan Cōcales de Men-doca.

Horat. Turſeli-nus hiſt. ædis Lauret.

place is that of *Lauretto*, where now it continueth in the *Marca of Ancona*. where it is very much frequented through the innumerable visitations of all sortes of Pilgrims, and for the multitude of miracles which are seene there to happen daylie. In the Chappelle of that place is an Image of our Ladie with her babe *Iesus*, deuoutlie carued out of Cedar wood. Also the pilgrimage to the church at *Mont-Serato* in the kingdome of *Cathalognia* in *Spaine* is very renowned, where the Image of the Mother of god is greatlie honored, which was there miraculouslie found within a caue, about the yeare of our Lord. 890. where by the intercession of our blessed Ladie haue bene wrought many assured miracles amply set downe, in a historie cõpiled therof and translated into french, and not long sithence dedicated to the french king now raigning.

Fetcol Marian pag. 105

Anno 1606.

THE SECOND CHAPTER.

A ND to the end wee occupie not our selues in forraine matters only. These low Countreis haue in semblable
manner

manner(& that in many places) the memories of the glorious *Virgin Marie* honored with diuers miracles: And to begin
with *Henault: Tongre,* a village hard by
the Towne of *Ath* hath an Image of our
Lady, the which in the yeare 1081. was
three tymes placed there, and notwithſtanding that it was diuers times caried
to other places, yet was it ſtil miracu-
louſlie brought thither back againe.

In the Abbay of *Cambron*, (which is of
the *Ciſtertian order*) is kept a certaine
Image of the Mother of God, painted
vpõ a wall, the which in the yeare 1232
being wounded with a bore-ſpeare by a
Iew, yeelded great aboundance of blood,
the markes wherof are to be ſeene to this
preſent day. Wee read the like to haue
hapned euen in our dayes in the yeare
1595 in the Duchie of *Sauoy* nere to a
towne called *Mountaruie,* where there
was an Image of our ladie, which hauing
receaued certaine gaſhes with a ſwoord
of a Caluiniſt, yeelded incontinentlie
blood, wherwith many blynd, deaf,
lame, and other diſeaſed were cured.

In like máner our Lord hath wrought
many meruelous thinges by the inuocation

tion of his holie Mother in a litle towne
of *Henault* called *Chieure* , since the yeare
of our lord 1326. the which also continueth euen to our daies.

And in speciall sorte in the same prouince the said blessed virgin is much honored in the towne of *Hall* where is an
Image of her, placed by *S. Elizabeth* daughter to the king of *Hungarie*, singuler deuotion being there vsed in regard of the miracles which are seé there to happé vnto
those who either go thither in pilgrimage
or els vow to go. Whereof the great lear
ned *I. Lipsius* hath of late cóposed a book.

In the Countrey of *Arthois* and in the
Citie of *Arras* is a wax taper brought
thither miraculoustie by the Mother of
God in the yeare of our lord 1105 in the
tyme of *Lambert* Bishop of *Arras*. And this
was donne to heale a disease called the
fyri-burning. This Candle is kept with
great care in the foresaid Citie and is vsed
verie souerainlie for the curing of many maladies: neuer consuming although
it be often tymes lighted; and that they
haue made many little candels of the
drops of the wax that haue been powred
from the same: not vnlike vnto that
candle

Ioan
Molan.
nat. SS.
Belg. 6.
Febr.

Ioannes
Moscus
in prat:
spirit.

candle of *Iohn the Heremit* dwelling in *St. thus* neere to *Hierufalē*, the which he had in his caue burning before an image of our lady, and which he was wont to recomend to the Mother of God, to the end she would ftil keep it burning for her honour, fo often as at any tyme he went to any place thence in pilgrimage. And although he was fometymes from home. for the fpace of two, three, yea of fix moneths together, yet he alwayes found it at his return whole and cleerely burning as before he left it. Lykwife many great workes and liberal gifts of God are feen to proceed from him, in the duchie of *Brabant*, by the intercefsion of the glorious virgin his mother.

At *Laken* nere to the citie of *Bruxels* a faire Church hath bene built, to the honor of our Lady, wherin (as it is well knowne to the world) many haue receiued help and remedie from the hand of God. So as the woorthines of this place confirmeth fufficientlie the ancient tradition, that the firft model or paterne of thefaid Church was fet downe by our Lady herfelf and honored with her vifible prefence.

In the

In the Citie of *Bruxelles* in a Chappel of our Ladie cal'ed the Sablon an Image of her was there sette in the yeare of our Lord 1348. by a very deuout woman called *Betrice Soetkens*, the which Image is thought to haue bene painted by miracle, and in this place many miracles were wrought vntil the yeare 1580.

Antiqu. M.S. ex bibliot Rubreæ vallis.

In certaine old written bookes in the Collegial Church of *S. Peters in Louaine* are contained sundrie miracles which haue in times past hapned before an Image of our Lady which is yet there, and these haue continued since the yeare 1442. euen vnto our time.

In *Viluord*, in a Cloister called of côfort where the Religieuse women of the Carmelitan order dwel, is an Image of our ladie the which Dame *Sophia* wife to duke Henry the second of *Brabant* receaued from her mother *S. Elizabeth* Countesse of *Hessen*, which she lefte there for the comfort of certaine old Matrons that then lyued in a congregation in that place, wherupon it hath still retained that name.

It is not needful to recount here the miracles which our Lord woorketh day

G   lie by

lie by the inuocation of his blessed mother in the Church of our lady of *Hanf-
wick* at *Macklin*, *Alfemberg* and *Sichii* nere
Bruxelles, at *Lede* by the towne of *Aloſ*, at
Haſſelaire by *Audenard* in *Flaundres*, at the
Chappel of our ladie in the market place
of *S. Omers* in *Arthois*, at the Chappel of
our ladie of grace nere to the Citie of
Lile, And it is thought that there is no one
prouince in theſe low Countreis, which
hath not, or had not, ſome place dedicated to the Mother of God, wherin his
diuine bountie hath not wrought or yet
woorketh not ſometimes miracles, wher
of there are both particuler and publike
teſtifications in great number.

THE THIRD CHAPTER.

B Vt amongſt all, that is very wounderful which wee ſee and heare to
happen daylie at the place of *Mountaigue*
nere to the towne of *Sichē*, in the Duchie
of *Brabant*, beeing of ſuch importance &
admiratiō that through the fame therof
within the ſpace of ſix or ſeaue mōthes
many thouſandes of Pilgrims from all
partes haue reſorted thither. And to the
end

end that in a matter so latelie knowne &
in such abundance of miracles amongst
the bruite of so-many incertainties, the
truth may perfitly be seene, wee haue
resolued to make here a particuler and
faithful rehersall of such thinges as hitherto haue come to our knowlege,
aswel concerning the place & the Image
as of the miracles. Which haue hapned, according to the informations gathered by the authoritie of the right Reuerend lord the Archbishop of *Macklin,*
howbeit through the diuersities of times
and distance of places wherin the persons dwel vnto whome God hath imparted his fauours, it hath bene impossible
to come to the perfit knowlege of ech
thing that hath besalne them, which
notwithstanding wee hope may be discouered in time, & come to light, whereof as yet we haue no knowlege, partly
through the negligence or simplicitie of
such as haue experimented them in them
selues, & partly for that many are (perhaps) ashamed to publish their secret ac-
cidentes & maladies, although they haue
bene miraculously cured therof.

G 2   T H E

THE FOVRTH CHAPTER.

BVt before, wee proceed any fur-
thes it wil not be imperrinent (confidering in this affaire the g eat prouidēce
and goodnes of God) to examine a litle
the particuler circūstances of the place,
of the Image, & of other thinges apper-
taning to this matter. It is a thing much
to be noted, that seeing in many rich and
mightie Cities & other places of strength
in these low Countreis , there are many
statelie Churches dedicated to the glorious *Virgin Marie,* and that she hath in so
many places her Images in gold & siluer,
and painted or carued with great art and
woorkmanship, yet notwithstanding
our Lord God (who is the greatnes of the
humble) & our blessed Lady the mother
of humilitie, would make choise of this
rude and desert hillock, in the territorie
of *Sichen,* a very poor towne, amongst a
company of poor and ruyned people, at
a small Image made of a sillie peece of
wood of the height of a foot and a half or
litle more, painted & set foorth verie simply, placed in an old Oake, & that vpon
the

the frontiers of those that are enemyes &
rebelles to our Princes.

The which things seem to mee ful of
many misteries, And first that what
soeuer concerneth the place and Image, is
very base and abiect. What other thing
doth it signifie, then that which the Prophet *Dauid* saith, *That the high lord respecteth
the things that are humble?* And that which the
*Apostle saith, Our lord hath chosen the abiect
things of this world?* And that our Lord
Iesus Christ did meane that this place
which he had appointed for his owne &
his mothers honour should be like to
the places of their habitation in this
world, where he made choise of two very low places, to wit, the one, that of
Nazareth for his incarnation and aboad,
and the other that of *Bethlem* with the
poor cribbe, for his natiuitie. How poor
and miserable that quarter of *Sichen* hath
bene, with how many mishaps and calamities it was wholy ruined and brought
to desolation, will not be impertinent to
declare, for the comfort of those poor afflicted people the inhabitants therof.

The towne of *Sichen* before these troubles had a faire parish Church dedica-

G 3   ted

red to S. *Euflate*, wel furnifhed with diuerfe aitars , ornaments and goodly belles. Moreouer it had a Cloifter of Religioufe women of the order of S.*Auftin*, with their Church and faire buildings accordingly. And now this towne is fo ruined , that at this prefent there is not fomuch as one bell, The Church & fteeple are for the moft part vncouered, There are few altars , and verie fmall ftore of ornaments that haue bene faued out of the fire, The Cloifter is all burnt downe, fauing one Chappell,& one litle hows which before was built for the fick. Moreouer thefaid towne had about twelue or thirteene hundreth Burgefes, many of them were welthy and all of competent meanes and abilitie, where at this prefent it is hard to fynd 300. foules therin,or in the places which are dependant of thefame, and all thofe are fo needie and low brought that there is not one of them of that abilitie as to entertaine his friend with a decent lodging.

This towne here-to-fore had many faire houfes built with brick and now they are all made with mudde , & thatched with ftraw in forme of a village, which

which is no wounder yf you confider
what the towne hath fuftained during
thefe troubles and ciuil garboiles.

After the defait of *Gemblours* which
hapned in the yeare 1578. and the 28. of
February the Towne and caftle being well
manned with a ftrong garrifon was befieged by the fouldiers of the Catholike
king, and after battrie beeing entred by
force, the fouldiers of the garrifon, were
either put to the fwoord, or drowned, or
hanged, many of the Burgefes flaine, &
the towne giuen ouer to fire and pillage.
Not many yeares after, it was taken
againe, fometymes by the rebells, fometymes by the kinges people. It was fix
times fpoiled, and once confumed euen
to afhes. Befides all this it was grieuou-
flie afflicted with the plague & wholie
deuowred and eaten vp with the great
garrifons which lay thetin continually.
And not onlie the Citie, but the Countrey round about was brought to fuch
defolation by the ranging vp and downe
of fouldiers theeues and murderers, that
the Countrey, (for fome myles) is fo pe-
ftred with woods, hedges, and bufhes,
that it is not onlie not habitable, but alfo
                              trauailers

trauailers cā scarcelie fynd any way or
paſſage thereunto, in ſuch ſort as I am
perſwaded that there is no one place in
all theſe low Countreis which hath endured ſo many miſeries calam ties and
aduerſities as this place hath. And notwithſtanding that the people are ſimple
and ſtill hold the faſhion of the ancient
Brabanders, yet haue they alwaies continued in the obſeruances of the Catholike faith, ſo as euen during the ſway of
heretiks, there was not ſo much as one
found amongſt them that changed his
faith, whereby may be ſeene the great
mercy and loue of God towardes theſe
miſerable & afflicted people, the which
being brought vnder ſo many calamities
he vouchſafeth to comfort now againe
by demonſtration of his wounderful
woorks amongſt them.

THE FIFT CHAPTER.

WHat ſhould be the cauſe why
our Lord vouchſafeth to woork
miracles in ſuch a parte of the Countrey
of *Brabant*, we may imagine (vpon apparent reaſons) that he doeth it for two
causes,

causes, vpon apparent reasons I say wee may imagin (*for who is he that knoweth the mynd of our Lord, or who is he that hath bene his counseller*) first it hath bene the custome of his diuine prouidence when he chastiseth any people for their correctiõ and not for their destruction and vtter ruine, to send them at tymes some comfort by miraculous woorkes of his power and mercy. The people of *Israel* was afflicted by the seruitude of *Egypt*, by the stinging of serpents, by the inuasion of the *Madianits*, and by other like aduersities, but to the end they might think that God had not altogether forsaken them, he comforted them by transporting them ouer the redde sea, he cured them by the beholding of the brasen serpēt, by staying of the Sunne vnder *Iosue*, by couering the fleece with dew lying on a dry place in the tyme of *Gedeon*, and by many other miracles. The Countrey of *Italie* was afflicted by a cruel warre betwixt the *Guelphes* and the *Gibbelines*, but our Lord vouchsafing to shew that he would send them a speedie deliuerãce translated thither miraculouslie the hows of our Ladie of *Lauretta*.

Euen

Euen so wee verilie hope that by these fauours and miracles, the diuine bountie of God hath giuen vs to vnderstand that he being moued with pitie & compassion vpon these poor low Countreis, wil take away very soon the scourge of his ire and indignation, to the end that wee should not think our selues wholly by him abandoned through the throng of so many oppressions and miseries, and therefore he sendeth vs now these tokens and presages of some deliuerance neer at hand.

The other reason may be that those holy Saints which haue dwelt and bene borne in this Countrey, and specially in *Brabant* haue by their merits and prayers obtained this grace of God that this place which they whiles they liued had in their possession as their inheritance and patrimony wherin they were wont to serue his diuine maiestie, or vnto which they vsed to resort, being deliuered from the furie of heretikes should be one day honored with so great miracles.

For this territory was once the patrimony of the first Saints of *Brabant*. It is wel knowne that *S. Bauo* had in his possession

Molan.
Nat.SS.
Belg.

seſsion the greateſt part of the *Haſbaine* of *Brabant*. It is alſo certaine that *S. Pipin* first duke of *Brabant* had his aboad in the towne of *Landen* wherupon it beareth the ſurname; in the ſame place and with him liued his wife *Iduberga*, from whence proceeded that holy offspring *Gertrude* and *Begga*, and of this *Begga* the great *Charlemaine* with his iſſue is deſcended. In this ſaid quarter alſo dwelled being of the blood of the foreſaid *Pipin S. Amillerga* mother of the holie virgins *Raynildis*, *Pharaildis*, and *Gudula*, and long before all theſe, *S. Ermelinde* a virgin right famous for her ſanctitie. Likewiſe *S. Trudo* in his daies poſſeſſed many places in the *Haſbaine* and in the *Campignie*, where he had preached the holie ghoſpell, His mother *Adela* renowned for miracles reſteth in a place called *zelhem* neer to the towne of *Dieſt*, which place heretofore apperteined to her, and is but two miles diſtant from *Montaigue*. Add herunto that our Lord hath remēbrāce of the zeal & magnanimitie of the old dukes of *Brabant*, who a thouſand yeares agoe did ſo valiantlie maintaine and aduance the Chriſtian Catholike faith againſt the inſidels Pagans,

Ian. 4.
Feb. 21.
Mar. 17.
Iul. 10.
& 16.
Octo. 1.
& 29.
Noueb. 23.

Deceb. 17.

Molin. lib de ſac. milit Duc. Braban.

Pagans, and heretikes. And that it seemeth that the Countrey of *Brabant* shal-
erelong be whole restored and setled
againe in the Catholike faith, and in
that glorious state wherin once it florished.

THE SIXT CHAPTER.

THat these things are donne vpon
a Mountaine is not without reasõs,
in regard that man being borne into this
world to retire his mynd frõ earthlie to
heauenlie things, our Lord, both in the
old and new testament was allwayes
woont to doe his most speciall and principall woorkes vpon Mountaines. Vpon
the Mount *Moria* *Isaac* was saued, and
Abraham receaued the benediction. Vpõ
the mount *Sinay* the law was deliuered
vnto *Moyses*. Vpon the mount *Horeb* *Helias*
saw God almighty somuch as a mortall
man was euer able to see him, vpon a
Mountaine our Lord was wont to
preach, vpõ the Mout *Thabor* he was trãs-
figured, vpon the Mount *Oliuet* he prayed
and vpon the mount *Caluary* he was crucified, and accomplished our saluation.

More-

Moreouer the most famous places of the
world where the holie Mother of God
is honored, are wyld Mountaines and
ful of wood, very much resembling this
our Mountaine. They which haue written the historie of *Laureto*, affirme that the
little hovvs wherin the incarnation of
our Lord was first wrought and which
was had in honour in the towne of *Naza-*
reth, vntil the yeare of our Lord 1291.
(because *Siria* was conquered by the *Sar-*
racens) was taken from that place and
transported into *Europe* into the Countrey
of *Dalmatia*, and there sette vpon a litle
Mountaine or hil nere to the Towne of
Tersactum. And forsomuch as in that place
they did it not that honour which was
conuenient, it came so to passe that 4.
yeares and 7. monthes after, thesaid litle
hovvs was by Angels transported into
the marca of *Ancona* in *Italy*, and set vpon a
Mo ntaine or hil in a wood hard by the
Citie of *Recanato*, and a litle while after
that, because the pilgrims were hindred
to go freely thither (through the multitude of Theeues and Robbers which
made the passage dangerous) it was miraculouslie set vpon an other hil belonging to

ging to two breethern, who being fallen
at variance for the offrings which were
there made and our Lord being offended
with their controuersies and couetoufnes, made the sayd litle house to be placed
vpon an other litle Mountaigne not farre
from thence in the yeare of our Lord
1294. where our good God woorketh
(euen to this present day) continually
many miracles and graces, to the comfort & strengthning of all good Christians. What place is there in *Spaine* more
honorable and more renowned for miracles, then that Mountaine in the kingdome of *Catholonia* not farre from *Barce-
lona* called *Mount-ferrato*? because it seemeth to haue bene cut with a saw, and
fitted for the seruice of the blessed virgin
Marie, The which Moūtaine (according
to that which many credible persons
haue written) was in time past inacces-
sible through the wyndinges and troublesome passages which it hath had: and
not habitab'e for the rockes & craggie
stones which it contained, but at this
present, it is seemlie set foorth with 13.
hermitages & a goodly great Monastery
of *S. Benedicts* order, with many faire
                                        buil-

buildings, and a merueilous multitude
of Pilgrims. In which place since the
yeare 801. vntil the yeare. 1599.
there hath bene wrought 381. miracles,
wherof a great part are approoued and
confirmed by publique and authentical
testifications.

THE SEVENTH CHAPTER.

NEither seemeth it to want reason
that our Lord would haue his Mother to be honored by her Image placed
in an Oke, for the holie scriptures informe vs that our Lord God hath wrought
many miracles vnder diuers Okes: For
vnder the Oke of *Mambre* according to
the Hebrew text he cocluded his league
with *Abraham*, and there promised him a
sonne by his wife *Sara*. In thesame place
the Angels appeared in forme of me, di-
uerstymes renewing in the name of God
the foresaid promise, and foretelling the
destruction of the inhabitants of *Sodome*.
Vnder an Oke nere vnto *Siche Iacob* buried
the Idols. Vnder thesame Oke *Iosue* renewed the aliance betwene God & the
people of *Israel*, as before we haue declared. Vnder the Oke in *Ephra* the angel ap Iud.
                                    peared

peared to *Gedeon* whome he appointed
Captaine and leader of the people of *Israel*, promising to free the out of the feruitude, of the *Madianits*. Yea our Lord
Iesus chrift wrought our faluation vpon
the wood, of the croffe which (as Doctors affirme) was framed of Oke. The
Pagans were wont to call the Oke, great
and holy, and dedicated it vnto *Iupiter* their chief God, becaufe in the beginning of the world men made their
food of acornes, which is the fruit therof
and the Romaines had a cuftome to giue
him a crowue of Oken leaues that in
warre had faued the lyfe of a Citizen of
Rome. Of Okes the Poet writeth, prophe-
fying of the golden world out of the ver-
fes of the *Sibilles* faying.

The tyme wil come of peace and plentie fo,
That from the Oke the honie fweet fhal flow.

When therefore wee cöfider the forefaid examples of the old teftament why
fhould we not hope that nere vnto this
oke by *Sichen* through the prayers of holie
and deuowt people. God may be inclined
to make a nevy alliance and reconciliatiö
betvvixt himfelf and thefe lovv countreis, that he vvil fend the Angel of vvif-
dome

dome amongſt vs, bring the Idols of he-
reſie and impietie to nothing, raiſe vs vp
ſome valerous *Gedeons*, graunt vs victory
ouer theſe *Madianites*, ſend comfort to the
loyal ſubiects , ſtrengthen both our
ſoules and bodies, & powre downe vpô
vs the dew of his heauenly graces.

THE EIGHT CHAPTER.

THat our Lord hath choſē this place
ſo nere vnto our enemyes which
is ſcarſe ſix or ſeauen hundreth paces
diſtant from the riuer of *Demer*, beyond
which riuer all the Countrey is ſubiect
to the contributions robberies and exa-
ctions of the enemies, ſo as vpon a clear
day one may ſee ſix or ſeauen miles into
the countrie held by the heretiks & rebelles, wee may therby thinck that the
wiſdome of God hath ordained it, that
not only the Catholiks might haue occaſion to exerciſe their piety, and ſeek for
mercy at the handes of God but alſo that
he might bring back againe thoſe which
are in error into the boſome of the Catholik Church, by the meanes of theſe
miracles: for that ſo great miracles and
H   ſuch

such abundance should be wrought in a place so nere the hereriks noses, what other thing may wee iudge it, thē a plaine demonstration that the honnor doone to images, inuocation of Saints, and pilgrimages made to holy places, are things very pious and right acceptable to the maiestie of God: notwithstanding whatsoeuer blasphemies and scoffings, of all the rablement of hereriks to the cōtrary.

Blessed be therfore the father of mercy and God of comfort, which comforteth vs after this manner in all our tribulatiōs, who in the doleful estate of these Countreis, by the wonderful woorks of his mercy yeeldeth ioy and consolation to the godly, confirmeth those that either stagger or doubt in their faith, and confoundeth the malice of hereriks (God graunt it may be to their saluation) with a light of such vnspeakable brightnes. Blessed be also the Mother of mercy, which procureth such fauours for vs poor wretches. God graunt that her goodnes will so dispose of vs, that as at the arriuall of her hows from *Nazareth* to *Italy*, that Countrey (which was thē oppressed with a long and cruel warre) gained

gained peace and concord by her prayers
to our Lord, so likwise by this new deuotion of Catholiks at *Mountague*, the blessed
virgin and mother of God being moued
to compassion, by the prayers teares and
deuout sighes of good people, may obtein
at the handes of God, for these low
Countreis scourged with so long a ciuil
warre, and welnigh brought to vtter
ruine, that the Idols of our synnes may
be buried vnder this Oake: that the heretyks may be reduced to the vnion of the
holy Catholyke, Apostolyke, & Romaine
Church, & our rebelles to their due obedience of their natural princes, that wee
may all of vs with one mouth, and in the
same Catholike faith, vnder one Prince
in earth praise and honor our God, three
persons in *Trinitie* and one in vnitie, & the
blessed virgin *Mary* mother of our Lord
Iesus Christ.

THE NYNTH CHAPTER.

BVt to come to our history. In *Brabāt*
there is a place ful of hilles & woods
and altogether vnhabited called in the
Duitch tongue *Scherpen-heuuel*, in French

Mountaigue. in Englifh *The fharpe or rough hil,* in regard of the roughnes and barennes of the place, fituated by the towne of *Sichen,* and litle more then a quarter of a dutche mile diftant from thence , and a good mile from *Dieft.* Vpon this place (beeing a hil fomewhat higher then the reft of the ground lying nere therunto) grew an old Oke, which was fomewhat great, wherunto a certaine Image of our lady was faftened, and there is a certaine report and old tradition amongft thofe people which liue in that quarter, that a hundreth yeares and more fithéce, there was a certaine Shepherd who feeding his flock along that *Mountaigne* fownd the fore faid Image of our Lady lying on the grownd, the which he determined to cary home with him, but the Image miraculoufly became fo heauy that he was neither able to cary it, nor to lift it, yea himfelf became fo immoueable that he had no power to ftirre out of the place, in fuch forte as he could not driue his flok homeward.   The farmer his Maifter much woundring at his Shepherds vnaccuftomed lingring, went himfelf to feek him, And hauing vnderftood the caufe of his

of his ſtay, perceaued forthwith that the
Image which the Shepherd mēt to haue
caried home, was theſame Image which
men vſed to honor at the Oke of *Mountaigue*. Wherefore he took it and without
any empeſchment or reſiſtance placed it
againe in the Oke. And the Shepherd as
though he had bene vnlooſed and vnfet-
tered went his way home with his ſheep
without any further difficultie. By the
report of this miracle, the people that
neighboured thereabout being excited
to deuotion, began to yeeld reuerence to
the place and Image, & repaired thether
very often to craue help of the bleſſed
virgin, eſpecialy againſt agues. The
which things the moſt ancient inhabitants of the place haue auowched vnder
their ſolemne othes, that they haue hard
their parents and ancetors report : to
witte, *Arnould* of *Eeynde* beeing foure-
ſcore yeares of age, *Iohn Swinnen* beeing
of 70. *Iohn Membors* of 60. and *Allard* of
Bogard alſo of 60. yeares of age, all beeing
inhabitants and Eſcheuins of *Sichen*. But
foraſmuch as wee haue this only by traditiō of certaine old people without any
further authentical proof (although wel

deſeruing credit heerin) wee meane not
ſo to affirme their reports as altogether
aſſured therof. But wil proceed to ſuch
other things, wherof wee can aleage ſo
authentical and aſſured proofs, as none
can iuſtly doubt therof.

THE TENTH CHAPTER.

IT is certaine and wel knowne that
the foreſaid Image remayned in the
Oke vntil the yeare 1580, but ſhortlie
after and till the yeare 1587. was no

Ioſſe vā
Arttic
vvho
yet li-
ueth
hath af-
firmed
vnder
his othe
that he
vvas
healed
of a lõg
quar-
tain agu
in the
yeare
1583.

Image at all in that place, as wee ſynd by
information of ſundry perſons who in
that tyme (to be cured of their agues)
although with euidēt danger viſited that
place, many being reſtored to health notwithſtanding (as is aforeſaid) no Image
was then there, wherby it may appeare
that not only the Image, but alſo the very
place is dedicated to the ſeruice of God,
and to the honor of his bleſſed Mother.
How this firſt Image was loſt wee yet
know no certainty, but it is coniectured
that it was deſtroyed by heretikes who
from the yeare 1578 vntil the yeare
1586. ranged daylie in thoſe partes pil-
ling

ling and spoyling the Countrey.

Afterwards in the yeare 1587. a good old man beeing a Burgeſſe & Eſcheuin of *Sichen* (of humilitie not willing to be named) conſidering the great concourſe and deuotion which people had to this place, and knowing that the firſt Image was loſt, went vnto a deuout and godly widow dwelling in *Dieſt*, called *Agnes Fredericks* hauing the cuſtody of the Church of *Allhallowes* in the ſuburbes of theſaid towne of *Dieſt* who had in her hows an Image of our lady made of wood, placed in a litle frame or tabernacle, which vpō erneſt entreaty ſhe giuing vnto him, he caried to *Mountague*, and cauſed it to be ſette vp in the foreſaid Oke, in the place of the other which was loſt; where it continued vntill lent in the yeare 1602. at which tyme Sir *Godfrey of Thienx* incle Paſtor of the Church of S. *Euſtace* in *Sichē*, took theſaid Image out of the Oke, and ſet it in a litle Chappel made of wood of ſix foot long and fyue broad, hard by the ſaid Oke. And theſame he did in regard of the great deuotion which he ſaw the people had that came thether to be cured of a vehement head-ache then

H 4   raigning,

raigning in thofe parts wherof very many found amendment. In which litle
Chappel the faid Image remayned vntil
fuch tyme as it was placed in the new
Chappel which now is built of ftone.

THE ELEVENTH CHAPTER.

LEt vs now therefore fpeak of the
miraculous and liberal cures which
our lord hath vouchfafed to woork vpon
thofe that haue honoured his bleffed
mother in this place.

From tyme out of mynd the people &
inhabitants of *Sichen* & places therabout,
were wont to fynd finguler help by our
Lady at *Mountague* fo often as they found
themfelues attainted of any agues.

Of which thing *Sir Godfrey* of *Thien-
vvincle* Curat of S. *Euftace* in *Sichen*, doth
fufficiently teftify: who remēbreth that
(fifty yeares paft) he being then about fix
yeares old, was caried by his parents to
Moūtague, where he was cured of an ague
which he had at that time,

Alfo at fuch tyme as the Spanifh fouldiers were in mutiny in the towne of
Dieft and that theyr Captains remayned
in the

in the towne of *Sichen* attending whyles the layd fouldiors were payd, there was a certaine Spanifh Captaine lodged in a Burgeife hows who was fick of an ague for the fpace of a whole yeare, and by reafon of his ficknes was fo wayward & troublefome as none could content him. It came to paffe that the good wife of the hows told him that if he defired to be freed of his ague, it were good he fhould vifit our lady at *Mountague*, feeing fo many were there cured : wherupon moued partly by her and partly by perfuafion of his owne feruants, he went thither, & accomplifhing there his deuotion, was there cured, and wholy deliuered of his ague, behauing himfelf afterwards fo modeftly and peaceably as he feemed to haue altered his nature.

Moreouer as the whole towne of *Sichen* can teftifie, there is fcarce therein one houfhold wherof fome one or other hath not receaued help at *Mountague*. The Curate and efcheuins of *Sichen* affirme affuredly that in the yere 1598 at what time the Irifh of the regiment of *Sir VVil-iam Stanley Coronel*, were lodged there, many of the were wont to vfe no other

phifik

phisik or remedy for their diseases, but to make their prayers at the foresaid place of *Mountague*, amongst whome very many were healed, in such sorte that *Father VValter Talbot* an Irish priest, one of the *societie of Iesus* (who at that tyme was their preacher and ghostlie father) was wont oftentimes to say with great admiratiō that this place was in very singuler manner chosen by God to aduance there his Mothers honour, for which cause he was moued to go thither sometymes deuoutly in procession, accōpained with thesaid Irish and the townesmen of *Sichen*. Wherof he wrote to Father *Thomas Salius*, who was the Superior of the fathers of the societie, which attended vpō the Catholik kings army in the low Countries. Many also affirme that the like cures haue hapned to diuers souldiers of other nations, which came thether in pilgrimage, both of the garrison of *Dieft* and *Sichen*. And some are of opiniō, that the bruite and fame of *Moūtague* was principally diuulged by thesame souldiers, in other Cities and places vnto which they repaired.

THE

THE TVVELFTH CHAPTER.

THe which bruite by Gods difpofition, in fhort tyme grew to be fo
grear, that it moued an infinit number of
people which haue flocked thither vpon
deuotion from all partes, wherof many
haue bene holpen and conforted, as may
appeare by fo many crutches, ftaues,
bands and other things (which the fick
perfons vfed in their maladies) left and
hanged about the Chappel, For in the
beginning of the month of *October* in the
yeare 1603. there were reckned vp, to
the number of 135. Crutches and legges
of wood, of fuch as were lame, and they
were brought thether within the fpace
of 4. or 5. monthes, without numbring
the bands and truffes of fuch as were
broken, and the fhooes which vvere vnderlayd belonging to fuch as limped,
vvherof the number vvould haue bene at
this prefent double, if (through the negligence of thofe vvho ferued the place)
they had not bene caryed avvay by other
pilgrims & paffengers. All vvhich things
vvere vndoubtedly left there by them
vvho

who receaued either cure or notable eafe
of their maladies. And to the end we
may fpeak a woord touching the number
of pilgrims, it is knowne by the relation
of diuers credible perfons, how that vpō
the eight of *Septēber* in the forefaid yeare
1603. being the feaſt of the *Natiuitie of
our Lady*, there were about twentie thowfand pilgrims, and vpon other dayes there
haue come thether many thowfands, &
daylie yet cometh thether a great nūber
from all Countreys and quarters, & they
not only of the common forte, but alfo
diuers Princes, Earles, Lordes, Gentlemen and Ladies, the reherfall of whofe
names would here be too tedious.

The XIII. Chapter.

THe fame is alfo confirmed by the offrings, in Siluer, Coyne, Candles,
Imazes of filuer, and of other matter reprefenting the limmes and perfons of
thofe who there haue either found cure
or eafe. The precious beades and other
guifts in filuer, and very rich veſtures for
the Image of our lady, wherof the nūber
is very great. And it will not be from the
purpofe

purpose to specifie and name some of thē:
First the Magistrates of the Citie of *Bru-*
xelles (wherin at that time the plague was
very hotte) sent in the month of *Septēber*
1603. to the honour of our lady of *Mount-*
ague a faire crowne of siluer guilt, with
this inscription in latin: *Regina Cælorum*
SS. Dei Matri B. Virgini Mariæ, Bruxella mor-
bo afflicta supplex obtulit. Anno 1603. Which
is as much to say. *The Citie of Bruxelles being*
afflicted with the pestilent disease, in hūble mãner
offieth this Crowne to the Queen of heauen, to
the most holy Mother of God, the blessed virgin
Marie: in the yeare 1603. And very many
of good credit did note, that after that
tyme the contagious disease that had raig
ned all that summer began to decrease &
by litle and litle to be aswaged.

The Magistrates and people of *Antwerp*
(who haue of old bene much obliged &
affectioned to our ladie their patronesse)
made a present vnto her at *Mountague* the
eight of *December* 1603. being the feast of
her conception, of two siluer candlesticks
very cunningly wrought with these ver-
ses and inscription.

Suscipe Sancta Parēs ex voto Antwerpia munus:
  Quod dat, ne pestis crescat acerba lues.

                                    I must

I muſt not forget the moſt honorable & deuout Princeſſe Dame *Dorothe* of *Loraine*, widow to the Duke of *Brunſwick*, who vpõ the eight of *October* in the yeare aforeſaid 1603. offred at theſayd place vnto our Lady, a faire ornament to hang before the Altar, recommending vnto our bleſſed Lady her iourney, which ſhe took out of theſe low *Countreis* into *Loraine*.

The noble lady *Dame Eleonor Henriq: ez de Guzman*, widow to the Earle of *Vſeda*, Chief Chãberlaine of the moſt gracious Infant of *Spayn*, the lady *Iſabella Ducheſſe of Brabant*, preſented there a faire gilt cuppe.

Omitting to make métion of a goodly foundation made to the Chappel of our Lady, by a principal perſon of the court, who deſired his name ſhould be conce-aled: and of many other guifts & offrings made there by diuers others, whoſe reward is like to be great before God.

THE FOVRTENTH CHAPTER.

OVr moſt gracious and deuout Prin-ces *Albertus* and *Iſabella* are not to be omitted:

omitted: for first the *Archduke Albertus* returning frō raising the siege of *Boisleduke*, which was beleagred by the rebels of *Holland*, and going to *Bruxelles* came to *Mountague*, on the tenth of *Nouember* 1603, where he gaue thankes to our lord for his victorie, and there did honour to his holy Moother, and some few dayes after, he went thither another time from the said Citie of *Bruxelles*, together with the Duchesse his wife, and all his Court, & very many lords and gentlemē: where beeing arriued vpon the twentith of the-said month of *Nouember*, the said Archduke & Duchesse, as right deuout Princes, with all the lords and ladies of their trayn, made their prayers vpon their knees for a long space, aswel for their owne as for their countreis welfare: and from thēce they went to lodge in the towne of *Diest*, which is distant a duitche mile & a half from that place. And after they had made their preparation by fasting and confession, to receaue the sacred communion, returned the next day (which was the feast of the presentation of our Lady) to *Mountague* on foot, and all their trayn, and there deuoutly hard three masses, at the

first

4. english myle & a half.

first wherof the Princes only did communicate, at the second all the ladies of estate & gentlewomen of honour to the Princesse, and at the third all the rest of the Court. And to the end their prayers might be of more force the Princes added a good almes therunto. The most gracious *Infanta Isabella* three daies immediatly one after another, at euentyde offred a most precious roabe, imbrodred with gold and siluer and most precious stones, the which roabes for the most part were wrought with her own hands. And besids this, the most gracious *Archduk Albertus* caused a notable almes to be giuen ouer and besides that which he had offred at his returne from *Boisleduke*. And vpon the fourth day the sayd Princes returned to *Bruxelles*, where they surceased not to haue care of the good ordering & adorning of the foresaid place of *Mountague*. And amõgst other the Archduke of his owne inuentiõ ordayned a very faire forme and maner to plant there certaine orders of trees in proportion, amongst which there should be built fourteene litle Chappelles or stations, to represent the ioyes and sorrowes of the holy mother

An exãpie of a deuout court.

ther of God: and this to be contriued in
such order and fashion that all the hil
should seeme to appeare in forme of a
starre, which signifieth the name of the
virgin *Mary*. And moreouer it is to be prouided of a hedge and ditch round about
that it may be *Hortus conclusus, a Garden roūd
enuironned*: a name which the holy scripture affordeth to our Lady. And besids all
this our sayd Princes haue made there an
oblation of a meruelous sumptuous ornament, together with a Chesuble and
Copes for the Deacon & Subdeacon to
celebrate diuine seruice therein.

THE XV. CHAPTER.

BVt to come to the miracles: let vs begin with the entrance of the yeare
1603. and some moneths before; after
which tyme especially about *Easter* the
principal of them hapned. And we wil
set them down according to euery moneth, so far foorth as they came to our
knowlege, adding vnto thē those which
afterwards insued, as also those wherof we haue gotten information since
the first publishing of this historie: pla-
I   cing

cing euery one in their due order, according to the tymes in which they came to
pas: to the end that our Lord (who
vouchfafed to worke thefe things by the
intercefsiō of his Mother) might receiue
the honor and glory which vnto him is
due, and that all Chriftians as wel thofe
which are mifguided and in error, as
others might confider and touche with
their fingers, where the light of truth
hath her abode, and where is the true
fheep fold, wherein they may expect and
hope to obtaine their euerlafting faluation.

Of a blynd woeman which was cured.

About
the
month
of May
or Iune
1602.

PEtronel Riders wyfe to Lambert Bauduin fometyme foldier, and launcier vnder the Lord of Grobbendonck in the Country of Brabant, in the yeare 1602. being at Dieft had a great defluction of humors, which fel vpon her eyes, and a great and vehement grief infued thereupō as if her eyes had ben gnawne with fome vermin: which increaced fo much that fhe vtterly loft her fight: notwithftanding

standing that many medicines were applyed vnto her both by the aduise of surgeons, as others, of which she receiued
no help at all: in such sorte that she could
not see or decerne any thing in the world
which continued more then eight or ten
dayes. At which tyme a certaine woman
seeing her in this plight, aduised her to
goe vnto our Ladie at *Montaigu* where
many had ben cured of their agues, hoping that there she should fynd some
help for her disease. Moreouer she coun-
selled her to wash her eyes with the
water which is behynd the Chappel of
the foresayd *Montaigu*. Whereupon the
sayd Petronel resolued to goe thither in
pilgrimage, and hauing sought out a woman in *Diest* to leade her, shee walked
(stark blynd) towards the said *Montaigu*
about the Moneth of May or Iune, in the
sayd yeare 1602: but assoone as shee
began to goe vp the hil towards the
chappel, she felt the accustomed griefs
of her eyes to be much asswaged, & with
all her self to be much inwardly comforted. Which alteration after shee had
perceiued, shee would needes trye whether shee had recouered any thing of

her

her fight or no, fo that with her fingers
lifting vp her eyelids, fhee perceiued that
fhee began to fee (as it were through an
obfcure mift) the graffe and bufhes of the
Mountayne, and a little afterwards fet-
ting fomewhat forwards, fhee perfectly
fawe the little chappel of wood where
the Image of our Ladie was placed, and
hereupon fhee fpake to the woman
which led her, and thancking her for
her paynes told her that fhee needed her
help no longer, for that fhee had nowe
recouered her fight: and fo the fayd
Petronel went alone without any other
ayd towards the forefayd water, where
hauing wafht her eyes, fhee fel to her
deuotions in the Chappel of our Ladye,
rendring thancks to God and her, for
this worck of mercie: and fo returning
whole and merrie to her hows at *Dieft*
hath euer fince inioyed perfectly her
fight, and hath been free from al her former paynes, and yet fo remayneth to this
prefent day, as it appeared vpon the fix
and twentith of Iune in the yeare 1604.
when in the citye of *Bruxelles* before the
Magiftrates there by folemn othe fhee
affirmed all that hath been fayd, conformable

mable to an act framed thereof subsigned P. *Numan* Secretaire, & sealed with the seale of the sayd Citie.

How blood was found, vpon the lips of the Image of our Ladie.

VPon the third of Ianuary in the yeare 1603. diuers Magistrates and other persons were met together at *Sichen* from the next villages about some affaires appertayning to that quarter. Amongst others *Mattew Oudenrogge* Escheuin of *Bekeuort*, *VValter Vnkelen* Escheuin of *VVanrode*, *Henry Reymakers* Escheuin of *VVerslecke*, *Barthelmew Schellens*, & *Laurens of Canien* were there preset. Who after they had ended all their busines at *Sichen*, returning homeward, and passing by *Montaigu*, they did their deuotions in the Chappel of our Ladie ; and whilst they were in prayer, the sayd *VValter Vnkelen* espyed a drop of blood vpon the lip of the image of our Ladie, whereupon drawing neere to the image, he wyped of the drop with his finger, & he found that it was perfect blood, and incontinently an other like drop returned, the

I 3   which

The third of Ianuary 1603.

which was wyped away by *Mathew Ou-denrogge*: and as an other the third tyme appeared, it was wyped of by *Henry Rey-makers*: and the foresayd *VValter Vnk.len* seeing the fourth drop of blood to ap-peare vpō the lip, tooke a cloth or hand-kerchief, and dryed it, and found a marck of very blood in the same, euen such as might issue out of the body of a lining man: whereupon they were meruelous-ly astonished: and the next morning this *VValter* looking vpon his hand-ker-chief, found the sayd drop to haue spred it self as large as an Inglish groate, and somewhat bleaker of colour then it was the day before. These aforenamed per-sons whyle yet they were in the Chap-pell, looked diligently on euery syde, to see whether the Image might re-ceiue any moisture through the roofe, but they found no signe at all of any such thing: for it was a very faire and cleere Sunne-shyny day, and there was neuer any paynting or colour layd on the pi-cture so farr as any mā could remember. And all this which hath ben sayd, was auerred by the foresayd persons, vnder their solē othes before the Magistrates

of

of the town of *Suken*, in the presence of
many witnesses, as appeareth by a wryting made hereof, and subsigned *L. van
Ogernen*, and sealed with the sea'e of the
sayd town: and it is very certaine, that in
the first three monethes of this accident, to witt, in the holy weeke before
Easter, the sayd picture by reason of the
oldnes thereof, by the appointmēt of the
Curate and Church-wardes was newly
painted.

How a lame mayde was healed.

MArie *Lenkens* daughter of *Francis* ⟨In April 1603.⟩
Lenkens & *Catharin Vermosen* beeing
ten yeares of age, had an accident that
hapned her in her right leg, in the yeare
1599, in such sorte that the sayd leg was
shrunck vp and became three fingers
shorter then the other, and withal smal-
ler and slenderer, in which sorte shee cōtinued for three yeares space together, although with great anguish and payne,
and the third yeare she was not able to
goe therewith in any sorte, whereupon
her mother resolued toe go with her in

I 4   pilgri-

pilgrimage to our ladie of *Montaigu* : the which she did vpon the feast of the Annunciation of the virgin *Marie*, in the sayd yeare 1603 , putting her daughter on horsback, and being come to the riuer of *Demere*, neere to a place called *Tysselt*, where by hors they were notable to passe they sent the sayd hors back again, & they both walked together on foot towards *Montaigu*, the poore lame mayden halting downright, and often falling to the ground, before they could arriue at the Chappel of our Ladie : Where being come exceedingly weerie, they did their deuotions: which being ended, the mayd recouered so much strength, that she returned home with her mother on foote, without any molestation payne or wearines neither at that present tyme , or euer after : and since that tyme her leg by little & little grew of æquall bignes & length with the other , in such forte that she now walketh without any difficultie , wheresoeuer she pleaseth, as wel as any other. Al which hath ben affirmed by her mother vnder her solemn othe before the Magistrates of the town of *Arschot*: and *Marie vander Nuit* widowe of
Christian

Christian vanden Vinne dwelling in *Arschot*, who accompanied them in their pilgrimage, together with *Henry Godfrey Michiels*, who was neighbour vnto the sayd mayd, did in lyk sorte vnder their othes auouch before the sayd Magistrates, that they had seen and known the foresayd mayde lame and impotent, and afterwards to haue ben miraculously cured, as hath ben sayd: all which appeareth by an act made thereof by the sayd Magistrates, bearing date the xxix th. of March in the yeare 1604, subsigned P. *Aelbrechts*, and sealed with the seale of the town of *Arschot*.

How a man sick of the palsey was healed.

PEter of *Honsberg* Escheuin of *Merbout* in the *Campignie*, being of the age of one and fiftie yeares, fel suddainely into a great disease, in the end of the Month of Ianuarie 1606, the which continuing for ten or twelue dayes space, thereupon ensued so great a palsey, that he was depriued of the vse of his armes and legs, & of all his other mebers, his head eyes and tongue onely excepted, which he

was

In April, 1603.

was able to moue. And befydes this, he had a grief that was fo vehement & continual, that he could neither fleepe or reft day or night: in fuch forte that from Palmefunday till eight dayes after Eafter he was faine to haue euery night at leaft two, fometymes three or fower of his familie to watch with him, and to adminifter vnto him his necefsities, fometymes to carie him to the fier, and prefently back to his bed again. Who albeit he had vfed the counfel and receiptes of fome Phyfitions for his recure, yet felt he no eafe at all, but rather increafe of his grief which made him wholy to giue them ouer. And whereas certain of the inhabitants of *Merhout* had related vnto him that by the inuocation of Gods Mother many miracles were wrought at *Mōtaigu* neer to *Dieft*, he entring into a feruent & zelous refolution, to take her for his refuge, and to goe in pilgrimage to that place: & withall to *Boxtele* in the *Campignie*, where the miraculous blood of the holy Sacrament of the altar is referued; in the mean whyle with many teares & grones calling vpon the glorious virgin Mary, and with great defire expecting

the

the feaſt of the Annunciation of our Ladie, (which was very neere, & was that
yeere tranſlated til after the octaues of
Eaſter, for that it fell in the holy week;)
& ſo much the more becauſe he had vnderſtood that diuers of his neighbours
were reſolued that day to go in pilgrimage to *Montaigu*, which day of the An-
nunciatiō when it came , he cauſed himſelf to be caryed in a waggon to the foreſaid mountaine, cōtinually afflicted with
the palſey & impotēcie of all his limmes:
ſaue onely that ſome two or three dayes
before his departure , and whylſt his
ſeruants made readie thoſe things which
were neceſſarie for his voyage , he began
a little to moue his fingers. Beeing therefore the ſame day arriued at *Montaigu*, he
found ſuch a thrōg of people , that he
could not in any wyſe come neere vnto
the Chappel. For which cauſe, to ſatiſfie
his deuotiō, they brought him the image
of our ladie to the waggo where he lay,
the which with much reuerence he kiſ-
ſed: and after the preſſe of the people
was paſt, his wyfe with one of his ſeruants and two others caried him three
tymes about the ſayd Chappel : and no
                              ſooner

sooner was he put again into the waggon, but he felt in himself a great change
and eafe: in fuch forte that he thought
himfelf wholy cured: but trying to moue
himfelf, he found that he was as yet impotent & without the vfe of his limmes.
Notwithftading beeing returned home,
he felt that his palfey by little & little
from that day forward begã to decreace:
& euery day after he foũd himfelf better,
in fo much that in fhort tyme he recouered fo gɾeɑt force & health, that he coɩld
permit himfelf to be led through his
hows: and a little whyle after he walked
without any help of his crutches, which
alfo with in few daies he layd afyde, walking onely with a ftaf in his hand, & not
long after without either ftaf or any
other help at all: in fuch forte that this
Honfberge being reftored to perfect health
and ftrength, & vfe of his limmes, fayled
not to render thancks to God, & his holy
Mother: and vpon the eigth of the moneth of Septẽber next following beeing
the day of the Natiuitie of the glorious
Virgin, he departed from his hows on
horfeback, to offer vnto our Lady one of
his Crutches wherewith he was wont
to fup-

to support himself: and from the town of
Si.hen he went on foot to the Chappel
of *Montaigu*, where he did his deuotion,
& gaue God thancks for the mercie
which he receiued as hath been sayd. And
since that tyme he hath continued wel
disposed & healthie, as he is at this present And this that hath ben here sayd, is
set down in the Register of the sayd Chap
pel vpon the eigth day of *Septembre* 1603.
And as by the sayd *Honsberg* it was againe
declared (being sumoned thereunto) vnder his solemn othe before the court and
Magistrates of *Merhout*, vpon the seuenth
of *March* in the yeare 1604. Vpon which
day *VVillebrord Bosmans, Adrian Verhellen* &
Iohn Suinne Escheuines of the same place,
declared and auouched, that they had
diuers tymes seē & visited this *Honsberg*
whyle he was sick, and that they found
him altogether taken with the palsey and
impotent & depriued of the vse of his
limmes. Al which is conformable to that
which the magistrate hath set down,
dated as before, and subsigned *Iohn Trudo-
nius* Secretarie: & sealed with their seale.

A cure

A cure of one that was blynd and taken
With the Apoplexie.

In May
1603.

ANne *Vereyken* the wyfe of *Hubert VVellens* dwelling in the village of *Teſtelt,* not farr from the town of *Sichen* was in the moneth of *Februarie* in the yeare 1603. taken with the *Apoplexie,* and therewith alſo loſt her ſight in ſo much that her huſband was forced to carry or lead her to euerie place , whether ſhe would goe. And although many medicines were applied to cure her diſeaſe, yet ſhe foude no help or cure at all: wherfore ſhee took her refuge towards our Ladie, & made a promis to goe and viſit her at *Montaigu,* the which when ſhe had accompliſhed in the moneth of *May* next following, ſhe recouered her ſight and the intier health of al her bodie , and went vp and down whereſoeuer it pleaſed her, & alwayes afterward remained in good ſtate as ſhe is at this preſent. All this here related, was according to order of law declared both by her ſelf and her huſband before the Magiſtrates of *Sichē,*

as wel

as wel vpon the eleuenth of *May* in the
foresaid yeare 1603, as also vpon the one
and twentieth of *April* 1604. According to
a wryting framed hereof & signed *L. van
Ogernen* Secretarie, & sealed with the
towne seale.

The punishement of one that scoffed at the Pilgrimage of Mountagu.

A Certain townesman of *Diest* (whose
name for certaine causes we do not *In May*
set downe) began to mock at such as 1603.
went in Pilgrimage to *Mont'aigu*, and a
little after was stricke in his body, in such
sorte that he became lame, & altogether
depriued of the vse of his limmes, & sustained
such vehemet tormétes, that he was
constrained to keep his bed: & although
he had procured certaire medicines and
remedies to be ministred vnto him, yet
could he not be holpé. Wherefore at last
resoluing with himself to goe and visit
our Lady at *Montaigu*: & hauing obtained
some strength after this his resolutió, he
walked thither by little & little on foot:
and so soone as he had perfourmed his
pilgri-

pilgrimage, he recouered & was wholy cured, as it appeareth by the information hereof taken in the town of *Dieſt*, by certaine commiſſioners that were ſent thither by the Right Reuerend the Lord Archbiſhop of Maclin.

How a Chyld that was in a conſumption and blynd was healed.

In May 2603.

I Oane Maes the widdow of *Lewis Caſtele* dwelling in the town of *Dieſt*, had a chyld of one year old or thereabout: who was taken with a great maladie, which kept him in his bed more thē three whole moneths continually, wherby he was brought ſo low, that he had nothing left but ſkin and bones: he had moreouer a ſwelling in his throte, which by diuers ſurgeons was iudged to be ſome vaine that was broken, by others, that it was ſome euill matter or humour which was deſcended thither. And beſydes theſe he had an accident in his eye, the which being ſhewed to the ſurgeons, they were of opinion that the eye was broken out, and that the peece of the ſight was corrupted,

rupted, as in very deed the chyld could see nothing therewith; and they were perfuaded that he fhould neuer fee with it fo long as he liued: the which chyld was come to thofe termes, that his mother expected no other thing of him but that he fhould fhortly dy. Nowithftanding putting her côfidence in the mercie of God, and in the afsiftance of his moft facred Mother, fhe refolued to go with her Chyld, & to vifit our Lady at *Môtaigu* on three feueral Frydayes: and notwith ftanding that the mother was alfo fick, yet fhe accomplifhed her Pilgrimage in the beginning of the fômer, in the yeare 1603. And the firft day that fhe was at the Chappel, fhe layd her chyld vpô the altar, fo long as fhe made her prayer: which being ended, & returning home-ward, the chyld fel fweetly a fleep in her armes, and fo continued til fhe came to *Dieft*: and in this forte perfifting in her deuotions the two next frydayes following, the chyld was made whole and found, and by little and little reco-uered the perfect health both of his bodie and of his eie; with which he now feeth very cleerely, and remaineth in

very good plight. All this thofe of th
Court of *Dieſt* haue witneſſed, after the
hearing & examination of the a forefayd
Ioane, conformable to a writing that was
drawn thereof, bearing date the xx^th of
March 1604. ſubſigned I. *vanden Goeden-*
huiſe, and ſealed with the ſeale of thefayd
town,

One cured of the Iaunders and Squinancie.

THe Ladie *Francis de Mombeck*, Abbeſſe
of the Cloiſter of *Hoght* neere to the
citie of *Maeſtright* in the Dutchie of *Brabāt*
in the beginning of May, 1603, was attain
ted with the Iaunders, whereof ſhe became ſo ſick, that hauing had the aduiſe
of a certain Phiſitiō which dwelled at *Liē*
ge he was in diſpaire of her lyfe as he plain
ly affirmed to Dame *Catharin Cortilz*,
Religiouſe of theſayd Conuent, yet he
ſent the ſayd ladie Abbeſſe ſome herbes
with a certain drink, but it profited her
nothing and as her diſeaſe daylie increaſed, ſo that ſhe had little hope by any
way of Phyſick, ſhe committed her ſelf
vnto God almightie, and to the help of
the

the glorious *Virgin Marie*, promifing by
vow vnto God and her, a pilgrimage &
an almeſſe vnto the chappel of our Ladie
at *Montaigu*, and two or three dayes after
ſhe ſent thither her mayd *Oda Tymmer-
mãs*, the which was don vpon the xxviiir-
of *May* in the foreſayd yeare 1603. who
hauing ended her deuotion ſhe brought
her Ladie a piece of the Oke wherein the
bleſſed Virgins Image was ſet; the which
theſayd ladie Abbeſſe receiuing with all
reuerence and deuotion, cauſed it to be
applyed to euery thing that either ſhe did
eat or drinck: trufting in God, & hoping
through the interceſſion of his holy mother that ſhe ſhould fynd remedie therby, and from that day ſhe began to améd
and to recouer perfectly her health, without any humaine help: in ſomuch that a
little whyle after ſhe was made whole &
ſound. Afterwards there hapned vnto her
a great ſoreries and paine in her throate,
which Phyſitiõs call the *Squinancie*, wherby ſhe was brought again into manifeſt
peril of death, as the ſurgeon openly declared whome they had ſent for to help
her. Her tongue and throte were ſo inflamed, that they ſeemed altogether
K 2 black:

black: and although, they opened a vaine in her tongue, three or fowr tymes together, yet it helped nothing, for not one drop of blood would come foorth, which when the-sayd Ladie Abbesse had perceiued, & vnderstanding the danger wherein she was, she vowed an other pilgrimage to our Ladie of *Montaigu*, & sent thither again the foresayd *Oda*, and *VVindel Corenborst* her seruãts, who hauing ended their deuotions vpon the xxvj. of Iune 1603. the-sayd Ladie Abbesse recouered afterwards, and within fewe dayes returned to her perfect health. As it wel appeareth by her attestatiõ signed with her own hand, and sealed with her seale.

Of a lame and impotent man healed.

In May
1603. BErträd *de Loyarbre* locksmith dwelling at *Huy* in the cuntrie of *Liege*, was, (some three yeares past) attached with a vehement paine in his reynes, and about his hart, in such sorte that he could not follow his occupatiõ except very seldom and that fayre & softly : the which paine
continued

continued very long, and at one tyme for the space of six whole monethes: wherby he was brought so low, that he was constrained to keep his bed, from *October* 1602, vntil Easter eue 1603. and then (although he was very sick) he endeuoured to ryse, but he found his left beg (by the long and continual paines thereof) to be much shrunck vp, & by a good foot to haue become shorter then the other, whereby he was forced to take two crutches, and with them he walked in great paine and feeblenes. So it came to passe, that on the day of *S. Peter* and *S. Paul*, beeing the xxix. of *Iune*, in the foresaid yeare 1603. he hard some relate the miracles of our Ladie of *Montaigu*: wherby he was so moued, that he purposed with a great and feruent desyre to go thether on foot with his crutches, & alone without the assistance of any other: which he did, walking on verie slowly, although not without great grief and labour of his body: in such sorte, that within fowr dayes and an half he came to the Chapel at *Motaigu*, which for all this was not past ten myles distant from *Huy*: hauing his hands and fingers much swolne, and the

skinne worne of by the continual handling of his crutches, vvith had alfo much
opened or ftrained his arme pittes. And
beeing novv come before the Chappel,
he made there deuoutly his prayers vnto
God and his glorious Mother, which
beeing eded, he rayfed vp himfelf faire &
foftly without his crutches, and began to
vvalk praying about the Chappel, although not vvithout great paine: but at
the fecod tyme he felt a certain foudaine
puffe of vvynd, to come down as it vvere
from heauen vpon him, in fomuch as he
feared he fhould haue been throvvn
dovvne to the earthe, by vvhich vvynd
he felt a kynd of motion and fvveet heat
to enter in to his bodie, vvhereby he
thought his interiour partes vvere vvar-
med & vvholy altered : and fo going the
third tyme about, he foud himfelf intierly cured; and that his left leg (vvhich before vvas a foot fhorter then the right)
vvas novv made longer and æqual vvith
the other, and that he could vvel vfe it :
yea, he found it ftonger then his leg that
before vvas vvhole: vvherevvith beeing
much coforted, hauing redred thackes to
God, &his holy Mother, who had prayed
                                        for

for him, he left there his crutches, and
walked homeward to *Huy* on foot without them. And in *August* next following,
and an other tyme after that, he came on
foot to *Montaigu*, in memorie & gratitude
of the fauour he had there receiued: & thē
he was much eafed of the paine he felt
about his hart, which he had very long
indured. All this which here hath beē fet
down, this *Bertrād* declared at *Mōtaigu*, before *M. Iames de Caftro*, doctor of diuinitie
& *Deane of the Chriftiantie* of *Dieft, Sir Gōd-
frey Thiē winckle* Curate of *Sichen*, Maifter
Ioachim de Bufchere Secretarie of the Coūcil
of *Brabant, Peter de Hem* Notarie, & many
others who were then prefent: & after
this againe it was all affirmed and verified vnder a folemne oth by the forefayd
Bertrand (beeing fummoned thereunto)
before the fworne Bourgemaifters and
Council of the faid town of *Huy*, as it appeareth by their atteftation made vnder
their feale, and figned by the fecretarie
of the fame town, dated the xvij.th of
Ianuarÿ 1604.

of

Of one that had a withred hand, and how it was afterwards healed.

In Iune 1603.

Marie I*sertant* the daughter of *Andrew* I*sertant,* dwelling at *Esselveke* neer to *Mousson,* hard by the Citie of *Aken,* was in the yeare 1603. surprised with a great malladie, whereof she feeling her self abettred, endeuoured to go into a caue of the hows to fetche somthing thence, and beeing come to the last step, was suddainely taken with a certain kynd of *Appoplexie*: which made her fall down to the grownd, hauing much hurt her self on her left syde, and especially her hand and foot on that syde, in such sorte that she could do no manner of woork: and was forced to walk with a crutch, for other wyse she was not able to goe & in this manner she continued ten whole weekes.

In the meane whyle, hauing hard reporte of the miracles which by the inuocation of our Ladie, were wrought at *Mõtaigue* she resolued lykewyse to go thither for the recouery of her health : and
arriued

arriued at the place vpō the xx^th of *Iune*,
in the same yeare 1603. and so soon as
she drew neer to the mountayne, she
began to feel a great, yea an intollerable
gnawing, in her left hand, which was so
lame, fast closed together, and dead, that
she had no feeling thereof, no not when
they pricked it with any sharp pointed
thing. When with certaine of her neighbours she was come vp to the Chappel,
they went about it some tymes on foot,
some tymes on their knees, making their
prayers very deuoutly: and foorthwith
her dry and dead hand opened of it self,
to the great admiration & comfort both
of her self, & of all those that assisted her.
For more proof whereof, withdrawing
her self into a cottage which was in that
mountaine, made her self redy & dressed
her head, as wel with the one hand as
with the other, & this in the sight of very
many: which for the space of the foresayd tē weeks she was neuer able to do:
and thus returning whole to her home,
she continued euer after very wel, as
she remaineth at this preset x^th of *March*
in the yeare 1604. On which day she affirmed and auouched all that hath byn
                                        sayd,

sayd, in the forefaid citie of *Aken* in the
prefence of Maifter *Peeter Henfenius* Licē-
tiate in diuinitie, Curate of S. *Foillie̅*, *Steue̅
Radermaker de Kelmis* maier of *Eneburg* neer
vnto *Eſſelbeke* , *Leonard Loop de Kelmis* and
Brice Iſertant brother vnto this *Marie*, all
which laſt three did in like māner aſſirm,
that they had ſee̅ theſayd *Marie* attainted
with the *Apoplexie* & palſie , as hath been
ſayd, conformable to a wryting framed
heer of bearing the date aboue ſpecified.

Of a lame young man cured.

In Iuly
1603.

HEnry *Capenbergh* ſonne of *Iohn Capenbergh* dwelling neere vnto *Kerck-
raid* , in the territorie of *Shertogen-rode* in
the Cuntrie beyond the *Meuſe,* was lame
of both his legges, & ſo had continued
eight yeeres continualy, in ſuch ſorte, that
he could hardly go with crutches : and
although his father had cauſed all māne̅ r
of remedies & medecines to be applied
vnto him , yet could he ro procure him
any help or eaſe at all. But after he had
hard tel of the miracles which were
wrought at *Montaigu* , he took his way
thitherward with his crutches, to performe

forme there his deuotion, hoping, that the glorious Mother of God would not faile to afsift him, and to pray for him. At which piace he arriued the fecōd of *Iulie* 1603. beeing the feaft of the Vifitatiō of our Ladie, and there offered vp his prayers right deuoutly before the Chappel: which beeing ended, he felt himfelf much eafed & in better order thē before: and as he returned homeward, pafsing by *Akē* & there praying to the *Virgin Marie* in her church which is in that citie, he foūd himfelf fo much bettered, that there he left and offered vp one of his crutches. Neuer-the-leffe once again he returned with one crutche to *Montaigu*, in the end of the aforefayd moneth, where hauing renued his prayers, he found himfelf perfectly whole & recouered, fo that leauing his other crutch at our Ladies Chappel, home he returned fafe and found, with out the help of any to afsift him, as he ftil continueth, & was fo vpon the xviij^th. of *Februarie* in the yeare 1604, on which day he declared & affirmed the forefayd particularities, before rhe Magiftrates of *Akē* as is to be feen by a wryting penned thereof, fubfigned **Nicolaus Munfterus** Secretarie

cretarie, and sealed with the seale of the
sayd Citie.

Of a woman that was cured of many straunge accidents.

In Iuly
1603.

IOane Cas, wyfe vnto VVilliam de Bois
dwelling at Iatez in the suburbs of the
Citie of Namures. was broken on b   h ly-
des, each rupture coming foorth as bigg
as ones fist: the which she had endured
for the space of eleuē or twelue yeares.
And in the yeare 1601. in the moneth of
May throwing hay out of her loft, down
she fell, & broke her right legge, to the
cure whereof she ēploied many remedies
and medcines, but she could not be so
wel holpen but that she remained lame
and impotent on that leg: in such sorte
that she was constained to walk with
a crutch, and her legge remayned very
ful of paine. Moreouer in the yeare 1603,
in the moneth of Iulie, her stomack swel-
led as great as a mannes head, whether it
was by any inward rupture of that part
which Physitions call Peritonæū, in which
the bowels are contained, or by some
other

other accident, so it was, that it bred in her such a disease and vexation, that she was brought to such extremitie, that she was reddy to giue vp the ghoste, and this according to the iudgement of her Curate, and of Maister *Hermes Petit* Doctor of Physick in *Namures*. The patiēt beeing in these termes, it happened that a certaine woman of her acquaintance called *Catharin Meurisse* came to visit her, who seeing her in such anxietie and danger, counseled her, & sayd, she might do wel to vow some Pilgrimage to our Ladie at *Montaigu* neere to *Sichen*, affirming that she her self by this meanes was cured of the grauel wherewith she had been long tyme afflicted. Which when thesayd patient had hard, whith great deuotion she sayd, that she did promisse to go that Pilgrimage through the grace and assistance of almightie God. And on thesame day about some three howers after she had thus promised, the aforesayd *Ioane Cas* foūd her self intierly whol and cured, as wel of her *Ruptures*, as of the swelling of her stomack: & so rysing out of her bed, she begā to walk vp & down her hows, not onely without her cruch

where

wherewith fhe was wount to help herfelf before, but alfo without any ftick or
ftaffe or any other thing els to fupport
her. And frō that day forward fhe could
go with one fhooe vnderlayd and made
higher the bredth of ones hand, becaufe
her broken legge was become fo much
more fhorte thē the other. And in *October*
following, fhe accomplifhed her pilgrimage to our Ladie at *Montaigu* as before
fhe had vowed; which when fhe had
performed, fhe felt greater eafe in her
leg thē before, in fomuch that her fhooe
is now but of an inch highe, which was
of a handbredth high before. And all this
that hath been here fet down, the *fayd*
Ioan Cas declared and verified vnder her
folemn othe, in the hands of *C. Remys* Notarie, in prefence of the Reuerēd *Sir Giles*
Bofman Chanon & *Archprieft* of the Bifho-
prick of *Namures*, and *Pierchon Pimperneau*
witneffes, cōformable to a publick wryting framed hereof, and fubfigned by the
fayd Notarie and dated the ix^{th} of *April*
1604.

How

How a wenche was suddainely healed of many soares.

WAlter *Gilton* glasier and *Marie de Raueschot* his wyfe, burgeses and inhabitants of the Citie of *Louaine* had amongst other children a daughter of thirteen yeares of age, called *Catharin,* which chyld in the year 1600. fel into an infirmitie and disease which is cōmonly called *the kings euil,* or the euil ofs. *Marcoul,* which broke out into more then an hundred holes, rūning with matter down all her bodie, hands, armes, neck, face, eies, belly, legges & feet, before & behynd & on euery syd: and her mouth was swolne as bigge as three mouthes, and in lyke manner was her nose and all her face, & her eyes were so swolne & ful of paine, that she was scarce able to see: and shee became so weak that she could not liue, and yet she could not dy: beeing sometymes in such pitiful sorte afflicted, that for the space of three moneths she could not stirr out of her bed, neither could she moue either hand or foot: and further

more

In Aug. 1603.

Because that sainct in France doth heale this disease in such as at his tombe commēd them selues to his holy intercessiō

more when so euer she rose vp out of
her bed, she could not go one step without the help of a staffe. To remedie
which disease, her parents vsed the aduise and Counsel of many Doctors of
Physick, and Surgeons, who had prescribed her many drincks and drugges, but
all was to no purpose or profit at all. Afterwards an other very skilful & famous
Surgeon dwelling in that Citie of *Louaine*
called M. *Rembold Walters*, beeing much
commended vnto thē, they couenaunted
with him for a certaine sōme of mony,
that he would take in hád to cure theyr
daughter, wherein he took great paines,
visiting and imploying his labor & skill
about her, twyse euery day, for six moneths space, & yet for al this could he not
obtaine his desyred purpos. These things
hauing thus continued for the space of
three yeeres, and this poor *Catharin* hauing hard reporte of the miracles of our
Ladie at *Montaigu*, and amongst others
how a certaine lame woman was there
cured: she importuned her parents, that
they would vouchesafe to go with her
vnto that place of pilgrimage : to which
her request they yeelded, and promised
they

they would so do : and where as her father intended to carie her on his back the
chyld would not permit that, but rather
resolued to goe thither her self on foot,
saying that shewould force het self thereunto : and she hoped that she should per-
fourme that voyage on foot, and so vpon
the second of *August* 1603. they made the
selues reddie for their iournie, & they put
on their daughter a cleane smock, taking
from her that which she had worne , the
which (be it written with reuerence to
the reader) was stif with the filth and
matter, which did yssue out of the soares
of her bodie : and putting a staffe in her
hand, after they had dyned they depar-
from *Louaine*, hauing in theyr companie
Iames Coremans & his wyfe, *Martin Lau-*
iens and others of their neighbours : and
that night they went and lodged at a village called *Thielt*, with is distant some
three myles from the foresayd Citie, hauing much stayed by the way, by reason
of the great difficultie thesayd wench
had to go. The next day in the morning
notwithstanding that it rained (which
was verie troublesome to the patient)
they took their way forwards towards

L   *Montaign*

Montaigu, where they arriued before midday, and there did their deuotion at the Chappel of our Ladie, from the tyme of their arriual til after dinner, and there offered vp a chyld made in wax: and hauing continued their prayers for one howers space, they retyred themselues into a booth or cottage hard by, and there reposed themselues, expecting til the raine (which stil continued) would cease: but when they saw it ceased not, they all set forwardes on foot with the little mayd, to returne home againe. In which their returne the patiet (although she had alredie gon so much that day) walked with better courage, then she had donne before, wherat all those of her companie were much astonished, and the sayd patient passed on her way singing sometymes certaine sonnets which the children of her yeares are wount ordinarily to sing. And being now come within half a mile of *Louaine* the Father seeing his daughter to wax somwhat werie, he carried her on his back vntil he came to the citie gates: & so soon as they were at home, the mother put the chyld into her bed as she was accustomed to doe: and

doe: & she passed that night very quietly, but the next morning the mayd arose
and put on her apparel without any help,
and came down, and tould her mother
that she had no filth or matter on her
smock, & that she felt no grief at all in her
bodie, but that she found her self wholy
cured. Whereupon her Father & Mother
searched her with all diligence, & found
her smock faire and cleane, without any
spotts at all, and which was more, they
foūd al her fores, which were very many
to be wholy cured and shut vp, and especially on her belly (where her grief was
greatest before) and that all was strong
& quite gon: yea leauing very few scares
behynd: in such forte that her mother
finding her thus cured made no diffict le
to let her ly that very nyght following
with the rest of her Children who were
wel in health: the which for three yeares
before she durst neuer haue permitted.
After this shee remained whole & wel,
not troubled with any grief in the world
and so she continueth euen to this present day. And since her cure she hath
been twise at *Montaigue*, once on foot,
and another tyme by waggon, to render
thancks

thancks to God and his glorious Mother
for so great and singuler a benefit. All
this that hath been sayd, was affirmed
and auerred by both the parents of the
chyld, before the Magistrates of the sayd
citie of *Louain*, vpon the xxvj[th]· of Iune in
the yeare 1604, and vpõ the selfsame day
the aboue named next neighbours of the
foresayd *Walter Gilten*, made their ap-
paréce before thesayd Magistrates, who
did in semblable manner affirm and declare, that they had sundrie tymes seen
the foresayd wench, both before & after
her Pilgrimage to *Montaigu*: and that before she was in the a foresayd euil case,
and that afterwards she miraculously &
perfectly was cured, as hath been sayd. As
it appeareth by the attestation of the a-
foresayd Magistrates and dated as aboue,
subsigned R. *le Prince*, and sealed with the
seale of the same citie.

---

*How a man whose legges were eaten with the
canker was healed.*

In Aug.
2603. **H**Enry *Loycx alias de Visschere* beeing of
75 yeares of age, dwelling in the
Village

Village of *Berthem*, neere to the Citie of
Louain had about midsomer 1603. his legs
and feet so grieuously swolne, that he
could put on no shoes, the paine was so
excessiue which he endured: and in the
moneth of *Iulie* in thesame yeare there
burst out in each of his legges a hole
neere to the ancle and instep of the foot:
the which holes within eight dayes
grew so bad, and became so large and
deep, that on the one syde a man myght
put in his three fingers, and on the other
syde there was dead fleshe of the length
of ones finger: and the patient affirmed
that he felt such paine thereof, as yf it had
bin gnawn by dogges. The which some
iudged to be the caker, for that the edges
of the wounds were ful of dead black
flesh: and that fró the bottom the blood
alwayes issued out with so terrible a
stentche, that no creature was able to
indure it: and as they perceiued that the
poor patient found no help by any thing
that he applyed, he was counseled by
some person, to go and visit our Ladie at
Montaigu: which he promised and vowed
to do, in hope there to receiue some consolation, and he neuer left to proceed in
                                     his

his intent, vntil he was caried thither: but
for so much as he was so sick and weak,
none durst take the matter vpon them,
except he were first put in the state of
grace, for feare least he should haue
dyed in the way as he went. The which
thing after the patient had vnderstood,
he caused himself to be caried to the
Church of *Berthem*, where he made his
confession, and comunicated, the blood
running from him by the way as he wet.
And a few dayes after, to witt vpon the
fift of *August* in the aforesaid yeare 1603.
he made himself to be caried in a waggon vnto *Montaigu*, where at our Ladies
Chappel he did his deuotio : & a certaine
Priest that then was there, couseled him
that he should make twise more that
voyage, and that for this purpose he
should make choice of the Fryday, and
that he should haue a good confidence
in the assistance of the Mother of God.
The patiet being returned home he soud
his legges much lesser and vnswolne, and
the paine thereof much more tollerable
then before. Whereupon following the
Counsel that was giuen him, he returned
again the secod tyme by waggo to *Mont-*
aigu,

aigu, vpon the feaſt of the *Aſſumption* of our Ladie : and after he had ended his prayers, he found much more eaſe then before. And vpon the next friday, beeing the xxij of theſame moneth, he was brought thither the third tyme, and did his deuotions as before, and hauing at euery of theſe tymes been led thriſe about the Chappel, not without effuſion of his blood, which rannc from his legges vpon the earth, together with a very great ſtenche as diuers of *Montaigu* reported, who then were preſent. And from'thece beeing come home, he fel into ſo great weaknes & ſuch a ſwouning that euerie one thought he ſhould haue foorthwith giuen vp his ghoſt : the which beeing ouer paſſed he affirmed that he felt a great and notable amendment of his legges & after that day the two great wouds in his legges were by litle and litle cured and filled vp of themſelues, and all the dead and corrupte fleſh became good. So as th ſame patient remaineth cured euen at this preſent, hauing nothing left him but the ſcarres of the ſoares, which are eache of the of a ſpan in greatnes. All which is wel known by an authentical

L 4   atteſta-

atteſtatiõ made before the Curate, Maier & Eſchewins, of theſaid village of *Berthe*, vpon the xxij. of *Februarie* 1 6 0 4. and ſealed with the ordinarie ſeale of that village.

The healing of a bunche.

In Aug. 1603.

In this monaſte rie a ver tuous & venera ble cõ pagnie of En gliſh gentle wwomen are pro teſſe d.

SIſter *Betrice Ieroons* a lay ſiſter profeſſed in the Cloiſter of S. *Vrſula* or of the eleuen thouſand Virgins, in a place called the *Halffstreet* in the Citie of *Louaine* contracted vpon the yeare 1 6 0 2. a cer̄:ainc accident, betwixt the right pap and her ſhoulder before, which was a kynd of bunch that happened her (as ſhe thought) by continual caſting her armes, in throwing of water with a wooden diſh vpon linnen, which they are woũt to bleache in that Cloiſter: which bunch was as great as ones fiſt, and it was not fleſhy or ſoft, but rather ſtiffe & hard as a bone, which grew (as it ſeemed vnto her) euen out of the ſhoulder bone, yet not hauing any different colour from the other partes of her bodie, neither was it any whit paineful, but onely when ſhe

preſſed

pressed it, and then somtymes it happened that she cast blood out of her mouth
The which she sustained (without
applying any remedie thereunto) about
one yeare and a half. But when she had
heard of the miracles which were donne
at *Montaigu* by the inuocation of our ladie,
she began to haue a desire to goe thether
in pilgrimage, and to pray that she
might be cured, much confiding that the
glorious Virgin would assist her herein.
And hereupon hauing obtained licēce of
her Superiour she took her voyage to
the sayd *Mōtaigu*, in the begining of *August*
1603. where she did her deuotion in
the Chappel of our Ladie, from thence
she went to lodge at *Sichen*, which is distant a little half duitche myle from that
place, where she perceiued that her aci-
dent began to wax better : and the next
morning returning to *Montaigu*, whyles
she was there at her prayers, she felt certaine stretchings and straynings from
her head to her right arme, and towards
the place where her bunch did grow:
but beeing that day returned to *Louaine*,
the next morning as she arose she found
her accidēt wholie cured and the bunch

L 5   to

to haue become of the same euennes
with the other partes of her bodie, so that
there was no difference thereby at al,
and from that tyme she hath remained
without all pain or whatsoeuer accidēt,
as thesayd Religious woman auouched
in the presence of her Mother or superiour & others of thesayd Conuent, vnto
whome the euil which the sayd sister
sustained, and from which she was now
freed, was wel known: and lykewyse in
the presence of the Venerable Fathers in
God sir *Iames van Ghele* Priest and Doctor
of Diuinitie, and *Sir Iames de Beer d'Oister-*
wijck, also Bacheler in Diuinitie, and Re-
ligions in the Conuent of the Iacobins in
Louain and of *M. Roland le Prince*: Secretarie of the sayd Citie, vpon the xxviij.th
of *October* 1603. and vpon the vj.th of Ianuarie 1604. according to an act that by
thesayd Secretarie *le Prince* was framed
hereof,

How a man that was sick of the falling
euil was cured.

In Aug.
1603.

Mathia Paçgen sonne of *Gaspar Paç-*
gen of *Horbagh* borne at *S. Laurens-*
bergh

berg in Cuntrie of *Iuliers*, neere vnto *Al-den-houen*, came vnto *Montaigu* in the beginning of *Auguſt* 1603.to make there his petition to our Ladie, that by her interceſsion he might be freed frõ the diſeaſe &infirmitie of the falling ſicknes, wherewith for ſeuen yeares paſt he had been troubled,for that he had vnderſtood that our Lord did many miracles at the inuocation of his holie Mother in that place. And ſo remaining ſome eight or té dayes at theſayd Moũtaine,he made his prayers deuoutely before the Chappel of our Ladie:during which tyme he was aſſailed ſix or ſeuen tymes euery day (as accuſtomarily he was wount to haue been)with three ſortes or kyndes of the falling euil: with ſuch a rage and vehemencie, with ſuch knocks hurling and cryes,that euery one thought he would haue been burſt, or that he ſhould haue dyed, which was a moſt pitiful ſight vnto all the Pilgrimes that were there preſent: who alſo endevoured by their prayers and almes to obtaine of God his cure and amendment. And vpon the eue of the *Aſſumption* of our Ladie in theſayd moneth of *Auguſt* , this *Mathias* perſeuering in his prayers and devotions uotions, found himself in perfect health and quyte deliuered from all these maladies: in such sorte that the next day euery one might manifestly see, that not onely he was deliuered frō his falling sicknes, but that there withall he had recouered a faire & liuely colour in his face, which before was very dead and pale, and his bodie much swolne, as many who had seen him at *Montaigu* whyle he had his disease, and afterwards when he was healed, affirmed. Thus the sayd *Mathias* returned in good plight to his hows by *Aldenhouen*. And in the beginning of *Februarie* in the yeare 1604. he repaired an other tyme to *Montaigu*, to render thácks vnto God and his glorious Mother for the benefit whichhe had there obtained, wherewith at yet he continueth most certaine & assured. Afterwards (to witt, vpon the xiiij. of the sayd moneth) he returned thither once againe, & brought with him the attestation concerning his maladies geuen him by the Curate of *Aldenhouen*, and also by the Magistrates of the Imperial Citie of *Aken*, dated vpō the xviij. of the aforesayd moneth of *Februarie*, and subsigned *Nicolaus Munsterus* Secretary

cretary and sealed with the seale of the
same Citie.

Of a spice of Leprosie which was there cured.

MAthew Croisier sonne to *Reynold Croi-* In Aug.
sier dwelling in the town of Huy 1603.
in the Cuntrie of Liege, beeing about
twelue yeares old, in the yeare 1603. became so ful of scabbes and botches running down along his bodie, that by the
Curate and Curch-wardens of Sainct
Steuens Parish in the same town, he was
presented before the Magistrates of *Huy*,
for a leper, and hereupon they made him
to be more diligently serched in the Citie
of *Liege*, to the end that yf he were found
a leper indeed they myght prouide for
him some necessarie entertainement, and
so to seperate him from the companie
and conuersation of other men.

For which cause the Magistrates appointed that they should deliuer him as
from the town, a bushel of corn for his
food, vntil such tyme as they were fully
informed of his maladie. In the meane
whyle this youth was visited by M. Thomas

mas d'Orbaix, and maifter *Nicolas de Palude*
Surgeons of thefayd Citie, who found
him full of botches, fcabbes, and deep
fores, wherein he had no feeling at all:
and yet could they not certainely iudge
what euil it was: as appeareth by the atteftation of the fayd Magiftrates giuen
vnder their feale vpon the xvij. of *Ianuarie*
1604. But the father of this youth hauing
been in Pilgrimage at *Montaigu,* and hauing feen and known the miracles which
were there donne by the inuocation of
the glorious Virgin *Marie,* he caufed his
fonne to be brought thither, in hope to
fyndthere fome help for him, and this
was about the middeft of *Auguft* in the
yeare 1603. Now as the youth was carried round about the Chappel of our lady
he began to cry out, that he was burned
within his bodie, & after they had ended
their deuotions, they caried him in-to a
booth or cottage hard by; where he refted very quietly that night, and in the
morning they found fome of his botches
healed, and all his foares and holes fhut
vp, and continuing there his denotions,
within two or three dayes all his other
foares and botches of his bodie were
cured

cured of them-selues, nothing remayning
but certaine red spottes as large as half a
philip daller, and those were to the number of fortie or fiftie. Moreouer this youth
was broken in such sorte, that his secret
partes were swolne as big as bothe ones
fists: of which rupture he was also cured
at that tyme, without any humaine help
or assistance: and hereof many persons of
credit who were then at *Montaigu* do
beare good testimonie, and namely M.
Iames de Castro Doctor of diuinitie, Archpriest or dean of the Christianitie in *Diest*,
Sir Iohn Hanegreaf Curate of *Testelt*, Maister *Ioachim Buscher* Secretarie of the Cou-
sell of *Brabant*, *Peter de Ham* Notarie, resi-
ding at *Diest*, and *Iohn Baptist Zangre* sworn
Printer in the Citie of *Leuaine*, of which
persons some visited the yong mancs naked bodie, and considered the perfectió
of his sayd cure, with the scarres that remained. And thesame yong man coming
afterwards to *Bruxelles*, was visited by a
skilful Surgeon, and found whole, and
quyte deliuered of his rupture, and from
all other diseases whatsoeuer.

Ho𝔂

How a man bruised with a fall was cured.

In Aug.
1603.

Cornelius *Fox* inhabitant of the town of *Diest* one day going about his af-faires, and passing betwixt the villages of *Bekeuort* and *Meerbeke* by *Diest*, happe-ned to stumble and to fall vpon a stump of wood lying in the way: so that he in-wardly grieuouselie hurt himselfin his breast, & for the space of six whole weeks was grieuously sick thereof, and after he had vsed the help of a Surgean, who had applyed diuers remedies and oynt-ments about him, yet found he no amed-ment at all: where vpon he purposed to go and visit our Ladie at *Montaign*, where in *August* 1603. hauing done his deuotion and washt his brest with a certain water which is in the sayd mountaine, he was immediately deliuered from all his paines and griefes, & neuer after felt any of the. And all this was solemnly sworne & auouched by the foresayd *Cornelius* be-fore the Magistrates of *Diest*, vpon the xxth. of *March* in the yeare 1604. and an instrument was formed & made thereof

and

and ſigned I. *vanden Goeden-huiſe* and ſealed with the ſeale of the aforeſaid town.

The Palſey Cured,

Leonard *Teeters* dwelling at *Beringen* in
the Cuntry of *Liege* was ſick of the
Palſey, and ſo taken in all his limmes, that
he could moue none of them, but onely
his head and tongue: the which hauing
continued thus a yeare and a half, fynding no help in any of the receiptes or
medicines which were imployed for his
cure, and being at the length aduertiſed
of the miracles which were wrought at
Montaigu, he reſolued to cauſe himſelf to
be caried thither, hauing great confidéce
to fynd ſome help by the interceſſion
of the glorious Virgin *Marie.* The which
he performed, and was caried thither in a
wagon wherein he was to be taken vp
and layd down euen as a verie infant:
when he had finiſhed his deuotion at the
chappel of our Ladie, he cauſed himſelf
to be caried home back againe, in the
ſame wagon, without perceiuing as yet
any amendment, but ſome two or three

In Aug.
1603.

dayes

dayes after, he begá to moue his limmes and to creep vpon his hands and feet about the hows. An other tyme after that he had a great desire to goe againe to visit our Ladie at Mótaigu wherfore he caused a wagō to be prepared for him , and he had now recouered somuch strégth that he could goe from his hows to the place where the wagon was, and hauing the second tyme dōne his deuotion vnto our Ladie, he obtained so much ease, that he left there one of his crutches, and with the other and the help of the wagon he returned home, in better disposition, and with more force then he had before. But fifteen dayes after he came thither againe the third tyme, and walked thither on foot only with one crutch & seiourned at Montaigu for the space of fifteen dayes, dooing there his daylie deuotions: & returned home againe with his crutch, but with more strength & in better health and disposition of his bodie then the two tymes before: and sithens he hath euery day found more ease & amendment. Al this that hath here been sayd this Leonard Peeters declared and testyfied vpon the xv.th of August 1604. in the presence of Sir

Godfrey

Godfrey of Thienwinkele Curate of *Sichen*, Sir
Iohn Rosa Prior of the *Iacobins* in *Louaine* &
Licentiate in Diuinitie, Brother *William
Siluius* procurator of the same Conuent,
Maister *Anthonie Bouckhout* Maier of *Sichen*
and *Iohn Baptist Zangre* Printer: as also afterwards he auouched thesame vnder his
othe solemly made before the Eschouter,
Maier and Escheuins of the aforesayd
town of *Beringen*, as it may be seen by
their attestation sealed with their seale,
and subsigned *Henricus Cillenius* secretarie.

The Healing of a certaine disease called the Scuruies.

Elizabeth *Vander Hoeuen* wyfe vnto
Zacharias van Anroy, dwelling in the
village of *Grasen* neer to *Bets* in the territorie of *Diest*, was in the lent 1603. taken
with an accidēt and maladie which bred
great prickigs in euery parte of her body,
together with many black spottes of the
bignes of a phillip daler whereby she
became not onely so weake & impotent
that she could do no manner of work but,
more ouer she had such vehement paine

In Aug. 1603.

M 2   that

that she could rest neither night nor day:
so that she did nothing but runne out of
her bed and presently runne thither
back againe, as yf she had been depriued
of her wittes: yet called she continually
vpō the name of the blessed *Virgin Marie*,
to the end she would pray for her in this
her affliction: which continued vntil *Au-*
gust, in the sayd yeare of our Lord 1603.
And then hauing hard some speak of the
miracles which were wrought at *Mont-*
aigu, by the intercession of the Mother of
God, shee deuoutly resolued to make a
pilgrimage to that place, the which she
performed: and praying at the Chappel
of our Ladie, immediately as she had ended her prayers, she felt a great amendment, and that the foresayd prickings and
stingings ceased: and from that tyme forwards she began to be better: whereupō
she was moued to return again vnto
Montaigu to render thancks to the *Virgin*
Marie, for the help she receiued by her
meanes, after which iourney (being very
soone after the other) the same *Elizabeth*
went home in perfect health and strēgth,
and became so strong and able of bodie,
in so much as she affirmed that she neuer
felt

felt her self better in all her lyf. According to her attestation of all the premises which iudicallie passed before the Eschouret and men of law of the foresayd Lordship of *Grasen* vpon the thirteenth of March 1604.

How a mayd was healed of her legges that were swolne and ful of paine.

M*artha vander Tay* being of two and fortie yeares of age, mayd-seruant in the hows of M. *Iohn Vāden Perre* Clarck in the Counsel of *Brabant* in *Bruxelles*: had a disease and accident in her legges, which hapened her in the yeare 1603, whereby they became very great and swolne, and so ful of ache that she could doe no kynd of labor, yea she could not so much as goe without extreme grief and shedding of teares, neither could she repose in the night through the vehemēcie of her paine which neuer stinted: but continued for the space of more then three monethes. Her Maister beeing desirous to help her, vsed the counsel of a certaine Fhisit.on dwelling in thesayd Citie, and afterward

In Aug. 2603.

ward of certain other men and women
practitioners in phisick: and they appointed her a number of diuers receiptes, as
of bathes, fomentations, ointments and
other such lyke, but all in vaine and without any help at all. Whereupon her
sayd maister (seeing her past hope to be
cured, and that yf she were cutt she
should remaine a cripple, and miserable
all the residue of her lyfe, as not able any
wayes to gaine her liuing) entred into a
deliberation to place her and to prouide
for her in some Hospitall, where she
might be maintained. But whē the fame
of the miracles of our Ladie at *Montaigu*
began to be bruited abroad, he resolued
at the last to send her thither, hoping that
there she might be holpen. And so about
mid *August* she was sent by waggon to a
Cloister called *Terbanck* neer to the Citie
of *Louain*, wherein a sister of the sayd
Clark liued: & from thence also by waggon she was conueyed to *Diest*, that the
next morning after she might goe to
Montaigu. In which voyage this *Martha*
began alredy to fynd some ease in her
legges. Hauing rested one night in *Diest*,
she made her self readie in the morning
to goe

to goe on foot vnto *Montaigu*, but it seemed vnto her a thing vnpossible, and so she stood in a doubt what she might doe: which whē the wyfe of the hows where she lodged perceiued, she bad her be of good courage, and exhorted her to goe not onely on foot, but barefoot also, for that there was but one good myle to the place, which seemed vnto the sayd *Martha* a thing altogether out of her power: not withstanding beeing much animated by the womans exhortation, and with the hope which she gaue her that the Mother of God would not permit her to return without comfort, on she sett forward barefoot, and as she went, she begā to feel that her legges waxed better & better. And beeing arriued at our Ladies chappel whylst she was at her prayers, she felt all the swelling and paines of her legges and feet to ceaſe and quite to be gon, euen as yf one should feel some thig to be vntied & looſed which before was bound and made faſt : and when her prayers were ended she returned again barefoot vnto *Dieſt*, beeing whole and maruelouſly comforted : and from *Dieſt*

M 4   by

by waggon (he went back to *Louain*, & fo
to *Bruxelles* fynding herfelf very wel in
all her bodie, as fhe is now euen at
this prefent. And all this that heer hath
ben fet down, was verified and auouched by herfelf, vnder her othe folemnly
made before thofe of the law in thefayd
Citie of *Bruxeles*, vpon the xxvith of *April*
1604. as may be feen by their atteftation
giuen hereof, fubfigned *Numan*, and
fealed with thefayd Cities feale.

A meruelous cure of an incurable Wound.

In Sept.
1603.

L Eonard *Stockueau* born at *S. Georges*, in
the territorie of the town of *Huy* in the
countrie of *Liege*, about fome fourteen
year ago as he trauayled one day through
the foreft of *Soigne* neer to a village called
Waterloos not farr from *Bruxelles*; was af-
failed by a theef and murderer : who
handled him fo cruelly, and gaue him fo
manie woundes, that he left him for dead
in the place: and amongft others he gaue
him a gafh on the left hamme, in fuch
forte that he cut in funder his finewes,
and it paffed euen to the bone. In this cafe
was

was he brought to an Hospital in *Bruxelles*, that there he might be seen vnto:
& within a certaine tyme al his wounds were healed saue that of his hamme, the which because the sinewes were cutt, euery one estemed as incurable, wherfore bee ng dismissed out of the Hospital he was forced to goe with two crutches : yet through the abundance of humours , which somtymes had thither thir cours there ensued many new sores and issues round about the principal wound: and although he vsed diuers medicines of certain Phisitions, yea and had perfourmed diuers pilgrimages, yet he found no heip at all. At the last in the moneth of *September* 1603 he went to visit our ladies at *Montaigu*: where hauing cōtinued nyne dayes, and daylie washing his sores with a certaine water that is in that moūtaine not far from the chappel, he found that the lesser sores cured of themselues , and when the nyne dayes were expired , he perceiued that the cut & interessed sinewes of his leg, were grown & made fast within to the bone of his sayd leg, and that they were roūd about couered with flesh, and a new skinne. yet the place of
the

the great wound remained hollow, and
with so great a hole, that one might easilie put his fist therein. And thus this *Leonard* was perfectly cured, without any
impediment or grief, walking, going
and assisting himself, with the sayd leg
euen as he himself pleased, and as any
other man that is whole and soud might
doe: hauing afterward made on foot the
way betwixt *Montaigu* & *Louain*, which is

dutche
miles.

fiue good lōg miles, and this he did in the
moneth of *October* next following. All
which the sayd *Stockneau* declared and affirmed vnder a solemn othe which he
made before the Curate Maier & Esche-
uins of *Sichen* the xxi[th.] of *April*, 1604. according to an instrument formed the-
reof, signed I. *van Ogernen* secretarie, and
sealed withe the seale of the sayd town.

How an o'd man was cured of the falling euil.

In Sept
1603.

GY'es *Libens* beeing seuentie yeares of
age dwelling at *Attenhouen* by the
town of *Landen* in *Brabant*, was vexed
with the falling euil aboue fiftie yeares
together, and he was tormented therewith

with especially vpon Sundayes and Holydayes, hauing but little ease of it vpon other dayes. This aged man beeing mooued by the miracles wrought at Môtaigu, purposed with himself to go thither in Pilgrimage, & there to intreate the blessed Virgin to obtaine for him that he might be healed: the which he performed vpon the seuenth of *September* in the foresayd yeare 1603. & hauing there finished his deuotions, he returned whole & in good plight, without euer after feeling any molestation thereof: as he affirmed before the Maier & Escheuins of the sayd Lordship of *Attêhouen* vpon the xxij.th of *March*, in the yeare 1604. & an instrument was drawn therof, subsigned *Nicolaus Nicolai* Secretarie, and sealed with the seale of the sayd Lordship.

How a man was healed of a rupture

IOhn *Hagels* Carpéter dwelling at *Adeuoort* by *Heylihsem*, neer *Tilemont*, in *Brabant*, being threescore & fower yeares old, in the yeare 1602, & in the moneth of *August* trauailing in reaping of corne in the

In Sept. 1603.

in the fields between the villages of
Veude & Raisbeuen, foũd that he was inwardly burſt by ouermuch labor: wherupon enſued a very great and exceſſiue
paine, which continued a whole yeare,
notwithſtãding that he had aplied many
remedies in vaine, at the laſt hauing hard
of the miracles of our Ladie at *Montaigv*,
and how by her interceſſion diuers had
ben healed of the lyke accident, he went
thither with great deuotion and confidence, vpon the eight of *September* 1603,
being the feaſt of the *Natiuitie* of our lady,
and hauing made his prayers at the
Chappel, he foũd much eaſe of his paine,
for which cauſe within ſome weekes after he returned twiſe thither againe, and
at the third tyme he found himſelf perfectly cured of his Rupture : & leauing
there his truſſe wherewith he was accuſtomed to ty hiſelf, he neuer after felt any
the leaſt paine or hinderance thereby. As
vnder his ſolẽ othe he auouched (beeing
ſummoned thereunto before the Curate,
Maier & Fſcheuins of the Vilage of *Neder
heylighſem*, vpon the eleuenth of *Februarie*
1604. according to their atteſtation
ſubſigned *Seruatius Roſeus* Curate, *Guil-*
laume

laume van Meeusele Maier, and G. Persoōs
Secretarie, and sealed with the seale of
the sayd Village.

The Curing of diuers accidents.

Maister *Francis Eland* Curate of the
Church called the *Chappelle de nostre
Dame* in the Citie of *Bruxelles*, was much
troubled with a flux of the *Hemorhoides*
commonly called in French *les troches*
which he had long tyme indured. Besydes
this he was *Astmaticque*, that is to say much
stratened in his breast, & short breathed,
in somuch as euery one thought he could
neuer recouer, notwithstanding that he
ordinarily vsed the coūsel of sundry physitions: who can wel witnes, how that
within one week he lost aboue thirtie
ounces of blood. The which disease continuing thus for diuers yeares, there followed vpon it a great swelling in his
feet and legges like vnto a dropsie, and
this cōtinued for fower yeares together,
notwithstanding that many remedies
were vsed about him, as bathes, fomentations, ointments, and other such like,
so that

In Sept. 1603.

so that he fel into such an infirmitie and
weakenes, (beeing now come to the
threescore & three yeare of his age)that
the Phisitions despaired of his health and
lyfe: hauing so lost his speach and memorie, that they thought he should neuer recouer the due vse of his speache so long
as he liued: and this they held as assured,
that at leastwise he would neuer be fitt
to execute his office of Pastorship again,
Wherefore at last he resolved to goe &
intreat our Ladie at *Motaigu* for his health
and so he caused him self to be carried
thither in *September* 1603. where hauing
donne his deuotions, and returning back
towards *Bruxelles*, he felt a certain kynd of
itching or byting, and alteration in his
legges, and besydes this, a new strength
and ease in his sinewes : and beeing
come home, he found that all the former swelling in his feet and legges
was gone, in such sorte, that from that
tyme he hath vsed no further remedies,
ointments, or receiptes, fynding himself also free from all his other accidents
as wel of the *Hemorhoides*, as of the debili-
tie and impotencie into which he was
fallne : yea he had gaigned so good a sto-
mak

mak, and is become so liuely, in somuch
as he auoucheth and affirmeth that now
beeing threescore and fower yeares old
he feeleth himself more strong and able,
the he was at the age of sortie or fistie, the
which he also approoueth by his outward carriage, perfou ming againe h's
office of paltorship more l uely ar d dex-
terously then euer he did before. And all
this (as he acknowledgeth and affirmeth)
by the intercession and assistance of the
glorious Virgin Marie. As of all the premises he hath giuen a sufficient attestation, written by his own hand in memorie of the benefit which God belto-
wed vpon him.

How an old man was healed of a great rupture

Daniel Smith Sextane of the parish
church of the town of *Vilvord*, neer
vnto *Bruxelles*, beeing threescore & seuē
yeares old, was some twenty yeares before broke on the right syde of his belly,
as big as both ones fistes, which happened
as he thought by riging the belles of that
Church. For the remedying whereof, he
did onlie ty himself with a trusse, made
fitt

fitt for the purpose: yet for all that he felt
very often such vehement paine, that he
thought he should haue lost his sences,&
in this manner he went vp and down
with great difficultie. But about the moneth of *August* 1603 , he was seased vpon
with a long and grieuous disease, where
by he thought he should fall into a dropsie
sie beeing very feeble , hauing no appetite to his meat, and vnable to do any
thing without great paine and trauaile,
which continued a whole moneth space.
In which tyme his wyfe hauing hard
talk of the miracles which by the intercession of our Ladie were wrought at
Montaigu, she resolued to goe thither, and
to pray there for her husbands recouerie,
or at least for the mittigatio of his paines,
and especially of his *Rupture* , wherewith
he was so cruelly tormented: the which
she performed not long after. Beeing the
come to *Montaigu,* vpon an euening at the
tyme of *Salue* , this *Daniel* beeing in the
Church at *Viluord,* told certain persons
that were neere vnto him , that he felt
himself at that very tyme much eased of
his malladie, which had continued now a
whole moneth as hath been sayd:& that
he felt

he felt in himself an appetit to his meat,
the which he never had all the tyme before: And from that instant his diseaseleft
him, so as he was no more therewith
troubled afterwards But his wyfe beeig
returned from *Montaigu*, he enquired of
her at what tyme and houer she did
her deuotiō at the Chappel of our Ladie,
and he vnderstood that it was in the euening about fiue of the clock, at thesame
tyme & instant that he found himself
eased of his disease as we haue sayd. And
about the middest of *September* thesayd
Daniel determined in like manner to go
vnto *Montaigu*, partly for deuotion, and
partly to giue thancks vnto God and his
most holy Mother,for the fauour he had
alredy obtained: and after this his deter-
minat on(although it was three dayes before hee took his iorney) he found himself so much eased and amended of his
Rupture, that to him it seemed in a māner
cured. Finally departing from *Viluord*, in
the cōpagnie of others of the same town,
who were also to go to *Montaigue*, not
wearing any trusse as hee was accustomed; and there hauing made his prayers
to our Ladie, in returning home on foot,
N found

foūd himself very luſtie, not feeling any
paine or impediment by his *Rupture*,
either in going or coming, but rather
eaſe & help:& beeing returned home, he
found himſelf not onely perfectly holpē,
but in ſo good a plight and diſpoſition of
bodie, as yf he were twentie yeares yonger then he was, in ſuch ſorte that euer
ſince he hath remayned free of all grief
and paine,& although he vſed no truſſe,
yet his *Rupture* neuer appeared. All theſe
thinges theſayd *Daniel* & his wyſe haue
ſolēnly auouched vnder their othes,be-
fore the Eſcheuins of *Viluerd*, vpon the
xxiij^th of *April* 1604.as it appeareth by the
informations taken thereof, and ſigned,
I. *Gheerts* ſecretarie of theſame town.

An admirable cure of diuers running ſores

In Sept.
1603.

MIſtris *Martha de Roſenberge*, daughter
vnto the Lord *Maximilian* Baron of
Roſenberge, in *Styria*, widdow vnto M.
Mathias Wortzelman, ſometyme Captaine
of a companie of foot,in the ſeruice of his
catholike maieſtie in the low cūtries, indured for two yeares ſpace a great accident

dẽt in her right leg, wherein there were
three open ſoares, which occupied her
whole thigh, from the very top thereof
to her knee, half an el in length, and a
quarter in breadth, as appeared by the
plaiſters which ſhe was wount to apply
thereũto. Betwixt each of the ſores there
were twelue holes or iſſues, which proceeded of certaine cold and ſharp humors, that diſcended thither frõ her head:
all which happened through the miſerie
and pouertie which ſhe endured, while
ſhee laboured in the court of B uxels, for
payment of ſuch monny as was due vnto
her huſband for his ſeruice. For the curing of theſe ſoares ſhe had taken the
counſel of diuers, together with diuers
remedies which ſundrie particuler per-
ſones had preſcribed her, without makíg
her caſe known to any Phiſition or Surgeon, & this vpon too much ſhame and
baſhfulnes that withheld her. But when
ſhe ſaw that all which ſhe did profited
her nothing, ſhe was in fine conſtrained
to put her ſelf into the hands of ſome
ſkilful Phiſition or Surgeon, for the recouery of her deſyred health, and there-
vpon ſhe intreated *M. Peter Paulſon* a ger-

mane

mane surgeon, and one of the guard to
our moſt gracious Prince and Soueraine
the Archduke *Albertus*, to help her : who
took vpon him to cure her, and for this
purpoſe let her blood three or fower tymes, and withall gaue her a purgation,
and took her into his hows the better
to adminiſter vnto her there the diet : ap-
plyíg to her ſoares all the remedies which
according to the arte of ſurgerie he was
able to inuent: yet could he for all his labour effectuate nothing, but onely that
her paines were ſomwhat appeaſed, and
ſometymes her ſoares were ſhut vp, but
they continued ſo not paſt a day or two,
for foorthwith they broke out againe as
before, and could neuer be conſolidated
or ſtrengthned. But at laſt this gentlewoman hauing hard in *Bruxelles*, of the miracles which were daylie wrought by the
inuocation of the Virgin *Marie* at *Montaigu*, ſhe had a great deſyre to goe thither
vpon deuotion, with hope and truſt, that
our Ladie would procure her her health:
and theſame night after that ſhe had
made this determinatiõ betwixt waking
and ſleeping, it ſeemed vnto her that ſhe
ſaw the Image of our Ladie of *Montaigu*,
with

with the wood that grew thereabout, &
she felt as it were an inward motion and
incouragemét to make the foresayd voyage. Wherevpon the next morning following (which was the xxij^th. of *September*
1603.)she beseeched our Ladie that she
might fynd some that would accompany
her to *Montaigu*. And afterwards going
to the hows of M. *Anne de la Croix* her gossip who somedayes before had talked
with her about her going to our Ladies,
she inquired of her when she purposed
to depart: vnto whome the other answered, that she intended to goe euen that
very day: whereof this Gentlewoman
Mistris Martha was very glad, and so
went with thesayd *Anne de la Croix* to
heare masse in the Church of S. *Gudula*
in *Bruxelles* , and soon after they set on
forewards in their way towards *Louain*,
and the day following towards *Montaigu*
In the way the sayd *Mistris Martha* felt
so great paine in her leg, and withall she
became so wearie, that she thought she
should neuer come to the Chappel not-
withstáding taking a good courage she
went on so wel , that she came to a certaine pathway where (the direct way to

Dieſt beeing left) people vſe to turn on
the left hand towards *Montaigu* , into
which way ſo ſoon as they were entred
ſhe perceiued the paine (which ſhe ſuſtained from the top of her head all alōg
her ſore leg) to decreaſe , and by little
and little to leaue her, and that all her
wearines ſurceaſed therewith : and ſo
beeing arriued at the chappel of our lady,
they made there their prayers:afterwards
hauing reſted and warmed them ſelues
in a litle hows thereby,they ſettled them
ſelues that night again to their prayers,
at which tyme this M. *Martha* began to
feel herſelf much better , and without
paine:whereupon (hauing felt this alteration) ſhe looked vpon her leg, and ſhe
perceiued that her ſoares began to wax
whole,in ſuch ſorte that taking away the
clothes & plaiſters which were applyed
thereunto, ſhe put them into her maud:
and the next day thoſe that had ſeen her
the day before affirmed,that they perceiued her to be much altered & amended,
both in her cullour and coutenance. And
the ſame day(after ſhe had giuen thacks
to God and his holy mother) they returned to *Bruxelles*,ſhee feeling in her way
                              the

the increase of her force and health: and when she was come home she found no more but one hole or issue in her leg, the which some two dayes after was perfectly shut vp of it self: in such sorte, that since that tyme she hath not onely inioyed intiere and perfect cure of her leg, but also she hath found a great force & strégth in all the interiour and exteriour partes of her bodie: and the places of the soares where the flesh was eaten away & consumed, were restored and filled vp again with new flesh. And all this which here hath bin set down, the foresayd M. Martha declared, and vnder her othe solemnly auouchd, before the Magistrates of the sayd Citie of *Bruxelles*, vpon the xvjth day of *October* 1603. Before whome also M. *Peter Paulionne* appeared, who being examined of the premisses, he likewise affirmed vnder his othe, that he had thesayd Mistresse *Martha* in hand seuen or eight Moneths continually, to cure her of her disease before specified, and what industrie he had vsed, as wel by blood-letting purging, diet, as otherwaies, according to the arte of surgerie: & that he compassed no other thing thereby, but to assuage in

N 4 some

some sorte the grief of her great sore, and
of the other yssues that were about it, and
that somtymes he had shut them vp for a
day or twaine, & yet that they afterwards
opened again, by reason of the continuall
defluxions that descéd dither: which
sores yeelded so great & terrible a stench,
that often tymes it forced his wife to
swoune. And that after this Mistresse
Martha was returned from *Montaigu*, he
hauing hard that she was perfectly cured,
was much amazed thereat: & thereupon
would needes see & visit her sayd sores,
& the places that were annoyed, & foúd
that verily all the holes, yssues, and sores
were perfectly healed vp, & that those
parts where the flesh was eaten away &
consumed, were filled vp againe with
flesh, and made æqual, and that onely certaine spottes and scarres remain d afterwards. The which the sayd M. *Peter Paul-*
sonne (cósidering the greatnes of the sore,
together with the multitude of the running issues & their sudaine cure) thought
could neuer naturaly or by any humaine
meanes be brought to pas, but onely by
the allmighty hand of God. All which
may be seen by the attestation of the.
sayd

sayd Magiſtrats, ſealed with the ſeale of theſayd Citie of *Bruxelles*, & and ſubligned P. *Numan Secretarie.*

An Admirable cure of a perſon betwitched, and ſore grieued with the bloodie fluxe,   In Sept. 1603.

Magdalē Preudhomme widow of *Baudechon Alatt* , beeing about the age of threeſcore yeares, dwelling in the Citie of *Bruxelles* , by trade a ſeller of old garments, went together with her daughter at the tyme of harueſt in the yeare 1593. to a certaine village neer to *Louaine* called *Berthem*, to reap corn, for that ſhe vnderſtood that ſome profit was there to be made: and hereupon ſhe there felto trauaile amongſt diuers others. At which tyme it happened that a certain huſbadman dwelling in that village, deſired her to haue an eye that none took any of his corn, which he had lying vpon a peece of land thereby. But ſhe hauing perceiued that a womā of that village was ſo hardy as to take ſome of his corne, this *Magdalen* aduertiſed him thereof: who going to the womans hows took away his corn
thence

thence by force , and in spyte of her brought it home to his own nows, although she was maruelousely agry therewith. The next day they beeing met againe in the field, this woman rebuked the sayd *Magdalen* for that she had accusd her , saying that she would pay her home for it. At night she returned to the Village, and lodged neer to the hows of the foresayd woman, who came and presented her with a trencher ful of fryed Romaine beanes, saying that she had bin in a great coller with her, for that she had accused her, but it was now past and gone, & that she made no account thereof : and although this *Magdalen* had no great appetit to her beanes, yet she receaued them, and did eate some few of them , and that night she set a certain grudge of an ague, but that withheld her not from going the next day to labour in the field, as she was wount to do before: where after she had been for some short tyme , she was taken with a very great ache in her head, and she began so to whirle about her bodie, as yf she had bin out of her wittes: in such sorte, that at night of force she must be conducted to

th 3

the vilage, by the assistace of an other wo
man, where she was suddainly take with
a vehement & welnigh continual flux:
which when the inhabitants of the vilage had vnderstood, they rebuked this
Magdalen for lodging so neere the sayd
woman, for so much as she was reported to be a witch: wherof this *Magdalen*
was not a little aston shed, & seeing that
she was not able to woork any longer,
by reason of the grieuousenes of her disease, she retnrned the next day faire and
softly towards *Bruxelles*, where she indured continually her sayd maladie: notwithstanding hauing a good hope that it
would not long continue, she placed her
self in the hows of one of her acquaintance called *Simon*, dwelling neere to the
place of the *Sablon* in *Bruxelles*, there to
haue care of his hows. But when this
flux would not cease, she was costrained
to depart from thence: which also in like
maner happened vnto her in diuers other
howses where she hyred her logings to
dwel in, & much a doe she had to synd
any harbour, because euery one abhorred
to admitt so filthie a creature into their
howses, for that her disease continued
long

long tyme without any intermiſſion,
although ſhe had vſed many remedies,
both by the aduiſe of a certaine Doctor
of Phiſick, as alſo of an other expert ſurgeon, who was alſo very wel ſeen in
Phyſick, beſides the counſells of very
many other particuler perſons, who had
adminiſtred vnto her diuers medicines,
but all was in vaine and to no purpoſe.
She hauing now ſuſtained this for diuers yeares, hauing euery night and day
ordinarily thirtie or fortie ſtooles, ſhe
became exceedingly weake and feeble,
not knowing what couſel to take wherby
to help her ſelf: wel at laſt ſhe remem-
bring that the woman of *Berthem* which
had giuen her the beanes was held for a
witch, ſhe therfore purpoſed to goe vnto
her, that ſhe might take away from her
the inchauntment (a thing wherein many now a dayes very eaſily permitt them
ſelues to be abuſed) but it was told her
by thoſe of the village, that not long after theſame woman went from thence,
and that ſome had vnderſtood that ſhe
was afterward by order of iuſtice executed for ſorcerie. Afterwards it was repor
ted, vnto this *Magdalen* that neere vnto
                                    the

the town of *Hall* in *Henault* there dwelled a certain man which took vpon him
to help thofe that were bewitched:wher
vpon fhe went thither fomtymes on foot,
fomtymes being caried,but he hauing vifited & examined her , told her that her
grief was incurable,and that fhe fhould
continue in this forte all the reft of her
lyfe: counfeling her notwithftanding to
make fome offering to our Ladie at *Hall*
and to wafh her legges for fome nyne
dayes with *Aqua vitæ*, the which fhe did,
without any ayd or help thereby,her fayd
flux induring ftil night & day as before:
whereby fhe became oftentymes fo fick,
that fhe was forced to go with crutches,
& fometymes in her hows fhe crept vpõ
all fower , and for a yeares fpace fhe
voyded in her ftooles cleer blood. At
length fhe was aduifed to feek vnto a cer
tain woman dwelling in *Bruxelles*, neer
vnto the Court, who was fkilful in ad-
miniftering certaine herbes againft forcerie. Who going and declaring vnto her
her neceffitie,thefayd womã gaue her to
drink certain fpoonfulles of wyne,with
certaine ftamped herbes, and with this
fhe returning to her lodging,and coming
                                    neer

neer to the Cloister of the Capuchines,
where she dwelt at that tyme, she felt
her self very ill and (be it spoken with
reuerence) she cast forth by way of vo-
miting eight little beastes, like vnto
myce new littered, hauing tailes & very
litle hair on their backs, & beeing alyue.
And a day or two after she took againe
of the former herbes, but then she voyded nothing at all. Hauing at the third
tyme receiued again the foresaid drinck,
she cast out two little beastes like vnto
fishes which liue in the water and are
called millers thūbes & withall three or
fower thinges lyke other fishes, and finally a great worme lyke a litle snake.
After she was deliuered of this filth, she
found her self a little eased about her
hart, but her flux neuer ceased either by
night or by day so that (be it spoken with
reuerence) she voided her meat euen in
such sort as she did eat it, without any
disgestion thereof at all: and so soon as
she had eaten or drunk any thing were
it neuer so little, she was incontinently
forced by siege to voyd it. In such wise,
that she was constrained to swathe her
self as women are wount to do their
little

little children , that she might gayn her
liuing by working in the houses of some
of her acquaintance, because the former
passion neuer ceased or stayed. And thus
she cōtinued with thesayd flux three or
fower yeares after she had cast out of her
bodie those things before mentioned,
without applying any other remedie,for
wel she found that she could not any
wayes be cured. At the last, in the yeare
1603. after this flux had continued welnigh ten yeares , she was aduised by
some ofher frendes to make a pilgrimage
to our Ladie at *Montaigu* , in hope that
there peraduenture she might recouer
her health,seeirg that many others were
at the same place miraculously cured.
The which she determined to do. But
hauing vnderstood that the wyse of *Ge-*
rard Monck trumpetour to the most gracious Arc'duke Albertus and thesayd *Gerards*
sister (who were of her acquaintance)
intended to go thither, she resolued to
stay til they were returned home againe,
that she might the better vnderstand by
them the manner ofthe way and diuers
other circūstances . They beeing returned this *Magdalen* wē. foorth with to see
them,

them, and whereas the trumpeters sister had brought home with her some of
the wood of the oake, in the which in
tymes past the Image of our Ladie was
placed, she gaue her a little piece thereof,
counseling her to put it in water, and to
drinck it in honor of our Ladie, & there
withall to put her confidence in God.
But *Magdalen* taking the wood, went pre
sently to the Church called the Chappel
of our Ladie, which was not far from
thence, and there putting her self vpon
he knees before the altar of the Virgin
Marie, she began to gnaw and eat the
foresayd piece of wood, deuoutely beseeching the Mother of God that she would
obtaine for her her health, and so soon
as she had swallowed it, she found her
self much eased, feeling in her bodie a
certaine heauie grosse matter to descend
from her stomack down to the left syde
of her belly. In that Church she continued in prayer till she had heard one
masse, and a part of an other, at which
tyme she perceiued that her former passion ceased, beeing neuer after troubled
with her accustomed flux, but onely that
she felt the thing that sunck down into
                                    her

her belly to be hard, and as great as the
two fistes of a má, whereby beeing very
much comforted, fhe went too thwith
to aduertis the trompeters wyfe hereof,
declaring vnto her how fhe felt herfelf
abettered. And herevpon a day or two
after fhe made her felf redie to goe in
Pilgrimage to *Montaigue*, together with
Derick vander Schure burges of thefaid Citie
of *Bruxels*, with his wyfe, & a yong mayd,
and with *Benedicta Hendrick* wyfe vnto
Hughe Notfer: and thus departing together
from *Bruxelles*, vpon the eue of *S. Mathew*
in *September*, in the forefayd yeare 1603,
they went and lodged that night at *Louain*,
thefayd *Magdalen* feeling nothing of
her former paffion: and the next day
they wét forwards all on foot to *Môtaigu*,
and the more fhe went the better fhe felt
her felf: but beeing now come neer the
moûtayne, at a place where the gibbet ftá
deth, *Magdalen* began to feel fuch vehemét
grypings in her belly, as though fhe had
byn in the trauaile of chyldbirth, in fuch
forte that fhe was conftrained to ftay
behynd, letting the others goe on, and no
bodie remayning with her but her own
daughter, and the wyfe of the aforefayd
O   *Derick*

Derick, and through the vehemencie of
the paine holding vp her self with her
hands against a tree, she was deliuered
as it were by way of chyldbirth of a
skinne or bladder as great as an ordinarie pynt pott, and it passed from her
with a kynd of noyse or souck the which
bladder was full of filthy matter, mixt
with yelow, green, blew, and black, as
they beheld it, thrusting and breaking it
with their feet and staues, wherewith
they trauailed. After that she was deliuered of this burthen, she felt her self incontinently much eased and comforted,
insomuch that she ran after the rest of
her companie, who were now gone a
good way before. They beeing all now
come to the chappel of our Ladie, they
prayed there a good whyle, and after
they had ended their deuotions, they returned theself same day on foot, & came
to a place which was but one half myle
distant from *Louain* : insomuch as the sayd
Magdalen had gon some tenne duitch
myles that day, without any paine or
hindrance at all by her former flux: and
the next day returned to *Bruxelles*, where
euer sithens she hath continued in as
good

good health and disposition of her bodie as euer she was in all her lyfe, and so she is euen at this present. And all this she hath affirmed vnder her solemne othe (beeing diligently examined thereof) before the Magistrates of the aforesayd citie of *Bruxelles* on the eyght of *April* 1604. and vpō the twelfth of the same moneth the aforsayd *Derick vander Schuren* and his wyfe made their appearance before the sayd magistrates, who in like manner vnder their oathes declared and testified, that some nyne or ten yeares before they knew the sayd *Magdalen*, and that they alwayes held and esteemed her, and haue hard that others also haue reputed her for an honest woman, and one worthie to be credited : and that in the tyme of her former maladie she had often complayned vnto them that she was bewitched, and that she had cast vp the myce and little fishes, and other such trash as before hath been declared. Moreouer they sayd, that they knew how for some eight or ten yeares she was continually afflicted with the flux : during which tyme they had seen her often tymes very sick & weak, & that the cullour of her.

O 2   face

face was verie yellow & vgly to behold.
And the wyf of this *Derick* declared that
this *Magdalen* had made the voyage to
our Ladies at *Montaigu* in her companie,
in the côpanie of her husband, & others
before mentioned, and she wel remem-
bred, that at such tyme as they aproched
neere the Mountaine about the place
where the gibet standeth, she complai-
ned of a paine which she felt in her belly,
and that she voyded in thesame place a
certaine thing which she would haue
shewed vnto her gossip, but she regarded it nothing, saying that it was some
ordure not worth the looking on, and so
going towards the Mountaine, she wel
perceiued that after she had been discha-
ged of the foresayd filth she walked on
very merrilie, and seemed more strong
and in better disposition of her bodie,
then before: returning on foot thesame
day that they departed from *Loraine*, to a
place with-in half a myle of the same
Citie: & that euer since she hath remained
in very good health. All which is to be
seen by a publick act made thereof vnder
the seale of thesayd Citie, of *Bruxels*, and
subsigned *P. Numan.*

Of a

Of a lame man that was cured.

IOhn *Gyles* dwelling at *Myanoie*, in the countie of *Namures*, beeing about threescore yeares of age, was suddenly taken with a great maladie in the moneth of *May* 1602, wherewith he became so impotent that he could moue neither his armes nor legges, feet nor handes: and continued thus keeping his bed for the space of three mon ths and an half: but afterwards beeing somwhat recouered, he went a whole yeare (though with great difficultie) vpon crutches. In which tyme he hard talke of the miracles which were donne at *Montaigu*: whereupon he was mooued to make a vow to goe thither, and there to visit our Ladie, and to pray for his health: after which vow thus made, he began to feel more strength in his legs & armes then before. And about the feast of.*S. Remigius* in the yeare 1603. he went to *Montaigu*, whether when he was come, hauing hard a masse in our Ladies Chappel, and finished his other deuotions, he found his legges & armes

In Sept. 1603.

The feast of this Saint is vpo the first d y of Octo-ber.

O 3 perfectly

perfectly cured, and all his bodie in so good disposition and order that there he left his crutches, and returned whole to his own hows without any ayd or help, neuer feeling after that tyme any grief: in somuch as at this present he is able to goe six or seuen duitche myles euerie day. All which thesayd *Iohn Gyles* affirmed & aduouched on the xvj.th. of Iune in the yeare 1604. in the presence of *C. Remy* Notarie resident at *Namures*, and Maister *Gyles Besman* chanon and Archpriest of *Namures*, and *M. Iohn Gisoulle* witnesses, according to an instrument compiled thereof, dated and signed as aboue.

How a Religious woman that was two and fortie yeares lame was cured.

In Oct. 1603.

MAistris *Catharin Tserraerts* daughter vnto Sir *Anthony Tserraerts*, Lord of **Hadoght**, and of the Ladie *Anne de Bailencourt* his wyfe, now Professed amengst the Religious women in the monasterie of the white Ladies in *Louain*, was lame of her left leg euen from her infancie; the which leg was fiue or six inches or an hand

hand-bredth shorter then the other:
her huklebone was not in the right place
but rather towardes her back, and made
there such a buntch that one might wel
perceiue it through her clothes, the knee
of that leg was crooked and pressed inwardly against her right thighe, in so
much that she could not separate the one
leg from the other: moreouer in regard of
the shortnes of the sayd left leg she was
constrained to weare a pantofle or shooe
vnderlayd vnder the heele with corck
some fiue or six inches highe, and for all
this it came not to the ground, but she
went still vpon her toes, as one might
easilie perceiue by the vpper lether of her
shooe that was ful of wrinckles. And of
this all her kinsfolkes and frendes can
beare witnesse, who haue seen her in this
sorte, as also Iames Ma ck Shoomaker, who
fitted her with shooes Yea furthermore
all the Religious of the foresayd conuent
of the white Ladies amongst whome
shee was professed ful seuenteen yeares,
as she also was scholler amongst them,
when shee was but eight yeares old. To
help this accident her paren es laboured
and spent much, whyle she was in her

O 4 tender

tender age, in somuch as they made her
weare for a long tyme together vpon her
flesh a peece of armour couered with
cloth or canasse, that by this meane they
might make her hanche returne into the
proper place which grew backwards as
hath been sayd, and this they did while
she dweiled in the hows of M *Maximilian*
Tsenraerts Esquyre, and Burgomaister of
the Citie of *Bruxelles*: vnto which place
her parents caused a certaine famous surgeon to come from *Harentales*, who
indeuoured to help her, and by stretching out her bodie with certaine kynd
of instruments made for that purpose,
thought to put her ioynts in their right
places. But when they saw that this profited her nothing, they permitted her to
goe for diuers yeares without any shooe
vnder-layd, or without any other help,
hoping that in tyme by forceing herself to goe, and by setting all her whole
foot on the ground, her left leg would be
stretched foorth longer, and become
equall to the other. But this did no more
help her then the former remedies, for
this *Catharin* remained lame, and in the
same case as she was before. Hauing afterwards

terwards a desire to imploy her self in the seruice of God in some order of Religion, and beeing for this end presented by her parents to certaine Religious womé of the whyt ladies, in the town of *Huy* in the cuntrie of *Liege*, they refused to admit her, for that they saw her so lame, which also happened vnto her at the Cloister of *Cortenberge* as the Ladie *Magdalen de Niuelle* Abbesse of thesame place cófessed, when she afterwards hard talke of thesayd Mistris *Catharin*. Notwithstanding all this, some yeares afterwards she perseuering in this her good purpose became religious in the foresayd conuent of the white Ladies in *Louain* on the xv. of *October* in the yeare 1585, where she first liued whilest she was but a little one as before hath been sayd. Hauing now been in this Cloister for the space of xvij. yeares, and stil so lame that she could not goe one foot, nor stád vpright, nor yet so much as step out of her bed without her shooe that was vnderlayd, (which she was cóstrayned to vse againe a good whyle before) and this her accident was very painefull vnto her, especially when she was to stand for any lóg

space

space in the quier, and she could neuer
kneel but onely on her right knee, as all
the Religous there did auouche; &
that ordinarilie they were forced to put
a step or piece of wood vnder her left
knee to make it æqual with the other.
But hauing hard talk of the great miracles which our Lord wrought by the inuocation of his holy Mother at Montaigu,
vnto which place all the world went in
pilgrimage, and many receiued help and
ayd in their infirmities and necessities,
she also began to haue a desyre to go thither, and to proue yf peraduenture it
pleased God to heale and cure her: but
she could not obtaine leaue of her superiour, who thought it no way expedient
for her. Notwithstanding she continued
in her former deuotion, hoping (that if she
should not be cured of her halting) she
should at leastwyse obtaine some spiritual profit for the saluation of her soule:
and hereupon she ceased not now and
then to renew her sute, and to request her
leaue that she might make the sayd voyage, & namely she intreated the Reueréd
Father in God M. *Iames Iansonius* Doctor
of diuinitie and Superior or Superinten-
dent

dent of that Cloister, who liking not the
sayd Religious womans request, endeuoured to persuade her to hold her self
content, and to beare patiently for the
loue of God this her infirmitie, and that
this would be a cause of her greater humilitie & more merit. Vpon which reason she remayned quiet and contented.
But whereas the Prince Marquis of *Ha-*
uregh was come to *Louain* vpō the xxvij^th.
of *September* in the yeare 1603. and intended to goe to salute our Ladie at *Mōtaigu*
this mayd Mistris *Catharin Tserraertes* laboured so much by the intercession of
some of her frendes that thesayd Lord
Marques obtained her licence of thesayd
Iansonius, that she might goe & performe
her desired deuotion in the aforesayd
Mountaine, and hereupon Mistris *Anne de*
Wamel procuratrix of thesayd Conuent
was appointed to accompanie her, with
whome and with some other Pilgrimes
she departed from *Louain* by waggon towardes our Ladies, and they arryued
there vpon the xxviij^th. of thesayd moneth of *September,* and vpon the xxix^th. in
the morning she did her deuotions in the
Chappel, whether also thesayd Lord Marquis

quis came from *Dieſt*, where he had lodged that night, and he intreated theſayd two Religious women to goe vnto *Dieſt* with him, which they did, and there were lodged in the Cloiſter called *Mariendale* and two dayes after (to witt vpon the tuiſday and weddenſday) they returned againe in companie of theſayd Lord Marquis to do their deuotions at *Montaigu*, theſayd Lord beeing in coache, by reaſon of his indiſpoſition, and the Religious with him in regard alſo of her accident , but all the reſt of his houſhold and companie went on foot, with their prayers and ſpiritual ſongs , and other ſuch lyke deuiſes inciting to deuotion. Some of this companie and amongſt others theſayd Religious put themſelues in the ſtate of grace , & receiued the holy Communion in our Ladies chappel, and did other their particuler deuotions . Vpõ weddenſday in the morning whylſt the holy ſeruice of the maſſe was ſaying in *Montaigu*, theſayd Miſtris *Catharin* began to feel a certaine paine neer vnto her left eare, the which begã to paſſe through all her bodie euen from her head down to her lame leg, but ſhee knowing not
                                      what

what this should meane, nor yet much regarding it, she made her prayers to our
Lord, more for the good of the Cuntrie,
and the weale of her soule, then for the
healing of her leg, except it pleased God
to increase his glorie thereby. And on the
same weddensday (beeing the first of *October* in the foresayd yeare 1603) she returned to *Louain* in the companie of the
sayd Lord Marquis and beeing entred
the Conuent (for it was now late)
hauing giuen the good-night to her superiour she retyred herself to her chamber there to repose her: but as she went
vp the stayres, she felt that her shooe
which was vnderlayd did so hinder her
that she could not wel go therewith, in
such sorte that beeing in her chamber,
shee put it of her foot, and withall she
perceiued that without any help of her
shooe she was able to stãd vpright vpõ
her legs, and to walk along her chamber,
feeling a marckable stretching and pluc-
king within her hip, and throughout all
her left leg: whereat she beeing much
amazed, and praysing God for this his fauor and the Glorious Virgin who had
prayed for her health (as she now felt
by her

by her own experience) she settled her selfe to her prayers, intending to perseuer therein all that night: but beeing somwhat weary, both through her iorney as also for that sleep came vpon her, after she had sayd some deuotions she betook her selfe to her rest. Vpon the next morning rysing out of her bed, she found her selfe so wel, and in such forte altered, that she needed no longer her shooe that was vnderlayd, but walked vp-right in the Conuent onely with a paire of pantofles, synding no more difficultie in setting both her feet on the groud, the aforesayd stretching from her hip vnto her leg stil continuing not-withstanding that at that tyme the bunche of the sayd hip (which was behynd her and out of the right place) was very much lower and lessened.

The Lord Marquis beeing aduertised of this miracle, sent some of his howshold and diuers others who had gone with her on this voyage to visit her, who al found this admirable change in her person, seeing her now vpon the second of *Octo'er* to walk with much ease, without any high shooe or other supporte.

Whereupon

Whereupó thesayd Lord Marquis(being meruelouſely glad of the grace which our lord had wrought in this Religious) obtained leaue to carrie her with him to *Bruxelles*, there to ſhew her to the moſt gracious Infante of *Spayne* Duches of *Brabant* our Princeſſe: which ſoon after he perfourmed; hauing moreouer cauſed a ſolemn Maſſe to be ſung before the holy Sacrament of miracle in theſayd Citie of *Bruxeles*, in way of thanks-giuing for this ſo notable a benefit. At which tyme her leg much meded, waxed greater,& increaced in ſtrength: inſomuch as the bunch before mētioned became altogether euē & equal, her leg turned right, & her heel ſtretched to the due proportion, in ſuch ſorte that ſhe could walk without any lett, or ſtand vpright, or ſeperate her legs as ſhe thought good, and ſet her ſelf down equally vpon both her knees, the which ſhe was neuer able to do in two and forty yeares, that is, in all her lyfe before: as theſayd Religious womā (who was euer reported to haue beē a vertuous mayd, and one that feared God) declared all theſe particularities to diuers perſons, as well gentlewomen

This bleſſed Sacrament is myraculous as wel for the manner thereof, as for the miracles it worketh of which miracles a Chanō of that Church, hath lately publiſhed a book.

a q

as others, which had beē with her at this
voyage, & there kept her companie, who
hard it fiō her own mouth. And whereas the Lord *Mathias Houius* Archbiſhop
of *Maclin* was at that tyme in *Bruxelles*, &
had known theſayd religious from her
youth, and had often ſeen her lame, he
cauſed her to come before him vpon the
fourth of *October*, that he might vnderſtād
the manner of this alteration euen from
her own mouth: and then in his preſence
and vpon her profeſsion ſhe declared in
ſubſtance all that which we haue alredy
ſayd: and at that very tyme that ſhe was
before theſayd Lord Archbiſhop, ſhe felt
her leg to ſtretch and pull with a forcible
interiour working: walking in a chāber
in his preſence with out any ſhooe that
was vnderlayd, & ſetting both her heeles
equally vpon the ground, as appeareth
by her depoſition, written by the hand
of theſayd Lord Archbiſhop, & ſubſcri-
bed by her ſelf. And for more aſſurance
of all this, the aforeſayd Doctor *Ianſonius*
cauſed all the religious women of the
Conuent of the whyte Dames in *Louaine*
to be aſſēbled together vpon the xv.th of
October, in the foreſayd yeare 1603 & exa-
                                    mined

mined punctually thesayd mistris *Catharin Tserraert*s in their presence, touching the curing of her leg, vnto whome she answered the very self same that we haue here set down: all thesayd religious women auouching that they had seen her lame as we haue sayd, all the tyme that she had dwelled in their Conuent, & she now walked without any vnderlayd shooe, and that far better then euer she did, as she the shewed very effectually, walking in their presence along the chamber, vpon shooes of æqual height, & not vnderlayd, so that none can see that she any wayes bendeth her bodie by halting towards the left leg (as before she was wount to doe) although as she her self declared, she feeleth somtymes the aforesayd operation and inward moouing, & that very liuely, as appeareth by the attestation of thesayd *Iansonius*, bearing date as aboue.

How a mayd was cured of an incurable accident.

MAgdalen van Horen a mayd of one & fiftie yeares old, dwelling at *Bruxelles*,

P

el'es, in the yeare 1600. vpon a certaine
day by ftretching her bodie fo ouerftrai-
ned her felf, that fhe was inwardly hurt
very grieuoufly, and there hanged out
of her bodie a peece of flefh as big(fo farr
as fhe could iudge it) as ones fift, in fuch
forte that fhe was conftrained to weare a
truffe or band made purpofely to hold it
in. Together with this fhe had a vehemēcy
continuall paine, which fometymes fo afflicted her, that fhe could fcarce goe, or
fo much as fit. Phyfitions call this kynd
of euil *Procidentia vteri* and they efteeme
it incurable, or at leaft-wyfe very hard
to be cured. This fhe endured about fome
three yeares, vntil the moneth of *Octobcr*
in the yeare 1603. But as people fpake
much of the miracles which were
wrought at *Montaigu* by the interceffion
of the glorious *Virgin Marie*, fhe was moued thereby to goe thither, in hope and
confidence that the bleffed Mother of
God would pray for her: & fo fhe went
by wagon to *Montaigu* in the forfayd moneth of *October*, in the cōpanie of Miftris
Agatha Reygers with whome fhe fometymes dwelled with Miftris *Margaret de
Merode* Miftris *Ioane Iacops* & fome others:
and

and beeing come to thesayd mountaine
not without great paine, that night they
did in thesame place their deuotions, and
hauing lodged afterwards in *Sichen*, the
next morning they went on foot to the
Chappel of our Ladie, where again they
prayed, hard masse, & comunicated, at
which very tyme thesayd *Magdalen* receaued so great ease and amendment, that
she found her self deliuered of her old
paines and griefes, & altogether altered,
in somuch as beeing returned to *Bruxelles*
she could goe and walk whether soeuer
she pleased, without any impediment or
grief, and without any band or trusse,
feeling thesayd peece of flesh to be wholy retired within her bodie. Vpon the
xviij.th of *Noueber* in thesame yeare 1603
she went again vnto *Montaigu*, with an
other companie, there to render thancks
to God and his holy mother, and offered
vp there one of her bands which she was
accustomed to weare, and although in
this last iorney shee had gon fiue duitche
myles on foot, yet for all that she felt no
paine or appearance of her former grief,
beeing whole & sound as shee is at this
present. All the aforesayd things this

P 2   *Magdalen*

Magdalen declared and auouched solenly ynder her othe, before the Magistrates of *Bruxelles* ypon the nyne and twentith of *March* in the yeare 1604. Vpon which day the foresayd Mistris *Agatha Reygers* and Mistris *Margarit de Merode* making also their appearance before thesayd Magistrates, declared and affirmed that they knew very wel that this *Magdalen* had indured this accidet for three yeares space, or thereabout, & how that after she had made the first voyage to *Montaign* she remained perfectly whole, & in good disposition of her bodie, which wel they might perceiue and know, forsomuch as thesayd *Magdalen* came often to their howses, because she had been seruant vnto Mistris *Agatha*, as hath been sayd. And vpô the seuenth of *April* following, *Anne vã Snick* Beghine dwelling in *Bruxelles*, and there for xxv. yeares practising the arte of surgerie appeared before thesayd magistrates, who vnder the like othe, declared and assured that she had in cure this *Magdalen*, but she could not help her: shewing moreouer how at thesame tyme (through the assistance of God) she had healed many wounderful diseases

and

and accidents, but she held that (which this *Magdalen* had) hardly euer to be cured by any naturall meanes or work of man. And al this that hath been sayd, is to be seen by an instrument and Act which pafled before the Magistrates of *Bruxelles* as wel vpon the forefayd nyne & twëtith of *March*, as vpon the feuenth of *April* 1604, fubfcribed P. *Numan* Secretarie, and figned with the feale of thefayd Citie.

Hew a certaine man was cured of the falling euill.

HEnry de Keerfmakers a baker and citizen of *Lbuain* was attainted with the falling ficknes, which he had indured about 4 yeares. It took him both in his hows, as alfo in the Churches & ftreets to his great confufion and callamitie. But vnderftanding of the miracles which were donne at *Mōtaigu* by the intercefsiō of our Ladie, he refolued about the feaft of *S. Iohn* in the yeare 1603. to go thither in Pilgrimage, with confidence that the Mother of God would afsift him, & that fhe would obtaine that his difeafe might

In the end of Iulie, or beginning of August 1603

P 3   be hol-

be holpen. About which tyme setting
forwards barefoot on his way he did his
deuotions at the Chappel of our Ladie, &
the next day returning towards *Louain*
he felt himself somwhat eased, and to
haue recouered more strength then before, as he told them that were in his cōpagnie, with this amendment he continued for eight dayes without feeling his
accustomed disease, but onely some
signes thereof, and a litle stretching of his
limmes. Eight dayes after he went thither again barefoot, and hauing made his
prayers to our Ladie as before, & beeing
come home he foūd himself very free frō
his former passion. Whereupon eight
dayes after he returned thither again
the third tyme also barefoot, in company
of some fower or fyue others, amongst
whome were two Religious men, Cordeliers of thesayd Citie of *Louain*, but
beeing come within two myles of thesayd *Montaigu* he was taken again with
a fit of his old disease, & that for the space
of half an hower, but returning to him
self, and beeing holpen by thesayd Religious men, he was for some parte of the
way led to the Chappel of our Ladie,
                                    where

where that euening he did his deuotions,
& remained for that night in the Mountayn. The next day he returned again to
his prayers in the Chappel, whether the
foresayd Religious men (who had lod-
ged in a Cloister of *Cordeliers* in *Dieft*) also
came, and one of them sayd masse, beseeching our Ladie for the health of this
poor patient: and after the office was ended, he returned with some others towards *Louain* very merry and pleasant,
without any wearines in his trauaile, to
the great wounderment of all those that
were in his companie. And after this third
visitation which was now more then a
yeare since, he was neuer taken or troubled with his maladie, but he is become
more healthy and in better disposition of
his bodie, then euer he was before, acknowledging that herein he hath receiued a singuler benefit and fauour of
the Mother of God. And since his cure he
hath been fower other tymes barefoot at
Montaigu, there to render thancks to our
Lord and to the blessed Virgin.

And all this that hath here been sayd this
Henry de Keersmaker hath deposed and affirmed vnder his solemn othe, before the

Magiſtrates of the Citie of *Louain* vpon
the xxiij.th of *October* 1604. Vpon which
day appeared alſo *M. Laurēs Boeſem* procurator, and *Lewis vanden Vyuere* grocer,
both Burgeſes and inhabitants of theſame Citie, who vnder the like othe affirmed and teſtified, that they had often
frequented and kept companie with the-
foreſayd *Henry*, (and eſpecially this *Lewis*
who had dwelled ſome fower or fiue
yeares in a hows iuſt ouer againſt his)and
thereby they knew very wel that ſome
yeares ſithens this *Henry* was much troubled with the falling ſicknes, which took
him ſometymes ſitting at table with thē,
ſometymes in the Cloiſter of the *Iaco.ins*,
yea and ſometymes in the very ſtreet as
he went with them to gather almes for
theſayd Religious *Iacobins*, in ſomuch
that to auoyd peril & confuſion, this
office was taken from him. And how
th t after he had made the Pilgrimages
to *Montaigu* as hath been ſayd, they neither ſaw or hard that for the ſpace of a
whole yeare he was euer taken with the
ſayd diſeaſe: wherat they theſelues much
merueiled, ſeeing him ſo wel and in ſo
good health, as he was at that preſent.All
which

which is manifest by the atteftation of thefayd Magiftrates, made thereof and dated as aboue, and fealed with the feale of *Louain* figned R. *le Prince* Secretarie.

A miraculous cure of a certayn grief and languifhing difeafe.

SIfter *Anne Laureys* beeing threefcore yeares old or there about, born in *Bruxelles*, and profeffed in the Conuent of the Religious women called of the Annunciatæ in *Louain*. In the yeare 1 5 8 4. whyleft fhe fung in the quier with fome other of her religious fifters who had very ftrong voices, and fung very high, forcing her voice to follow them in finging, felt that fhe had hurt and indamaged her head, hauing a paine therein fo vehement and ftrong, that it feemed vnto her as yf her head had been cleft in twayn : which paine dayly increaced: and befides fhe felt in her head a noyfe & continuall founding like a clock, which fhe indured for a long fpace, vntil the xxvjth of *October* in anno 1603. and fo for the fpace of xviij. yeares: fo that no day
paff d

paſſed without great grief and paine, and for the moſt parte ſhe was conſtrained to abſent her ſelf from the diuine ſeruice and office with the other Religious, becauſe ſhe could not indure to heare them ſing, no nor ſomuch as any words that might be ſpoken alowd, & when thoſe of the Conuent had their recreation, ſhe was forced to get her ſelf out of the companie, becauſe ſhe might not be troubled with their voices, and ordinarily euery night it was very long ere ſhe could ſettle her ſelf to ſleep. To cure this grief ſhe had vſed the counſells of many perſons, and many remedies, without any profit at all. Finally hauing vnderſtood of the miracles that were wrought at *Montaigu* by inuocating vpon our Ladie, ſhe turned her ſelf with all her hart vnto her, hoping that by her interceſſiõ ſhe might obtain help. And for ſo much as the Religiouſ women of that Conuent (acording to their rule) neuer go out of their Monaſterie, they reedified an old Chappel which was in their garden, and they placed therein an Image printed acording to that of *Montaigu*, to the end in that place they might exerciſe their deuotions

uotions, and doe honor to the Mother of
God becaufe it was not lawful for them
to goe vnto *Montaigu.* Vnto this Chappel
thefayd fifter *Anne* went vpon three
fundry dayes, inftantly befeeching the
Virgin *Marie* to procure her her health,
with intention that fhe her felf would
haue gon to the miraculous place, yf it
had been lawful. And vpon the third day
(beeing the xxvj^th. of *October* 1603.) betwixt fiue and fix of the clock at night,
hauing ended her third Vifitation, fhe
felt her felf much eafed, and withall to be
much inwardly cõforted: and after com-
pline hauing retired herfelf into her chã-
ber, fhe refted that night very wel, not
hearing any noyfe or founding in her
head, and waking about eleuen of the
clock thefame night, fhe found herfelf
fo wel and healthie, and fo free from her
maladie, that fhe went with the reft of
the Religious to matines: and fo continuing better and better, fhe neuer after
felt any paine or trouble in her head, but
inioyed her perfet and intier health. All
which here is fayd may be feen by the atteftation of fifter *Clare Leyen* her Superiour, Sifter *Anne Smits* the vicareffe of the
fayd

fayd Conuent, and by the o he of the fayd
Sifter *Anne Laureys*; made in the hands of
the Reuerend Father *Anthonie de Bergaigne*
Confeffor of thefayd Conuent , vpon
the xx^(th.) of *Ianuarie* 1604. and after that
again vpon the xvj^(th) of *March* in the fame
yeare, in the prefence of the Magiftrates
of thefayd citie of *Louaine*, before whome
alfo her Superiour appeared , who in
like manner declared and auouched that
fhe knew right wel how that thefayd
Religious had the a forefayd paffion and
grief fo long as hath been fayd, which
partlie fhe had feen & partlie had hard
of her felf. And all this is conformable
to the atteftation of thefayd Magiftrates,
bearing date as aboue, and figned *R. le
Prince* Secretarie, and fealed with the
feale of thefame Citie.

---

*How a Religious woman of the order of S. Clare
was fuddenly healed of the palfey.*

In Oct.
1603.

SIfter *Anne de Bruyn* daughter of *Iohn de
Bruyn van Aelft* , marchant & inhabitát
of the citie of *Antwerp*. in the ftreet called
Kipdorp, was profeffed amongft religious
women

womē in the Cloiſter of S. Clare in Antwerp commōly called of the poor Clariſſes, in the yeare 1593. ſhe beeing xxii. yeares of age, healthie and ſound of al her limmes, going, ſeruing, & labouring as the reſt of theſame Conuent: but in the moneth of October in the yeare 1597. ſhe was taken with a great diſeaſe, in ſuch ſorte that twyce they gaue her the extreme vnctiō and they did the recommēdations of her ſoule in the quier, as is the cuſtome to doe vnto Religious perſons that are in dying. But hauing been ſomwhat recouered of this diſeaſe, ſhe regained ſomuch ſtrength that ſhe could walk with the ayd of a ſtaf, & by holding vp her ſelf againſt the wall, which continued for ſome ſix weekes or there about: but a little after this ſhe was ſo taken with the palſey, and became ſo impotent, that ſhe could neither goe, kneel, or ſtand, and ſo remayned for the ſpace of ſix yeares in the infirmarie of theſayd Conuent, hauing ſo loſt the vſe of her limmes, that when any would remoue her, they were conſtrained either to carry her, or to draw her, ſometymes by one of the ſtrongeſt of the Religious & ſometymes by two of thē,
                                    although

although she did also help her self with
her staff. And it hapened sometymes that
her hands became so impotent, that they
were constrained to feed her lyke a chyld
and to put her meat into her mouth. In
this six yeares space the poor patient vsed
diuers sortes of medicines, drincks, cha-
sings, bathes, & other deuises that were
thought good against the palsey and impotencie, and this, first by the assistance
of M. VVilliam Peters Doctor of Phisick, &
after his death, of M. Godfrey Verreyken
Phisition of the Citie of Antwerp, as also
of M. Cornelius van Velsen Sutgeon dwelling in thesame place, yet neuer felt she
any ease remedie or diminution of her
euil. In somuch as thesayd Phisition and
surgeon iudged her disease to be an ouer-
growen & incurable impotencie, so sur-
ceasing to apply any other thig vnto her,
as thesayd Doctor and Surgeon auouched
solemnly vnder their othes in the handes
of the Reuerend the Vicar and Official
of the dioces of Antwerp, vpon the fifth of
Nouem'er in the year 1603. and vnder the
lyke othe before the magistrates of thesame Citie vpon the fourth of December in
thesame yeare. This Religious woman
                                        ther-

therfore beeing destitute of all humain ayd and remedie, setled all her confidence in God:& hauing hard of the great miracles which our Lord dayly wrought by the inuocation of his holy Mother at *Montaigu,* she began to haue a desire to send some thither to visit our Ladie for her, and to pray for her health yf it were expedient for her soule.

Whereupō she intreated her Superiour Sister *Cornelia Gyllis* that she would send to *Montaigu* one or two lay sisters to present her prayers & deuotions to our Ladie for her, the which thing was graunted her, and so Sister *Anne Groelens* and Sister *Elizabeth van Immerzele* were sent thither, and to them was deliuered the staff wherewith the impotent patient was wount to assist her self, & withal a peece of money to offer there in signe of her desyre and intention to implore the ayd of the Mother of God: and thus departing from *Antwerp* together with the Mother of Sister *Anne Groelens,* vpon a thursday beeing the 23th. of *October* in the sayd yeare 1603. and passing by *Bruxelles* and *Louain,* they arryued at *Montaigu* vpon Saterday, beeyng the xxvth. of the same moneth:

moneth: where they, performed their deuotions and prayers for her health, as by thesayd Sister *Anne de Bruyn* they were willed : which also they continued vpon the Sunday and Moonday following. At which tyme also the Religious of her Conuent at *Antwerp* sayd some prayers to that end. And vpon the xxviij[th.] of thesame moneth (beeing *SS. Symon* and *Iudes* day) thesayd Sister *Anne* awaking soon after fower of the clock in the morning and fynding her self in her accustomed impotencie much sorrowed thereat, notwithstanding she resigned her self to the mercie of God, neither was she yet out of hope of the recouery of her health. Beeing in these conceites suddenly she had a desyre to ryse out of her bed, and to goe to the quier to giue thancks vnto God; and although she felt no strength in her bodie yet notwithstanding she took a staff which stood hard by her bed indeuouring therewith to rayse her self, and beeing faire and softly come out of her bed, and standing on her feet, she began to feel some strength in her legs : whereupon leauing her staff, & signing herself with the signe of the crosse, with

a great

a great confidence which she had in the glorious Virgin *Marie* she began to walk alone, and beeing come into the middest of her chamber which at that tyme was in the infirmarie, she felt a certain turning in her head, in such sorte that she thought she should have fallen to the ground: but calling vpon the name of God to graunt her force & strength, shee went forward til she came to an other chamber hard by, where vpon the great comfort & ioy which then she conceaued, she cast her self thryce vpon her knees, to yeeld thancks vnto God, and by little & little beeing come into the quier, she kneeled down before the *Blessed Sacrament,* where she prayed & sayd *Te Deum.* From thence she went into the dormitorie, and awaking the Mother Abbesse or Superiour, she told her that she was cured, whereat the Superiour much meruailing commaunded her to goe forthwith to the quier, whether afterwards she came with all her other Religious, and there yeelded thancks to our Lord and his holy Mother, beginning again the aforesayd song *Te Deum,* at which tyme thesayd sister *Anne de Bruyn* stood stil

Q   and

& vpryght in her seat as wel as the rest,
hauig also bin but a little before for a long
tyme on her knees before the *Blessed Sacrament*, and the altar of our Ladie: which
she was neuer able to haue donne for six
yeares before. After this thesayd sister
Anne walked alone freely, without staffe
or other stay throughout all the Monasterie. Vpon the very self same day came
to these Clarisses Father *Iohn Pelkins* Cor-
delier, their Confessor, who found this
sister *Anne* in good health, and walking
without any thing to help or support her,
whereat he was much amazed, and thanked the Almighty for this his mercie:
saying some prayers to thesame purpose,
and incontinently thesame sister *Anne*
came down without any help to the
confession seat, to which place she could
not goe for seue yeares before: but either
her confessor was forced to goe vnto the
infirmarie (where she remained continually) to heare her confessions, or
otherwyse they must carrie or draw her
to the grate or confession seat. After she
had confessed, thesayd Father *Iohn Pellens*
after masse administred vnto her the blessed *Sacramēt* of the altar, in way of thanks
giuing:

giuing: for the receiuing whereof she put
her self on her knees without any difficultie, arose, did reuerence, and departed thence, without any to help her : and
that so reddely as yf she had neuer been
sick. Vpon the xxx[th] of thesame moneth
of *October* the two Religious that were
sent to *Montaigu* returned again to *Ant-*
werp, where they found thesayd sister
Anne whole and in good health, as she is
euen vnto this day, to the great admiration of all those which before had seen
her, & especially of the Citizens & inhabitants of *Antwerp*, who in great number
came to the Monasterie to see and vnderstand the mercie which it pleased our
Lord to shew to this Religious woman,
by the inuocatiō of his holy Mother, thā-
king and praysing him for thesame. And
all this which we haue here set down
was solemnly examined, auouched, and
wittnessed vnder their othes, first before
M. *Iohn del Rio* priest, Archdeacon and
Chanon of the Collegial Church of our
Ladie in *Antwerp*, beeing the Vicar general and Official of the Dioces there,
and afterward again befor M. *Iohn vander*
Noot Escheuin, and M. *Dionis vander Neesen*

Q 2   Secre-

Secretarie of thesayd Citie, apointed in commiſſion for this purpoſe by the Magiſtrates, according to a reſolution and decree of the ſecond of *December* in thesayd yeare 1603. ſubſigned *I. vanden Kieboam,* where all was verified vnder the othes of euery one, ſo farr as might touch them, and according to their knowledge : to witt, by the foreſayd ſiſter *Cornilia Gylis* Mother Abbeſſe of the Cōuent, Brother *Iohn Pellens* the Confeſſor, Brother *Anthony de Panteghen* his aſſiſtent, ſiſter *Agnes Reyns* keeper of the infirmarie, who had the care of theſayd ſick perſon for a long tyme : the ſayd ſiſter *Anne de Bruyn,* ſiſter *Anne Groelins,* ſiſter *Elizaveth van Immerzele,* who went in pilgrimage for her : and M. *Godfrey Verreyken* phyſition of theſame Citie, M. *Cornelius van Velſen,* and *Iohn Watrinx* Surgeons, who had aſſiſted this impotent Religious woman during her maladie, and for many yeares had laboured to help & cure her. In like manner *Iohn de Bruyn van Aelſt,* Father of theſayd ſiſter Anne, and *Miſtris Sara vander Weelde* her Mother in law, who had diuers tymes viſited and frequented theſayd Religious woman, in the tyme of her infirmitie and palſey, who on

the

the next day after the feast of SS. *Symon*
& *Iude*, foūd her whole & cured, againſt
all mannes hope: as is manifeſt by their
othes as before hath been ſpecified.

How a Religious woman was cured of the Cancker.

SIſter *Margarit vāden Perre* born in Antwerp and there profeſſed a lay ſiſter
in the Cloiſter of the third order of S.
Francis, beeing thirtie yeares old, had the
cancker in her breſtes, for the ſpace of fower moneths, as diuers Phiſitions and
Surgeons iudged, who had her in cure: to
witt, two men, and two women, and yet
ſhe could not fynd any help for all their
labor: yea on the cōtrarie her euil waxed
dayly greater and wors: in ſuch ſorte that
all thoſe that viſited her ſayd plainely that
it was incurable, for that the patient had
her breſtes as hard as a ſtone, reddiſh, ble-
wiſh, and ſo vgly that it was a grieuous
thing to behold them. Her right pap was
ſwoln euen vnto her arme-pit and from
thence her grief paſſed vnto her back,
where it ſeemed that it would haue burſt
out. Vnder the other pap was a great ſwel

In Oct.
16 03.

Q 3   ling,

ling, and out of her nipples issued somtymes a certaine kynd of matter, somtymes verie blood, and so it did somtymes also out of her eares. Thus the poor Religious woman was so full of paine, and in so miserable an estate, that for a whole yeares space before her cure she was not able to doe any manner of woork, neither could shee ly, but was constrained to sleep sitting, & that with very great paine: and sometymes one of her armes became so stiff that she could not lift it to her head. And to be healed of this accidēt shee repaired to a skilful woman called *Magdalen*, dwelling in the *Brestraet* in the sayd Citie of *Antwerp* : who for the space of some six moneths took in hand to cure her, applying certaine plaisters of herbes vnto her: but whē in steed of helping her she became wors, she left that cunning woman, and vsed a certain plaister which a famous Surgeon dwelling the town of *Harentals* called M. *Peter,* had prescribed her, who also helping her nothing thereby, & perceiuing her self to be past all hope to be cured, she left him also. Afterwards an old Portuguez Surgeō, called *Vento Rodriguez,* counseled her
                                        to make

to make an issue in her arme, to draw out
thereby the humor of the canker : but all
was in vaine, and to no profit at all. After
that again she applyed diuers remedies
which some of her neighbours & freinds
taught her, but without any further successe. After a certain tyme she permitted
that her brestes might be visited by an el-
derlie mayd, who exercised her self in
surgerie called *Anne Cammarts*, alias
Abacucx: who hauing visited her twice or
thryce, and perceiuing that her disease
was incurable: she gaue her no other coũ
sel, but that she should take a purgation twice or thryce euerie yeare: which
she tryed for once or twice, but durst not
proceed therein, in regard of an other accident which she had, to witt, a rupture,
which also she had sustained for the space
of viij yeares. At the last she shewed her
impediment again to an other cunning
woman called *Gertrude Munters*, who foũd
that the canker was not onely in both
her brestes, but that it had pass'd euen
vnto her back, where also shee felt a great
hardnes : and this woman did nothing
els to her but rub her back with a certain
kind of ointmẽt, which shee could hardly
Q 4   indure

indure, causing her to apply vnto her breastes certain plates of lead, and faire linnen, counseling her furthermore to tamper with no more physick, but to commend all vnto God, for so much as there was no other way to help her. And in this manner this Religious woman was abandoned and forsaken of all humaine help, euerie one foretelling her that visited her that ere long she should come to that miserie that would be most lamentable for any to behold. In this tyme so vehement and excessiue great were the paines which this Relig ous woman indured, that often tymes she consumed whole nightes in teares and lamenting.

But some three moneths after hauing vnderstood that Sister *Anne de Brum, the Clarisse* was miraculousely cured by the inuocation of our Lady of *Montaigu*, she turned her self with all her hart towards our ladie, beseeching the mother or superior of the Conuét that she might make a voyage *to Montaigu*, to recommend there her health vnto the Mother of God.

Which was graunted her, vpó the fourth day of *Nonember* in the yeare 1603: & from
the

the very tyme that she had obtained her
sayd leaue, she began to feel some ease in
her self. And vpon the next day she departed frō *Antwerp*, together with Sister
Marie Clemens, gardian of the sick , who
had assisted her during the tyme of her
maladie. They hauing past by *Bruxelles* &
arriued at *Louain* the patient beeing not
able to indure the shoggíg of the waggō,
went from *Louain* vnto *Montaigu* on foot.
Whether when they were come, they
did their deuotions that very day in the
Chappel of our Ladie. The next day
(beeing the nynth of the aforesayd moneth) they hard three masses, at the first
masse thesayd patient was very weake &
sick , but hauing receiued the blessed Sacrament of the altar she began to feel in
her self a notable ease,as wel in regard of
her disease of the cancker as of her rupture,and at the third masse she found herself perfectly whole : for it seemed vnto
her that she felt a hād strokíg ouer her &
therewith to wype away all her paine.
And from that tyme feeling herself perfectly whole, she gaue thancks to God,&
to his most holy Mother , leauing in the
Chappel the lead and cloathes which she
vsed

vfed before. And thus returned with her
companie to *Antweip* whoe and found.
And beeing come home, thefayd fifter
Marie Clemens vifited her breafts, & foud
them perfectly cured and in good ordet:
where as before they were fo miferable
and deformed, that none could behold
them without horrour: fynding alfo that
the end of her teat was clofed vp , & that
there was no hardnes in all her bofome
but a very little in her left pap, which
within three or fower dayes after was
gone and ceafed.

So that fince the tyme of this vifitation
fhe remained quyte deliuered and free of
the cãcker, as alfo of her rupture, which
fhe had indured for eight yeares fpace, as
hath been fayd: and fo fhe fettled herfelf
to labour and trauaile againe with the
other Religious in thefayd Cloifter, as before fhe was accuftomed. Some dayes
after her return fhe was vifited again as
wel by the aforefayd *Anne Cammarts*, as
alfo by *Gertrule Munters*, both expert in
furgerie as we haue fayd, who to their
great admiration foud thefayd Religious
intyrely and perfectly cured, as wel in
her breafts, as in her arme-pitts & back,
                                    with

without any apparence or signe of any
hardnes, or of any other disease, but that
she was whole, and very wel in all her
bodie. All this here set down was affirmed and verified by their solemn othes,
made in the hands of the aforesayd Vi-
care of *Antwerp*, vpon the xxj. of *Nouember*
1603, and vpon the iiij. of *December* in the
same yeare. The like solemn attestation
was made thereof before these commis-
saries: M. *Iohn vander Noot* Escheuin, & M.
Denis vader Neesen secretarie of thesayd Citie, by these persons here named: to witt,
by *Sister Ioane de Herde* Mother or Superiour of thesayd Conuent, by the fore-
named *Sister Margarit vander Perre*, *Sister
Marie Clemens*, mistris or gardian of the
infirmarie, *Sister Hester de Mompere*, & *Sister
Marie Perez*, all Religious women of thesame Conuent: who at sundrie tymes had
assisted this *Sister Margarit*, and had seen
her diseases, who also knew her rupture,
whereof together with her cancker she
was healed, as hath binsayd. Also the a-
foresayd Anne *Cammaerts alias Abacucx* &
Gertrude Munters affirmed thesame vnder
their othes: who in tymes past had care
of thesayd Religious woman, and had visited

fited her breafts, both before & after her
fayd cure, as is manifeft by an inftrument
framed thereof, and dated as aboue.

The curing of a fore which was fifteen yeares old.

In Nou. 1603.

Ioane *Ruts* the widow of *Iohn Strobant*, of about fiftie yeares of age, dwelling in the lordfhip of *Campenhout* in the Maierdome of the Citie of *Bruxelles*. In the year 1599. got an accident in her left leg, vpõ the ankle of her foot, whereupon grew a fore or iffue as great in compas as ones hand, and a finger or more in length: wherein fhe felt fuch vehement & continual payne, that fhe could neither by night or day take any reft: and fhe was very often fully mynded to haue cutt of that leg, beeing forced for the moft part to keep her bed, or to fit in a chair, beeing not able to go in any manner, except it were fometymes with two crutches, or whith a ftaff, or els creeping on all fower vpon the ground. And although fhe had applyed diuers remedies, yet could fhe receiue no eafe, and her euil was acounted

red incurable. But in the yeare 1603. ha-
uíg hard of the miracles which our Lord
did woork by the inuocation of his holy
Mother at *Montaigu* thesayd *Ioane* made a
vow to go thither in pilgrimage : and
whereas through her great paine, de-
bilitie, & weakns she was not able to go,
it happened that a certain person mooued
with compassion of her estate, carried
her in a waggon vnto *Montaigu*, in the
moneth of *October* in the aforesayd yeare
1603. Where beeing in the Chappel of
our Ladie she did there her deuotions,
with firme hope and confidence to be cured: and returuing home caried with her
some of the water which is behynd the
chappel in thesayd Moütayne, the which
(that it might last the longer) shee mixed
with riuer water, and she daylie washed
and made cleane her leg therewith, whereby incontinently she perceiued a great
alteration and ease in her sore, and without applying any thing els thereunto it
healed vp of it self, and within few moneths was perfectly whole, in such sorte
that at this present she goeth & walketh
lustely whethersoeuer she pleaseth, not
feeling any paine or grief, beeing now
able

able to go three or fower duitche myles
at a tyme, whereas before (though she
might thereby haue gayned all the world)
she was not able to go one myle. And in
thankfulnes for this benefit, the sayd *Ioane*
went an other tyme in Pilgrimage to
Montaign, within the Octaues of the *Af-
sumption* of our Ladie, in this yeare 1604.
and this she performed on foot, and
went thither on one daye, and returned on the next, without any impedimēt
by her former accident. As the sayd *Ioane*
declared & auouched all these thigs vnder
her othe, solemnly giuen before the chief
Maier and Escheuines of thesayd Lordship of *Campenhout*, vpon the nynteenth
of *October* in the sayd yeare 1604, according to their attestation giuen thereof, &
sealed with the seale of thesayd Lordship, and subsigned R. *Hermans* Secretarie.

How a Chyld beeing broken was cured.

In Nou. **F**Rancis Addiers of fower yeares and an
1603. half old, the sonne of *Francis Addiers*, &
of *Anne vande VVinckele* his wyfe dwelling
in *Bruxelles*, was broken on the left syde of
his

his bellie, & this hapned him when he
was but six weekes old, so that from that
tyme they made him weare a truffe, becaufe thefayd rupture appeared of the
bignes of a turkeys egge, & neuer kept
in, but vvhê they put on his truffe: & oftê
tymes it was feen in his fecret partes,
whereby he indured great pain, efpe-
tially twife or thrife euery moneth at
the change of the moone. And although
his mother had applied diuers medicines
both by the aduife of fome furgeons as
of others, yet fhe nothing preuailed.
But hauing heard the fame of *Mont-*
aigu, & of the miracles that were there
wrought by the inuocation of our Ladie, fhe refolued to carrie thither her
chyld, and there to pray vnto our Ladie for his health, which fhe performed
about the middeft of *October*, in the
yeare 1603, & remained there for three
dayes, praying daylie in thefayd Chappel: & after the third day fhe perceiued
that her chylds difeafe was much amended. Whereupon fhee left there his truffe
in memorie thereof: and beeing come
home fhee perceiued that his rupture
appeared again't, but after that tyme her
chyld

chyld was perfectly cured, so that since
thesayd pilgrimage he neuer needed
either truſſe or any other remedy, beeing much altered in his bodie, ſo that
he became fatter & ſtronger, going, running, & playing, as othe chilarei othis
age are without to do, not feeling any paine
or impediment by thesayd rupture: which
things his mother solenly affirmed vnder
her othe, in the preſence of the Magiſtrates of *Bruxelles*, vpon the eleuenth of *December*, in thesayd yeare 1603. Vpon
which day alſo *Arnold Addiers* vnder burge-
maiſter of thesayd citie declared and affirmed vnder the like othe before thesaid
Magiſtrates, that he had ſeen thesayd
chyld thus broken, when he was but ſix
weeks old, as hath been ſayd: and that he
had made inquirie after all ſortes of remedies to cure him, yf it had been poſſible, and yet nothing would help, ſo that
the ſurgeons were of opinion that the
chyld was to be cutt, whereunto neither
he nor any of his kinſfolks and frendes
would agree, ſhewing more ouer that
he knew right wel how that thesayd *Anne
vanden Winkele* his daughter in law went
with thesayd chyld to viſit our Ladie at
                                    Montaigu

Montaigu, and how that after her return the sayd chyld was found to be cured, as now he is. And all this is manifest by the attestation of the Magistrates, subsigned P. *Numan,* and sealed with the seale of the same Citie.

A suddain cure of a laguishing disease:

SIster *Michielle Blyleuen,* daughter of M. *Thomas Blyleuen* Sergeant Maior of the Citie of *Louain,* professed Religious of the Conuent of the *Annunciate* in the sayd Citie, in the yeare 1603 fel into a great disease, which lasted for the space of six moneths, together which a perpetual pensiuenes at her hart, and a shortnes of breath; which was so great that she lost all her strength, beeing so feeble & faint, that six or seuen tymes euery day the sweat issued violently out of euery parte of her bodie, & the teares out of her eies; and for two whole moneths she was not able to go in any sorte, but as she was led by some one of the Religious, at which tyme she so lost her appetite, that she would receiue no meate, but vpon force

In Nou. 1603.

R   and

and her superiours commaundment. In
such sorte, that she was forced to vse the
counsel first of *Doctor Vilerius*, and afterwards continually of *Doctor Fienus* both
professors of Physick in the Vniuersitie
of *Louain*. But for all that they had prescribed her receiptes at diuers tymes, yet she
found no profit or ease thereby. Whereupon hauing now for two moneths space
left all vse of Physick, she determined to
go and pray three tymes at the Chappel
which they had accomodated in their
garden, in the honour of our ladie, and in
memorie of the miracles which by her
intercession were wrought at *Montaigu*:
with a desyre to haue done the same in
the place it self yf it might haue been permitted her. Going therefore to the sayd
Chappel, with great paine & labor, vpon
a saterday beeing the xv.th. of *Nouember* in
the sayd yeare 1603 : & hauing there dōne her deuotiō, she began to feel a great
ease and alteration in her bodie, recoue-
ring a notable force & ablenes in her self,
in so much that on the same day she did
read the mattines of our Ladie on her
knees, which for fiue moneths before she
was not able to do. On the night following

wing she beeing in the quier with the
rest of the religious, & reading her howers, at the very instant that mattines
was ended by the song of *Salue Regina*, the
sayd *Sister Michelle* felt as it were a had
vpon her shoulder which seemed to haue
pressed her down , & this was in so euident a manner that she felt & perfectly
discerned the very fingers; whereby she
started, & looked back to see the person
that touched her. After Mattines she
went to repose her, and rysing again in
the morning she found herself merue-
loully amended, & so strong, that immediately after, she went to the Chu che to
be present at diuine seruice with the rest
of the Religious, with whome she sung
so lowd & liuely that they were greatly
astonished thereat, not knowing what
voice it was that sounded so shrill. And
from that tyme afterwards she hath remained healthie, & in good plight, singing and asisting at the ordinarie ob-
seruances as the other Religious : who
auouch and testifie , that they neuer saw
her so strong & in so good lyking as she
hath been since the tyme aboue mentioned. And the Superiour and Vicaresse of
R 2　　　　thesayd

thesayd Convent haue giuen attestation & certified vnder their seales, that all this is true that hath been here related. Likewise thesayd religious hath also affirmed thesame in the hands of the Reuerend Father *Antonie de Bergaigne* their ghostly father, vpon the twentith of *Ianuarie* 1604, and after that again in the presence of the Magistrates of thesayd Citie of *Louain* vpon the xvj. of *March* in thesayd yeare 1604. Vpon which day also thesayd Superiour Sister *Clare van Leyden* appearing before thesame Magistrates, declared that she knew very wel that thesayd Religious was so long tyme sick, and in the aforesayd plight, as hauing seen it partly with her own eyes, and partly hauing vnderstood somuch from thesayd Religious herself, as it is to be seen by the attestation subsigned *R. de Prince* Secretarie, and sealed with the seale of thesame Citie.

The cure of a rupture.

In Nou. 1603.

FRancis de Alarcon one of the houshold of the most gracious Archdukes *Albert* and

and *Isabel* Dukes of *Brabant* our Princes,
happened to be inwardly broken in managing & conducting a froward and
stubborn hors, & the rupture came foorth
as big as ones fist, who hauing indured
this euil with much paine for three
yeares and an half, & hauing vsed diuers
remedies, by bads, trusses, as other wise,
yet without any proffit: at last he went
in pilgrimage to our Ladies at *Montaigu*,
where hauing prayed a whyle in the
Chappel, he foud himself perfectly freed
and healed of his *Rupture*: inso much as
he left of his band or trusse which he
had worne before, as appeareth by his
attestation giuen vnder his own seale.

How a wench that had the palsey, and was depriued of her wittes was healed.

ANgela *Wouters* daughter of *Elizabeth*   In Nou
van *Herp* the wyfe of *Mathias Lesteens*   1603.
cooper, dwelling in the old *Corne-market*
in the Citie of *Antwerp*, about thirteen
yeares old, was in the moneth of *September*
1603. attainted with a certain kynd of
Apoplexie, especialy in her armes, and in
    R 3   her

her right syde and leg, with so great a stretching and trembling that she could not go, & at certaine tymes she became dumme, in such sorte that none could vnderstand her when she indeuoured to speake. At last she wholy lost her speache besydes this, she was depriued of her wittes, & became so weak, that she could not apparel herself, no nor so much as put her meat into her mouth. Her parents caused Maister *Bennet Rutten* sworn Doctor of Phisick for the Citie of Antwerp to be sent for, who visiting the mayd, let her blood in the foot, and afterwards gaue her a purge, for he was of opinion that her malladie proceeded of some interiour motion, which Philitions call *Motus connulsius*: which take their beginning of some venemous matter gathered in the braine: but after he had visited her twise or thrise, he let her parents sufficiently to vnderstand that he had little hope of her recouerie, counseling them to make some pi'grimage or to vse some other kynd of deuotion with their child, & to call vpon the help of God for her. Which when her parents had heard they resolued that one of them should go with
her

her to *Montaigu*, there to salute the *Virgin Marie* and this was to be performed so soone a the winter was past. But vpon the xxj. of *Nouember* (beeing the feast of the Presentation of our Ladie) the sayd *Mathias* ryling in the morning, aduertised his wyfe of the feast ; and counseled her to go with her daughter to our Ladies Church in the sayd Citie of *Antwerp*, to heare masse, and to pray there for her health: which shee did, and after she had heard masse she bought a wax taper, commaunding her daughter to light it, & to set it on the candlestick which stadeth before our Ladies altar , which she did with the hand that had the palsey, assisting and lifting it vp with the other had, her mother beseeching God to help her, and the blessed Virgin to pray for her health , exhorting her daughter to call vpo the Mother of God, that she would vouchsafe to pray for her: and immediately the sayd candle (although it was very wel lighted) wet out of it self. Beeig the secod tyme lighted , out it wet again, as it happened also the third tyme, yet she caused it stil to be lighted again, & that the mayd (by her help should put it on

R 4 the

the forsayd candleſtick, perſuading her
ſelf that it would be a thing right pleaſing
to the *Virgin Marie* that the chyld her ſelf
ſhould offer vp the candle vnto her. This
donne, home ſhee returneth with her
daughter, ſynding for all this no alteration that day in the mayd: but the wench
ariſing the next day (beeing the two and
twētith of theſayd moneth) early in the
morning, down ſhe cometh all apparailed, whereat her Mother was much
abaſhed, and enquired of her who had
apparailed her: & when ſhee had heard
her anſwer that ſhee alone had dōne it,
and on the other part ſeeing her daughter
to goe ſo perfectly wel, ſhe began to
thanck God and his holy Mother for it,
beeing ſingulerly glad to ſee in her this
alteration. And from that day ſtil afterwards theſayd wench remained whole
and ſound, going, ſpeaking, and performing all her bodily functions as wel as
euer ſhe had dōne before: Where as during her foreſayd diſeaſe ſhe was neuer
able to put on her clothes, to walk, to
ſpeak, or to do any kynd of work, but ſhe
ſat alwayes trembling, and drawing in
her limmes, and ſometymes for the ſpace

of

of three dayes together a great quantitie
of froathie spettle ranne cōtinually out
of her mouth. And the aforesayd M.
Bennet Rutten coming some certaine dayes
after to visit the mayd, found her suddainly healed as hath been sayd. And all
that hath beē here related is to be seen
by the information takē hereof vpon the
fifteenth as also vpō the last of *December*,
in thesayd year 1603. by M. *Iohn vander*
Noot esquire and Escheuin, and *Maister*
Denis vander Neesen Secretarie of thesayd
citie of *Antwerp*, appointed by Magistrates
in commission for this matter. Who
vpon these things examined vnder their
solemn othes thesayd *Mathias Lesteens* her
Father in law, and *Elizabeth van Herp* her
Mother, the aforesayd Doctor *Maister*
Bennet Rutten, and with these *Father Michel*
van Ophouen licentiate in Diuinitie, and
Religious in the Cloister of the *Iacobins*
in thesame place, who was kinsman to
the chyld, and had also seen her first
sick, and afterwards miraculously cured.

The

The cure of a Rupture.

In Nou.
1603.

MAister *Balthazar van Rossum* esquire, sometymes coronel of a regiment of Allemans in the king of *Spayne* his seruice, beeing of the age of eight and fiftie, in the yeare 1597. as he was in the Citie of *Luxemburg* he found himself burst on the left syde, the which accident he caused to be visited by diuers surgeons, both in the sayd Citie of *Luxemburg*, as also afterwards in the Citie of *Doüay*, who iudged it to be a very *Hernia* or *Rupture*: and after he had vsed diuers helps and remedies, at last he was constrained to weare a trusse fitted for the purpose, not knowing any other way whereby, to help himself. But in the yeare 1603. hauing heard of the miracles of our ladie at *Mötaigu* he made a secret promis to goe thither in pilgrimage, and to pray for his health, with good hope to fynd there some help and fauor. And he accomplished this his deuout voyage thryse, about the moneth of *September* in the foresayd yeare, and after a whyle one day in *Bruxelles*

elles taking of his truſſe which he vſed to weare, he found himſelf perfectly healed, neuer hauing any feeling thereof afterwards, verily aſſuring himſelf that he had obtained theſayd cure, onely by the fauor of God which he had found in theſayd pilgrimage : for ſo he declared and auouched theſame vnder his ſoléne othe vpon the xth of *Iulie*, in the hands of M. *Iohn Bricx* Notarie in the Citie of *Bruges*, and in the preſence of *Andrew Vermeulen*, and *George* the ſonne of *George Modan* wittneſſes : as appeareth by a publick inſtrument diſpatched hereof, dated and ſigned as aboue, together with the ſubſcriptiō of theſayd *van Roſſum*, with his own hand.

How a Religious woman was ſuddainely cured
of a ſtrange and incurable diſeaſe.

SIſter *Barbara de Berges*, the daughter of M. *Gerard de Berges* in his lyfe-tyme Phiſition of *Antwerp*, beeing ſix and thirty yeares old, made her profeſſion in Religion in the Cloiſter called of the ſick leapers in theſayd Citie, where ſhee was taken with a grieuous malladie, which forced her to keep her bed continually

for

In Dec.
1593

for the space of six yeares and three moneths. Of this her disease no man could
giue any iudgemēt what it should be, some
saying as mamely D. *Emanuel Gomez* Portugues (after that he had applyed vnto
her many remedies) that it was an inward
cancker. Others as M *Bennet Ratten* sworn
Phisition of the sayd Citie, that it was
Melancholia hypochondriaca, proceeding from
the splene & left syde, accompained with
diuers other accidents and infirmities, as
the beating of the hart, & a certain kynd
of anguish which took her so often as any
person touched her bodie, though neuer
so litle: and this with such a faynting
and feeblenes, that it seemed that death
it self would immediately haue ensued
thereof. In so-much that they could not
past twyse or thryse in a yeare take her
out of her bed: and yet euery tyme she
would fall into such qualmes & fayntings
that they thought she would haue dyed,
and at one tyme amongst others beeing
taken out of her bed, and layd vpon an
other on the ground, vntil such tyme as
her owne was made redie, shee became
so feeble by this touching and remouing
her, that they were forced to let her so ly
on the

on the ground for fifteen dayes continually before she could returu again to her
self. Whereof many were wittnesses, as
hereafter shallbe set down: and amongst
the rest the Reuerend. M. *Gosuin Batson*
Chanon of our Ladies in *Antwerp*, & other
Religious wome who had assisted in that
tyme of her sowning. And although she
became very cold lying in this manner
on the ground, yet she could not indure
that any should apply any hote napkins
or clothes to warme her bodie, for then
would she fall agai into her former sowning and fayntings, that euery one looked
for nothing els but that she should dy.
Yea, which is more, yf any did but onely
touch the bed wherein she did ly, or so
much as the curtaines, she took such an
apprehension thereof, that she sowned
incontinently, and for this cause, they re-
mooued her out of her bed but twise or
thryse in a yeare, as we haue declared.

And the Religious women that attended her were constrained to put good
store of thornes round about the pillers
of her bed. to the end that none might
touche it whereby the patient might not
fall into her strange swownings. And it is

to be

to be noted, that for the space of six moneths before she was healed she had neuer been out of her bed, and she could neuer sit vpright therein, either to eat or drinck, or to do anythingels: moreouer the sinewes of her left leg were so shruck vp, that it was shorter by a foot then the other. Again for these six yeares this poor religious person had vsed the counsel and help of many Physitions, and had tryed many medicines, receiptes, and remedies, which rather made her wors then better: insomuch as the Phisitions plainely affirmed that they knew not how to help her. Some fower yeares before she was cured they made her an yssue, and they thrust a great red whore pack needle through the skin of her left side, drawing through the same a corde made of silk, the which (for the space of three moneths) they drew dayly vp and down to make a way, through the which the bad humors might passe: and although hereby she suffered much paine, yet it profited her nothing at all: yea she rather felt her self woors then before. Now this Religious seeing there was no hope in man, she armed her self with patience the best
                                                      she

she could, and she had for some yeares
before vpon deuotion determined that
when she had thus lyen seuen yeares,
she would either visit or cause some to
visit our Ladie of *Hanswyck* in the citie
of *Maclin*, in hope by way of prayer to
obtaine her health. But in the meane
while hauing heard of the great miracles
which were wrought at *Montaigu* by the
inuocation of the glorious *Virgin Marie*,
she had a great desire to visit that place,
and she beseeched God to affoord her so
much strength that she might be caried
thither. In the meane tyme sister *Anne van*
Calster Superiour of that Conuent hauing
compassion of the desolate poor creature
promised her, that she her self would go
and visit our Ladie at *Montaigu* for her,
and that there she would pray for her
health: the which thing she fulfilled: and
beeing returned home, she went to see
the sayd Religious whome she found in
the self same state, who told her Superior that she thought it good to go
thither thryce & that she had beseeched
our Lord that shee her self might be the
third person that should there visit our
Ladie. It happened not long after that the
aboue

aboue named Chanon *Batſon* (who diuers tymes vpon charitie viſited & comforted the patient in her afflictions) had ſayd maſſe in theſayd Conuent: at which tyme he recommended her to God, and at that very tyme determined to make a pilgrimage vnto *Montaigu* in her name, & there to pray for her health. After the maſſe was ſayd he went vnto the ſick perſon, and declared vnto her his intention: the which when ſhe had heard, ſhe was inwardly altered, and ſeemed to be exceedingly glad thereof, as theſayd M. *Batſon* wel perceiued: whereby he felt himſelf the more incited to accompliſh theſayd promeſſe. Vpon this reſolution he departed from *Antwerp* with *Sir Vulmare Schetz* Paſtor of theſayd Conuent, paſſing by bote on the riuer of *Scaldis* vnto *Willebrook*, from thence they went on foot vnto *Montaigu*, & in lyke manner returned back again on foot afterwards. Beeing at *Montaigu* vpon the third of *December*, in theſayd yeare 1 6 0 3. which was the eue of *S. Barbara*, they both calebrated maſſe in the Chappel of our Ladie, and prayed vnto allmightie God by the interceſſion of his holy Mother to vouchſafe to

reſtore

restore this poor and miserable Religious woman to her health. Vpon the self same day that the holy sacrifice was there offered for her, the sayd Religious womā beeing in *Antwerp* in her bed felt her self to be much amended, and to haue obtained a new strength, and immediately afterwards she felt so great payne in her bodie, that she fell into an ague. The next day (beeing the feast of *S. Barbara*) at eleuen of the clock about noon she began again to feel her strength much to increase, and she spake to the Sister that kept her that she would reache vnto her her hād, which when she had taken, she raysed vp her self by her self, vpon her feet vpon her bed: whereat the sister beeing much astonished cryed out for feare, and the sayd Religious fel down heauily again vpon her bed, not sustaining for all this any alteration or faintnes hereby, whereas before she was woūt to fal into sowning and that almost to death, when any did so much as but touch her, yea although it were neuer so softly, as hath been sayd. And the sayd sister *Barbara de Berges* remayned all that day in her bed, although she thought that after dinner

S she

she was strong enough to walk vp and down her chamber. But vpon the next day following which was fryday & the fifth of the aforesayd moneth of *December*, she craued to haue her apparell deliuered vnto her, which was giuen her, and she put it on alone by her self without any to help her, beginning first with her left arme, on which syde all her disease had been, which arme none might touch before, no more then any other part of her bodie without the daunger of falling into her accustomed faintenes: and so hauing apparailed herself shee came cheerefully out of her bed: and signing her self with the signe of the crosse, down she cast herself vpon her knees, & lifting vp her eyes to heauen, she gaue thancks to our Lord and sayd: *Praise be to the O Marie.* Which when the other Religious wome saw who were in the chamber with her, they powred out teares of ioy: and Sister *Michielle de Bergues* the natural Sister of thesayd *Barbara* fel into a swoune, vpon tender affection & astonishment which she had conceiued. After this thesayd Sister sat her down in a chaire by the fyer for an hower or two, where as before

fore she could not indure any fyer, no not
so much as that her clothes should be
warmed. Sitting thus before the fyer she
sayd that she felt such a force & strength
in her bones and marow, from her head
down to her feet, as yf some had powred
somwhat from aboue vpon her, & she
began to walk all alone about the chamber. Whereupon the religious women
who were there present sang *Te Deum* in
way of thancks giuing, and after that the
Hymne A*ue Maris stella*, the sayd patient
inioying the health and good disposition
of her bodie going & walking vp and
down whether so euer she pleased reco-
uering also her appetite which so long
tyme before shee had lost, in so much that
foorthwith shee dranck a good draught
of wyne, and some other sustenace shee
also receiued, and that with a very good
stomack, whereas in times past she had
no desyre to her meate, and she could
not so much as swallow down a little
wyne although it were drop after drop
without great paine and difficultie. And
vpon thesame fryday at night came
home from Mo*taigu* the sayd maister B*arso*,
and the Pastor, and coming into thesayd
religious

religious womans chamber, they found
her sitting before the fyer, who arose incontinently of her self and gaue them the
welcome home, shewing vnto the how
that all her accidents and diseases were
perfectly cured. And so became dayly
more strong, and in better plight: in such
forte, that vpon the next day she heard
three masses, with the rest of the Conuet,
at the which she afsisted for the most
part vpon her knees. Some two or three
dayes after the feast of *S. Barbara* the a
foresayd Doctor *M. Benedict Rutten* was
sent for by the Conuent; to visit thesayd
religious woma, whome he foud whole
and strong, going vp and down the monasterie without any crutch, staffe, or
any humaine help. And all this that hath
been here fayd was verified & solemnly
auouched before Maister *Iohn vander Noot*
Esquire and Escheuin, and maister *Denis
vander Neesen* Secretarie of thesayd Citie
of *Antwerp* appointed in commission by
the Magistrates for this matter as hath
been sayd, acording to the information
taken hereof, & put in wryting: and this
by diuers persons of good: credit, who
at diuers tymes had visited and afsisted
thesayd

thesayd patient in her grieuous malladie, and afterwards found her thus suddenly cured: to witt, thesayd Sister *Anne van Calstere* Superiour, thesayd Maister *Gosuin Batson* Chanon, & Maister *VVlmare Schetz* Pastor, thesayd Sister *Barbara de Bergues* the sayd Doctor *Benedict Rutten*, and Sister *Michielle de Bergues* vpon the last of *December*, in thesayd yeare 1603. And this same religious was afterwards in very good and perfect health of bodie vpon the last of *May* in the yeare 1604, beeing visited by him that hath written these things and in the moneth of *Iulie* she personally went in pilgrimage to our Ladies at *Môtaigu*, as she herself had before prayed our Lord, and verily trusted that she should be the third that was to go thither in pilgrimage for herself: a thing to all the world very strange and wounderfull.

A long deafnes cured.

DAme Adrian *de Goux de wedergraet* In Dec. Prioresse of the Cloister of *shertoginnen dale* or valley of the Dutchesse at *Oudergem* neere to the Citie of *Bruxelles*: 1603.

S 3   some

some thirtie-eight yeares agoe became deafe of both her eares, in such sorte that she could not heare when the Riligious did sing, yea although they did all sing together in her presence, hearing nothing but a certain little sound as yf it had been a farr of, and the lyke was of the sound of the belles of thesayd Conuent. Besydes this, she had an exceeding cōtinuall payn in the top of her head, with a certain noyse in her eares, as yf it had been of a water mill. And although she had applied diuers remedies, as wel by the aduise of hysitions, as of others, yet she receiued no benefit by them: but that sometymes after she had vsed these medicines, and receiptes, she felt her self a little amēded, the which lasted for some one, two, or three moneths, but she fell again incontinently into her accustomed deafnes: and thus passing many yeares therewith, she abandoned all physick, wholy resigning herself to the wil of God. But at last vnderstanding of the miracles of *Mōtaigu* she purposed to send some thither to our Ladie in pilgrimage: and about the feast of S. *Remigius* in the yeare 1 6 0 3, she sent thither M. *Iohn wailart* a religious man,

man, and *Antonet Hazard* her mayd, with an almes, & she sent thither afterwards the sayd *Antonet* alone. The which pilgrimages beeing ended, it happened vpō the first Sunday of Aduēt that the sayd Dame *Adrian* hauing been that night at Mattines with tȳe other religious womē: & returned thence to take her rest, she began to dreame, and beeing betwixt sleeping and waking it seemed vnto her that she saw before her an image of our Ladie, the which opening her eyes she beheld: at which sight at the beginning she was affraied, but taking courage she beseeched the glorious Virgin *Marie* that she would vouchsafe to pray for the cure of her deafnes: and soorthwith the sayd Image stretched foorth the hand, and touched her vpon the temples and eies, saying vnto her certain words: whereof she hath as yet perfect memorie. And so vanishing away, vpon the next day, the sayd Prioresse perceiued that she begā to heare better then before, and afterwards by litle and litle within the space of seuē or eight dayes she perfectly recouered her hearing: in so much as at this present she not onely heareth the soūd of the belles,

S 4   or the

or the song of the religious, but she can perfectly and distinctly heare what any speaketh, as wel as any other, not hauing the former paines or noyse in her head. As the sayd dame Prioresse hath testified & auouched all this that here hath been sayd vnder her own seale, & the seale of her Côuét, as also vnder their seales the like hath been donn by Father *Iohn Molemans* Confessor, Sister *Marie vander Lindē* Subprioresse , Sister *Elizabeth Houture* , Sister *Marie Beck*, Sister *Elizabeth du Terne,* and Sister *Anne vā Diene* all religious women of this Conuent: who haue seen and noted the sayd dame Prioresse, to haue had the aforesaid deafenes, and now to inioy her perfect hearing, according to an instrument framed thereof, subsigned & sealed as aboue, vpon the xxvj of May 1604.

How

How a lamce Wench was cured.

IOhn *Nyemegens* Apoticarie dwelling in
the *Keeftrate* in the Citie of *Antwerp*, had
a daughter called *Margarit* about thirteē
yeares of age, who from the tyme that
fhe was fix woneths old had a lame foot,
in fuch forte that her right leg was fhorter then the other by a good hand bredth;
wherevpon they were conftrained to
vnderlay her fhooe, and make it higher,
& for all this fhe went with great paine
vpon her toes, for that her heele could
not reft vpon her fhooe, as appeared to
the commiffaries according to the information which they receiued thereof.
This wench hauing heard what was reported of the miracles which by the interceffion of the glorious Virgin Mother of God were wrought at *Montaigu*,
fhe neuer ceafed to intreat her Father to
permitt her to goe thither vpō deuotion:
but her Father telling her yf fhe defyred
to be cured, that thereby fhe might be
more pleafing & acceptable to the world,
that then infallibly her prayers would
                                    neuer

In Dec
1603.

neuer be graunted. She answered him
that she intended no such thing, but rather that her intention was good and
holy: and thereupon he yeelded vnto her
that she might go that voyage , sending
with her an auncient mayd seruant, called *Anne van Poyer*: and they both departed
together from *Antwerp* vpon the xxvj^{th.}
of *Nouember* 1603. & arriued at *Diest* vpon
the xxviij^{th.} and then vpon the next day
beeing the xxix^{th.} they went to *Montaigu*,
where they remained two dayes: to witt
the xxxth of thesayd moneth of *Nouember*,
and the first of *December:* lying one night
at *Montaigu* and the other night at *Sichen:*
dayly performing their deuotions at the
Chappel of our Ladie: & vpon the third
day at the end of the second masse which
they hard , thesayd *Margarit* perceiued
that her foot was amended , telling the
foresayd seruant, that she thought she
could go wel enough without her high
shooe, and thereupon she began to stand
vpon her feet, and to walk vpright. And
beeing returned from thece to *Diest* they
bought her an other paire of shooes of
æqual higth, which she put on, and she
perceiued that her legges were now become

come æqual, and the one as long as the other. And thus vpon the fifth of thesayd moneth of *December* they returned to *Antwerp*, thesayd *Margarit* beeing deliuered from her accustomed halting, now, walking on both her feet with shooes of æquall higth, becauſe her legges were become of æquall length. All which was verified & auouched vnder their ſolemne othes, both by the aforeſayd *Iohn Nyemegens*, and by *Marie Vermeulen* his wyfe, as alſo by theſayd *Anne van Poyer*, *Philippes vanden Brook* and *Iohn de Ram* Almoner of theſayd Citie and neighbour vnto theſayd *Iohn Nyemegens*, before the aforeſayd M. *Iohn vander Noot* Eſquire and Eſcheuin, and Maiſter *Denis vander Neeſen* Secretarie of theſayd Citie of *Antwerp*, put in commiſſion about this affaire : all which aboue named perſons knew this wench to haue been lame euen from her infancie, and to haue been miraculouſly cured as hath been ſayd : as in lyke manner theſayd *Margarit Nyemegēs* declared theſame in the preſence of the former perſons, comformable to an information taken thereof vpō the xij^th. of theſayd moneth of *December* 1603.

The

The sore eyes of a chyld suddainely cured.

ELizabeth *Verbiest* daughter of *Peter Verbiest* Sopemaker dwelling in the Citie of *Antwerp* vpon the *Zant*, and of *Marie Speekaert* his wyfe, beeing seué yeares old, about Chriftmaffe in the yeare 1603. had an accident in her eyes for the fpace of fiue or fix dayes, her eyes beeing verie read and inflamed, in fo much that fhe could not indure the day-light nor any other light, and through the paine thereof fhe could reft neither by day or by night, & one of her eyes was fwolne as big as a great nut, and although her parents ceafed not to apply diuers remedies to them, yet no amendment infued thereby. It happened that on a certain day the chyldes mother met with one *Iane Gouarts* the wyfe of *Iohn Bertells* a bleacher of linné cloth, dwelling in *Antwerp*, & talking with her of thefayd accident, thefayd *Iane* gaue vnto her a little peece of the Oke of our Ladie of *Montaigu* to vfe it againft the aforefayd difeafe. Which thefayd mother receiuing, putting

ting her hope in the help of the *Virgin Marie* shee steeped thesayd wood in a little rose-water mixed with raine water, and a little holy water, and with this water she washed one morning her daughters eyes, who the next night rested very wel, not feeling any paine at all, and vpon the day following in the morning, she awaked as perfectly whole and cured as euer she was before the foresayd disease had happened vnto her: in so much that she went to the schoole the very self same day, feeling afterwards no manner of grief in her eyes. As her father and mother auouched thesame vnder their othes before the Magistrates of the Citie of *Antwerp*, vpon the nynth of *March* in the yeare 1604, according to an act framed thereof, and subsigned *Vander Neesen* Secretarie of thesayd Citie.

The cure of a sore that was fiue and twentie yeares old.

A Nthonie *vanden Velde* keeper and officer of the forest of *Soigne*: dwelling in the village of *Terhulp* three duitch

In Dec. 1603

myles

myles frō *Bruxelles* was attainted with a
quartain ague in the yeare 1575. which
continued about three or fower yeares,
whereby he became so weak and leane
that he was but onely skinne and bones.
Moreouer his left leg became so great
that he was not able to walk thereon:and
this hauing continued long, and fynding
no help although he had applied many
things thereunto by the aduise and counsel of some apothecaries & others , vpon
a day as he went vnto a certaine surgeon
in hope to be holpen by him, who intending to giue some ease to the patiēt, with
a corrisiue medicin made a little hole in
thesayd leg , whereby some water and
moisture began to yssue out of thesame,
but nothing els: and after a whyle sundrie other yssues began to grow in diuers
partes thereof, somtymes on the one syde
somtyme on the other syde of that which
was made by the barber. In somuch that
in short tyme al these yssues gatherig into
one, they made a sore of the greatnes &
compas of an egge: and this vpon the
shinne aboue the ankle, beeing very red,
and burning hote, and so ful of corruption that many thought the very bone
                                    had

had perifhed and decayed. And as the
patient indured intollerable payne, he
caufed diuers other remedies to be applied thereunto, but all in vaine and to
no purpofe. He alfo went in pilgrimage
to diuers deuout places, and yet obtained he no eafe at all thereby. At the laft
in the yeare 1 6 0 3. in the moneth of *December*, in the beginning of *Aduent* hauing
heard fome talk of the miracles which by
the intercefsion of the glorious *Virgin
Marie* were wrought at *Montaigu*, the fayd
Anthonie much defyred to get fome peece
of the wood of the Oake wherein the
miraculous picture had wount to haue
been fet: and hauing by the meanes of a
certain frend obtained a peece, & withall
a filuer medall of our Ladie of the fame
place, he put them both into cold water,
and therewith he wafhed his fore for
the fpace of nyne dayes, adding fome
few prayers vnto God, and to the glorious *Virgin Marie*. And from the very
tyme that he began to wafhe his leg, he
perceiued that the fore (which he fuftained for fyue-and-twentie yeares together, with much paine weakenes and
extenuation of his bodie) began to clofe
vp

vp, and euery day to become leſſer and
leſſer, in ſuch ſorte that when the nyne
dayes were expired, it was quyte ſhut vp
and healed, and ſince that tyme, he hath
remayned in good plight, not feeling
therein any ſwelling or payne, declaring
that from that tyme he hath found his
bodie in good diſpoſition and health, that
he ſeemeth to himſelf to haue become
yonger then he was before. All which
that here hath been ſayd he auouched vnder his ſolemne othe before the Magiſtrates of the Citie of *Bruxelles,* vpon the
xxj^{th.} of *Oƈtober* 1604. And vpon theſame
day appeared alſo before theſayd Magiſtrates *Miſtris Gertrude Ianoteau* wyfe of
VVybert Valle, dwelling at the Inne called *du Kennebutin* in theſame Citie, and
with her *Bertrand vanden Velde* brother and
Anthonette Baſton wyfe of theſayd *Anthonie
vanden Velde*, who vnder the lyke othes
affirmed that they had often ſeen theſayd
ſore, the which was very foule and vgly to behold: to witt, theſayd *Miſtris
Gertrude* ſome eight yeares ago, and theſayd *Anthonette* euer ſince it firſt began.
As alſo they had ſeen theſame ſore after
he had waſhed it, and they had found it
                                                   whole

whole and cured as hath been fayd: as also at that very tyme thefayd *Anthonie* shewed it to the magiftrates them felues, who found it to be intiere and whole, according to their atteftation made hereof, fealed with the feale of thefayd Citie, and figned P. *Numan* Secretarie, and dated as aboue.

The punifbement of a foldier that determined to hinder the Pilgrimage of Montaigu.

IT wil not be from the purpofe to declare in this place, how that a certain foldier of the gheufes and rebelles of *Holland* had determined one day with tweluie other companions to fwim ouer the riuer of *Demiere*, & fo to come and kil fuch Pilgrims as went towards our Ladie of *Montaigu*, and therewithall to rob the iewels & donaries that were offered there. And for this purpos they had fitted themfelues with certaine fuites of canuas, that they might be the fooner dry. But meaning firft to vndertake fome other exploit with thefe his mates, he was

In Dece 1603.

T wounded

wounded through both his legges by an
harquebuse, in such forte that his determination was dashed. As he himself
(acknowledging his bad intention) declared the same to a certain perso of good
credit, whose name we here conceale for
that he liueth amongst the enimies. And
to say nothing whether this ought to be
esteemed for a miracle or no, yet is it
worthy the consideration, to see God his
euident prouidence in this matter.

How a lame woman was cured.

C Atharin Mosnier wyse of Iohn Bailly
dwelling in the town of Arb in the
countrie of Henault, beeing in chyldbed,
was taken with a certain disease which
caused in her the palsey, & stretching of
her sinewes on her left syde, whereby
shee became altogether lame, and when
she walked it was with great paine.
Whereupon her husband resolued to go
in pilgrimage for her to our Ladie at
Motaigu, to obtaine there of our ladie his
wyues health. The same voyage beeing
made and his deuotion ended, the sayd
woman

In Dec.
1603

woman was perfectly cured of her
halting and lamenes, as it appeareth by
the attestation of the Magistrates of the
sayd town of *Ath*, dated vpon the last of
December 1603. signed *I. le Merchier*, and
sealed with the seale of thesame town.

---

*How a possessed person was deliuered by wood
of the Oke of our Ladie.*

CAtharin de Bus daughter of the late *In Ian.*
John de Bus dwelling in the Citie of *1604.*
Lille in the Coutie of *Flauders*, in the yeare
1601. beeing sixtee yeares of age or therabout was found to haue been possessed
of the deuil, who by diuers sleightes tru-
peries and promises had deceiued & cir-
cumueted her: insomuch that she could
be scarse a quarter of an hower in peace,
without beeing seased vpon vexed and
troubled by the enimy : which made her
speak (to the purpos) diuers sortes of languages, as Hebrew, Greek and Latin : as
maister *Michiel le Cadel* Pastor of the Parish
of S. Sauiour in the Citie of *Lille*, & Maister
Siluester Denis priest of thesame Church
solemnly auouched, as hauing heard and
T 2   exorcized

exorcized the sayd patient. Who besydes
the speaking of these strange languages,
did in furie things aboue all naturall
and humaine force : so that it was necessarie to haue fiue or six men to hold her:
who notwithstanding were much troubled to keep and hold her down. For
when they came neere vnto her with the
Blessed Sacrament of the altar she wrythed
& wrested herself strangely, both with
her legges, armes, and back , as with her
neck and head, with a terrible countenance, gnashing of her teeth, and grisely
drawing of her mouth. The parents &
frends of this wench labored so much
that she was diuers tymes exorcized,
sometymes by certain fathers of the
order of the Capuchins, sometymes by
other Priestes, vnto whome the wicked
spirits answered in diuers languages,
confessing at that tyme that they were
seuen in number, they spake diuers iniurious and scandalous things, & told the
faultes of diuers that were present. So
that one day whyle this *Catharin* was
exorcized in a Chappel of our Ladie
built in the honour of the hows of our
Ladie of *Loretto* (which was after the
feast

feaſt of *All Sainctes* in the yeare 1603)
there was a reporte in the Citie of *Lille*
that the town of *Oſtend* (which as then
was kept by the rebelles of *Holland*, and
aſſieged by the armie of our Princes)
was ſurrendered: the enemie was ſo bold
as to ſay by the mouth of the wench that
it was not trew, & that they ſhould ſee
ſo much ere it were long, and that thoſe
that had bruted it abroad were certaine
theeues that came from robbing the *Ci-*
boire of the *Bleſſed Sacrament* in the town of
Newport the which they had as yet in
their bagge, and that the great maiſter   A note
compelled them to ſay ſo much to accuſe   for
their ſinne. Which was afterwards found churche
true. For vpon the ſelf ſame day two   robbers.
ſoldiers Suiſſers were caſt into pryſon in
the ſayd Citie of *Lille*, who had blazed a-
broad the report of the aforeſayd rendring of *Oſtend*, and the ſayd Cibo r was
found amongſt them, the which they
had ſtolen out of *Newport*, whether afterwards they were carried, & there put
to death by order of Iuſtice The prieſts
cōtinuing the ſayd exorciſines, after ſome
ſower moneths the patient was deliuered of one of thoſe wicked ſpirits, and

T 5   after

after a whyle successiuely again of other
three, giuing to wer euident signes of their
departure, by breaking or cracking diuers
panes of the glasse windoes as otherwise.
Hauing firt and before they departed
throwne out at the mouth of the patient
sometymes brimstone, sometymes pin-
nes in great number, a bowed peece of
siluer of fiue sous, and a great naile of the
length of ones had. After that againe thesayd exorcismes were continued by thesayd Sir *Siluester Denis*, both by the intrea-
tie of the wenches parents, as also by the
commaundement of the Lord Bishop of
Tournay, and in the space of two moneths
by the ordinarie exorcismes of the Catholik Church two other of the enimies
were cast out: & a moneth or fiue weeks
after, again on other, And although now
seuen wicked feendes (according to the
number which they themselues had difcouered) were departed, yet thesayd Sir
Siluester perceiued that the enemy had
lyed, and that thesayd wench was not yet
cured. Wherefore he ceased not to continue the exorcismes vntil the beginning
of the yeare 1604, within the octaues of
the *Epiphanie* of our lord: when on a tyme
thesayd

Sir *Siluester* exorcising the patient in the
presence of a great multitude of people:
the deuil began to cry out; and speak to
one that was there present these words.
Arte thow there also? I know wel
enough from whence thou comest; and
what thou hast brought with thee: thow
arte one of them that hath been visiting
Marie of *Montaigu*. It was true that the
parents and frends of thesayd wench had
made a vow to goe in Pilgrimage to our
Ladie at *Montaigu* to pray there for her
cure. At these words the people began to
look about them, who he should be of
whome the enimie had spoken; & there
was found a man that was come from
Montaigu, and had brought with him a
peece of the Oke of our Ladie. Whereupon Sir *Siluester* took thesayd pecce; and
made the patient to eat it, and immediately after she had swallowed it, the enimie (who called himself *Houillu, Clicquet*,
and *Clinquart*) shewed himself in her
throit, crying out that he scorched and
burned, because of the wood which was
eaten: & he added, that he was copel-
led to depart, and that there remained in
her as yet three : & beeing demaūded by

exorcist by whose merit and intercession
he was to depart? The wicked seed answered; of *Marie* of *Montaigu*. And afterwards beeing demaunded what signe he
would giue of his departure? He sayd: he
would burst a glasse of the Church window. And immediately after, two of thé
departed with thesayd signe of bursting
the glasse, & the third saying that he was
the last of tenne, cryed out (in going
foorth) with a lowd voice. *Viue N. Damé
de Montaigu, qui nous faict sortir. Honour be to
our Ladie of Montaigu, who maketh vs to depart.*
He beeing compelled to speake these

Mar. 1. words (as wth reasó we may presume)by
Marc. 3. the maiestie & soueraine power of God;
Luc. 4. euen as we haue in the Gospel, that the
Act. 16. deuils in their departing gaue testimonie
that our Lord Iesus Christ was the sonne
of God. And in going he plucked out a
great naile that was fastned deep in the
wall, the which he threw against the
window, but yet touched it not.

And from that day afterwards thesayd
Catharin remayned whole and perfectly
free from the possession and vexation of
the enimie: inioying all her limmes and
sences as freely as euer she did before.

And

And about the beginning of *May* thesayd *Catharin* accompained with thesayd Sir *Siluester Denis* and *Peter du Trieu* her vncle went towards *Montaigu*, where she remained for nyne dayes, going to confession and communion, and dayly visiting the Chappel of our Ladie, yeelding thacks to God, and to his holy Mother for the mercie which she had receiued. And all this that hath here been sayd is manifest both by the deposition and attestation of thesayd *Catharin*, of thesayd Sir *Siluester* & *Peter du Trieu* made ynder their othes before the Pastor of *Sichen*, Maister *Anthonie de Bouckhout* Maier, and Sir *Bartholmew Thichon* Chaplain of our Ladies: as also by another attestation made and passed ynder the othes of thesayd persons, and with them of Sir *Michel le Candel*, and *Marie du Bus* wyfe of the aforesayd *Peter*, before the Magistrates of the Citie of *Lille*, vpon the first of *Iune*, in thesayd yeare 1604. according to a wryting composed hereof, dated as aboue, sealed with the greate seale of thesayd *Citie* and signed P. *Mouton*.

How.

How a Chyld that was burst was afterwards cured.

GErard van Omel wyk-maister of the Citie of Antwerp, and Susan VVagemakers his wyfe, had in the yeare 1903. a chyld called Lewis, who from the tyme that he was fower moneths old was foūd to be burst, in-so-much as his parents were constrained to bynd him with a trusse fitted for this purpose: because the rupture came foorth oftentymes as big as a great ball, which put the chyld to much paine, and his parents to great sorrow. At last about the end of April, or in the beginning of May, in the yeare 1604. the said Susan resolued to go in pilgrimage with her chyld to our Ladie of Montaigu, to pray there for his cure: which shee performed at the same tyme. But beeing in the Citie of Louain, and reddie to depart thence to Montaigu, there came tydings that the troupes of the muteners were not farr from Diest, and Tillemont, committing there many outrages and insolencies. Whereupon some dissuaded her

her to go any further as she did not, but stayed at the sayd Citie of *Louain*. And so perceiuing that shee could not accomplish her pious intention at *Montaigu*, went with her chyld to *S. Peters* Church in thesayd Citie, and there shee caused a masse to be sayd at our Ladies altar in the honour of God, and this shee did in lieu of her desyred pilgrimage: which masse shee did heare deuoutely, praying for her chyldes health. This donne she departed thence, and returned home to *Antwerp*, where after a day or twain taking from the chylds bodie his trusse, shee found him perfectly healed: insomuch that shee neuer needed to bynd him therewith afterwards, for so much (I say) as the chyld remayned in perfect health, as beeing intierly cured. As this *Gerard* and his wyfe testified and declared ynder their solemn othes, before the Magistrates of *Antwerp* on the thirteenth of *October* in thesayd yeare 1604. on which day lyke wyse appeared *M. Francis van Maldere* surgeõ, dweling in thesame citie, who ynder the lyke othe affirmed that he had seen thesayd chyld, and that he knew him to haue been burst, and how that at this present

present he is perfectly healed, for the aſſuráce whereof he had viſited & ſerched him. Lykewiſe *Cathariu Briers* widow of one *Simon Maes* appeared there, who auouched that ſhee had often ſeen & viſited theſaid chyld whyleſt he was burſt, and made for him certain truſſes, and how ſhe fyndeth him now healed: as manifeſtly may be ſeen by the information that was iuridically taken hereof, & ſubſigned *D. vander Neeſen* ſecretarie of theſayd Citie, and dated as aboue.

How a blynd man recouered his ſight.

In May. 1603.

ANthony *de Groote* born at *Eyckeren* neere to the citie of *Antwerp*, beeing nyne and twétie yeares old, in the yeare 1597. in lent, had a great defluction of a catharre which fell down vpon his right eye beeing then a ſoldier vnder Captain *Bourey* in the forte of *Damlrugge*, neere to theſayd citie. Whereupon he withdrew himſelf to an hoſpital in *Antwerp* to be there healed and aſsiſted: in which place they applyed vnto him diuers remedies, & amongſt others, he had an yſſue made him

him in the nape of the neck, the which he
did beare for six weekes; but he profited
nothing thereby: yea he lost quyte the
sight of that eye. About some two yeares
after seruing again as a soldier vnder captain *Grysperre* in a forte neere to *Callo* by
Antwerp, there happened him an other
defluxion in his left eye, whereby he lost
that eye within the space of eight dayes,
in somuch as the he became stark blynd,
and thereby was forced to forsake his seruice, and to cause himself to be led to
Antwerp, where hauing sold all that he
had, he sustained his lyfe very miserably,
and at last he was brought to that extremitie, that he had no other meanes
wherby to lyue but by the charitie and
almes of good people: making himself to
be led vp & down the streetes of the same
Citie for many yeares. But hauing heard
of the miracles which were wrought at
Montaigu, he resolued and made a vow
to go thither, there to do honour to the
glorious Virgin *Marie*, and to pray vnto
her that he might recouer his sight, yf it
were for his soules health. And thus afterwards vpon the xxviij^th of *April* in the
yeare 1604. he departed in boate from
Antwerp

Antwerp to the Citie of *Macline*, accompained with a boy that did lead him, and with *Vincent vanden Hout* a lame man: and hauing continued at *Macline* vntil the first of *May*, they went together to *Montaigu*, and arriued there vpon the next day after dinner, beeing Sunday the secōd of the sayd moneth. Vpō that day they did their deuotions at the Chappel of our Ladie of *Montaigu*, and so vpon the moonday, & tuisday following thesayd blynd man still praying for his sight and washing twise euery day his eyes with the water which is in thesayd mountayne. Vpon moonday he began to feel great paine, shootings, and prickings in his head, and especially about his eyes. Vpon tuisday he went to confession to Sir *Bartholmew Tridon* Chapein of thesayd place, and receiued the blessed Sacrament of the altar: and after dinner vpon the same day beeing the fourth of thesayd moneth of *May*, about the tyme of *Salue* whyle this *Anthony* was praying in the Chappel, and creeping vpon all fower about the altar, saying some prayers, he felt as if certain strings had been broken in his eyes, and therewithal he recouered his sight, being

able

a little after to marck and know
euery thing, and so became better and
better: in so much that he could perfectly see and know all sortes of figures and
cullours, read, and discerne peeces of
money, and go whether soeuer he pleased, without any to lead him, euen as he
was wount before that he fel into thesaid blyndnes. The which thesayd *Anthony*
declared, and affirmed solemnly vnder
his othe, before the Magistrates of the
Citie of *Bruxelles* (returning from *Montaigu* towards the Citie of *Antwerp*) vpon
the seuenth of thesame moneth of *May*, in
this yeare 1604. Before whome also vpõ
thesame day appeared *Vincent vanden Heur*
who vnder the lyke othe declared that
for fiue yeares he had seen and known
this blynd man in thesayd Citie of *Antwerp*: and how with him he had made
the voyage to *Montaigu*, where he had
miraculously recouerd his sight, as thesayd *Vincent* had seen, hauing been neere
to him in thesayd Chappel of our Ladie.
All conformable to an act of thesayd Magistrates composed thereof, and dated
vpon the seuenth of *May* 1604. signed P.
Numan, and sealed with the seale orthe-
sayd

fayd Citie. And vpon the xiij.th of thefaid moneth this *Anthony de Groote* beeing called into the full affembly of the Magiftrates of the citie of *Antwerp*, and examined concerning his cure, declared vnder his folemn othe all that he had fworn before the magiftrates of *Bruxelles*, adding moreouer, that at what tyme he began firft to fee in the Chappel of our Ladie, euery thing did feeme vnto him to be of a yellow cullour, which notwithftanding paffed quickly away, and immediately after he enioyed his perfect fight. Vpon thefame day appeared before the Magiftrates of *Antwerp Rombold* of *Mansdale* Lord of *Ofterlant*, who vnder the lyke othe declared that for many yeares agoe he had known this *Anthonie*, as hauing fomtimes been his feruant, and that he knew right wel that for fiue yeares or thereabout he was ftark blynd, & beeing blynd had been diuers tymes at his hows for almeffe: hauing feen him often led through the ftreetes, & to haue been with other beggers before the Church doores. Befides *Clement Ionkers Tifferand* appeared before thefayd Magiftrates, who declared and auouched that

some-

some fiue yeares a goe this *Anthonie* had complayned vnto him euen with teares how that he had lost his sight, whereupō he gaue him counsel to repaire vnto a certain surgeon that dwelt at the golden hand in *S. Anthonies* street of *Antwerp*, to craue his help, and yet for all that he remained stil blynd. Also the Almoners of the sayd Citie appeared before this assembly, who affirmed how they had seē for some yeares this *Antonie* beeing the blynd to haue been led through the streetes, & to beg for almesse: and how that somtymes they had sent for him to their chamber of the poor, giuing him some assistance for his entertainement. And how that beeing brought to the same chamber ypon the xxvj.^th of *April* in the sayd yeare 1604 he gaue them to vnderstand that he was determined to goe in pilgrimage to our Ladies of *Montaigu*, to beseech God that by her intercession he might recouer his sight: whereupon they wishing him the help and assistence of God, caused the portion to be deliuered vnto him which he was woūt to receiue weekely: and how that since his return hauing been with them they saw and

V   knew

knew that he enioyed his fight, for which they praysed & thancked God, giuing vnto thesayd *Anthonie* an extraordinarie almesse. Finally thesayd Bourguemaifters, Escheuins and counsellers of the communitie of thesayd Citie of *Antwerp* (beeing collegially assembled) auouched and certified vpon thesame day that for some yeares they had seen this *Anthonie*, blynd, and begging almesse in diuers places, both at the gate of our Ladies Church as els where. All this beeing manifest by the attestation of thesayd Magistrates dated vpon thesayd xiij, of *May* 1604. subsigned D. *vander Neesen*, & sealed with the seale of thesame Citie.

How a man being nyntie yeares old was cured of a rupture.

In *May.*
1604.
IOhn *Montady* born in the Cuntrie of *Angolesme* in *France* , beeing nyntie yeares of age, dwelling in the Citie of *Bruxelles*, in the yeare 1602. serued as a soldier in the companie of Captain *Anseau*, in the Regiment of Count de *Busquoy*: beeing at the siege of *Ostend* in the Coutie

of

of Flanders, which town at that tyme was held by the rebelles againſt our Princes, ſtanding one night ſentenel vpon ſome part of the trenches, it happened that a canon ball beeing ſhott from the town caried away with it a great peece of wood that was not farr of from the place where this Motady ſtood, which came ſo neer vnto his bodie, that foorthwith he felt himſelf to be inwardly burſt by the wynd and ayre of theſayd peece of wood: as a little afterwards the rupture ſhewed it ſelf vpon his left ſyde: and it ſo increaced that within three dayes ſpace it was as big as a mannes head : in ſo much as he could not poſsibly go but with two crutches, the which he vſed for two yeares together. And the weight of theſayd rupture was ſo great, that the ſkin which was about it began to ſlit, and was as it were rent in twain. Vpon a tyme before eaſter in the yeare 1604.he ſeiourning in the Citie of *Lille*,& hearing what was recounted of the miracles of our Ladie of *Montaigu*, he purpoſed and vowed to go thether to pray for his health. And he departed which his crutches from *Lille* at the end of the moneth

V 2   of

of *April*: and passing by the Citie of *Bruxe-
elles*, vpon the viij. of *May*, he set forward
on his way towardes thesayd *Montaigu*:
and he hath affirmed that so soone as
he was departed from *Lille*, he felt his
strength to increace, and perceiued that
he went more strongly then he was accustomed. Beeing arriued at *Montaigu*
vpon the tenth of thesayd moneth, he
settled himself to his deuotions for some
dayes at our Ladies Chappel, vntil the
twelfth day, vpon which day praying
vpon his knees at the tyme of *Salue*, he
felt his said rupture to moue in his bodie
as if a chyld should stirr in his mothers
wōb, & once or twise making a noise, it
caused in him so great paine that he was
forced to cry out, at which cry came
to him Sir *Barthelmew Tichon* Chaplain
who raised him vp, and standing vpon
his feet, he foūd himself whole & cured:
insomuch as there he left his crutches, &
offered them to our Ladie, walking with
out them and any other help whether
soeuer he pleased, not feeling any further
grief or paine: the rupture withdrawing
it self wholy in-to his bodie, without
leauing any marck or signe thereof. As
                                    thesayd

thesayd *Iohn Montady* avouched and testified solemnly vnder his othe, before the
Magistrates of the Citie of *Bruxelles*, vpō
the twentith day of thesayd moneth of
May. Vpō which day also appeared before
the Magistrates *Anthonie Capello* citizen
of thesayd Citie, who declared and affirmed vnder the like othe, that for the
space of two yeares before he had been
very wel aquainted with thesayd *Iohn
Montady*, and had holpen him with some
almesse : yea & that diuers tymes he had
seen his accident of the bignes of a mannes head, as hath been sayd, at which tyme
he went with two crutches, whereas at
that present he saw him go without
either crutch or staff: and hauing at thesame instant visited the place of thesayd
rupture, he found it altogether retyred
with-in his bodie, & whole. All which
may appeare by the attestation of thesayd Magistrates, signed P. *Numan* & sea-
ldd with the seale of thesayd Citie.

How

How a yong wench was cured of the rupture.

In May. 1604.

CHristina *van Schobeke* daughter of the late *Christian Schobeke* and of *Antoneta van VVeghelen* his wyfe, dwelling in the Citie of *Antwerp*, was foūd to haue been brooken on both her sydes, euen from her cradel, and from the tyme that she was but three weekes old. Whereby she had infinit incommodites and paines, & principally in her infácie: in such sorte that to yeeld her some help her parents made her weare a trusse, such an one as is wount to be applyed vnto those that are broken, and she continued thus for eight yeares : to witt, vnto the yeare 1604. At last her mother hauing hard great reporte of the miracles which were wrought by the inuocation of our Ladie of *Montaigu* she resolued to carrie thither her daughter, & there to pray for her health: the which she did, and beeing arriued at the place, vpon the xix. of *Iune* in the sayd yeare 1604. they did their deuotions at our Ladies Chappel, and the

mother

mother offered that which by vow she
the had promised: & after that she went
to wash her daughter with the water that
is in thesayd mountain. Vpon the next
day(which was Sunday) they continued
their prayers & washing as they had dón
the day before, and afterwards beeing
come to an Inne to take their refection,
the wench began to complain, that she
could weare her trusse no longer, and
that she felt it much to wring her bodie:
which whē her mother heard, she carried
her again to the Chappel, there to pray
for her: but so soon as they were entred
in,the band or trusse did break in twaine
of it self, & fel down to her feet: of the
which her mother caused the Paſtor to be
aduertiſed by *Gertrude VVoeſt* wyfe vnto
Iohn Eghens draper dwelling in Antwerp,
who was at that preſent in the Chappel.
And ſo perceiuing that her daughter was
healed, she returned with her towards
the Citie of *Antwerp*, & theſayd *Chriſtina*
(beeing but eight yeares old (went ſix
duitch miles on foot without feeling any
pain or rupture whereas before her en-
trailes were wount to come foorth on
both ſydes vpon neuer ſo little labor or
V 4   wearines

wearines, as hath been ſayd.

All this which hath been here related was auouched and affirmed vnder her ſolemn othe by theſayd *Antonet van VVeghelen* mother of that broken chyld, before the Magiſtrates of theſayd Citie vpon the laſt of Iune in theſayd yeare 1 6 0 4. Vpon which day alſo appeared before theſayd Magiſtrates ſiſter *Cicilie Cappels* dwelling in the Hoſpital, and *Marie Matthys* widow to *VVilliam vanden Boſſche* who vnder the like othe affirmed and declared that they knew very wel that theſaid *Chriſtina* ſome yeares ago was burſt, beeing brought diuers tymes by her mother to theſayd Hoſpitall of *Antwerp* to be holpen yf it had beē poſſible: where ſhe was looked vnto & fitted with her truſſe by theſayd ſiſter *Cicilie*: theſayd *Marie Matthys* affirming that this *Chriſtina* with her mother had dwelled in her hows more then eight yeares ſpace, in which tyme ſhe had ſeen her continually with this rupture, vntil the tyme wherof we haue ſpokē: & that ſhe was miraculouſly cured. All this beeing manifeſt by the atteſtatiō of theſayd Magiſtrats of *Antwerp*, dated as aboue, ſealed with the ſeale of theſayd the sayd Citie, & signed D. *Vander Neesen*.

How a Woman Was cured of a Rupture.

GVdula Schinck widow to one *Martin* In Iune.
Alart, who in his lyfe tyme was a 1603.
Notarie in the Citie of *Bruxelles*, beeing
threescore and fiue yeares old some two
and thirtie yeares before was broken on
the right syde, by ouerstrayning her self
through lifting vp from the ground a
bucket of water, she beeing at that tyme
great with chyld: and the rupture came
foorth of the bignes of a goose egge, insomuch that she was forced to weare ordinarily a band fitte for such diseases. In
which thirtie two yeares space she endured continually grieuous payn, and she
applyed thereunto diuers remedies, but
yet they little profited her to her cure. At
last hauing heard of the miracles which
were dayly wrought at *Montaigu* by the
intercession of the glorious *Virgin Marie*,
she resolued to go thether in Pilgrimage, with very great hope to recouer
her health. And so at *S. Iohns* tyde in this
yeare 1604. she caused herself to be carried thether by waggon, and hauing
spent

spent there some dayes in prayer, she
found her self so wel, that she left her
trusse behynd her, and offered it to our
Ladie, & so returned in very good plight
to *Bruxelles*. not feeling any paine or grief
afterwardes. Some fower or fiue weekes
after that, thesayd *Gudula* made an other
voyage to *Montaigu* on foot, and returned
homeward again on foot the rupture
neuer appeering: and so she remaineth
perfectly cured, feeling no manner of
paine through her former disease: she hauing declared and auouched these things
here set down, and that solemnly vnder
her othe, before the magistrates of the
Citie of *Bruxelles*, vpon the twelfth of
August in thesayd yeare 1604, Vpō which
day also appeared *Mistris Agatha Reigers*, &
Margarite de Merode, as also *Anne van Ni-*
nerzele their mayd, who vnder the lyke
othe affirmed and auouched that they
knew very wel how that thesayd *Gudula*
had been burst as hath been sayd, because
she was wount to come often tymes
vnto their hows, as also for that they had
often visited and afsisted her in her malladie, & when she was much tormented
with thesayd disease. All which s con-
for¹mable

formable to the attestation of thesayd
Magistrates of the citie of *Bruxelles*, dated
as aboue, and subsigned P. *Numan* Secretarie.

A very hard disease Cured.

MASter *Adrian van Asbrook*, sworn In Iune
clarck of the Amman office, and 1604.
of the Criminal court in the Citie of
Bruxelles, and Mistris *Catharin Verbeke* his
wyfe, had a chyld called *VViliam*, who in
the yeare 1602. beeing three moneths old
became ful of a certain kynd of eating
scabbednes, which the phisitions call
Herpes exedens, or corrodens, or exulcerans : in
French *Feu volaige graz*, in English, the
wyld fier, and his bodie was spotted
therewith in diuers parts and especially,
most of all in his face, eares, the top of his
head, and in his left arme: his forhead &
all his face beeing so ouer spred with
scabbes sore wheales & blisters, yeelding
foorth a certain corrupt and filthie matter, that there was no place of him free
but onely his mouthe, in so much as he
seemed to haue his face al couered ouer
with

with a hard and il fauourd bark, and
therewithal it had a certain kynd of inward gnawing, which was so intollerable, that the chyld stil scratching his face
made the blood together with the filthie
matter to run out thereof : a thing
so hiduous and horrible, that euery one
was much abashed to behold it : and thesayd chyld had such continual vehement
prickings and pain, that he would not
permit any of the hows to rest, either
day or night:& he continued in this sorte
more then two yeares together: at which
tyme his parents caused infinit remedies
to be applyed vnto him, both by the aduise of Surgeons as of diuers other persons : somtymes of such men or women
as took vpon them to cure and heale the
lyke accidents: and somtymes of such as
had tryed their receiptes either vpon the-
selues or vpon their children : and those
persons were not onely of the Citie of
Bruxelles, but also of other Cities neer
about, as of *Antwerp*, and *Maclin*: from
whence diuers sent vnto them sundrie
receiptes, wherby an hundreth and an
hundreth persons had been holpen : yea
such as had indured the disease twentie
                                    yeares

yeares together. But they found no remedie or amendment at all, in all the
care & diligéce that euer was employed.
And this accident became so great and incurable, that it did eat away not only the
skinne, but also the very flesh to the bone,
which they beheld often quyte bare, both
in his armes, as about the temples of his
head, insomuch that the parents were
not without feare that the disease would
turn into a leprosie. And they considering how that no help or inuention of
man could profit them, they took their
recourse to the mercie of God, and to
the assistance and gracious fauour of the
glorious *Virgin Marie*. And hereupon this
Asbrook and his wyfe went with their
chyld to *Montaigu* vpon the fyue & twen-
teth of *Iune*, in the yeare 1604. & hauing
donne their deuotions for somedayes at
the Chappel of our Ladie, home they
came again to *Bruxelles*, not perceiuing
that the malladie was any whit amended. Notwithstanding stil confiding in
God, and in the assistence of the glorious
Virgin Marie his blessed Mother, they applyed vnto him afterwardes no other remedie or medicin nor any of the receipes
which

which they were wount to vſe about
him : leauing the chyld euen as he was,
yet after a whyle they began to ſee and
perceiue how that ſince theſayd viſitation
of our Ladie theſayd chyld began daylie
to wax whole , and that all the ſcabbes
botches and bliſters went away of themſelues, without any exterior help, inſomuch that at the end of fifteen or twentie dayes, the diſeaſe was quyte gone, the
holes and open ſores were healed vp, and
the chyld was cured : and his ſkin and
fleſh throughout all his bodie both on
his face neck eares as other parts became
ſo faire aud clean as of any chyld in the
world, no ſpottes or ſcarres remaining
afterwards, as was manifeſtly ſeen vpon
the day when this was dated. And all that
here hath been ſayd was auouched and
verified vnder their ſolemn othes in preſence of the Magiſtrates of the Citie of
Bruxelles vpõ the twelfth of *Auguſt* in the
ſayd yeare 1604. by theſayd Maiſter
Adrian van Aſbrook, his wyfe, *Francis van
Aſbrook* his daughter: Maiſter *Iohn Huioel*
lieftenant to the Aman of theſayd Citie ,
and by *Helena vanden Eeckhout* wyfe of *Iohn
Moſſelman*? who all affirmed to haue ſeen
theſayd

thesayd chyld in so miserable a plight as
hath been sayd: yea that they had seen
diuers tymes how the flesh was eaten a-
way euen to the very bones: and the sayd
Helen declared moreouer that she had endeuoured for the space of six moneths or
more to cure this chyld, and that with
such remedies wherewith she had holpen aboue an hundreth persons, & yet in
this she could no whit améd him. There
appeered also vpon the same day before
the sayd Magistrates *Arnold Addiers* vnder
Bourguemaster of the sayd Citie of *Bruxelles*, the Ladie *Marie de Carondelet*, widow
of the late Lord de *Chassegnies* the Ladie
Catharin de Carondelet, widow of the late
Coronel *Bostock*, Mistris *Margarit de Bock-
bout*, wyfe of Coronel *Balthazar van Rossum*
Mystris *Agatha Reygers*, Mistris *Margarit de
Merode*, and Maister *Lewis VVinnocx*, Surgeon, all dwelling in the same Citie: who
auouched vnder the lyke othe that they
had sundry tymes seen the sayd chyld in
such miserable state as before hath been
declared, they hauing administred vnto
him all the receptes and remedies that
they could deuise, and yet without any
help or profit at all. And how that some-
weekes

weekes after the sayd pilgrimage of our
Ladie, they found him throughly whole,
and so perfectly cured as yf he neuer had
been touched with any euil in the world.
All which is manifestly to be seen by the
attestation of the Magistrates of the sayd
citie, dated as aboue, and signed P. *Numan*
Secretarie.

A lame hand cured.

In Iulie.
1604.

IOhn *Courtois* Commissarie of their
Highneses, dwelling in the Citie of
Antwerp some fifteen yeares ago beeing
in the Lordship of Hoghstrate in the *kē-
pinia* was vpon a day wounded in the
right hand hard by the wrist, with a
blow of a sword, by which blow which
passed through half his arme his sinewes
were cut in twain: and about the same
place he had receiued also a thrust. Whyle
these hurtes were in curing it happened that the wyld fyer entred into the
same arme, and it was inflamed therewith euen to the arme-pitt, where-
vpon the Surgeons resolued that the
arme should be cutt of, or els the hurt
man

man should lose his life : but he would neuer consent thereunto, rather chusing to dy then to be brought vnto that extremitie, and thereupon calling vpō the ayd and help of the *Virgin Marie* he vowed to make a pilgrimage to our Ladie of *Hall*. After which vow within the space of fower or fyue dayes he recouered in such sorte his strength & health, that he arose out of his bed, got on horseback, and so came to *Antwerp* feeling daily his arme much amended : from *Antwerp* he went on foot to the sayd town of *Hall* and there accomplished his promis, & so recouered the intiere cure of his sayd arme saue onely that it was lame on the three last fingers and on the thumb, his hād remayning crooked and his fingers stiffe. And vpon the fourteenth of *Iuly* in the yeare 1604 he going to *Montaigu* there to offer his honour & prayers to our Ladie he put himself in the state of grace, cōmunicated, & after some Masses he was presēt at the processiō in which the miraculous Image was carryed round about the Chappel, & so beseeching our Lord moste instanly and his glorious Mother that he might be cured of the sayd lamenes of

W   his

his hand, he gaue his beades to the Prieſt
to touch the Image therewith, which
the Prieſt did, who reſtoring them again
vnto him he with great confidence receiued them with his ſayd lame hand, the
which euen by the very touching of the
ſayd beades he perceiued to bee forthwith cured beeing able to moue & ſhutt
it as he could haue donne before that he
became lame: and from that tyme his
ſayd hand continued very wel, & it ſerueth him as fittly as dothe the other.
All this he himſelf declared and auouched vnder his ſolemn othe, before
the Magiſtrates of the Citie of *Antwerp*,
vpon the fourth of *Auguſt* 1 6 0 4. vpon
which day alſo apeared Maſter *Paul van
Aſſeliers*, Eſchoutet of the ſayd Citie, and
Miſtris *Ioane Courtois* his wyfe, who vnder
the lyke othe aſſured & witneſſed that
they knew right wel that the ſayd *Iohn
Courtois* their brother was ſome fifteen
yeares before lame of his right hand, in
the manner as before we haue declared,
and how that after the ſayd voyage to
Montaigu he was cured, and now hath the
vſe of his ſayd right hand as wel as of the
left, the which was neuer hurt. All which
is

is conformable to an attestation of the
sayd Magistrates of *Antwerp* dated as
aboue, subsigned D. *vander Neesen*, and
sealed with the seale of thesayd Citie.

The cure of a Rupture or Hernia.

Elizabeth *VVouters* alias *Gooskens* Be-
guyne in the Beguinage of the town
of *Dieft*, in the yeare 1601 drawing water
out of a wel she vsed such force that she
burst herself on both sydes, where the
rupture first apeared of the bignes of a
turkies egge and afterward of a mannes
fist, insomuch that she was constrained
to weare a trusse. induring often tymes
much paine, and sometymes she kept her
bed for the space of one two or three
moneths together: and although she had
vsed many medicines & remedies, yet for
all that, she felt no amedmet. Finally cō-
sidering that she fond no help by humaine
meanes, and fearing withal that this disease would hinder her from beeing admitted to her professiō in the Beguinage,
for so much as she was as yet in her yeare
of probatiō, she took her refuge to the

In Iulie.
1604.

W 2   Mother

Mother of God: and in the yeare 1604.
(hauing endured this accident for the
space of almoste fower yeares) she purposed to go three tymes to visit our ladie
at *Montaigu* to the end she might obtaine
thereby her health. And so vpon the eue
of *S. Marie Magdalen*, to witt, vpō the one
and twentith of *Iuly* in thesayd yeare, she
made her first Pilgrimage, & she felt
some amendment: vpon the day next
following thesayd feast she returned
the second tyme, and hauing ended her
deuotiō at the Chappel and going down
the hil towards *Diest* where she dwelt,
it happened that the point wherewith
her trusse was tyed on the right syde,
broke of it self, notwithstanding that it
was both strong and new, which when
she had perceiued she mended it & tyed
it againe, and so went on somwhat forward in her way: but by and by againe
she beeing not yet at the bottom of the
hill the other point on the left syde did
break, which likewise was new, & this
did neuer so happen vnto her before.
Whereat beeing much amazed, & thinking with herself that our Lord had bestowed some grace and fauour vpon her
she

fhe returned in hafte toward our Ladies
Chappel, & fettled herfelf again to her
prayers. In which place fhe felt herfelf
fo wel that taking from her bodie her
truffe fhe left it there for a memorie. And
from that day fhe found herfelf perfectly
whole and cured of her rupture, not feeling afterwards any grief or hindrance
thereby. Whereupon fhe returned on
the morrow following for the third time
in way of thanks-giuing, and caufed a
maffe to be fayd, praifed God and the
glorious virgin *Marie* who had obtained
for her this fauour. All which was declared by thefayd *Elizabeth* vpon the fourteenth of *October* in thefayd yeare 1604 in
the prefence of Mafter *Haymo Timermans*
Paftor of thefayd Beguinage *Sir Michiel*
VVouters, and *Lambert Bouwens*, Chaplanes
as witneffes, and Miftris *Catharin Maes*
Beguin of thefayd place in *Dieft*, with
whome thefayd *Elizabeth VVouters* doth
dwel. And vpon the twentith of thefayd
moneth of *October* thefayd *Elizabeth* appearing before the magiftrates of the
town of *Dieft* did fweare vpon her profeffion that all the premiffes were true.
And vnder the like othe haue witneffed

W 3   thefame

thesame, first Mistris *Catharin* that she knew right wel that this *Elizabeth* was burst, and had often kept her bed, hauing liued with her for the space of two whole yeares. And *Anne Shertogen* a Beguine, lykewise affirmed that thesayd *Elizabeth* had sworn the truthe which shee knew for that she had accompanied her in the foresayd Pilgrimage to *Montaigu*. All which is euident by the attestation of the Magistrates of *Diest*, dated as aboue, subsigned *P. van Zille*, and sealed with the seale of thesayd town.

How a yong man that was borne lame, and of a monstrous shape was cured.

In Iulie. 1604. IOhn *Clement* the sonne of *Iames* of the Citie of *Lucerna* in *Zuitzerland*, beeing at this present three and twenty yeares of age or thereabout, came into this world with a verie deformed and imperfect shape, hauing his legges wholy fastned against his bodie, and his knees thrust so fast against his breast, that none could so much as put a finger betwixt them, from the tyme of his birth vnto the

the tyme of his cure. Moreouer his thighes and the calfes of his legges were fastned together and couered vnder one flesh & skinne, together, with his belly and breast: insomuch that he could not stretch out his legges in any sorte. And as some Germaines told him (who had heard it from his Father) that his Mother dyed in her trauaile of him, and she was cutt vp and opened to saue the chyld, His father seeing this his defect and disproportion indeuoured by al meanes in his chyldhood to help and cure him: & for this effect caused him to be caried to diuers bathes both in highe *Germanie* as also in the kingdome of *Hungarie*, and yet could he obtaine no help. It happened in the yeare 1594 (at what tyme *Ernestus* Archduke of *Austria* was gouernour of the *low Cuntries*) that a certain noble mã of the kingdome of *Polonia* called *Tobias Metzka* hauing a desyre to see the *low Cuntries* and other prouinces, admitted the father of thesayd *Iohn Clement* into his seruice, to serue him as an interpreter, because he was skilful in sundrie languages, for so much as he had followed the warres in diuers Cuntries: & so the-

W 4 sayd

sayd *Iohn Clement* was carried by his father
amongst this noble-mannes baggage : &
coming neere to the Citie of *Boisleduke,* he
fel sick in a village called *Vlyemen* : in so
much as his Father beeing constrained to
passe forward with his Lord was forced
to leaue him there, vntil such tyme as he
recouered, deliuering him some money
for his entertainement. Hauing dwelt in
this village for the space of fifteen moneths, and beeing at last restored to his
health, he was sent for by his Father to
come to Bruxelles, where thesayd Lord
Tobias Metzka as then remained.

Whereupō he set himself on the way towardes his Father : but vnderstanding
how that there were certain famous bathes neere to the Citie of A *ken,* he caused
himself first to be carryed thether, that
he mighthaue the vse of them as he passed by, to trie yf he might fynd any help
againſt his euill, and so he remained for
three weekes at the bathes of *Bourssct*
neere to thesayd citie : but for all this he
receaued no ease at all thereby. And from
thence continuing his iourney forward
towards *Bruxelles* he found that his father
(beeing sent into *France* by thesayd Lord
Metzka

Metzka about some busines) had fallen into the hands of certain theeues and robbers by whome he was murdred. Whereupon he remained in *Bruxelles* entertaining himself for the space of two or three moneths, partly with the money which his father had left him and partly by the almesse which certaine gentlemē and others had giuen him. After this by boat he went to *Antwerp*, where lykewyse he liued by that which charitable people bestowed vpon him, for so much as he was not able to gaine his liuing by reason of his lamenes, and the want of his limnes. Whyle he liued after this mānet in *Antwerp* certain *Holland* mariners (who were at that tyme there) asked him yf he would go with them, they would carrie him to a place where he should be wel entertained, & haue good meanes to lyue, Who consenting thereunto was carried by them to the Citie of *Dort*, where he lodged in a stret called *den Crommē Elleboge* in the hows of *Iohn de Spellemeker*, and from thence he went to *Rotterdam* and so to many other Cities of *Holland*, as *Delf*, *Leyden*, *Harlem*, and the *Haghe*, alwayes going vpon his hands with two
litle

litle ſtiltes of a hand bredth or half a foot
in heigth, touching onely the earth with
the toppe of his feet which did hang before his bodie, & they were verie little,
& his legges not three inches thick vnder his knees, and after this ſorte had he
gon all the dayes of his lyfe. Whyle he
was in theſayd town of *Haghe* he dwelt
for the ſpace of a yeare in the hows of a
Scotiſh-man who was a labourer vnto
briclayers, dwelling in a place called *opden
geeſt*, & in this hows he did ly in a cradle
for ſo much as when he did ly in a bed
(hauing no vſe either of his feet or legges
and for that his bodie was round lyke a
bowle) he did ordinarily tumble down
to the beddes feet. From hence he went
by boat to many other townes of *Holland*,
as alſo of *Zeláď*; as *Fluſhing*, *Camfere*, *Armú*,
& *Middelborow*, where he lodged at a hows
of a widow called *Marie d'Oſtend*, who
dwelled behynd the Princes court. Alſo
in the Citie of *Breda*, where he lodged in
a widows hows that ſold ſmall wares,
called *Catharin*, dwelling at *Mone-uelt* neer
to the priſon: he was alſo in *Berges* vpon
Zoam, and whereas betwixt this town &
Tertole there was a forte vpon the *water*
wherein

wherein there serued certain Almans in
garrison, he found the meanes to enter
into their acquaintáce, becaufe he fpake
their language, in which place he liued
on free coft for a tyme: which was in the
yeare 1 5 9 6. at which tyme the Archduke *Albert* (who at this prefent is our
Prince) befieged the Citie of *Hulft*. Vpon
a day he beeing gon out of this forte, and
going with his hand-ftilts to a farme
hows in the cuntrie to beg his victualles,
the Coũt *Manrice de Nassow* accompanied
with the Count of *Hollach* and others,
chanced to paffe that way, with certain
waggons, and thefayd Count *Maurice*
feeing him fo monfterous & miferable,
demaunded of him whence he was, and
how he fell into that impotencie, and hauing heard the particularities, he gaue
him fome fower or fiue peeces of gold in
almes, and they were french crownes fo
farre as he can wel remember; in lyke
manner the Count of *Hollach* gaue him
fome peeces of filuer, and thefayd Count
Maurice commaunded him to caufe himfelf to be carried to the *Haghe*, promifing
to prouide him of fome entertainement:
& although he went thether afterwards
yet

yet he made no great sute for the sayd entertainement, but rather liued of that
which those carles had giuen him and
of that which daylie he receaued of good
people. And so going from one Citie to
an other in *Holland* for the space of two
yeares and a half or there about, at last he
came to the Citie of *Vtreght*, where he
lay at a place called *Opt Sant* in the hows
of one *Elizabeth van Dort*: and as he there
frequented certain Catholiks, they
couseled him not to stay in *Holland* where
Heretickes commaunded, but rather to
return to *Beuxelles* from whence he came:
& that there he might fynd how to liue,
and better meanes of entertainement,
both for his corporal lyfe, as for the exercise of his faith : and religion, by the
good assistance of the gentilitie and other
good persons in that Citie. Which admo-
nition was of that force with him, that
he following their counsel, resolued to
return thither: and thereupon he caused
himself to he carryed to the Cities of
Bommel, *Heusden*, and the aboue-named
village of *vliemen*, and at length to the
Citie of *Boisse duke*, where the Curate of *S.
Iames* vpon charitie entertained him for
the

the space of a whole winter. And the winter beeing ended, he procured that he might be carried by waggon to the Citie of *Graue*, and to *Venlo*, and from thence he came to *VVaghtendonck* whereof the Lord of *Gelain* had the commaunderie, who nourished and entertained him for the space of six moneths Afterwards thesayd *Iohn Clement* made himself to be carryed to *Aken*, where again both in thesame town as also in the aforsayd *Bouisset*, he vsed the baths for nyne or ten dayes together, but yet nothing aduanced his cure thereby. From thece passing by *Maestright. Tongres*, and other Cities, he came to *Bruxelles*: where he made his stay, entertaining himself vpon almes, and by cutting little wooden crosses & tooth-pickers which he sold. His limmes stil remaining in thesame monstrousnes and disproportion as they were euen at the beginning, creeping vpon his hands with his little stilts vpon the ground as hath been sayd, sittyng daylie at the foot of the staires which mout vp to the Princes pallais, where for many yeares together, thowsands and thowsands, of people haue seê & known

him

him in the aforesayd plight, and assisted him with their almes, as they passed by. At last in the yeare 1601, certain persons of thesayd Citie moued through charitie and compassion towards him, found meanes to haue him learn the art of painting, that therewith in tyme ro come he might gaine his liuing: & this was donne by the assistance of the Almoners of the Church of S. *Iames* in *Couberghe* and by other charitable people, procuring him moreouer that she should haue in certain howses euerie day a meales meate, Hauing been therefore about some two yeares & a half in the hows of *Anthony vãder Meren* painter, to learne that art, and hearíg ofté the miracles recouted which by the intercessió of the glorious mother of God were wrought at *Montaigu*, he had a desyre to go lykewise thether in pilgrimage, and to offer his prayers to the *Virgin Marie* that she would procure him the cure of his bodie, or at leastwyse that he might go with two crutches, or rather that he might haue some better vse of his limmes, and that he might not be forced stil to draw them along the groúd as to that tyme he had donne, whereunto

also

also diuers of his frends exhorted him. And about some two moneths before he took vpon him this iourney lying at that tyme in the prince of *Orange* his stable, twyse in one night, either in vision or in sleep, he thought that he had been at *Montaigu*, and that he could haue stood vpright vpon his feet, which did breed in him a greater desyre and deuotion to go thither then before: & so he asked leaue of his Maister, who verie willingly yeelded thereunto. But whylest he was in doubt by what way or meanes he might go thether, by reason of his vnablenes, soone after an occasion was offered: for that *Michiel vander Hagen* keeper of the wyne-seller in their Highnesses pallais in thesayd Citie of *Bruxelles* had receiued some store of wynes from *Cullen*: whereupon thesayd *vander Hagen* commended him to the carters, that when they returned they would take him vp into one of their emptie cartes. and so carrie him to the town of *Diest*: which they did, vpon the third of *Iuly* in the yeare 1 6 0 4. and they lodged that night at the Emperour in the Citie of *Louain*: and vpon the next day following they took their way to
Diest,

Dieſt, together with theſayd lame yongman. And beeing come to a certain place called *Hulſterbos*, where the way of *Montaigu* is deuided from that of *Dieſt*, the carter that had brought him thether took him down, thinking that he would eaſely haue foúd out the way, and ſo forwards towards *Dieſt* they wét with their cartes: but after they had gon awhyle on their way one of theſayd carters called *Laurens Donner* inwardly moued with cópaſſion, and fearing that God would puniſh them for their little charitie vſed towards this miſerable creature who (beeing not able to go but onely creeping with his little hand-ſtilts) might fall in daunger to be deuoured by wolues, dogs, or other wyld beaſtes, he felt ſo great a remorſe of cóſcience, that he ſpeedily returned with his cart, and hauing found him almoſt in the place where they left him, vp he ſet him again, and carried him to *Dieſt* to the Inne of the Swan: as the ſame carters beeing afterwardes returned with new loding to *Bruxelles* declared to diuers perſons of credit. Vpon the day following which was moonday and the fift of *Iuly*) in the morning the hoſt of the ſwan

fwan procured tbat he fhould be carried
to the Chappel of our Ladie at *Montaigu*,
where beeing entred into a certain lodging or cottage, the mafter of the hows
as he beheld him in this monfterous and
ftrange fhape, beeing much amazed
thereat, begã to fay that he much woun-
dred that fuch an one as he would come
thether vpon any hope to be cured : not
for that he doubted of the power of God,
but becaufe it feemed vnto him a thing
verie extraordinarie to obtain the cure
of fo admirable an accident. For all this
thefayd *Iohn Clement* went incontinently
to the Chappel, where he heard two or
three maffes, after he went to confeffion
and communicated, and about an hower
after he had communicated he began to
feel a faddenes and feeblenes at his hart,
and withal certain grieuous & excefsiue
paine in all the partes of his bodie, in fo
much that the fweat iffued out of him
euen from his head down to his feet: and
thincking to go out of the Chappel to
take the ayre he became much weaker:
whereupon he returned and remained
in prayer all that day. In the mean whyle
his paines increafed continually vntil

the euening after the *Salue*, at what tyme
beeing before the altar of our Ladie in
his deuotions, he felt himself inuisibly lift
vp from the ground, & his legges which
before were fixed & fastned to his bodie
and shrouded within his dublet as hath
been sayd, fel down, and of themselues
violently opened thesayd dublet, and so
he found himself standing vpright vpon
his feet, whereat he was much astonished, and ceased not to prayse God and
his holy mother for the mercie that was
shewed to his vnwoorthinesse. And as
he happened to be somwhat faint in this
alteration, he fel with his handes against
the altar, but was holpen by those that
were there present and placed in the
confession seat, whylest they brought
him some apparel, and especialy bree-
ches, because at what tyme his legges fell
down & that his dublet was opened by
force, in lyke sorte that peece of cloth
wherewith he was wont to couer his
bodie below and whereupon he did vse
to sitt, was torne in peeces also. Moreouer at thesame instant thesayd *Iohn Clement* was healed of a wound in his head,
which he had gotten some fifteen dayes
before,

before, and was not healed vntil that
very tyme, hauing at his departure from
Bruxelles brought with him six plaisters
to applie thereunto, the which at the
very self same tyme was found so wel &
perfectly cured and healed, that there was
no need that any should put their hand
thereunto. And all this happened in the
presence of many persons, who came frō
diuers places, and can beare wittnesse of
this suddaine and vnexpected cure. A
litle whyle after, the sayd *Iohn Clement* was
was led (by two or three persons for so
much as he was very weak) to the Inne
of the Angel, going vpright vpon his
legges and feet, which he was neuer able
to do in al his lyfe before: feeling a certain
force and vigor to discend incontinētly
into his legges, yea and a certain augmen-
tation thereof. And the host of the aforesayd Inne repenting himself of his former
opinion, took foorthwith the mesure of
the legges of the sayd lame youth, & some
two howers after he measured them a-
gain & he foūd that betwixt the tyme of
the first and second measuring, his legges
were grown bigger and grosser by three
inches: and after that tyme they began to

X 2   espy

espy his snewes and vaines to appeare in
his legges, which were neuer seen there
before. And so leauing his sayd hadstills
in the Chappel for a memorie, he resolued to stay there for the space of nyne
dayes, going dayly to the sayd Chappel,
and there hearing diuine seruice : walking the first two dayes with a staffe, but
on the other dayes without either staff
or other help: A day or two after the sayd
cure this *Iohn Clement* hauing got a clean
shert, and looking vpon the places where
his legges did hang from his bodie he
found that the holes and pittes within the
which his knees did rest and hang against
his breast, began to be filled vp with
flesh, & where his thighes were fastned
there the cullour was as red as blood, &
it put him to paine at what tyme so euer
he touched it: but after a little whyle all
this payn passed away. And during the
tyme that he remained at *Montaigu* he was
visited by diuers persons from *Diest* (who
before had seen him so miserably lame
and deformed) and now saw him go
vpright: and amongst others he was twise
visited by Count *Frederik vanden Berghe*, to
his great admiration at so notable a miracle.

racle. And vpon the fifteenth of *Iulie* he returned by waggon to *Bruxelles,* at the entrance of which citie he went some part of the way on foot vntil he came to the Church of the *Couberge ,* where *Te Deum* was sung and thancks geuen to God for this maruelous woork, which it pleased him to woork in this perso by the intercession of his holy Mother. And vpon the eighteenth of thesayd moneth, this *Iohn Clement* was present with a whyte wax taper in his hand at the procession of the *Holy Sacrament of miracle,* the which is yearely made vpon that day: & he walked vpright before the blessed Sacrament in the sight of many thowsads of people who at that tyme were in thesayd Citie of *Bruxelles,* yet he went but a part of the way because he was yet weak and with payn in his legges, wherein he felt a continuall stretching, and an inward working in his snewes and vaines, his legges and feet still growing, & howerly increasing both in flesh and strength. Vpon thesame day beeing sent for to appeare before the right reuerend Father in God, the Archbishops grace of *Maclin,* who at that tyme was in thesame Citie,

all

the contents hereof were read vnto him,
the which vnder a solemn othe he affirmed to be true, in the presence of the sayd
Lord Archbishop, of M. *Peeter Vinckius*
Deane of the Christianitie of *Bruxelles*,
Master *Theodore Sammelius* Dean of the
Christianitie of *Aloft*, Master *Iames de Saf-*
segem, & Master *Martin Huelet* Chaplaines
to the sayd lords grace, also of Master
Euerard van Enffe droffard of Coeuord and
Master *Herman van Enffe* his brother. And
vpon the nyne and twentith day of thesayd moneth of *Iulie* the same *Iohn Clement*
appeared before the whole court of the
Magistrates of the Citie of *Bruxelles*,
where in the presence of the Bourgema-
sters, Escheuins, Receauers & Counsel
of the sayd Citie, Collegially assembled,
he auouched again vnder his solemn
othe all that we haue here related: thesame hauing been once more read vnto
him by the Secretarie.

And vpon the same day appeared before
this assembly Master *VVilliam de Coninck*
an inhabitant of the Citie of *Bruxelles*, and
practitioner of phisick and surgerie, who
after they had shewed vnto him this *Iohn*
Clement, he affirmed and declared vnder
the

the lyke othe that some three yeares and
a halt past or there about going with his
wyf towards the Court or the Princes
Pallace in thesayd Citie, he found him
sitting at the foot of the staires there, and
considering how strangely he was lame
and impotent, he had a desire to behold
more particulerly his accident, and thesayd *Iohn Clement* vnbuttening his dublet
& shewing vnto him his bodie, thesayd
master *VVilliam* found that his legges
(which were very little and slender) did
hang against his bodie and that his knees
were thrust & made fast against his breast
he saw moreouer (for that he had curiou-
sely searched him with his hands) that his
thighes and calfes of his legges did grow
all vnder one flesh and skin together to
his bellie, and the foreparte of his bodie
against which parte his sayd thighes were
fastned: and his feet did hang *right down*
to the ground, thesayd *Iohn Clement*, hauing
standing hard by him two litle stiltes
wherewith he did help himself as he
went vpon his hands, and so he giuing
vnto him an almesse and the best comfort
he could, departed and went forward on
his way. There appeared also onthesame

X 4   day

day and in thesame place Master *Anthony vander Meren* Painter, who vnder the lyke othe declared that for the space of some eight and twenty moneths thesayd *Iohn Clement* had learned vnder him the arte of paintíg in which tyme he had caused him twyce or thryse to open his dublet, and to shew him his bodie thereby to see his defect: and he had found that his thighes were fast in one flesh and skinne with his bodie, & that he could not moue his legges, but onely that he could open and seperate the one leg a litle frō the other, setting or laying them toward the one or other arme-pit, and that he neuer went but vpon his hands with his two little stiltes of wood. Moreouer there appeared at thesame hower and place *Iohn de Grieck* who learned to paint of this Master *Anthony*, and also vnder his othe affirmed, that during the tyme that thesayd *Iohn Clement* was his fellow prentice, they had been twyse at two seueral tymes at the riuer called la *Senne* to wash and bathe themselues (the lame youth alwayes holding fast to the banck of the riuer,) and thereby he had seen his naked bodie, and perfectly beheld that his thighes and

calfes

calfes of his legges, were faftened vnder thefame flefh & fkinne againft his bellie and breaft, fo that he could not ftretch out his legges. At thefame tyme alfo appeared before thefayd affembly of thofe magiftrates *Michiel Hardy* painter dwelling in thefame citie, who vnder a folemn othe declared that he had wrought for fome tyme in the hows of Mafter *Anthony* with thefame *Iohn Clement*, whome he knew to haue been fo lame and impotent that he could not go but onely vpon his hāds with two litle ftiltes. And how that fower or fyue tymes he had been with him at the riuer to wafh themfelues: vpon which occafion he had feen his naked bodie, and wel and perfectly marked and confidered that his legges (efpecially about his thighes) were faft and faftened to his bodie before with the felf fame flefh and fkinne, his leggs hanging down his bodie, euen as a womans pappes hang from her breaft, in fuch fort that he could neuer ftretch them foorth; the which he had marked diuers tymes. There appeared alfo vpon thefame day & in prefence of the aforefayd Magiftrates *Catharin de Tournay* the wyfe of *Andrew van Zeele* dwel

ing

ling in thefayd Citie, who lykewife affirmed & declared vnder her othe that thefayd *Iohn Clemēt* had lodged for fome monethes in her hows, during which tyme
fhe had feen three or fower tymes his legges, & fhe had foûd that they were faft, &
hanged from his bodie: his thighes hauing
but one flefh and fkinne with his bellie
and breft, infomuch that he could not
ftretch them forth : whereupon he was
forced to walk and creep vpon his hands,
holding two little ftilkes of wood, as
verie often fhe had feen him. Vpon thefame day alfo appeared before thefayd
Magiftrates *Francis le Febare*, wyfe of *Frācis
van Schuttepit*, painter, who vnder thelyke
othe affirmed and teftified that thefayd
Iohn Clemēt had lodged in her hows for the
fpace of fower or fiue moneths : lying in
a hutch or cheft wherein they had made
bread : in which tyme fhe had at two
fundrie tymes feen and perfectly beheld
his legges which were verie fmalle and
flender, and hanged hard to his bodie, &
his thighes were faftened to his bellie
with the felf fame flefh & fkinne, fo that
he could not poffibly ftretch them foorth
at length. Declaring moreouer that vpon
the

the fifth of *Iulie* in this yeare 1604. shee
came from *Bruxelles* to *Montaigu*, and that
after dinner vpon thesame day that this
Iohn Clement arriued there in the morning
from *Diest*, and whereas he was miracu-
loully healed that verie euening, she with
some others ayded and assisted him in his
necessities, affirming that immediately
after his cure he withdrawing himselfe a
syde, shewed vnto her the peeces of skin
which remained hanging from his bodie
about the places where his thighes had
been fastned, as hath been sayd, he inqui-
ring of her whether he should cut them
a way or not: whereupon she answered
him that he should let them remaine
there still, expecting what God would
dispose thereof. And vpon the second day
of *August* in thesame yeare 1604. there
appeared before the Magistrates of the
Citie of *Louain Iohn de Soethem*, the host of
the Inne at the signe of the Emperour in
thesayd Citie, who vnder his solēn othe
declared and auouched how that vpon
the third of *Iuly* in thesame yeare through
the commendations of *Mychael vander
Hagen*, a certain young man that was mō-
sterously deformed called (as he vnderstood)

stood) *Iohn Clement* came to lodge in his hows whome when he saw to be so monsterous and deformed in his limmes that he went vpon his hands with two little stiltes, he desired to see his accident, and hauing made him to open his dublet thesayd host found that the legges of the lame youth were not past three inches thick, so far as he could remeber (whose legges not-with-stading at this present are more then fourteen inches about) & that they were fast and hanged by his thighes against his brest aud bellie, and were so farre thrust in & that with a certain kynd of hollownes that none could put his hand, no not so much as his finger betwixt, and that his knees did ly against his brest & were couered with the skin of his brest as he had seen and felt them with his hands. Affirming moreouer that as this serche was made in the presence of the carters who had brought him from *Bruxelles*, they made a mockery that thesayd lame fellow would goe to *Montaigu* with any hope that our Ladie would obtaine any cure for him: telling and persuading him that it was a friuolous matter: yet for all this he continuing in his good

good purpose, procured himselfon the
next day following to be conuayed to
Diest and from thence to *Montaigu* as hath
been sayd. All these premisses beeing manifest by the attestations & publik wry-
tings both of the Citie of *Bruxelles*, subsigned P. *Numan* Secretarie, as also of *Lo-*
vain subsigned R. *de Prince* Secretarie, dated
respectiuely vpon the xxix. of *Iulie*, and
the second of *August* 1 6 0 4. and sealed
with the seales of the sayd Cities.

Wel here I must needes call vpon you
(Christian brethren) who vnder pretéce
of following a reformed Religion, haue
left the assured foot-steppes of your forefathers, and that royal way wherein so
many Martyrs and Confessors, so many
holy Bishops and Doctors, so many Priestes, Eremites, Monkes, and Religious
people, and so many honorable soules
haue walked : whose moste holy memories yet replenish the world. You (I say)
that haue forsaken the liuely fountaine &
haue digged to your selues stincking pittes and cesternes, who haue left the fat &
fertil pastures of the auncient Churche,
and raunge vp and down the barren de-
settes of your own nouelties, and who in
                                    steed

steed of eatyng the delicious frute of the tree of lyfe , gnaw on the dry bark of your subtil though vain inuentions. Behold the glorious brightnes of the Catholik Churche: and withal behold the place of our own abode, and consider with your selues , yf you haue not forsaken the hows of God, & haue not gone to adore in *Bethel* and *Galgala*, there to serue the Idols of our own obstinate opinion : wherby you persuade your selues, that for the space of a thowsand yeares & more, there hath been no faith or right beleef or true churche in the world, wherein the fathful might hope or procure their saluarion: but that all was depraued corrupted and marred vntil some fiftie or threescore yeares ago, whe first forsooth was brought in the reformation & heauenly light, contrary to the woord of our Lord who sayd when he firit planted his Church, that the gates (to witt , all the power and pollicie) of hel , should neuer preuaile against it. Faith welbeloued is not as a proclamation or as a text of the ciuil law, which euery one may explicate and interpret at his pleasure, and which may bee altered & realtered vpon euery

euery occafion, & according to the diuer
fities of tymes. Faith is the marck wherewith euery one muft prefent himfelf
before his eternal Iudge at the laft dreadful day, yf you be detectiue herein, there
fhalbe graunted you no appeal, you fhal
neuer after be able to remedie or repaire
the fault, but all fhal be quyte loft for all
eternitie. O terrible etetnitie o dreadful
word, O incomprehenfible eternitie, O
infinit depth and profunditie either for
weal or wo, either for glorie or paine,
and yet you make no more difficultie to
change your faith and religion then one
would make to change his fhert or coat
What affurance, what teftimonie, what
proof, haue you of your pretended reformation? In the Catholik Apoftolik Ro-
main Churche we haue the markes of the
true & fincere doctrine, we haue the affured feales of the truthe : miracles (I fay)
the heauenely teftifications and impref-
fions of the foueraine hand of Almighty,
God. Whome ought one rather to beleeue, the chatting of a babling tongue,
fortified with nothing els but the credit
and tradition of one crept out of the fhel
but yefterday, and the antiquitie of half a
                              hundred

hũdred yeares, or rather those who teache
a doctrin of sixteen hundred yeares old,
and the woords of those which wee see
daylie to be confirmed by certain admirable supernatural woorkes of almighty
God, who doth vouchsafe vs thé. These
are the true proofs vnto which our lord
referred the Iews when they would not
beleeue him. Vnto these proofs, vnto
these woorks (Sirs) we remitt you in
lyke manner : consider here the hand of
God, beleeue heerby that the true Church
is not perished & decayed, as you dreame,
and withal vnderstand, how you haue
embraced darknes in steed of the truthe it
self: I know that the hoatest & flesshliest
companions amongst you wil say that
all this is but coosenage, sorcerie, and the
woork of the deuil: but this was & is the
old song of the Iewes heretikes and pagás,
against the Christian & Catholik Church
in euery age, when you shalbe able to do
somuch be it by what force or vertue
soeuer, we wil also make esteeme of your
argument: in the meane whyle you shal
contét your self with the answere which
Mat. 12. our Lord gaue to thesayd Iewes when
Mar. 3.
Luc. 11. they in lyke sorte reproched him: for
                                      thereby

thereby the euer-lasting wisdome of
God thought that he had giuen a sufficient solution for such an obiection. But
I beseech you (bretheren) lay asyde for
a whyle the fume of your passions which
transporte you. Enter into your own
consciences, and ponder with your selues
yf you haue not occasion to thinck that
we walk in the right way of the truthe
(seeing that God yeeldeth such ample
proofs and cōfirmations thereof amōgst
vs) and that you are in danger to incurre
the perdition of your own soules, and of
your euerlasting saluation. Can it be possible that all these admirable things can
be the woorks of the deuil? Cā he restore
the sight to the blynde? the hearing to the
deaf? is he able to cure the afflicted with
the palsey? in a momēt to make the canc-
kers, botches, and other incurable diseases
to vanish away? Hath he the power to
creat new limmes, flesh and blood in
the bodies of creatures? as you may see in
the cure of the lame youth of three and
twenty yeares old, who had no legges to
walk vpon. Truly yf his power could
reach vnto this, he had dōne it many ages
a go, and so the true miracles of our Sa-
                    Y   uiour

uiour and of his Apostles should haue
had no force to woork the conuersion of
the Gentils, but all would haue been turned into vanitie and ridiculous foolerie,
when the deuil should haue donne as
much for his own parte, as Christ
and his Apostles had donne for their doctrine, that so the world should not haue
been conuerted, which he held vnder his
tyrannicall yoke. No it is too grosse an
error to haue such a cogitation, and it
maketh that miserable damned creature
equal to the souerain God of heauen.
And what commoditie could this sworn
enimie of mankynd draw out of this his
proceedings: Is it lykely that he wil do
any thing whereby the world should be
incited the more to honour and serue
God; beare reuerence to the *Virgin
Marie*: and adict it self to works of vertue and sanctitie? Is there any man in his
right wittes that doth beleeue this? It is
no other, it is no other (frendes) but
the woork and mercie of God, who in
these latter dayes amongst so many shel-
ues and rockes of errors setteth before vs
a *Pharus* or Beacon, a light from heauen,
a *Cynosura* or celestial star, an infallible
mark

mark by the stedfast contemplation whereof we are to direct the course of our nauigation in this lyfe, yf we wil not vtterly perish. It appertaineth vnto vs to yeeld him infinit thancks for thesame, and in such sorte to frame our liues that he wil vouchsafe to continue & increase towards vs this his mercie, It is your duty (brethren) to open your eyes and to behold the sunne which ryseth so brightly shyning, for yf (notwithstanding all this light) you wil perseuer in the obscure night of your darcknes, you shalbe iudged inexcusable, and are lyke one day to feel the terrible and heauy hand of the Almighty vpon you for thesame.

The Cure of a flux of long continuance.

SIster *Marie Heytmeyers* a Conuers Religious woman of the Cloister of *Herkenroy* in the Coūtie of *Loon*, in the cuntrie of *Liege*, was taken with a flux which continued without cease for the space of more then a yeare & a half, in somuch that shee kept her bed for a long tyme. For the remedie whereof shee vsed first

In Aug. 1604.

Y 2   the

the counsel of the mistris of the infirmarie, and of other religious women of
her Conuent, and afterwards the aduise
& counsel of Master *Henry van Roy* Doctor
of physick, dweling at *S. Trone*. Afterwards of Doctor *Herman Griffenroy*, who
came from the citie of *Liege*, of an other
Doctor in the town of *Hasselt* called *Some-*
rius, a certain Surgeon called M. *Noel d'Ar-*
thois of an other of *Sittert*, of a certain
woman of the sayd citie of *S. Trone*, by the
aduise of all these she took many drincks,
receptes, and medicines, but all in vaine,
& without any profit, the sayd flux stil
continuing without cease, beeing for the
most parte of blood; & she thought she
should haue voyded all her bowells,
hauing had and that very often tymes,
aboue thirtie stooles within the space of
a day and a night. Whereby perceiuing
herself past all hope of recouerie by any
humaine meanes, she took her recours to
almightie God, and to his holy Mother
the *Virgin Marie*, and so in the yeare 1604
she promised to go in pilgrimage to *Mont-*
aigu, to which place she transported herself within a little whyle after, and there
hauing donne her deuotions, she returned

n ed homeward with some more ease thē
b efore, howbeit shee was not perfectly
cured. But beeing come home to her
Conuent, and continuing her deuotions
towards the *Virgin Marie* for some nyne
dayes space, settling her hart and intentiō
towards the miraculous place of *Mōtaigu*,
vpon the nynthe day (which was in the
moneth of *August*) after dinner, she felt a
maruelous and miraculous alteration in
her bodie, in so much that she thought
s hee had as it were a new bodie, & from
that instant thesayd flux ceased, and thesayd religious woman remained perfectly whole and cured. After which cure
she hath been twyce at *Montaigu* to thank
God for his fauour, and his holy Mother
for her assistance, the patient daylie re-
couering her strength. All which appeareth by the attestation of the Maier and
sworne men of the place & Conuent of
Herkenroy, who had the examination of
the s yd Sister *Marie*, and of other witnesse that could wel testifie thesames: dated vpon the twelfth of *October* in the
sayd yeare 1604. & sealed with the seales
of the ladie Abbesse and of the mayer
& sworne persōs of the aforesayd coūet.

How vpon the seuenth of September the place of Montaigu was inuaded by the Rebells of Holland.

OVr Lord therefore thus daylie continuing his miracles and maruelous woorks, whose glorious beames did not only shine in *Brabant*, and in other neer neighbouring contries, but did shoot out euen vnto *Holland*, and other places held by the heretikes & rebells against our Princes, and the enimie of mankynd perceiuing that by this way his kingdom began to be troobled, and that by these so euident and infallible testimonies not only they who in some sorte wauered, or doubted of their Catholik fayth were confirmed, but that those also who were misled & erred in their Religion, would thereby come to the knowledge of the true faith, and so forsake those darck mistes of error wherewith they were enuironed. This our ghostly enimie (I say) inflamed with anger &enuie against the holy Mother of God, indeuoured so much that he incited certain Captaines

and

and cheefs of the rebells that vpon a suddaine (and whylst our armie and men of warre were employed in the countie of *Flāders* both about the taking in of *Osted* as also in resisting the rebelles who were planted before the town of *Scluse*) they might go to surpryse, burn, and destroy the Image and Chappel of our Ladie of *Montaigu*. And so hauing assembled together some eight hundreth or a thowsand hors from the Cities of *Breda* and *Bergues* vpon *Soam*, they came vpō the eue of the *Natiuitie* of our Ladie, beeing the vij^{th.} of *September*, 1604. in the night to the bank-syde of the riuer of *Demere*, through the which they hauing waded at a certain place not far from the town of *Sichen*, (the water beeing then verie low) they thought to haue surprysed the place and al that was therein a little after midnight, before that any should discouer them: but whereas an hower or two before they passed ouer the riuer, those of *Montaigu* were aduertised of their enterprise, they had opportunitie to saue the miraculous Image, and the best vestures and ornaments of the Chappel.

When

When the Heretikes were arriued at *Montaigu* they began to belch out infinit blasphemies, & horrible iniurious words againſt the Mother of God; and caſting themſelues furiouſly into the Chappel, they broke the images, pictures & painted tables that remained: they burnt the foormes, cheſtes, ſeates of confeſsion, and other thinges that were of wood, and yet the Chappel took no fyer, allthough they laboured to burn it alſo. And taking no compaſsion at the teares and waylings of the poor inhabitants, cõſumed with fyer all their, howſes cottages and baraques in the moũtayne, they robd certain women (that were come thether in pilgrimage, and had remained there all that night to the end that on the next day they might the better atteñ́d to their deuotions) ſpoyling them of their rings, iewels, money, and ſuch lyke ſtuff, and ſome men they took whome they carried away with them, but thoſe were very few. And ſo making their retreat with the glory of ſo honorable an exployt they paſſed further within the countrie and ſo returned into the *Campigne* and from thence euery one to his own quarter, with ſmal gayn
and

and bootie, but yet with the honorable tytle of howsburners, Image-breakers, and persecutors of the Mother of God, and of her who brought vs foorth our æternal saluation, & who with her own flesh and blood nourished the bodie and flesh of the Sauiour of the world, by which he saued & redeemed vs. A woork which at that great day of iudgement must expect of the soueraine Iudge (who is her sonne) such a guerdon and recompence as any man of iudgment may wel imagin : seeing amōgst mortal men there is none so simple or base mynded that can behold his own mother abused and vnworthelie iniuried without some inward feeling thereof. Which thing all they who haue any way consented or assisted vnto ought seriously to consider. Also the reporte is (not that we affirm it for an assured truthe) that many of these gallants haue alredy experienced the renenging hand of God vpon them. And truely yf this be not come vpon them alredie, let them assure themselues, that by how much the later it is before they feel the hand of God, by so much the heauier wil it fall vpon them. But what hath the

deuil

deuil gayned (thinck you) by this affront;
but onely that the affectiō & deuotion of
good Catholiks is grown much greater,
and more feruent towards the glorious
virgin Mother of God, and that the visitation of this holy place hath been sithēs
as much frequented andcontinued as euer
it was before, and that in steed of a few
poor little sheddes and cottages now you
may see diuers good complete howses.
And without all doubt Satan laboureth
in vaine to extirpate and root out that
which hath been planted by the hand of
the Almightie: let him spyte at it, and let
him gnash his teeth as much as he wil
againſt it, his mallice shal be turned vpō
his own head, and this glorious woman
this Ladie whome euough we can not
pryze, whome we serue and honour, shal
by the holy frute of her womb crush the
head both of him and of all his adherents
and consortes.

A Cure of the Dropsy and other diseases.

In Sep. 1604. MArie Gerbrants, the daughter of Ger-
brant Heſſels, dwelling in the Citie
of

of *Amsterdam* in *Holland*, was for the space of more then three yeares afflicted with the dropsie, and for two whole yeares she was in that case that she could not walk in any manner, neither without crutches nor with them, hauing all her bodie ful of water, her legges swoln and as stiffe as stakes, and so grosse that her heeles could not be seen. Besydes this, shee had an accident in her right syde aboue the hip, as yf some of her sinewes had been ouerstrained & ouerwrested, causing the place to swel as big as ones fist, which did much trooble her. And although she had vsed the aduise of a certain Doctor of phisick, and that for a whole yeare, yet he could do her no good, insomuch that he told the patient plainly that he knew no meanes wherby to help her. Afterwards in the yeare 1604. about Easter hauing heard of the miracles which were don at *Montaigu* she was very desirous to go thither, & to pray there vnto our Ladie for her health, And at last she set her self on the way in the companie of one *Bernard Adrianson* the ordinarie messager of *Amsterdam*, with whome she came to *Antwerp* vpon the seuenth of *September* in the same

yeare

yeare 1604. and lodged in the hows of mistris *Angela de Poriss*, at the whyte flowr de luce in the *Keyser strate*, and vpon the same day, she taking boat departed towards the Citie of *Maclin*, together with two yong maydes whose names were *Susan vader Schueren*, & *Anne de Duyue*. From *Maclin* by wagon they went towards *Mötaigu* where they arriued vpō the seuenth of thesayd moneth, beeing the eue of the Natiuitie of our Ladie. On thesame euening thesayd *Marie Gerbrants*, wēt to confession with intention to communicate vpon the next day, and to performe her deuotion, and for this purpos she remained that night in the mountayne : but whereas on thesame night the soldiers of the heretical rebells of *Hollād* had passed ouer the riuer, and were come to destroy and ruine the place, and that our people were aduertised of their coming, thesayd *Marie* (about two of the clock after midnight) with her companie put themselues quickly into the wagon and with all speed possible fled to saue themselues in the Citie of *Louaine*. And they beeing in the wagon the patient perceiued that the swelling and accident in her hip

was

was gone and cured, feeling verie little paine ther of: & on they went the next day to *Antwerp*, where thesayd *Marie* continued vntil the fifteenth of thesayd moneth of *September*, & then again fhee took her way towards *Montaigu*, hauing in her companie thesayd *Anne ae Duyue*, and *Ioan Fierlincx*, and on the day following they arriued there, vpõ which day they confeffed and communicated, praying deuoutely in the Chappel of our Ladie, & that euening they wẽt to lodge in *Dieft*, thefayd *Marie* at that tyme going with two crutches. Vpõ the day followig they returned to *Montaigu*, and againe they did their deuotions in the Chappel. And as the patient prepared her felf to go to the altar to receiue the bleffed Sacramẽt fhe foũd herfelf fo conforted & ftrẽgthned that fhe went thether without any help of her crutches. They hauing ended their deuotions put themfelues into their waggon, towards the which fhe alfo walked without her crutches, leaning onely vpon thefayd *Anne de Duyue*. And on the next day (which was faterday) beeing in the citie of *Maclin*, thefayd *Marie* was fo ftrong as that fhee went without either

either crutche or any other help from her lodging to the Church of *S. Rombold* , where shee was present at our Ladies masse. Vpon the same day shee arriued at *Antwerp*, and daylie euer after she found her self better and better, & all the swelling of her legges and bodie ceased and went away, shee not hauing any kynd of eiection or voyding of the water that was therein, insomuch that the bodies of her coate which before her cure could not be drawn together, was found that by a quarter of an ell it was afterwards too great for her. Together with this grace which shee receiued at *Montaigu* shee also obtained an other, which was the curing of a certain disease called *Schuerbuyck* (a malladie wel known in *Holland*) wherewith at the very selfsame tyme she was grieued. In somuch as within seuen or eight dayes she was perfectly cured of all her accidēts, as she is euen at this present. Wherefore vpon the last of thesayd moneth of *September* shee returned the third tyme to our Ladies at *Montaigu*, in the companie of the aforesayd Mistris *Angela de Portis* to render thancks to our Lord, and his holy Mother for this his

woork

work of mercie, & for a memorie, there
fhe offered vp her crutches. All which
appeareth by the teftimonies and othes
folemnly made before the Magiftrates of
the Citie of *Antwerp*, both by thefayd
Marie Gerbrants, and *Anne de Duyue*, as alfo
by Miftris *Sufan vander Schueren*, & Miftris
Angela de Portis, according to an information taken hereof vpon the feuen and
twentith of *Septemb.r*, & vpon the fourth
and xxj^{th.} of *October* in thefayd yeare
1604. Subfigned D. *vander Neefen* Secretarie of thefayd Citie.

A Rupture cured.

Godfrey Ruthinck of *Borkelo*, recea-
uer for their highneffes in *Geldres*
had a fonne called *Lubert*, of the age of
twelue yeares, who in the yeare 1604.
was fo beaten and & trodden vnder foot
by an other boy in *Geldres*, that he was
burft on both fydes: wherewith his parents much agrieued caufed M. *Iofe Kinck*
furgeon inhabitant of thefayd town to
bee fent for, that hee might help and cure
the chyld yf it were poffible, who hauing
                                        vifited

visited him, applyed for the space of three
weeks certain oyles and plaisters vnto
him, which are good againtt that difeafe.
But his parents perceauing that nothing
profited him they took their refuge to almightie God, and to his holy Mother:
promising to make a Pilgrimage to our
Ladie of *Montaigu*. And hereupon the
wyfe of thefayd *Godfrey* went thether
with her chyld, and arriued there vpon
the térh of *August* in thefame yeare 1604:
and hauing for fome tyme donne there
her deuotions, as fhee returned home towards thefayd town of *Geldres*, fhe perceiued in her way that her chyldes difeafe was amended, and beeing come
home fhee caufed the forefayd furgeon
M. *Iofe Kinck* to be called for, to fee the
chyld. Who hauing feen and viſited the
place of the difeafe in the prefence of
diuers perfons, he found him perfe&-
&ly healed, as he is euen at this prefent. The which both thefayd *Godfrey*
& his wyfe, & thefayd M. *Iofe Kinck* Surgeon auouched and affirmed ynder their
folemn othes, before the Magiftrates of
the town of *Geldres*, as it appeareth by the
atteftation of thefayd Magiftrates giuen
hereof,

hereof, and dated vpon xx^{th.} of *October* in the same yeare 1604. subsigned *L. Richard*, and sealed with the seale of the sayd town.

How a lame woman was cured.

Marie Martin widow of *Iohn Thiry*, dwelling in *Ligny* neer to *Fleru* in the County of *Namur*, beeing fiftie and fower yeares old, some fiue yeares ago in a night became so lame that shee could not moue her self, and this happened her especially in her left leg, in such sorte that shee was forced to vse two crutches, for without them shee could not go. And to the end shee might be healed, shee went in pilgrimage to diuers places of deuotiõ as wel in the cuntrie of *Henalt*, as of *Liege*, & els were, & yet could shee obtain no ease. At last hauing heard of the miracles of our Ladie at *Montaign*, shee went thether vpon her crutches about the beginning of *Nouember* in the yeare 1604, & beeing in our Ladies Chappel she sayd her prayers there vpon her knees: afterwards intending to go to the priest to con-

In Aug. 1604.

Z

to confession that she might also communicate, suddainly as shee arose shee felt in herself such an alteration, that shee went to her Confessor without any help of her crutches, and hauing ended her deuotions shee departed onely with the help of a staffe, and left her crutches in the Chappel for a perpetuall memorie of the benefit which shee had there receiued, and so returned home, where shee remaineth increasing daylie in her strength and force, going at this present to the Church, & in her hows without any support what soeuer: as appeareth by her deposition made vnder her othe before the Maier and Escheuins of the court of the Lordship of *Ligny*, vpō the seuenth of Ianuarij 1605, subsigned I. *Dacos* Secretarie.

A cure of a sore leg.

Nicholas *Crummens* a yong man borne in *Vaels* hard by the Citie of *Aken*, as some seauen yeares since hee serued one *Martin Lomans* in a farme appertayning to the Chanons of *Aken* where hee was
imployed

imployed in tilling the ground and to
look vnto certain horses, hee felt on a
day about Whitsontyde a kynde of grief
and gnawing in his left leg, and afterwards an issue broke out of thesame leg,
the which increasing by litle and litle
waxing as broad as the palme of ones
hand, it began to yeeld out a kynd of yellow water and moisture, and it much
hindred him in his labor, and somtymes
he was in that case that he could not go
out ofthe hows. Whereupon he transported himself to thesayd Citie of *Aken*
there to take the counsel and aduise of a
certain surgeon called *Henry Pauon*, in
whose hows he remained about some
three weekes for this purpose: but he
profited him nothing for al that he could
apply vnto him: and in steed of one issue
there ensued an other. Afterwardes he
was couseled by some to go to the hagman of the Citie, who had him in cure
for the space of fifteen dayes, and yet he
was nothing holpen by him. From thece
he caused himself to be carried to the citie
of *Maestright*, where for the space of six
moneths he put himself into the hads of
the Barbers and Surgeons, and namely

Z 2   of

of M. Iohn Cornille, Iames Hutain, and Peter Crommens: who all by diuers medicines & remedies endeuoured to cure him, but they atchieued no more then the others before: his leg remaning with the former soares, and was very much swoln, so that the patient was forced to go with two crutches. And in this plight he remained for a long tyme, beeing not able to go somuch as one or two steps without his crutches. Whereby being at last brought to that pouertie that he was cōstrained to procure his liuing by the almesse of good folk, he was counseled by some to goe vnto the great Hospital of *Bruxelles* there to be healed and assisted. Where beeing admitted, he continued for some fower moneths and an half, and albeit that he was daylie visited by M. *Iohn Bierens* sworn Surgeon of the Citie, and by the Religious women of thesayd hospital, yet they could neuer cure him. Whereupon leauing *Bruxelles*, he went to *Antwerp*, where he was again in the Hospital for fourteen weekes, and he was assisted and dressed by two Surgeons, whereof the one was called M. *Cornelius* and the other M. *Iohn*, & although

both

both they and the Physitions which visited and frequented him, had vsed all their diligence to heale him, yet they profited nothing, so that all that they did was in vaine. In somuch as beeing out of all hope to be cured, he departed out of the Hospital, and went vp and down a beggig going alwayes with his crutches. Afterwards coming to the Citie of *Maclin* he put himself into the Hospital to try yf there he could be holpen : where for the space of six weekes he was in the hands of the surgeon of that Hospital, dwelling neere to our Ladies Church, who also spared no paynes to cure him: but all was frutelesse, and procured him no ease, the poor patient continuing stil in thesayd state, hauing his left leg drawn backward, and very crooked, and so stiff, that he thought none was able by any force to make it right again. And so seeing all the remedies that he applyed there vnto did no good, he remained stil lame, not medling any more with phisick or surgerie, saue onely that he took some plaisters now from one, and then from an other to preserue his leg from rotting. It happened that in the beginning of the

Z 3   yeare

yeare 1603. he hard folk tel of the miracles which were wrought at *Montaigu*
through inuocation of our Ladie, whereupon he wet with his crutches thether
from the aforesayd village of *Vaels*, where
he was at that present, and he continued
for a certain tyme in the moútayne, there
daylie praying, and yet at that tyme he
felt no ease at all. But wheras afterwards
he perseuered in going often tymes in
pilgrimage to thesayd *Montaigu*, and in
visiting our Ladies Chappel: at the last
betwixt Easter and Whit suntyde in the
yeare 1604. seiourning for some tyme on
thesayd mountayn, and dooing his accustomed deuotions at the Chappel, he also
took of the water that is in thesayd place,
and daylie washed his leg therewith:
wherein he found incontinently amendment, and perceiued that the two soares
of his leg (which were now turned into
one and was as large as both ones hands)
began to heale, and by litle and litle to
decrease. Vpon which euét beeing to depart from thence, he furnished himself
with a good quantitie of that water in a
pot, where with he continued to wash
his leg as before, and so by litle and litle
the

thesayd sore was made perfectly whole,
and the swelling of his leg went away.
And in the beginning of *December* in thesayd yeare 1604. he came again to *Mont-*
aigu with his crutches (although he had
alredy felt so great ease that he vsed them
not) and stayed there vntil the twentith
of thesayd moneth, daylie washing his
leg in the order as before we haue sayd:
& at that tyme it became very right, strõg,
and free from the former euil, insomuch
that he left his crutches at our Ladies
Chappel, going and walking as perfectly as any other: and from thence he
went on foot without any painé or grief
to the Citie of *Bruxelles* vpon the xxijth of
thesame moneth : where before the magistrates of thesayd Citie he affirmed and
vnder his othe solemnly auouched the
thinges that here haue been declared, as it
apeareth by the attestatiõ they dispatched
heerof, dated thesame day, and subsigned,
P. *Numan* Secretarie of thesayd Citie.

Laus Deo beatæque Virgini Dei Geni-
trici Mariæ.

4   The

THE
CONCLVSION OF
THE TRANSLATOR.

Eere, and with thefe
(Chriftian Reader)
I thought good for
this prefent to end, al-
though Almightie God
through his goodnes of
thefe miraculous wor-
kes as yet maketh no end. The addition of
thofe miracles which at our *Montaigu*
this laft yeare haue been wrought,
after due examination are now vnder
the printers hands, whereof in tyme (by
Gods help) I wil make thee partaker.
Meane whyle with the deuout Euange-
lical woman make thy profit of thefe
which here thou fyndeft: and with her
not onely inclyne thy hart to beleeue,
but alfo lift vp thy voice to profeffe and
confeffe the happines of this facred Mother,

ther, at whose intercession they are wrought, and withall the infallible assured authoritie of the Catholik Apostolik and Romane Church, in which onely, and for whose onely comfort, credit, and confirmatiō they are atchiued. Remēber who they were that would haue killed *Lazarus*, and in deed killed our Lord and Sauiour *Iesus Christ*: whome therfore they should haue beleeued and honored, whē they saw by his most doubtles signes the truthe was so manifested and theyr impietie detected. Beware thou turn not with them to the reason of state, and earthly pollicie, saying: *Ne veniant Romani* or such like, thereby diuerting thy self from that which principally thou art bound to regard, least through the iust iudgement of God, that which thou now most fearest apprehend thee, and that which should be thy soueraine obiect, hereafter faile thee. Doost thou not see how our Catholik doctrin by thesame powerful hand at this present is vpholden and fostered, by which at the beginning it was planted and took root? Read read, and see. Yet for thyn own good I am to intreat thee, to auoid all curiositie in thy reading.

reading, as thou seest how I haue auoided
it in my translation: endeuouring rather
truly then trimly to expresse my Author,
as he hath labored purely & punctually
to deliuer vs the truthe. Lykewyse be
thou careful, not curious in learning
the truthe, and Christially couragious in confessing the truthe,
that in the hower of thy
chiefest peril the
truthe may de-
liuer thee.

Hæc translatio miraculorum beatissimæ Virginis Mariæ in colle acuto ex Gallico in Anglicum idioma facta, piorum ac bonorum virorum (quibus sicut mihi ipsi fido) iudicio sincera & catholica inuenta est. Poterit ergo imprimi ad multorum oppressorum catholicorum solatium. Dedit 21. Ianuarij 1606.

Egbertus Spitoldius S. T. L. Canonicus & Plebanus Antwerpiensis librorum censor.

Cum Gratia & Priuilegio ad Sexennium.

Buschere.

Faultes escaped in the printing.

In the translators preface.

For sf. *read* of.
For paryer. prayer.
For comfort, consort.
    In the preface of the author.
For the pietie of princes,
Read, the pietie of our princes.
Pag. 22. *for* reaons *read* reasons.
Pag. 26. *for* acotnes *read* acornes.
Pag. 175. *for* depar *read* departed.
Pag. 190. *for* calebrated *read* cele-
                brated.
Pag. 250. *for* Carles *read* Earles
    Consider (courteous Reader) our
difficulties in vsing printers that are
strangers, and at thy discretion vouch-
safe to correct these and such lyke
faultes.